AMERICAN REGIONALISM

by

HOWARD W. ODUM
Author of *Southern Regions*
and
HARRY ESTILL MOORE

REGIONALISM, the things cultural and physical which give character to geographical areas, is a topic of increasing importance in recent American literature. It has been the subject of such widely divergent books as *Middletown, You Have Seen Their Faces* and *Rich Land, Poor Land*. But *American Regionalism* is the first *comprehensive* treatment of this subject. Here are presented complete analyses of what the authors designate as Natural, Culture and Service Regions. The treatments involve examinations of every aspect (aesthetic, governmental, economic, social, etc.) in its relation to every region.

The book is an excellent framework for the consideration of all New Deal programs and trends of modern society, and provides a critical interpretation of many moot points. It is at once valuable as a work of scholarship, provocative as new material on subjects of current controversy, and inspiring in its plea for a richer Americanism.

Howard Odum is widely known as a writer, lecturer, and director of the Institute for Research in Social Science at the University of North Carolina.

As Dr. Carol Aronovici, the well-known authority on city planning and housing, says, "Dr. Odum's first-hand experience as an investigator and his technical skill in gathering and organizing such material should place this book in the first rank in sociological literature."

AMERICAN REGIONALISM

A CULTURAL-HISTORICAL APPROACH TO NATIONAL INTEGRATION

BY

HOWARD W. ODUM

AND

HARRY ESTILL MOORE

NEW YORK
HENRY HOLT AND COMPANY

IN CANADA, OXFORD UNIVERSITY PRESS

PRINTED IN THE
UNITED STATES OF AMERICA

CONTENTS

Part III

THE REGIONAL DEVELOPMENT OF A CHANGING NATION

INTRODUCTORY NOTE

AMERICAN REGIONALISM attempts to present a general picture of contemporary regionalism in the United States interpreted in the light of its historical and theoretical backgrounds. The book has grown logically out of "the day's work" and therefore reflects the limitation of the workshop product. Parts I and III are the outgrowth of many years of regional study and exploration, more particularly in the Southeast and the Southwest, but comparatively also in the Middle States and the Far West with some first-hand observations in all of the six major regions. Part II is the result of the more recent recognition of the rich and undeveloped field of the historical and theoretical backgrounds of regionalism and of the importance of historical evidence in the testing of practical efforts.

This workshop nature of the book is apparent in both its general objectives and in the methods and procedures through which these objectives have been sought. For some time it has been clear that there was needed a working compendium of the extraordinary amount and variety of materials on regionalism to the end that clarification and unity of the great diversity of regional approaches might be attained. Such a compendium was needed, further, not only as inventory, but to serve as testing media for regional research and planning in the light of realistic situations. Another objective was to focus upon regionalism as a cultural-historical approach to national unity and to translate the older historical sectionalism into a dynamic doctrine of national development. It was desired further to explore the extent to which regionalism might serve not only as a tool for progress but as a medium for portraying the new pluralism of the American nation and for interpreting its growth through the orderly processes of the people and their institutions within the living geography of a natural and cultural heritage. There was need also to explore the possibilities of regionalism as a medium for the co-operation and co-ordination of the social sciences in their joint approach to the study of realistic contemporary society.

The student, as well as a critical but generous public, will recognize the volume as illustrative and representative rather than as exhaustive and critical. Illustrative of the diversity of the regional approach are certain apparent contradictions and inconsistencies in the use of the term region and in the special emphasis which we have placed upon certain specific aspects of regionalism. Thus, the metropolitan region is, on the premises of our definitions, a minor and specialized region and often appears as contradictory to the major tenets of national regionalism. Yet because American regionalism had its rise and incidence in metropolitan regionalism and because it has constituted an almost complete field of its own, we must present the picture in reality as one of the chief types.

So, too, in our presentation of the states as tools for regionalism it must be clear that the states are utilized, not because they are political entities but because they are measurable units which combine essential indices, and because through their outer borders must be found some arbitrary margins for the region. Thus, the group-of-states region implies no essentially exclusive reference to a political or purely administrative entity, but on the contrary to a minimum-maximum region in which delimitation can be implemented in realistic terms. If there were natural subregions, which could actually be delimited in terms of realistic boundaries and units susceptible of social implementation as major regions, they would be preferably utilized. But they do not exist. The states do exist and under the American system must continue to exist and are therefore essential units. Besides, the states are cultural and societal as well as political and, in regional groups, they comprehend many of the natural subregions.

In much the same way the older authentic literary regionalism stands in direct opposition to our premise of regionalism as a constituent part of the whole and as a tool for national integration of all parts of the nation. Yet the exponents of this pattern of regionalism have appeared at times to excel all others in the presentation of the merits of their case. Accordingly, no contradiction appears in presenting their viewpoint as not only representative of American regionalism but as an outstanding example of the diversity and complexity of the total regional structure. This does not mean that we accept the literary concept of regionalism. Nor does our advocacy of the reintegration of agrarian culture in American life through the regional approach indicate agreement with the agrarians. At best, our rural regionalism must be interpreted primarily as analogy for a very real something for which, as yet, we have no accurate designation. And, finally, our cataloguing of the multiple *district* or purely administrative or service areas as *regions* is in character with current usage rather than acceptable definition.

Both the merits and the limitations of the plan of the present volume are illustrated in the arrangement of the three parts. In general, each of the parts—namely, Part I, dealing with the general rise and incidence of American regionalism; Part II, giving the theoretical-historical story from the viewpoint of the social sciences; and Part III, illustrating the American scene—is intended to provide a relatively complete unit in itself. For this reason, as well as for the purpose of featuring certain recurring motifs, there is some repetition of ideas and concepts along with their application to the actual scene.

But there are certain dilemmas for which there is no satisfactory way out. One of these is the impossibility of presenting a sixfold regional division which will be satisfactory to everybody for all purposes. The answer here is, of course, approximation of the largest number of agreements with the smallest number of contradictions and limitations, on the one hand, and on the other, an actual beginning, through which uniformities may be approximated and revisions continued. The basis upon which this sixfold division rests and the procedures by which conclusions are reached, as set forth in Chapter XVIII, should be appraised in relation to both the general merits of the case and in comparison with other possible divisions.

A second dilemma follows logically—namely, a similar impossibility of presenting satisfactorily even a preliminary inventory or descriptive picture of each great region and, by the same token, the regional totality of the nation in so limited a space and methodology. The answer here is not even approximation but illustration and outline, basic to further adequate separate regional analysis. There has appeared to be an almost unanimous agreement among both students and the public that there should emerge, as soon as possible, authentic inventories and studies of each of the great regions. The chapters dealing with the several regions, in addition to the purposes already stated, will serve as an exercise in this direction. They may well serve further to point up the dynamics and the realism of historical, economic, and cultural regionalism of the nation too often overlooked in the past. Apology, not excuse, must be the final answer to the unevenness, incompleteness, and imperfections of presentations which cry out for thoroughness and appeal.

Other dilemmas are self-evident. One of these is found in the assumptions of regionalism which, it must be made clear beyond misunderstanding, is not a panacea, a "plan," or a "cause," or an inflexible societal arrangement superimposed upon the nation, but rather the inevitable product of a natural process which emerges as an organic part of the great totality of the national scene. It may be envisaged as economy or new frontier, or utilized as tool or motivation, but it takes its place as only one of the organic structural parts of the nation, capable of functional implementation. This will be clear from our attempt to catalogue some of the standard problems and dilemmas which face the nation and the degree to which the regional setting is of some importance to them. The great significance of regionalism, then, in addition to its explanatory value, is its logical place in the next natural steps in the development of the nation such as to obviate unrealistic all-inclusive mechanical "isms" and plans so often offered as substitutes for fundamental processes and extensions of the American order.

> In the presentation of the material, we have utilized a few special technical arrangements. One of these is the blocked paragraph, as illustrated in this note. Such an arrangement serves several purposes: *to cite authorities, to feature quotations and sources, to give emphasis and vividness, to shift viewpoint and method, to illustrate.* The paragraphs thus arranged are often analogous to the printed tables in a statistical

study, and they also afford a greater opportunity to support the text with details in the language of the original writers.

In the case of the maps and charts we have featured full-page illustrations, more or less analogous to photographs, primarily supplementary to the printed page. In general, these maps and charts do not repeat or duplicate the text, so that in Part III, for instance, the picture of the several regions will be found, not only in the brief outline portraiture and analysis but in the maps, charts, and tables. In both the selection and arrangement of the maps, we have made the dimensions of all maps and charts such that they can be printed on the vertical page. *All maps are superimposed over the base map of the six regions of the nation, the heavy black lines indicating Northeast, Southeast, Northwest, Southwest, Middle States, and Far West, while the shaded lines denote the particular regional divisions described.*

It is desired to acknowledge indebtedness to a larger number of sources than can be satisfactorily done. First must be listed certain seminars and classes at the University of North Carolina, the University of Illinois, the University of Texas, and in the summer sessions of the University of Southern California and of Columbia University, where courses on regional problems and planning have been given. Over a period of years, it is scarcely possible to thank the large number of graduate students at the University of North Carolina by name. While their earlier work, as acknowledged in *Southern Regions of the United States*, was primarily in the field of regional studies, they have also helped greatly to point up these general studies of regionalism. For special assistance, however, Margaret Jarman Hagood, John Maclachlan, Lee Coleman, should be mentioned. At the University of Illinois, Ella Courter, W. G. Piersel, Dwight P. Flanders, Hugh Brodgen, and Alleyne Baumgardner; at the University of Southern California, Mildred Rubin Minter and Edwin Morganroth; and at Columbia, Eugene P. Link.

Special acknowledgment is due Bernice Milburn Moore for her assistance in many ways, and especially for her co-operation in building up several of the chapters and for reading much of the manuscript and checking source titles. For reading and criticizing a number of chapters and for various co-operation, encouragement, and criticism, we are indebted to our colleagues: at the University of North Carolina, Ernest R. Groves, T. J. Woofter, Jr., Guy B. Johnson, Katharine Jocher, Harriet L. Herring, Harold D. Meyer, Roy M. Brown, Lee M. Brooks; and especially to James W. Fesler and Rupert B. Vance for reading the manuscript and for many valuable suggestions. Martha Edwards compiled the digest on population backgrounds. Eugene P. Odum assisted in the chapter on Ecology. A. E. Bevacqua prepared most of the maps. For their unusually proficient secretarial assistance, special thanks are due Belle Mooring and Treva Williams Bevacqua. At the University of Texas, we are indebted to Carl M. Rosenquist, Warner E. Gettys, and Clarence E. Ayres.

Special appreciation is also expressed to Marshall E. Dimock and Lewis Mumford for the reading and criticism of the revised manuscript, to the Institute for Research in Social Science at the University of North Carolina for its continuing support and for permission to use some of the materials of *Southern Regions of the United States*, and to Katharine Jocher for her supervision of the preparation, checking, and reading of all the manuscript.

H. W. O.
H. E. M.

Part I

THE RISE AND INCIDENCE OF AMERICAN REGIONALISM

VARYING CONCEPTS OF THE REGION

A region may be regarded as a spontaneous expression of physical and psychological differences.[1]

Regions are genuine entities, each of which expresses, both natural and cultural differentiation from its neighbors.[1]

An area within which the combination of environmental and demographic factors have created a homogeneity of economic and social structure.[2]

In an area like France with an ancient civilization, a geographical region is defined by an *ensemble de rapports* between man and the natural millieu.[3]

Any one part of a national domain sufficiently unified physiographically and socially, to have a true consciousness of its own customs and ideals, and to possess a sense of distinction from other parts of the country.[4]

A region is an area . . . delineated on a basis of general homogeneity of land character and general homogeneity of occupance.[5]

Regions are areas within which there is significant homogeneity in one or several respects.[6]

A region is a natural-economic unit, and is an expression of areal differentiation in the physical and cultural landscapes.[7]

An area or unit in which the economic and social activities of the population are integrated around a focal and administrative center.[8]

Physical regions, like organic regions, are of many different kinds and may be classified by their individual characteristics such as geologic, geographic, climatic, or ecologic.[9]

A governmental region is an area in which the people are objectively bound together by ties of governmental authority. Its limits have been set by law.[9]

. . . organic regions may be defined roughly as areas within which a higher degree of mutual dependency exists than in relationships outside that area.[9]

A "region" is the geographer's term for an "environmental type" in which "the geographic elements are combined in certain definite and constant relations." [10]

. . . an area, wherein there has grown up one characteristic pattern of human adjustment to environment, one general class of human use of resources and locus,—is a region.[11]

Every region is a domain where many dissimilar beings, artificially brought together, have subsequently adapted themselves to a common existence.[12]

Every region has its unique character to which contribute the features of the soil, atmosphere, plants and man.[13]

. . . an area throughout which a particular set of physical conditions will lead to a particular type of economic life.[13]

. . . geographic areas which have become unified culturally, unified at first economically and later by consensus of thought, social patterns of education, recreation, and other forms of action which serve to distinguish it from other areas.[23]

The dominant theme is the expression of the individuality of the region as the site of a particular group of people and their work.[24]

. . . a complex of land, water, air, plant, animal and man regarded in their special relationship as together constituting a definite, characteristic portion of the Earth's surface.[25]

A region may be described loosely as an area of which the inhabitants instinctively feel themselves a part.[9]

Our personal region is bounded by the environs of our daily life.[9]

Our region is a familiar place, where we know, to some extent, the lay of the land, the traits of the people and their resources, needs and problems.[9]

Region is a name for man's concept of the entity of an area.[9]

The regional concept is based on natural or unrestricted relationships between places and people, as distinguished from political or governmental relationships.[9]

In its inherent nature, and in the common meaning of the word, a region is a territory of indefinite extent.[9]

The regional concept thus embraces two distinct kinds of areas—geologic, geographic, climatic and other physical characteristics and organic regions or areas of human life and movement.[9]

An organic region may thus be described as an area whose people are bound together by mutual dependencies arising from common interests.[9]

Geo-physical regions may be described as areas bounded by definite physical conformations or areas having similar physical characteristics, such as rainfall, temperature, climate.[9]

. . . the region is distinguished by the use to which it is put by its occupants.[14]

A natural region may be defined as any portion of the earth's surface whose physical conditions are homogeneous.[15]

. . . the region as a culture area, "an assemblage of such forms as have interdependence and is functionally differentiated from other areas.[24]

. . . an area which is characterized throughout by similar or closely related surface features, and which is contrasted in these respects with neighboring areas.[17]

. . . those areas that show within their boundaries essential uniformity in dominant physical conditions and consequently in dominant life responses.[18]

It is this tendency of all tribal traits of culture to coincide with economic traits that gives a regional character to culture as a whole.[19]

. . . the region is comprised of a constellation of communities.[20]

A region is generally considered to be an area exhibiting homogeneity in one or more of its aspects, and thus it represents an areal or spatial generalization.[21]

. . . an area where many dissimilar species of inhabitants adapt themselves to a common existence so that the ecological community as a whole keeps on.[22]

A *region* may be defined as an area where nature acts in a roughly uniform manner.[26]

Between the continent and the historic village is an area sometimes larger, sometimes smaller than the political state. It is the human region.[27]

My conception of a region is one in which the vegetation, animal and human life have acquired a character due to a permanent association; to the fact that the struggle for existence had brought about some sort of equilibrium among the competing and co-operating organism.[28]

The above concepts indicate both diversity and a certain agreement with reference to the meanings of regionalism. The authors are: 1. George T. Renner, 2. T. J. Woofter, Jr., 3. Isaiah Bowman, 4. Josiah Royce, 5. R. S. Platt, 6. W. D. Jones, 7. G. H. Smith, 8. R. D. McKenzie, 9. V. B. Stanbery, 10. B. A. Botkin, 11. American Society of Planning Officials, 12. P. Vidal de la Blache, 13. R. E. Dickinson and J. R. Howarth, 14. R. H. Whitbeck, 15. Wolfgang L. G. Joerg, 17. Nevin M. Fenneman, 18. Mabel C. Stark, 19. Clark Wissler, 20. Carl A. Dawson and Warner E. Gettys, 21. National Resources Board, 22. Radhakamal Mukerjee, 23. Kimball Young, 24. Carl O. Sauer, 25. A. J. Herbertson, 26. Stuart Chase, 27. Lewis Mumford, 28. Robert E. Park.

Chapter 1

THE IMPLICATIONS AND MEANINGS OF REGIONALISM

THE theme of American regionalism is, after all, essentially that of a great American Nation, the land and the people, in whose continuity and unity of development, through a fine equilibrium of geographic, cultural, and historical factors, must be found not only the testing grounds of American democracy but, according to many observers, the hope of western civilization. How the new regionalism may be the key to a better understanding of the past and the richer development of the future, to the theoretical study of our society, and to the practical planning of its new frontiers, constitutes the more specific theme of this volume.

Basic to all this is, of course, the new science of the region, a science descriptive of how all societies grow, fundamental to realistic planning, and important in the interrelation and co-ordination of the social sciences and the new co-operation between the physical and the social sciences. The implications and meanings of such regionalism are manifold. From the American viewpoint, it interprets the living society of the historical nation and the quest for political, cultural, and spiritual autonomy. In the generic sense, it magnifies the meaning of the local group in relation to the whole and features the folk-regional society as basic to the growth of cultures. It emphasizes the new realism of the people as the scientific as well as symbolic basic element in modern civilization. From a more practical viewpoint, namely, that of the inventory and planning of modern society, regionalism emerges as an equally definitive economy of balance and equilibrium between conflicting forces. It goes further; it offers a medium and technique of decentralization and redistribution in an age now being characterized as moving toward over-centralization, urbanism, and totalitarianism.

When we come to define the concept of "regionalism," there is the twofold dilemma of interpreting the many concepts and of focusing upon an adequate meaning which is both authentic and realistic. First of all, of course, we assume certain broad societal implications of regionalism such as that it implies "the regional framework of civilization," "the pluralism of America," the natural origins and quality of all folk-life and culture. In this general sense we recall that regionalism is a symbol of America's geographic as opposed to occupational representation; of popular as opposed to class control. It is, therefore, a fact, both product and process, and not something new, arbitrarily fabricated as a panacea. Regionalism, in this general sense, is envisaged for what it is rather than for what it does.

These general meanings are of the greatest importance to the public. "Is there a regional history of America?" asks one group of students. The historians answer that there is. "Is there a regional psychology?" asks another. The literary and governmental folks have found out that there is. "Is there an average America?" asks still another group. Our foreign visitors and the statisticians tell us that there is not. "Is the answer to this question of bigness and technology in relation to the problem of freedom and opportunity in any way bound up in the implications of regionalism?" The regionalist answers that it may be.

Yet we need to go further than this. We need to test the validity of the term "the new science of the region," by which we have in mind a considerable and growing body of knowledge about the region gathered through tested methods of research and study. We have, therefore, presented samplings from the geographers, the anthropologists, the ecologists, the economists, the historians, the political scientists, and the sociologists. On this assumption, then, regionalism through the co-operation and co-ordination of the efforts and techniques of the several sciences and social sciences may actually approximate a methodological approach. Implied in this science of the region is the universal twofold motivation of all science, namely, to discover truth and to attain mastery, both of which are inherent in the new regionalism which, perhaps more than anything else, explains the nation, and may be now utilized in its further planning. This twofold objective of science is implied throughout the book in the dichotomous arrangement—first, the historical and theoretical, and then the illustrations and application through which implementation is assumed. It is in this area that the efforts and techniques of the different sciences may be examined and co-ordinated.

The significance of regionalism as the key to equilibrium is reflected in an extraordinary wide range of situations, such as the conflict between nationalism and internationalism, between sectionalism and federalism, and the imbalance between agrarian and urban life, between agriculture and industry, between individuation and socialization in governmental trends, between a quantity civilization of standardizing forces and a quality world, between machines and men. The significance of regionalism as a technique of decentralization and redistribution is reflected in an equally wide range of examples. Some of these are basic to the decentralization and redistribution of population, of industry, of wealth and capital, of culture, of social pathology, and of bigness, complexity, and technology in general. In all these aspects of regionalism, it is important to note that, whether in the historical explanation of society, in the broader meaning of economy, or in the more specialized meaning of technique, *regionalism assumes no all-inclusive or single exclusive force or panacea; rather, as a comprehensive tool, it assumes approximation and direction in the sum total of achievements of which it is itself a part.*

More immediate and vivid, however, than the science of the region is the reality of actual American regionalism in the United States. Regionalism is no longer merely an academic subject. The theoretical and historical aspects, therefore, become essentially phases of practical importance. For the nation has already been divided into numerous regions for many and varying purposes. There are regions of earlier historical significance. There are regions of newer administrative functions. There are regions of convenience and of necessity. There are regions of government and regions of commerce. There are regions of literary achievement and regions of agricultural adjustment. There are regions of land and of water, of forests and of minerals, of flora and of crops. There are regions of educational institutions and football arrangements; regions of wholesale trade and of Rotary and Kiwanis. There are regions within regions, subregions and districts. Within and among all these and many other manifestations, regionalism becomes a realistic frame of reference for research and study and a practical framework for planning and for adjustment in such areas as population development and policy, standards of living and work, the increase of wealth and well-being, the changing status of race and minority groups, the equalization of opportunity, the development and mastery of new "social frontiers."

Much of the realism of this "American" emphasis upon regionalism flows naturally from the historical backgrounds of the nation which must constitute a chief thread throughout the volume. Rupert B. Vance sees arising from such background "great hordes of America's regions, the number and variety of which are limited only by the frames of reference chosen. On the frontier emerged zones of exploration, of military control, of missionary activity, of the 'long hunter,' fur trapper, Indian trader and squatter. Spanish frontier, French frontier, Indian frontier, Puritan and Tidewater, Fall Line and Appalachians, Old West and Old Northwest, Southwest and Middle Border, California and Oregon County, these are the regions the pioneer process carved out of a virgin continent. Natural areas change into culture-made areas, drainage basins become hydroelectric power zones, biotic areas become types of farming areas, harbor indentations become the zones of port authorities and the list continues *ad infinitum.* Today one may take his choice of physiographic areas, trade areas, types of farming areas, census areas, railroad nets, superpower zones, army corps areas, Federal Reserve Districts, newspaper circulation areas, voting maps, or any of the multitudinous indices gathered by statistical agencies to delimit his regions." [1] Now comes the author of *The Great Plains* challenging America to relegislate so as to adjust its economy to what he calls "the North, the South, and the West. Each will be shown to have a history of its own, a distinct way of life determined by the character both of its inhabitants and of its physical environment, and a fundamental economic structure, which the political, economic, and financial expansion of this country has tended to accentuate." [2]

So abundant are the evidences, so wide the range of application, so far-reaching the implications, so varied and diverse the meanings

[1] Rupert B. Vance, in E. W. Burgess and Herbert Blumer, Editors, *Human Side of Social Planning*, pp. 91-92.

[2] Walter Prescott Webb, *Divided We Stand*, p. 4.

and discussions of this new cultural economy called regionalism that it makes little difference from which angle we approach its general treatment. Perhaps the best approach will be through some current illustrations and through certain rather broad assumptions, prefatory to later characterization and definition. Closely paralleling such illustrations and assumptions will be the organic relationship which regionalism shows to the continuing evolution of man and culture. They will be followed with abundant evidence of the vitality and realism of American regionalism as found in a very large and growing body of literature, in important national, regional, and state developments, and in the increasing importance of regionalism as tool and technic in social planning. Frequent recapitulation will emphasize, alongside current developments and implications, the historical and theoretical foundations with their extraordinarily wide range of documentation basic to the understanding of present postulates and movements.

Perhaps we may best begin with current examples of popular interest and practical implications. Thus our assumption that regionalism is in reality a national economy may be illustrated by William Allen White's characterization of the Supreme Court issue, national of all national issues, as essentially one of regional elements. Pointing out that the United States has more conflicting interests and claims than any other nation, he continues: "First of all, they are questions of region. From the beginning, regional differences have required a compromise." And, again, pointing up certain areal problems of the North, the South, the West, the pioneer frontiers, he continues: "These regions are not merely colored places on the map. They present different views of life. Justice for one region is not justice for the other. Yet a rough approximation of justice for each region must be worked out if all these regions are held together in the bonds of a continental commonwealth." [3] A similar illustration may be cited from the many current realistic discussions of the southern regions of the United States, commonly called "The South." Thus, Dorothy Thompson, speaking before the Union League in New York and pointing to the past isolation of the South as well as to its historical, economic, and cultural conditioning since 1865, is "convinced that the fate of this vast region is the central problem in our whole national

[3] William Allen White, "Supreme Court—or 'Rule by Impulses,'" *The New York Times Magazine*, April 25, 1937, p. 3.

economy."[4] Referring to the historical side, she points out how any policy which leads to the enrichment of one section at the expense of the other, as was the earlier case of the "North" against the "South," must eventually threaten the total economy, and she appeals for national-regional policies to minimize the dangers of a revolting, impoverished mass of people. Pointing to the future, she emphasizes the similar danger of developing these regions, without design, in unwise competition with other regions. So, too, recent filibusters in Congress have accentuated and made vivid the very problem of continuing reintegration of all regions into the changing national fabric. The action of the New York State Legislature turning aside from its own problems to pass the resolution demanding legislation for Florida or Mississippi is sectionalism equally with that of the filibustering senators. The revival of sectionalism in the New York mayoralty campaign of 1937 was illustrative of the same problem. It was perhaps with many of these problems in mind that Mr. Justice Brandeis has expressed the thought that in these southern regions may be found our greatest national problem.

Illustrations of the regional-national approach are abundant. One is that of experimental regionalism in which a given area may be set up as a testing field for the nation. The example which has most frequently been cited, as a way of testing such a postulate, is the TVA. Further illustrations of the growing realization of the significance of regions in the total national economy may be found in many of the proposed experiments and policies advocated by the national government. One is found in the advocacy of planning for river valley regions described in Chapter IV. Another is found in the studies of the Great Plains and the Dust Bowl. Still others are found in the search for satisfactory administrative regions for governmental functions, many examples of which will be cited later. A specific illustration of an unofficial type is that of Secretary Wallace's characterization of the problems of the northeastern agricultural program in the first major agricultural regional conference of his administration. The twelve states of the Northeast, he pointed out, can greatly increase their agricultural efficiency through their own co-operative endeavor. But especially, he pointed out further, they are dependent upon the purchasing power and co-operation of

[4] Dorothy Thompson, address before the "Ladies Night" dinner of the Union League Club, published in *New York Herald Tribune*, April 26, 1937.

other regions of the nation. Citing the great increase of shipments from the Northeast to the Southeast of producers' goods, he pointed out how the purchasing power of the southern farmer and the southern textile worker, for instance, affect the prosperity of the northeastern farmer through the increased production and purchasing power of the manufacturers and people of the Northeast who supply the goods to the purchasing region.

In the subsequent characterization of the several regions of the United States, presented in Chapters XIX-XXIV, many more examples will appear. These bare samplings are adequate for the present to illustrate, perhaps in over-simplified current terms, the general assumptions of regionalism in the practical affairs of the nation. We proceed then to a still broader assumption with reference to both the practical and theoretical significance of regionalism.

Once in every generation or so, in every new period of development, there arises some new movement or economy or motivation through which next stages of development are evolved or through which impending crises are met. So, too, in the broader fields of scholarship and research, of experimentation and study, new concepts arise or old concepts are expanded and revivified in the effort to construct sound theory upon which to base realistic endeavor. The assumption here is that the new regionalism may provide such an economy, technique, and concept at the present time, granting a new science of the region in general, and in America a new realism of the region. These assumptions may be supported by a number of larger implications of regionalism in the present American scene.

Continuing the assumption that regionalism is a key to balance and equilibrium, it is important to note that these constitute not only the motif of social planning but the basic need for all social reconstruction. Such equilibrium is needed not only between and among the several diversified areas of the nation, but between industry and agriculture, between urban and rural life, and between and among the various groups of people who constitute the democracy, since the aim of that democracy is to offer not only each individual but each demotic group full opportunity and representation. Mumford points this up vividly when he headlines these three problems: "the problem of tempo; the problem of equilibrium; the problem of organic balance; in back of them all the problem of human satisfaction and cultural achievement—

these have now become the critical and all-important problems of modern civilization. To face these problems, to evolve appropriate social goals and to invent appropriate social and political instruments for an active attack upon them, and finally to carry them into action: here are new outlets for social intelligence, social energy, social good will." [5]

In the search for this equilibrium, regionalism represents both a philosophy and a technique of opportunity and representation. The geographic and areal, the local, the racial, the civic representation in an enduring democracy must be somehow co-ordinate with individual representation. Democracy assumes opportunity and representation for the individual, but it is too often overlooked that the same guarantee applies to the group or state or race or region. This is especially significant in the problem of the distribution of wealth, in which regional capacities and regional needs are of the greatest importance.

In this connection there may be mentioned the rigorous demand for rural representation and agricultural parity in the new national planning. The conscious desire for representation of the rural regions was well illustrated in an incident which occurred soon after the passage of the Wagner Labor Act. An enthusiastic and distinguished speaker over the radio was eloquently congratulating the nation upon the fact that now at last capital and labor, employer and employee, would move arm in arm down the halls of time dictating America's new destiny. To which the leader of one of the great farm organizations replied: "The heck you will; agriculture must certainly have something to say, won't it?" Thus is set in new perspective rural regionalism over against urban and metropolitan regionalism. The principle of equalization of opportunity, wherever found, is always valid in the democratic process.

Regionalism, again, to point up motivations of the past, represents the philosophy and technique of self-help, self-development, and initiative in which each areal unit is not only aided, but is committed to the full development of its own resources and capacities. This, on the one hand, is in contrast to dependency by any region upon the nation or to submarginality as compared with other regions; and, on the other hand, to exploitation from any sources from with-

[5] Lewis Mumford, *Technics and Civilization,* pp. 430-433.

out. It assumes that the key to the redistribution of wealth and the equalization of opportunity will be found in the capacity of each region to create wealth and, through new reaches of consumption of commodities, maintain that capacity and retain that wealth in well-balanced production and consumption programs.

> Regionalism is thus essentially an economy not of scarcity but of abundance, to the end that all the people may have access to adequate food, clothing, housing, tools, occupational opportunity—an accomplishment to be made possible through regional techniques of use as well as production. Special adaptation to resources and people will be the key to both production and consumption. Furthermore, regionalism represents an economy of specialized industry as well as decentralized industry, an economy offering an opportunity for the several regions not only to realize upon their own peculiar resources, but also to do so with minimum competition with other regions. Thus, if the Southwest can grow cotton and tung trees and can evolve new industries for developing its resources and increasing its wealth without competing with the great states north of it in cattle and corn and hogs, the benefits are apparent. If the Southeastern states can create millions of dollars of new wealth through hundreds of processing plants to make starch from sweet potatoes, paper pulp from pines, and other products now imported or representing scarcity, then regionalism becomes a very realistic and practical national economy.

Another broad assumption is that decentralization is inherent in regionalism. If this is true, one implication of regionalism may well be the opposite of the present tendency toward urbanism, centralization, and concentration of power and wealth. Regionalism as the natural mode of decentralization rests upon the logic of earlier evolutionary processes. Cultures grow from beginnings outward. The margins of bigness are the occasion for redistribution. An economy of decentralized industry is usually cited as the most common example of decentralization. Here regionalism offers what many students consider the best "way on" in so large and complex a nation as the United States. It is not merely decentralization as found in metropolitan regionalism. It comprehends also the foundation of small industries—industries adapted to village and town—and, through farm chemurgic and other inventive aids, it promotes a wide distribution over the nation. It comprehends part-time industry and planning. It is not merely the regional mercantilism of Professor Gras and others; it is not merely Stuart Chase's solution of "rich land, poor land," through economic regionalism, or Lewis Mumford's economic regionalism in *Technics and Civilization.* It is all of these and more, a totality in which all past historical experience —including such lessons as are provided by French, German, and Polish regionalism—is utilized in the projection of regional planning of the future.

> Of great significance is the culture economy of regionalism through which the decentralization of people, of culture, and of pathology, may be attained in the new frontiers of American life. Here are involved the dilemmas of megapolitan culture emphasized by Geddes and Spengler and the more immediate crises of unemployment and relief in great cities. Yet, again, such decentralization does not apply only to the metropolitan regions or the planned towns and communities 'round about the great cities. It takes into account the whole phenomenon of the new mobility of people, the migrations to and from cities. It comprehends movements to and from farms, providing technical ways for the reintegration of agrarian culture in American life. It points to the development of new frontiers of American culture, which may provide new centers of health and recreation, of opportunity for urban decentralization where surplus wealth may be expended or normal cultures develop in the new Southwest or the changing Northwest with their great water resources, or the great playgrounds of New England and the Southeast, or in the multitudinous parks and playgrounds and public domains of a great nation. Regionalism is, therefore, the essential symbol of the new American physical and cultural frontier.

Again, regionalism provides an economy for the decentralization of political power and administrative procedure in government and business. As such, it transcends the older "pure" states' rights and safeguards the people from federal over-centralization. In administrative procedure it provides for economy and efficiency in governmental and social services as well as representative opportunity for production and distribution of goods. Thus, Burdett G. Lewis says, "Regionalism strikes an effective and natural medium between uncontrolled individualism among the states and complete centralization of administration at Washington." Regionalism represents also an economy of essential flexibility so fundamental in an American democracy.

From the historical and cultural viewpoint regionalism is reflected in Sir William Beveridge's verdict concerning the United States. Said he: "If I had to sum up my impressions, I should think in terms of drama; I should choose a parody from Pirandello: 'Six Americas in search of a faith.'" Our six great regions, he decided, are characterized by "profound divisions of race and history, with opposed economic interests, with different ways of life and thought." So, regionalism represents an essential minimum tool for planning, through which not only administrative balance and efficiency may be attained but the contributions of science, of engineering, of chemurgy, and of all the new evolving social techniques may be tested in living, areal, cultural laboratories.

Finally, a study of historical developments and of the universal patterns of societal evolution will show the supreme practical validity of regionalism. This does not mean only that in America the nation has grown and grown from expanding domain and has evolved from earlier local and sectional patterns to current regional and national design. It means this and more. It means also that all cultures and civilizations have evolved logically from regional beginnings. The local regional group represents the elemental unit in all societies whether that of the oriental city, the medieval city, or the empire. Cultures and peoples, nations and empires grow from regional sustentation areas out into expanded entities. It is not possible, therefore, to understand or to direct society except through the regional approach. Somewhere within the realistic bounds of regional science and arrangement will be found both the elements and tools of any great totality and unity of national development.

The broad assumptions of this theory—and it should be reaffirmed that the most practical thing in the world is dependable theory—may be supported by studies made in wide and varied fields. We may mention, as evidence of the distinguished heritage of the concept of regionalism in both the natural and the social sciences, the organic and functional regions of the geographers, the structural and functional regions of the ecologists, the culture regions of the anthropologists, the cultural determinism of the sociologists, the mercantile regionalism of the economists, the administrative regionalism of the political scientists, the aesthetic and literary regionalism of the arts, in addition to that large cataloguing of composite world regions and peoples symbolic of man's long, hard, historical road up to now.

We have presented enough of this broad sweeping picture of the range and implications of regionalism to indicate something of its organic nature and significance and to show that *regionalism is in reality the opposite of its most common interpretation, namely, localism, sectionalism, or provincialism.* We have yet to approach more specific and authentic definitions of regionalism, first through the cataloguing of its general attributes; second, through illustrative definitions of the many types of regionalism; and, third, through the cataloguing of the many concepts which are *not* regionalism. First, then, we continue the further characterization of regionalism by pointing out certain attributes of the region, regionalism being defined here generally as the science of the region or the culture economy of which the region is the basic unit.

Beginning, then, with the elemental factor of space, the region is, of course, first of all an area, a geographic unit with limits and bounds. Regionalism is, therefore, an areal or spatial generalization. This is true, whether it be the geographer's region, the geologist's region, the ecologist's region, the anthropologist's region, or any other. This attribute may be illustrated by a large number and variety of definitions from authentic sources, samplings of which will be presented subsequently. Yet, in the second place, the region differs from the mere locality or pure geographic area in that it is characterized not so much by boundary lines and actual limits as it is by flexibility of limits, by extension from a center, and by fringe or border margins which separate one area from another. Climatic zones, the range of rainfall, the gradually changing types of soil and configuration of land, and the diversity of natural resources are examples showing how relative and flexible regional delimitation is. So, too, in the economic, political, and cultural life of a nation, the region finds its boundaries overlapping state lines or rivers and valleys in accordance with the nature of the common indices basic to the regional homogeneity in question. R. D. McKenzie points out that a region "may or may not conform to the boundaries of a natural unit. The base of the region becomes tenuous and changeable with variations in influence from the center." [6] The third attribute of the region is some degree

[6] R. D. McKenzie, in National Resources Committee's *Regional Factors in National Planning and Development*, December 1935, p. 147.

of homogeneity in a number of selected characteristics. This is true of the geographic region, which is characterized by closely related surface features and is contrasted in these respects with neighboring areas, or which shows essential uniformity "in dominant physical conditions and consequently in dominant life responses."[7] Likewise the cultural, economic, administrative, or other region is one which exhibits homogeneity in a clustering of selected units of measurement or aspects of its life. Even the simplest of spatial regions must be characterized by some limiting quality or qualities.

The definitive nature of the region and the aspects of its homogeneity will be determined by the fourth attribute of the region, namely, some structural or functional aspect or aspects through which the region is to be denominated. Sometimes the "function" or purposive nature of the region seems little more than a "class" of similarities. Yet the geographer's region may be delimited not only by homogeneity in climate or rainfall, but by land use or by research objectives in which the region serves as a workable unit of inquiry. The economic region may be characterized not only by resources but by accessibility, transportation, power. There may therefore be, generally speaking, as many regions as there are purposes or functions available.

Yet there must be a limit to the multiplicity of regions, so that in general a fifth attribute must be found in the relative, composite homogeneity of the largest number of factors for the largest number of purposes in view, to the end that the region may be a practical, workable unit susceptible of both definition and utilization. This is manifestly of the greatest importance and may be illustrated in the case of, let us say, the geographic regions of the world or the administrative regions of a great nation which must have a reasonable limit as parts of a whole, regardless of the possibility of academic delineation through manifest homogeneity of a very few characteristics. It is possible to catalogue seven or eight hundred soil regions in the United States, yet for all practical composite purposes such a classification is not practicable.

This brings us to the two final and key attributes of the region. The geographic area, characterized by a large degree of homogeneity in selected traits, does not in itself constitute a region in the more

[7] Cf. Radhakamal Mukerjee, *Regional Sociology, passim.*

comprehensive and scientific sense. The geographic area, on the one hand, may find its chief characteristic one of isolation and separateness, and, on the other hand, it may be a specialized area devoid of the joint indices of geography and culture or the frame of reference for societal study or planning. A key attribute of the region is, therefore, that it must be a *constituent unit in an aggregate whole or totality*. Inherent in the region as opposed to the mere locality or the isolated section is the essence of unity of which it can exist only as a part. Thus, "the regionalist sees the region as a unit, a microcosm of society, a set of factors combining to form a regional pattern; and believes that these elements can be understood only when conceived as a part of the whole." [8] In this more vital sense urbanism or metropolitanism is not regionalism in so far as urban centers seek their own ends regardless of relationship to other great centers or in opposition to national or rural ends. In agreement with this view, Lewis Mumford points out that "regionalism is the antithesis of false cosmopolitanism." This point is manifestly of the greatest importance. If some of the social scientists posit the thesis that progress consists in the urbanization of the nation, and if others protest concentration and urbanism, it must be clear that there is conflict worthy of more study than we yet have. Here regionalism will have considerable significance in the interrelation of the sciences in such research. Regionalism is also important in the realistic breaking away from the old sectionalism in American life—a radical departure necessary to the attainment of equilibrium and unity in the national culture on what are often called the social frontiers.

The final key attribute is found in the organic nature of the region. A region has organic unity not only in its natural landscape, but in that cultural evolution in which the age-long quartette of elements are at work—namely, the land and the people, culturally conditioned through time and spatial relationships. Thus, Professor Aronovici defines regionalism as "the study of the relation of man to geographic areas, and the potentialities which this relation represents in terms of human welfare and progress. The history of tribes, nations, and races is one long record of regional realism, in terms of security and productivity, sought through expansion and contraction of regional

[8] Cf. Harry E. Moore, *What Is Regionalism?*

boundaries."[9] So, too, Clark Wissler writes that "one cannot read anthropological discussions without becoming aware that the procedure is based on a belief in regional differences in social behavior and that social evolution itself is regional."[10] From such an organic implication it seems possible to characterize regionalism as a cultural *Gestalt*, in which are balanced all the constituent factors of culture in the making.[11]

Before turning to the further support of these assumptions and implications, attributes and illustrations, with authentic definitions from other sources, it is important to emphasize the great diversity of usage and meaning of the concept of regionalism in recent literature both in professional journals and in popular discussions. Although these will be discussed at length in the several respective chapters, it may be well to call attention here to three or four of the most common examples. The multiplicity of conflicting meanings and their varied application give emphasis to the need for as clear a presentation of the subject as possible.

A common usage is the very general one of making metropolitan regionalism synonymous with the total comprehensive, organic regionalism which has evolved so rapidly within recent years into a new national economy. This is illustrated in perhaps more than half of the articles dealing with regionalism and regional planning listed in current bibliographies, including some of those current in 1937. This is pointed out well by Carol Aronovici, who says: "It is unfortunate that in this country the terms region and regional planning have been loosely used, so that metropolitan planning has become interchangeable with regional planning. Metropolitanism and metropolitan planning apply only to the relation between a given center of population and its outlying areas, while regionalism and regional planning should embrace the study and development of all geographic entities. . . ."[12]

A second type of usage has been that which assumes that regionalism and sectionalism are synonymous and that the essence of regionalism and regional planning is to be found in the objectives of local and provincial study or in the practical ends of local development,

[9] Carol Aronovici, "Regionalism: A New National Economy," *Columbia University Quarterly*, December 1936, p. 268.

[10] Clark Wissler, "The Culture Area Concept in Social Anthropology," *American Journal of Sociology*, XXXII, p. 882.

[11] Cf. Harry E. Moore, *op. cit.*

[12] Aronovici, *op. cit.*, p. 271.

or at most in a sort of regional mercantilism. Professor Turner's pioneer work on sectionalism is often cited as the record of American regionalism. Manifestly, as will be shown in Chapter II, this is an unfortunate confusion of meanings. This distinction between regionalism and sectionalism is of the greatest importance at the present time. By regionalism we mean a new American social economy and societal determinism, as opposed to the early American sectionalism and geographic, economic determinism. Such regionalism is also opposed to the traditional literary localism. Indeed, perhaps the first distinction between the new realistic regionalism and the older sectionalism is that regionalism assumes first, last, and always a totality composed of the several areal and cultural units, a great national unity and integrated culture in which each region exists as a region solely as a component unit in the whole. Sectionalism, on the other hand, always assumes isolated, segregated areal divisions with potential completeness in themselves and looked upon as separate entities. This was the magnificent picture of Frederick Jackson Turner's sectionalism in American life. This was James Truslow Adams' *America's Tragedy*.

A third popular usage is that found almost universally in the discussions of literary regionalism, which usually connotes location and provincialism, as will be pointed out in Chapter VII. Manifestly, such regionalism is in reality a sort of sentimental romanticism for the local area or for the historical period. No matter how much there is of this sort of thing or how real or how productive of certain results, it is not scientific regionalism. A notable exception to this has been the constant reiteration of William Allen White that, for instance, the great American novel, as a representative of the great American totality, must logically be a regional product. Here it is clear that the significance of the local area or culture in regionalism is found in its contribution through delimitable phenomena and interrelated study to the larger study of society and cultures. Regionalism involves the local; but much more. It involves the past, but not merely the past. The local becomes a medium for the understanding and characterization of the universal. The past becomes material for the study of the present and the future.

We have already implied that another basis of confusion has grown up through the various conceptions of geographic and cultural areas as symbols of geographic determinism or economic determinism, whereas genuine regionalism is in reality a larger societal determinism in which all the factors of life are balanced in harmony with the natural heritage. As such, it affords new living laboratories for the study of culture and for the development of peoples.

Professor Franz Boas gives a clear critique of this phase of regionalism when he writes: "Political theories have also been built upon the assumption that single forces determine the course of cultural history. Most important among these are the theories of geographical and economic determinism. Geographical determinism means that geographical environment controls the development of culture; economic determinism that the economic conditions of life shape all the manifestations of early culture and of complex civilization. It is easy to show that both theories ascribe an exaggerated importance to factors that do play an important part in the life of man, but that are each only one of many determinant elements. The study of the cultural history of any particular area shows clearly that geographical conditions by themselves have no creative force and are certainly no absolute determinants of culture." [13]

We come now to our next task of presenting further representative and authentic concepts and definitions of the region and regionalism in support of our previous assumptions and characterizations. We select only a few under each general division, citing for more exhaustive study the catalogue of concepts blocked in on page 2. First, the geographic area comes nearest to epitomizing the physical region. That is, it is an area in which natural features constitute the determining criteria within spatial limits.

Thus, Joerg defines the natural region simply as "any portion of the earth's surface whose physical conditions are homogeneous." [14] So Herbertson characterizes the region as "a complex of land, water, air, plant, animal, and man regarded in their spatial relationship as together constituting a definite portion of the earth's surface." [15] Fenneman's region is "an area characterized throughout by similar or closely re-

[13] Franz Boas, *Anthropology and Modern Life*, p. 229.

[14] Wolfgang L. G. Joerg, "The Subdivision of North America into Natural Regions," *Annals of the Association of American Geographers*, IV, 56-57.

[15] A. J. Herbertson, "The Major Natural Regions: An Essay in Systematic Geography," *Geographical Journal*, XXV, 300.

lated surface features, and which is contrasted in these respects with neighboring areas."[16] Another good definition is one from Professor Aronovici, which combines the areal and homogeneity indices. The term regionalism, he says, used in its broadest implications, refers to "a geographic area or areas which a given civilization-standard of a people seems to require for the fulfillment of its aspirations through material resources."[17] Two others are selected from the many excellent characterizations of the geographic region by Isaiah Bowman. In the first example he points out that "most branches of knowledge have to deal with *area.* From this simple fact and its multiplied bearings flows one of the most important values of geography in studies that deal with mankind. In going from the abstraction, *area,* to specific regions, geography provides: (1) a framework of physical facts, region by region, the world around; (2) unifying explanations of physical phenomena in terms of laws evolved through experimental methods or by the elaborate testing of hypotheses following both inductive and deductive methods; (3) an identification of regional characteristics, physical and human, through detailed statistical methods and by field notation; (4) a comparison of regions with the object of widening the generalities of physiography and human experience that have their bases in local and detailed observation."[18]

The geographers have long set up the region as a divisional means for study. A second quotation from President Bowman reinforces the relational significance of the geographic region to the study of culture. "We generalize real men and real places," he writes, "by grouping them according to likenesses of function or location. To think of groups is at once to be aware of the relationships between groups. A given group has, like any one of its members, a limited and particular set of conditions to face. These conditions are spread over an area or region. It is the purpose of the geographer to study limiting or significant environmental conditions in their regional association, basing his understanding upon physical examinations on the one hand and upon human reactions or relationships on the other."[19] This concept leads to the twofold objective of seeking knowledge of both land and men, of areas and cultures.

[16] Nevin M. Fenneman, "Physiographic Boundaries within the United States," *Annals of the Association of American Geographers,* IV, 86.

[17] Aronovici, *op. cit.,* p. 268.

[18] Isaiah Bowman, *Geography in Relation to the Social Sciences,* pp. 145-146.

[19] *Ibid.,* p. 24.

An excellent characterization of this interpretation may be found in V. B. Stanbery's studies of regional planning. In one of these he distinguishes between the geo-physical and the organic region, defining each as follows: "Geo-physical regions may be described as areas bounded by definite physical conformations or areas having similar physical characteristics, such as rainfall, temperature, climate. Physical regions, like organic regions, are of many different kinds and may be classified by their individual characteristics such as geologic, geographic, climatic, or ecologic." On the other hand, "organic regions may be defined roughly as areas within which a higher degree of mutual dependency exists than in relationships outside that area." "An organic area," he says further, "may thus be described as an area whose people are bound together by mutual dependencies arising from common interests. In its inherent nature, and in the common meaning of the word, a region is a territory of indefinite extent. Its boundaries cannot be sharply delineated; nor its essence captured by categorical definition. Human activity is not confined to any one area, and, hence an organic region cannot be entirely self-contained." [20]

Next, a few definitions of the functional character of the region will indicate both the nature of regions and the methods of their delimitation. This functional characterization may be based upon research or administrative factors or upon economic character or purpose or upon as many functions and characteristics as may be desired. Thus, McKenzie considers "a region to be a geographic (areal) unit in which the economic and social activities of the population are integrated around a focal economic and administrative center." [21] Two statements from the findings of the American Society of Planning Officials will point out other functional aspects of regionalism. Thus, "Regionalism, as a *motif* for planning, seems to offer manifold promises, the road to which involves several definite steps: (a) identifying the regionalism which is present; (b) demarking the area which encompasses it; (c) determining the needs of this area; (d) making a plan and fitting it to the area in question; (e) implementing the plan in terms of state and federal sovereignties." Again, ". . . our main concern is to identify the fundamental regionalism which is the core or nucleus of the area. Similarly, our major

[20] V. B. Stanbery, *An Approach to Regional Planning*, pp. 6, 7, 4, 3.

[21] R. D. McKenzie, in National Resources Committee's *Regional Factors in National Planning and Development*, December 1935, p. 146.

objective becomes that of preserving the area's essential unity and homogeneity as a frame for program formulation and for the execution of those programs. Thus the paramount emphasis is placed upon the problem area and not the states, although the sovereignty of the latter is not impaired."[22]

Further discussion of the structural and functional nature of the region will be found in the several chapters dealing with metropolitan regionalism, administrative regionalism, river valley regions, the economist's region, the ecologist's region, the political scientist's region, and others. So, too, the functional nature of the region appears in our catalogue of types of regional planning on the functional level, such as land planning, water planning, conservation planning, economic planning, cultural planning, in each of which the regional implications and variations constitute a fundamental part. Still further illustrations of the unity, compositeness and organic nature of the region may serve also to recapitulate the various characterizations and definitions of the region already given. B. A. Botkin, searching for the total background of regionalism upon which to base a general literary regionalism gives the following summary: "A 'region' is the geographer's term for an 'environmental type' in which 'the geographic elements are combined in certain definite and constant relations.' From the concept of the natural region—physiographic, geological, climatic, biotic, etc.—the human geographer, correlating social with organic and inorganic factors, has developed the concept of the cultural landscape and the human use region. From human geography, in turn, the sociologist and the ethnologist have derived the concepts of the sociological region and the culture area. In the natural, social, and engineering sciences, 'regionalism' as a discipline has not only opened up new research leads but supplied the technique of regional planning."[23]

Marshall E. Dimock, in his studies of the regional factors in national planning and development, characterizes regionalism as "a clustering of environmental, economic, social and governmental factors to such an extent that a distinct consciousness of separate identity within the whole, a need for autonomous planning, a manifestation of cultural peculiarities, and a desire for administrative freedom, are theoretically recognized and actually put into effect. Regional-

[22] *Planning for City, State, Region and Nation.* Proceedings of the Joint Conference on Planning, 1936, pp. 108, 110.

[23] B. A. Botkin, "Regionalism: Cult or Culture?", *The English Journal*, XXV, No. 3, p. 181.

ism is something which remains to be realized and further developed, as well as a phenomenon which has already appeared and taken form. In one sense, and perhaps the best one, regionalism is a way of life; it is a self-conscious process."[24] In another contribution, he points out that "political boundaries, sectional loyalties, climates of opinion are just as real (although admittedly more complicated and less predictable) as water, land and vegetation. . . . Regional factors are in part measurable and predictable; in part they are traditional, contrived and emotional. Whether regionalism results from the growth of a sense of community, in turn dependent upon common traditions, interests and aspirations, or whether it results from man's rational analysis of economic and governmental problems needing solution, it is none the less regionalism."[25]

So Lucien Brocard points out that, "To an even greater extent than the nation as a whole, the regional economy depends for its complete development upon continuous contact with other regions, so that, by co-operating with them, it may facilitate the movement of commodities and men. It is necessary to combine with the complex economic development already discussed a certain geographical specialization of industry, by means of which the various communities may accentuate the prosperity of one another and of the whole nation."[26] Still two other types of characterization are those of Lewis Mumford on artistic regionalism and R. K. Gooch on French regionalism. Mumford features "a soundly bottomed regionalism [which] can achieve cosmopolitan breadth without losing its integrity or virtue; it is only a sick and puling regionalism that must continually gaze with enamored eyes upon its own face, praising its warts and pimples as beauty marks. For a genuine regional tradition lives by two principles. One is, *cultivate whatever you have*, no matter how poor it is; *it is at least your own.* The other is, *seek elsewhere for what you do not possess;* absorb whatever is good wherever you may find it; make it your own."[27] Gooch's regionalism of France "stands somewhere between administrative decentralization and federalism. It touches on both; and if a more rigid logic envisages three schools of thought and three movements, a basic similarity none the less exists and a common princi-

[24] National Resources Committee, *Regional Factors in National Planning and Development,* December 1935, p. 138.

[25] Marshall E. Dimock, unpublished manuscript.

[26] Lucien Brocard, "Regional Economy and Economic Regionalism," *Annals of the American Academy of Political and Social Science,* CLXII, 84-85.

[27] Lewis Mumford, "Orozco in New England," *The New Republic,* LXXX, 235.

ple underlies all three. In this perspective, French Regionalism, which has been called *un fédéralisme très atténué*, is only a special, though a very important, manifestation of world federalism." [28]

It yet remains to point up two other aspects of regionalism basic to the general picture. The one is the rise of American regionalism through the chronological and evolutionary development of the nation from area to area, from frontier to frontier, and ultimately from section to region. The other is to focus upon American regionalism as a tool and area of planning, especially as it has been featured by the National Resources Committee in *Regional Factors in National Planning* and in the analysis of regional factors involved in much of the federal program within recent years. Since both of these aspects will be treated adequately in separate chapters a few illustrations will suffice to present the case.

We may begin with the historical development of the nation in which its Atlantic seaboard states early tended to divide themselves into North and South while the great diversity of the land made regional entities a natural product. Thus, James Truslow Adams points out: "The Northeast of rolling hills and low mountains, wholly covered with forest and dotted with a thousand gem-like lakes, had nothing in common with the waterless cactus-spotted deserts of the Southwest; nor had the Southeast of low-lying sandy pine barrens, humid swamps, and slow-moving mud-brown rivers with the Northwest of bright cascades, snow-capped mountains, and highlands reaching down to the blue Pacific. There was equally striking contrast between the wide horizons of the ocean-like plains and the endless complexity of the barren and forbidding western mountains. The climate was also of infinite variety, from the tropical and moist heat of the low-lying gulf coasts to the dry air of the high western plateaus or the long cold of the Maine winters and the blizzard-swept plains of the northern central valley." [29] So New England "is the geographical region east of the Hudson valley. It is the historical region of the Yankee. It is the ethical region of the New England conscience and of Puritanism. It is an industrial region separate from all other industrial regions, a recreational region of rugged coast, tumbled mountains, crystal clear streams and lakes, sloping orchards, and white-pine forests." [30] Again, Lewis Mumford has pointed out the natural evolution of regional

[28] R. K. Gooch, *Regionalism in France*, p. 17.
[29] James Truslow Adams, *The Epic of America*, p. 5.
[30] W. R. Greely, "Regional and City Planning in New England," in James Truslow Adams, *et al.*, *New England's Prospect*, p. 408.

units in the nation. He says: "Before the Civil War there had grown up in the United States a number of differentiated regions, each of which had its characteristic polity and art and way of life. New England, Virginia, South Carolina, Louisiana, had distinct and special traditions, and in New England and New York particularly the poetic cycle of regionalism had begun: Hawthorne, Thoreau, Emerson, were New Englanders first; and Americans by the grace of certain political connections which they neither repudiated altogether nor over-valued; and although Whitman and Melville were in their conscious political philosophies identified with 'these states' as a unity, one sees in their work the local influence of the brisk cosmopolitan part of New York, adventuring out to other parts of the world, or, on shore, welcoming each new cargo of men and goods." [31] Finally, to select one other example, A. B. Hulbert continues the picture of the ever westward movement of regional frontiers: "The story of the American Republic, territorially speaking, has been the story of the planting of one 'West' after another, from the Atlantic to the Pacific; and, in a measure the political history of our Republic has been the story of reactions of 'Wests' on 'Easts,' or vice versa, with reference to almost every problem of national life. Therefore what was 'West' and what was 'East' was almost always, and is yet, a matter of personal viewpoint. To many a typical 'Down Easterner' anything beyond the Hudson is the 'West' today; to the sons of the Middle Border nothing is really 'West' until the Great Plains are reached; while a friend of mine, hailing from Bellingham, Washington, remarked to me within the year: 'When I cross the Rockies and get off the train at Denver I can tell where I am by my nose–it just *smells* East.' " [32]

The classical story of American sectional development is, of course, found in Frederick Jackson Turner's contributions on the influence of both the frontier and of sections in American life. Since a separate chapter will be devoted to the general theme of sections and regions, it is necessary here only to point up Professor Turner's portraiture of the nation as a series of sections to the end that the historical picture may be clear and that the fundamental difference between sectionalism and regionalism may be emphasized.

"The frontier and the section are two of the most fundamental factors in American history," wrote Professor Turner. "The frontier is a moving section, or rather a form of society, determined by the reac-

[31] Lewis Mumford, "The Theory and Practice of Regionalism," *Sociological Review,* Vol. 20, p. 137.

[32] A. B. Hulbert, *Frontiers, the Genius of American Nationality*, pp. 127-128.

tions between the wilderness and the edge of expanding settlement; the section is the outcome of the deeper-seated geographical conditions interacting with the stock which settled the region. Sections are more important than states in shaping the underlying forces of American history. . . . The West was a migrating region, a stage of society rather than a place. Each region reached in the process of expansion from the coast had its frontier experience, was for a time 'the West,' and when the frontier passed on to new regions, it left behind, in the older areas, memories, traditions; an inherited attitude toward life that persisted long after the frontier had passed by. But while the influence of the frontier permeated East as well as West, by survival of the pioneer psychology and by the reaction of the Western ideals and life upon the East, it was in the newer regions, in the area called the West at any given time, that frontier traits and conceptions were most in evidence. This 'West' was more than 'the frontier' of popular speech. It included also the more populous transitional zone adjacent, which was still influenced by pioneer traditions and where economic society had more in common with the newer than with the older regions." And again: "We must remember that each of the sections of this continental nation—New England, the Middle States, the Southeast, the Southwest, the Middle West, the Great Plains, the Mountain States, the Pacific Coast—has its own special geographical qualities, its own resources and economic capacities, and its own rival interest, partly determined in the days when the geological foundations were laid down." Once again, "We in America are in reality a federation of sections rather than of states." Yet, "American sectionalism has been very inadequately dealt with by our historians. Impressed by the artificial political boundary lines of states, they have almost entirely given their attention either to national or to state history, or to the broad division of North and South, overlooking the fact that there are several natural, economic and social sections that are fundamental in American historical development. As population extended itself, it flowed into various physiographic provinces, some of them comparable in size and resources, not only to the greater nations of Europe, but even to some of the great empires that have from time to time been formed by combinations of these nations. The American physical map may be regarded as a map of potential nations and empires, each to be conquered and colonized, each to rise through stages of development, each to achieve a certain social and industrial unity, each to possess certain fundamental assumptions, certain psychological traits, and each to interact with the others, and in combination to form that United States. . . ." [33]

[33] Frederick Jackson Turner, *The Significance of Sections in American History*, p. 183.

It may be pointed out here, too, that sectionalism in the nation is analogous to nationalism in the world at large, each signifying isolation and self-sufficiency as opposed to co-operative participation and unity. Thus, Professor Hayes' characterization of the evils of nationalism might well apply to sectionalism. The attributes which he ascribes to nationalism include an intolerant attitude and behavior; belief in the imperial mission of one's own nationality; carrying a chip on the shoulder; dwelling on the memory of past wars; a willingness to be led by self-styled patriots; a diffidence about thinking differently from others; a spirit of exclusiveness; ignorance of others; and gross pride.[34]

The significance of the new trend from sectionalism to regionalism is reflected also in the growing recognition of the reality of the region in all national planning. Thus, regionalism and regional planning often become synonymous, so that through the concept and techniques of regional planning we may recapitulate again various aspects of American regionalism. Frankfurter and Landis emphasize the factor of equilibrium and balance between the states and the federal power: "The overwhelming difficulties confronting modern society must not be at the mercy of the false antithesis embodied in the shibboleths 'States' Rights' and 'National Supremacy.' . . . Our regions are realities. Political thinking must respond to those realities. Instead of leading to parochialism, it will bring a fresh ferment of political thought whereby national aims may be achieved through various forms of political adjustment."[35]

John Orchard in *Regional Factors in National Planning and Development* describes the region for planning purposes: "As I see the problem, the optimum region for social and economic planning should possess certain characteristics: (1) There should be some unifying core (problem or interest); (2) its area should include all the territory tributary to the core; (3) there should be an absence of serious conflicting interests within the areas; (4) the region should not be so diversified that it will place too great a burden upon the ability and training of the planners. It seems that the geographic region most

[34] Carlton J. H. Hayes, *Essays on Nationalism*, p. 275; see also his *The Historical Evolution of Modern Nationalism*.

[35] Felix Frankfurter and J. M. Landis, "The Compact Clause of the Constitution," *Yale Law Journal*, XXXIV, 729.

nearly includes the above characteristics." [36] Benton Mackaye characterizes regional planning in terms of the composite region: "Regional planning . . . consists in the attempt at discovering the plans of Nature for the attainment of man's ends upon the earth; it visualizes industry as the servant of culture; and its chief concern is the guidance within a region of 'the flow of civilization.' . . . This flow may consist of electric fluid, of lumber, of wheat, of beef, or dairy products." It may consist of the "flow of population, . . . of housing and living facilities." [37] Another characterization from *Regional Factors in National Planning and Development* points out that: "It is patent . . . that the whole meaning of regional planning is to devise a cultural pattern which will fit a large areal unit, and that the qualities inherent in the area not only dictate in large part the features of that plan, but also its territorial extent." [38] The region for national planning should represent organic relationship as well as organic unity in such fields as transport, land use, recreation, power, use of water, redevelopment of forests, conservation of mineral resources, etc. Finally, two popular passages from Lewis Mumford give varied interpretations of regional planning: "Regional planning asks not how wide an area can be brought under the aegis of the metropolis, but how the population and civic facilities can be distributed so as to promote and stimulate a vivid, creative life throughout a whole region—a region being any geographic area that possesses a certain unity of climate, soil, vegetation, industry and culture. The regionalist attempts to plan such an area so that all its sites and resources, from forest to city, from highland to water level, may be soundly developed, and so that population will be distributed so as to utilize, rather than to nullify or destroy, its natural advantages. It sees people, industry and the land as a single unit. In sum, regional planning does not mean the planning of big cities beyond their present areas; it means the reinvigoration and rehabilitation of whole regions so that the products of culture and civilization, instead of being confined to a prosperous minority in the congested centers, shall be available to everyone at every point in a region where the physical basis for a cultivated life can be laid down." [39]

All these and other aspects of regionalism will be discussed and illustrated in the chapters which follow. It remains to emphasize at

[36] John Orchard, in National Resources Committee's *Regional Factors in National Planning and Development*, December 1935, p. 148.

[37] Benton Mackaye, "Regional Planning," *Sociological Review*, XX, No. 4, pp. 298-299.

[38] National Resources Committee, *Regional Factors in National Planning and Development*, December 1935, p. 20.

[39] Lewis Mumford, "Regions to Live In," *Survey*, Vol. 54, No. 3, pp. 151-152.

this point the importance and difficulty of delineating the major composite regions of the United States through which the greatest degree and homogeneity for the largest possible purposes may be attained. These regions, flexible and susceptible to adjustment, may then constitute the basis for uniform study and planning and for the vivid portraiture of the nation both for scientific and practical purposes and for creating popular interest and for giving a satisfying sympathetic understanding of the nation's dilemmas and progress.

Since the term region has been used in such a variety of ways, it is necessary to note these meanings and to interpret them in relation to the relatively specific usage in the present work. Exclusive of the popular usage which denotes any sort of areal subdivision and of such specialized natural regions as those of the plant and animal ecologists, the geographers, and the soil classificationists, there have been five general types of regions commonly discussed in the United States. From these we develop one which may well be defined as the major composite societal region, as opposed to the limited specialized region. Such a region is selected as embodying the fewest contradictions, the greatest flexibility, and the largest degree of homogeneity for all purposes of study and planning. Within the framework of such a region there must also be provision for overlapping, flexibility, and the inclusion of other areal units, such as subregions, districts, specialized areas and zones. These five types of regions are: *first*, the natural region, such as mountain range, river valley, great plains; *second*, the metropolitan region, where the city is the center and focus of the radiating territory adjacent; *third*, a general loosely used designation which implies the section or provincial locality from which loyalties, patriotism, folkways radiate; *fourth*, the region for convenience, such as administrative divisions of natural organizations or governmental departments; and *fifth*, the group-of-states region, which, if state lines be primarily the arbitrary margins of measurement, may comprehend in varying degrees most of the other types.

Each of these types of region has a distinguished heritage in historical development or authentic usage. Thus, the *river valley region*, brought so much to the forefront by the National Resources Committee and President Roosevelt's proposed seven regional planning agencies, has long-standing advocates in the persons of the geographers. Perhaps the first of distinction was Vidal de la Blache, who envisaged an economy in which societies would be organized around river valleys. Burgess, the political scientist and founder of Columbia's graduate school, thought state lines should be determined by mountains and not rivers. More recently the TVA, the Mississippi River Valley, and the Ohio River Valley Committees and many illuminating studies of water problems and planning have given precedence to river valley regions. So, too, the "Dust Bowl," the Great Plains, the Belt of Drought areas have all featured the natural region as the unit for planning. The *metropolitan region*, perhaps in America the "Dean of Regions," has been featured notably through such major reports as those dealing with New York and its environs, the St. Louis region, the Washington-Baltimore region, and others. Likewise, the metropolitan region has been emphasized in the regional arrangements suggested by the National Resources Committee for Federal Administration, whereby such major region finds its genesis and definition in the urban center. So, too, the proposals of Charles E. Merriam and others for the city-state and urbanism studies of the Chicago human ecologists inquiring into territorial aspects of the city have given considerable distinction to the concept. The *section*, of course, finds its most distinguished heritage in Frederick Jackson Turner but it has been given great emphasis also by James Truslow Adams, William E. Dodd, Charles A. Beard and others. *Literary and aesthetic regionalism*, symbol of local color and culture, has had a long and distinguished record. *Administrative regionalism* finds ample documentation and usage in the hundred and more administrative divisions of the Federal Government, and similar divisional arrangements of educational, religious, and commercial organizations. *The group-of-states region* is found as a technical tool in most of the administrative units of government and as an attempt at co-operative effort across state lines in such recent experiments as the New England Planning Board, the Northwest Planning Board, certain interstate compacts, and in many voluntary organizations. To some extent also the TVA has consistently catalogued the seven contiguous states as areal boundaries of its experimental and co-operative concern.

"Region" in this volume means the *composite societal region* combining a relatively large degree of homogeneity measured by a relatively large number of indices available for a relatively large number of purposes or classifications. This means it must comprehend both the natural factors and the societal factors which must, of course, include the American states and prevailing historic, economic, and culture traits. The region may be, therefore, a "major" region not because of its geographical size but because of the number and importance of classifications of functional or cultural units. The Northeast is such an area, having the smallest area of any of the six major regions of the nation, yet having the largest and most complex population and industry, the largest ratio of wealth, and the largest number of national agencies and organizations. Yet the size of the area is an important factor in determining practical limitations within the measures of homogeneity. In some such way as the astronomer's region is the space that can be explored with existing telescopes, so our region must assume reasonable maximum distances for travel, organization, study, administration. This is illustrated again by Lewis Mumford's dictum that for a region "it is necessary to take an area large enough to embrace a sufficient range of interests, and small enough to keep these interests in focus and to make them a subject of direct collective concern." [40]

Composite societal regions are of two sorts: *the major region* and *the minor region*, which we designate as the *subregion*. Both of these are clearly differentiated from single-purpose, isolated, specialized areas, such as organizational or administrative units including districts, provinces, centers, zones, and the like. Within this frame of reference, both major regions and minor regions may be of two sorts, namely, the *natural* or *physiographic region* and the *societal* or *cultural region*, and, of course, in the exceptional case they may approximate both.

The nature and importance of the *subregion* may well be illustrated in the case where both the physiographic and the societal region are combined. Such instances may be found in the classifications of J. Russell Smith in his arrangements of regions jointly characterized by "men and resources." Thus he says: "This point of organizing by regions is made clear if we think of the State of Minnesota. Northeastern Minnesota is a sparsely peopled land of forest and swamp, nearly all too rough and rocky for good farms. This part of the state had long been called the *Upper Lake Region.* Western Minnesota is a grassland now famed for its farms. It is one of the levelest, smoothest, softest lands in the world. Its smooth levelness makes it the perfect land for the operation of large-scale agricultural machinery. It

[40] Lewis Mumford, *The Culture of Cities.* Quoted by permission from proof sheets.

has long been known as part of the Spring Wheat Region. Very few things can be said about both of these two sharply different sections of Minnesota. But there are many things that can be said about the *Spring Wheat Region* and the *Upper Lake Region* because each area has a unity that enables us to tell things about the whole of it. Now, it so happens that this Spring Wheat Region extends into South Dakota and North Dakota and into Canada where it stretches across the three prairie provinces of Manitoba, Saskatchewan, and Alberta. How foolish it would be to describe the Spring Wheat Region three times for each of the three American states and three more times for each of the three Canadian provinces. And how clear other wheat-growing regions of the world become if you think of them as regions similar in climate and soil to western Minnesota."[41]

The "American" Region, further, as used in the present work is the *composite group-of-states major societal region.* For those composite areas or minor regions in which it is necessary to cut across state lines the term *subregion* is used. For the societal subregion which must ignore state boundaries but which manifestly must have arbitrary boundary lines for measurement, the counties and smaller civil units assume the same sort of role as the states in the major region. For group-of-county subdivisions within states or for mere administrative areas, *district* rather than region is the characterization which is used. For still more specific delimitation of functional or administrative areas defined by legislative fiat, the term *zone* is available. These do not preclude the specialized usages which are in general synonymous with the district, namely, such terms as division, area, station, branch, center, field office, section, territory. The term *district*, however, is adequate for all of these, and *zone* is a very specialized term, so that the threefold delineation of *region, subregion*, and *district* is quite ample for all purposes.

In substantiation of this classificatory arrangement certain further considerations are timely. One is in contrasting the group-of-states region with the natural region, in which certain contradictions might appear to exist. Thus, the great Appalachian Mountain natural region, extending from near the Lower South up almost into Canada, might be a *larger* area than, let us say, the Southeastern States. Yet its classification units for the purposes of societal study or planning are so much

[41] J. Russell Smith, *Men and Resources,* Introduction, pp. vi-vii.

fewer than for the group-of-states region that it becomes a minor or subregional area. If it is a natural subregion it will be appraised in units of topography, situation, soil, rivers, and mountains. If it is a societal subregion it will be appraised as was the case in the survey of Gray and his associates, in county units with such special subregional concentrations as may be devised. For, because of its great heterogeneity of temperature and of topographical relationship to the society of the nation, it must be broken up into numerous subregions. The same is true of the Mississippi River Valley Region which is far larger, let us say, than the group-of-states region designated as the Middle States, yet because of the limited and specialized classification purposes and its great heterogeneity in so many natural, economic, and cultural indices, it cannot qualify for the composite major societal region. On the other hand, within the group-of-states region may be incorporated numerous subregional arrangements to provide for both natural advantages and for cutting across state lines. The socio-economic-natural subregion may again be illustrated in the case of areas in which there is a clustering of a large number of socio-economic traits which are no respecters of state lines, such as the Cotton Belt, the Black Belt, the Dairy Region, the Winter Wheat Subregion, and the like.

All of these considerations and others lead to the conclusion, therefore, that the group-of-states major region will qualify best as the composite region which approximates the largest number and variety of indices available for the largest number of purposes or classifications. In the projection of American culture into the next frontier developments, it seems clear, too, that it is the societal region with which the nation and its changing civilization is primarily concerned. By the same token, then, it would seem that the natural region, no matter what specialized advantages it offers, cannot qualify as the key major region not only because it cannot be made to coincide with the societal or cultural region, but because it is not practically realistic. Range of climate, topography, historical and cultural diversity militate against its use as a composite culture region. Such regions do not, therefore, approximate adequacy without ignoring the legal, sovereign, cultural foundations of the nation. More important, however, as the irreducible criterion of reality is the historical, constitutional, and organizational status of the 48 states, which are the very warp and woof of the national fabric. Natural regions can be utilized for new political and sovereign arrangements only by changing the American form and spirit of government and by ignoring the sweep of technology. Furthermore, to urge the formation of new regional states, based on natural regions, is to repeat the imperfect arrangements of the present states, or to set up too many new states, or to leave out of the picture innumerable border areas not comprehended in natural regions of approximate homogeneity. The natural region, therefore, as found in the United States, cannot qualify as the major societal region in the present American scene. On the other hand, this accentuates the importance of the natural region as one of the key subregional tools for every desired specialized concern and especially for interstate co-operative efforts and for co-operative arrangements between the nation at large and the states and regions.

Applying this test of the composite group-of-states region and keeping in mind also the greatest possible flexibility for future trends as well as adaptation to as large a number of natural subregions as possible, we have set up for exploratory purposes and for a comprehensive frame of reference for research and planning, a sixfold regional America to comprehend the *Northeast* and the *Southeast*, the *Northwest* and the *Southwest*, the *Middle States* and the *Far West*. These are realistic extensions of the earlier historical "sections." They represent two "Souths," two "Norths," and two "Wests." Still more historically literal, they represent one "East," one "South," and four "Wests." These are *major* regions approximating a greater degree of homogeneity measured by a larger number of indices for a larger number of purposes and classifications than any other regional framework that has been utilized or than any other that, on the basis of our data and premises, would appear possible. *The basis upon which this classification rests is stated fully in Chapter XVIII, "Measures of American Regionalism."*

Chapter II

FROM SECTIONALISM TO REGIONALISM

IN the previous chapter, we have pointed out the tendency in the past to confuse sectionalism with regionalism, and we have called attention to a considerable usage which still assumes sectionalism and regionalism to be synonymous. To the extent to which such usage has become common, it is necessary to trace the development of sectionalism as basic to the evolution of regionalism rather than coinciding with it. The way will then be open to point up fundamental differences in meaning and implications.

That which was Frederick Jackson Turner's magnificent sectionalism and James Truslow Adams' *America's Tragedy* had its rise and incidence in the historical and geographical development and expansion of a great frontier nation. The great range and variety of the physical resources and topography of America constituted the basis for a many-regioned nation. America became, in reality, a nation of varied *sections* due to the incidence and vicissitudes of economic development and cultural conflict. The story of the nation is in one sense essentially the story of this sectional development. The thesis of this volume is that the promise and prospect of the nation in the future is, in another sense, to be found in the substitution of a realistic and comprehensive regionalism for the older historical sectionalism.

The story of sectionalism in American life is a fascinating one and may be glimpsed through several avenues of approach. First, there are many authentic concepts and definitions of sectionalism; second, there is the story of its rise and incidence through the naturally expanding domain in which geographic regions become articulate sections because of economic incidence and cultural conflict. Next we may examine some of the fundamental distinctions between sectionalism and regionalism. And, finally, we may explore the possibilities which inhere in the implementation of this transfer from sectionalism to regionalism through this emerging economy of regionalism.

Frederick Jackson Turner has made the most significant contribution to the understanding of sectionalism in American life, and his premise is adequately supported by most of the works dealing with the historical development of the United States. In Chapter I we have already cited examples of the ever-expanding nation and of its earlier sectional divisions. Professor Turner's premise was that "the economic, political, and social life of the United States, even its literature, psychology, and its religious organizations, must be described by sections, . . . In spite of similarity of traits and institutions throughout the nation, it is also a congeries of sections." Professor Turner points out further that "arising from the facts of physical geography and the regional settlement of different peoples and types of society on the Atlantic Coast, there was a sectionalism from the beginning." So, again, contrasting the East with the West, he points out that "from the beginning East and West have shown a sectional attitude."[1] Evidences of this were numerous: the condescension of the East toward the upland folk; the disrespect in which the West was held by the East and the East by the West; the story of the grangers, populists, anti-monopolists, progressives, farmers' bloc, and others. This was illustrated by movements so to fix the number of representatives from the Atlantic States that the eastern quota would always be greater than the number from the West.

This comprehensiveness of American sectionalism is fundamental both to the understanding of the nature of American institutions and dilemmas and to the further ordering of the nation in the next period of development. "Sectionalism in American history," wrote Professor Turner, "has been so commonly conceived by historians as the struggle between North and South over slavery, that the much more complicated sectionalism, involving all the various geographic provinces of the United States . . . has been neglected."[2]

[1] Frederick Jackson Turner, *The Significance of Sections in American History*, pp. 183, 22, 25.

[2] *Ibid.*, p. 193.

Evidence that the South and the Civil War constituted only a part of the issue of American sectionalism is supplemented richly, not only by Turner, but by Charles A. Beard, James Truslow Adams, William E. Dodd, Arthur Schlesinger, and many other historians. The Civil War, as Turner pointed out, "was only the most drastic and most tragic of sectional manifestations, and in no small degree the form it took depended upon the fact that rival societies, free and slave, were marching side by side into the unoccupied lands of the West, . . ."[3] So, too, the physical divergence between the East and the West was accepted as evidence of potential separateness. "Nature," said Rufus King, "has severed the two countries by a vast chain of mountains, interest and convenience will keep them separate, and the feeble policy of our disjointed government will not be able to unite them." Even if the West should become a part of the nation, "the Western States, multiplied in numbers and augmented in population will control the interests of the whole."[4] It was inevitable that the West, resenting both the conceptions of the East and the attitudes manifested would, as Turner points out, take "the attitude of a section itself." Thus quickly, in undesigned and rapid growth, grew three great sections, the East, the South, the West, so that Turner concludes that "throughout our history, then, there has been this sectionalism of West and East and this eastern conception of the West as recruiting ground merely for the rival Atlantic Coast sections."[5]

Yet this East-West-South sectionalism did not stop with the earlier history, or with the earlier struggle for priority in lands and canals and railways. William E. Dodd points out the gigantic sectional struggle which followed the Civil War between certain factors of East and West, and which constituted a continuing or revivification of sectionalism. "Here were two powerful sections of the nation, the South and the West, which had formerly supported each other in national affairs. They each had grievances. If the South were readmitted to the Union, southern and western men would inevitably unite their strength and arrange a national policy which would serve their interests. Andrew Johnson, in spite of his loud talk during the early months of his presidency, represented the promise and guarantee of such a combination. Hence the bitter struggle to impeach him. Industrial men succeeded by a campaign of hatred both in

[3] *Ibid.*, pp. 26-27. [4] Quoted from *ibid.*, pp. 28, 29. [5] *Ibid.*, pp. 30, 33.

defeating Johnson and in holding the South out of the Union for a decade. Meanwhile, industrialism made its position secure." [6]

Dodd pictures vividly the place of industry and economic development in the forming of sections seeking their own interests. "From Boston to Minneapolis stretched this vast industrial domain," in which, he points out, "railroads tied the mines and the farms of the rest of the country to the nerve centers of this busy, smoke-blackened region. National, state, and private banks fed the industries, the railroads, and the other ancillary businesses with the necessary capital which was borrowed from Europe or from the savings of the country. Real estate rose in value beyond the wildest dreams of its owners because industry brought millions of tenants; bank and industrial stocks doubled and quadrupled both in volume and in price because vast populations gathered in the cities increased the consumption of goods. Rich men grew to be millionaires and millionaires became masters of hundreds of millions of wealth." To the economic factors were added sectional patterns in politics in three decades of powerful development. Thus Dodd points out that: "From 1866 to 1896, the process went on almost without interruption. The opposition, led in the beginning by members of Congress from the Middle West, called itself the Democratic party. It consisted in a solid South voting against the East whether in good or ill repute and the provincial West. The provincials of America could not see that it was a blessing to cover the earth with great plants and wide-flung mill settlements so long as cotton, corn, tobacco, and all other products of their lands declined in value. Their sons ran away to the cities to swell the enormous tide of newcomers from Europe, both of which masses of men added to the representation of the industrial districts in Congress and made the more difficult the election of any leader of the farming groups to the presidency. Every year the country regions not touched by industry became less attractive. Houses took on a tumbledown appearance. The South became a waste. Planters became farmers; farmers became tenants; and tenants took places as day laborers or emigrated to the city. There was no help for it. Old America that lived upon the land and talked of liberty and equality was vanishing." [7]

So came the powerful forces which were to contrast the earlier rural regions of America with a great urbanism which was to constitute a new and powerful "sectionalism" in the sense that urban and

[6] William A. Dunning in William E. Dodd, *Woodrow Wilson and His Work*, p. 61.

[7] William E. Dodd, *Woodrow Wilson and His Work*, pp. 62-64.

industrial regions, in conflict with rural interests, were bent on self-interest more than national development. And what could the rural regions, the Southeast, the Southwest, the Wests, do except to fall in line and set the pace for a new nation. Says Dodd, "Country merchants far and near endeavored to have their names on the books of these elect of the world; little bankers in every town and city scraped together as much money as possible in order to maintain big balances in Wall Street; clergymen learned the law from real masters rather than from musty books said to come from a certain mountain in ancient Palestine; and universities were very loth to fall into ill favor with the only men of power in the country. What else could men do? They were caught in a system, as the people of the old South had been caught in the slavery system." [8]

Returning now to our examination of the basic factors of sectionalism, we may cite Turner's statement that, unlike France and Germany, "the United States has the problem of the clash of economic interests closely associated with regional geography on a large scale." On this basis he predicted the certainty of sectional clash of interests in which "sectionalism will hereafter be shaped by such new forces. We have become a nation comparable to all Europe in area, with settled geographic provinces which equal great European nations. We are in this sense an empire, a federation of sections, a union of potential nations." [9]

Herein lies the essential quality of sectionalism; inherent in it is the idea of separatism and isolation; of separate units with separate interests. It must be clear that, since the very definition of regionalism implies a unifying function, it must be different from sectionalism as everywhere defined by the historians. Here the distinctions are clear between the divisive power of self-seeking *sections* and the integrating power of co-ordinate *regions* fabricated into a united whole. The premise of the new regionalism goes further and assumes that the United States must not, either because of its bigness and complexity or because of conflicting interests, become a federation of conflicting sections but a homogeneity of varying regions. Professor Turner, warning of the likelihood of an increase of sectionalism and

[8] *Ibid.*, p. 68.
[9] Turner, *op. cit.*, pp. 36, 37.

pointing up multiple bases for this trend rather than the tendency toward a wholesome regionalism, points out "the danger that the province or section shall think of itself naïvely as the nation; that New England shall think that America is merely New England writ large or the Middle West shall think that America is really the Middle West writ large and then proceed to denounce the sections that do not perceive the accuracy of this view as wicked or ignorant or un-American. This kind of nationalism is a sectional mirage."[10]

The Turner warning, of course, was logical. So, too, Professor Turner's nearest approach to the ideal of national unity, though a projection of a possible regionalism through homogeneities of states and resources, now appears to be one of the most important trends in American life. In this approach he recognized the cultural significance of regions when he pointed out the fallacy of generalizations which may ascribe to a single geographic or economic or other interest alone the compelling explanation of sectionalism. "There are," he wrote, "also the factors of ideals and psychology, the inherited intellectual habits, derived from the stock from which the voters sprang. Some of these ideals carry the voters into lines that contradict their own interests. But as a rule there has been such a connection of the stock, the geographic conditions, the economic interests, and the conceptions of right and wrong, that all have played upon each other to the same end."[11] This is transition from sectionalism to regionalism, in which the nation will avoid "the insistence upon the particular interests and ideals of the section in which we live, without sympathetic comprehension of the ideals, the interests and the rights of other sections. We must shape our national action to the fact of a vast and varied union of unlike sections."[12] This substitution of regional units is the basis for regional planning in the nation. This is the challenge which comes also from James Truslow Adams' dictum: "Sectionalism, whether of the North and the South, that of the East and West, or others, is still a living force molding our destiny."[13]

Others warn of the continuing danger of sectionalism. Thus, H. G. Roach writes in the *American Political Science Review:* "Sectionalism is a fundamental and persistent factor in American politics. In the shaping of Congressional legislation and even in the formation of the platforms of our national parties, the influence of conflicting sectional interests is of prime importance. . . . A study of the period

[10] Turner, *op. cit.*, pp. 45-46. [11] *Ibid.*, pp. 48-49. [12] *Ibid.*, p. 51.
[13] James Truslow Adams, *America's Tragedy*, preface, p. v.

from the early 1870's to 1890 shows that sectionalism at that time was in large measure the product of the interaction of two movements in our national development,—the rapid expansion of Western settlement, particularly the trans-Mississippi Middle West (the West North Central States) and the Mountain region, and the marked intensification of industrialism in the older sections of the country, especially in the North Atlantic States." [14]

> Perhaps we need give only a few other characterizations of sectionalism before we contrast it further with the current emerging regionalism. The spirit and motivation of the old sectionalism has been well described by Waldo Frank. "Each part," he points out, "believed itself whole. Kindred or adjacent parts joined loosely to create a Section. And now America was a crazy-quilt of sections. There was the section of Puritan New England, the section of more conservative New York and New Jersey, the feudal section of the South, the dissident section of the southern mountains, the section of the Jacksonian Mississippi. Each section created a sectionalism of its very own: a rabid rationalization of its specific interests; and the idea of each was a sprawling makeshift pieced from splintered Europe. Within the section, there was no harmony. The religious and rationalist fanatics of Boston dwelt askance together. Farmers and town mechanics in New York spoke no concordant words. There was only a minimum of accommodation; only the fulsome rhetoric of the politician to make them at least drunk together. Between the great sectionalisms—the North, the South, the Wests—there was the hostility that turned to bloodshed." [15]

The most clearly stated measures of sectionalism, however, are still those of Professor Turner's criteria. Thus he says: "I shall recognize as tests of sectionalism all of those methods by which a given area resists national uniformity, whether by mere opposition in public opinion on the part of a considerable area, or by formal protest, or by combining its votes in Congress and in presidential elections, and also those manifestations of economic and social separateness involved in the existence in a given region of a set of fundamental assumptions, a mental and emotional attitude which segregates the section from other sections or from the nation as a whole. Sooner or later such

[14] H. G. Roach, "Sectionalism in Congress, 1870 to 1890," *American Political Science Review,* Vol. 19, No. 3, p. 500.

[15] Waldo Frank, "Rediscovery of America," *The New Republic,* LIII, 345-346.

sectional influences find expression in politics and legislation, and they are even potential bases for forcible resistance." [16]

Professor Turner's political sectionalism finds some sanction also in Stuart Chase's distinction between regionalism and sectionalism. Says Chase: "A *region* may be defined as an area where nature acts in a roughly uniform manner, . . . The Old South is a section, but the land is cut into several natural regions . . . a region provides a major basis for economic planning, a section a basis for political uproar." [17] Turner's political sectionalism was delineated in four ways: First, in a group of states contending with other groups or with the nation; second, in a congeries of congressional districts mapped by homogeneity of congressional votes; third, by approximation of areas delimited by presidential and state elections; and, fourth, by sectional homogeneity denoted by the mapping of election precincts.

We have now traced something of the rise and significance of sectionalism and pointed out enough of its characteristics to enable us, on the background of Chapter I, to contrast sectionalism with regionalism. We have already pointed out the analogy between sectionalism in the nation and economic nationalism in the world at large. We have pointed out certain conflicting factors between metropolitan regionalism and the more comprehensive national regionalism now emerging, and later we shall contrast the interests of urban and rural areas as possible bases for "sectional" conflict. We may now turn to the further examination of five important distinctions between sectionalism and regionalism which we have previously discussed.

> In the first place, we have pointed out, regionalism envisages the nation first, making the national culture and welfare the final arbiter. It is, therefore, essentially a co-operative concern. On the other hand, sectionalism sees the region first and the nation afterwards. It is, therefore, essentially a competitive emphasis. In the second place, sectionalism emphasizes the autonomy inherent in political boundaries and state sovereignties. It confuses the state as a unity in the regional or national whole with the state as a separate entity. It emphasizes technical legislation, provincial interests, local loyalties. Over against the co-operating group-of-states region it sets up a confederation of states "with common interests, menaced by federal action." Where

[16] Turner, *op. cit.*, p. 288.
[17] Stuart Chase, *Rich Land, Poor Land*, pp. 10-11.

sectionalism features separateness, regionalism connotes component and constituent parts of the larger national culture. Another way to look at sectionalism is to liken it to cultural inbreeding, whereas regionalism is line-breeding. The most common illustration of this terminology is probably found in the criticism of educational institutions for too much "inbreeding," that is, utilizing their own graduates almost exclusively.

Inherent in the new concept and practice, by the very nature of its regional, interregional, and national co-operative processes, in the fourth place, is the implication of more of the designed and planned society in regionalism than in sectionalism, which is the group correspondent to individualism. Finally, one of the most critical aspects of sectionalism is the fact that it must have its counterpart in a potential and, in the full flowering of its development, an inevitable coercive federalism, which is contrary to the stated ideals of American democracy.

Some such comprehensive distinction between the two is well stated by Hedwig Hintze: "Regionalism must be distinguished from nationalism in that it recognizes a higher national unity and superior national interests transcending the attachment to the local region. It must be distinguished also from mere sectionalism in that it is not based exclusively on regional economic or class interests, but involves certain ethnic factors, such as cultural, traditional or linguistic peculiarities, which provide a basis for what is often termed a subnationality." [18]

The assumptions of this volume are that these distinctions, so far from being merely academic, are realistically fundamental in theory and practice. Regionalism is organic, basic to the evolution of all culture. Sectionalism is mechanical and is basic to specialized and temporary ends. We may, however, at this time examine Donald Davidson's alternative characterization in which he thinks that on matters of general culture, traditions, and perhaps economics, regionalism may be a reality; but that when tested by political arrangements it is still sectionalism. Davidson is quite willing to help work out the reality of regionalism if it can be done, but he feels that the historical and structural sectionalism is so firmly ingrained that we shall have to keep it. Thus he writes: "The sectional peculiarities of the major divisions are now thoroughly intrenched in differences of climate, population, specialized economy, and cultural tradition. In older sections like the South the differences go so deep as to seem practically ineradicable, and they beget loyalties that cannot be over-

[18] Hedwig Hintze, "Regionalism," *Encyclopedia of the Social Sciences*, XIII, 209.

ridden without damage to the human spirit. To enlist these loyalties rather than to over-ride them would seem to be among the pressing obligations of the new regionalism; for without loyalty no nation, however perfectly planned in theory, can endure. To persuade and guide sectional loyalties is a task that regionalists have not yet undertaken. But it must finally be undertaken; and the practical name of such persuasion is politics." [19] This viewpoint would seem to correspond to Turner's political sectionalism and is, therefore, still "historical."

Davidson seems to sense this point. He continues: "It is evidently becoming necessary—for the political scientist, if not for the sociologist and economist—to work out a kind of Federalism which will officially acknowledge the existence of sections and discover the means of adapting the national polity to permit their healthy functioning within it. We have never had that kind of Federalism. The Federalism of the constitution makers, who were intent upon building a nation out of bodies that claimed separate sovereignty, took only the states into legal regard. Partly because of that too limited regard the old Federalism came finally into trouble, since it was difficult to frame a sectional reciprocity that would be both legal and satisfactory under a governmental instrument that did not recognize sections. The post-bellum Federalism crystallized an old error and allowed the East to dominate West and South. It was a false Federalism and is perishing before our eyes. What kind of Federalism will emerge from the New Deal remains to be seen. If it is a centralization more drastic than we have yet known, which will be heedless of sectional differentiations, it will not be the right kind of Federalism and will bear the seeds of its own failure. In advocating respect for sectionalism, I should not be understood as having any disrespect for regionalism, but rather the complete contrary. If the regionalist in action often turns out to be a sectionalist, the reverse is equally true: the sectionalist, in analyzing the problems of his section, inevitably turns regionalist. My intention has been to show a necessary relation between sectionalism and regionalism and to correct a prevailing impression that there is something dangerous and vindictive about sectionalism, and that regionalism, by contrast, is safe, orderly, and affectionate. Both are 'isms,' both are natural and reasonable, both have vices and explosive possibilities as all human phenomena must have." [20]

[19] Donald Davidson, "Where Regionalism and Sectionalism Meet," *Social Forces*, Vol. 13, p. 30.

[20] *Ibid.* See also Davidson's new volume, *The Attack on Leviathan: Regionalism and Nationalism in the United States.*

Davidson argues that sectionalism has as many conservative as destructive tendencies. On the one hand, it is conservative in the Jeffersonian sense, providing an automatic check against over-centralization. Furthermore, he thinks the existence of sections diminishes the possibility of violent revolution and guarantees that changes in the social order must adapt themselves to democratic institutions. On the other hand, in sectionalism is the possibility of realizing the values which come from regional study and of the great system of regional study now being planned. The sectional units, he thinks, may be the tools for regional enrichment.

Appraising further the fivefold distinction between sectionalism and regionalism, which we have presented, he resumes: "Although I should not agree with every detail of this description of differences, I should say that the general lines of this distinction are correct. The distinction must be granted so long as regionalism operates only as a technique of social study. But when regionalism goes into action and becomes not only a study but a working force, or even a doctrine, the distinction tends to break down. In the field of action the two terms are far from being opposed. They are complementary aspects of the same thing. Sectionalism is the political approach, and regionalism is the economic and cultural approach to an identical set of facts. Under a democratic government, regionalism will hardly avoid developing sectional features as soon as the conclusions drawn from its studies begin to be applied. When regionalists declare against sectionalism, they mean that they want to escape the embarrassment of dealing in the old sort of politics. For that desire they are not to be blamed. But where there is democratic government there must be politics. We cannot shut up large-scale social experiments in a vacuum and expect Americans not to exercise their suffrage pro and con; or if not their suffrage their age-old habits of jockeying and manipulating, in blocs and lobbies. Or, if by some extraordinary means politics is ruled out of regionalism, we shall then have to abandon our present political society and substitute for it the scientific society. As matters now stand, we cannot escape the political implications of our actions by invoking the spirit of science, by insisting on the name of regionalism, or by talking of the general good of society. The hope of the regionalist should be for his studies to achieve the kind of political instrumentation that will realize their latent possibilities. That kind of politics will mean sectionalism, though not the kind of sectionalism which tyrannizes over other sections, like the old sectionalism of the

North; or the warlike, seceding sectionalism which was the answer to it. Experience teaches us that it is fatal to ignore the existence of sections and sectional interests in a nation so large and diverse as ours is. If we again ignore them, we will once more invite disaster, and the wholesome purposes of the New Regionalism will stand in danger of defeat before they have had a fair trial." [21]

What Davidson appears to overlook is the fact that regionalism connotes unity in a total national composition, while sectionalism with its separatism is inherently different. This is true even more in a federation of states. He overlooks the fact that administrative regionalism is a very small part of the total construct of regionalism. It is important to note also that the habits of a people do change with relative rapidity and that, as the nation is knit more closely into a unit by economic interdependence and the efficiency of communication facilities, there arises a new situation which in and of itself demands new modes of action and at the same time brings an acute awareness of this need to the public consciousness. Equally, the separatism of sectionalism retards the expansion and growth of the units involved and the broader services of the nation to these units. Lewis Mumford's interpretation describes most effectively the situation and the problem.

The re-animation and re-building of regions, as deliberate works of collective art, is the grand task of politics for the opening generation. It raises anew, in a form that now has fuller human significance, the fundamental questions of human interrelationship across the ethnic, ideological, and cultural boundaries that have been carried over from the past. And as the new tasks of region-building imply shifts in the population, migration into more favored areas, and the building up or reconstruction of a multitude of new urban complexes, the politics of regional development become of critical importance. Not merely must we define and express the region: we must work out, by deliberate experiment, the areas for interregional co-operation and for super-regional authority. . . . What we have to conceive and work out is a federal system of government which shall be based upon a progressive integration of region with region, of province with province, of continent with continent: each part loose enough and flexible enough to adjust to the continuing changes in local and transregional

[21] Donald Davidson, "Where Regionalism and Sectionalism Meet," *Social Forces*, Vol. 13, pp. 24-25.

life. Once such a structure has been outlined, it will tend to make effective that concentric regrouping of political, economic, and cultural functions, whose absence is today a severe handicap to co-operative effort. . . . Political consolidation, in indifference to regional realities, has met with unexpected obstacles: under the even whitewash of "national unity" the colors of the underlying geographic, economic, and cultural realities are beginning to show through. Not the least important sign of this new regime is the recognition accorded under Lenin in Soviet Russia to the principle of cultural autonomy. The fact is that real communities and real regions do not fit into the frontiers and the ideological pattern of the national state. The state is usually too big to define a single region, with its political, economic, and social elements in symmetrical relationships, and it is too small to include a whole society, like that of Western Europe or the North American Continent, which must ultimately become the sphere of a larger system of co-operative administration. The limits of functional authority, such as is involved in the organization of a continental railroad system or the steel industry, cannot rest effectively within the fortuitous boundaries of the state: the larger relationships need a larger framework of authority, and the more intimate relationships require a narrower field of effort. This is no less true of art and science and religion, which are by nature part of the common stock, not of a region, a province, or a state, but of a whole society. There is no way short of tyrannical repression in which the interests of a scholar, a man of letters, or a member of the Catholic Church can be kept within the boundaries of the national state.[22]

In his *Roads to Social Peace*, Professor E. A. Ross featured "The Avoidance of Sectionalism" in a separate chapter.[23] While "the new regionalism" had not emerged at the time he was writing, his emphasis upon realistic ways and means of avoiding social conflict within the nation may well serve to interpret from another angle the fundamental importance of changing from the old order of sectional conflict to national co-ordination through regional integration. We may debate the question whether the difference between sectionalism and regionalism is an academic matter, but the realities remain that the difference in ideals and objectives is so great that, academic or not, the old sectionalism must be transcended by the new regionalism if the nation is to avoid the old mistakes. Just as there is need for

[22] Lewis Mumford, *The Culture of Cities*. Quoted, by permission, from proof sheets.

[23] E. A. Ross, *Roads to Social Peace*, ch. I.

decentralization through regional divisions, there is also need for minimizing the narrow, local, state dominance through enlargement into regional homogeneities. These will be the buffer between the state and the federal power.

Illustrations of the national-regional and regional-national approach, as opposed to the sectional, are abundant. One type of illustration is that of federal grants and equalization funds for the use of states, the nature and amount often being determined by the regional nature of the need and problem. Land grant colleges represent the joint efforts of federal and local agencies working together on a unified basis. Through this sort of co-operation a new era in American education and agricultural development may be ushered in. Federal public health services, road building, vocational education, and social security represent other federal-regional techniques of co-operation.

Many of the more recent federal-co-operative arrangements represent the national-regional ideal, although a few have appeared to focus so much on federal control as to endanger genuine regionalism by fomenting sectional antagonisms. However, there are ample illustrations of the positive sort, leaving the discussion of the negative ones for our last chapter. Of the federal illustrations, the TVA is an excellent sample. Manifestly, it promotes the regional well-being through the development and enrichment of both physical and human resources. It does not, however, limit itself to southern employees or southern ideas, neither does it reject southern people or southern ideas. Manifestly it overlaps state boundaries, but in no sense assumes to take over or dictate the ways and rights of the seven states involved in the river valley region. Manifestly, it is national in so far as it sets up an experiment which might be helpful to other similar regions of the nation. Manifestly, it would run contrary to soundly bottomed regionalism if and when it should transcend the rights and freedom of the people within the region either by manifestly intentional organization or by subterfuge.

So, too, many of the agricultural adjustment policies are based upon the realities of regionalism. Obviously, the adjustment acts which take cognizance of wheat and cotton and corn and hogs and tobacco get their specifications from the regional needs and settings. So, too, it is possible to project a federal equalization fund in education with a view to balance and equilibrium between and among the regions and with a view to equalizing opportunity for rural and urban or for whites and Negroes. Again, some of the great dams which provide irrigation and power are of the greatest importance in enriching regional cultures where they are and adding to the national total, rather than attempting to starve them out or move the people from the areas involved.

> These are adequate to illustrate the case in general. We may cite a more specific example utilized in the study of the southern regions. One of the best illustrations may be found in the problem of race development and relations in the South. The evidence all indicates that it is not possible to make adjustments or work out solutions on any purely "southern," sectional basis, which logically would have in mind primarily the interests of the white South. On the other hand, in view of the dominance of folkways over stateways, of the actualities already existent, and of the cultural and historical backgrounds of the several regions and of the American principles of government, it is not possible to effect immediate readjustments through complete federal coercion and control, which would be analogous in many ways to the extreme sectional viewpoint. What is needed is a comprehensive approach looking to the facts and welfare of the nation, of the North and the South, of white and Negro, all according to the regional-national approach inseparably bound together both in ultimate ends and in methods of attainment. There are fundamental differences involving both cultural and technical difficulties based upon sound historical and philosophical grounds.
>
> "A specific illustration of a real regional-national approach as opposed to the earlier narrow sectional [viewpoint] may be found in the upbuilding of Negro institutions of higher learning in the South, in which southern institutions are being developed through interregional co-operation and aid, approximating mutual satisfaction to the South, the North, the Negroes, and the whites, as nearly as is possible under the circumstances. Thus the most eminent Negro men of science and letters in the nation have come to southern Negro colleges to develop a new era. This new educational statesmanship is a maturer development than the earlier limitations set by the South, in which it sought little education for the Negro, on the one hand, and the missionary spirit of the philanthropists from the North, on the other. It also represents the best thought and effort of the Negro race, whose personnel, skill, and training are being brought more and more to bear upon the problems in hand. A similar illustration might be cited in the case of

public and elementary education in many of the southern states, in which such out of the region funds as Rosenwald, Slater, and Jeanes have contributed to a richer regional culture and a broader interregional contact." [24]

The other side of the question, apart from the advantage to the area involved through its richer development and better national integration, reflects important advantages for the nation as a whole. As its regions are in wealth and welfare, on the one hand, or in poverty and conflict, on the other, so will the nation reap or lose. If the Southeastern Region sends its millions of people into all parts of the nation, there will be enrichment in proportion as these people are well educated and equipped. In times of stress and depression these assets and liabilities are especially demonstrable as also in time of war the national unity must be geared with the national wealth. So, too, other phases of the national-regional aspects are apparent in the development and conservation of natural resources. We shall, therefore, examine next something of the regionalism involved in the natural regions of the nation.

This problem of natural resources and their development will prove one of the most important corollaries to regional concepts and practices. One of the most important of the new implications of regionalism in the nation reflects a trend contrary to what has often been predicted and finds a sort of counterpart in the increasing tendency toward economic nationalism. This is the basis for new difficulties and obligations in the way of the new regionalism. It had been freely predicted that modern communication, technology, and standardization processes would tend to minimize regional and national differences. There is, however, the important fact that certain economic aspects of both regionalism and nationalism have been accentuated by modern technology. Communication, transportation, and invention bring regions and nations closer together, but they may also solidify groups and standardize production. In the older days, for instance, the manufacture of finer fabrics, cloths, and paper was centered in northern and eastern regions of the United States. The progress of science and invention later made it possible for the South to compete on more favorable terms. Continued development easily leads to competitive rivalries which accentuate regional or sectional interests. The same sort of thing is likely to apply in other regions

[24] Howard W. Odum, *Southern Regions of the United States*, p. 255.

and to other commodities, setting, for instance, the Middle States and the Southeast in regional rivalry in furniture-making and the dairy industry, or the Southwest and the Far West in citrus fruits, or the Southwest and the Southeast in cotton growing and manufacture. It applies also to other nations—the production of cotton and cotton goods, of oil, of many things originally imported or exported; so that a new type of economic planning will be necessary to gear together interregional and international programs. The assumption is that science has broken down the old division between manufacturing countries and raw material countries and is reducing the number of raw materials which come primarily from nature. The further assumption is that general cultural factors, science, ideas, literature, travel, recreation, should be international, but that goods, finance, economic processes, should be primarily national. The same presumptions are applicable to regions within the nation, changing many of the earlier assumptions.[25]

Finally, an important distinction between regionalism and sectionalism is found in the recent rapid rise of regionalism in America. The very urgency of river valley and other natural regions for planning and development, through which the national whole is envisaged as being better promoted by regional rather than state action, implies a definite meaning of the region quite different from the section. No one uses the term river valley sections, or natural grass sections, or winter wheat sections, or soil sections. This test of the meaning will be seen further in the next two chapters.

Few themes are more abundantly supported in the best of the popular and authentic historical writings than this sectional-regional development of the American republic. In addition to Turner's *The Significance of Sections in American History* and *The United States, 1830-1850*, a wealth of materials and interpretation is found in Beard's *Rise of American Civilization;* Adams' *Epic of America*, *America's Tragedy*, and especially in his *Provincial Society* and his *History of American Life Series;* Schlesinger and Fox's edited series of volumes on *A History of American Life;* Morison and Commager's *The Growth of the American Republic;* and Buck's *The Road to Reunion.* Some of the evidences from these historical interpretations will appear in the chapters that follow, and especially in the chapters dealing with the six major regions of the United States, each of which reflects much of the sectional constituency of the United States.

[25] Adapted from *ibid.*, pp. 248-249.

Chapter III

NATURAL REGIONS: SOIL, TOPOGRAPHY, CLIMATE

We have called attention to the several types of regions and in particular to certain contrasts between the "natural" regions and others which combine certain arbitrary characteristics with natural regions—such as metropolitan regions, administrative regions, and the group-of-states regions—and in which the historical, legal, and cultural units must constitute the basic indices of statistical research and planning techniques. In so far as the historical background of states and other legally constituted units is in conflict with the physiographic factors, the final margins must be found in the administrative and cultural balance of man and institutions. Perhaps the clearest statement of the first policy is that of Mr. V. B. Stanbery who insists that the natural organic region should be the basic unit with which planning has to deal. Planning, he believes, should be regional in concept whether the regions be large or small, interstate or substate. True areal planning should be regional planning whether it be carried out under authority of city, county, state or federal agencies. Yet, he is inclined to make the region synonymous with the "natural" region.

"In establishing boundaries and headquarters for planning administration," he writes, "a distinction should be made between purely administrative districts and natural regions. We should clearly distinguish between areas arbitrarily delimited for administrative purposes and slowly evolving organic entities. The term 'region' should not be degraded through loose and indiscriminate application to administrative areas. In planning terminology, 'region' should be reserved for areas exhibiting the distinctive characteristics of true regionality, irrespective of political or administrative boundaries. In contradistinction to 'region,' the word 'district' is particularly appropriate f… designating areas of governmental jurisdiction, since a district is an area arbitrarily delimited for specific purposes rather than one which has evolved through natural growth."[1]

As a matter of reality, America's regions, and even its sections, find their basis in the bigness and areal divergence of the continent. This is, however, the beginning and not the end of regions. To think of America is to think of bigness. Extending from ocean to ocean, from a North so cold that man has been unable to introduce profitable farming to a South so hot that winter is almost unknown, with a variety so great that the wildest flights of imagination are quite likely to be true of some particular area, with expanses so level they remind of the sea, with mountains so high they seem to reach into heaven itself, with soil so fertile there is little that cannot be grown and soil so arid that life can scarcely subsist, with forests merging into grass lands, which in turn shrivel and die under a rainless sky, America presents pictures of untold variety, natural regions of infinite diversity.

There are so many regional divisions and aspects of this great America that an entire volume would scarcely catalogue and describe them. They range all the way from six or seven hundred agricultural subregions to three great regions designated by Walter Prescott Webb as three fairly distinct cultures, each of which he thinks can be "with reasonable accuracy marked off geographically and adequately described." However, he calls these regions—the South, the North, the West—sections, and the keynote to his *Divided We Stand* is couched in terms of a question: "To the thoughtful man or woman living in the South or the West the question often occurs, Just how united are these United States?"[2] So, too, Stuart Chase, in his popular *Rich Land, Poor Land,* sets off on his exploration with a graphic picturization of what he calls "between two oceans," attempting to break down a continental America, which extends for 3,000 miles from the Pacific to the Atlantic and 1,200 miles from the Gulf to Canada, covering 3,000 square miles, with

[1] V. B. Stanbery, "That Planning Administration Should Distinguish between Administrative Districts and Natural Regions," memorandum especially prepared for *American Regionalism,* August 3, 1937.

[2] Walter Prescott Webb, *Divided We Stand,* p. 3.

a high point of 14,500 feet above sea level and a low point of 276 feet below. Without adopting these regions as definitive, he uses the Van Hise regional classification as a premise for the study of the continent. These eight regions include the Atlantic and Gulf Plains, the Eastern Plateau, the Appalachian Mountain Country and the Ozarks, the Great Lakes Plains, the Prairie Plains, the Great Plains, the Rocky Mountains and the Western Plateau, and the Pacific.[3]

As far back as 1898, Franklin Henry Giddings, in an elementary textbook on sociology, approached the scientific study of habitable areas through a regional framework of North America, which he termed the Grainless North, the Western Desert, and the Region of Fertility. More specifically, then, he studied local areas, and, within the larger regions, set up for the premises of research eight natural regions within his third region of fertility. These were the Coast Swamps, the Atlantic Plain, the Piedmont Region, Mountain Regions, the Great Plateau, Timber and Lake Regions, the Southern Alluvial Region, and the Prairie Region.[4]

Perhaps the best and most recent illustration of the premise that the nation can be studied adequately only in terms of regions and subregions, with the physiographic regions as the base for the study and understanding of men and resources, is found in the twenty-nine regions of the geographer J. Russell Smith, in his study of North America and its place in world geography. In these regions he characterizes, on the one hand, the general physical nature of the region and, on the other, something of its perspective to resources and society. The regions themselves are an object lesson in the appraisal of the nation. Land of Codfish and Glaciation: *New England-Canadian Maritime Region;* Land of Lakes and Forest: *The Northeastern Highlands;* The Metropolitan City: *New York;* A Thoroughfare and a String of Towns: *The Hudson Valley, Erie Canal Belt, and Buffalo;* A Sandy Land of Low Fertility and High Productivity: *The North Atlantic Coastal Plain;* Rolling Hills, Clay Soils, and Blue Grass: *The Northern Piedmont;* Long Strips of Land: *The Appalachian Ridge and Valley Region;* Forests and Fuel: *The Appalachian Plateau and the Upper Ohio Valley;* A Cool Island of Climate in a Warm Land: *The Blue Ridge and the Carolina Mountains;* An Island of Hills in the Great Central Plains: *Ozark Plateau and Ouachita Mountains;* Long, Warm,

[3] Stuart Chase, *Rich Land, Poor Land*, pp. 6, 10-12.
[4] Franklin H. Giddings, *The Elements of Sociology*, pp. 13-18.

Moist Summers–Changeable, Rainy Winters: *The Cotton Belt;* Subtropical Coasts: *The Gulf Coast and the Florida Peninsula;* Chaparral and Irrigated Oases: *The Lower Rio Grande Valley;* Land of Meat and Bread: *The Corn Belt;* Rolling Hills Divided and United by a Great Waterway: *The Lower Valley of the Ohio;* A Land That Blows Away: *The Winter Wheat Region;* A Frontier with a Dwindling Population: *The Spring Wheat Region;* Land of Cow and Silo: *The North Central Dairy Region;* Heavy Trade and a Great Thoroughfare: *The Lake Region;* A Land That Man Has Yet to Understand: *The Dry West and the Great Plains;* Islands of Forest and Farms in a Sea of Pastures: *The Rocky Mountains;* Great Distances, Few People: *The Southwestern Intermountain Plateaus;* An Enemy That Advances and Retreats: *The Great American Desert;* Deserts with Cold Winters, and Oases: *The Great Basin;* A Land of Serious Problems and Mighty Plans: *The Columbia-Fraser Basins;* Moist Mild Winters, Dry Summers, Tourists, and Moving Pictures: *Southern California;* A Great Valley and a Great Mountain Chain: *Central California;* An American Region with an English Climate: *The Puget Sound and Willamette Valley;* Fish and Forests: *The North Pacific Coast and Mountains.*[5]

The most natural divisions of a country so vast are those of forest, river, mountain, plain, and coast land; soils and climates. Soils are, of course, the fundamental factor in a natural division of the nation, since soils plus rainfall plus climate enable the agriculturalist to utilize the various regions and determine the course of his utilization. Nevertheless the occurrence of minerals, woods, and streams which we have learned to use in our particular culture is also of vital importance. All of these factors serve to distinguish one region from another and to lay the foundation for many distinctive ways of life. Such regions are not only original natural areas before an age of science, communication, and technology, but continue to influence the cultural landscape. We shall, therefore, in this chapter recall the main physiographic regions according to topography, climate, and soils, leaving for a special chapter the great river valley regions, and for the chapter on Rural Regions the classification of agricultural regions.

Physical conditions have been the principal influences directing agricultural development in the modern world. Temperature and moist-

[5] J. Russell Smith, *Men and Resources: North America and Its Place in World Geography,* pp. xi-xii.

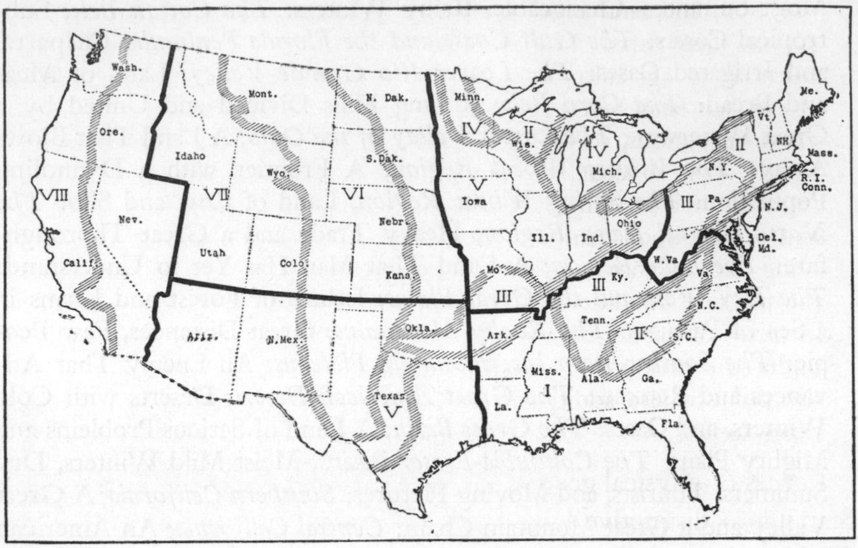

TWO OF THE MOST INTERESTING VARIATIONS OF NATURAL REGIONS ARE HERE ILLUSTRATED

Above: Land Regions adapted from Van Hise's *The Conservation of Natural Resources* and Webb's *The Great Plains.*

Below: Time Belts, as used to determine the several "Standard" times of the United States.

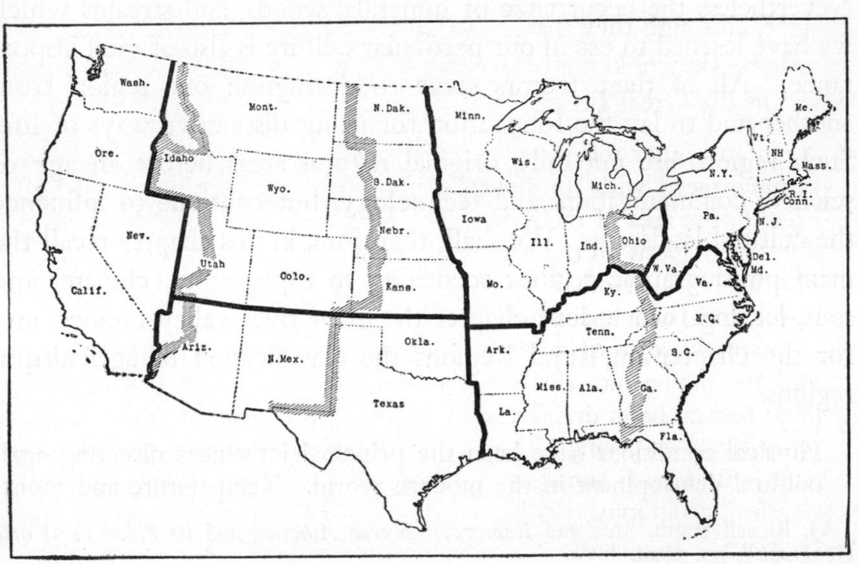

ure, soil, and land relief or lay of the land or topography—all have played their parts. In general the protection of life and property, so essential to agricultural development throughout the history of the world, has been better maintained during the last century than during previous periods, so that the results of natural forces have been constantly more evident. Population has continued to increase, although recently at a lessening rate, thus pressing upon the natural resources, and urging upon mankind the necessity for understanding the underlying factors that condition our agricultural life. The influence of the physical conditions may be altered, but this alteration is expensive in terms of capital or labor or both. These physical conditions yield under the pressure of man's technic, but soon the resistance reaches the point where additional pressure becomes unprofitable and sometimes futile.[6]

Forces of physical geography have carved the surface of the United States into distinctive landscapes, dependent in large part upon the various factors of geologic formation, rainfall, wind, temperature, elevation, and steepness of slope, working in conformity with the vast movements of the earth's surface by which enormous blocks are raised or lowered, often to the accompaniment of faulting or volcanic action. More recently man has been added to this list of geographic factors, since his activities profoundly affect the other forces at work reshaping the surface of the earth. His work, however, has been in progress such a relatively short time that its effects are still somewhat meager, although they may be of vital importance to his own welfare, as witness the choked stream beds of the South and the encroaching desert in the Great Plains.

As in any other scheme of regionalization, the physical geographer is at once faced with the question of how many regions are advisable. Clearly, the area of the nation may be divided into as many or as few different regions on the basis of surface features as may be demanded. But, again as in other schemes of regionalization, there are certain major areas which display a cohesiveness which seems to stamp them as "natural" regional divisions. The simplest of such plans would divide the nation into three major regions, the Atlantic watershed, the great central basin drained by the Great Lakes and the Mississippi and other rivers emptying into the Gulf of Mexico, and the Pacific slope. Such a division is simple and is based on one of the great agencies of physical geography, drainage. It has been made the basis of many

[6] O. E. Baker, "Introduction" to *American Atlas of Agriculture, 1936.*

generalized descriptions of the area. Another system utilizing the same criterion would divide the great central basin into two major provinces, one drained by the Great Lakes and the other by the streams emptying into the Gulf. This scheme is also utilized by some writers, but by others it is objected that the divide between the Great Lakes and the Gulf drainage areas is so low and poorly defined that the division is rather arbitrary.

"The arrangement of the major physiographic divisions of the United States is unique. The interior consists of vast plains bound on the east and west by two extensive mountain systems. On the east rise the low plateaus and ridges of the Appalachian Highlands; and on the west the Cordillera, a belt of mountain ranges, plateaus, and basins, over 1,000 miles wide in places. The trend of these two mountain systems converges toward the south. Between, at their nearest approach, is interposed an interior highland, composed of the Ozark Plateaus and Ouachita Mountains. In the north, around Lake Superior, the Interior Plains merge into the Laurentian Upland, which extends far into Canada. Along the Atlantic and the Gulf Coast, from Long Island southward into Mexico, the Appalachian Highlands and Interior Plains are bordered by a Coastal Plain. In the Cordillera three major divisions are recognized—the Rocky Mountain system on the east, the Pacific Mountain system along the Pacific Coast, and the Intermountain Plateaus and Basins between these exterior mountain ranges." [7]

Surface relief, through its influence in the formation of a more or less favorable natural environment for human occupancy, necessarily has influenced land settlement. Population distribution on the basis of elevation above sea level alone shows marked differences. Of the nation's population about 95 percent inhabits land that has an elevation of less than 2,000 feet, whereas the area of such land comprises about 57 percent of the total land area of the United States. Climatic conditions arising from the relief features account in part for their distribution. As a factor in influencing land utilization and agricultural development, land relief is as basic as climate or character of soil. Moreover, land relief determines in large measure the climate and the soil.[8]

The appearance of any land mass, as W. M. Davis has demonstrated, depends primarily on the original activities by which the area was formed, or *structure*, the destructive erosional *processes* by which it has been changed, and the degree to which these destructive processes have advanced, or the *stage* which the form has reached in its cycle of construction or destruction. Such a method of descrip-

[7] F. J. Marschner, "Land Relief," *American Atlas of Agriculture, 1936,* p. 3.
[8] *Ibid.,* p. 6.

tion is primarily historical, but affords a ready basis for the division of a continent, especially when mapped in terms of present realities rather than of former structures which may have been largely obliterated by the processes of erosion. But when this is true, the former structure gives a basis for distinguishing one region from another.

This was the basis used by a committee of the Association of American Geographers who undertook the task of dividing the area of the United States into districts or regions of which "the maximum number of general statements may be made with the minimum necessity for considering details and exceptions," with the added criterion that the resulting divisions should "be useful in the consideration of the effects of topography on human affairs," so that their study "looks both ways —backward to geology and forward to geography."[9] This discussion is followed, in general, in the description of physiographic regions here presented. But even with highly specialized scholars working on relatively objective data, it was found that it was not always possible to reach agreement as to the exact boundaries of regions, so that some of the delimiting lines were chosen arbitrarily and others were left indefinite, while all such limits were generalized either because of indefiniteness of the true boundaries or because of the interpenetration of forms characteristic of contiguous regions, or, as in some cases, the appearance of small areas differing greatly from the surrounding terrain. In spite of these difficulties as to detail, there is general agreement, expressed by the committee mentioned and by geographers in general, as to the major divisions of the United States.

We begin with the eastern shore of the continent which is composed of the Atlantic Plain, a geologic structure of comparatively recent origin. This plain is submerged from about the site of the city of New York northeastward, though Long Island and Cape Cod are generally thought of as being part of this province. The boundary of the province is marked along the Atlantic seaboard by the "fall line," the point at which the streams leave their more rapid upper courses and debouch onto the lower, more level lands; further westward the line of demarcation is not so well marked, but swings northward through central and western Alabama, follows closely along

[9] N. M. Fenneman, "Physiographic Divisions of the United States," *Annals of the Association of American Geographers*, VI, 22-23, 25. This work is made the basis of the physiographic regions used in *American Regionalism* since the conditions under which the areas were mapped would seem to give it the stamp of authority by the present-day geographers of America.

the valley of the Tennessee River to the southern borders of the Ozark and Ouachita highlands and then along the Balcones escarpment to the Rio Grande. Thus this region includes much of the territory which was settled early in the history of the nation and the level lands into which the southern migrants found easy access. Its western limits are fairly close to the boundary of the social and cultural region known as the South.

The contrast between this great natural region and the cultural regions within its domain may be envisaged by comparing "northern" and "southern" cultures and also by examining its physical subregions and their cultural diversification. For the province is often divided into districts, the embayed section extending from the northern limit of the province southward through North Carolina, the sea island section extending from that point to Florida, the peninsula of Florida, the eastern Gulf Plains, stretching westward to the flood plain of the Mississippi, the alluvial plains of that stream, and the western Gulf Plains, which occupy the territory from the Mississippi alluvium to the Rio Grande, and beyond.

Scarcely less typical of the contrast is the second major natural region. Roughly parallel to the Atlantic coastline, back of the plains, lies the Appalachian highland region, comprising the Piedmont, the Blue Ridge system, the Appalachian Valley, the Appalachian Mountains, the Adirondack Mountains, and the New England area. These major units of the region are in their turn divided into numerous smaller areas, but the broken character of the uplift gives a common characteristic to the large territory lying between the coastal plains and a line running near the southern shores of Lakes Ontario and Erie through central Ohio, Kentucky and Tennessee, and well into Alabama. The Hudson and St. Lawrence valleys form a continuation of the Great Valley of the Appalachians. *Thus, the entire New England area is, strictly speaking, a continuation of the Blue Ridge and Piedmont divisions of the Appalachian uplift. Though this region shelters some of the most backward peoples of the nation, it has also been utilized for some of the most intensive areas of development.* The New England industrial district is within the region, the cities of New York, Philadelphia, Pittsburgh, Cleveland, Baltimore, Atlanta, and Birmingham are included or lie close to the borders and have most of their hinterlands within the region.

> Of social importance is the great valley of the Appalachians which seems to have formed something of a natural highway along which migrants found their easiest route in settling the hills of the eastern part of the nation. Gaps through the mountain masses have exerted strong influence on the location of transportation lines and have thereby aided in deciding the fate of cities on tidewater to the eastward. The swift waters of streams descending to the plains have been made the basis of manufacturing along the eastern slope and the Tennessee Valley Authority is now attempting to introduce a similar exploitation of natural energy along one of the major streams flowing westward from this same uplift. The plateau which forms the western flank of the mountains has proven a source of wealth through supplying our modern culture with its essentials of iron, coal and petroleum.

By far the largest physiographic region of the country is that known as the Interior Plains, which together with the Gulf Plains from which it is separated by a more or less arbitrary division, occupies all that vast area from the break of the western plateau of the Appalachians to the foothills of the Rocky Mountains, with the exception of the intrusion of a small area of the Canadian Laurentian Upland in northern Wisconsin. Within this area are found the famous bluegrass sections of Kentucky and Tennessee, the fertile corn lands of Indiana and Illinois and Iowa, the dairying section of Minnesota, Wisconsin, Illinois, and Ohio, the wheat fields and the cattle ranches of the more arid portions lying within the rain shadow of the high western mountains. Here a great empire lay waiting for the Anglo-American pioneers, and they were not slow to grasp it. Indeed the rate at which this region was populated, up to the edge of the Great Plains with its forbidding bareness, is one of the outstanding achievements of humankind. Here, again, mineral resources of iron, coal, and petroleum, combined with ease of construction of transportation routes, have encouraged interaction so that the region is often declared to be the most typically American.

> Here again, a vast area is divided into a number of subregions, although the relatively simple geologic structure has kept the number of these at a minimum. The bluegrass regions of Kentucky and Tennessee

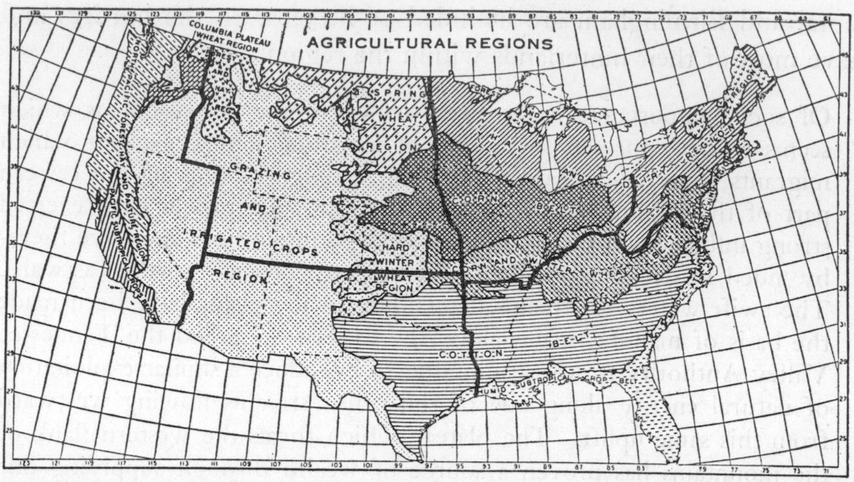

TWO OF THE MOST COMMONLY USED ILLUSTRATIONS OF PHYSIOGRAPHIC AND NATURAL REGIONS ARE THOSE OF NATURAL VEGETATION AND AGRICULTURAL LAND USE REGIONS

Above: Major Agricultural Regions.

Below: Natural Vegetation Regions, both adapted by permission from the Bureau of Agricultural Economics of the United States Department of Agriculture.

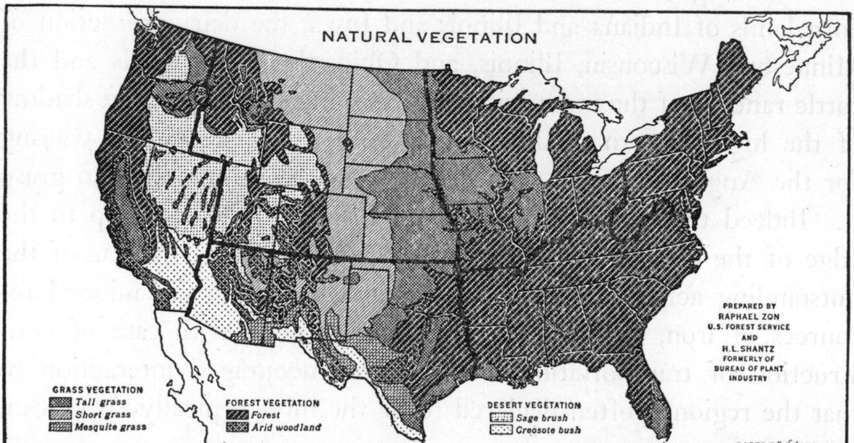

with their surroundings of higher lands form the interior low plateaus; the badly eroded Black Hills and the still more greatly eroded Texas Hills stand out as remains of an older order in the area. Otherwise the entire region is composed of rock strata lying almost horizontal, covered with deep soils and drained by lazy-moving rivers. The upper portions of the region have been glaciated heavily, with the result that drainage is poor and lakes abundant, affording recreational facilities of great value. South of this area is found the till plains, also glaciated but better drained, which run in a broad belt through Ohio, Indiana, Illinois, and Iowa into Kansas and Nebraska, the best-known agricultural region of the country. The southern boundary of this region lies close to the Ohio and Missouri Rivers, until the latter turns northward above Kansas City. An extension of the region follows along the western flank of the Ozark and Ouachita mountain systems through Kansas southward into Oklahoma and Texas before it gives way to the final subregion, the Great Plains area.

The Great Plains area is large enough to warrant a separate discussion, but is geologically and physiographically a part of the Interior Plains system. The line setting it off from the more central plains is often purely arbitrary, from the geologic point of view, though in most places the transition is marked by bold escarpments. But the decisive factor is rainfall. By common consent the area between the lands receiving twenty inches of rainfall annually and the foothills of the Rocky Mountains are known as the Great Plains. This line runs very near the 100th meridian and so divides the continent almost exactly. Structurally the Great Plains are similar to the lands to the east; the altitude rises so gradually that the traveler may not notice a change. But the absence of sufficient rainfall to enable mankind to carry on his traditional mode of life made the region a place of terror for decades, a situation only partly mitigated by the introduction of windmills by which water might be secured from deep underground sources, and barbed wire which permitted agriculturists to continue their practice of enclosing their fields. East of this area American culture rested securely on three supports—land, water, and timber. Here two of those supports were withdrawn,[10] and the

[10] Walter Prescott Webb, *The Great Plains*, p. 9 and *passim*. *The Western Range*, Senate Document 199, 74th Congress, 2nd Session, is a recent and authoritative discussion of the problems of this area.

bitter experiences of recent years have raised anew the question of whether the area is habitable as a densely populated farming region.

Lying between the Gulf Plains and the Interior Plains are the Ozark and Ouachita highlands, separated by the valley of the Arkansas River. The Ozark region is really a plateau, badly eroded on its borders, while the Ouachita are true mountains, due to folding of the earth strata as in the Appalachian system, of which it is thought they may be a detached portion.[11] Both areas lend themselves less easily to human use than do the surrounding territories and so are classified as "backward" areas.

Rising from the Great Plains are the Rocky Mountains, which give their name to one of the major physiographic regions of the nation. It is this mountain system which forms the continental divide with its lofty peaks. These mountains reach from beyond the Canadian border southward to the neighborhood of Santa Fe, New Mexico, where they give way to the Intermontane Plateaus which form the highlands of southern New Mexico and Arizona and extend southward into Mexico. The mountain system proper is divided by the Wyoming Basin, a relatively low plateau in which are found the headwaters of both the Platte River, draining into the Mississippi and thence to the Gulf of Mexico, and the Colorado, running southwest to the Gulf of California and the Pacific. Topographically the Wyoming Basin is an extension of the Great Plains area, although structurally it is a part of the mountain system. Below the basin lie the Southern Rocky Mountains, while to its north lie the Northern Rocky Mountains, or as Powell prefers, the Stony Mountains.[12]

Between the Rocky Mountains and the Pacific Mountain system lie the Intermontane Plateaus, composed of the Columbia Plateau, the Colorado Plateau, and the Basin and Range province. This entire region has been subjected to great changes in altitude in which huge blocks have been raised. Volcanic action has also been great so that immense lava beds are characteristic. This process has given rise to a broken topography which is furthered by the steep-walled canyons cut by the major streams flowing through the region. The Colorado River drains the lower portion of the region; waters falling on the

[11] A. P. Brigham, *The United States of America,* p. 37.

[12] J. W. Powell, "Physiographic Regions of the United States," *National Geographic Monographs,* I, 87.

northern areas find their way to the sea through the Snake and Columbia Rivers, while in the central Great Basin portion the rainfall is so slight that scattered and often temporary lakes care for the drainage.

Still farther west lies the Pacific Mountain system, mountains resulting from block faulting, folding and volcanic action much after the fashion of the Intermontane region, but reaching a higher altitude. As in the case of the Appalachian system a somewhat irregular valley extends north and south between higher ground. In the north this valley is represented by Puget Sound and the valley of the Willamette. Further south, after being broken by the Calapooya Mountains, it reappears in the valleys of the Sacramento and San Joaquin Rivers. These valley systems were former gulfs of the Pacific, and owe much of their utility as agricultural areas and as sites of ports to this fact.

Rainfall, cloudiness, and fog, length of growing season, prevailing winds and ocean currents, humidity, and the range of the diurnal and seasonal variations—all of these combine into a totality which gives each major region of the United States a distinctive climate. This is true whether the regions considered are the six used by the present writers, or are selected on the basis of any other set of criteria. With so many variable factors, indeed, it is possible to find an almost unlimited number of distinctive climatic areas in a body of land as large as this nation. But as with other regional criteria, the climatic indices merge slowly into each other, in most instances, so that the problem of marking definite limits to one type of climate is very difficult. This is perhaps the chief reason for the variety of climatic provinces outlined by various writers on the subject. This diversity is explainable, also, as the result of the different amounts of emphasis placed on the various climatic factors by different students.

However, the climatic forces, like other forces of nature, work in combination, interweave themselves into patterns which give distinctive characteristics to large areas. In the United States, and more particularly in the western portion of the country, *the broad east-west temperature belts have cut across the rainfall zones and so checkerboard the nation into natural regions which vary from damp and hot in the Southeast to semi-arid and cold in the northern rain-shadow of the western mountains.* Temperature and rainfall are the two prime factors in denoting climate. In this country, temperature decreases, in general, with the latitude, while rainfall decreases with the approach to the Pacific Mountain system. But there are important exceptions and modifications of these generalizations which must be noted in any study of the subject.

It is true, for instance, that the lines connecting points of equal surface temperature tend to cross the continent in an east-west direction. But such lines bend far southward as they cross the eastern mountains, and in the western third of the continent seem to lose all sense of direction as they twist and curve through the broken country. Further, such lines tend to crowd together in winter and to separate in summer, since the northern portions of the nation are subject to much greater variations in annual temperatures than are the southern states. This range of temperature is greatest in the area between the Rocky Mountains and the Great Lakes, near the Canadian border. Here the difference between mean summer and winter temperatures approaches 60 degrees. Along the Gulf Coast it is less than half that amount. Along the western coast of the country both rainfall and temperature are greatly affected by the winds from the ocean, so that temperature lines tend to parallel rainfall lines, both following along the coast, and both having high gradients as the nearby mountains are reached. Further, 50 to 60 percent of the rains fall at night, when evaporation is lessened. In general the eastern portion of the country has rainfall well distributed throughout the year, the central areas receive most of their rain during the warm months, and the Pacific Coast area has most of its rain during the early months of each year.

From the human point of view the humidity may be almost as important as the actual temperature. Charts showing this factor of climate indicate that the Atlantic Coastal Plains and the northeastern section of the country are humid to the point of "mugginess," while Utah seems to be the center of an area of low humidity. A secondary area of low humidity often appears over West Virginia and the surrounding territory. These areas are important factors in the development of certain health and recreation facilities; newer aspects of the social frontiers may be examined at length in the study of the several regions. These and other cultural elements are closely correlated with the amount of sunshine received.

For the year as a whole the least relative amount of sunshine in the United States is received along the north Pacific Coast, where the averages are only about 40 per cent of the total hours from sunrise to sunset, and in portions of the Great Lakes region and the central and northern Appalachian Mountain districts, where somewhat less than 50 percent of the possible amount is received. In the remaining districts east of the Mississippi River and in the northern border states from the Great Lakes westward to the Rockies the average annual sunshine ranges between 50 and 60 percent of the possible amount, except in portions of the Southeastern States, where it is somewhat higher, especially in the Florida peninsula. Between the Mississippi River and the Rocky Mountains the annual percentage is mostly between 60 and 70 which is true also of the central portion of the Rocky Mountain and Interior Plateau regions. The maximum amount of sunshine in the United States occurs in the far Southwest, including extreme western Texas, and portions of New Mexico, Arizona, and California. In southwestern Arizona and the adjoining portion of California the sun shines on the average for the year in nearly 90 percent of the total number of hours from sunrise to sunset.[13]

Temperature is sometimes utilized as a standard index of cultural as well as physical regions. Compare Huntington's regions of efficiency and of temperature. Yet there are varied aspects which may be observed. Of particular importance to the agricultural interests of the nation is the number of frost-free days in the year. The southern tip of Florida and the extreme lower Rio Grande Valley in Texas are practically free of frost. The cotton belt lies within the area which has approximately 200 days free of frost, and indeed is partly determined by this factor. This line would run close to the northern border of the Southwestern Region as the altitude increases. From this line northward the growing season gradually lessens until it becomes less than 90 days in the northern Rocky Mountains and ranges between that figure and 120 days along the Canadian border.

In conjunction with other factors, the prevailing winds are important climatic elements. The effect of the winds on temperature along the Pacific Coast has been mentioned. Since most of the winds are from the land to the ocean on the eastern shore of the continent, the Atlantic Ocean has little effect on climate. The fact that the winds generally blow from the west also accounts for the rain-shadow desert and semi-desert conditions prevailing to the eastward of the mountains along the Pacific Coast and the Rocky Mountains. This same climatic

[13] Joseph Burton Kincer, "Sunshine and Wind," *American Atlas of Agriculture, 1936*, p. 31.

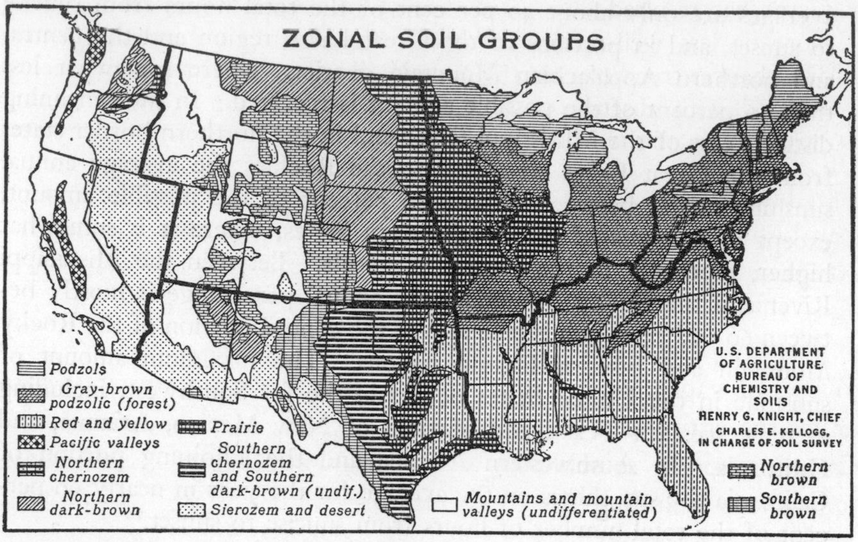

Another example of the great variety of natural regions and of their complicated features is found in the comparison of the great zonal soil groups with the major agricultural regions and with temperature and rainfall. Upon many of these features will depend the details of regional planning. Adapted by permission from the Bureau of Agricultural Economics of the United States Department of Agriculture.

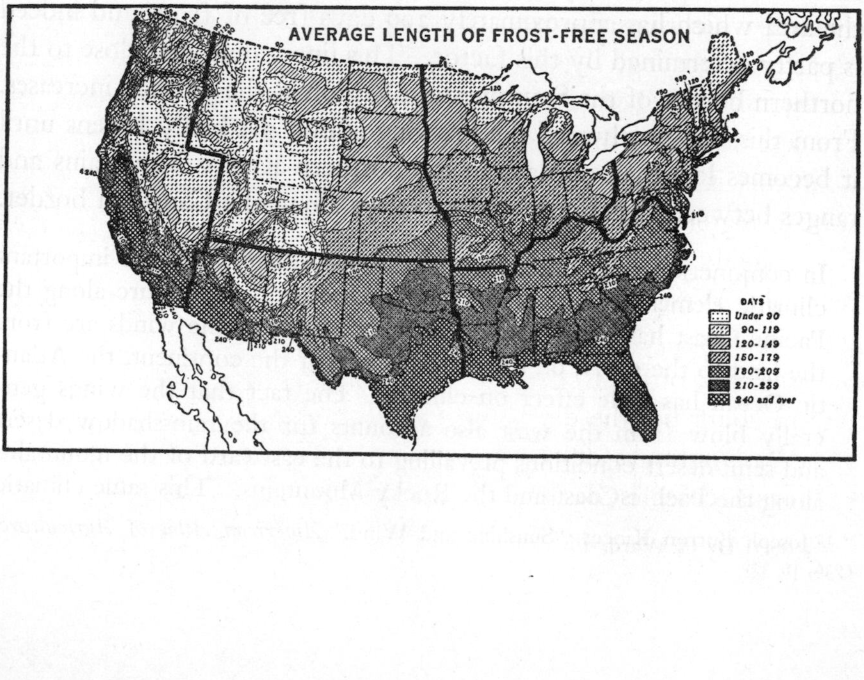

factor has resulted in a general eastward movement of storms along more or less well-recognized paths. In general, it seems that these disturbances trend toward the New England states. These movements, coupled with absence of east-west mountain ranges, make for great variations in the weather of the United States.

In combination, these various climatic conditions and tendencies may be made the basis of climatic regions of the nation. With the exception of the minor disturbing element of the Appalachian Mountains, the eastern portion of the United States has a climate of great uniformity, making due allowance for latitude and distance from sources of vapor for rainfall. So great is this uniformity that Ward unites the entire area east of the isohyet of 20 inches into one great climatic region. A subordinate region along the Gulf Coast is distinguished, including the lower portions of the states of Georgia, Alabama, Mississippi, and Texas and the entire states of Louisiana and Florida. The Great Plains climatic province is made to extend from the line of 20-inch annual rainfall to the crests of the Rocky Mountains, the Plateau region extends from this point westward to the crests of the Sierra Nevada-Cascade ranges, while the Pacific Coast province includes the remainder of the nation.[14] The three western divisions are divided into north and south regions along more or less arbitrary lines.

Renner describes the area east of the Great Plains and north of a line drawn through Virginia, North Carolina, Tennessee, Missouri, Oklahoma, and Texas, as humid continental. An extension of the line just described through northern New Mexico and Arizona into California is made a boundary between continental and subtropical climate regions. Thus the area south of the eastern portion of this line, roughly coinciding with the cotton belt, is labeled humid subtropical. West of the line of 20-inch rainfall, i.e., a line through western Texas, Oklahoma, Kansas, Nebraska, and the Dakotas, and on either side of the Rocky Mountains lies the dry continental region. To the south lies the dry subtropical region. The coast of Oregon and Washington is described as being temperate marine, while the California coast is designated as Mediterranean subtropical. The

[14] Robert De C. Ward, *The Climates of the United States*, pp. 19 ff.

southern tips of Florida and Texas are within the monsoon tropical regions, while the mountains are left undifferentiated.[15]

On the basis of types of rainfall, Kendrew divides the North American Continent into ten climatic areas.[16] The first of these extends along the Pacific Coast in a narrow strip as far east as to include the Cascade Range from northern California to the western tip of the Alaskan peninsula. Rainfall in this area is very abundant with a pronounced maximum in the late autumn or early winter. An indication of the variation in seasonal rainfall is given by figures for Olympia, where there is an average of less than one inch in July and August as compared to more than nine inches in December.

Most of the state of California forms the second major region. Here the cold off-shore currents effectively dry the winds in summer so that there is practically no rainfall. During the winter months precipitation varies from almost five inches during December and January at San Francisco to between one and two inches at San Diego.

East of the coastal ranges of mountains and west of the Rockies the scanty rainfall is more evenly distributed throughout the year, but tends to be concentrated during the colder half of the year with a secondary peak in late spring and early summer. Further south, in Arizona and New Mexico, the intense heat of summer produces thunder showers so that July and August become the rainiest months, the amount varying from one to three inches for each of these periods.

East of the Rocky Mountains and extending as far east as the mouth of the Rio Grande and Lake Michigan the Plains type of rainfall predominates. This is almost an exact reversal of the distribution found on the Pacific Coast. Winter is relatively dry, but rains begin in early spring and reach their maximum in June. Such a distribution is ideal for farming purposes, of course.

Most of the remainder of the country is classified as Gulf type, and is characterized by a late summer maximum rainfall, although there is considerable rainfall throughout the year. Within this area, and extending from the Mississippi River to and including the southern

[15] Cf. Map, "Climates of the United States," National Resources Committee's *Regional Factors in National Planning and Development*, December 1935, p. 171.

[16] W. G. Kendrew, *The Climates of the Continents*, pp. 262-299.

Appalachian ranges, is a region in which rainfall gradually decrease throughout the year until November, when it begins to increase toward its maximum in March.

Along the St. Lawrence Valley and the Atlantic Coast north of Chesapeake Bay and west of the New England coastal strip, the rainfall is remarkably uniform throughout the year, though there is usually a slight rise in volume in late summer following a slight subsidence in spring. On the New England coast the conditions are again reversed. Although the amount of rain falling varies only slightly during the year, the late spring and early summer months are the driest, while the maximum fall comes during the winter months.

Since, in the last analysis, rainfall is the only source from which we may expect to secure water for agriculture, for power generation, for navigation, for sanitation, for any of the innumerable uses to which we put it daily, its importance to our culture can hardly be overestimated.

> "One cannot imagine man separated from water any more than one can imagine him separated from land. Water is an essential part of his being. He uses it in innumerable ways; and because in areas of dense population he has been favored with it, frequently he spends it recklessly, thinks of it as he thinks of air as an unlimited requisite of existence and gives little heed to its value. In drier regions water is held of greater value, and stringent laws governing its use are formulated. The place of water in the lives of people in arid lands may be partially realized by the frequent rain ceremonies of the Hopi Indians and by the repeated references in the religious literature of desert peoples, as the Bible and Koran, to water as a blessing and to paradise as a place where there is abundant water." [17]

In terms of the sixfold regional division of the United States it is possible to characterize climatic types. Thus the *Northeast* has strongly contrasted seasons, short growing season, steep temperature gradients, little moderating effect of the ocean, plentiful rainfall well distributed throughout the year, frequent changes due to the passage of cyclonic storms. The *Southeast* has a more equable climate due to the effect of the Gulf of Mexico, the temperatures are higher and the range less, though diurnal changes are greater. Changes in weather are also less frequent. The rainfall is heavier and tends to a peak during the summer months.

[17] *Ibid.*, p. 287.

The *Middle States* have little protection from the cold winds from the north, and so have wide temperature variations, though not so wide as found in the Northwestern Region, which is still more exposed. The rainfall tends to be heaviest in the spring and early summer months and is considerably less than in the Northeast or the Southeast. However, rain falls more often in the neighborhood of the Great Lakes than in any other region of the country. As in the Northeast, a large portion of the precipitation is in the form of snow. Tornadoes tend to replace the thunderstorms of the more eastern and southern regions.

The lower rainfall is the distinguishing characteristic of the *Northwestern* and *Southwestern* Regions. These two regions differ mostly in temperature due to differences in latitude. Both lie in the rainshadow of mountains and both suffer alike from that fact. Temperature range here reaches its maximum in the Northwest States. The Northern Region has a very short growing season in its upper reaches, while the Southwestern Region has a range of from 120 days to more than nine months, the great variation being due to differences in altitude. Cold waves and "northers" are frequent, due to the low relief. The rainfall distribution is particularly favorable both from the diurnal and seasonal points of view; most of it comes during the nights of the growing season. Humidity is at a minimum.

The *Far Western* Region contains such a variety of climatic conditions that any attempt at synthesis seems impractical. It may be remarked, however, that the range of both rainfall and temperature is extreme, the first varying from less than 10 inches in southern California to more than 100 inches on the northwestern coast. The greatest amount of this rain comes during the winter months in the southern part of the region, while the northern portion is visited by almost continual rainfall, with the peak during the winter months. The temperature changes along the coast are much less than in any other region of the nation, though across the mountain barriers this range is increased greatly. Thunderstorms are rare, but winds from the north often do damage in the longitudinal valleys. The climate along the coast is largely controlled by the ocean, but this condition rapidly disappears as one proceeds eastward into the mountains, and the summers are extremely hot in the interior valleys of the southern portion of the region.

Minerals are the most "natural" of the products used by man in that they are formed, so far as is known, only by processes which take exceedingly long periods of time and in that man is apparently incapable of affecting these processes. Minerals may be mined and used, seemingly they cannot be created. Hence the region which lacks the minerals demanded by our modern culture is at a great disadvantage in comparison to those in which these products occur. This truism takes on added significance from the trend toward increased use of metals and inanimate forms of energy, the bases of western civilization.

> Mineral deposits are among the most highly prized treasures of any nation. They are the basic resources through which nations achieve industrial greatness and through which they are able to maintain their supremacy. With them the national foundations are laid for a rich industrial evolution; without them no nation can hope for a sustained industrial and commercial advance. The country without the basic minerals is inevitably destined for a lesser rank and is almost sure to be outstripped in economic progress by others more favorably supplied. Indeed, the cultural complex of a nation is, to a very high degree, mirrored in the per capita consumption of minerals, both as to quantity and variety. The extensive use of minerals, and metals particularly, is also the element which most clearly differentiates the complexity of the highly developed modern, high-precision measurements necessary for the highly technical products which add so much to our well-being, comfort and satisfaction. We are definitely living in a mineral age, and our cultural development is definitely a mineral civilization.[18]

The United States had an exceptionally abundant heritage of minerals. Just what the present stock is, no one knows, but it is certain that it has been greatly depleted. Large deposits of almost any of the useful minerals are not likely to be discovered in the future, but new technologies may bring into value minerals not now utilized. Hence speculation as to our ability to meet future needs is partly futile, though interesting and important from the point of view that we have no assurance of either new discoveries or changes in existing technology.

> A brief survey of the occurrence of the most valuable mineral products indicates wide variance in presence and value and thus goes far to explain differences in regional economy. Coal, the most important of the minerals used in our modern culture, is found within the United States in four major belts. The eastern mountain system provides coal

[18] William H. Haas, "Our Mineral Treasures," *Our Natural Resources and Their Conservation* (A. E. Parkins and J. R. Whitaker, editors), pp. 409-410. See also Chapter II in *Recent Social Trends in the United States.*

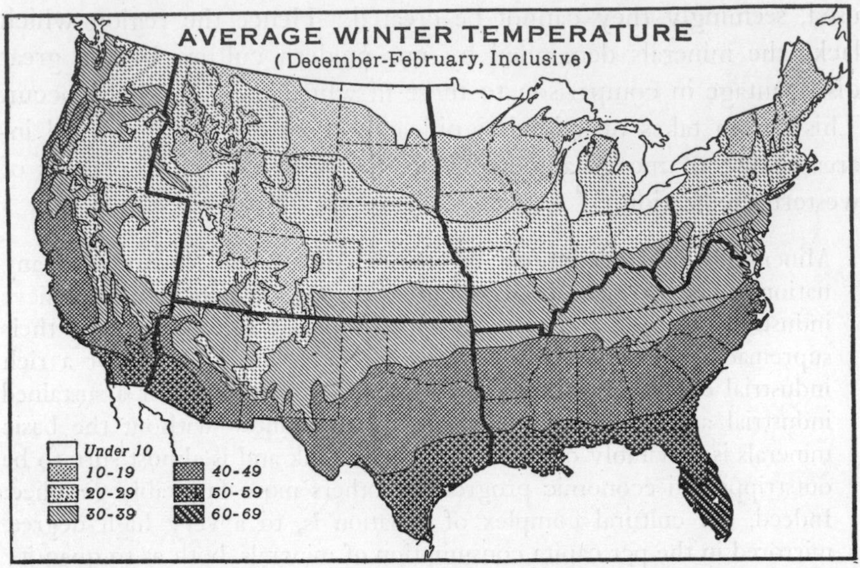

One of the best illustrations of the contradictions involved in natural regions is that of temperature as contrasted, for instance, with natural vegetation zones, rainfall, and river valleys, the former running north and south, the others, east and west. Adapted by permission from the Bureau of Agricultural Economics of the United States Department of Agriculture.

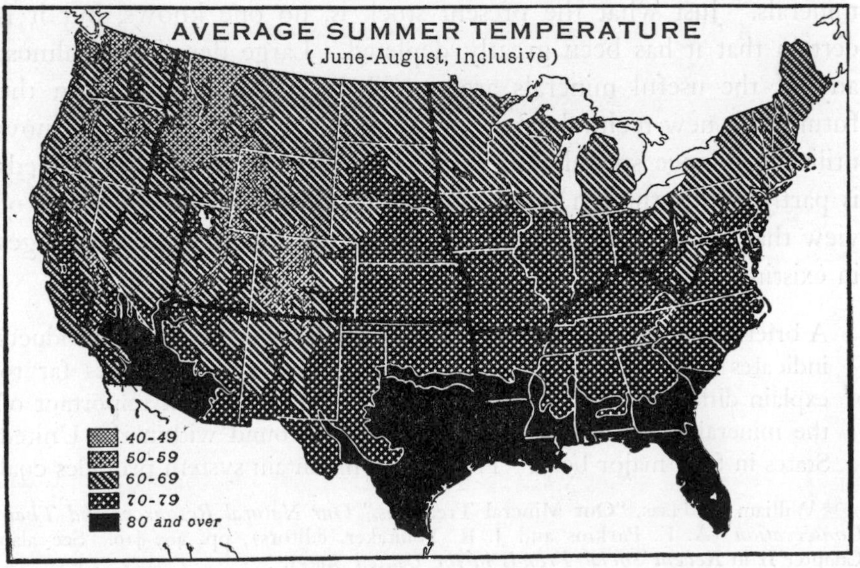

of both the anthracite and bituminous varieties, the only area in which both sorts are found. This coal belt includes parts of the Northeast, the Middle States, and the Southeast. Another belt, of doubtful value except in scattered spots, extends across lower Alabama, Mississippi, Arkansas, Louisiana, Texas, and on into Mexico. Of probable future value, this deposit is of little present importance. The mid-continental area of coal deposit lies on either side of the Mississippi River, in Indiana, Illinois, Missouri, eastern Kansas, and Oklahoma, with a detached area in northern Texas. These fields supply a large portion of the industrial coal used in the central portion of the nation. The Northwestern States have coal supplies in North Dakota, Montana, Wyoming, Colorado, Utah, and New Mexico, all in relatively small and scattered areas. The Far Western States have small and relatively inconsequential coal beds in each of the three coastal states. Iron is found in several of the same localities as is coal. This is largely responsible for the growth of the smelting industry in this country, although since its development the industry has begun to draw much of its supply of iron ore from the Lake Superior Region, at a considerable distance from the coal supplies. The Appalachian Mountains contain iron ore throughout most of their extent. Aside from the Lake Superior Region, other deposits are somewhat scattered and of little commercial value at this time. However sizeable ore deposits are known in Missouri, Texas, New Mexico, Colorado, Wyoming, Montana, Idaho, Washington, and California.

Petroleum is becoming more and more important as a source of energy in this nation and again the distribution is scattered among the various regions. A map of the oil production shows four or five fairly well-defined petroleum regions. The first petroleum was produced in Pennsylvania and this region is still one of the major producing areas. This general area extends from western New York and Pennsylvania westward through the Lake States and Kentucky to the Mississippi. The mid-continental field extends from southeastern Kansas through Oklahoma and Texas and includes the southeastern portion of New Mexico. Oil wells along the Gulf Coast are usually included in another region because of differences in the geological structures from which the oil is taken, but geographically may be assigned to the mid-continental field. The Rocky Mountain oil fields extend along the mountains through Colorado northward into southern Montana. The Far West is supplied with petroleum from the California fields, extending in a broken series from near

San Francisco to Los Angeles.[19] The discovery of the enormous east Texas oil field has given the mid-continental area a definite lead in the production of this form of energy within the past few years, but all of the other regions are of importance. The remaining metals of primary importance, gold, silver, lead, zinc and copper, are found mostly within the western portion of the country, though small deposits appear also in the eastern regions, and important quantities of lead and zinc are mined in the area about the juncture of the state lines of Missouri, Kansas, Oklahoma, and Arkansas.

> If we live in an era of minerals, certainly not the least of these in importance are the inanimate forms of fuel. By our modern technology we have learned to exploit these minerals for energy formerly supplied by much more laborious methods. "Formerly man depended upon his own muscular strength, supplemented somewhat by that of domestic animals and to a slight extent by water power, to do the work needed to produce crops and other goods. This had been the situation for centuries, and productive progress had been slow indeed. The productive capacity per man was probably nearly as high in the days of Grecian greatness as it was during colonial times in America. Then came the use of steam power, with coal as the source of energy. The changes resulting came slowly at first. During the latter part of the eighteenth century and early part of the nineteenth, man had not learned how to utilize this new-found source of energy on a big scale, and hence his progress was slow. However, by the middle of the nineteenth century, inventive genius had responded with machines or rapidly increasing efficiency. By means of steam engines and power-driven machinery, the energy latent in coal could then be utilized readily. Soon other sources of energy were discovered in the forms of petroleum and natural gas, electricity made water power more practicable, and thus the modern industrial era sprang into vigorous being. Within a few decades greater mechanical changes occurred than had taken place during several preceding centuries."[20]

On the bases of these resources mining and industrial regions have appeared, the steel region from Pittsburgh to Chicago, the "Silver States" bloc in Congress as examples. So, too, the Birmingham area, the petroleum interstate compacts, and other economic and social

[19] C. R. Van Hise, *The Conservation of Natural Resources* (Edited by Loomis Havemeyer), *passim.*

[20] Nels A. Bengston, "The Mineral Fuels," *Our Natural Resources and Their Conservation* (A. E. Parkins and J. R. Whitaker, editors), p. 437.

arrangements indicate that these regions are cultural as well as geologic.

Since soil gives man an opportunity to utilize many of the factors of physical geography, it is perhaps the most fundamental of the natural resources in spite of its relative loss of importance as we have turned more and more to minerals and inorganic fuels. Certainly land has been the base of America's wealth. Until the beginning of the modern age practically all of man's energy was secured through the soil, either through the direct appropriation of growing plants or through indirect appropriation via animals which in turn existed on growing plants. Thus, Sumner and Keller have posited the man-land ratio as the index of culture.

Soils are the products of the environmental conditions under which they have developed or are developing. These conditions in turn are the products of geologic, topographic, physiographic, climatic, and biologic factors.

The range of differences in environmental conditions within the United States is wide. This is due not only to the great area included, but also to the large number of possible combinations of environmental factors. Of the factors named, the climatic and biologic are active or dynamic and constitute the forces operating in any given spot in developing the soil. The others are passive and accelerate, retard, or modify in some other way the action of the dynamic factors. Any given association of environmental factors producing an environment would occupy, theoretically, a point only on the earth's surface, since in general each factor has a different strength of expression or a slight difference in character in different localities. In the practical consideration of environment as soil building agents, however, a range in strength of expression or of character of each factor is accepted as a unit rather than a single absolute value. An association of these value-ranging units, producing an environment, will occupy an *area* rather than a *point*.

Although the number of possible environmental units is large, many individual units extend over large areas. This is fortunate, since the expression of these conditions in terms of organic life and of that group of bodies, the soils, which are neither wholly organic nor wholly inorganic, may therefore be studied over large areas. The occurrence of similar physical conditions over large areas facilitates the study of the relationship of these conditions to the character of the soils, plants, and animals existing and developing under their influences. The physical conditions in the United States offer unusual advantages for the study of the relation of organic life and of soils to the physical environment.[21]

It is possible to group soils into two major groups, on the basis of more than one soil feature. For example, it would be possible to group them into well-drained soils and poorly drained soils, into dark-colored soils and light-colored soils, and, as we shall see, on at least one other basis. The arguments for and against one or the other of these bases cannot be stated here. It can be stated, however, that after mature consideration of all the factors involved it has been decided that the best basis on which soils can be classified into two major soil groups is that of the presence, in one of the groups (the Pedocal group) of a zone of lime carbonate accumulation in some horizon or layer of the soil profile, regardless of the character or composition of the parent rock, and the absence of such accumulated material in any horizon of the soil profile in the other group (the Pedalfer group). This seems to be the most permanent and most tangible basis on which to effect this result.[22]

Until recently soil was considered a geologic product. Soil surveyors busied themselves with a description of the nature of the rocks whose disintegration produced soil, the size of the soil particles, and similar properties. Since 1915, however, soil experts have tended more and more to include other elements, particularly the effect of biologic factors. The result has been a sharp distinction between the geologic nature of a bit of earth and its soil characteristics, though inevitably the two are closely related. This distinction is made clear by a consideration of the differences in the earth at the surface, the soil, and the earth at a depth of a few feet, which represents the parent material of the soil without the modifying effects of other factors. This distinction is also shown by the contrasts in maps of the soil regions of the country with maps of the parent materials of such soils.[23]

In terms of the characteristics of the soil itself, the United States may be divided into two major soil regions. A line drawn near the 100th meridian, or the eastern edge of the Great Plains Area, roughly divides the soils containing carbonate of lime and those lacking this important element. This division is partly geologic and in part the result of differences in rainfall. Geologic forces have placed the lime in the western soils and scant rainfall has prevented its being leached

[21] C. F. Marbut, "Soils of the United States," *Atlas of American Agriculture, 1936*, p. 11. This work is followed closely in the present discussion.

[22] *Ibid.*, p. 14.

[23] *Atlas of American Agriculture*, Part III, Plates 2 and 4, soils section.

out by percolating ground waters. The pedocalic soils, those containing the lime matter, are in general also much richer in organic material than the pedalfers, or soils in which the lime is missing. The pedocals have lost little of the mineral content of their parent rocks, while the reverse is true of the pedalfers. Economically, this difference is shown in the sales of artificial fertilizers in the two major divisions.

Each of these major divisions is subdivided into several major areas, which may be subdivided still further almost at will. However, on the basis of community of factors, the Bureau of Chemistry and Soils of the United States Department of Agriculture has outlined the major soil provinces of the country. The pedalfers are divided into the podzols, gray-brown podzolic soils, red and yellow soils, northern prairie soils, southern prairie soils. The pedocals are subdivided into northern chernozem, southern chernozem, northern and southern dark brown and brown soils, northern and southern gray desert soils. The mountain regions and the Nebraska sandhills are excluded from the regional classification. The Pacific Coast valley area has soils of such varied nature occurring within such narrow limits that it is treated as a separate province.

In the northern Lake Region, the Adirondack Mountains, the northern portion of New England and the hills of Pennsylvania, the eastern coast of New Jersey, are soils associated with low temperatures, abundant rainfall, and a covering of coniferous forests and other acid-tolerant growth. The soil consists of a layer of partly decayed vegetable matter overlying a gray or whitish stratum from which a large portion of the mineral and vegetable matter has been leached. The subsoil often contains a higher amount of these minerals. The topsoil thus has a high silica content. These are called podzols.

The gray-brown podzolic soils are closely related to the true podzols, but are distinguished by differences in color indicated by the name, due to a thin layer of humus material. The top layer indurated with humus is thicker, the subsoil is heavier and has no admixture of vegetable matter, though iron and aluminum compounds have been carried into it by the leaching which is the common attribute of both these soils. These soils are found in areas formerly occupied by deciduous forests with few conifers. This soil group occupies most of the North-

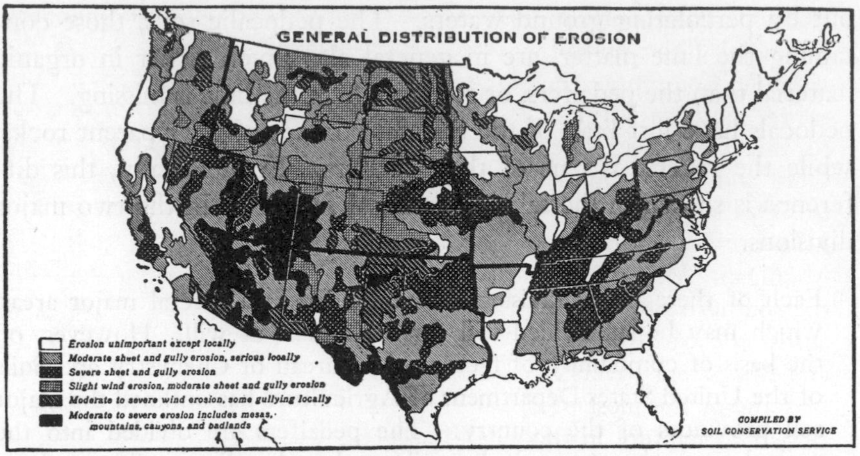

"RICH LAND, POOR LAND" WAS STUART CHASE'S WAY OF MAKING VIVID THE WASTE OF LAND AND RESOURCES

Above: The Regional Picture of Soil Erosion and

Below: The Regional Variation of Rainfall. Adapted by permission from the Bureau of Agricultural Economics of the United States Department of Agriculture.

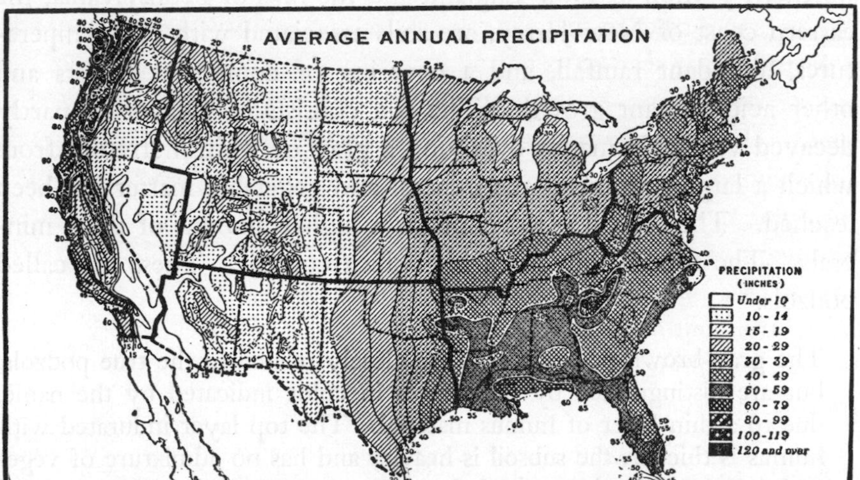

east and a large portion of the Middle States. The northern boundary is fixed by the podzol region. The southern boundary leaves the Atlantic Coast near the southern end of the Chesapeake Bay, runs across southern Virginia, western North Carolina, southern Tennessee to the Tennessee River, along that stream to the juncture of the Ohio and Mississippi, southwestward to include most but not all of the Ozark Region, and then swings eastward near the mouth of the Missouri River across Illinois into northwestern Indiana and Lake Michigan. West of that lake there is a tongue of the region covering the southern portion of Wisconsin and extending for a short distance across the Mississippi River. Other tongues extend up the Missouri and Mississippi Rivers from their junction. Thus this soil is the basis of some of the most prosperous as well as some of the most poverty-ridden agriculture in the nation. This is possible, of course, because of minor variations in the soil composition and the great differences in farming skill from one portion of the region to another.

Most of the Southeast is covered by the red and yellow soils, the most thoroughly leached soils of the nation. This leaching is due to the high rainfall and the generally sandy texture of the soils. The differences in color seem to be relatively unimportant, but the reddish soils are found on the higher grounds, while the lowlands are characterized by the more yellow soils. The depth of the ground water appears to be correlated with the difference in color. The red designation is incorrect in that the mature soil never displays a red surface. The red fields seen so often in the region indicate either immature soil or denudation of the grayish or yellowish surface, usually the latter. These soils have developed under forest conditions closely approximating the gray-brown podzols, but under higher temperature and more ground water, which explains the higher degree of leaching. The area covered by this soil group is about the same size as that occupied by the gray-brown podzolic group, extending along the southern boundary of the latter region well into Texas. Small areas along the Texas-Louisiana coast and a crescent of prairie soil in Alabama are to be excluded from the region.

Just to the west of the gray-brown and the red-yellow soil regions is found the prairie soils. These soils have developed in regions of high rainfall, but have not suffered leaching as would be expected normally, due to their thick cover of grass. This has resulted in a large amount of humus in the upper layer of the soils which gives them a black or dark brown color. The underlying material is also brown, with about the same fine-grained texture. The gray-brown soil prongs along the rivers, described above, in this soil region, represent the development of this underlying material after erosion has taken its toll, or, perhaps, they are transported materials. The southern section of this region is distinguished from the northern on the basis of somewhat greater leaching, due to less thickness of the grass cover or to higher rainfall. The areas along the Texas-Louisiana coast and in Alabama mentioned as "islands" in the red-yellow region, belong with the southern prairie soils.

The above four soil regions comprise the great pedalfer soil area of the nation. In general, and with the partial exception of the prairie soils, they may be characterized as having a topsoil from which at least some if not most of the mineral and vegetable content has been dissolved, to be deposited in the subsoil, or second stratum. High rainfall and abundant growth of vegetation seem to have been the dominant factors in creating these soil types.

From the western edge of the prairie soil region the rainfall grows less and the vegetation more sparse. It is in this area that the pedocalic, or lime-carbonate-bearing soils, have developed. The notable exceptions are undeveloped soils in some portions and the occurrence of pedalferic soils at moderate elevations in the Pacific Coast Region. The influence of climate and vegetation is shown in the fact that while the soil regions of the eastern part of the United States run in a general east-west direction, the divisions in the western portion of the country trend in a north-south line. The relative abundance of vegetable matter and its influence are indicated in the growing lightness in color of the soils as one proceeds from east to west to the western edge of the arid area.

The *Atlas of American Agriculture* divides the soils of the Great Plains Area into three regions, the Chernozems, the Dark Brown, and the Brown. The division is made on the distinction in color as the rainfall and the vegetable cover and humus content become more scant. However, along the foot of the Rocky Mountain range there lies a narrow strip of soil which is darker than that to the eastward. All of these soils show a profile similar to that of the prairie soils, but have a zone of concentration of carbonate of lime at depths varying from little more than one foot to three feet or more. In the western portion of the area, in the brown soils, there may be a mantle of two or three inches of loose, wind-blown material overlying the matted grass roots which gives the soil its characteristic color. Save for these minor differences the three soil regions might well be combined into one, it seems.

West of the strip of chernozem soil, the dark-brown and brown soils tend to interlock due to local differences in relief and rainfall. Some small areas of chernozem soils even occur at the foot of the mountains and in the Columbia Plateau Region. However, in general the plateaus and basins of the Rocky Mountain Region are occupied by brown soils.

Between the Rocky and Sierra Nevada-Cascade mountain ranges lies the great area of arid basins and mountains with its characteristic gray soil. Due to the low agricultural importance of this land little soil mapping has been done, but it is assumed that the typical profile consists of loose gravel material over a crust of very fine gray or whitish material in which other small rocks may be embedded. Below this crust lies the brown or reddish brown soil which contains the roots of plants. Below this stratum is the zone of concentration of lime carbonate characteristic of all the soils of that portion of the country. Although the Intermontane Region is divided into a northern and southern portion, the soils of the entire area from southern Idaho and Oregon to the Mexican border are essentially of this character so far as is now known. Of course much of the region is rough country and, therefore, not included in descriptions of soil types.

In the mountain sections of the Pacific Coast Region little information on the soils has been collected, but since this area is similar in climate and vegetation to the mountains of the eastern portion of the United States, it seems likely that investigation will reveal the presence of pedalferic soil structures here. This supposition is furthered by the presence of soils resembling the pedalferic gray-brown soils of the east in the Puget Sound Region. A somewhat similar situation exists in the Willamette Valley in Oregon. Although the mature soils of the California Valley display the dark color and the zone of calcium carbonate concentration characteristic of the pedocals, these soils are overlaid in many places with alluvial fans of soil material which has not yet developed a definite profile. Further south, in the neighbor-

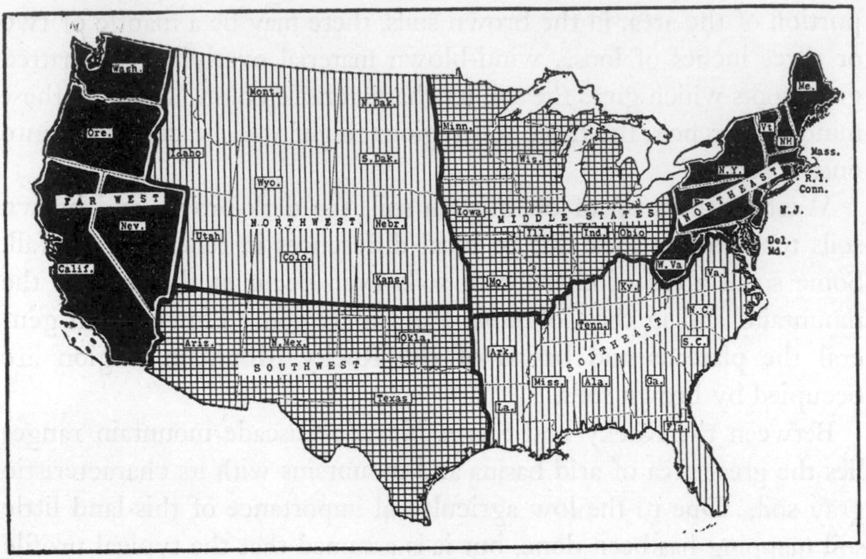

Above: The Six Major Societal Group-of-States Regions utilized in *American Regionalism* as approximating the largest available degree of homogeneity measured by the largest number of indices available for the largest possible number of purposes.

Below: The map below illustrates the no-man's land of border lines and states and indicates how the regions would be flexible and modified if it were not necessary to utilize state lines. The Southwest, for instance, would follow popular usage and include parts of Utah, Colorado, and Kansas, as would the Middle States extend over to the tree belt line of Nebraska and the Dakotas. West Virginia would classify in three regions.

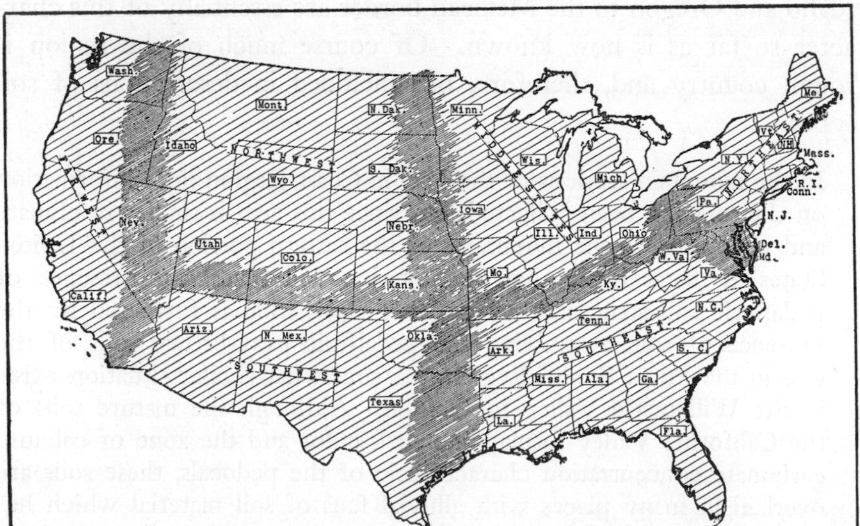

hood of Los Angeles, the soils are noncalcareous. The soils of the Imperial Valley are recently deposited alluvium and have not developed soil profiles. It is evident that more detailed work is required in the Pacific Coast Region before accurate classification is possible. The *Atlas of American Agriculture*, soils section, recognizes this situation by lumping all of the cultivated soils of the region into one category, "Soils of the Pacific Valleys."

The mutual interdependence of soil and climate is revealed in the regions of natural vegetation. Indeed these areas gain admission to a discussion of "natural" regions because they are such sensitive indicators of the factors of purely physical geography; but they also have the further great human value of indicating the sorts of agricultural use to which man may put the lands.

The vegetation of the United States may be broadly divided into forest, grassland, and desert shrub.

The forest vegetation forms two broad belts, one extending inland from the Atlantic Ocean and the other inland from the Pacific Ocean. The eastern is relatively continuous, while the western is broken by many interspersed areas of nonforested land. In the region east of the Cascade-Sierra the forests are confined largely to mountain tops and high plateaus. The eastern portion of the western forest extends down over the Rocky Mountain range and divides the unforested portion of the United States into two broad strips, one of which lies east of the Rocky Mountains and the other between the Rockies and the Cascade-Sierra. Of these two belts the eastern constitutes the great grassland area, while the western constitutes the desert-shrub area. The desert area broadens out toward the south, and along the Mexican boundary forms a continuous strip extending from the Pacific Ocean to the Gulf of Mexico, interrupted only here and there at higher elevation.[24]

Each of these various regions has been made the locus of a particular type of agriculture varying from the forestry and grazing of the cold northern tongues of the Canadian provinces, which extend southward into this country, to the Mediterranean agriculture of Florida, the Rio Grande Valley of Texas, and southern California. But crops raised, animals tended, the forms through which soils are exploited are more cultural than natural. Hence a discussion of agricultural regions is postponed to the chapter on Rural Regionalism.

[24] H. L. Shantz and Raphael Zon, "Natural Vegetation," *idem*, p. 3.

Chapter IV

NATURAL REGIONS: RIVER VALLEY REGIONS

NEATLY conforming to the realities of regional planning as recommended by those who advocate "natural" regions, are the river valley regions. If the nation had been organized and its cultural areas developed on the basis of physiographic regions and if the world of transportation, communication, and technology had not changed, the river valley areas would afford an approximation to the perfect regions unless indeed they tended too much toward the sectional economy or toward Turner's subnational conflict. From any viewpoint they afford effective subregions through which state lines may be transcended in adequate co-operative planning ventures without violating state priorities or changing the form of government. Such subregional divisions afford perhaps the most usable of all natural regions through which to implement the co-ordinating of federal and state functions. River valley regions in America, as in other parts of the world, combine resources with realism in their role in the historical development of civilization and in their continuing but differing significance in the modern technological world. The biographies of the Nile or of Ole Man River or of the Blue Danube or the Silvery Rio Grande are no more romantic and powerful in their stories of earlier culture than are the new rivers of waters in their dramatic and realistic part in power and irrigation, in flood and conservation, in sanitation and navigation in present-day civilization.

This has been pictured in a hundred ways. Thus, the Mississippi and its valley, the river and its relentless flow from the North to the South, carrying its burden of soil and fortunes of land and men has been portrayed. "From as far west as Idaho and as far east as Pennsylvania,

4,500 miles from Canada, the river flows to the Gulf. . . . Water from the glaciers of the Rockies, and from the turkey ridges of the Alleghenies: water from two-thirds of all the rivulets, creeks, streams and rivers of the nation—the Mississippi. Down to St. Louis: down the Milk, the Cannonball, the Sioux and Cheyenne; down the Chippewa, Rock, Wisconsin and St. Croix, the Republican, the Platte and the Niobrara. Down from Pittsburgh, a thousand miles to Cairo: the Monongahela, the Allegheny and the Kanawha; down the Wabash, the Hocking and the Muskingum—the Kentucky, the Cumberland and the Tennessee. Down the Ohio a thousand miles to Cairo. Down a thousand miles from Cairo: down the Wolf, the White and the St. Francis; the Yazoo, the Old Red and the Big Black; down the Ouachita and the Arkansas, a thousand miles to New Orleans." [1]

The phenomenal rise of the automobile and the new modes of rapid transportation and communication have obscured for most Americans the important aspects of the nation's physical wealth as found in its hundreds of rivers. Yet to counteract this is the new dominance of power in which streams are again keys to wealth and development. These are inseparably related to countless little lakes which dot the landscape and the Great Lakes, like inland seas, with the limitless reaches of another 5,000 miles of gulf and ocean water front. What the Lakes to Gulf development might be is still problematical, as are the new reaches of development upon the Tennessee, the Cumberland, the Ohio, the Colorado, the Columbia, and the others listed in this chapter. There are in the nation four great rivers which will average more than two thousand miles in length; another four, more than a thousand miles; and four score and more are navigable, capable of adding richly to the fertility and to the scenic beauty and commercial assets of the nation.[2] Pictures of showboat and river romance are lost in the past, yet the modern picture is more dynamic: power dams and factories, rivers of waters with towns on their shores, barges on their bosoms, big rivers laden with commerce, little rivers and creeks, mountain stream and lake, water reservoir for the cities. Yet it is unfortunate that the nation has forgot what these rivers have been in the romance and the techniques of earlier developments, whether as practical routes of discovery and

[1] Adapted from "The River," condensed from *McCall's* for May, 1937, and reprinted in *Conservation*, vol. 3, No. 3, p. 11.

[2] Cf. Lucien Lehman, *The American Illusion*, p. 30.

commerce or travel ways for intrepid trappers whose trading posts penetrated far into the depths of the forest frontier.

This importance of rivers has recently been re-emphasized by many students and writers. Stuart Chase writes vividly about rivers. "Man has long addressed his survival to great rivers–the Nile, the Tigris and Euphrates, the Hwang Ho, the Ganges, the Danube and the Volga. With their co-operation civilizations rise, the wheat springs, trade flows, great cities grow. If their laws are forgotten or neglected, civilizations fall, floods roar, silt chokes the channels, bread fails, drought spreads. North America is no exception to this ancient rule. The continent has given us much and will give us more, if we work with her. But if we continue our neglect and contempt for her land and waters, she will exact a calamitous penalty, and all the laboratories, all the machines, all the banks, will not offset it."[3]

Returning again to historical America, it is an interesting commentary upon the regional expansion of the United States that the decisive factor in the significant westward movements was not land but rivers. Thus, when there was protest to those who sought the Oregon lands, traveling through areas of rich and fertile soils, the reply was always about rivers in Oregon. Land there was here in the rich prairies, but in the farther West there was to be also land where farms could border on rivers whose transportation services would connect them with markets at home and abroad.

Horace Greeley thought the emigration of a thousand souls to Oregon wore "an aspect of insanity." In a burst of indignant eloquence he exclaimed: "Why do they brave the desert, the wilderness, the savage, the snowy precipices of the Rocky Mountains, the weary summer march, the storm-drenched bivouac, and the gnawings of hunger?" But the Oregon emigrants were not insane. They could give the editorial pundit a very sound answer, namely: "You say our wagon wheels in going to the Willamette carved ruts across millions of acres that are fully as fertile as what we find here. True enough. But what good is land if the means of getting its products to market do not practically exist? In the Willamette Valley a navigable river flows by every settler's door, and the ocean is only a short distance away. Similar situations in the Middle West were no longer easy to find. Therefore, we headed for Oregon to insure to ourselves and our children really valuable farm homes."[4]

[3] Stuart Chase, *Rich Land, Poor Land*, p. 17.
[4] Joseph Schafer, *The Social History of American Agriculture*, pp. 3-4.

Again, it is well known how the "Western Waters" were the key to these earlier "wests," from which the nation was to develop its frontiers and achieve new regional expansion. If the story of the early nation is essentially a story of the "wests," it is important to note how the several rivers were instrumental as the gateways to further expansion. Thus, Frederick Jackson Turner pictures four river systems basic to the earlier migrations.

> There was "The New River, rising in North Carolina near the head-springs of rivers that flowed to the Atlantic, tore a defiant course through the Blue Ridge and the Alleghenies to join the Great Kanawha in West Virginia. Another tributary of the Great Kanawha, the Greenbrier, rising near the sources of the Monongahela, skirted the western edge of the Alleghenies in its southward flow. Here, on the upper waters of the Ohio, was the physiographic basis for a state, a natural unit, rudely cut by the Pennsylvania boundary line, and apportioned between that state and Virginia, in spite of the veto of the Alleghenies." Next and "near to the springs of the New River were the many streams that flowed between the ridges of the Cumberland Mountains and the Alleghenies to join the Tennessee. These affluents of the Tennessee–Powell's River, the Clinch, the Holston, the French Broad, the Nolichucky, and the Watauga–walled in to east and west by mountains, made another natural unit. Here Virginia's southern line ran right across these river courses, and left the settlements at the head of the Holston in Virginia, while their neighbors lower on the river were under the jurisdiction of North Carolina; and between these settlements and the parent states ran the Allegheny wall. It would be strange if these physiographic facts did not produce their natural result." Once again, "passing through Cumberland Gap at Virginia's southwest corner, the pioneer reached another area of Virginia's back lands, the greenswards of Kentucky. This land was bounded on the north by the Ohio, while to the south was the Cumberland, forming a natural boundary, but severed for the most part from the political bounds of the region by the same unreasonable Virginia line that had cut in two the settlements on the Tennessee. These Kentucky fields constituted another natural economic area." And, finally, "across the Ohio lay the wide Northwest, between the Mississippi and the Great Lakes, its ownership in dispute between Virginia, Massachusetts, and Connecticut, under their charter bounds, and New York, through her protectorate over the Six Nations." [5]

[5] Frederick Jackson Turner, *The Significance of Sections in American History*, pp. 93-94.

It has often been pointed out that the traveler today, across the wide expanse of the great West, whether by rail or by automobile, may well observe the earlier routes of river valley and mountain pass. Certainly the romance of the Colorado and the Rio Grande thrill the tourist as dominant factors in the whole terrain. If the tourist will study his history, he will find that no less marked by river valleys than the earlier "wests" was the continuing further westward movement of later years.

> A. B. Hulbert points out that "Beyond the Mississippi, the Missouri, Platte and Arkansas Rivers were the keys of transportation to the Rockies; at the head of the Platte (near Casper, Wyoming) the Sweetwater Valley offered a passageway through famous South Pass, beyond which the Green and Bear presented fertile oases for those who were pressing on by way of the Snake River and the Blue Mountains to Oregon, or by way of Raft River and the Humboldt to the Carson River passageway across the Sierras to California. At the head of the Arkansas the Purgatoire (called 'Picketwire' by cattlemen) led to Raton Pass and, beyond, the trail ran down through the wide levels and uplands of New Mexico, taking the traveler or wagon train to curious old Santa Fé. Gaining thus the Rio Grande River, a California path diverged from the valley below Socorro and led by later Cooke's Spring (near Deming, New Mexico) through the modern Apache Pass to Tucson and the Gila River; crossing the Colorado and the sand hills, the parched (now luxurious) Imperial Valley opened the way either to San Diego or the pueblo of Los Angeles."[6]

The best picture of the nation today in terms of river valleys is that which has been presented by the National Resources Committee through its special studies of *Drainage Basin Problems and Programs.* It constitutes an extraordinary picture of the nation in terms of natural valley regions as well as an inventory of the problems and the potentialities of the multiple and rich natural resources as found in the rivers of the nations and the natural regions created by them. The total picture is envisaged through seventeen river valley regions, which in turn comprehend approximately one hundred sub-river valley regions, which again comprehend a thousand tributaries, many of which include among them the most beautiful as well as the most significant streams in the nation.

[6] Archer Butler Hulbert, *Frontiers, The Genius of American Nationality*, pp. 165-166.

The seventeen river valley regions comprehend:

1. The New England Drainage Basins with the Maine Rivers, Merrimack, Eastern Massachusetts, Thames-Blackstone-Taunton, Connecticut-Housatonic.

2. The North Atlantic Drainage Basins with the Hudson, New Jersey-New York Coast, Delaware, Susquehanna.

3. Middle Atlantic Drainage Basins with the Upper Chesapeake, Potomac, Lower Chesapeake, James-Roanoke-Chowan, Carolina Coast (Tar-Neuse, Cape Fear, Peedee, Santee, and Edisto).

4. Southeast Drainage Basins with the Savannah-Altahama, St. Marys-Suwannee, St. Johns, Southern Florida (Kissimmee, Tampa, and Everglades), Appalachicola-Chattahoochee, Eastern Gulf (Aucilla and Escambia), Mobile.

5. Tennessee Valley with its Tennessee River.

6. Ohio Drainage Basins with the Ohio General: Ohio Eastern Tributaries (Upper Ohio, Beaver, and Kanawha), Ohio Northern Tributaries (Muskingum, Scioto, Miami, and Wabash), Ohio Southern Tributaries (Big Sandy, Kentucky, Green, Cumberland, and Lower Ohio).

7. Great Lakes Drainage Basins with the Great Lakes: Superior, Michigan, Huron, Erie, Ontario, St. Lawrence, Champlain.

8. Upper Mississippi-Red River of the North, with the Red River of the North, Mouse-Devils Lake, Rainy, Mississippi Headwaters, Minnesota, Upper Eastern Tributaries, Upper Western Tributaries, Wisconsin, Rock, Iowa-Cedar, Des Moines-Skunk, Illinois, Western Tributaries-Keokuk-Alton, St. Louis, Kaskaskia-Big Muddy.

9. Missouri Drainage Basins with the Missouri Headwaters, Yellowstone, Upper Western Tributaries, Upper Eastern Tributaries, Cheyenne, White-Niobrara, Platte, Kansas, Lower Missouri, Chariton-Grand, Osage, Gasconade.

10. Southwest Mississippi Drainage Basins with the Upper Arkansas, Cimarron, Canadian, Central Arkansas, Neosho-Verdigris, Lower Arkansas, Upper White-Black-St. Francis, Upper Red, Washita, Lower Red, Ouachita.

11. Lower Mississippi Drainage Basins with the Cairo-Memphis, Lower Mississippi, Yazoo-Black, Pontchartrain, Pearl-Pascagoula.

12. Upper Rio Grande, above Fort Quitman, Texas.

13. Western Gulf Drainage Basins with the Sabine, Trinity, Brazos-Colorado, Guadalupe, Nueces, Lower Rio Grande-Pecos.

14. Colorado Basin with its Colorado River.

15. The Great Basin, Central and Northern, Sierra Nevada, Great Salt Lake, and Humboldt.

16. California Drainage Basins with the Northern California-Klamath, Central Valley-San Francisco Bay, Central California Coast, Southern California Coast.

17. Pacific Northwest (Columbia River-General Plan) with the Snake, Upper Columbia, Middle Columbia, Lower Columbia-Willamette, Puget Sound, Oregon Coast, Washington Coast.[7]

The special significance of the river valley regions in the present era may be indicated by the proposal of the President to set up a number of federal authorities, supplementary to the TVA and the Mississippi River Valley Committee, with a view to organic planning for the nation's future. This proposed regional arrangement will be further discussed in a later section. The basis upon which the study of *Drainage Basin Problems and Programs* (from which the recommendations grew) was undertaken included three main objectives. These were: "(1) to determine the principal water problems in the various drainage areas of the country, (2) to outline in broad terms an integrated pattern of water development and control designed to solve those problems, and (3) to present specific construction projects and investigation projects as elements of the integrated pattern or plan, with general priorities of importance and time."[8] The regional and national implications of river valley areas may be examined further from both the general statement of problems and objectives and from the specific problems involved in the several valleys.

Thus, the Committee interprets the problem broadly by pointing out that in the past people have been concerned primarily with a single or immediate interest. Accordingly, "With respect to water, people have been concerned, for the most part, only with their own immediate interests in particular types of problems. In planning the storage of water for irrigation in the arid West, the possibilities of concomitant power development have not always been emphasized. In planning the drainage of lands for agricultural use in the humid East, the possibility of injury to other interests affected by the behavior of water commonly has been ignored. Far too often in all sections of the country the control of a stream subject to destructive floods, the improvement of a river channel for navigation, the procurement of water from a stream for municipal and domestic use, the disposal of sewage and industrial waste in a drainage channel, or other concern in the use or control of water, has been treated as an isolated problem, in disregard both of the inherent relationships between various types

[7] National Resources Committee, *Drainage Basin Problems and Programs,* December 1936, pp. 103-104.
[8] *Ibid.,* p. 1.

of water problems and of the possibilities of multiple-purpose development. Too often, also, specific water problems have been treated solely in terms of particular localities, urban or rural, with resultant injury to other localities on the same river system. Water development in general has been haphazard."[9]

One major objective of co-operative regional planning is to point up the need for change from the old ways of utilizing resources to better ways and means for both conserving and developing for further use. The Committee points out that "during the last few years it has become increasingly apparent that such orderless, unintegrated treatment of water problems, however natural and excusable it may have been under pioneer conditions, should no longer be tolerated."[10] The Committee points out further that, although water is at times a merciless enemy of man, it is nevertheless perhaps the most precious natural resource of the nation. They remind us that the supply of available water for essential purposes is strictly limited, and that even so it varies from time to time at a given place as well as from place to place at a given time. The report emphasizes the fact that the further development of large areas in all sections depends on the extent to which the supply of water can be increased by various techniques of storing surface water or pumping ground water, or by other means. They warn that wasteful use of water must cease and that also the maximum supply of water that can be made regularly available in each drainage area must be put to its best co-ordinated use.

"Under these circumstances," they continue, "it would be unwise to depend solely on the long-run tendency of economic conditions to bring about the use of water in the places and ways in which it would have greatest value. The process would be far too slow and far too costly. Moreover, the sum total of individual and local interests in the waters of a drainage area may differ greatly from the best interest of the public at large in their use. Still further, continued unco-ordinated development of waters might presently preclude in many basins their later control and utilization in an orderly, balanced manner conducive in greatest measure to the general welfare. The inherent conflict of interests in water, between private users, between private and

[9] *Ibid.*, pp. 1-2.
[10] *Ibid.*, p. 2.

public organizations, and even between public agencies, increases year by year. From every point of view, a practicable water development program that can be put into action promptly is needed in each river basin of the country. A plan without action is useless; continued unplanned action would be foolhardy." [11]

In Chapter XI we discuss the various functional and administrative levels of regional planning. Perhaps in no phase is the "problem" aspect more clearly demonstrated than in that of water planning. The total problems envisaged in the national program have been grouped under eleven divisions, each varying, of course, with the several regions. The major problems of water use and control listed by the Committee are: bank and coastal erosion control; domestic and industrial water supply; drainage; flood control; generation of electric power; irrigation; navigation; recreation; soil conservation and forest development; waste disposal and pollution abatement; wildlife conservation.[12] Something of the regional variation of problems and programs may be seen from the description of the chief problems in the several regions.

Thus, in New England the problem is strikingly in contrast to that, let us say, in the Colorado or Rio Grande River Valley regions. In New England, flood control is uppermost and "must be approached not as an isolated problem, but as one of several benefits, including power development, improved sanitation, enhancement of recreational opportunities, and betterment of streams for navigation, that may result in combination from the construction of storage reservoirs to collect flood waters and release them later in relatively dry periods. The necessity for approaching the problem in this manner arises from the fact that reliable studies of the frequency of floods and of resultant damages indicate the latter may not alone justify the cost of the reservoirs needed to eliminate such damages. This is true despite the availability of many favorable sites for new reservoirs and the possibility of utilizing for storage numerous lakes and ponds, by controlling their outlets. Storage reservoirs accordingly must be built both for power and for flood protection consistent with provisions for adequate financing and reimbursement for project costs, where material power development does ensue. Experience in New England has confirmed the value of power-storage reservoirs in this respect. It is assumed

[11] National Resources Committee, *op. cit.*, December 1936, p. 2.
[12] *Ibid.*, p. 4.

that such reservoirs would be intelligently and adequately operated under the direction of a suitable agency."[13]

To take an example of great contrast, in the Colorado Drainage Basin, there are the multiple problems of storage, recreation, irrigation, and navigation. Thus, the Boulder Canyon Dam is a multiple-purpose project, with extraordinary possibilities and almost exceeding the imagination, involving navigation, flood control, available water for municipal use as well as for irrigation, the development of power. Consequently the future development of civilization in the basin is involved.

The Committee points out the importance of silt as one of the more serious problems of the basin, since, they remind us, "the Colorado River has carried annually 200 million tons of sediment to the Gulf, and every reservoir built upon the system will be slowly robbed of its storage space unless remedial measures are applied."[14]

Furthermore, the Committee emphasizes the necessity of knowing the facts. "The Colorado River compact makes the consumptive use of water (diversions less return waters) the measure and limit of allocations of the waters of the river. The several states involved must allot among themselves the blanket apportionments specified by the compact. This cannot be done without full knowledge of the water consumed in irrigation, of evaporation from reservoirs, of the water that can be economically exported from the basin, and of the contributions and consumptive uses by each state under past, present, and final conditions of development. Data essential for the solution of the many problems involved must come from studies and measurements of erosion, the quality of water, stream flow, underground waters, the consumptive use of water, the effect of forests on water supply, and from surveys for reservoirs, irrigation projects, power sites, and trans-mountain diversions. The water resources of the Colorado Basin have been studied heretofore largely in terms of state and municipal interests. They should be studied likewise in terms of the basin as a whole, in terms of interbasin relationships, in terms of national welfare, and in terms of international relations, with due regard to the various interests involved and in the light of all relevant economic and cultural conditions. The fact, for example, that diversions of water from the

[13] *Ibid.*, p. 9.
[14] *Ibid.*, p. 85.

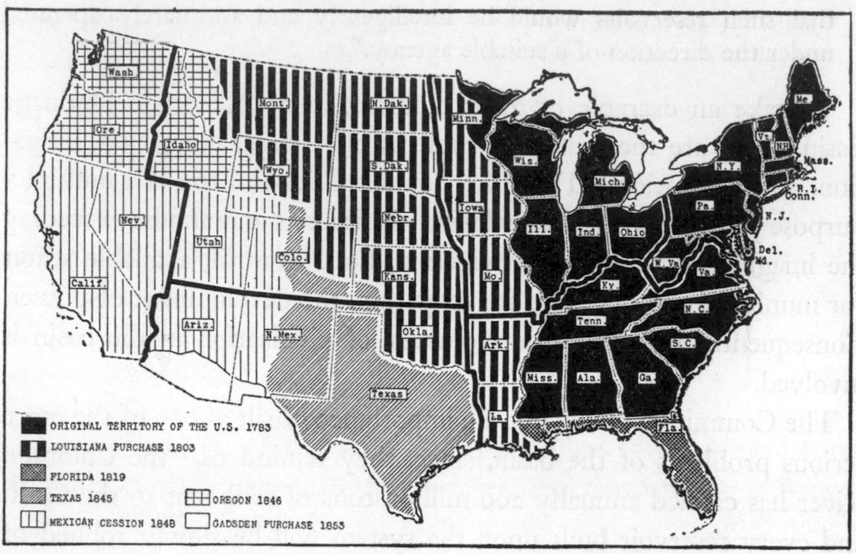

Above: Historical Development of the Nation. Adapted from J. S. Bassett, *A Short History of the United States.*

Below: The Seventeen Major River Valley Regions. Adapted from the National Resources Committee, *Drainage Basin Problems and Programs.*

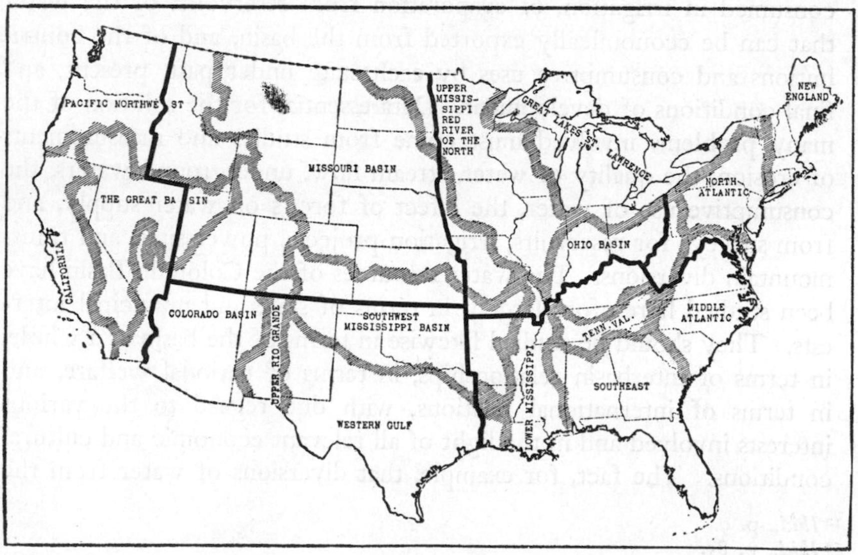

basin that have been made or proposed amount to several million acre-feet annually, raises questions of interregional and national scope." [15]

Contrast, again, the California area in which the region must depend ultimately for its further expansion upon the development and utilization of all available water, with, let us say, the Southeastern Region, which has too much water in some seasons and some areas. Thus the outlook for the California area with its fast-growing population, variously predicted to increase from its more than six millions to from ten to twenty millions, must necessarily depend upon the supply of water that can be made regularly available for essential purposes. Here, as in other western areas of new social frontiers, agriculture will be conditioned by the supply of water for irrigation, industries will depend for power on hydroelectric energy, and consequently cities and farm lands and rural life, communities and factories, will be conditioned almost entirely by the supply of water available to them. All of these basic factors are more important than the usual minor problems of "the need for better water through abatement of pollution, the need for additional river improvements in behalf of navigation, the need for further development of water bodies for recreational use, and the like." [16] Contrasted with the East, the Ohio, the Mississippi, the Cumberland, the Connecticut Valley, the flood problem, though urgent in some localities, "is less fundamental than the requirement for more water to replenish or replace underground supplies for irrigation and to provide adequate domestic supplies for the areas of denser urban population." [17]

The romance of the Oregon trail or of the multiple transcontinental highways and railroads is no more romantic nor realistic in frontier realism than the nearly completed 249-mile aqueduct to divert water from the Colorado River over the mountains to Los Angeles. So, too, what were formerly vast desert wastes now blossom with Edens of crops and flowers and beautiful homes, thus creating new regional worlds for the enrichment of the new frontiers. Still contrasting with these are the river valleys of the Great Pacific Northwest and of the multiple mountain and valley streams of the Southeast where power and industry are at stake.

[15] National Resources Committee, *op. cit.*, December 1936, p. 85.
[16] *Ibid.*, p. 93. [17] *Ibid.*

Two or three further examples will suffice. Thus, the most pressing problem of the Pacific Northwest at present in relation to power "is the development, through stimulation of power-consuming industries and otherwise, of markets for the output of projects now under construction, particularly those at Grand Coulee and Bonneville. The proposal to add greatly to the height of the dam under construction at Grand Coulee is intended not only to increase the output of power, but also to promote irrigation and in so doing create a market for power. Some of the power made available by the higher dam could be used to pump water to irrigate ultimately 1,200,000 acres of fertile land above the proposed reservoir and otherwise to serve settlers on the land reclaimed. The long-term relationships of the High Dam should receive further study. The dams at Grand Coulee and Bonneville are the uppermost and lowermost members of a system of 10 dams by which it is proposed to utilize ultimately 92 percent of the 1,300-foot fall of the Columbia River in its 750-mile course from the Canadian border to the sea for power plants with an aggregate installed capacity of more than 10,000,000 horsepower. The objective challenges admiration, but construction of additional units of the system should not get out of step with the regional requirements for power. The system of dams proposed would provide, with associated channel improvements, for sea-going ships to The Dalles, 190 miles inland, and for modern barges to Priest Rapids, 400 miles inland. Decades undoubtedly will pass before the development of the Columbia River for power, irrigation, and navigation is completed."[18]

The elements of variety and contrast are here emphasized both to indicate the availability of river valley regions for specialized functional planning and also to show how fundamental it is to permit of regional specialization. Still further, the extraordinary variety and diversity of physical characteristics indicate the difficulty of subjecting cultural development and social organization to river valley regional administration. Note, for instance, how once again the problems in the lower Mississippi Valley contrast strikingly with those of the Far West. The problems differ within the states and even within counties and metropolitan areas.

Thus, they "relate chiefly to protection against surplus waters and to their disposal, rather than to the conservation of water for man's use. . . . Below Cairo, the flood problem is of paramount importance. There the Mississippi channel and flood plain, as developed by natural

[18] National Resources Committee, *op. cit.*, December 1936, p. 97.

processes, formed a huge trough by which storm waters from the Ohio River, the upper Mississippi, the Missouri, and numerous southern tributaries, both large and small, were conveyed to the Gulf of Mexico. In order to occupy and utilize parts of the rich flood plain, the construction of levees was begun early in the eighteenth century and has continued to the present. Until 1917 it was carried on by many diverse interests. In 1883, a tentative grade line was established for the top of the levees all the way from Cairo to the mouth of the river. In 1898, a new grade line, averaging some 5 feet higher, was established. After the floods of 1912 and 1913 demonstrated its inadequacy with tragic force, a third line was adopted in 1914 several feet higher than the 1898 grade. In 1927 the levees, which had been brought almost everywhere to the standard 1914 grade line, were again broken in many places and the greater part of the valley was flooded with appalling loss of life and property. In 1928 the Congress adopted a new plan of protection involving still higher levees supplemented by a system of emergency floodways. Additional works provided in the act approved June 15, 1936, are designed to afford protection against floods from lower tributaries and, by means of a floodway system of more generous capacity, to care for floodwaters in excess of the safe carrying capacity of the leveed course of the main river. Security appears now to be reasonably assured. Reservoir systems on the Tennessee, Ohio, and other tributaries of the Mississippi will add to the security otherwise in prospect by increasing the freeboard on the levee system along the lower Mississippi and by reducing the frequency and duration of floodway use." [19]

Yet the building of levees and the guarantee of security against flood, alike at Louisville and Cairo, and numerous way places, do not make similar the farm and culture of the vast number of communities throughout the 1,000 miles of Ole Man River, nor justify standardized arrangements for social and economic life. How specialized this planning is may be seen from a further examination of the proposed programs. In addition to the emergencies involved in flood control for the most powerful of all American waters there are other needs. Among the needs pointed up by the Committee are: "Marked improvement of land-drainage conditions, involving the redesign and reconstruction of hundreds of independent drainage works and their integration into a few well-planned, unified systems is a need of prime importance from the standpoints of agriculture and the elimination of

[19] *Ibid.*, p. 73.

malarial conditions. The magnitude of the task involved has made local endeavor ineffectual in most sections. Co-operation is necessary between adjoining districts and between states."

Further, "there are large areas normally subject to backwater from the Mississippi at high stages which cannot be made safe and suitable for human occupancy through flood protection, drainage, and associated measures. Most of these lands are forested and they function effectively during floods as huge natural retarding basins. This represents their best use for the greater good of the greater number. They might well be incorporated in national forests to insure perpetuity of the important service they render, to form wildlife refuges, and to obviate further ill-advised attempts at their reclamation and agricultural occupation. It may be added that flood control and drainage for any other partially developed or undeveloped portions of the alluvial valley should be associated with a program of land development, occupation, use, and ownership that will insure a notably higher standard of living than now prevails there."[20] In contrast, once again, is the nearby region of the Arkansas River and the Southwest Mississippi Basin. Thus "The prime water need of the upper section of the basin is more water for lands now irrigated. More water may be made available by further conservation of existing supplies and by transmountain diversion from drainage on the western slopes of the Rocky Mountains. Storage of water on the Canadian River, in New Mexico, ultimately will put under irrigation some 60,000 acres, most of which is new land. Proposals for storing floodwaters on the Cimarron in New Mexico and Oklahoma involve smaller irrigation developments, which, if used for production of forage and subsistence crops, may harmonize satisfactorily with the best comprehensive land-use economy."[21] And still again, note the striking contrast to the problems of the upper Mississippi, where "The principal uses of the Mississippi River above St. Louis relate to disposal of wastes, to navigation, to municipal water supplies, and, to a limited extent, to water power. The river serves as a sewer, and is seriously polluted below certain large cities. As a result, fish life, water-supply sources, and recreational facilities are greatly impaired. Wastes from an urban population of about 8,000,000 affect the stream from which various municipalities draw their water supplies."[22]

The significance of the natural river valleys may be examined again in the reports dealing with the great composite Mississippi River

[20] National Resources Committee, *op. cit.*, December 1936, p. 73.
[21] *Ibid.*, p. 65.
[22] *Ibid.*, p. 47.

Basin with its major tributaries. This gives a broad but less detailed picture of the one greatest natural river valley region in the nation. Indeed, it comprehends two-thirds of the states of the nation. Such a region, sometimes characterized by the engineers and by Mr. Ickes as a great homogeneous area, was examined by an earlier committee on the Mississippi Valley. The picture may be envisaged in terms of the five great sub-basins, which are characteristic of the nature and range of the river regions. They both contrast and recapitulate the points of emphasis already made. We shall, therefore, merely point up a few elementary facts. First, is the Upper Mississippi Basin, which comprises that sector of the drainage area of the Mississippi River north of the junctions of the Missouri and Ohio Rivers, not inclusive of the drainage areas of these two tributaries, each of which is itself a great system. This upper basin is about 185,000 square miles, or 15 percent of the entire Mississippi area, and the related Great Lakes and Hudson Bay drainage areas about 95,000 square miles. The area under consideration includes practically all of the states of Illinois, Wisconsin, and Minnesota, the eastern two-thirds of Iowa, somewhat more than the northeastern third of North Dakota, the Upper Peninsula of Michigan, corners of Missouri and Indiana, and a few square miles of South Dakota. Second is the Ohio River Basin, which is the longest, largest, and most important tributary entering the Mississippi from the east. Measured from its source in the glacial hills of southwestern New York to its junction with the Mississippi River at Cairo, Illinois, the Ohio River has a length of about 1,300 miles.

Third is the Missouri Basin which presents a quite different picture from the two previous regions. The seven and one-half million inhabitants are distributed into three major zones of human occupation, each representing a distinctive group of adjustments to conditions of the natural environment. The eastern third of the basin is characterized by moderately dense settlement, a relatively stable and diversified agriculture, and an increasingly important urban life based in considerable part on the manufacture and distribution of commodities used and produced in the middle and western zones. This is the "Commercial Front" of the Basin. The more effective planning for utilization of forests and forest lands for water conservation, control of soil erosion, lumber, and recreation is a matter of urgent importance. In the western zone, western Montana and on the Colorado Piedmont, there are few concentrations of population, which with their complements of cities and radial alignments of transportation facilities, are founded chiefly on mineral industries or irrigation agriculture. A dependable and adequate supply of water is required in these oases not alone to insure consistent harvests of cash crops, but also to provide sufficient feed for livestock grazed on the pastures of the surrounding plains and mountains. Here, planning for irrigation, water supply, electricity, and recreation stands out as the big need of the region. Between the eastern and western zones of the basin lies a vast middle zone that is characterized by a relatively sparse and unstable population. Efforts to exploit and occupy this middle zone have depended chiefly upon the agriculture. Some settlers have turned to irrigation farming. However, this zone remains a land of great economic hazard, especially in times of water shortage. Manufacturing is of slight importance, and there is little foundation for its development. Mining is of significance chiefly on the slopes of the Black Hills Uplift.

Fourth is the Southwestern Basins, comprising four principal rivers and their tributaries, which present for study 280,000 square miles of land, mostly fertile, possessed of varied natural resources and capable of extensive development. As agriculture and industry are developed in the basins, their population, now comparatively sparse, will increase correspondingly. The Southwest is a promising field for local initiative in flood control and water resources development. The steep gradients of the rivers in the upper reaches, while aggravating conditions that make for floods, at the same time afford opportunities for hydroelectric power development that sooner or later will play an important part in the life of the region.

This great basin constitutes almost one-fourth of the area of the Mississippi River Basin, and is made up of four rivers—the Red, Arkansas, White, and Ouachita Rivers. Each of the four basins may roughly be divided into two parts for the purpose of water planning. In the upper parts, the problem is mainly one of conservation and augmentation. There the stream flow is inadequate to meet the future, or even the present, needs of the region. Conservation by storage reservoirs becomes necessary. In the lower parts of all four basins, the scene changes. Control and utilization of excess water becomes the paramount factor on these rivers. Flood control, power development, and perhaps the regulation of low flow for navigation constitute the main problems. Nearly half of the population lives on farms. With the development of industries, the provision of cheap power, and the protection of the land against floods, there should be an inflow of settlers, attracted by the better living conditions. Of the 650,000 farms in the basins, 5 percent have electric lights, 25 percent have telephones, 11 percent have radios, 51 percent have automobiles, and 6 percent have water piped into the houses. Such meager conditions of living show the possibilities of regional planning of this kind.

Finally, the Lower Mississippi Basin is still a different problem. The population of the Lower Mississippi Region was approximately 3,905,000 in 1930. Of this number, 60 percent lived in the alluvial valley, or Delta, as it is commonly called, and 40 percent lived in the Uplands. In the Delta and the Uplands alike, about two-thirds of the population is rural, and about half the total depend directly upon commerce rather than industry. Here, planning for flood control and water use stands out as a vital factor in looking to the future.

The most critical and wide-spread water and land problem is that of soil erosion. Forestry and conservative grazing represent the best uses for most of the hill lands of the basin, since without a protective cover of trees or of sod, denudation will continue active to its final stage. The plan calls for the Federal Government to continue purchasing eroded lands there with the view to plant forests, control grazing, and check gullying. The protected parts of the Delta have a clean and dependable supply of water either from the Mississippi River, or from the artesian wells and reservoirs that underlie the entire region at from 300 to 2,000 feet. Because of the ease with which upper ground waters are polluted, the surface supplies of water are not satisfactory. The plan for this basin calls for federal aid in financing the construction of water supply and sewage disposal works in urban areas in which the problem of public health is concerned.[23]

The potency of river valley planning has already been indicated in the arguments from the Committee report already quoted. Perhaps the best illustration of all the river valley regions is that of the Tennessee Valley, which is the basis for the nation's most realistic experiment in regional-national planning. In the work and plans of the TVA may be recapitulated many of the ideals and methods for the development, conservation, and utilization of natural resources

[23] Cf. Gordon R. Beers, Unpublished Report on The Mississippi Valley Project.

through more effective planning and co-operation between state and federal forces.

The integrated plan of the TVA has been fully described in a 1937 report, *Tennessee Valley Authority—1933-1937*. Parts of the summaries will illustrate the case. Thus, "The most characteristic physical factor of the Tennessee Valley is obviously the Tennessee River. In a state of nature this river is one of extremes—of violent floods that erode its banks, menace towns and cities, and increase the destructive high-water crests of the Ohio and Mississippi Rivers; and of periods of drought, when the waters run very low, navigation is impossible, and power development is largely nullified. The Tennessee River is much larger than any other Ohio River tributary and therefore it contributes the largest volume of floodwater to Ohio. Potentially the Tennessee River is a great waterway for navigation. Dams on its tributaries will aid navigation and flood control on the Ohio and Mississippi. The same works which are useful for navigation and flood control can be employed to generate a very large amount of electric power, and the three purposes can be achieved by a single co-ordinated program much more economically than though each purpose were pursued without relation to the others. Thus it is proving to be possible to work out a single plan for an economical development of the Tennessee River system so that floods will be tamed, a great system of navigation made possible, and the natural power of the river rendered available. In addition other very important values almost automatically come into being, such as the development of one of the outstanding recreational areas of the nation." And again, "By statute and by necessity the twin purposes of navigation and flood control must be served by any dams built on the tributaries, and these requirements dominated the location and design of such dams. Hence there was again no room for dams designed for power only, which were the only kind which private enterprise could be interested in building and operating. The Federal Government should locate, design, and build all the new dams on the main river and the major dams on the tributaries if it is to meet its explicit responsibility for navigation and its implicit responsibility for flood control. It should likewise operate such dams, because it should be free at all times to hold back water or to release water for its own primary purposes. The Federal Government, and the Federal Government alone, could operate the dams as co-ordinated units for river control." Still again, "To sum up, the engineering development of the Tennessee River creates not merely multiple-purpose dams but a multiple-purpose system of river control, and under an integrated plan the several purposes can be made to supplement and support each other. No unit smaller than the entire Tennessee River system would make this fully possible. Nothing less than a single authority exercising at least some of the powers of government could develop and operate this unit."[24]

Concentration which can both ignore and respect state lines and authorities is in accordance with the stated principles of American democracy. Thus, the Authority emphasizes the fact that the release of the energies of the people is also a function and that planning must be the democratic labor of many agencies and individuals. The role of states, cities, counties, districts is enhanced, so the Authority believes, by the federal recognition of interests and jurisdiction.

Yet the great significance of the TVA is not primarily in its techniques for developing a valley of great resources as a unit. Important as this is, it is not the major function of government. The chief significance must be found in the TVA as a great experiment in the twin motivation of developing and utilizing both the physical and human resources and as a type of subregion.

> It has been pointed out in *Southern Regions of the United States* that in the Tennessee Valley, with its TVA, may be found all the elemental factors of the new American regionalism. In area touching seven states, in near physical contiguity bordering on four more states inseparably linked through wealth and welfare; within the bounds of a circle radiating four hundred miles from Muscle Shoals, parts of still other states; comprehending all told a population aggregating more than half the people of continental United States. In regional homogeneity the Valley ranks high, yet with such extraordinary range and variety of resources, people, and institutions as to afford ample subregional divisions and to constitute the perfect laboratory for social experiment and social planning. The Tennessee Valley now represents no mere river basin, but the skill and planning of a nation, the imagination of the people many times divided, and the on-goings of engineers, planners, educators, economists, sociologists, critics and patrons, politicians, manufacturers, dreamers and schemers, reformers and statesmen, common folks in the South and out. In the Valley are possible also most of the dangers and most of the virtues inherent in a great regional-national experiment. Here, too, are dangers and difficulties symbolic of the range and power, or the failure and futility of a possible abortive American regionalism. Here are measures of what

[24] *Tennessee Valley Authority—1933-1937*, pp. 2, 3, 4, 5, 7.

civilization has done to a people and by the same token what civilization should do for them in another era. Here is test for the southern people and test for the nation in a dozen fundamentals of economic and social reconstruction. For the Tennessee Valley is but a gateway to the great Ohio Valley and the greater Mississippi Valley, comprehending two-thirds of the nation. It is but one of the scores of river valleys of the Southeast where the engineers have estimated the possibilities of dam construction to cost not 50 millions, not 100 or 200 or 300 millions, but 3,000 millions out of a national possible aggregate of 8,000 millions, for flood control and power and irrigation and restoration. Even the 42,000 square miles of basin territory is less than half as large as the Appalachian regions themselves. The three-fold significance, therefore, of the Tennessee Valley as a subregional symbol is: first, its availability for a national-regional laboratory, revolutionary in its methodology, heroic in its sweep; second, its tremendous significance in the framework of realistic regional analysis and planning; and, third, its reality as a type of actual subregion of the national scene.[25]

Finally, we note two recent major occasions for the re-examination of the river valley regions of America. One is the new series of volumes on American rivers and American folk, which has been described elsewhere. In this series, it is assumed that the story of the American people can best be told in terms of rivers and their romance. In the second volume of the series, for instance the one dealing with the Upper Mississippi,[26] the story of the great Northwest and something of the later "Middle West" is told with reality and charm, in which, however, authentic historical data from Larson, Adams, Bond, Fox, Craven, and others are skillfully interwoven into the epic of the upper Father of Waters.

The other occasion is the recommendation to Congress of President Franklin D. Roosevelt that there be established at least six additional river valley regional planning agencies in the nation. The assumption is that these agencies will be somewhat similar to the Tennessee Valley Authority, since the purpose of the bills introduced into Congress is to "provide for regional conservation and development of the national resources, and for other purposes." In addition to the TVA,

[25] Adapted from Howard W. Odum, *Southern Regions of the United States*, pp. 163, 167.

[26] Walter Havighurst, *Upper Mississippi.*

there would be agencies comprehending *the Atlantic Seaboard*, *the Great Lakes-Ohio Valley*, *the Missouri Valley*, *the Arkansas Valley*, *the South-Western*, *the Columbia Valley*. This represents a considerable consolidation of the seventeen major river valleys described in the report of the special committee from the National Resources Committee.

The relative merits of these proposals are discussed in relation to states and regions in Chapter IX. The implications are far-reaching and may afford opportunity for great constructive measures of reconstruction or may retard realistic planning for the better integration of the regions and the people. It is, therefore, necessary here only to point out the fact that the great value of such agencies will be found in their attack upon special subregions of the nation which overlap state lines and at the same time to preserve the American principles of sovereignty and democracy. Contrariwise, the great danger would be in the subtle changing of the American Constitution through the indirect undermining of local autonomy and administrative democracy. Inherent in this danger is the possible overemphasis upon economic and material matter and upon engineering and technological processes as against human and cultural fundamentals worked out through social assignments that are democratic and that look to the development and conservation of the people and their freedom. It is not enough to say that the real objective, after all, is the welfare of the people, since this welfare cannot be achieved without economic well-being. Neither can it be attained through the mere assumption of technological determinism which would guarantee to increase wealth and conserve and develop the natural resources of the country. The objectives of the bills are clearly focused upon the natural resources. "To develop, integrate, and co-ordinate plans, projects, and activities for or incidental to the promotion of navigation, the control and prevention of floods, the safeguarding of navigable waters, and the reclamation of the public lands, in order to aid and protect commerce among the several states, to strengthen the national defense, to conserve the water, soil, mineral, and forest resources of the nation, to stabilize employment, and relieve unemployment, and otherwise to protect commerce among the states, provide for the national defense, and promote the general welfare of the United States." If these great authorities can be established within the framework of sound finance and politics and can function after the manner of the TVA at its best, and if they will not transcend the more important composite social planning boards of the major regions, the assumption seems justified that they may constitute epochal units in the nation's economy of the future.

Chapter V

CULTURE REGIONS: METROPOLITAN REGIONALISM

IN the past, American regionalism has been more commonly identified with metropolitan regionalism than with any other of its phases, with the possible exceptions of "sectionalism" and literary regionalism. This limitation has been one result of metropolitan planning. Like sectionalism, its connotation was local; and the concept of metropolitan regionalism as THE regionalism thus paralleled closely that of social planning which, beginning with town and city planning, rapidly expanded to national and regional planning in the larger sense. From a local technique of arrangements both have come to comprehend broader philosophical and political meanings and applications.

Harold Buttenheim in discussing trends in planning, in *Planning and Civic Comment*, in 1936, points out that "the National Conference on City Planning was ten years old before Regional Planning appeared in its program as an annual meeting subject. At the Conference held at Niagara Falls and Buffalo in that tenth anniversary year—1919—the opening paper on 'Regional Town Planning' was presented by Thomas Adams, then Housing and Town Planning Adviser of the Canadian Government. Regional planning had, of course, been discussed and some progress made in various parts of the country in earlier years, the Boston Metropolitan Park District having been organized as early as 1893. As the term regional planning was understood in 1919 and during the following decade, it involved the planning of metropolitan areas. Such areas might penetrate two or more states, but they did not embrace groups of entire states. A more recent trend, which was given much emphasis in 1935, has been the enlargement of planning areas beyond the city or the metropolitan region and their decentralization as related to national planning, so as to cover all or large parts of several contiguous states." So, too, this specialized meaning of metropolitan regionalism and its continued usage is indicated in the special report on urbanism of the National Resources Committee. Thus, the metropolitan region is "a logical outgrowth of the expansion of cities and proliferation of modern technology, [and] promises to be even more significant in the twentieth century. In the course of the industrial revolution the whole of Western civilization has been profoundly transformed. Urbanism, by which is meant the concentration of large masses of people into relatively limited areas together with the technical and human problems that arise out of this mode of living, is one of the latest and most significant products of this development." [1]

The most noteworthy examples of metropolitan regionalism in America are those of the St. Louis Metropolitan Region and of New York and its environs. In the case of the St. Louis region, the St. Louis Regional Planning Commission has acted as the central organization for all of the types of planning beyond the city or other single jurisdiction and has proposed a "metropolitan area." This metropolitan area or district is included within a 20-mile radius from the central business district and comprises 840 square miles. As described by the National Resources Committee, the larger "region" embraces three entire counties in Illinois and two townships and part of a fourth county, while on the west side of the Mississippi it includes all of St. Louis County and portions of three adjoining counties. Practically all of the region is included within 35 miles from the central business district and is roughly 3,200 square miles in area. These two districts contain a great variety of land and water scenery and resources varying from the Great Flat of the Mississippi bottom lands to the rugged country on the edge of the Ozarks.[2]

The best-known example of metropolitan-regional planning in the United States, however, is that centering around New York City. This region contains 22 counties in the states of New York, New Jersey, and Connecticut. The planners attempted to include "all that territory in which people's ways of living and working are directly affected by the presence of the metropolis." In pursuing

[1] National Resources Committee, Research Committee on Urbanism, *Interim Report to the National Resources Committee*, July 1936, p. 1.
[2] National Resources Committee, *Regional Planning, Part II–St. Louis Region.*

this aim they enclosed an area which includes more than 400 separate municipalities and approximately 10,000,000 persons. In geographic terms, the region consists of approximately 3,500,000 acres or 5,528 square miles.

> The task of integrating the life of the region is visioned by the planning committee as including six major factors: "First, transit and transportation, which are in the hands of regulative private corporations, or, as in the case of the City of New York, of governmental bodies acting as corporations; second, harbor and waterway improvement, bridge and tunnel projects, and the like, which come under the jurisdiction of such bodies as the Port Authority; third, county highways, loop roads, parks and parkways and similar proposals which involve the state, county, and local authorities; fourth, highways, parks, zoning regulations, and other proposals in New York City; fifth, such special projects as the development of Jamaica Bay and the Hackensack Meadows, requiring special legislation, agreement between public authorities and owners of land, or the creation of special joint authorities where existing political jurisdictions overlap. Finally, there are the suggestions which the Regional Plan puts forward for the architectural development of the city, whether to be carried out by public authorities or private enterprise."[3] It is emphasized that this plan must be kept plastic to meet the growth of the city in the future.

> Such planning efforts have important implications for state governments. "Within the United States, six interstate metropolitan regional planning organizations are now in operation, centering in Washington, D. C., New York City, Philadelphia, Chicago, St. Louis, and Kansas City. There is much in common among these planning enterprises; their origin, purposes, and work are, for this investigation quite similar, although some of them are further advanced than others. In each of these six projects the initiation of regional planning was due to an increasing need for co-ordination among the many governmental units having jurisdiction within the region. In each case, the distinctly regional problems, and hence the regional area, were found to overlap state boundaries. The New York, Philadelphia, and Chicago regions lie in 3 states, the St. Louis and Kansas City regions in 2 states, while the Washington region includes the District of Columbia and parts of Maryland and Virginia . . . these metropolitan regions include areas somewhat larger than that of the central cities themselves, but at the same time much smaller than the territory which may be con-

[3] R. L. Duffus, *Mastering a Metropolis*, p. 261.

sidered 'tributary' to these cities. Generally speaking, the regions include only the metropolitan, urban, and suburban areas."[4]

In 1937, there were 1,073 city and town planning boards in the United States. The remarkable interest in such work is evidenced by the growth of the number of such boards. In 1922 there were only 185. Metropolitan and city planning seems to be centered in the states of New York, Massachusetts, and California, in each of which there are more than one hundred such organizations.[5]

Regional planning and much of the interest in regionalism has grown out of such activities. Indeed, the term "region" a few years ago was commonly used to designate a portion of a city. A little later it connoted planning of a city and its immediate environs. Now its common usage is to indicate larger units; usually including or cutting across several states whether dominated by a metropolitan center or not. Thus the meaning of the term has undergone a rapid expansion. At the end of 1936 there were 506 metropolitan planning agencies which included territory outside the city limits, often being coterminous with the county in which the city was located. Many county and inter-county agencies have also come into being. The National Resources Committee reported on May 15, 1937, that there were at least 27 such bodies. In addition, all the states of the union save two, Delaware and Maine, had set up state planning boards.[6]

So long as America was a land of river valleys, it was doomed to sectionalism; when the industrial revolution cast its net of steel rails over the continent it gained the possibility of becoming a series of integrated regions. This is true simply because the interests of inhabitants of valleys draw them down the slopes and away from their neighbors across the ridge, whereas railways lead out and on across physiographic basins from one valley to the next, from the section to the nation of unified regions.

The railways created the city as we know it today.[7] Into these focal points of our culture it brought men and machines to receive

[4] National Resources Committee, *Regional Factors in National Planning and Development*, December 1935, p. 14.

[5] National Resources Committee, *Status of City and County Planning in the United States*, May 15, 1937.

[6] *Ibid.*

[7] G. C. Quiett, *They Built the West.*

and transform the products of the area lying about in all directions, not merely along the valley at the mouth of which the older city had grown up. Ridges were no longer important barriers, though mountains still remain so. A new form of organization began to take place, a union of diverse elements from different valleys. Homogeneity was broken down. Awareness of the rest of the world was forced into our consciousness. While holding to our traditions and localisms and developing new ones to meet new situations, we became citizens of a wider world, too. We have modified our traditions and the institutions growing out of them in the light of a wider experience.

The regional importance of the city lies in the fact that it and the surrounding country have always been one in fact if not in feeling. The growth of the city has depended upon the hinterland—upon the farms and villages with their raw materials from field and mine and forest and home. These products the city has received and traded for the needs of the hinterland, thus making itself necessary to the region as a whole, forming its center and focus.[8] This tendency has been accentuated by the tendency of regions to specialize in certain products—in wheat, or iron, or fruit, for instance—thereby increasing its dependence on other regions for other necessities. Transportation facilities radiate from these centers; communication agencies are there concentrated. The cultural surplus of the area tends to be gathered there in the form of schools, hospitals, entertainment facilities, etc.[9] The result has been that the city has come to represent its surrounding territory.

Cities bear definite relationships to physiographic factors, but here as elsewhere, as culture accumulates geographic conditions come to be of less relative weight. After man learned to make boats and use waterways as highways, cities were located along the rivers. Since ocean transportation has become a dominant factor in our civilization, there has been a steady movement, still observable, of cities to the deep water. Cities have also grown up where valley meets plain; or where the topography of a region made it necessary to change the

[8] Kimball Young, *An Introductory Sociology.*

[9] J. M. Gillette, "Urban Influence and Selection," *Publications of the American Sociological Society*, XXIII, 1-14.

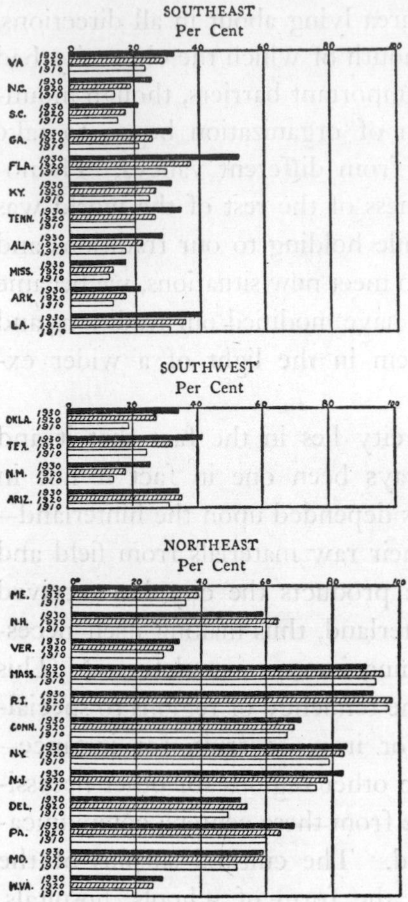

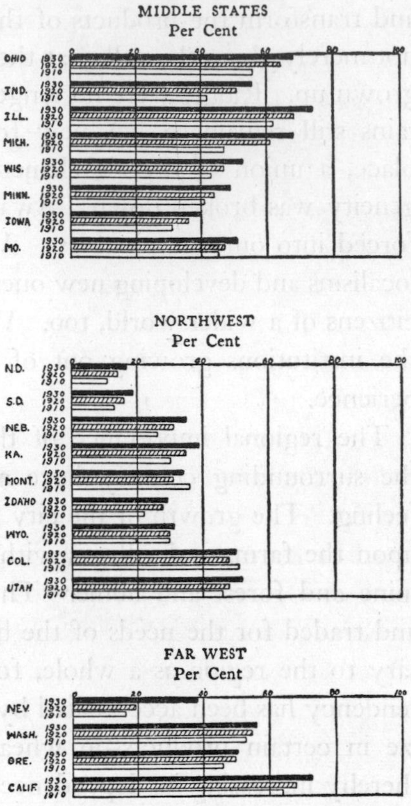

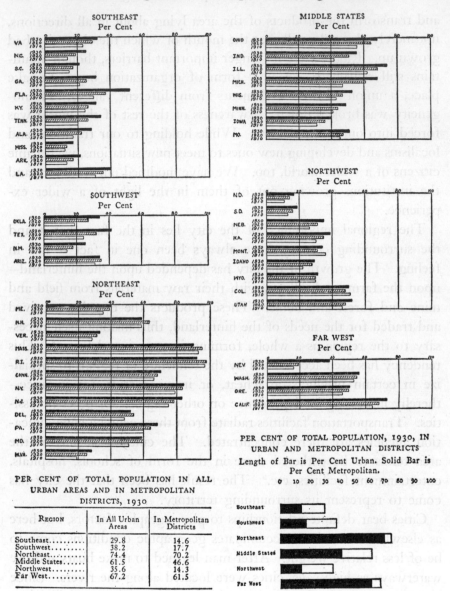

PER CENT OF TOTAL POPULATION IN ALL URBAN AREAS AND IN METROPOLITAN DISTRICTS, 1930

Region	In All Urban Areas	In Metropolitan Districts
Southeast........	29.8	14.6
Southwest........	38.2	17.7
Northeast........	74.4	70.2
Middle States....	61.5	46.6
Northwest........	35.6	14.3
Far West.........	67.2	61.5

PER CENT OF TOTAL POPULATION, 1930, IN URBAN AND METROPOLITAN DISTRICTS

Length of Bar is Per Cent Urban. Solid Bar is Per Cent Metropolitan.

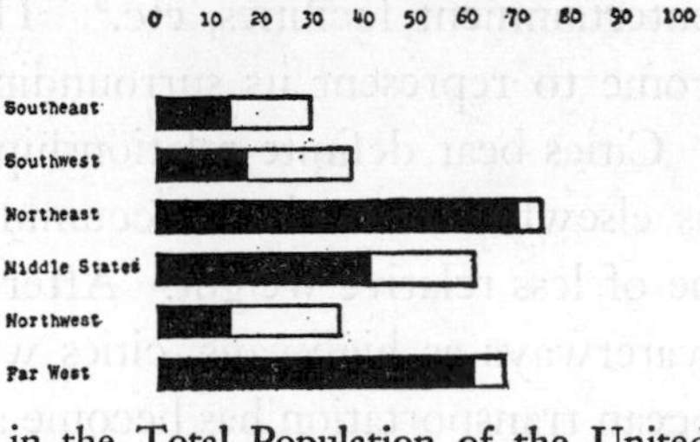

Percent of Urban Population, by Regions, in the Total Population of the United States, 1910-1930. Adapted from *Southern Regions of the United States.*

mode of transportation. And here is the key to the location of the city. The city is born of the transportation system provided by the culture.[10] It follows, then, that a change in the technique of transportation has, and will, result in a change in the location and the sphere of the city. In the United States the railway has been the dominant form of transportation for almost a century. And American cities are the products of the rail system. We have reorganized our national life since the spread of the rail net.

If the railway has been one of the dominant factors in the emergence and organization of the metropolitan region in the past, the motor vehicle seems to supply the key to understanding what has happened during the last twenty years and what is likely to happen in the near future. The inflexibility of the rail system gave the city and its region a rigid, compacted form in which the city differed greatly from the surrounding areas. The elasticity of the automobile and motor truck are changing this to one of loosely nucleated, highly specialized and therefore interdependent, communities. This specialization seems to be mostly functional, some of the services vital to the region being concentrated within the city even more than in the past, while others are being placed in locations with particular advantages or are even being dispersed throughout the region in branches which keep close contact with their central directing agency at their focus of dominance. This has also given rise to the satellite city, which may be of considerable size but which depends upon the central metropolis and on other specialized centers for its existence.

As the railways pushed their way west of the Mississippi and faced the problem of gathering profits there arose a system of zoning freight rates which in its turn gave rise to a series of "gateway" cities, where favorable rates forced a concentration of commercial and industrial firms, along with the financial houses they demanded. This system gave such cities virtual economic sovereignty over large areas of the nation. Distinct, but distinctly subordinate, small cities and villages were strung along the railways, all facing the metropolis.[11]

[10] C. H. Cooley, "The Theory of Transportation," *Publications of the American Economic Association*, IX, 40-42.
[11] N. S. B. Gras, *An Introduction to Economic History*.

But the actual rail facilities are no more important than the cost of service over them. McKenzie has dramatically illustrated this by using the first-class freight rate between New York and Chicago as a base and then mapping "freight rate distances" from Chicago, as the railroad hub of the nation, and various other cities. Such a map shows the New England cities drawn westward, since they enjoy advantageous rates, while cities to the south and west have their distances greatly increased; Los Angeles and San Diego are thus located somewhere in the neighborhood of the Hawaiian Islands. In percentages of cost, on the same base as 100, other cities in various parts of the nation vary from 92.4 (Boston), to 274 (Fort Wayne). The variation is somewhat affected by the distance, the general rule being that short distances carry high rates per miles, while long distances are accompanied by lower per-mile cost. But such variations clearly give the favored cities a critical advantage in securing and holding dominance over regions.[12]

Since the turn of the century, however, this picture has once more been repainted. More than 25,000,000 motor vehicles were in use in 1930, everyone of which was in some degree a competitor of the older transportation devices. Almost three quarters of a million miles of highway had been provided for their use. Since local funds supplied most of the early highways, these new ties between city and country clustered thickest about the most prosperous cities, tending to fray out and disappear rapidly as the poorer areas were reached. In this, highway construction followed closely the pattern of early railway building, when ambitious cities undertook the construction of lines purposely designed to tap valuable hinterlands. But the railways soon became national or at least regional in character; those crossing the western plains built cities rather than served them. Something of the same sort has taken place with the highway net; since state and federal funds are being depended on more and more for their construction they are being designed to draw together distant areas and to furnish through routes rather than concentrate smaller areas about the larger cities as was the case at first. Intercity connections are receiving more attention. As traffic is diverted from the older railway to the newer motor way small cities which derived their importance from their function as local distribution

[12] R. D. McKenzie, *The Metropolitan Community*, pp. 150-156.

points are finding themselves stranded, while other such centers with poor rail facilities in the past are using the truck to extend their trade territory and to tap areas formerly subject to competitive centers. In the case of the larger cities this effect is not so noticeable, since such centers commonly have access to both the rail and highway nets. However, the large cities have gained by the growth of the motor services. These routes bring products directly into the city which formerly went to smaller towns. They also serve as feeders to the railways, giving quick connection between city and formerly isolated areas and thereby enabling a more intensive exploitation to take place. All of this means that the motor vehicle has made toward a greater concentration of control in the metropolitan district.

Although it is still too early to come to any conclusions as to the effects of air travel and freight upon city growth, it is already evident that this will be a factor of considerable importance. Up to now, however, it has been important principally because it has forced all cities to provide airport facilities, not so much because of the importance of their use to the city as for fear that other cities will subsidize such travel and thereby gain an advantage which will be of great value in the future. Small towns have also rushed to provide landing fields in an effort to secure some advantage over their rivals.

The growth of the rail system has tended to throw consideration of the water transportation facilities into the background. However, it must be remembered that most of the large cities of this nation have water as well as rail communication, and that rail freight rates are tempered by water-borne competition. The construction of the Panama Canal illustrates the significance of this factor very well. Before traffic began to use this waterway, cities in the western portion of the country built their connections with the midwestern or eastern metropoli. The Pacific Coast cities had practically no hinterlands. But when the canal was opened and regular shipping services established, the lower freight rates from the eastern seaboard to Pacific ports made it possible for these cities to develop as supply depots for vast inland areas. At the same time, the slight advantage enjoyed by the Middle States was wiped out, and cities along the Atlantic took over this business. A new market was opened for products of the Far

West, especially of those areas near the deep water. Thus, this engineering feat shifted a large amount of control from the Chicago area to the eastern seaboard, and at the same time gave the Far West an entirely different orientation.[13]

The discussion of the city thus far has been mostly in terms of commerce and trade. This is because the town and city are first of all market places. Other institutions cluster there, it is true, but the reason for the existence of most cities is their ability to handle trade and financial relationships for a larger or smaller area. This was recognized some time ago, and has never been seriously disputed. Warren H. Wilson defined the community in terms of team haul in 1912 in one of the first scientific community studies made.[14] Galpin followed the same technique in his study of "The Anatomy of an Agricultural Community," published as a bulletin by the University of Wisconsin extension service. More recently the human ecologists have applied this principle to the study of metropolitan areas. Their efforts have been warmly seconded by the commercial associations, chambers of commerce and similar organizations which have been concerned with delimiting the trade areas of their cities.[15]

From these studies it has been demonstrated that the influence of the city tends to fade and disappear with time, cost, and distance, or time-cost-distance, which, again, is largely a function of the transportation devices in use. The automobile has greatly extended this range of influence so far as retail buying is concerned, while the truck has had a similar effect on wholesale territories. Competition with other centers also serves to limit the range and particularly the direction of this dominance.[16]

Thus it appears that the influence of the metropolis over the region is not uniform but varies in intensity with the distance from the center. Some functions are confined almost wholly to the city itself, while others are scattered throughout the region. But most have a gradient character, gradually fading as the outer limits of the region are reached. This means that the degree of participation in the metropolitan culture, and the resulting conditioning, are not the same for all the people of

[13] McKenzie, *op. cit.*, pp. 154-157.
[14] Warren H. Wilson, *The Evolution of the Country Community.*
[15] McKenzie, *op. cit.*, p. 77.
[16] *Ibid.*, pp. 77-78.

the region. Those who live within the city proper have fullest opportunity for participation; those who work in the city, but live in suburbs, a little less; those who live in satellite cities and make frequent visits to the center, still less; those in small cities and towns at some distance get most of their participation in the form of reading supplemented by occasional visits, while the rural dweller may be almost free of immediate and direct influence of the metropolis. However, indirect influences through contact with persons who are in more intimate connection with the city, through the effects of freight rates, market conditions, financial connection, radio, etc., do carry the influence of the city even to persons who are totally unaware of any such effect on their lives.

These lines of influence follow closely along the lines of transportation and communication so that the intensity of the city's influence would be mapped as a multi-pointed star, the number of points being the same as the number of lines of communication. Between the zones along these lines would appear areas which might be in close physical proximity to the city but at great social distance.

In general, William J. Reilly found that the drawing power of a city is in direct ratio to its population and in inverse ratio to the square of the distance—that is he finds that the law of gravitation applies to trade areas as well as to migration and physical masses. However, the trade pull exerted by a city depends on a variety of factors and further varies with the commodity considered. Reilly lists these factors as: lines of transportation, lines of communication, class of inhabitants, density of population, proximity to larger market, the nature of the businesses in the city, social and amusement factors, nature of competition offered, population of the city, distance and psychological attitude toward distance, topographic and climatic conditions in area, and leadership of store owners and managers.[17] The degree to which specialty shops will appear also varies directly with the size of the city, and this factor has an important bearing on the distance from which customers will come. Thus, Reilly estimates that a town of about 60,000 is necessary to a successful store selling only men's hats. Standardized, frequently bought goods sell readily in the smaller cities, but highly stylized or unusual articles require the larger population of the city and its trade area to become the basis of exclusive shops. By a study of the amounts spent for food, general merchandise and

[17] *Methods for the Study of Retail Relationships*, University of Texas Bulletin Number 2944.

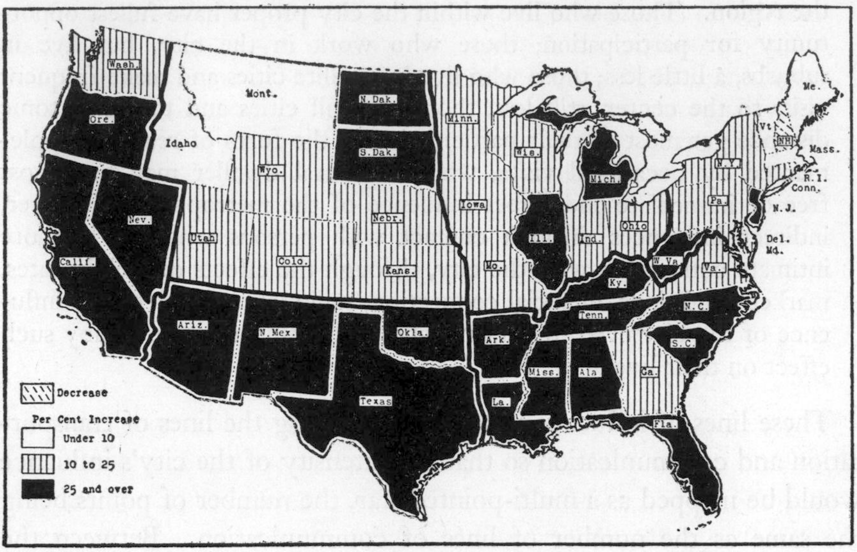

Above: Percent Increase in Urban Population, 1920-1930.

Below: Urban, Metropolitan Village and Metropolitan Unincorporated Population by States, 1930. Note urbanization trend of the Southeast and Southwest.

STATE AND REGION	Census Urban (1)	Metropolitan Village (2)	Metropolitan Unincorporated (3)	New Total Urban Sum of 1, 2 and 3
Southeast.....	*7,616,831*	*36,489*	*558,228*	*8,211,548*
Alabama.......	744,273	5,611	72,279	822,163
Arkansas.......	382,878	2,092	12,064	397,034
Florida.........	759,778	4,965	42,787	807,530
Georgia.........	895,492	5,252	94,533	995,277
Kentucky.......	799,026	14,420	69,452	882,898
Louisiana.......	833,532	....	22,544	856,076
Mississippi......	338,850	....	....	338,850
North Carolina..	809,847	....	....	809,847
South Carolina..	371,080	....	....	371,080
Tennessee.......	896,538	4,149	135,307	1,035,994
Virginia........	785,537	....	109,262	894,799
Southwest.....	*3,467,701*	*17,094*	*167,502*	*3,652,297*
Arizona........	149,856	....	....	149,856
New Mexico....	106,816	....	....	106,816
Oklahoma......	821,681	5,088	36,428	836,197
Texas..........	2,389,348	12,006	131,074	2,532,428
Northeast.....	*28,296,202*	*369,980*	*2,258,844*	*30,925,026*
Connecticut.....	1,131,770	8,534	265,381	1,405,685
Delaware.......	123,146	3,031	32,363	158,540
Maine..........	321,506	....	....	321,506
Maryland.......	974,869	1,877	129,965	1,106,711
Massachusetts...	3,831,426	....	175,554	4,006,980
New Hampshire.	273,079	....	....	273,079
New Jersey......	3,339,244	127,336	248,559	3,715,139
New York......	10,521,952	55,976	484,801	11,062,729
Pennsylvania....	6,533,511	168,628	840,293	7,542,432
Rhode Island....	635,429	....	20,939	656,368
Vermont........	118,766	....	....	118,766
West Virginia...	491,504	4,598	60,989	557,091

STATE AND REGION	Census Urban (1)	Metropolitan Village (2)	Metropolitan Unincorporated (3)	New Total Urban Sum of 1, 2 and 3
Middle States.	*20,890,935*	*214,734*	*897,065*	*22,002,734*
Illinois.........	5,635,727	74,086	116,013	5,825,826
Indiana........	1,795,892	19,774	86,022	1,901,688
Iowa..........	979,292	1,352	19,285	999,929
Michigan......	3,302,075	14,353	137,297	3,453,725
Minnesota.....	1,257,616	12,854	30,750	1,301,220
Missouri.......	1,859,119	13,061	151,773	2,023,953
Ohio..........	4,507,371	76,097	294,109	4,877,577
Wisconsin......	1,553,843	3,157	61,816	1,618,816
Northwest....	*2,626,940*	*15,485*	*98,493*	*2,740,918*
Colorado......	519,882	10,789	24,131	554,802
Idaho.........	129,507	....	....	129,507
Kansas........	729,834	....	29,813	759,647
Montana......	181,036	....	....	181,036
Nebraska......	486,107	809	11,995	498,911
North Dakota..	113,306	....	....	113,306
South Dakota..	130,907	....	....	130,907
Utah..........	266,264	3,887	32,554	302,705
Wyoming......	70,097	....	....	70,097
Far West....	*5,569,345*	*55,485*	*612,954*	*6,237,784*
California......	4,160,596	36,888	482,909	4,680,393
Nevada.......	34,464	....	....	34,464
Oregon........	489,746	9,129	45,431	544,306
Washington....	884,539	9,468	84,614	978,621
United States*	68,467,954	709,267	4,593,086	73,770,307

*District of Columbia is omitted.

clothing in cities near Chicago and Los Angeles, McKenzie found that the local centers sell as much or more food per capita than do the large cities, but that for the other classes of goods, the nearby cities sell very much less, the amount sold increasing with the distance from the metropolis. The assumption is that the residents of these smaller cities go to the metropolis for these services.[18]

Much the same situation is reflected by studies of wholesale distribution. The *Chicago Tribune* asks all visiting buyers to register. These registrations show a rapid falling off with distance, 61 percent coming from towns within a radius of 200 miles and only 12 percent coming from 600 miles or over.[19] A University of Illinois study of banking relations shows the same trend. Here there was a consistent decline of banks having correspondents in Chicago up to the 1,200-mile point, after which the number rose again. This rise was explained by the number of banks in other metropolitan centers maintaining connections with Chicago banks, but not being in a subordinate position, as were most of those at lesser distances.[20]

In the field of industry, the tendency toward division of processes in various factories for later assembly plus the desire to exploit all sources of labor have also favored the metropolitan community. With speedy and certain communication there is no reason why parts of a machine should not be manufactured in highly specialized factories located at some distance from each other. On the contrary there are many advantages of such division. But such highly specialized plants select only one class of labor and often the selection is made on a sex basis. Other industries are quick to see the advantages of offering employment to persons who are in the community because of family ties, but are without a market for their activity. The desire to benefit from the skills developed in other plants and to use by-products also leads to the erection, or congregation, of industries within trucking distance of each other, thus forming industrial agglomerations. Such areas may be said to be centralized, but not concentrated. That is, they have a focal point about which they arrange themselves in orderly patterns, but their organization is not so compact as it would have been before the introduction of the motor truck.

[18] McKenzie, *op. cit.*, pp. 74-75. [19] *Ibid.*, pp. 76-77. [20] *Ibid.*, pp. 77-78.

National advertising in magazines and newspapers, the motion picture and the radio, aided by good roads, have kept the small town customer up with, if not ahead of, the small town merchant and, thus, have become factors in the concentration of trade in the larger cities. Of these factors the newspaper is by far the most important in regionalizing relationships. This is partly the result of the character of the American newspaper. In this country the emphasis is on news rather than on opinion and on locality rather than on the nation as a whole. This means that the newspapers are highly localized, or at most regionalized. The newspapers published in the metropolitan centers circulate throughout the region dominated by that center. As in the case of trade relationships, the extent of this circulation is in proportion to the size of the city and shades off with distance. In 1930 the *Chicago Tribune* conducted a study which shows that the circulation of Chicago morning newspapers is greater than those of newspapers in competing cities in almost exactly the same area in which more than half the rail traffic moves toward Chicago.[21]

> It is also noted that newspapers from metropolitan cities enter into active competition with those published in the smaller towns and cities, but that the reverse is not true to any great extent. Here again, the situation is very similar to the trading practices. That is, the metropolitan region has a news focus just as it has a trading focus, but it also has many subcenters, each of which is also a news center, as well as a trading center, for a localized area. The small cities have the function of acting as liaison agents between the metropolis and the rural areas. The more urbanized inhabitants insist on the metropolitan newspaper, while those of more localized tastes are content with the local daily or weekly which specializes more in the news of their friends and acquaintances.
>
> There is another factor which limits the circulation of newspapers of all sorts and which also explains, in part, the close coincidence between circulation areas and trade areas. The newspaper is primarily a purveyor of advertising. But what the advertiser buys is not space, nor even gross circulation, but the opportunity to place his persuasive argument before prospective customers. Some products which are highly standardized and are sold everywhere can be, and are, advertised without reference to the place of sale. But even in most nation-

[21] R. E. Park and Charles Newcomb, "Newspaper Circulation and Metropolitan Regions," *The Metropolitan Community* (edited by R. D. McKenzie), p. 106.

ally advertised products, a definite place at which the product can be bought is an essential part of the advertisement. Therefore, advertisers insist that the medium they choose be circulated among the people who will likely be interested and within the territory easily accessible to the store mentioned. Of course, this applies with much greater force for businesses, such as department stores, having only one outlet; and these businesses place the greater portion of the newspaper advertising. Hence a newspaper with a large circulation outside the trade area of the city in which it is published finds itself unable to charge for this circulation, since the advertiser insists on paying only for readers who are also prospective customers. And, since circulation, in itself, is not profitable to modern newspapers, the newspaper is not anxious to extend its circulation beyond its effective advertising limits. This is why the more progressive newspapers have been careful in recent years to make accurate measurements of the areas served by the merchants of their towns.

This has led the newspapers into a self-conscious attempt to further the interests of the cities in which they are published, and goes far to explain the close connection between newspaper publishers and executives of chambers of commerce.[22] This combination of cities, newspapers, trade organizations is, of course, analogous to sectionalism and localism.

That this perfect relationship between trade area and circulation area cannot be attained, however, is shown by the study of metropolitan regions as measured in newspaper circulation by Robert E. Park and Charles Newcomb and summarized by McKenzie.[23] This study was made on the assumption that the metropolitan region could be determined by measuring the area in which circulation of a morning newspaper from a selected list of metropolitan centers dominated. But when the areas were charted, it was found that no one newspaper dominated in some areas; that other areas within the metropolitan regions were dominated by newspapers published in fairly large cities, but that such areas were enclaves in the region, in that the metropolitan paper again dominated the region beyond the reach of the local paper. This would seem to indicate that such cities were important centers but still a part of the region and not entitled to consideration as separate entities.

[22] Cf. for example, George B. Dealey, "The Newspaper as a City Builder," *American City*, XLIII, 129-130.

[23] McKenzie, *op. cit.*, ch. VIII.

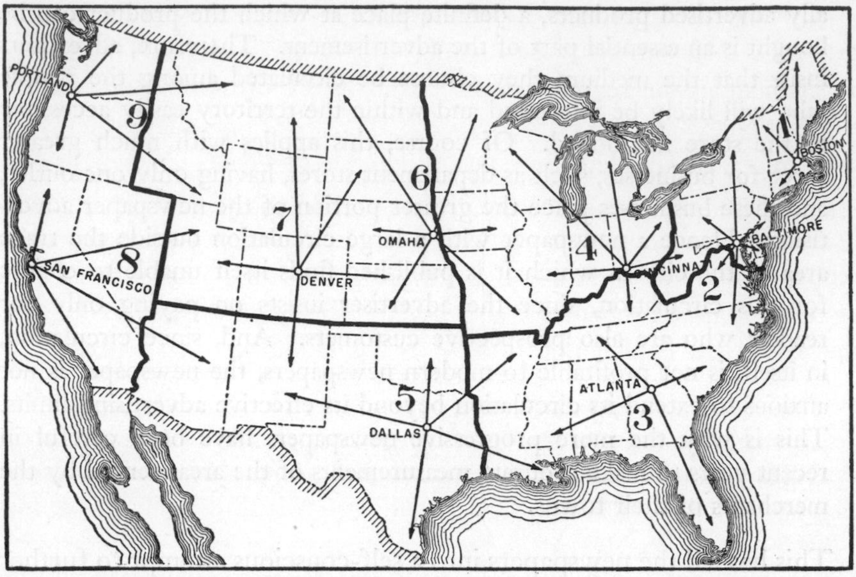

HERE ARE TWO ILLUSTRATIONS OF HOW ADMINISTRATIVE REGIONALISM MIGHT BE SET UP

Above: Actual Field Offices of the National Resources Committee as of 1937-1938.
Below: Possible Planning Regions Based upon Administrative Convenience. Both by permission of the National Resources Committee.

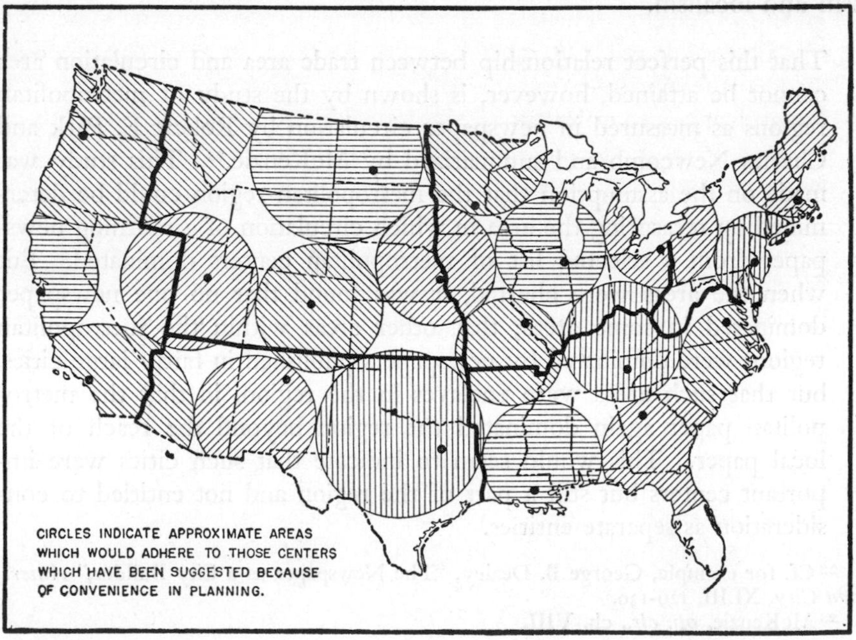

CIRCLES INDICATE APPROXIMATE AREAS WHICH WOULD ADHERE TO THOSE CENTERS WHICH HAVE BEEN SUGGESTED BECAUSE OF CONVENIENCE IN PLANNING.

Although holding that regionalization on the basis of metropolitan centers is "of somewhat doubtful validity," since the city is merely an element in the regional complex and not its fundamental outline, the National Resources Committee, in its 1935 report, maps the nation as it might be divided into metropolitan regions. The map has no official significance, of course, but is interesting in that presumably it represents the opinion of the men who would be asked to make recommendations were such a project undertaken at this time. As in other regional schemes the regions in the northeastern portion of the nation are smaller than in the South and West.

This means that the large cities of the eastern seaboard are seen as dominating relatively small, but populous, areas. Traditional New England loses the northwestern corner of Vermont and the southwestern corner of Connecticut in the Boston Region. These lost bits are awarded to New York along with all of the state of that name, the northeastern corner of Pennsylvania and northern New Jersey. The sphere of influence of Philadelphia is limited to eastern Pennsylvania, southern New Jersey and Delaware—one of the smallest regions in the nation for one of the largest cities. Detroit also has a small hinterland, being given dominance over not quite all of the lower Michigan Peninsula, the western edge of this body of land being given to Chicago. The state of Ohio is divided between three metropoli, Cleveland and Cincinnati within the state, and Chicago, which invades the northwestern corner. To Cleveland also goes western Pennsylvania—regardless of Pittsburgh—a bit of Maryland, and a little more of West Virginia. Cincinnati shares West Virginia with Cleveland and with Baltimore.

The other outlined regions stretch out more. Atlanta is given a region which includes all of the states of South Carolina, Georgia, Florida, Alabama and Mississippi as well as goodly portions of North Carolina, Tennessee, and some of the parishes of Louisiana. The St. Louis Region extends from eastern Kentucky westward to Colorado and comes south far enough to take in most of Arkansas and Oklahoma with a bit of the Texas panhandle. Chicago and Minneapolis-St. Paul have regions stretching far to the west, that of the first named city extending from within Ohio to the Wyoming boundary, and that of the Twin Cities beginning with the northern peninsula of Michigan and including the strip just south of the Canadian border as far west as Idaho.

The influence of the Rocky Mountains is seen in the regions assigned

Denver and Salt Lake City. Both have general north-south trends, that of Denver running from across the northern portion of Wyoming to a peak at El Paso on the Mexican border. The Salt Lake City Region extends as far north, but runs south only to northern Arizona. The Far West is divided between Portland, San Francisco and Los Angeles. The latter city has a region extending eastward to El Paso. San Francisco dominates northwestern Nevada, while most of Idaho falls to Portland.

The way in which state lines are crossed by these regional boundaries is interesting. Pennsylvania, Ohio, West Virginia, Kentucky, Indiana, Nebraska, Wyoming, Texas, New Mexico, Arkansas, Nevada and California all have parts of their domain in three distinct regions. Only Maine, New Hampshire, South Carolina, Rhode Island, Delaware, Iowa, North Dakota, Oregon, Washington, Georgia, Florida, Alabama and Utah are wholly contained in metropolitan regions. Only in the case of Delaware and the northern boundary of Missouri do the limits of the metropolitan regions coincide with state lines for any considerable distance.[24]

Action of the Federal Government in selecting cities as regional headquarters for various departmental and bureaucratic functions is, in a way, a recognition of metropolitan regionalism. These headquarters usually supervise only one function, although several, or even scores, of such headquarter offices may be housed in one city. The criteria for the selection of such centers varies with the department or bureau making the selection, but those listed by the Federal Reserve Banking Board in selecting the twelve cities for their districts would seem to apply in general: "(1) the mercantile, industrial and financial connections existing in each district, and the relations between the various portions of the district and the site selected for the location of the Federal Reserve Bank . . . (2) the general geographical situation of the district transportation lines, and the facilities for speedy communication between the Federal Reserve Bank and all portions of the district." [25]

The steady widening of the city limits, the awarding of police power to the cities for special purposes outside their territorial limits,

[24] National Resources Committee, *Regional Factors in National Planning and Development*, December 1935, p. 158.

[25] *Location of Federal Reserve Districts*, Senate Document 485, Sixty-Third Congress, Second Session, p. 361.

the movement for consolidation of city and county or for the autonomy of the large cities also indicate recognition of the very great difficulty, if not impossibility, of furnishing adequate governmental service to large cities under the present form of organization. This has led many theorists, notably N. S. B. Gras, Charles E. Merriam, Patrick Geddes, and Thomas H. Reed to predict that in the near future we will be forced to establish separate and distinct governmental areas for the metropolitan centers. That even the proverbial man in the street is thinking along this line is shown by the large number of articles making such suggestions, and by a contest held by the *Chicago Tribune* some years ago in which the contestants were asked to map a new arrangement of administrative areas. The winning map retained 31 of the existing states, created nine new ones by consolidations, and provided for the erection of ten city states surrounding the larger metropolitan centers.[26] Thus we have come to a metropolitan economy which bids fair to rival that of the nation. Where the town of the past served and was supported by an area a few miles across, where the medieval city had a hinterland of not much more than a score of miles in diameter, the modern metropolis dominates regions composed of groups of states. It was this growth, according to Weber, which produced the present national state.[27] It was primarily the demand for release of restrictions of trade within the empires of the Middle Ages which brought about mercantilism and political unity and supervision. These were necessary before regional-national economy could be realized. When wide areas had been freed of bothersome restrictions, the metropolis arose; London was changed from an agricultural market to the first commercial city of England, and then of the world.

This metropolitan economy is characterized by its ability to organize wider areas than had been possible in the past, and, in addition, by its function of bringing the rest of the world much closer to its hinterland. This allows for specialization within the subregions, secure in the knowledge that the things not locally produced may be secured from the metropolis, as well as for regional specialization in the case of homogeneous regions, for which the metropolis per-

[26] C. E. Merriam, *The Written Constitution and the Unwritten Attitude.*

[27] Adna Ferrin Weber, *Growth of Cities in the Nineteenth Century*, pp. 176-178.

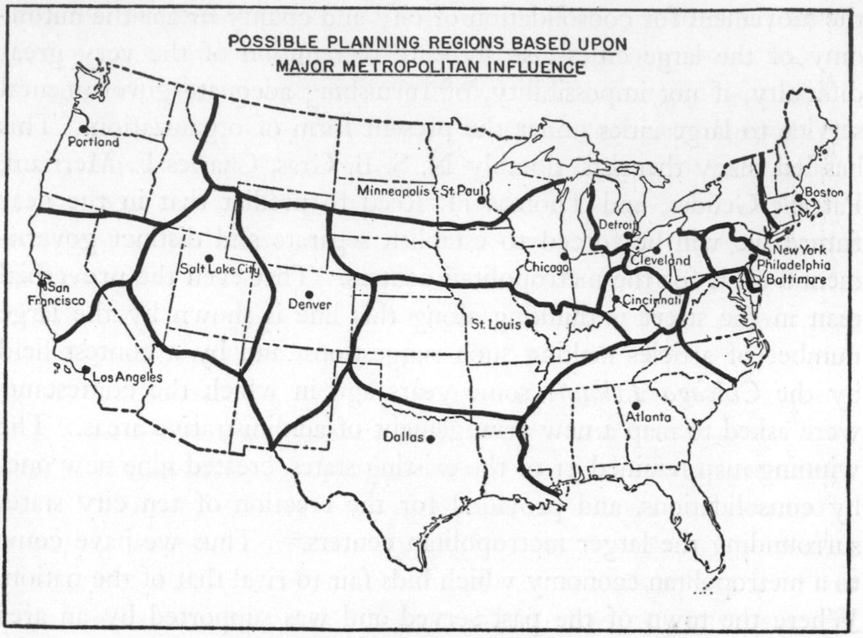

TWO TYPES OF SUGGESTED PLANNING APPROACHES

Above: If Metropolitan Centers Were the Basis of Planning Arrangements. Adapted from *Regional Factors in National Planning and Development*.

Below: Regional Distribution of National Parks and Monuments. Adapted by permission from the National Park Service.

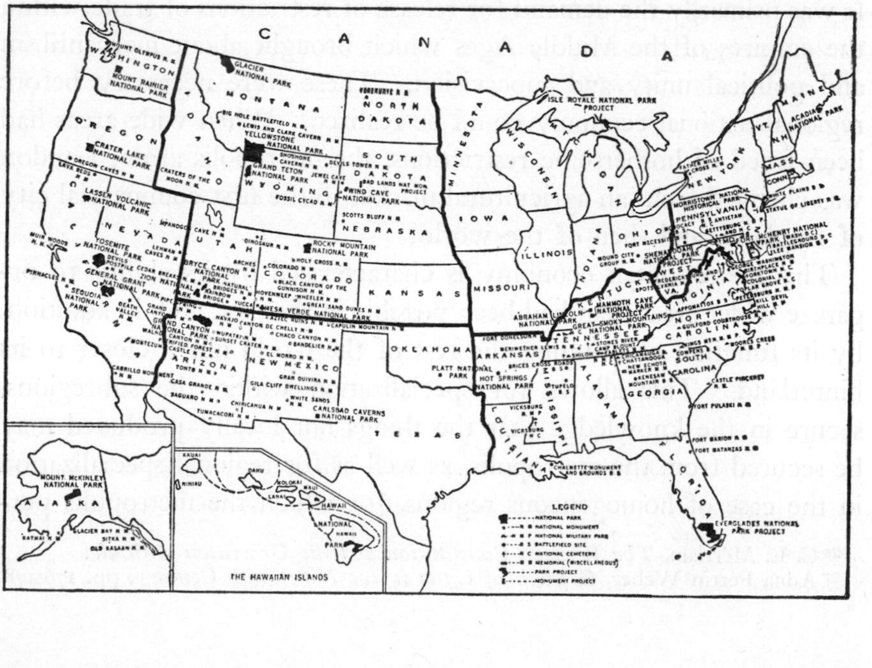

forms the same service. That is, the metropolis integrates and tends to regionalize, where the town and small city formerly sectionalized.

It is this integrating function that Gras stresses in his discussion of the metropolitan community. There, he says, are concentrated the wholesalers, the railways, motor-bus companies, express agencies, cold storage and warehouse plants and elevators. Above all, there are the financial institutions, banks, trust companies, insurance corporations which accumulate and disperse funds for the regional economic arrangements. This means that the number of such centers is limited. A wide free-trade area is the first prerequisite; but natural resources, transportation facilities both water and rail, a location far enough away from other metropoli, a climate not too hot and too humid—these are also required.[28]

Where these conditions are present, the great city forms a natural focus for a region, at once taking on the color of the surrounding territory and giving that territory a tone which is peculiar to it alone. The center and the hinterland are inseparable; together they form a unit and together they work out their destiny. The hinterland supports the metropolis. The metropolis integrates the hinterland and renders it services of marketing, accumulation of culture, connection with and interdependence on other regions, which was impossible before the rise of the great city.

Institutions have changed both their location and their nature in the reorganization which the city has brought about. We have succeeded fairly well in describing those changes, but we have not yet made any successful analysis of their role in social change. We know what they do better than we know how, or why. We know that this process is continuing, but we do not know how far, or in exactly what direction, it will lead us. We have come to realize that mere size is not an index of metropolitanism. There are many cities in the United States with more than 100,000 population which are not and never can become metropolitan because they are too highly specialized, or because they lie in the shadow of some well-established center. On the other hand there are smaller cities which perform most, if not all, of the metropolitan functions of integration and

[28] N. S. B. Gras, "Rise of the Metropolitan Community," *The Urban Community* (edited by Ernest W. Burgess).

dispersion. The size required for a city to become a metropolis varies with the density of population in the region it serves, although there is a minimum below which it cannot fall. There are also super-metropolitan centers, as London, New York, and perhaps Chicago, which cut across the areas of other metropoli and take from them some of their functions.

For regionalism the chief significance of the metropolis is that regions of distinct characteristics may be outlined as surrounding them and depending on them. One of the weaknesses of the method is that there remain large areas which do not seem to belong to any given metropolitan center and which are therefore not placeable in such a regional scheme. Also, there are differences in the city and its hinterland, often conflict between the two which seems to deny the homogeneity frequently considered an essential characteristic of regionalism. This subject of the relations between the city and the country needs more study than it has yet received, especially since it is generally agreed that the city will continue to grow for some decades at least. Thompson thinks it is quite likely that the United States will follow the lead of England and Wales and place three-fourths to four-fifths of its population in cities, leaving just enough in the rural districts to supply foods and raw materials.[29] However, authorities agree that these cities will not be the cities we know today, so far as structure is concerned. On the contrary they will be composed of a series of subcenters, polynucleated, centralized but not concentrated, spreading over an area whose extent will be determined by the efficiency of the intra-metropolitan transportation system. Such an organization will bring the city and the rural areas into closer contact and should result in better adjustment.

During the last census decade somewhere near twenty million rural dwellers migrated to the cities of the nation. Though techniques are lacking for measuring the effect these persons had on the urban way of life, it is self-evident that they did not shed their rural habits and philosophy when they crossed the line marked "City Limit." At the same time a somewhat smaller stream was flowing back to the country from the city. These people took to the rural areas city

[29] Warren S. Thompson, *Population Problems*, p. 320.

habits and philosophies, or better, the habits and philosophy of the particular city from which they migrated. These two movements inevitably have the effect of leveling off urban-rural differences, of making the total area from which and to which this migration takes place more unified. As mobility has increased, this leveling effect has been more pronounced.

All agencies of communication have worked to the same effect. The newspaper, the radio, the motion picture, the telephone and telegraph, the railway and the highway have all aided in this process. It is sometimes argued that this will result in a standardized, stereotyped culture extending throughout the nation. But when it is remembered that most of these agencies tend to cluster in relatively few centers; that the newspapers are primarily local, that most migrants do not leave the region, that the transportation and communication nets are fine-woven near the large cities and fray out toward the regional limits, it is evident that the intra-regional contacts are multiplied much more rapidly than are the interregional ones. The net effect, therefore, is that regional consciousness is intensified at the same time that regional interdependence is strengthened.

However, there will remain certain rural-urban points of difference. Just so long as the rural districts are dependent on the production of raw materials and foodstuffs for processing and consumption in the cities, it seems unlikely that economic conflict can be wiped out entirely. This is the fatal obstacle to the formation of farmer-labor political parties, it would seem. Also, in spite of better communication and transportation, there are fundamental differences in mores and folkways between city and country. It seems likely that these are of the nature of cultural lags and will disappear in time, but it is at least questionable whether their places will not be taken by other lags. The city is the center of change; and it seems, therefore, that some time must elapse before the rural areas accept the new ways of the city.

This question of the pervasiveness of the metropolis' influence on the region has been approached by William F. Ogburn in his study of intra- and interregional differences. Here the cities were compared with the rural areas within the region and with other cities outside the region in a series of characteristics: family size, school attendance,

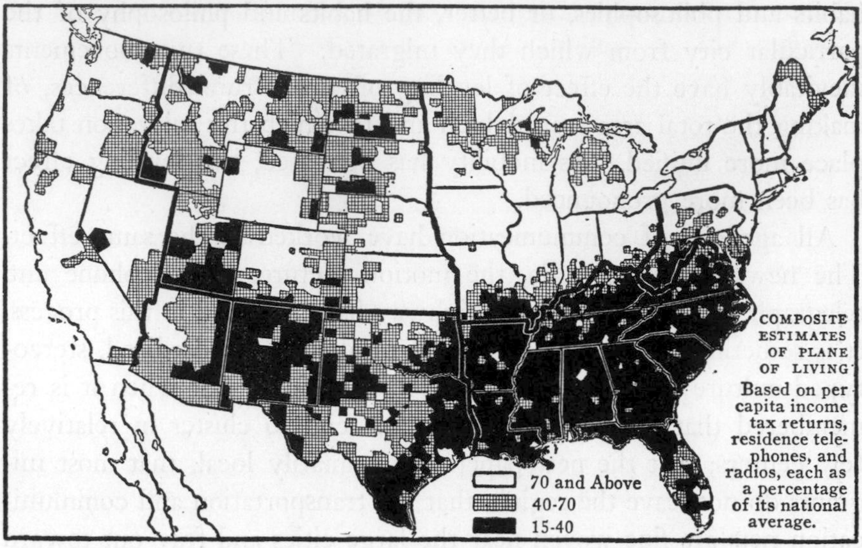

PLANES OF LIVING IN THE UNITED STATES ARE OFTEN MEASURED IN TERMS OF URBAN CHARACTER AND PURCHASING POWER

Above: Plane of Living by Counties. Adapted from Carter Goodrich's *Migration and Economic Opportunity*.

Below: Counties in the United States with a Density of 150 or More Persons Per Square Mile. From Census data.

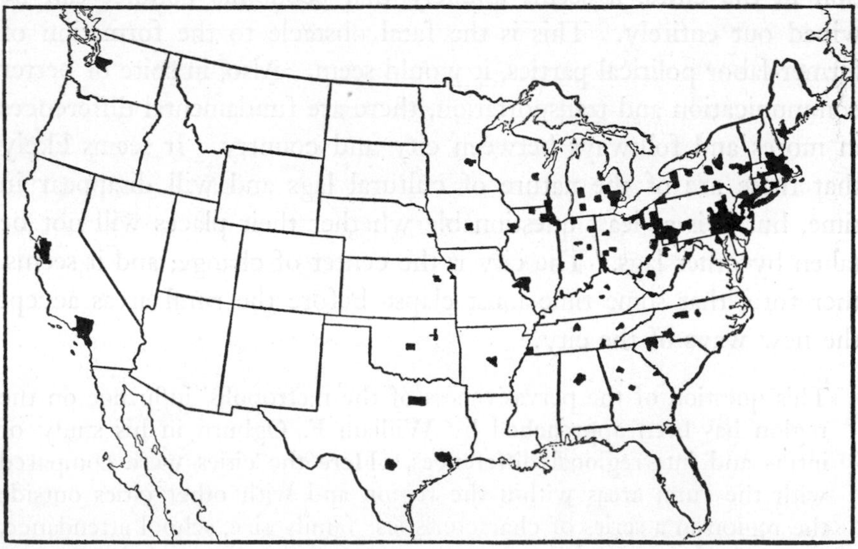

rent, percent married, percent widowed, home owners, income taxpayers, ratio of youthful and of aged to middle-aged persons, sex ratio, foreign born, birth and death rates, automobiles, telephones, postal receipts, radios, and church membership. It has been recognized for some time that there are important rural-urban differences in most of these characteristics. However, Ogburn concludes that the theory that cities are more alike than regions is not convincingly supported, but that there are important differences in the degree to which cities differ. This may be due, he thinks, to the fact that the cities are made up largely of persons from the surrounding areas. He rejects the idea that occupational specialization can account for the differences. However, his evidence is conclusive, on the basis of the criteria selected, that there are intra-regional differences which are greater than inter-regional ones.[30]

What Ogburn's study shows is simply that we are moving away from sectionalism and toward true regionalism. Sectionalism is characterized by such wide differences and attitudes that mutual adjustment is difficult and conflict results. As the city comes to exert more influence on its hinterland these differences will be mitigated. The entire area, as the city already has, will come to be less unlike other portions of the nation, but, again as the city has, will retain its own flavor, its own peculiarities, its own distinctive character. This, with the lessened differences which will make adjustment on the national basis both easy and essential, will give us a flowering of regionalism. But will the trend toward more likeness continue until all regional as well as sectional differences have disappeared? This seems somewhat unlikely. The incidence of cultural change seldom affects all areas alike as Ogburn remarks; and nothing seems to be more certain than that change will continue. Thus, it appears that we will continue to have minor differences in our major regions which will form the basis of the interstimulation needed for a healthy national life.

Two big questions remain to be answered by the metropolis. Can it integrate its territory and spread its culture so that participation will be approximately equal by all the inhabitants? Will the competition and conflict between metropoli give way to stable accom-

[30] "Regions," *Social Forces*, Vol. 15, pp. 6-11. See also his brochure, *Social Characteristics of Cities.*

modation in which variation will be preserved but hostility will be forgotten and the interests of the nation will take precedence over those of the area? Regionalism, as the term is used here, envisages a social order in which all the people will share in the benefits of all of our culture. The charge has been made repeatedly that the big city gathers unto itself most of the fruits of our civilization and hordes them away from the ruralite. This is only partly true, but the part truth of the statement casts doubt on the ultimate efficacy of metropolitanism. The growing efficiency of communication lessens the gap between the participation of city and country dweller. Can it mitigate it sufficiently to allow a healthy culture to grow up? The evidence of the past is not too encouraging.

As to the other question, it would seem that cultural and economic maturity will do much to lessen the conflicts between the big cities. At present it is true that the metropolis is too often arrayed against both the nation and the country. But these cities are growing rapidly, are trying to find their place in our social system. So long as there are unattached areas, or areas which may be easily detached from other cities, the struggle is likely to continue. When maturity is reached, when population has become stabilized, when traditions have become firm, when orientation is completed, it seems not unlikely that inter-metropolitan competition will be replaced by a trend toward accommodation. We are approaching such a state of equilibrium, indices indicate. That we shall never reach it, absolutely, seems fairly certain in a world in which change is our most stable factor.

> The dangers of taking the city as the regional center, of seeing regionalism as an illustration of metropolitan influence is summarized by the National Resources Committee in these terms: To construct regions which would adhere to cities rather than to the broader aspects of resources, economic patterns, and regional interests is to place the emphasis upon one factor rather than the total region. Upon such a basis regional planning tends to become an expanded form of city planning. On the other hand, it is by no means certain that planning has not arisen at least in part out of the necessity of preserving local rural culture and resources against chaotic economic and social forces emanating from the city. Even were cities themselves carefully

planned, this would still be true, for the city is an organism whose very nature places its nutritive processes above larger regional considerations.[31]

[31] National Resources Committee, *Regional Factors in National Planning and Development*, December 1935, p. 159.

Chapter VI

CULTURE REGIONS: THE RURAL NATION

THE term Rural Regionalism, more accurately the economy of rural areas and "Rural America," may be used by way of contrast to metropolitan regionalism as presented in the previous chapter. Literally, of course, there are no major rural regions except in the sense later described or compared with urban. Yet, if for no other reasons than the fact that large areas and large ratios of people are not included in metropolitan regions, and because of the significance of historical American rural foundations and their place in the national equilibrium, it is necessary to present the rural picture as an integral part of American regionalism. This is of special importance in view of the fact that many economists and population experts frankly predict that in the United States only enough people will remain in rural areas to produce the crops necessary for the nation. If commercial farming be projected as the next step, this would leave a very small number and would tend to relegate farming as a way of life to historical America. Equally important is the other school which holds that a new balance of rural culture in American life is organically necessary.

The study of realistic rural regionalism in American life may, therefore, be approached from many viewpoints. First, of course, is the understanding that the term is a relative and instrumental one. Perhaps the key point of view must be that of equilibrium and balance between agrarian and industrial life, the key again to rural and regional planning. Another viewpoint, and perhaps the most logical one in the present volume, is to contrast rural areas with urban and metropolitan regions. A third is to point up the numerical, quantitative, and areal ratio of America, which is rural. Still another is to appraise it in relation to the earlier historical agrarian America. A fifth is to view rural regionalism as a very important concept and planning technique in American life in so far as it may constitute the testing ground for farming and rural culture as a way of life, representing societies close to nature as opposed to urban aggregations and technology. A sixth aspect is found in the relation of land, minerals, water, and other natural resources to the total wealth of the nation. Consequently, the seventh aspect is that of the technic of planning for land and water conservation. The agricultural regions of the United States also serve to point up rural areas as frames of reference for commodity production, study, and planning. So, too, the regional division of the nation in terms of agricultural and land-use regions is basic to the development of rural America. And, again, as an economy of decentralization and distribution, rural regions may serve as areas for new agricultural and village frontiers and for reintegrating agrarian culture in American life.

> Strictly speaking, the terms rural areas and subregions will be more representative of our problem due to the difficulty of delimiting actual regions and to their multiplicity throughout most of the major regions of the United States. Yet most of the attributes of "the region" may be found in many rural areas. That is, they are constituted of spatial or geographic areas, yet with borders of zones rather than lines, fading into urban areas, and each rural region or subregion usually constitutes a unit in the total economy of the larger region or of the nation. The indices of rural regions might be easily determined, as for instance all those parts of the nation with less than 150 inhabitants per square mile, in opposition to the urban or metropolitan regions. A simple device for indicating rural regions might be to draw the areal lines around the chief metropolitan areas and centers as described by those who picture metropolitan areas. Those areas which are not included within the metropolitan regions would constitute the basis for beginning the delineation of rural regions. For this type of picture, see the maps showing number and location of counties having a density of 150 people to the square mile and the metropolitan centers set up by committees of the National Resources Committee.

If we wish to envisage the "rural region" as a larger entity, it is possible to illustrate with such great regions as the Northwest and the Southeast. In the picturization of and planning for these regions

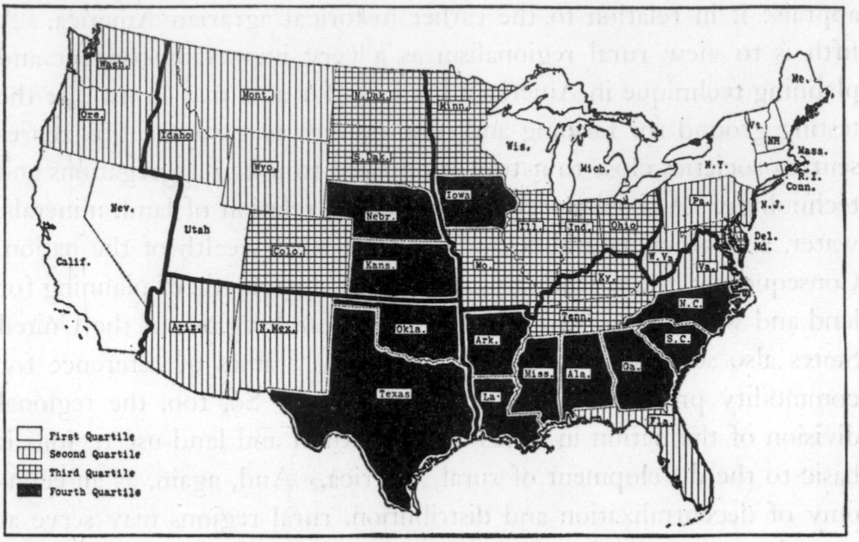

HERE ARE TWO OTHER REGIONAL PICTURES OF FARM TENANCY

Above: The Ratio of Farm Tenancy in Terms of the Highest to Lowest Percentages.

Below: The Same for Average Value per Farm of Land and Buildings Operated by Tenants in 1930.

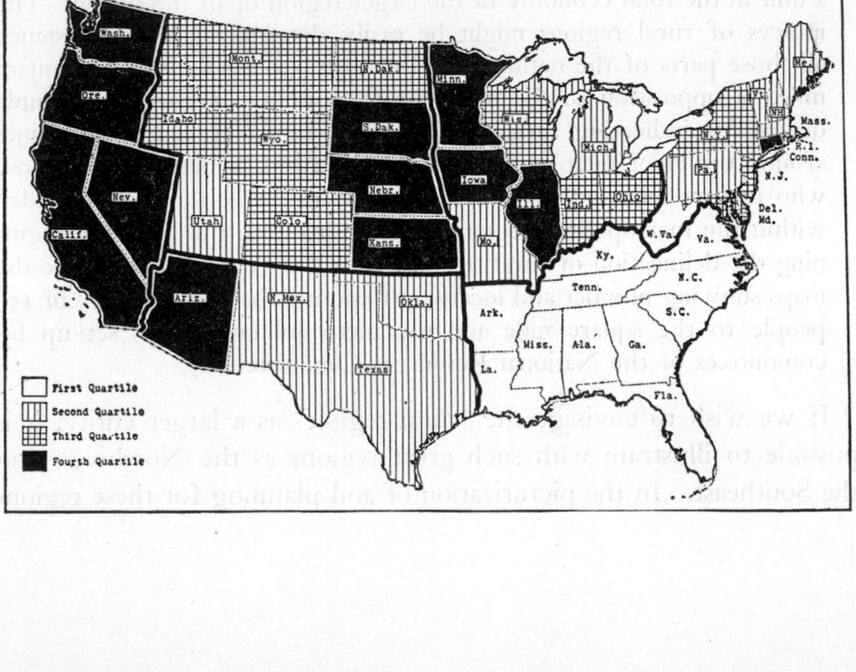

their metropolitan regions are incidental as contrasted with the Northeastern Region of the nation, where urban and industrial character dominate the region. Thus, we might illustrate in the case of planning for the milk industry through dairying, contrasting the great milk basins around New York and Boston with the diffused industry of the South. In the case of the Southeast, livestock and dairying would be set up as a chief economy for reconstructing the old rural cotton economy, for rebuilding lands, for attaining a well-balanced agriculture, and for the enrichment of the whole region through agricultural reconstruction and the increase of adequate diet and the raising of standards of living. In contrast, the problem of planning for the dairy industry in the Northeast is primarily one of a milk supply for the great cities and industrial centers in which the emphasis on farm or rural welfare does not appear except in the economic aspects of parity and prices.

Or the rural character of the regions can be illustrated through statistics of prevailing rural traits. Thus, the Northwest is primarily a rural region as measured by population density, occupations, agriculture, stock raising, land use, forestry, mining. There are only five metropolitan regions in the nine states, and only four states have urban centers with a population of over 50,000 people. Outside of Kansas and Colorado, there are only eight cities with a population of more than 25,000 people. A 1936 *Atlas of the World*, published for the Container Corporation of America by Rand, McNally and Company, on its Economics Activities Map shows only those colors depicting (1) forestry, hunting and fishing, (2) agriculture, (3) grazing, with only two small dots for manufacturing in the very eastern portion of the region on the Missouri River.

Of the six great regions in the nation, the Northwest with an area of 818,508 square miles is not only by far the largest of the regions but it has a larger percentage of the nation's total area in farms than any other region, namely, 27,833,000 acres, or 23.8 percent, and derives a greater proportion of its total income from agriculture than any other, all of the states having a percentage of 30 and more, with the exception of Utah and Colorado. Furthermore, though it ranks only fourth in the total number of farms it has the largest percentage of the large farms in the country, over half of the farms exceeding 500 acres as

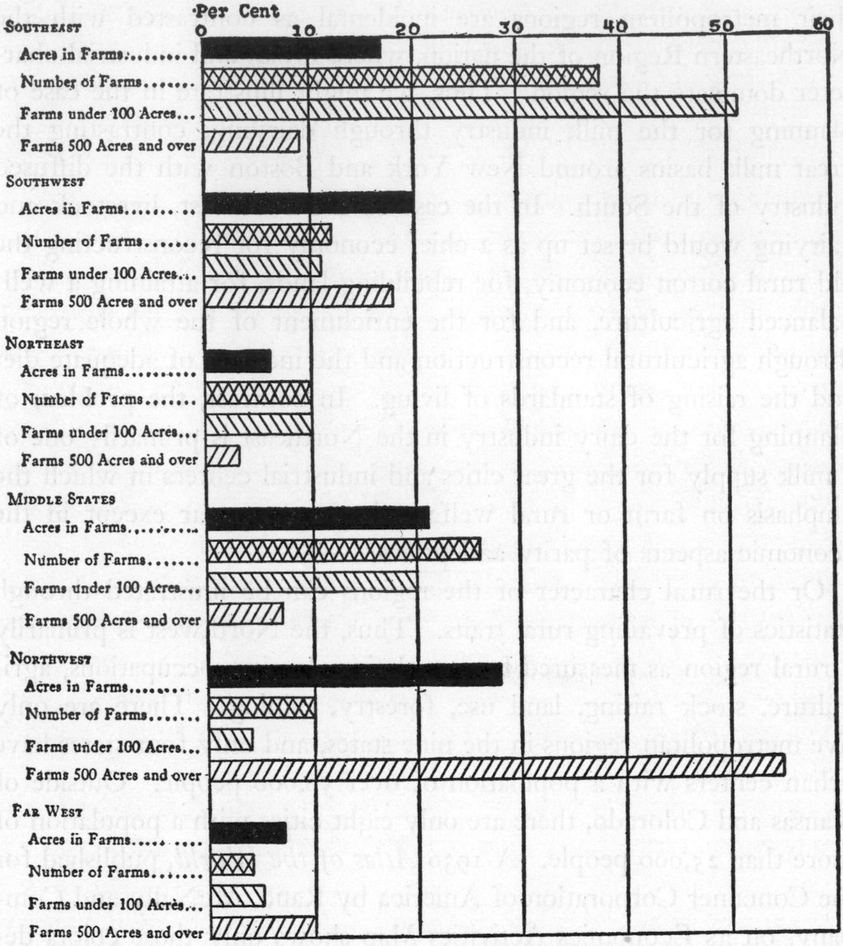

REGIONAL DISTRIBUTION OF ACRES IN FARMS, 1930

REGION	Per Cent of Total Crop Land	Per Cent of Total Pasture Land	Per Cent of Total Woodland Pasture Land	Per Cent Woodland not Used for Pasture	Per Cent All Other Land in Farms
SOUTHEAST	42.5	26.4	41.8	24.3	6.8
SOUTHWEST	27.3	69.9	14.6	0.9	1.9
NORTHEAST	40.2	38.0	32.5	16.4	5.4
MIDDLE STATES	57.9	32.6	34.3	4.0	5.5
NORTHWEST	43.1	52.4	4.7	0.4	4.1
FAR WEST	29.9	63 3	19.8	2.3	4.5

A Regional Classification of Farm Lands by Number and Size

compared with the 17.5 percent of the Southwest the next in rank, or the 2.6 percent of the Northeast. Correspondingly, it has the least percentage of small farms with its 3.6 percent as only one-fifth of its farms are under 100 acres. It comes second among the regions with its 43.1 percent total crop land and third in the total pasture land.[1]

So, too, the most realistic implication of the rural regionalism of the agrarian South, however, is found in the actual picture of the present Southeast. Here, again, the region is primarily rural, constituting in area almost the whole landscape; in people, three-fourths and more of the population, either in actuality or in experience and interest. The region ranks second only to the great agricultural Middle States in composite measure of its commodity production. Moreover, the Southeast receives more than 25 percent of its income from agriculture as opposed to about 12.5 percent for the nation. Its percentage of gainfully employed in extractive work, 45.7, is the highest of any region, as is its ratio of farm population to the total. The burden and implications of the rural South include further the processes of change and conflict reflected in a heavy migration cityward and the whole recent decade of country life bankruptcy. Likewise, part of the agrarian problem is that of attaining an enduring balance between rural and urban civilization. A part is the reconstruction of cotton economy. A part is the problem of securing the southeastern farmer in a normal procedure whereby he adapts his crops to climate, soil, transportation, human-use requirements, rather than primarily to a colonial, commercial agriculture. A part is the marginal standard of living and housing of five millions of the region's rural folk; a part is the prospect of a new sort of American peasantry. In fine and in sum, one of the key problems of *the region* is its rural economy.

It was pointed out in *Southern Regions of the United States* that "this pre-eminently rural Southeast enumerates a larger number of farm families than any other region of the nation. Of the 6,266,000 odd farms in the United States, the Southeast has 2,380,000 compared with the other regions: in round numbers the Far West, 265,000; the Northwest, 648,000; the Northeast, 618,000; the Southwest, 744,000; and the Middle States, 1,622,000. Mississippi alone has a larger number

[1] Adapted from Elma Courter, unpublished manuscript.

of farms than all of the great agricultural Far West. The Southeast is different, among other respects, in having the lowest average acreage per farm; namely, 71 acres. Mississippi averages only 53 acres per farm. A similar small farm division is found in the other 'plantation states'; in Louisiana where the average size is scarcely 58 acres; in Arkansas, only 66; and in Alabama, only 68. For the whole Southeast nearly 80 percent of the total farms are under 100 acres and less than one percent over 500 acres. Moreover, the size of these farms has been steadily decreasing since 1900. And before that time the break-up of the plantation system into small farms constituted an unprecedented revolution in the economic and cultural ways of the region." [2]

The rural region as an entity, with its implications for planning and for political and economic reality, may be further observed in the Southwest and in the dual, rural-urban Middle States, in which metropolitan regions like Chicago are set in dynamic contrast to lower rural Illinois. Such entities are also observable in certain rural countries of Europe. Thus, John Gunther calls attention to the Danube as a real frontier and border line between industrial Europe and the agrarian states of the Southeast, "between the complex mechanical civilizations of Germany and Czechoslovakia and the primitive agricultural societies of the Balkans which live on grain." [3] So, too, rural Denmark, Ireland, certain of the regions of France and Germany, represent examples of what might be termed rural regions, in contrast to industrial regions.

Another illustration of the deeper significance of rural regionalism is that of France, which "is essentially an agricultural country. Less than one-half of its population lives in cities of 2,500 or more. An urbanized population assimilates and loses its identity more rapidly than a population which remains close to the soil. As Ernest Lavisse writes: 'The robust rural constitution which climate and soil give to our country is a fact cemented by Nature and Time. . . . In that inheres, upon that is based, a solidity which, perhaps, can not be found in any country to the same degree as in ours; a French solidity. Among those peoples with an industrial civilization, who are our neighbors, we see today that, more and more, the inhabitants draw their subsistence from without; the earth, with us, remains the source of nour-

[2] Howard W. Odum, *Southern Regions of the United States*, p. 59.

[3] John Gunther, "Hazelnuts for Guns," *Saturday Evening Post*, Vol. 209, No. 4, p. 5 (May 1, 1937).

ishment for its children. That creates a difference in the attachment which it inspires.' This is one very important reason why the Frenchman tends to think of himself as belonging to a province or region rather than to the nation at large. It seems to me, moreover, in a consideration of French regions, that Paris is not just a city; it, too, is a region. It has a distinct culture of its own, just as do the provinces. The Parisian always thinks, not in terms of France, but in terms of Paris; the rest of the country is merely 'la province.' "[4]

There is, after all, an important organic, as well as economic contrast here, whether between the earlier rural and later urban America or between the ideals and objectives of the modern urbanists and others. Thus, many students of urbanism hold frankly that the greatest indications of progress in America are the evidences that all America is being urbanized. What might be more desirable from the viewpoint of the rural regionalist and in conformity with historical America might be the objective that all America, including as much as possible of the cities, would be ruralized in the very realistic sense of decentralizing congestion and technology into richer living in more natural societies.

Contrary to this assumption of progress as urban and technological is that of a considerable body of philosophers and students, typified by the Spenglerian theories of decline, that overurbanization is a universal index of decay and deterioration. Thus, the postulate is that as civilization grows more and more complex and urban, the city becomes the center of every creative activity, until, at the beginning of the decline, we have the megapolitan civilization in which man is no longer attached to the earth; he moves with the flux of the urban center. The folk changes into the mass. The city triumphs over the country, the intelligentsia over tradition, and money over policy. While early culture is characterized by rural exchange, with money as a means, the decline period is characterized by money as an economic function in itself. From the popular current viewpoint Dorothy Thompson writes that "We can't have a culture in this country so long as the most of the wealth is produced in a handful of centers. Our cities are monstrosities, full of corruption, crime and slums, places where wealth exists without amenities, and everything is available except integrity and fresh air."[5]

[4] Adapted from an unpublished study of French Regionalism by Mildred Rubin.
[5] Letter to the Editors in *Free America,* I, No. 11, p. 5.

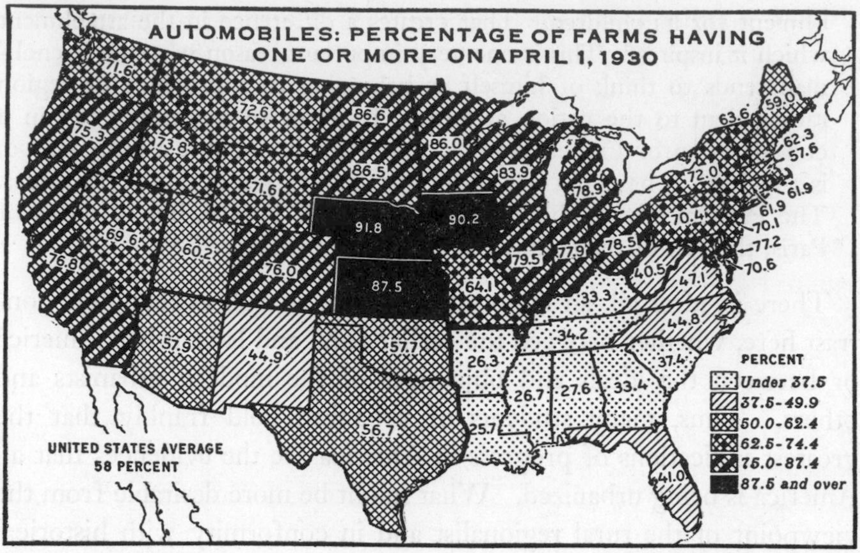

Note contrasting details in which regions having a small percentage of farms having automobiles must often pay a higher gasoline tax per acre. Adapted by permission from the Bureau of Agricultural Economics of the United States Department of Agriculture, and from their valuable series of graphic bulletins.

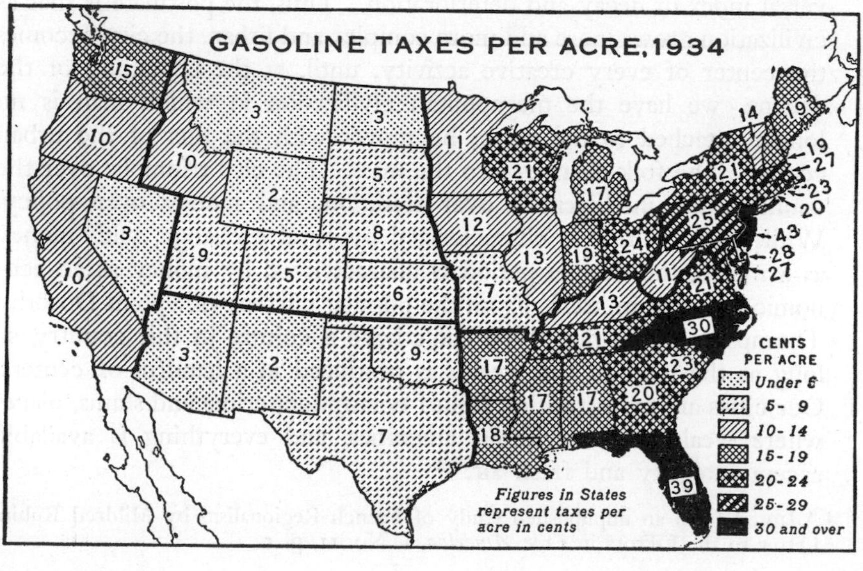

These conflicting theories are important in relation to the postulate that regionalism may be a comprehensive tool for the working out of a better balance and equilibrium between the too big and urban and technological society and the normal rural-urban. It is also important to note the fact that contrary to many assumptions the rural regions have dominated the cities and have set their character. Thus, Chicago as a city conditioned by a great midwestern agricultural region is contrasted with New York, the more self-contained world metropolis. Savannah is characterized by Ogburn, for instance, as more urban than Chicago, because of the rural conditioning of the great agricultural center of the Middle States. So, too, Ogburn shows a great variation in the characteristics of cities, sometimes showing less homogeneity than rural areas. Of these characteristics, they have been due in part to rural conditioning, now agriculture, now lumbering, now mining, now fishing. This is of the essence of an equilibrium between the folk and the land, between the primary and secondary occupations. When this balance is broken so that man does not live in harmony with his natural heritage, then, so the social ecologist holds, there is no enduring society.

This significance of differences between urban and rural regions is pointed out by Ogburn as being related to many aspects of national life. Thus, "there are several possible implications of the fact that in many traits cities of different regions resemble each other more than they do the surrounding hinterland. One is that it is probably not wise to make regional comparisons in regard to those traits, such as sex ratios, number of old people, etc., in which the cities of different regions are so much alike. At least when such comparisons are made the cities should be excepted. There is a good deal of loose, exaggerated talk about regional differences, whereas actually the cities of the different regions have many resemblances. At least it should be borne in mind that urban-rural differences very often overshadow regional differences.

"Another implication concerns the nature of representation in legislative assemblies, which is on a geographical if not a regional basis. A representative to Congress from San Francisco and one from New York may have nearer the same constituents in many traits than one or the other would have, respectively, with a representative from a rural region of California or a rural region of New York State. There is probably little to be done practically about changing the nature of representation, but a recognition of these resemblances and differences is important in interpreting representation.

"Above all, however, the data show that regional comparisons so common in the past have been upset to a degree by the appearance of cities, which cut across regional lines." [6]

This contrasting economy of rural and urban civilization is still of the greatest importance in the evolving America of the new cultural frontiers. We may examine these contrasts in several ways. One is to note the changing nature and tempo of rural life and civilization of the present and contrast it with the earlier agrarian culture. Thus, the present-day rural life comprehends a broader meaning than the earlier Jeffersonian America. Yet it is of the greatest importance to note that chiefest among the earlier authentic historical Americanisms was that of the agrarian culture. This brings us to the importance of reconsidering the basic and organic place which agrarian culture has in the national fabric and, therefore, the need for examining carefully the prospects of its continuing. This, then, leads inevitably to the deeper significance of "farming as a way of life" rather than primarily as an economic activity.

With reference to the current range of rural life and institutions, William E. Cole points up the expanding concept of "rural." "To the unmeticulous mind, 'rural' means the smell of freshly mown meadows, herds of cattle, fields of crops, quietude, a country store, a rural church and a school at the crossroads, farmers in overalls, wives in house gingham, and hired hands in the fields. True, these elements characterize one phase of the meaning of rural, but an ever-widening concept of the term is necessary in any consideration of planning procedures. Today, the rural environment includes many occupations besides farming, and many classes of people besides farmers. It includes many thousands of individuals who live in the country but who work in the town or city. It includes a constant daily flow of population between city and country. Homes with radios; farmers with stocks and bonds and automobiles; recreation at urban centers, and other similar cultural traits and patterns, all belong to rural environment today. Often it is so difficult, in fact, to differentiate between rural and urban that some have suggested the term 'rurban' to characterize adequately the cultural patterns of these two population groupings

[6] W. F. Ogburn, "Social Characteristics of Cities. VII. Urban Resemblances and Regional Differences," *Public Management*, XVIII, 203.

within the hinterland of metropolitan areas which no longer live as separate entities, but as an integrated whole. Rural, then, is an ever-expanding term, including more and more interrelationships between city and country and calling for an ever-expanding set of concepts for the consideration of the problems of urban and rural planning, and for an increasingly more inclusive definition of what is rural." [7]

Yet the student of culture, as well as of national history, recognizes distinctive traits that appear to be rural and are, therefore, of elemental importance. These differences center around community life and institutions, occupations, composition of population, cultural heritage, relation to land and nature and out-of-doors, and the composite differences due to physiographic environment and psychological processes.

Carl Taylor describes some of these differences: "We recognize that during the last 150 years, American agriculture has traveled steadily from the ox-cart and ox-team to the automobile and the tractor; from the cradle and the flail to the combine; from the tallow candle to the electric light, and from dire isolation to modern socialization. We recognize that there is a vast difference between types of agricultural production and their concomitant techniques, technologies, habits, and customs, and consequently of the thinking and purposing of the people engaged in agriculture. We recognize that there has been and is a difference in the parts played by the owner-operator, the tenant, and the hired man in these various processes and purposes of agriculture. We recognize that there are great differences among the various type-of-farming areas of the nation.

"But with all of these differences, there are a great many things that are common to farmers everywhere, whether they be intensive or extensive farmers, whether they are owner-operators, tenants, or hired men, and even whether they are producers of products for the market or for home consumption. And these things are not common to persons engaged in other occupations and living in other environments.

"The average urban worker on the one hand is very little influenced by direct contact with physical nature. The weather is excluded by walls and roofs, temperature is controlled by means of artificial heat and electric fans, and even daylight is no longer essential for work. The farmer on the other hand works out-of-doors, is compelled constantly to struggle against or co-operate personally with the forces of gravity, and must adjust his physical behavior to climate and season.

[7] William E. Cole and Hugh Price Crowe, *Recent Trends in Rural Planning*, pp. 1-2. (Quoted by permission of Prentice-Hall, Inc.)

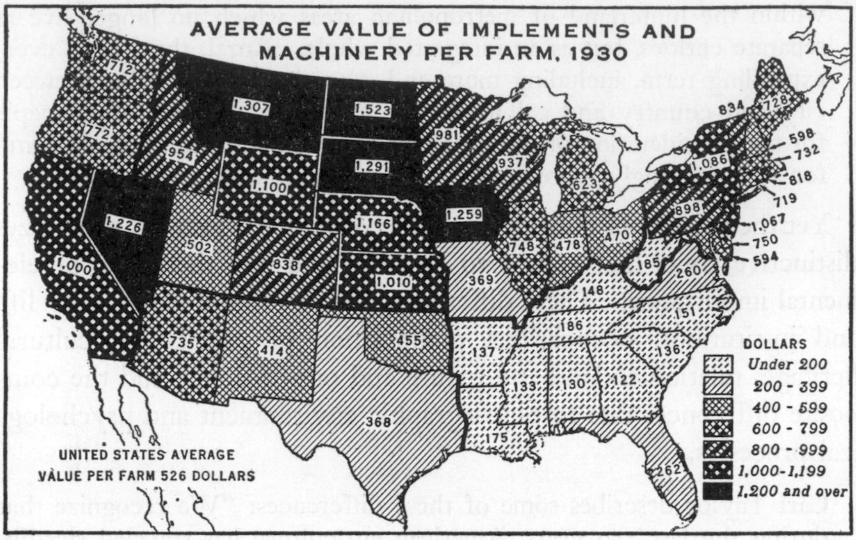

The question is being asked often now as to what will happen to agriculture in general when the South becomes more mechanized and in particular what will happen to the great body of white and Negro tenants. Maps adapted by permission from the Bureau of Agricultural Economics of the United States Department of Agriculture.

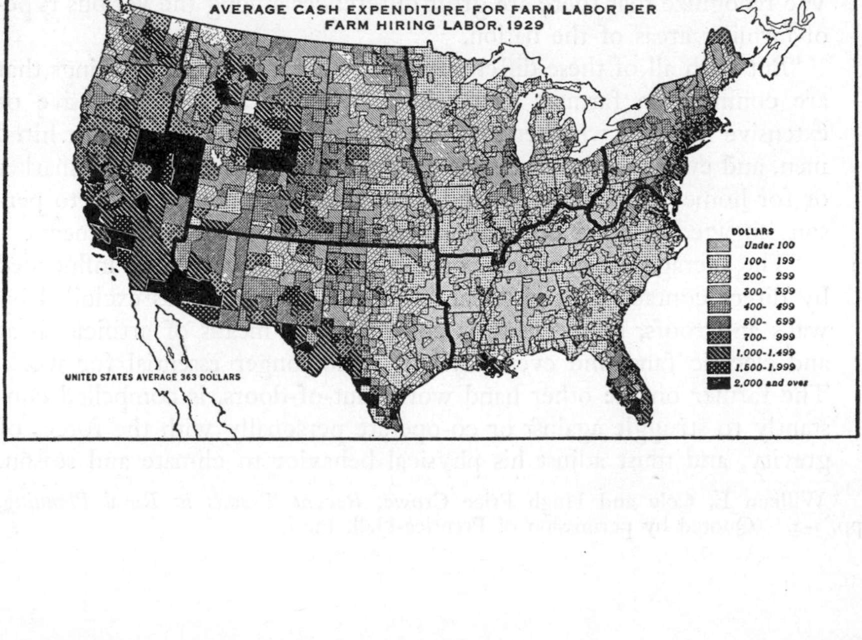

He works for the most part with tools and implements in a process of individual production rather than with giant power machines in mass production. He works many hours in solitude or associated with relatively few people, most often with members of his own family. He is a breeder, a husbandman, a nurturer, and a conserver, rather than a fabricator or a machine operator. He works with a high degree of initiative and judgment, not under the compulsion of the factory whistle or the edicts of someone higher up. His manual labor, his planning, his money-making, and his family life are all woven together in his day-by-day behavior and thinking."[8]

There is yet to be examined more carefully than has yet been done the significance of these differences. To many, rural life and urban life are considered as of differing degrees of accommodation to technology and density of population. To others, the difference is much greater.

Carl Taylor gives the arguments on either side of the new and the old rural situation: "Those who believe that the entrance of science, business, commerce, and mechanization into agriculture has been all to the good, point out the following as grounds for their convictions. They say that human labor per unit of farm product is much less today than it used to be; that increased application of science to agriculture has brought to all rural people a much more exact knowledge, not only of their day-by-day problems, but of the world at large; that the application of business criteria to the farm enterprise has facilitated the adjustment of population to the land base and the production of at least the major crops to areas in which they have a natural comparative advantage; that a relatively high material standard of living has been gained for the entrepreneurs of agriculture; and that there is a growing tendency to modernize all rural social institutions and thus give to rural people facilities and services which the farmers of yesterday did not have. Those who are inclined to the belief that most of this so-called progress has in fact been a net loss, argue that we have sacrificed the cohesiveness of family life, largely lost the homogeneity of rural community life, suffered a heavy depletion of folk culture, and developed widespread insecurity."[9]

We may point up this contrast with two other illustrations, the one having to do with the freedom and joy and richness of country life

[8] Carl C. Taylor, *The Restoration of Rural Culture*, pp. 3-4 (Address before the National Catholic Rural Life Conference, Richmond, Virginia, November 9, 1937).

[9] *Ibid.*, p. 7.

as a culture, and the other reflecting the Thomas Jefferson philosophy of America's destiny as he saw it. The distinction between what we are calling the ruralization of the city as opposed to the urbanization of the country may be envisaged in the following long catalogue of "things I love in the country," a symposium of several years of collecting by *The Progressive Farmer*. It must be clear that these are not merely sentiment, but represent units of measurement as specific and potent as tables of statistics. They are indeed presented as analogous to such a statistical array, and they contrast country life with city life. The following sample represents about one-twentieth of the selections.

> To see things grow . . . The happy expression on my boy's face as a martin goes into his gourd and hear him yell, "Time to go barefooted, Mother! Martin's in my gourd!" . . . The smell of clean-scrubbed floors and freshly washed fireplaces . . . The songs and the flashing color of the birds . . . The sweetness of yellow jasmine by the roadside, of lilacs in my garden, and arbutus in the woods . . . To dig in flower beds and plant seeds . . . Pastures carpeted with sweet young grass, elms that stand aquiver in frills of tender green, the rose mist of the red-buds, and the scent of wild plum blossoms in the air . . . The rippling, dreamily drifting river and the little marsh-surrounded islands and the high, green, white-capped waves that break on the uninhabited beaches of our sea-coast . . . The winter winds as they sing in the chimney, chanting a melody no one knows, and the March winds that bring in the birds and blossoms in a flurry . . . The frogs as they sing in the marsh on the first warm nights in spring . . . To inhale the perfume of a crabapple tree in full bloom . . . To smell fresh-plowed fields and walk in a drizzling rain . . . The superb optimism of wheatfields nestling beneath blankets of snow . . . Dark storms, leaden clouds, breath-taking gusts of sleet, frozen marshes, and streams with closed eye-lids . . . To do my chores at the close of day . . . The tap-tap of the ram as it pumps water up the hill to the tank in our yard . . . The clear ringing of the ax as the wood-cutters chop wood . . . The peep-peep of baby chicks in the spring . . . The cows standing knee-deep in hay on a cold day, eating to their hearts' content . . . The delicate, far-reaching aroma of sage, and the smell of mist, wood-smoke, and pine needles . . . The sound and sight of wild geese against the November sky . . . The nicker of a horse for his corn . . . The quiet solitudes, where one may steal away and be alone and yet not lonely . . . The valleys of golden-hued stubble, dotted with shocks of ripened grain . . . The wild

squall of a hawk before a summer shower . . . The friendliness of my country neighbors . . .

The Thomas Jefferson philosophy of American agrarian culture was based upon experience and ideals of a nation in which nine of every ten people were country folks as compared to one out of every three or four of the present time. Although there is no implication of a back-to-the-land movement, still the problem of the strain of the cities and the poverty of the rural areas is universally considered one of America's greatest dilemmas.

To state the contrast in a different way, "there was . . . the Jeffersonian democracy in which the farmer was the bulwark of democracy and there was the agriculture of the 1930's providing less than 13 percent of the nation's income. There was Thomas Jefferson proclaiming, 'The mob of great cities add just so much to the support of pure government, as sores do to the strength of the human body,' and there was the 1930 America with more than 60 percent of its people living within metropolitan areas, with 96 such regions each boasting over 100,000 population, with a single metropolitan region having twice as many people in it as all of Jefferson's beloved domain. There was Thomas Jefferson admonishing 'to let our workshops remain in Europe' and there was the America of the new crisis with more than 37,000,000 or 76.2 percent of all its working folk occupied in manufacturing, mechanical distribution, and social services. There was Jefferson idealizing that government as best which governs least and there was the amazing new NRA of America.

"Or to focus the two pictures in a slightly different way, there was the Jeffersonian small nation of rural states, of one or two regions of simple motivation, of homogeneity of people, of few occupations, with small individual fortunes centered chiefly in farm and forest, in land and homes, contrasted with the present very large nation of urban and industrial majorities, in greatly differing regions with complex motivation and heterogeneity of population, with hundreds of varied occupations, large individual fortunes, fabulous salaries, corporate holdings and wealth not only in farm lands and commodities, but in city real estate, factories, railroads, traction and steamship lines, coal and iron, stores and banks, utilities and amusements, food and tobacco, textile and furniture, rubber, and leather, and glass, and machinery, and automobiles, and metal, and petroleum, and power, and soap, and drugs, and multiplied consumers' goods." [10]

[10] Howard W. Odum, "The Case for Regional National Social Planning," *Social Forces,* Vol. 13, p. 13.

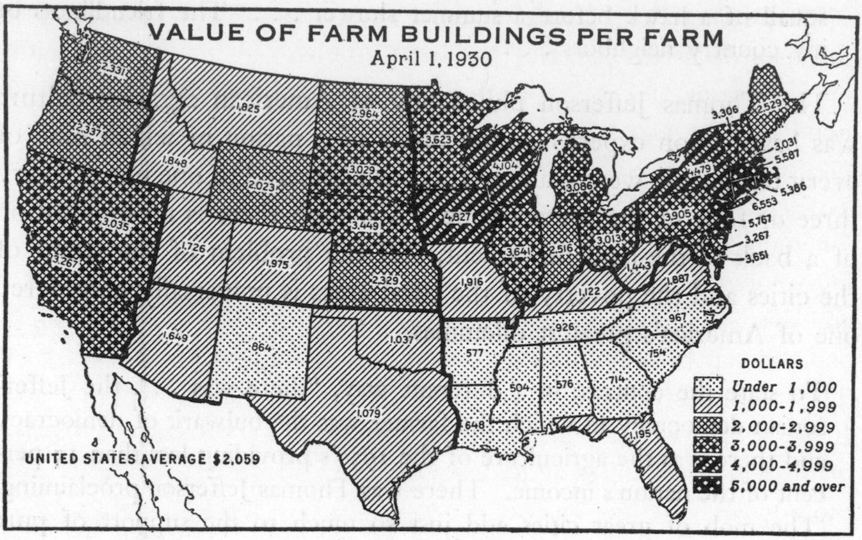

Regional variations in technical economic indices should be interpreted only for what they measure. Although, for instance, Nevada shows a very high ratio of value for farms and farm buildings its ratio of book buying is 1 to 50; while South Carolina is very low in the former it ranks about 2 to 5 in the latter. Maps adapted by permission from the Bureau of Agricultural Economics of the United States Department of Agriculture.

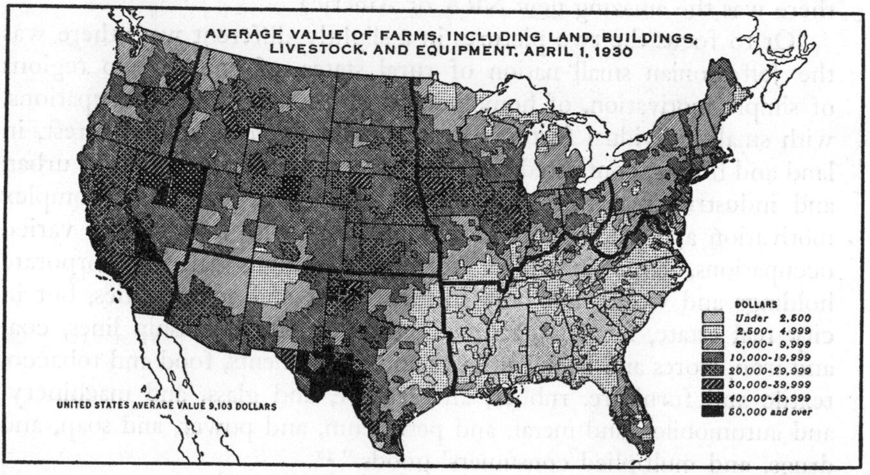

This earlier American picture of rural regions as contrasted with the present urban America has been emphasized by the Committee on Urbanism of the National Resources Committee in which they point out the fact that "The transition of the United States from a predominantly rural to an urban country has taken place in less than half a century. Whereas in 1880 the United States was still overwhelmingly rural with only some 14,000,000 of her people, amounting to about 29 percent of the total, in incorporated places of 2,500 and over, by 1930 the urban population had increased to nearly 69,000,000 representing approximately 56 percent of the nation's total. The number of urban places rose from 1,099 in 1880 to 3,165 in 1930. If we restrict ourselves to the larger urban places of 8,000 and over, or the still larger cities of 30,000 and over, the rate of increase in both the number of cities and the urban population is still higher. . . . If the degree of urbanization of a country is a measure of its maturity then the United States may be said to have come of age. The leading problem facing the United States today is no longer what it was in the early days of the nation when a concerted national effort was put forth to overcome the dependence upon the Old World of an undeveloped, agricultural, frontier community by encouraging local industries, and incidentally thereby the growth of cities. The issue of the present day seems to be, rather, how in the face of the uncontrolled growth of urban and metropolitan agglomerations a reasonable balance may be retained between the urban and the rural elements in the national economy." [11]

All this suggests a new regional balance of men and agriculture and a greater total ratio of agriculture and rural life in the nation's total culture. This is not only a mechanical matter of agricultural parity as compared with industry, for which it is necessary to plan more effectively than heretofore. It is undoubtedly one of the larger organic problems of American planning.

This problem is implied in our previous assumption that there must be a more effective reintegration of agrarian culture in American life than has been predicated by many of the economists and population

[11] Research Committee on Urbanism, *Interim Report to the National Resources Committee*, July 1936, pp. 2, 6.

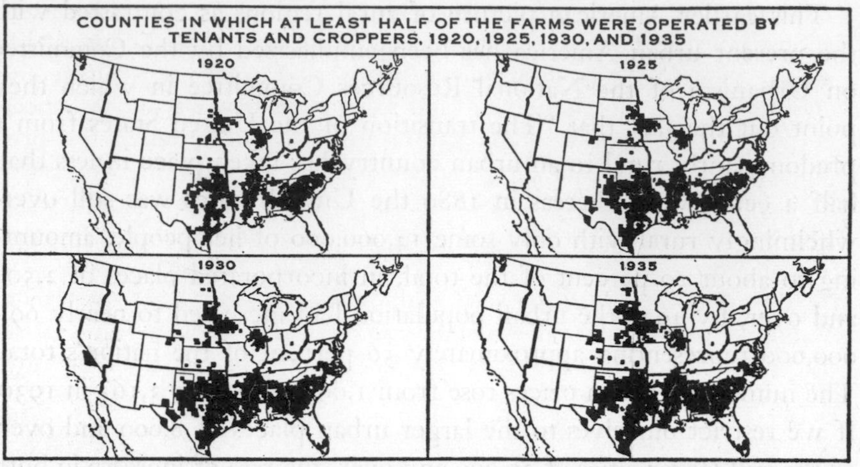

Alongside the tragic consequences of soil erosion increase has gone also a steady increase in farm tenancy in the nation. Three regions, the two Souths and the Middle States, show the greatest increase. Adapted by permission from the Bureau of Agricultural Economics of the United States Department of Agriculture.

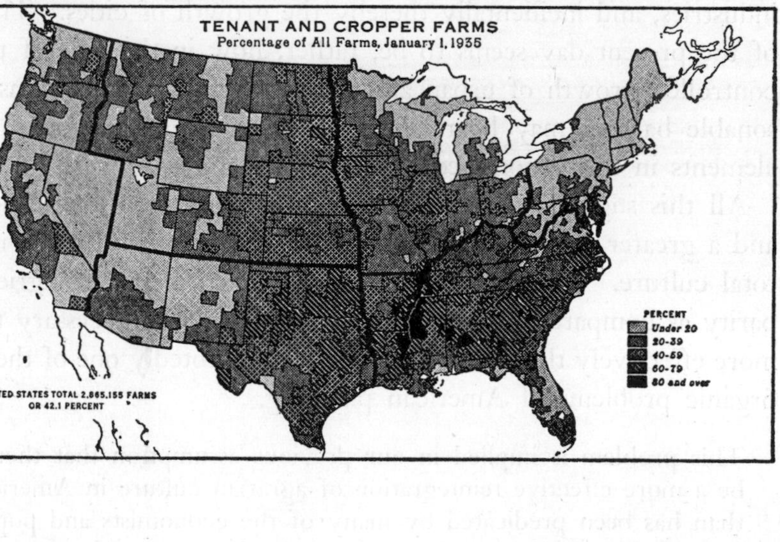

experts. We do not refer to the cult of agrarianism which bodes no industrial order, but to the increment of agriculture and country life in the total national fabric woven of a well-balanced agriculture and industry. It is not only that land is still the base of our American wealth. The greatest single natural resource is found in the productiveness of the soil. It is often pointed out that in contrast to "iron mines, coal mines, and oil wells, productivity may be conserved and even enhanced by wise and intelligent use. It is a possible heritage for all posterity." [12]

It is not only that the seed bed of the nation's population must continue to be in rural America and that therefore the quality of future America is conditioned by the quality of our rural culture. It is not only that the spirit and genius of early America were grounded in a vital agrarian culture, the nature of our laws and institutions assuming a continuity of such fundamentals. It is all of this and more. It is a matter of essential equilibrium and balance between agrarian and industrial culture, between country life and city activities, between physical resources and technology, between machines and men. It is, therefore, essentially a problem of progress and survival.

In order to make the matter more specific, we may call attention to many current predictions that in the next periods of American development agriculture and rural life, the land and the people on it, must recede yet further and further into such dangerous ratios as to make American democracy impossible of attainment. The assumption is ventured that the enduring equilibrium in American culture will not be found in less than a fourth of its people and their occupations in the rural-agricultural area but more nearly a third; that not a sixth or a seventh of the national income will be derived from agriculture and allied work, but nearer a fifth. Such a premise still assumes urban development and the increase of technology; but it also assumes new skills in land conservation and utilization, a nearer approximation to agricultural parity, the aid of agricultural engineering, the development of chemical service to agriculture, rural electrification and power development, the upraising of standards of housing, living, rural institutions; the function of agriculture as a great reserve economy in time of national depression, and the working out of national-regional and interregional balance and equilibrium.

The cultural and historical backgrounds of rural America and of rural life everywhere give some evidence to indicate that there is a very realistic organic relation of rural regions to the whole regional

[12] Cf. Howard W. Odum, "The Human Aspects of Chemurgy," *Farm Chemurgic Journal*, Vol. I, No. 1, pp. 60-71.

movement. Lewis Mumford maintains that the historical revival of regionalism was re-enforced by the notable movement which was bound up in the "Return to Nature." There is in America, in the revival of interest and publications and movements about nature and the conservation of land and wild life, perhaps a parallel movement.

> Mumford makes the earlier case as follows: "The cultivation of nature for its own sake, and the pursuit of rural modes of living and the appreciation of the rural environment became in the eighteenth century one of the chief means of escaping the counting house and the machine. So long as the country was uppermost, the cult of nature could have no meaning: being a part of life, there was no need to make it a special object of thought. It was only when the townsman found himself closed in by his methodical urban routine and deprived in his new urban environment of the sight of sky and grass and trees, that the value of the country manifested itself clearly to him. Before this, an occasional rare adventurer would seek the solitude of the mountains to cultivate his soul: but in the eighteenth century Jean-Jacques Rousseau, preaching the wisdom of the peasant and the sanity of the simple rural occupations, led a whole succession of generations outside the gates of their cities: they botanized, they climbed mountains, they sang peasant songs, they swam in the moonlight, they helped in the harvest field; and those who could afford to built themselves rural retreats. This impulse to recapture nature had a powerful influence upon the cultivation of the environment as a whole and upon the development of cities: but I reserve this for discussion in another book."[13]

Mumford maintains that "Movements as vast and complex as the migration of peoples from the seventeenth to the twentieth century" cannot be explained by the pressure of population-growth, nor by politics, nor by any single cause. Yet the combination of many causes focused upon the contrast between urban-industrial life and country life.

> Especially all these motives were in existence: "the desire to be free from social compulsion, the desire for economic security, the desire to return to nature; and they played into each other's hands. They provided both the excuse and the motive power for escaping from the new mechanical civilization that was closing in upon the Western

[13] Lewis Mumford, *Technics and Civilization*, p. 295. (Quoted by permission of Harcourt, Brace and Company, Inc.)

World. To shoot, to trap, to chop trees, to hold a plow, to prospect, to face a seam—all these primitive occupations, out of which technics had originally sprung, all these occupations that had been closed and stabilized by the very advances of technics, were now open to the pioneer: he might be hunter, fisher, miner, woodman, and farmer by turn, and by engaging in these occupations people could restore their plain animal vigor as men and women, temporarily freed from the duties of a more orderly and servile existence." [14]

So, again, Mumford points up the significance of rural regions in the rise and incidence of economic regionalism. He thinks the "prime examples of conscious economic regionalism up to the present have come from countries like Ireland and Denmark, or states like Wisconsin, where the occupations were predominantly agricultural, and where a flourishing economic life depended upon an intelligent exploitation of all the regional resources. But economic regionalism does not aim at complete self-sufficiency: even under the most primitive conditions no region has ever been economically self-sufficient in all respects. On the other hand, economic regionalism does aim at combating the evil of over-specialization: since whatever the temporary commercial advantages of such specialization it tends to impoverish the cultural life of a region and, by placing all its eggs in one basket, to make precarious ultimately its economic existence. Just as every region has a potential balance of animal life and vegetation, so it has a potential social balance between industry and agriculture, between cities and farms, between built-up spaces and open spaces. A region entirely specialized for a single resource, or covered from boundary line to boundary line by a solid area of houses and streets, is a defective environment, no matter how well its trade may temporarily flourish. Economic regionalism is necessary to provide for a varied social life, as well as to provide for a balanced economy." [15]

It remains to note the extraordinary range of rural problems which face those who seek next steps through regional planning. Agriculture and housing, small industry and part-time farming, villages and open countryside, soil conservation and rivers, forests and co-operatives—these and others constitute a long catalogue of problems for which distinctive rural and regional measures will be required. These aspects of rural regionalism may be studied further in the subsequent chapter on Regional Planning.

[14] *Ibid.*, pp. 297-298. (Quoted by permission.)
[15] *Ibid.*, pp. 388-389. (Quoted by permission.)

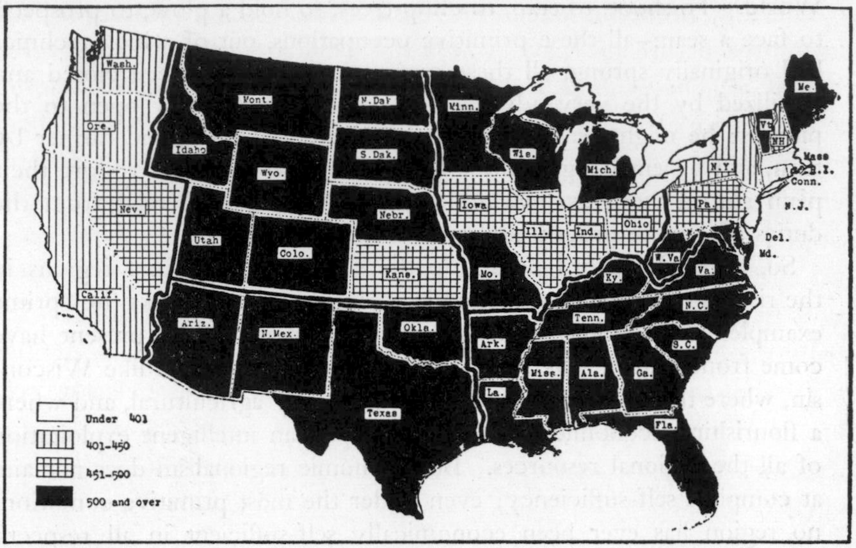

Above: Rural Farm Population Under Five Years of Age Per Thousand Women 15 to 44 Years of Age, 1930.

Below: Percent of Total Population Fifty-Five Years of Age and Over, 1930

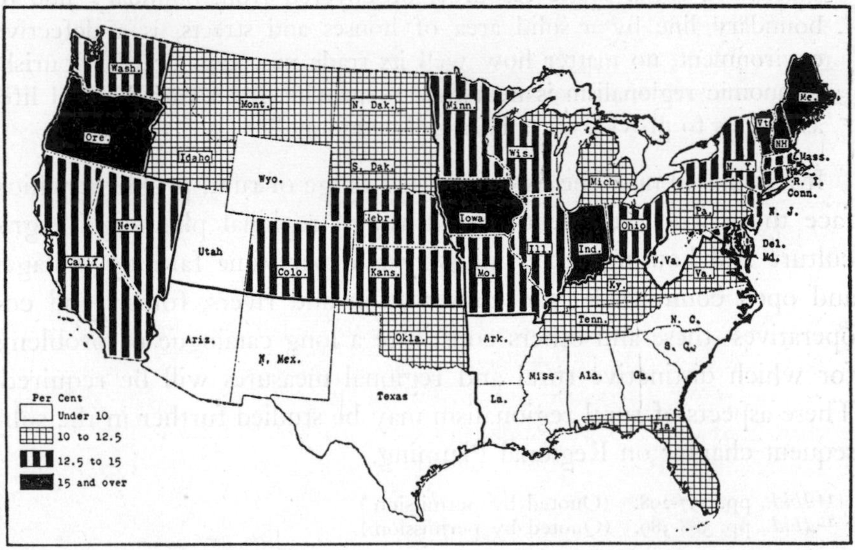

There is, however, one other basic consideration underlying the distinctive nature of rural America. This is found in the specific regions which combine soil, climate, crops, and people, commonly designated as agricultural regions. In these subregional divisions may be found not only indices of rural America, but such divisions represent an indivisible union of the physical and cultural aspects of civilization. It is clearly impossible to grow cotton in North Dakota; just as clearly is it possible in each region of the nation to grow other crops which are not grown or are grown only as curiosities. Actually the crop grown in a particular region will depend on a number of factors: soil, climate, slope of the land, density of population, traditions of the farmers and their readiness to accept new techniques of cultivation, varieties of plants, access to markets, efficiency as compared to other regions. We have customarily given great emphasis to the physical factors, but it seems that the cultural elements are fully as important. The importance of the cultural element in agricultural practice is indicated by the fact that the agricultural regions do not coincide with the physiographic, climatic, or soil regions of the nation. Further they vary from time to time and from student to student, within fairly low limits.

However, physical nature affects the agriculturists as greatly as any other occupational group, unless it be the miners, and the agricultural regions of the nation do coincide roughly with certain combinations of climate, soil, and topography. The scheme of regionalization on these bases worked out by O. E. Baker, of the United States Department of Agriculture, is the most commonly accepted and is made the basis of the discussion which follows.

> Along the coast of the Gulf of Mexico from the neighborhood of Corpus Christi, Texas, including the entire state of Florida and extending in a narrow strip up the Atlantic Coast to about Charleston, South Carolina, is an area known as Humid Subtropical Agricultural Region. The climate is hot and moist due to the presence of the warm ocean waters, the soil is sandy and badly leached, the topography is flat so that drainage is poor. Subtropical crops as rice, sugar cane, citrus fruits and early vegetables occupy most of the cultivated portion of the region, which includes only about twenty percent of the land surface. In the western portion of the region much of the land is used

as pasturage. An extension of the coastal plains along the Atlantic as far north as Cape Cod, similar to the Humid Subtropical Region except that rainfall and temperatures are lower, is known as the Mid-Atlantic Trucking Region. The crops grown vary somewhat with the latitude, but in general are those which may be sold in the cities along or near the Atlantic Coast.

The Cotton Belt as one of the major crop regions of the nation is at the present time of great importance in the crises facing the governmental planning for equilibrium between agriculture and industry and between and among regions. There are various subregions of this large belt. One great area is commonly called the Black Belt. However, the general division lies to the north and west of the subtropical and trucking regions described. The northern boundary is somewhat flexible, varying with the price of cotton, but in general runs from the neighborhood of Norfolk, Virginia, southwestward to include the Carolina Piedmont, near the Georgia-Alabama-Tennessee line, along the Tennessee River to cross the Mississippi just above the southern boundaries of Kentucky and Missouri, across the northwestern corner of Arkansas, the northern portion of Oklahoma, cuts southwest across the northwestern portion of Texas to include a small bit of New Mexico, and then follows the line of the Pecos-Rio Grande at a distance of about 100 miles to the Gulf. Almost half of the cultivated acres in this region are given to cotton, but only about one-fourth of the area is in cultivation. Corn is the crop of secondary importance, but cotton is so much more profitable that corn is grown only for local consumption. In the eastern portion of the region large acreage is devoted to tobacco. Climatic conditions largely outline the region. On the south the limit of profitable cotton culture is set by eleven inches of rainfall during the autumn, the harvesting season. On the north, the limit is set by the line indicating 200 frost-free days. On the west the limit closely follows the line of 20 inches annual rainfall.

To the north of the cotton region corn and winter wheat are the dominant crops and give their name to the agricultural region. This region includes most of Maryland, Virginia, Kentucky, and Missouri. The western portion of North Carolina, the eastern portion of Tennessee, a strip just north of the Ohio including the southern counties of Ohio, Indiana and Illinois and the eastern portion of Kansas, the northwestern corner of Arkansas and the northeastern corner of Oklahoma are also included. The limits on all sides of this area are vague and liable to shift. Cotton may invade from the south, corn from the north, or wheat from the west. Corn is the most valuable crop produced in the region, though wheat occupies the greatest acreage. Stock farming is also prevalent, especially in the limestone valleys, but not so important as in the Corn Belt.

The Corn Belt stretches westward from central Ohio, including most of Indiana and Illinois, all of Iowa save the northeastern corner, about half of Nebraska, a strip along the northern boundary of Kansas, the southeastern corner of South Dakota, and southwestern Minnesota. The climate is warm and moist and the land fertile, rain falls in spring and summer, the topography is almost level, so that this region is more intensively cultivated than any other in the nation. More than 90 percent of the land is in farms and more than 60 percent of it is cultivated. Almost half of the cultivated land is planted in corn. Large numbers of cattle and swine are grown or imported into the region and much of the grain produced is marketed in the form of livestock. The prosperity of the region is indicated by the fact that maps showing density of various farm conveniences and luxuries are uniformly shaded heaviest in this region.

Still further to the north lies the Hay and Dairying Region, comprising most of Minnesota and Wisconsin, Michigan, eastern Ohio, West Virginia, Pennsylvania, New York and central New England. In this region the summers are cool and humid. Recently glaciated, the land is often rough and is poorly drained so that lakes and swamps are frequent. Such conditions make pasturage and hay an easy method of exploitation, while the large number of cities to which the farmers have relatively easy access furnish ready markets for much of the milk produced. This same population factor is responsible for the fairly large, though scattered, production of vegetables. Still further north and including the upper portions of Wisconsin and Michigan, the Adirondack Region and northern New England is the Forest and Hay Region, distinguished from the region to the south by a colder climate, the greater abundance of forests, and consequently less agricultural use. The land is poor and it is commonly agreed that forests are perhaps the most productive use to which the region can be placed.

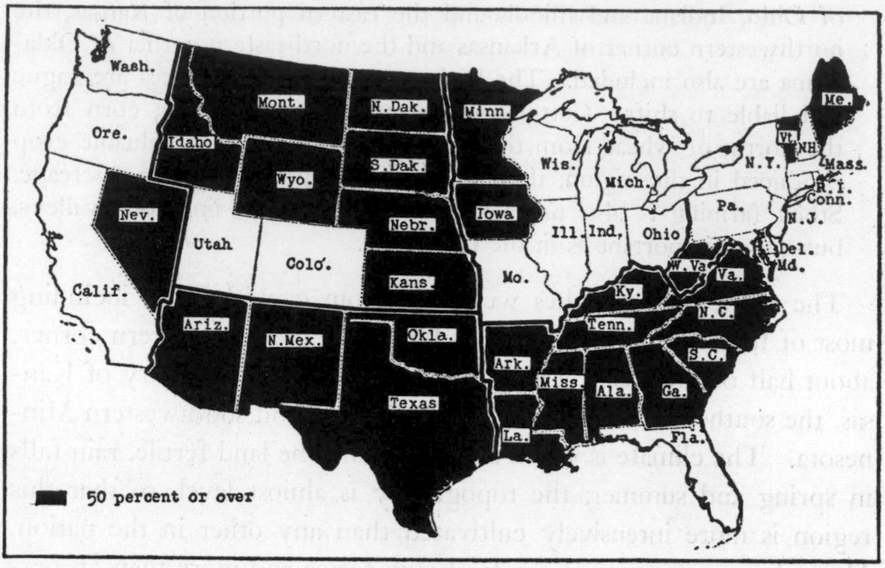

RURAL AND METROPOLITAN AREAS OF THE NATION

Above: States with Rural Population of Fifty Percent or Over.

Below: Metropolitan Districts of the United States, Having 100,000 or More Population in 1930. Adapted from McKenzie, *The Metropolitan Community*.

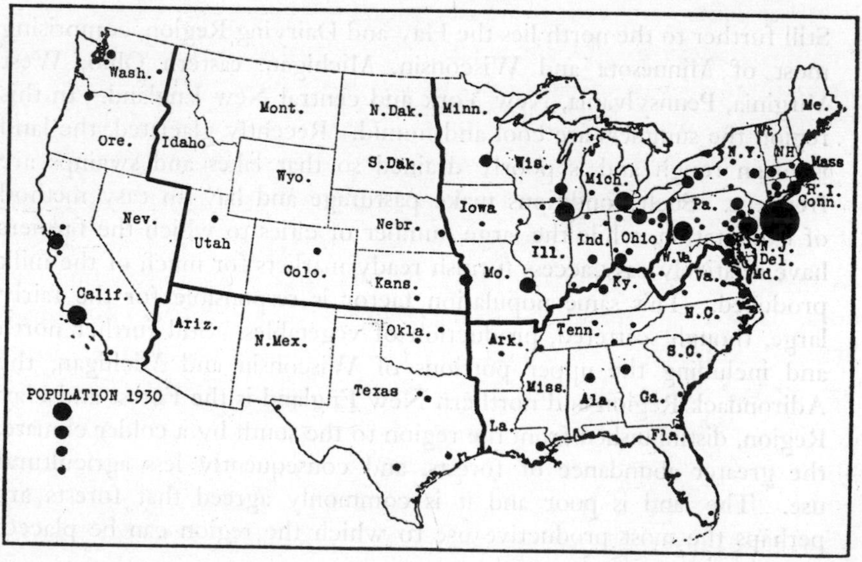

The regions described above, except for the Atlantic trucking region, run in a general east-west direction, the temperature variations being one of the major factors in their delimitation. Although temperature is also an important factor in the other agricultural regions of the nation, rainfall becomes more important, and finally decisive. Hence the regions either take on a north-south direction or consist of small, compact areas.

Wheat will grow in regions of relatively scanty rainfall and cool climate, so that it is to be expected that this crop would replace corn and dairying to the west. There are three small regions characterized as wheat growing areas: the Hard Winter Wheat Region, the Spring Wheat Region, and the Columbia Plateau Wheat Region. The first lies to the north of the Cotton Region in Oklahoma and Texas, covering most of Kansas and the northeastern corner of Colorado. The second occupies the famous Red River Valley of the north, the two Dakotas, and the northeastern portion of Montana. The third is found in the Plateau Valley of the Columbia River in central Washington. In all of these regions the land is relatively flat, the climate is cool to cold, the rainfall below thirty inches per year. The soils of the two eastern regions are similar, of the grasslands type with relatively high lime content. These characteristics are shared with the soils of the Columbia Plateau. Oats and barley are also grown on these lands, and there is a considerable production of flax, principally for the oil from the seed. The agriculture of the regions is mechanized to a high degree. The principal distinction between the winter and spring wheat regions is that in the former the grain grows through the winter, an indication of the milder climate.

Three other similar agricultural regions are found in the mountains of the western part of the nation, the Northern Forest and Brush Region, the North Pacific Hay, Pasture and Forage Region, and Forest and Hay Region. These lie in and along the mountains in Montana and Idaho, extending southward to about the northern border of Wyoming, and along the Cascade-Sierra Nevada ranges to central California. They are all characterized by forests and scanty agriculture limited mostly to meadow pasturage and forest range lands. The soils are poor and often undeveloped due to the steep slopes and fairly heavy rainfall, especially along the Pacific Coast.

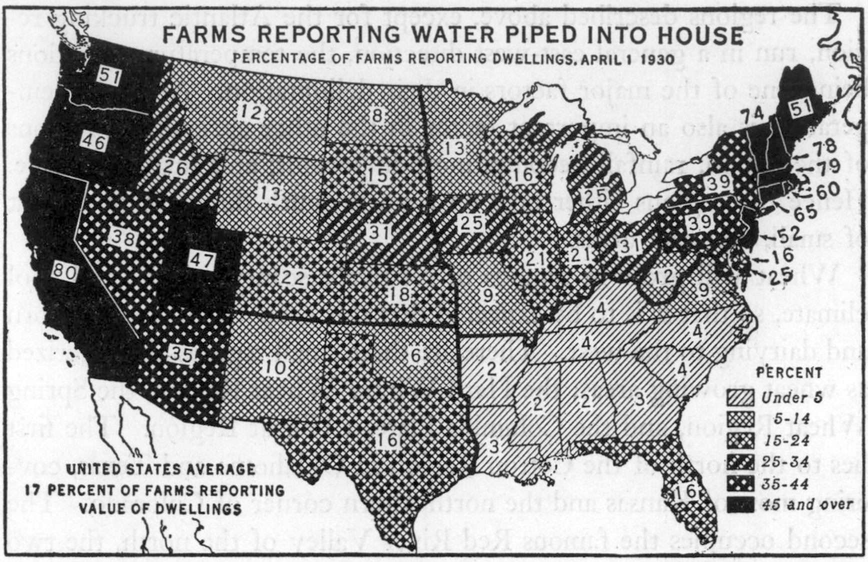

Examples of regional variation in rural-farm civilization in the United States. Note Northeast and Far West as Compared with the Southeast. Adapted from the Bureau of Agricultural Economics, Department of Agriculture.

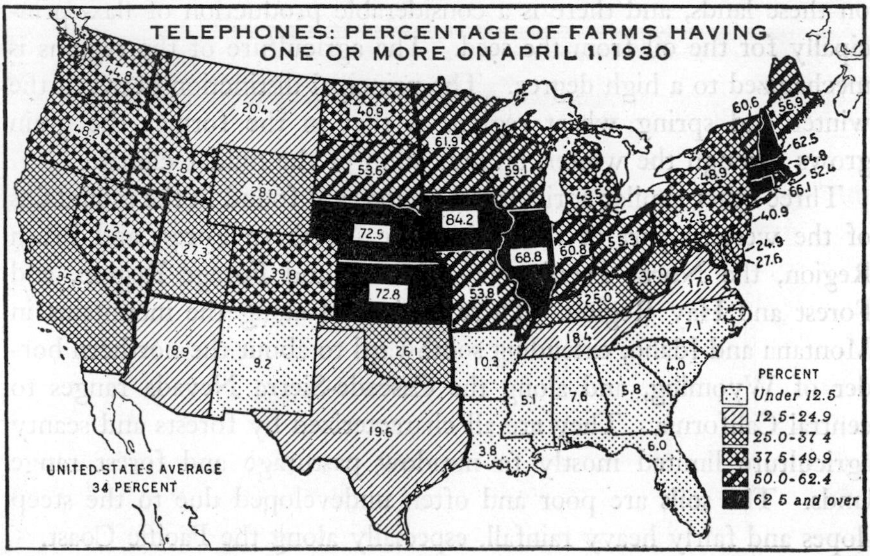

Between the western mountain ranges much of the land is not fitted for agricultural purposes. The soils are poorly developed due to lack of rainfall and vegetation. On the mountains soil is often missing, while in the valleys it is mostly wind-blown alluvium mixed with gravel. Hence this vast area is classified as range and grazing lands. In spots, however, irrigation has been developed and the land is productive. The most famous of such small areas is the Imperial Valley of southern California. This area includes most of Montana, Oregon, southern Idaho, Wyoming, Colorado, Utah, Nevada, Arizona, New Mexico, southeastern California, and Trans-Pecos Texas. The sandhills of Nebraska should also be included in this region.

The valley of California and the agricultural lands in the vicinity of Los Angeles constitute the Western Subtropical or Mediterranean agricultural region. Like the Gulf Coastal Region, temperatures are high, but unlike that region, the rainfall is scanty and comes mostly during the winter months, so that irrigation is needed. The crops are dissimilar, except that the Los Angeles section produces citrus fruits. Fruit and vegetables form the major crops, though much of the land is devoted to small grains. A somewhat similar agriculture is found in the Willamette Valley and the Puget Sound and Columbia Valley regions further north, though here the citrus fruits are replaced by peaches, berries, and other crops able to withstand freezing temperatures. These regions offer an excellent example of the way in which rural and village cultures are conditioned by the types of agricultural conditions in contrast, for instance, with the Southeast with its cotton and tobacco as single-crop, cash farming, which have colored that whole regional culture.

The further significance of agricultural regions may be studied through elaborate subregionalization in the form of types of farming areas in the United States, prepared by the Bureau of the Census, Department of Commerce, in 1930. There is listed a total of 514 such regions, to which should be added two or three hundred additional areas in the form of sub-subregions within these. This extraordinarily fine piece of work illustrates further the limitations of natural regions as administrative units as contrasted with the cultural and historical units of states, counties, and districts.

Special illustrations of rural and agricultural features within each major region will appear in Chapters XIX-XXIV. It is important here, however, to call attention to certain other aspects of rural development which are important in our continuing regional analysis. One of these is the "rural problem area" which has been studied by Woofter and others, in which the evidence indicates a considerable degree of consistency in the relation between poor land, poor farms, and depression needs. There are subregional areas susceptible to effective study and planning.

> Another special phase is that of rural land planning, which, while listed in our "levels of planning" in Chapter XI needs to be catalogued here as a part of rural planning. The best example of this is found in the TVA, where "The Rural Land Classification Program . . . produces a classification of land in the Tennessee Valley into five categories on the basis of those *economic conditions of the people* and *physical conditions of the land* that can be *observed in the field*. In addition to this relatively simple and generalized classification, the more significant substantiating data are being recorded. In this fashion we are gradually building up for the Basin a quantitative portrayal of the distribution of the five major classes of land and a quantitative portrayal of a considerable body of supporting information. The first will be of major significance in the broader aspects of land planning; the second, because it provides information concerning erosion conditions, slope conditions, types or farming, quality of farmsteads and equipment, and similar items, will provide relatively detailed understandings that are significant in the refinements of a broad land plan."[16]

Another aspect is the specialized techniques being developed for "rural planning." One of these is, of course, rural zoning, in which Wisconsin has pioneered. In their volume, *Recent Trends in Rural Planning*, Cole and Crowe include more than a dozen major categories, including land-use planning, land settlement, human resources and human welfare, rural electrification, together with various aspects of rural government, county planning, and rural health, crime, safety.[17] In each of these, the assumption is that special techniques will be needed as distinctive from city planning or general economic planning. We have included rural and county planning in the classification of our "levels of planning" in Chapter XI.

[16] From "Office Memorandum," *The Rural Land Classification Program*, December 1935.

[17] William E. Cole and Hugh Price Crowe, *op. cit.*

Finally, it is important to take into consideration the agrarian movement and to note the meaning of agrarianism, which in its purest form is quite in contradistinction to our present usage as implying a balanced economy as between agriculture and industry. Thus, Cauley defines agrarianism as "an economic and social system under which the chief method of making a living is that of tilling the soil, with a consequent rather wide dispersion of population and a relative meagerness of commercial intercourse. It is, probably, simply the antithesis of Industrial Capitalism." [18] Since the "agrarians" have made valuable contributions to the discussion of regionalism, which will be considered in our next chapter, it remains only to point up here the meaning of our term "the reintegration of agrarian culture in American life," which features, not the return to the simple life or agrarian culture, but the renewing of the elemental processes of agriculture and country life in the total evolving and changing technological world. Reintegration is integration and balance over and over again in an adequate "regional balance" of man and his work.

[18] Troy J. Cauley, *Agrarianism*, p. 3.

Chapter VII

CULTURE REGIONS: LITERARY AND AESTHETIC REGIONALISM

NEXT to metropolitan regionalism and sectionalism the rise and characterization of American regionalism has perhaps been more often identified with literary regionalism than with anything else. Indeed, by many of those who have written fluently upon the subject, the term regionalism has commonly been used as a synonym for literary localism. Thus the whole regionalist movement has often been described in terms of that regionalism discussed so effectively by the group commonly designated as agrarians. From this and from the fact that the public has been keenly interested in the portraiture of the various folk groups and differing localities in the nation, it has happened that the most common characterization of regionalism, as of sectionalism, has been that of provincialism, of local interest and color.

Over against this is, of course, the broader literary regionalism suggested by William Allen White who writes: "In the nature of things the Great American Novel must be a composite of regional novels. Always, since fiction began to appear in the United States, it has been regional fiction. Fashion in American fiction has changed, but its regional characteristics remain. Even Sinclair Lewis, who has written great American novels for his day and time, has written them with regional backgrounds. . . . Looking back a generation one sees in perspective that the American story of the day following the Civil War, was in all its regional phases a frontier story. Yet no one novelist could encompass it. Today the new story of the rise of American industrialism is essentially a regional story with a different epic theme for the same tragic circumstances in every regional landscape. . . ."[1]

[1] William Allen White, "Racy of the Soil" (Review of Arthur Pound, *Once a Wilderness*), *Saturday Review of Literature*, X, 607.

A variation of this theme is found in the "Heirs of the Pioneers," symbolism for a regional review by Oliver La Farge. He thinks that there "have been very few stories written that are not fundamentally sectional, with the exception of such panoramic works as Dos Passos' series. A certain urban provincialism similar to the attitude of a Parisian towards 'les provinces,' strengthened by our middle class's strong sense of security and unity, has led us to accept a novel laid in New York or Boston or some such center as being general, where one laid in Georgia is sectional. The American pattern is one of men reared in a locality of definite local flavor, whether city, country, or wilderness, who come to maturity to participate in the common experiences and activities of America as a whole. Perhaps one might define a truly sectional novel as one in which the larger part of the characters are unfamiliar to the people of the country at large. The bulk of American novels can be neatly divided according to this criterion. . . ."[2]

This assumption that the regional portraitures are only fundamental units in the great American literary fabric is of the utmost importance. In emphasizing the fact that the great American novel when it appears must necessarily be a story of American regions, Mr. White insists that each regional novel, "as all regional stories is only a part of American history." Thus, *Main Street*, *A Lantern in Her Hand*, *Cimarron*, *Come and Get It*, *Once a Wilderness*, *Gone with the Wind* are "racy of the soil" and essentially constituent parts of an aggregate American picture which must comprehend the whole of the national spirit and character. In so far as these novels have presented primarily the local, they fall within the genuine American picture. This may be illustrated in the case of Emerson and Thoreau and other New England writers who were primarily New England yet also American, in so far as they expressed the universal American character in terms of the New England culture and setting. The vitality of this theme of regional literature is evidenced by the extraordinary selling power which regional books have shown in recent years. It has also been in evidence in the Pulitzer awards and book club adoptions during the last ten or fifteen years.

Even though literary regionalism may at times connote the realities of local areas it is nevertheless of the essence of culture regions. And

[2] Oliver La Farge, "Heirs of the Pioneers" (Review of Archie Binns, *The Laurels Are Cut Down*), *Saturday Review of Literature*, XV, No. 25, p. 5.

still more than this it is of the essence of historical regionalism wherever the concept has been developed through the full flowering of all forces. Thus Lewis Mumford insists that "the revival of place interests and language interests, focussed in the new appreciation of regional history, is one of the definite characteristics of the nineteenth century culture." He continues, "This movement has gone through a similar set of stages in every country where it has taken place: in Denmark, in Norway, in Ireland, in Catalonia, in Brittany, in Wales, in Scotland, in Palestine, and similar signs are already visible in various regions in North America. There is, as M. Jourdanne has put it, at first a poetic cycle: this leads to the recovery of the language and literature of the folk, and the attempt to use it as a vehicle for contemporary expression on the basis of largely traditional forms. The second is the cycle of prose, in which the interest in the language leads to an interest in the totality of a community's life and history, and so brings the movement directly onto the contemporary stage. And finally there is the cycle of action, in which regionalism forms for itself fresh objectives, political, economic, civic, cultural, on the basis, not of a servile restoration of the past, but of a growing integration of the new forces that have attached themselves to the main trunk of tradition. The only places where regionalism has not been militantly self-conscious are places like the cities and provinces of Germany in which—until the recent centralization of power by the Totalitarian State—an autonomous and effective local life had never entirely disappeared.

"The besetting weakness of regionalism lies in the fact that it is in part a blind reaction against outward circumstances and disruptions, an attempt to find refuge within an old shell against the turbulent invasions of the outside world, armed with its new engines: in short, an aversion from what is, rather than an impulse toward what may be. For the merely sentimental regionalist, the past was an absolute. His impulse was to fix some definite moment in the past, and to keep on living it over and over again, holding the 'original' regional costumes, which were in fact merely the fashion of a certain century, maintaining the regional forms of architecture, which were merely the most convenient and comely constructions at a certain moment of cultural and technical development; and he sought, more or less, to keep these 'original' customs and habits and interests fixed forever in the same mold: a neurotic retreat. In that sense regionalism, it seems plain, was anti-historical and anti-organic: for it denied both the fact of change and the possibility that anything of value could come out of it." [3]

[3] Lewis Mumford, *Technics and Civilization*, pp. 292-293. (Quoted by permission of Harcourt, Brace and Company, Inc.)

The movement spreads to comprehend the national policy in relation to local units and decentralization. American literary regionalists therefore have an excellent precedent in French literature and policy.

Thus the trend of modern French literature is definitely in the direction of regionalism.[4] It may be pointed out here that most of the greatest masterpieces of French literature, already become classics, are in the form of epics of the provinces. Examples may be found in the novels of George Sand, of Stendhal, of Balzac, and of Flaubert. The most recent literature contains at least one work for each province. "The paradox of such a rich provincial literature side by side with a Paris, so absorbing, so magnetic, and in a state so highly centralized must be apparent."[5] M. Billy explains this curious phenomenon by saying that the earlier works dealing with provincial life were the purely objective studies of psychological curiosities. In modern times, however, the study of the province becomes subjective, because of the fact that "le tourisme" has reawakened the regional sentiment and that, as a consequence, the literary French have become enamored anew of their native provinces. M. Billy makes a distinction between the earlier provincial literature and the newer literature which he characterizes as regional. "The regionalist sentiment, which has developed especially since the progress of 'le tourisme' is different in the sense that it carries with it, more or less conscious and avowed, a prejudice and an apology" (in the sense of defense). "The provincial novel is generally pessimistic. The regional novel is optimistic in spirit."[6] Coincident with the almost unprecedented vogue for regional literature is the decline of the so-called Parisian literature. "Le tourism," which is a phenomenon so uniquely French that it admits of no adequate translation into English, has, until recently, been the most lucrative business of any in France. With the influx of travelers, particularly from the United States, the French have come to see new possibilities in their ancient monuments. Seeing the extravagant interest displayed by foreigners in each traditional province, they became conscious of the regions which had, heretofore, been an unconscious force in their cultural heritage. This awakening translated itself into modern French literature.

A similar historical development of French regionalism shows the earlier regions of "sentimental" or cultural regionalism as expressed in language, customs, literature but with the men of letters ultimately

[4] This summary is from Mildred Rubin's unpublished study of French Regionalism.
[5] *Ibid.* André Billy, *La Littérature française contemporaine*, p. 135.
[6] *Ibid.*

taking up the problems of economic and political regionalism. Thus, while the culture regions do come from the local areas one other example of the literary-artistic regionalism blending with the national fabric and thus transcending the purely local is that of Polish regionalism.

> Regionalism in literary production consists in presenting the human spirit in every aspect in correlation with its immediate environment. Man, language, landscape and the cultural riches of a particular region, considered as the result of the reactions of the individual—heir of certain peculiarities of race and tradition; these should be the topics of interest for literary regionalism. Its subjects are drawn from local legends, historical episodes, and all that popular tradition can furnish. In the domain of history and literary criticism, regionalism applies itself to disengaging the conditions of soil and race which make it possible for a particular region to participate more or less in literary production, and also studies the reasons that urge poets to celebrate particular regions in their works. In short, scientific study is made of the soil, the ethnographical peculiarities, and the idioms of the regions that have inspired poets and novelists. In the domain of the theater, regionalism seeks to utilize the legends, tales and superstitions attached to certain ruins, mountains and sites whose history—an individual history, so to speak—has remained long-lived in the memory of the people. The creation of a popular theater in Poland out of those elements, and the renaissance of the drama of manners by these means are the ideas which owe their inspiration directly to regionalism. In the plastic arts and architecture, regionalism indicates to them the wealth of motif and peculiarities in technique which distinguish local art, as well as historical art, which itself is born of a definite environment. Regionalism in music watches with special solicitude over musical ethnography, the collection and scientific elaboration of the melodies and musical instruments of the Polish people, and desires to make her folk music as accessible as possible, as well as the foundation for the musical powers of society in a national sense. In the domain of musical production, regionalism will exert influence on composers, inciting them to draw from themes pregnant with special territorial character and to present them in artistic form. Regionalism likewise encourages research in the history of music and musical culture in the diverse regions of Poland so as eventually to establish a synthesis of the history of Polish music.[7]

[7] Adapted from "Communications," *The Sociological Review*, XXIV, No. 2, pp. 197-198.

This brings us to point out that, like other aspects of regionalism, literary regionalism is a fact. There is, therefore, no need to debate the reality of the concept which is being discussed more and more. Irrespective of what the different sorts of literary regionalism may be, the concept of literary regionalism is one in the growing family of larger concepts of American regionalism. It follows, of course, that even as in other types of regionalism, there will be many varying forms, concepts, and ideas, ranging from mere localism to the larger reaches of genuine literary regionalism, through which the whole American literature and interpretation may be fabricated.

This conflict of ideologies is of the essence of regionalism. Thus B. A. Botkin presents the case well: "But apart from economic issues, certain cultural and aesthetic values emerge from the smoke of the regionalist conflict. The first and chief of these is the sense of a native tradition growing by folk accretions out of local cultures. In spite of the tendency of the provinces to substitute their local myths for the national myth of Americanism (the *ignis fatuus* of the 'national period' of our literature), regionalism has done much to destroy that 'all-destroying abstraction, America,' and to initiate a new period in American literary history.

"Aside from its importance to literary criticism and scholarship, the conception of a regionally differentiated and interregionally related culture has something to offer to literature, namely, a subject matter (the physical and cultural landscape, local customs, character, speech, etc.), a technique (folk and native modes of expression, style, rhythm, imagery, symbolism), a point of view (the social idea of a planned society and the cultural values derived from tradition as 'the liberator, not the confiner').

"Seen in this light, regionalism, properly controlled, becomes a valuable social adjunct to literature, along with ethnology, folk lore, and Marxist economics. In common with these disciplines, regionalism marks a trend away from the belletristic—pure literature and absolute poetry—toward a social and cultural art—from literary anarchy toward literary collectivism. In this development the regional movement has served to fix attention on the fact that, as individual character and action are inseparable from the social structure, so geographical relationships tend to modify both. Regional coherences exist, to be cultivated by the artist, not for a peculiar glamor of picturesqueness or quaintness or for the false security of 'limited solidarities,' but as a means to the end of social portraiture and the expression of personality with roots.

"In this regional literature a natural division of labor exists between the provincial writer, on the side of the rural and agrarian, and the metropolitan writer, on the side of the urban and industrial. But both are essential to a complete picture of the American scene and the American folk and to the new ideology and mythology emerging alike from our buried cultures and our submerged classes." [8]

One way of supporting this assumption of idealistic literary regionalism is simply to present the catalogue of actual regional output in the six major regions previously selected. That is, here are actual regions and here is extraordinarily vigorous literature which comes from or deals with such regions. This is, of course, a mere picturization of a very large and varied aggregate of literary productions, the nature of which reflects an extraordinary degree of regional character. Later on, these contributions may be subjected to critical analysis with a view to a classification within the more special meanings of regionalism. The first objective, however, of presenting the extraordinary arrangement of regional literature is primarily simply to give the picture and to emphasize the regional effect and implications of our recent regional literature. This is, after all, literary regionalism, basic to both the understanding of how our present usage has grown up and to analyzing the emerging regionalism of the future. Something of this actual catalogue of regional books will be presented in Part III as the picture of each region is presented.

It is necessary, however, first to present the main characterizations of that local literary regionalism around which recent discussions have raged. From the reviews of books, from articles and discussions in the *Saturday Review of Literature* and *The Bookman*, more lately *The American Review*, and from special studies, such as *New England's Prospect*, and *The Flowering of New England*, it is possible to obtain a fair "hearing" for the various viewpoints. First, there is the extremist's interpretation, such as that of James Gray, who writes of "The Minnesota Muse" and is hard put to find a realistic concept of regionalism. Says he: "That militantly American doctrine called regionalism, which has tended in recent years to make of local prejudice something vaguely resembling a religion, would probably hold that the heavenly Muse does herself over, with protean variability,

[8] "Regionalism: Cult or Culture," *The English Journal*, March 1936, p. 184.

each time that she crosses a state line. No doubt the conviction is strong in the true believer's heart that when one of the inspirational sisters finds herself in Minnesota, she wearily gets out her make-up kit and prepares for a lugubrious session celebrating the sorrows of the soil and of the soul. The costume assigned to the Minnesota Muse, in the regionalist's handbook, is a decent though shabby, Mother Hubbard. She sings exclusively of ruined wheat harvests and she sings of them with a strong Swedish accent." [9]

Another equally narrow concept of regionalism is that in which Paul Beath, seeking to catalogue four fallacies of regionalism, finds its rise and incidence in the southern agrarians. Thus, he claims that "The southern agrarian school led by Davidson, John Crowe Ransom, and Allen Tate initiated the current regional movement which has since spread to other sections, notably the Southwest and the Middle West. These critics have often been called, and I think rightly, unreconstructed rebels who are continuing the Civil War long after Appomattox. It is interesting to speculate on what the present situation would have been had the South won the war and determined the character of the civilization of America. Undoubtedly Mr. Davidson, Mr. Ransom, and Mr. Tate would have looked upon a southernized America and found it good. New Yorkers would have inveighed against the Nashville critics. The North, however, as a matter of fact won the Civil War and whether we like it or not put its cultural stamp on the nation. Resentment of this fact seems to me the motive power behind the regionalist movement. I doubt whether healthy, vigorous, and enduring arts and letters can come of anything so negative as resentment." [10]

> The further limitations of the same author's concept may be seen clearly from the statement of his four fallacies: "The first fallacy of regionalism is that so far it has based its theory on an inferiority complex. This is a harsh statement, but six years of active participation in the regionalist movement have convinced me of its truth. I qualify myself by inserting 'in its present state' and 'seems' in hope that this aspect of inferiority may be temporary or illusive. . . .

[9] James Gray, "The Minnesota Muse," *Saturday Review of Literature,* XVI, No. 7, p. 3.

[10] Paul Robert Beath, "Regionalism: Pro and Con. Four Fallacies of Regionalism," *Saturday Review of Literature,* XV, No. 5, pp. 4, 14.

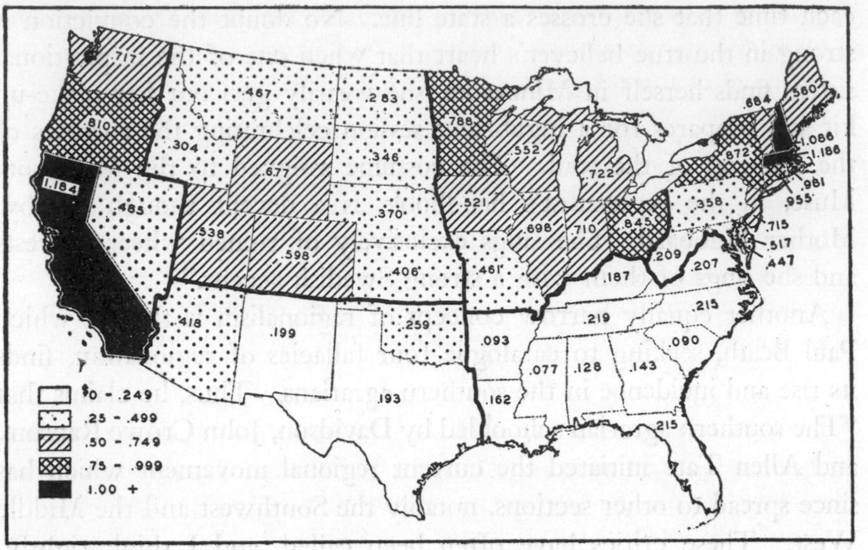

ILLUSTRATIONS OF CULTURAL DIFFERENTIALS IN THE SEVERAL REGIONS

Above: Per Capita Expenditures for Public Libraries, 1929.

Below: Percent of Population Registered as Library Borrowers, 1929. Reproduced and adapted from Wilson and Wight, *County Library Service in the South.*

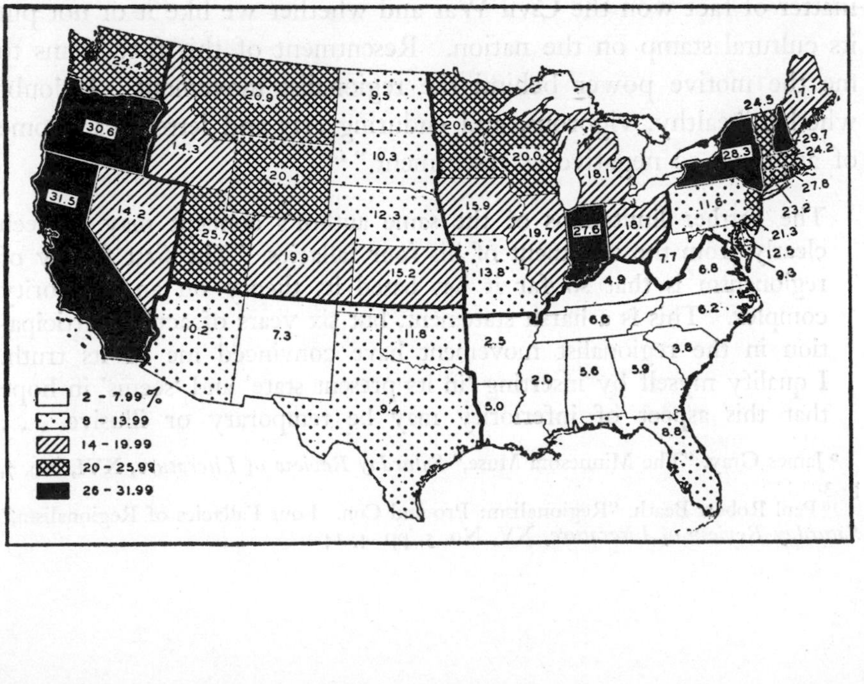

Jealousy is perhaps the chief ingredient of this state of mind. The highbrow regionalists are jealous of New York, because New York has more of the things highbrows value. On the other hand middlebrow regionalists in the great Middle West are jealous of California, because California has more of the things middlebrows value. The New York critic and the native Californian on their parts are quick to defend themselves and castigate the upstart Southerner and Midlander. Donald Davidson, perhaps the sanest of the regional critics, has repeatedly warned his readers against this small boy's 'my-dad-can-whip-your-dad' attitude. And yet Mr. Davidson himself in his exasperation with the metropolitan critics too often waves the Confederate flag and calls the opposition 'damned Yankees.' . . .

"The second fallacy of regionalism is its denial of the great tradition. By the great tradition I mean what Matthew Arnold meant: the best that has been thought and known in the world. One who has been educated in the great tradition becomes thereby a cosmopolite of the spirit. His intellect is not limited in space by his own environment or in time by his own generation. He is heir, as the saying goes, to the wisdom of the ages. There are certain aspects of American regionalism which tend to negate this tradition. In rejecting New York there is danger of rejecting Athens, Rome, Paris, and London as well. The more rabid regionalists say, 'Let's forget these foreign influences for a while and create something to take their place.' . . .

"The third fallacy of regionalism lies in its almost exclusive preoccupation with mediocrity, especially local mediocrity. This situation is all the more lamentable because most regionalists are highbrows. Highbrows are those who have been educated to consume the best ideas of the past and present. The best ideas in the past have gathered eventually in cosmopolitan centers and do so now. Regionalists, being highbrows, desire the cream of this cosmopolitan culture—a cultivated society, an atmosphere of wealth and affluence, entertainment by distinguished theatrical, musical, and literary artists. But—unlike middlebrows, the true regionalists, who contentedly live, work, propagate, and die oblivious to the great world—the highbrow regionalists continually fret and fume, publish little magazines, issue manifestoes, and generally go around with chips on their shoulders. . . .

"The fourth fallacy of regionalism is its exploitation of the rural folk at the expense of the urban folk. The pursuit of folklore is a legitimate and fascinating pursuit; and, contrary to the contention of the economic school of criticism, modern folklore does exist. The fallacy of the regionalists lies in dressing up folklore and peddling it in bookstores, in theaters, and on the radio." [11]

[11] Beath, *op. cit.*, pp. 3, 4, 14, 16.

In reply to these fallacies of regionalism Joseph E. Baker defends the idea of regionalism in terms of four arguments which have recently been advanced in its favor. Yet these arguments are essentially the statements of a localism, which authentic enough in common usage, are nevertheless contrary to a genuine regionalism, except in so far as he contrasts metropolitan New York dominance with the rest of the nation. "Regionalism," he writes, "at its best promises to be something very different from the folklore-and-mediocrity cult on which the critic fixes his attention. I would not for a moment defend such qualities and attitudes, but it is my hope that Regionalism may save us from those very vices; they are the vices of a culture centralized in New York. And so long as our culture is centralized in New York we are not likely to produce interpreters of our regions worthy to rank with Rabelais, Wordsworth, Dickens, Mark Twain, Hardy. In attempting to defend a thing hoped for—what a Platonist might call the Idea of Regionalism—I shall not rely entirely on my own views, but indicate the four arguments for Regionalism that have recently been advanced."[12]

His first argument, however, which is the historical, cites Turner's sectionalism as the chiefest of evidence for regionalism, a fallacy which we have already discussed. The second argument in favor of regionalism he gives as the political and cites again the southern agrarians as representing a plea for partisan representation, which again is the essence of sectionalism. Yet the regionalism of Tate and Davidson at its best will protest the extreme interpretations which its other-sectional critics give it as being limited to the local and selfish.[13] Thus, Allen Tate distinguishes between regionalism and sectionalism. "In any case," he writes, "the sectional writer has a point of view which is in some recognizable sense related to the beliefs historically identified with the community of his birth or rearing. Now literary regionalism, on the other hand, I think most people will agree, is less self-conscious, less abstract and philosophical; it is often a conscious program, but it is turned in upon itself; a cultivation of the local color, the local characters, the local customs, of the community for their own sake. Sectionalism, however, aggressively compares these features of itself with those of some other community. It is by necessity

[12] Joseph E. Baker, "Regionalism: Pro and Con. Four Arguments for Regionalism," *Saturday Review of Literature,* XV, No. 5, p. 3.

[13] *Ibid.*, pp. 3, 4, 14.

a doctrine, philosophical at its rare best, at its worst boastful propaganda. Sectionalism is thus a kind of politics, a set of social value; but regionalism is, or should be, self-contained and unaware of whatever value it may have. And, again, the effect of sectionalism in literature we have seen; it falsifies the creative impulse with the motives of social action, with motives that are vaguely political." [14]

Two other characterizations of literary regionalism are more generous in appraisal. One is that of Donald Davidson and the other that of the editor of the *Saturday Review of Literature*. Donald Davidson points out that "a regional literature, so-called, may thus very well be, among other things, a self-conscious expression of the life of a region. It may exploit intimate and local aspects of its scene, thus recovering the 'usable past' so much referred to; but it does not narrow itself to mere picturesqueness and antiquarianism except as a reaction to an overdose of metropolitan nationalism. The overdose and the reaction are both regrettable. But the pettiness or belligerency that they produce are not the inevitable features of a good regional literature, for a good regional literature needs only (to quote Allen Tate) 'the immediate organic sense of life in which a fine artist works.' . . . For some time to come our literature will not represent a uniform culture, but will be conditioned by the diverse regional cultures upon which it depends for its vitality." [15] And again, the other two arguments for regionalism, set forth by Mr. Baker, about which something will be said later, illustrate admirably Donald Davidson's verdict on the varieties of meanings of literary regionalism. "Like many other terms appropriated from the language of science, the words *region* and *regionalism* lose all exactness when they enter the literary vocabulary. . . . For one group of critics regionalism is a mere catchword which they use almost as a formula of dismissal for tendencies that they do not bother to take seriously. For another group regionalism is a battle-cry, the symbol of all they feel is worth fighting for in the reconstruction of American literature." [16]

[14] Allen Tate, "Regionalism and Sectionalism," *The New Republic*, Volume 69, pp. 158, 160.

[15] Donald Davidson, "Regionalism and Nationalism in American Literature," *The American Review*, V, No. 1, pp. 48, 53, 54.

[16] *Ibid.*, p. 48. See also Davidson's *The Attack on Leviathan: Regionalism and Nationalism in the United States.*

The editor of the *Saturday Review of Literature* wrote in 1934 that ". . . A new nationalism is sure to bring a new regionalism with it, and regionalism is already boomingly under way in this country. Those old enough to remember the vogue of 'local color' in the last century, will ask what is the difference between regionalism and 'local color.' 'Local color' was a pursuit of dying idiosyncrasies of character and dialect in a country rapidly becoming standardized and, not so rapidly, shaping its culture toward an internationalism which, it was believed, laissez-faire economics would eventually make politically possible. The war and the sequent crash of international capitalism ended all that. Our frame of reference has already ceased to be a world society in which the dialect of the southern mountaineers and the customs of Breton peasants are equally curious. Our frame begins to be a nation which, since it is also a continent, is a trading area large enough to be reasonably self-contained, a country where a central government plans a polity and an economy for diverse units in a (theoretically) harmonious whole.

"And within such a frame of reference the regions, the sections which are the true divisions of this country, assume a new importance and a new consciousness. They are no longer curious survivals in a standardizing world, but rather authentic components of an artificial unity—agricultural, industrial, commercial, to use economic terms; conservative, radical, liberal, fundamentalist, naive, sophisticated, traditional, to use intellectual or spiritual terms. The literature which springs (or should spring) from these regions and makes them articulate, is no longer romantic and quaint; it is the expression of an intellectual climate which demands its share in the nation's weather. Indeed, under the new system or even under the influence of such ideas as have been described above, regional novels, regional poetry, regional plays take on some of the functioning of a national literature. They assert the vitality of a part which is independent though indispensable to the whole. They are positive where 'local color' was negative, they are dynamic instead of archaeological and static, and, if they are good enough, may be of outstanding importance because this new state which we are developing is still far too abstract in conception and mechanical in operation to possess the blood of loyalty and the flesh of tradition and the nerves of passion so essential for literature.

"With this in view, the rise of regionalism in American literature, beginning perhaps with the poetic renaissance of before the war, and extending now into fiction and drama, seems more worth discussing than many of the quids and quiddities exercising the wits of critics and scholars in the literary and academic journals." [17]

[17] "The Boom in Regionalism" (Editorial), *Saturday Review of Literature*, X, No. 38, p. 606.

Returning to the argument for and against regionalism, Mr. Baker presents a more modified type of regionalism in his argument for art. Thus, he insists that "The regionalist who ignores the universal is at fault, of course; the life of his region is his medium of expression, not his message, and he should not make his thinking a mere search for the curious, the odd, and the picturesque—that was the error of the local-colorist. But the internationalists (to which, indeed, our present brand of nationalism must be referred) recommend to us a literature which gives neither the universal ideal of humanity at its best, nor the subtle essence of a local culture; but rather those elementary physical and economic interests which are common to man at his crudest in Atlanta, Manchester, and Hamburg—the lowest common denominator, not the profoundest human potentialities. We are much more likely to rise to a conception of man as fully human by contemplating his achievements as they flower in different regions—of America, and of Europe." [18]

Mr. Baker presents another argument for regionalism on the assumption that our great cities are not centers of culture at all and never will be. On the contrary, they are centers of technology and action and civilization. This theory, he thinks, "considers New York and Chicago to be late colonial offshoots of a European civilization already in decline when they were built. They lack the cultural past native to European cities, and bear no vital organic relation to our American culture, which is growing up now where cultures have always grown: in the smaller cities and the countryside. 'I view great cities,' said Jefferson, 'as pestilential to the morals, the health, and the liberties of man.' This view has been developed, with suggestions from Plato and Spengler, in such books as Agar's *Land of the Free.* It challenges the superstition that 'In rejecting New York there is danger of rejecting Athens.' On the contrary, when a people bows down before the gods of the 'world-city'—Imperial Rome, Babylon, Alexandria, New York, Chicago—they are rejecting the values developed in smaller cities, say the size of Athens, or Jerusalem, or Florence, or Weimar, or Concord, or Edinburgh, or Oxford, or Richmond.

"Regional art is not the only form of art. And each piece of regional writing must be judged on its own merits. But regionalism will perform a great service for America if it can free us from the four fallacies of New York: its aggrandizement of the 'proletarians'—

[18] Baker, *op. cit.,* p. 14.

by which I do *not* mean those who work with their hands,—at the expense of country gentlemen, town gentlemen, burghers, and artisans; its preoccupation with the brass mediocrity of New York—so much less tolerable than the golden mediocrity of the South; its denial of the Great Tradition (which still flourishes in Chapel Hill, Iowa City, and Princeton); and its inferiority complex, which leads the semi-educated 'nomads of the pavement' to make the most ridiculous assertions of cultural superiority, especially when in the presence of ideas that might be better than those which happen to have gathered in Manhattan." [19]

Turning again to the southern agrarians, they became the text for certain other interpretations of regionalism and for a critical review of *The Flowering of New England.* Thus, Mr. Austin Warren writes: "We of New England have looked with some envy upon the alert movement in progress among our brethren of Nashville and its circumjacent South. Long ago, *The Fugitive* took shelter with us; and the group whose wares it modestly purveyed seemed to us then, as still it does, the most important 'group' in our poetic present. When these ironists and 'metaphysicals' proved political economists also, as all good artists ought, we rejoiced that the 'War between the States' had not disappeared—to the furtherance of our national monotony, but had, salutarily, been transmuted from bullets to tracts." [20]

Continuing, "Our own 'region' had, under the style of 'local color,' a brief, mild, minor triumph in the short tales of Mary E. Wilkins, Alice Brown, and Sarah Orne Jewett, which portrayed the Yankee stock as petering out into spinsters and neurotics, delineated the shabby gentility of village ladies and the sapping solitude of back-road farmers. A sense of decay pervaded these tales as it did, for the most part, the poetry of Frost, Robinson, and Amy Lowell. Drained of its young men by successive migrations to the West and the cities, the country resigned itself to summer tourists. The industrial centers expanded, but their Yankee residents dwindled. Intellectually, Boston became a defunct capital, a thriving center for colleges, schools, libraries, historic 'shrines,' and cemeteries, a negligible factor in the imaginative and speculative life of America." [21]

[19] Baker, *op. cit.*, p. 14.

[20] Austin Warren, "Regional Retrospection," *The American Review*, VIII, No. 2, pp. 245-246.

[21] *Ibid.*, p. 247.

Yet, Mr. Brooks makes his own case for a fair regional-national interpretation rather than any merely local or provincial artistry. Thus, of New England, he says: "Here we have a homogeneous people, living close to the soil, intensely religious, unconscious, unexpressed in art and letters, with a strong sense of home and fatherland. One of its towns becomes a 'culture-city,' for Boston, with Cambridge and Concord considered as suburbs, answers to this name, which Spengler accords to Florence, Bruges and Weimar, as no other town has ever answered in either of the Americas. There is a springtime feeling in the air, a joyous sense of awakening, a free creativeness, an unconscious pride, expressed in the founding of institutions, intellectual, humanitarian, artistic, and—at first a little timid, cold and shy—the mind begins to shape into myths and stories the dreams of the pre-urban countryside. There is a moment of equipoise, a widespread flowering of the imagination in which the thoughts and feelings of the people, with all their faiths and hopes, find expression. The culture-city dominates the country, but only as its accepted vent and mouthpiece. Then gradually the mind, detached from the soil, grows more and more self-conscious. Contradictions arise within it, and worldlier arts supplant the large, free, ingenuous forms through which the poetic mind has taken shape. What formerly grew from the soil begins to be planned. The Hawthornes yield to the Henry Jameses. Overintelligent, fragile, cautious and doubtful, the soul of the culture-city loses the self-confidence and joy that have marked its early development,—it is filled with a presentiment to the end; and the culture-city itself surrenders to the world-city—Boston surrenders to New York,—which stands for cosmopolitan deracination. What has once been vital becomes provincial; and the sense that one belongs to a dying race dominates and poisons the creative mind." [22]

Concerning the "national" or "American" character of the great New England authors, Mr. Brooks points out that these authors, even as their political contemporaries, were "American" in that they thought of all America as to be New England extended. "They were as completely of their people as any authors of the oldest nations; and they saw, if not themselves,—for they were not self-conscious,—at least their profession as having a Promethean role to play. They were

[22] Van Wyck Brooks, *The Flowering of New England*, pp. 526-527.

teachers, educators and bringers of light, with a deep and affectionate feeling of obligation towards the young republic their fathers had brought into being. That New England was appointed to guide the nation, to civilize it and humanize it, none of them ever doubted, a motive that was evident in all their writings, from Emerson's early addresses to the table-talk of Holmes, from Longfellow's *Hiawatha*, in which an Indian myth conveys the poet's notion of his role, to the prophecies of *Uncle Tom's Cabin*." [23]

A broad and realistic interpretation of literary regionalism runs through the editorial pages of the *Saturday Review of Literature* from which numerous excerpts have been chosen to illustrate the several aspects. Thus discussing the pulse of the machine the editors take the position that regional literature comprehends the problem of the human race *vs.* environment, which must surely be as obsessing in the America of the 1930's as in the New England of the 1840's. And they hold that many recent American novels, "from such types of the best seller as Stark Young's *So Red the Rose* to the philosophic or economic or psychological or propagandist stories of Louis Adamic, James Farrell, Erskine Caldwell, etc., etc., are puzzled struggings with the victims or heroes of circumstance in the American scene.[24]

Further, "No one doubts (and British and French critics, for example, are free to admit) the virility and richness of these novels, especially those which deal specifically with regional life and regional problems, whether they be of the plains, of the cotton fields, or of the steel mills. . . . The books of the new regionalists lack essential rhythm because time, place, and people have not yet harmoniously met in our America. Perhaps they never will." [25]

"It was a sound instinct which led some literary critic to substitute the word 'regional' for the old nineteenth-century term 'local color.' It is much more than color which a region imposes on a race, indeed the 'color' of regional writing is too often no more than quaint details of speech or dress which the incapable author describes because he cannot grasp the real characteristics beneath, which are so different from his own.

"The influences which mold temperament, and therefore social rela-

[23] Brooks, *op. cit.*, pp. 528-529.

[24] "The Pulse of the Machine—II" (Editorial), *Saturday Review of Literature*, XII, No. 13, p. 8.

[25] *Ibid.*

tionships, religion, and art, and especially the art of literature, are still chiefly natural. Wind, rain, sun, plain, valley, mountain, in their combinations and permutations, are assuredly the sculptors of habit now as in the past, even in cities. . . .

"The importance of these regional distinctions in literature has been often discussed but seldom carried beyond an analysis of local peculiarity or a dubious statement of facts of resemblance between torrid heat and torrid expression, or drab horizons and drabness of thought." [26]

We have catalogued these viewpoints in much detail because they reflect on the one hand the changing attitudes in America toward regionalism and on the other there will be found in the detailed quotations an interpretation inherent in them which cannot be paraphrased. In the literary regionalism is to be found not only much that is synonymous with the popular concept but also much of the assumption of the intellectuals that what they conceive is the sum and substance of all else. These quotations, however, also reflect the contrariwise insight of many of those who write, notwithstanding the editorials in the *Saturday Review of Literature* and of William Allen White in which the total economic and cultural factors are recognized not only as the basis of regionalism but of literary interpretation of America.

We have pointed out the fact that there is no need to debate the question of whether there is a literary regionalism. It is a fact and reality beyond question and the problem becomes one of seeing it, of describing it, of correcting it and implementing it in its relation not only to literature but to other phases of American regionalism. When we say literary regionalism is a reality we need here illustrate with only a single major testimony, in addition to what we have presented. This is the actual achievement of literature within the last two decades in the field of regional portraiture or the sum of titles contributed by regional authors. In this sum total is America, thus qualifying the rich regional heritage as the genuinc constituent parts of the national literature. Restricting our titles to fiction and making the listings in *The Publishers' Weekly* our source, it is possible to catalogue more than two thousand regional titles which have ap-

[26] "The Pulse of the Machine" (Editorial), *Saturday Review of Literature*, XII, No. 12, p. 8.

peared during the last two decades. If we take the years from 1927 through 1936 or in round numbers the last ten years we find the following distribution. The Northeast leads with 449 titles, followed strangely enough by the Northwest with its "westerns" with 344, the Southeast with 281, the Middle States with 183, the Southwest with 138, and the Far West with 137.

These volumes themselves afford almost complete data for dramatic *personae* of the nation as well as for popular characterization. It is a rich field for many but of course a very special one. We may, however, indicate here samplings of the books which whether right or wrong, have received notoriety in the public appraisal. Strangely enough the Southeast has the largest number of Pulitzer prize winners and best sellers and has tended to give the best regional portraiture. Yet New England again lives and the "wests" become "American," too, and over again.

To begin with the *Southeast*, here are titles that drew attained distinction, Julia Peterkin's *Black April* and *Scarlet Sister Mary;* Thomas S. Stribling's *Bright Metal, Unfinished Cathedral, The Forge,* and *The Store;* William Faulkner's *Sanctuary, The Sound and the Fury;* Erskine Caldwell's *Tobacco Road, God's Little Acre;* Ellen Glasgow's *Vein of Iron, Barren Ground;* Robert Emmet Kennedy's *Gritney People;* Maristan Chapman's *The Weather Tree, The Happy Mountain;* Elizabeth Madox Roberts' *My Heart and My Flesh, He Sent Forth a Raven;* Mary Heaton Vorse's *Strike;* Fielding Burke's *Call Home the Heart, A Stone Came Rolling;* Paul Green's *This Body the Earth;* Grace Lumpkin's *A Sign for Cain;* Carolina Gordon's *Aleck Maury;* Zora Neale Hueston's *Jonah's Gourd Vine;* Stark Young's *So Red the Rose;* Margaret Mitchell's *Gone with the Wind;* Minnie Hite Moody's *Death Is a Little Man;* E. P. O'Donald's *Green Margins;* Charles Wertenbaker's *To My Father;* M. K. Rawlings' *South Moon Under. . . .*

The *Middle States* and *Northeast* follow next in order. In the *Middle States* the following: Ole Edvart Rölvaag's *Their Father God;* Phil Stong's *State Fair;* James T. Farrell's *Young Lonigan, Judgment Day, Gas-House McGirty, The Young Manhood of Studs Lonigan;* Sinclair Lewis' *Elmer Gantry;* Ruth Suckow's *The Bonney Family;* Margaret A. Barnes' *Years of Grace;* Albert Halper's *The Foundry;* Edna Ferber's *Come and Get It;* Dorothy Thomas' *The Home Place;* Howard Erickson's *Son of Earth;* Louis Bromfield's *The Farm. . . .* The *Northeast* included: Edna Ferber's *American Beauty;* J. Dos Passos' *1919;* Louis Bromfield's *Twenty-four Hours;* Mary Ellen Chase's *Uplands, Mary*

> *Peters;* Joseph Hergesheimer's *The Foolscap Rose;* James Boyd's *Roll River;* George Santayana's *The Last Puritan;* J. G. Cozzens' *Last Adam;* G. H. Carroll's *As the Earth Turns. . . .*
>
> Samplings from the other regions include in the *Northwest:* Bess Streeter Aldrich's *A Lantern in Her Hand;* Ole E. Rölvaag's *Giants in the Earth;* Sophus Keith Winther's *Take All to Nebraska;* Langston Hughes' *Not Without Laughter;* M. Ostenso's *There's Always Another Year. . . .* In the *Far West:* Oliver La Farge's *Laughing Boy;* Robert Cantwell's *Laugh and Lie Down;* H. L. Davis' *Honey in the Horn;* John Steinbeck's *Tortilla Flat. . . .* In the *Southwest:* Edna Ferber's *Cimarron;* Thyra Samter Winslow's *My Own, My Native Land;* Paul Horgan's *Main Line West. . . .*

Another index of regional variation may be found in the series of articles in *Scribner's* entitled "Life in the United States." Here was basic material for American picture *de luxe*, uneven, ragged, but good. To sample from Volumes 90, 91, and 92, for 1931 and 1932 we can catalogue a score or more that will probably represent the whole series adequately. Some of these articles were written in competition for awards. Many of them are by young aspiring authors making their first contribution. In this respect they also represent the American scene. The following are samples:

> Le Sueur's "Corn Village," and "Beer Town," Holt's "Drummer's Rest," Donnell's "Fragments from Alluvia," Wilson's "Red Cross and County Agent," McCrae's "Five Kids from the East Side," Francis' "The Saga of Joe Magarac: Steelman," Rawlings' "A Plumb Clare Conscience," Cimino's "Muscadines for Pink Corsets," Garrison's "Old Billy Hell," Francis' "The Ladies Call on Mr. Pussick," McKeanan's "In Defense of Kansas," Neely's "Yankee Cotton Planter," Gower's "Two Years," Prentice's "Oklahoma Race Riot," Cabell's "He-Rain," Hartwick's "Hills of Home," Irwin's "The Job of Reporting," Hazard's "And the Cops Got Their Man Including the Taxi Driver," Sister Mary Francis' "Nan's Diary," Francis' "Record Month," Autumn's "Diving for Abalones," James' "Blind Backer," Morton's "A Bride in a Box Car," Evans and Wetherill's "Death of a Medicine Man," Rodger's "Florida Interlude," Douring's "New York Lawyer," Dodge's "Old Ste. Genevieve," Boyden's "Finding of Domicile," Anonymous, "Lady Bootlegger," Bercovici's "A Radical Childhood," Bind's "To the Lifeboats," and Carmer's "Black Belt."

Chapter VIII

SERVICE REGIONS: GOVERNMENTAL

REALITY of regions and the need for their recognition in theory and in planning is shown by their actual use in many and diverse fields. Maps showing the nation neatly segmented are part of the standard equipment of executive offices throughout the United States. It is indeed rare that one enters an office of a high official of the government, of an industrial concern, of a manufacturing plant, or of a social or religious institution that his eye is not struck by some sort of regionalization of the territory in which the affairs of the office are carried on. We have "regionalized" our nation and subregionalized and districted our states, our counties, and our cities. This is one of the products of the exigencies of our bigness and administrative problems. More than a hundred bureaus, departments and other major agencies of the federal government have sets of regions of varying sizes and shapes as an aid to more efficient administration, or for other reasons sometimes not so apparent. Churches have divided the nation into conferences, bishoprics, or other divisions. Commercial and industrial executives have found it expedient to assign certain territories to certain subordinate headquarters, often setting up separate corporations for that purpose. Some schools are now awarding fellowships and other forms of aid on a regional basis, choosing so many students from each region. The large mail-order companies issue different catalogues for different parts of the nation. Regionalism, of a sort, is an almost universal practice as well as a social theory. The present chapter will review some of the aspects, recommendations, and uses of governmental service and administrative regions, leaving for the next chapter those dealing with non-governmental activities.

Governmental administrative regionalism, as commonly discussed, is of two sorts. There are the numerous proposals heard within recent years to eliminate the states, or to seriously reduce their present status, and to set up new forms of regional political sovereign administrative units. Other proposals are not so radical. They merely envisage combination and correlation of the functions now performed by the states and other governmental units through supervision on a regional scale. Both types of reorganization have won the adherence of recognized leaders in the field of political science and of popular writers.

This idea has also received the attention of members of the national Congress. We have already called attention to the popular contest of the *Chicago Tribune.* So, too, Delbert Clark, who has written political news for the *New York Times* for years, quotes an unnamed legislative leader as privately advocating nine groups of states instead of the present forty-eight. This scheme is more or less typical of others, and may be used as an illustration. On the basis of mutuality of interests, this division would set up the following regional "departments": New England, composed of the traditional six states; the Middle Atlantic, including New York, New Jersey, Delaware, Pennsylvania, and West Virginia; the South Atlantic Group of Kentucky, Tennessee, Virginia, North Carolina, South Carolina, and Maryland; the Great Lakes Department, composed of Michigan, Illinois, Indiana and Ohio; that of the Mississippi, of Arkansas, Louisiana, Mississippi, Alabama, Georgia and Florida; the Prairie Department, consisting of the Dakotas, Nebraska, Kansas, Iowa, Minnesota, and Wisconsin. The new Southwest would be made up of Arizona, New Mexico, Texas, Oklahoma, and Missouri; the Pacific Coast states of California, Washington, and Oregon, would form the department bearing that name; and Montana, Idaho, Utah, Colorado, Nevada, and Wyoming would form the Rocky Mountain Department.[1]

Other similar proposals will appear in the later chapter which discusses states, subregions, and districts as tools for regionalism, in which the administrative unit of government and the cultural unit of society are contrasted with the natural region as the most realistic basis for enduring regionalism. This movement for regional reclassification of governmental functions or at least for purposes of econ-

[1] Delbert Clark, "Nine Groups Instead of the 48 States," *New York Times Magazine,* April 21, 1935.

omy and jurisdiction is, however, grounded upon important considerations of perhaps four sorts. There are the geographic, territorial considerations, the historical influences, and the cumulative trend, resulting from modern communication developments, general postwar social tensions and centralization methods of administration, toward reorganization of nearly all forms of government and industry to conform to modern economy and technology. The fourth factor has been a trend toward decentralization as a sort of reaction to too much bigness and concentration. In all of these aspects, of course, time and change are dominant factors, contrasting the simple government of Thomas Jefferson in a small rural agrarian culture with the complex, big urban industrial technological world of Franklin D. Roosevelt. In most of these phases, too, social incidence of war and special epochs of national development have played considerable part.

Perhaps the development of French regionalism illustrates the combined factors as well as any other. Thus, as a result of historical development and of the great war there has been developing a strong trend toward decentralization. This is essentially the new regionalism, the theory of which is set forth very succinctly by an eminent French regionalist, M. Lucien Brocard: "In the field of public administration, as in that of business enterprise, excessive centralization is an obstacle to progress, since it paralyzes the activities of the region and places upon the shoulders of the central authority a burden which, by reason of its ignorance of local conditions, it is not fitted to bear. The inconvenience of such centralization grows in direct proportion to the number and the complexity of the regional activities administered, and it is to this fact that we must attribute the movement towards regional decentralization that has been evident, in greater or less degree, in all countries possessing a centralized administration." [2] There appear to be two schools of opinion on this subject. One believes that the government should remain essentially unchanged as to structure, since its foundation is in the Constitution, but that greater power should be given to departments and to communes so that they may act under local initiative for certain of their purely local functions. Apart from the advocates of this decentralization, or decon-

[2] Lucien Brocard, "Regional Economy and Economic Regionalism." Translated by F. Cyril James from an article appearing in *La Revue Economique Internationale*, November 1931, and reprinted in translation in *Annals of the American Academy of Political and Social Science*, July 1932, p. 87.

centration, there are those who can see no *raison d'être* for the departments, and who propose, therefore, to abolish them, and to establish regions. Most of the programs set forth indicate that the regional boundaries should conform as closely as possible to natural, economic, or to the traditional regions (the provinces). "In the course of the Third Republic, something like twenty-five serious parliamentary proposals have been made for complete regionalist reform of the administrative system."[3] As early as 1851 a regionalist program for administrative reform was proposed. The National Assembly of 1871, "called the most liberal assembly ever elected in France, contained a large majority of advocates of decentralization."[4] Therefore, decentralization and regionalism as one of its forms, has had governmental sanction. Regionalist leaders suffer no persecution for their views, although they are sometimes accused of separatism by partisans of the centralized state. In 1890 there was another important proposal which planned to group the departments into eighteen regions for local government. From that time regular proposals have been introduced in Parliament. In general, they have been very favorably received. Often the Prime Minister himself would speak in their behalf. One Prime Minister, M. Rouvier, "declared in the Chamber of Deputies in 1905 in a few sentences, interrupted by vigorous applause, that he regretted 'that there do not exist grand administrative regions,' since, if such regions did exist, 'they would permit of having a more intense local life, which would relieve the congestion of France and would at the same time make possible recruiting public functionaries with more care.'"[5] Later both Clemenceau and Briand were champions of the cause, although Briand believed rather in a federation of new units to replace the departments.[6]

In the case of Polish regionalism the principle is stated that equilibrium between the authority of the state and the liberty of the citizen and also between local interests and the needs of the country as a whole constitute the foundation of state unity. Regionalism is therefore the first essential. It is further held that the complete liberty of development for the special characteristics of the several regions of Poland form the basis for the national distribution of work and for the enhancement of both the creative artistic wealth as well as the total wealth and culture.

[3] R. K. Gooch, *Regionalism in France*, p. 56.
[4] *Ibid.*, p. 57.
[5] *Ibid.*, p. 62.
[6] From unpublished manuscript by Mildred Rubin.

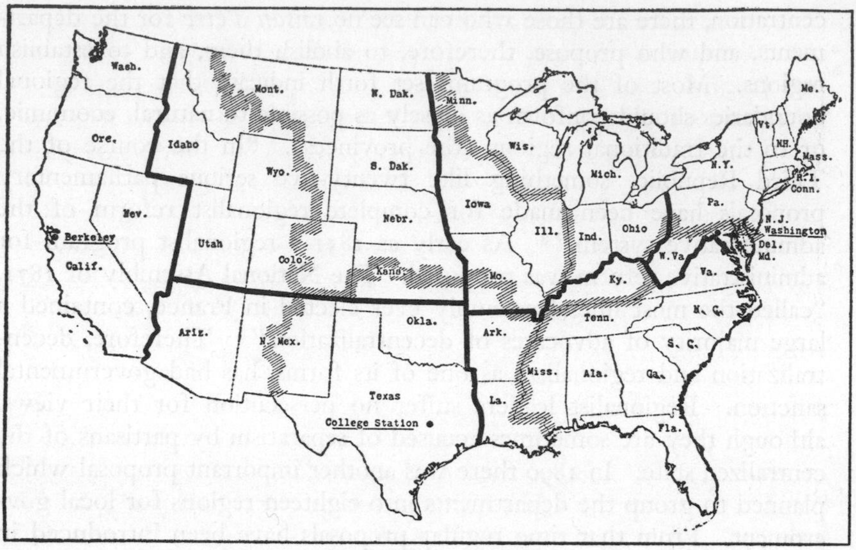

ILLUSTRATIONS OF VARIATION IN ADMINISTRATIVE DISTRICTS

Above: Soil Survey Districts, Bureau of Chemistry and Soils, Department of Agriculture.

Below: Water Resources Branch Areas, Geological Survey, U. S. Department of the Interior.

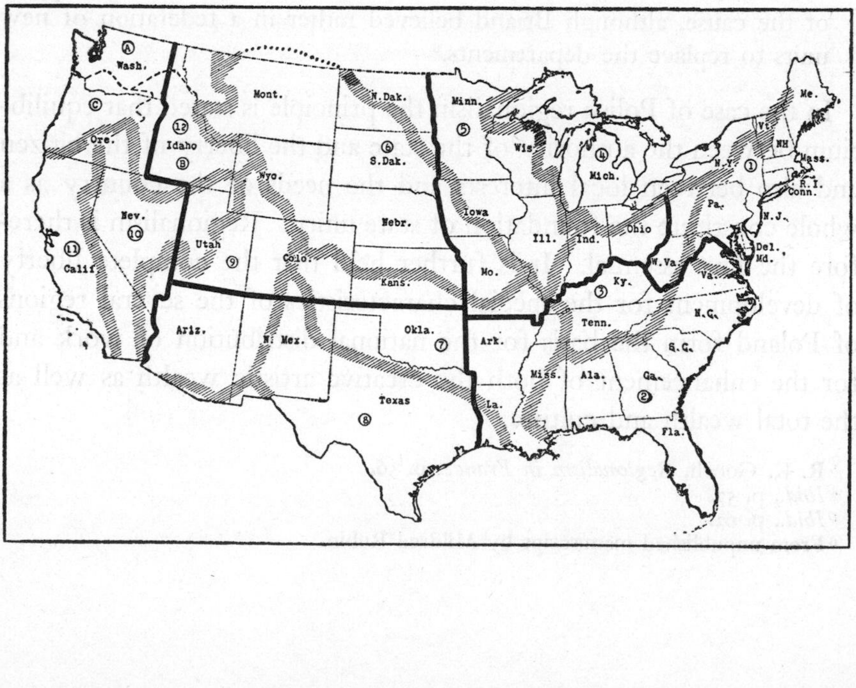

> Regionalism tends to give to the state an administrative structure which should assure the necessary development of the individual economic and cultural values in the separate regions. It is the internal decentralization of administration, without prejudice to the homogeneous and adaptable administration of the state as a whole, which best satisfies the stated object. A wide autonomous movement, collaborating with public administration, should extend its activity to all the essential problems on whose solution depends the development of the individual character of the local centers, both economic and cultural. Regionalism tends to supply public administration with legal regulations in a form individualized and made appropriate to local needs.[7]

Concerning the American situation James W. Fesler has pointed out the fact that American students of government have too long and completely ignored the significance of territorial definitions of jurisdiction, since in a country the size of the United States areal spheres are indispensable.[8] He shows the necessity for democratic agencies of federal jurisdiction and calls attention to regional grouping of states, to state compacts, to the proposal of the Council of State Governments to set up ten regions each with a permanent secretariat for regional jurisdiction.

> In the same paper, Fesler points out further "The significance of federal administrative regions for the political scientist which transcends mere considerations of efficiency and economy in public administration. The whole issue of regionalism is being increasingly posed by geographers, sociologists, and progressive students of polity. Regional geographers have demonstrated that state boundaries have slight relation to natural physical areas, and they have emphasized that social problems rest heavily on the physical environment. Sociologists have reached somewhat similar conclusions although using a different approach. They have analyzed social statistics (literacy, birth rates, crimes, proportion of urban to rural population, etc.) on the basis of which they have delineated social regions of the United States.[9]

[7] Adapted from "Communications," *The Sociological Review*, XXIV, No. 2, pp. 197-198.

[8] James W. Fesler, "Federal Administrative Regions," *American Political Science Review*, XXX, 257-268.

[9] See, for example, Howard W. Odum, *Southern Regions of the United States*. The journal, *Social Forces*, published at the University of North Carolina, frequently carries articles illustrative of the sociological approach to regionalism. See particularly the issues for December 1929, March 1934, and October 1934.

Students of politics have analyzed presidential elections and votes in Congress to prove that there are political regions.[10] The proposal of regional government is a rather radical adaptation to government of the discovery that states do not represent geographical, social, or (in a special sense) political unities. Several years ago W. B. Munro suggested the desirability of regional government.[11] W. Y. Elliott in his *The Need for Constitutional Reform* proposes that twelve regions be established by a 1936 constitutional convention, and that representation in the Senate should be from the regions, not from states.[12] Newspapers and periodicals have essayed to popularize the proposal to substitute regions for the states." [13]

As a matter of fact, regionalization of activities has long been a practice of the Federal Government; so much so that this may be considered the usual policy for such bureaus and departments as function throughout the nation. In 1935 it was calculated that there were some 108 such regional schemes then in use. Some of these agencies used states as their units of administration, others found the divisions along state lines impractical, since they are generally too small to use as regions, and too large to be used as divisions or subregions, and often bear little discoverable relation to the function performed by the federal agency. Fesler points out in his list of these administrative regions, as of November 1934, that more than three-fourths of the regional schemes then in use had less than seventeen regions.[14] However, there seems to be little agreement as to the optimum number of regions to use. Seven agencies have divided the country into four and nine regions, each, while nine agencies have set up twelve areas. Four agencies divide the nation into two parts, while one agency has 83 divisions.

Although regions are often formed by grouping states together, for obvious reasons of ease of co-operation with state officials, access to statistics, etc., the state of Pennsylvania was divided by 35 of the 106 agencies studied by Fesler. Illinois and Indiana were divided 27 times, each, while New York and Ohio each suffered mutilation 25

[10] Pre-eminently, Frederick Jackson Turner, *The Significance of Sections in American History*, and Arthur Norman Holcombe, *The Political Parties of Today.*
[11] *The Invisible Government.*
[12] *The Need for Constitutional Reform.*
[13] *Chicago Tribune*, December 8, 15, 22, 1929. *New York Times*, April 21, 1935, Magazine Section, p. 5. *Saturday Evening Post*, December 8, 1924, Editorial Page.
[14] Fesler, *op. cit.*

times. Maps of the various regional schemes disclose a tendency on the part of the governmental agencies to use smaller areas as regions in the North and East, in rough proportion to the population contained in the area rather than in accordance with the ease of transportation and communication within the region, though the latter factors were evidently considered and weighted heavily in the selection of headquarters cities. This tendency toward smaller areas in thickly populated sections is observable even in those regions having to do with physiographic factors. This is to be expected since these agencies usually have to do with law enforcement. Indeed, from the social and political point of view, the region takes on reality only as it is the locus of institutions and people served by them. That is, the actual regions as organized are based on ease of administration and a desire to equalize the amount of work done by each region more than on natural geographic or social conditions.[15]

The traditional regional units of the country suffer dismemberment at the hands of federal regional mappers more often than not. The case of New England, perhaps the most traditional regional unit in the nation and nicely set off by geographic features, is illustrative. Of the 93 schemes in use in this area, only twenty are composed of the six states east of the Hudson River. Thirteen others divorce all or a part of Connecticut from New England. Eleven other schemes divide New England into two or more regions. In 41 cases the New England States are grouped with larger units, sometimes with ten Northeastern States, sometimes with even larger groupings. Eight schemes cut across the New England boundary. It is also noteworthy that fifteen agencies which have regional divisions of the country have no administrative areas in this portion of the nation. In less well-recognized regions, the diversity is still more striking.[16]

The inevitable result of such heterogeneity in regionalization is an impossibility of co-ordinating the work of the Federal Government in any specific area. On the other hand, it is certainly true that different agencies can use different areas to best advantage, at least from their own point of view. The question seems to boil down to whether we wish a purely functional administration, or whether we

[15] *Ibid.*
[16] *Ibid.*

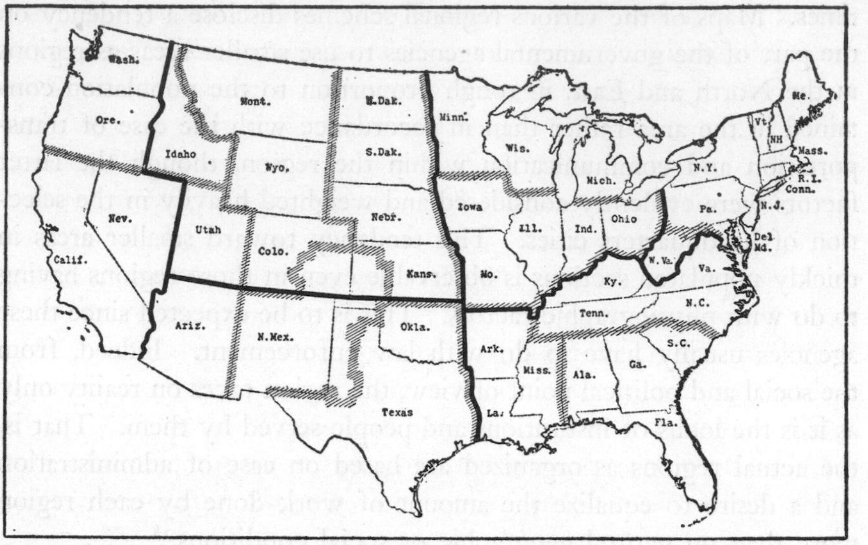

Above: Administrative Regions as Reported in First Annual Report of the Resettlement Administration, 1936.

Below: Maintenance Divisions as Utilized by the Bureau of Air Commerce, adapted from *Regional Factors in National Planning and Development.*

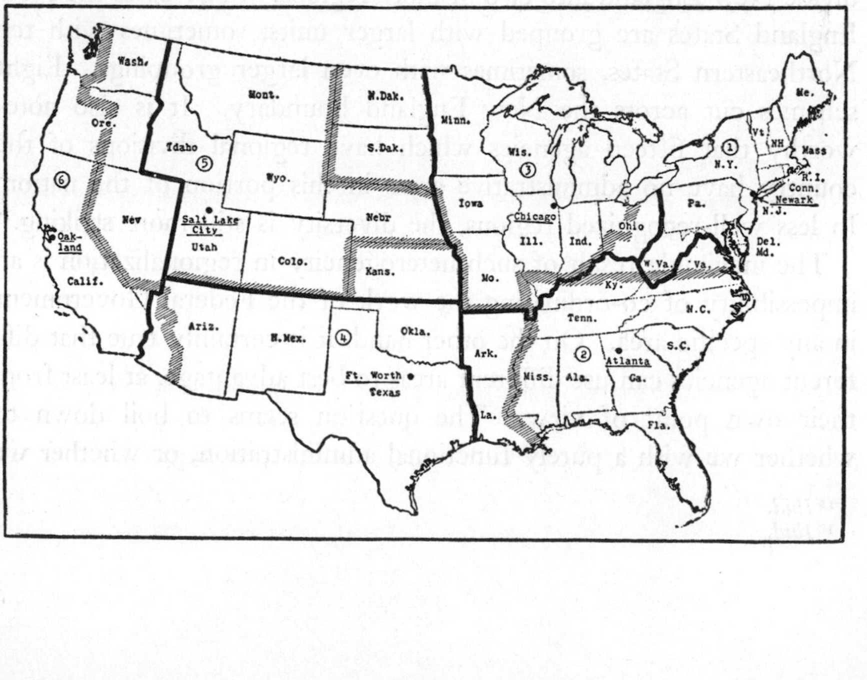

should hold to our older concept of geographic, areal, representation and administration. There are arguments, and no lack of proponents to present them, on both sides. Undoubtedly a large part of the diversity noted comes from the functional philosophy adopted, perhaps unconsciously, by the regionalizing departments and bureaus. The administrative regions we have are the results of efforts to secure divisions which would satisfy the demands made upon the agencies; demands seeking efficiency in some cases, in others perhaps based on desire for patronage; the idea that federal funds and employees should be well distributed throughout the states and congressional districts.

This lack of coincidence in federal regions invades the confines of single departments, or even the same function within the same department. The Federal Reserve Bank regions do not coincide with those of the Federal Land Bank in any single instance, though both functions are very similar. This is to be explained by the criteria adopted in delimiting these regions. The Federal Reserve System sought ease of communication and a high degree of homogeneity in its divisions, while the Federal Land Bank took the position that none of its regions should be characterized by dependence upon one crop or the same series of crops lest poor market conditions should bring disaster.

The above examples are adequate to indicate the range and nature of administrative regions, as well as the problems involved in their delineation and use. Perhaps the case still needs to be illustrated with further samplings. One of the best-known regional arrangements is that of the United States Census. "There were nine divisions of states: New England, Middle Atlantic, East North Central, West North Central, South Atlantic, East South Central, West South Central, Mountain, Pacific. There were paradoxical factors inherent in a division called Mountain, extending all the way from north to south and coinciding to a great extent with the agricultural region designated as grazing and irrigated farming country, and including much of the vast desert plains of America. Likewise, there was little in common between Delaware and many another state of the South Atlantic Division, such as South Carolina or Georgia. Certainly the District of Columbia is not 'southern.' Yet because of its decades of usage and because of comparative data this classification must remain the simplest standard mechanical subdivision."[17]

[17] Howard W. Odum, *Southern Regions of the United States*, pp. 263-265.

Keeping in mind the types of major regions already mentioned, it is important to explore further the tools of regionalism as found in the multiple subdivisions and their terminology and usage in governmental organizations. Thus it is possible to catalogue hundreds of divisional areas in terms of actual administrative usage. These include districts, centers, zones, sections, stations, territories and the like, and they serve to give reality to the American picture.

These subdivisions are classified under ten major governmental organizations, namely, the Departments of the Treasury, War, Justice, Post Office, Navy, Interior, Agriculture, Commerce, Labor, and Independent New Deal Establishments.[18] Beginning with the Treasury Department there are districts, agency districts, comptrollers districts, collection districts, special agents divisions, alcohol tax units, income tax units, divisions and field divisions, together with other districts in the Bureaus of the Mint, Narcotics, Procurement Division, Secret Service, and areas and recruiting stations of the United States Coast Guard. In the War Department there are Corps Areas, Procurement Zones, Air Corps, Chemical Warfare Service, Corps of Engineers, Medical Department, Ordnance Department, Quartermaster Corps, and Signal Corps in each of which there are procurement districts. In the Department of Justice there are Bureau of Prisons and Division of Investigation in which there are federal penitentiaries and field office districts. In the Post Office Department there are Central Accounting Post Offices, Inspection Districts, Supply Offices, Railway Mail Service Divisions. In the Navy Department there are Naval Districts, Naval Material Inspection Districts, Recruiting Divisions and Districts, Marine Corps. In the Interior Department there are Bureau of Mines, Bureau of Reclamation, Division of Investigation, General Land Office, National Park Service, Office of Education, United States Geological Survey in which there are regions, districts, and areas. In the Department of Agriculture there are Agricultural Adjustment Administration, Bureau of Agricultural Economics, Bureau of Agricultural Engineering, Bureau of Animal Industry, Bureau of Biological Survey, Bureau of Chemistry and Soils, Bureau of Public Roads, Extension Service, Food and Drug Administration, Forest Service, Weather Bureau, in which there are sections, districts and stations, divisions, regions and zones. In the Department of Commerce there are Bureau of Air Commerce, Bureau of the Census (Geographic Division), Bureau of Foreign and Domestic Commerce, Bureau of Navigation and Steamboat Inspection,

[18] National Resources Board, *Regional Factors in National Planning and Development,* June 1935, Appendix E, pp. 223-230.

Lighthouse Service, United States Shipping Board Merchant Fleet Corporation, in each of which there are districts. In the Department of Labor there is the Immigration and Naturalization Service in which there are districts. In the Independent Establishments there are Civil Service Commission, Farm Credit Administration, Federal Communications Commission, Federal Co-ordinator of Transportation, Federal Emergency Relief Administration, Federal Home Loan Bank Board, Federal Housing Administration, Federal Power Commission, Federal Reserve Board, Home Owners' Loan Corporation, Interstate Commerce Commission, National Labor Relations Board, National Recovery Administration, Public Works Administration, Reconstruction Finance Corporation, Securities and Exchange Commission, United States Employees' Compensation Commission, Veterans' Administration, in which there are districts, regions, zones, agencies and regional offices.

There remain two important aspects of the governmental administrative or jurisdictional regions to be examined. One is interstate co-operation, either the compact or other formal or informal territorial arrangements for co-operative efforts. The other is the historical background upon which the present clamor for the minimization of state lines and state authority rests. Graves lists five ways in which he thinks the interstate co-operation may be attained. These include congressional action, as in the case of the pure food and drug act; constitutional amendments giving the Federal Government jurisdiction over the particular problem which is vexatious; concurrent power, in which the Federal Government would set minimum requirements; indirect control through subsidies from the Federal Government, given if standards are maintained, but in which no state is compelled to accept the standards and the contingent subsidy; unofficial co-operation between state and federal officials; interstate compacts or other agreements.[19]

Of these, the first two result in centralization of more power in the hands of the Federal Government. The others tend in the same direction, with inducement being substituted for force. This is less true of the last, the compact method, than of the others, but even here the constitutional provision requiring the consent and approval of Congress gives the national government a large degree of super-

[19] W. Brooke Graves, *Uniform State Action.*

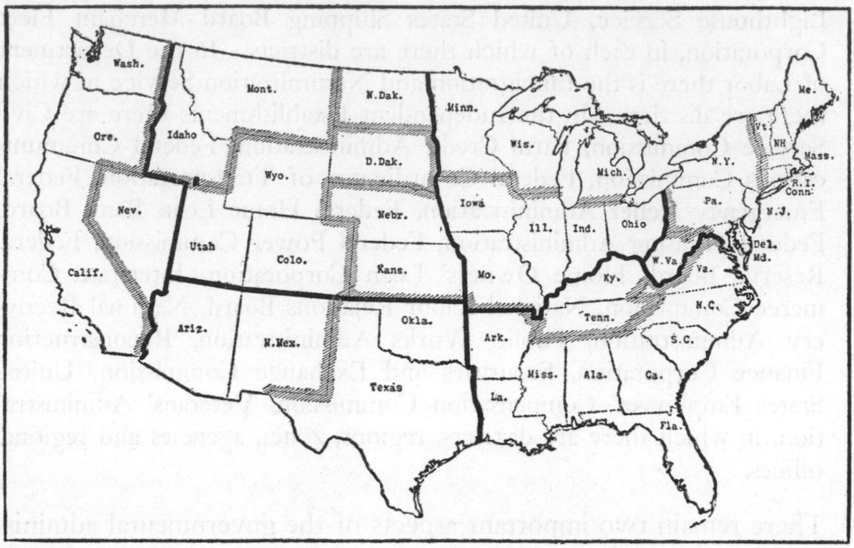

EXAMPLES OF VARIATION IN FUNCTIONAL ADMINISTRATIVE DISTRICTS OF THE UNITED STATES

Above: Forest Regions by States and Principal Forest Areas.

Below: Divisions for Meat Inspection Laboratories, Bureau of Animal Husbandry, Department of Agriculture. Adapted from *Regional Factors in National Planning and Development.*

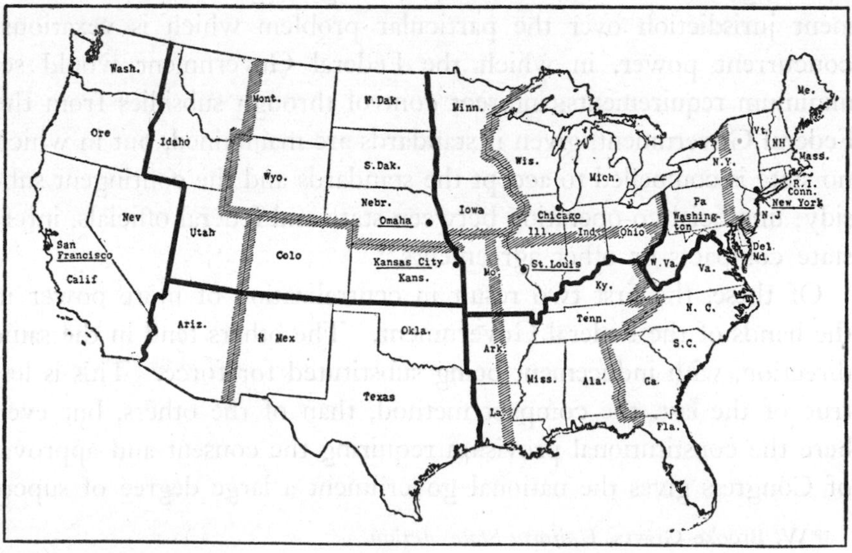

visory power. However, this is not necessarily a bad thing in itself. In fact, it seems to be perfectly apparent that if we are to have regionalism rather than sectional autonomy, we must have a central supervisory power. The rights of the nation must be maintained above those of the region.

The underlying desire in all of these methods is that of securing uniform state action to avoid the confusion and contradictions now found too often. To this end several organizations have worked for many years. Perhaps the best-known is the National Conference of Commissioners of Uniform State Laws. This organization has been promoting this idea since 1889. No state has adopted more than 27 of the 45 proposed uniform laws, while one state, Texas, has adopted only two of its recommendations. This would seem to argue that the states are pretty well determined that national uniformity of state laws is not essential or desirable; a conclusion one would expect after considering the wide variance in the situations actually existing in the several states. It is hard to imagine Utah and Massachusetts seeing eye to eye on any matter.

Actually, of course, uniformity of state laws is not needed or desired on all subjects. This conclusion was reached as long ago as 1891 by Henry C. Thompkins, who declared, "There is and there will continue to be, a difference in the character and surroundings of the people residing in the different portions of the Union that will require a difference in the law governing them. . . . And that uniformity is only desirable in those matters which affect all the people of the nation alike." [20] This latter category is of considerable extent, however.

In an effort to secure more uniform laws and more uniform administration of laws, state officials have formed numerous associations. But here again areal differences appear in the regional divisions of such organizations. Graves lists some 37 such regional organizations, along with eighteen pages of national organizations. Such associations range from governors' conferences to the International Pacific Salmon Federation, whose province it is to see that the salmon receive equal protection along the Pacific Coast.

[20] Thirteen Reports, *American Bar Association,* 247.

The American Legislators' Association is another organization of recent initiation in this field of interstate co-operation. This Association is representative of the state legislatures and was founded to secure co-operation between the states based upon sound research and reference service. The more recent Council of State Governments is an outgrowth of the Legislators' Association, but puts emphasis upon uniform administration rather than legislation. These organizations have all been valuable in promoting intelligent discussion of the possibilities of co-operation between governmental units on various levels. Of particular interest to the present discussion are the recommendations adopted at the conference held by these agencies in Washington, in March 1935. Among other things they recommended the establishment of regional secretariats since "Your committee feels that the establishment of such regional secretariats is vital to the development of harmonious state relationships and that such secretariats would prove to be effective agencies for improving interstate co-operation." [21]

Perhaps the most promising solution of regional problems in terms of state action is the interstate compact, through which the individual states delegate a specific portion of their authority to a regional entity for specific purposes. This device seems to have originated during the life of the Articles of Confederation as a means of settling boundary disputes between the semi-independent governmental entities of that time, but was carried into the new constitution through a prohibition of entering compacts without the consent of Congress. This device has been used forty-six times during the life of the nation, though Congress has authorized twenty-three other compacts, which for one reason or another have never been completed. Thirteen such agreements are listed by the Library of Congress as having been effectuated without specific authorization by Congress.[22]

But the interstate compact is a relatively new method, in spite of its history. Since 1900 Congress has granted the right to negotiate 44 such agreements, of which 30 have been effectuated since 1918. The subjects for which such covenants have been entered are revealing. They have been used in efforts to meet situations concerning boundaries, criminal jurisdiction over boundary waters, uniformity of legislation, interstate accounting, taxation, control of public utili-

[21] Quoted in National Resources Committee, *Regional Factors in National Planning and Development*, December 1935, p. 26.
[22] *Ibid.*, pp. 34-36.

ties, stream control, conservation of natural resources, law enforcement and setting standards of labor. It is notable that most of these uses are not directly related to social and economic problems, but are, rather, political in nature.

Boundary disputes have been the subject most frequently adjusted by this method, though court action has also been resorted to in such areas. The use of the compact where court action could not settle the dispute equitably is illustrated in the suit before the Supreme Court involving the Washington-Oregon boundary along the Columbia River. This line had been set at the center of the north channel of the river, but the south channel had become the principal branch of the stream. The court felt itself powerless to redraw the boundary line, but suggested that the states themselves take such action through an interstate agreement.[23]

The most famous case involving interstate debt was that resulting from the partition of Virginia during the Civil War. A compact assigned a portion of the debt of the State of Virginia at the time of separation to the new state, but litigation was necessary to secure payment. This case is also important in that the Supreme Court there took the position that Congress had power to enforce such interstate agreements, or to create necessary judicial remedies.[24]

In 1910 Congress passed a resolution giving the states of Wisconsin, Illinois, Indiana, and Michigan, or any two of them, the right to enter an agreement as to criminal jurisdiction over lake waters, and in 1934 went much further in granting a blanket agreement to compacts negotiated between any of the states for prevention of crime or enforcement of criminal laws. Even that most jealously guarded governmental prerogative, the right of taxation, has been made the subject of such an agreement, in the case of Missouri and Kansas covenanting not to tax the properties of municipal waterworks in the Kansas City region. In the field of public utilities one of the early compacts had to do with the construction of a canal between Maryland, Virginia, and the District of Columbia, and affecting Pennsylvania, while the numerous interstate bridges and the tunnels beneath the Hudson between New York and New Jersey furnish recent examples.

The first use of the compact in labor legislation resulted from a conference in 1934, when Connecticut, New York, Maine, Rhode

[23] *Washington vs. Oregon,* 211 U. S. 273.
[24] *Virginia vs. West Virginia,* 246 U. S. 565.

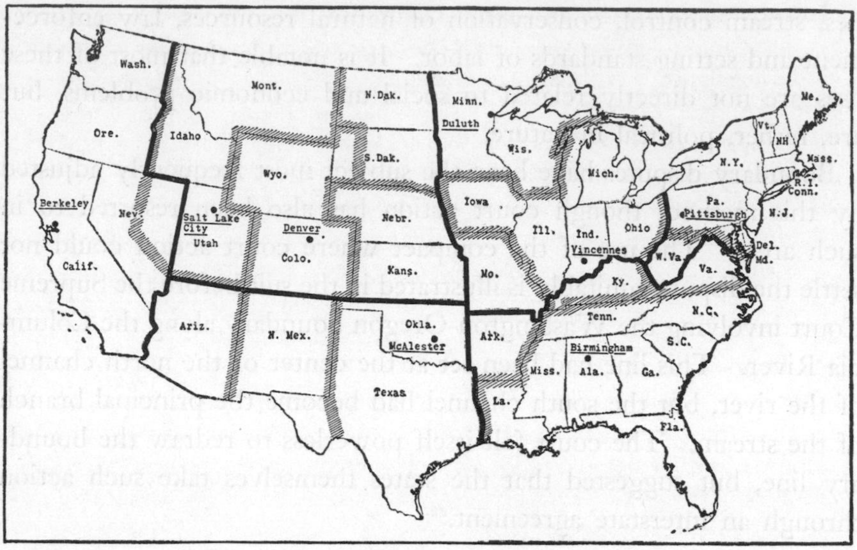

EXAMPLES OF VARIATION IN FEDERAL ADMINISTRATIVE DISTRICTS IN WHICH STATE LINES ARE IGNORED

Above: Safety Districts, Bureau of Mines, Interior Department.

Below: Safety Appliances Groups, Bureau of Safety, Interstate Commerce Commission. Adapted from *Regional Factors in National Planning and Development,* page 252.

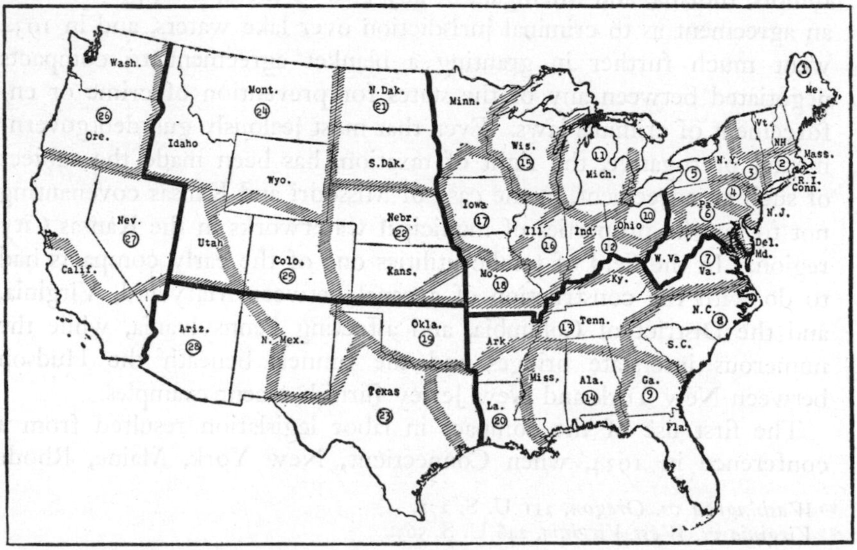

Island, Massachusetts and New Hampshire provided for a permanent commission to investigate and report to the various states on matters affecting labor. Although enforcement is left to the individual states, the compact contains a provision that questions arising from state laws adopted in conformity with the compact shall be referred to the interstate commission.[25] However, any action of the interstate body is advisory only. This is, perhaps, the fatal weakness of this method of dealing with such problems, as was demonstrated when, at a conference at Spring Lake, New Jersey, June 28 and 29, 1935, an attempt to secure agreement to a ban on child labor was made. Only the representative of Connecticut was ready to sign; the governor of New Jersey and the secretary of the Manufacturers' Association of that state solemnly warned against "precipitate action" and interference with "widely variant fundamental conditions of industry and labor"; and North Carolina was the only southern state to send a representative. Since industries using child labor are found in most if not all of the industrialized states it is evident that restrictions of this nature would upset the competitive system which is fundamental in our economic and political philosophy.

In the field of conservation of natural resources the interstate compact has also had a checkered career. In the major illustration of this problem, the Colorado River Compact, one of the interested states, Arizona, refused to accept the agreement and seriously delayed work through court action. The experience has been definitely disappointing to advocates of the compact method of settling regional problems. Somewhat the same result has followed efforts to conserve petroleum by means of interstate compacts. This is a distinctly regional problem in that the large oil fields lie in several states and flush production in one field may wreck the national market. Although states have established their right to limit production, the Supreme Court refused to uphold a law prohibiting the movement in interstate commerce of petroleum produced in defiance of such state laws. However, the adverse decision rested on the argument that no standard for the guidance of administrative officers had been set, so that the attitude on the purpose of the law remains in doubt.[26] The oil-producing states of the Southwest have since that decision

[25] National Resources Committee, *Regional Factors in National Planning and Development*, December 1935, p. 38.

[26] Northcutt Ely, *Oil Conservation Through Interstate Agreement* is a full discussion of this particular situation.

entered into a compact, but its success seems to be somewhat doubtful.

The interstate authority has no power to incur binding obligations and no provision was made for the financial responsibility of the states for violations of the compact; that is, it does not have the power requisite to success. Instead of being able to work out problems on a regional basis, it becomes the tool of states jealous of their prerogatives and niggardly in their grants of authority. However, it seems undeniable that many regional problems can and have been settled by this mechanism. Most such problems, it is to be noted, have been such that but one decision was required; they usually have not been continuing problems needing constant or frequent adjustment.

This review of interstate and state-national conflict and efforts at co-operation will serve to indicate the complexities of our present situation and the basis upon which some scholars have advanced the idea of regional authorities of various sorts to meet this situation. It suggests further, however, the historical background upon which the national development has taken place and the relative merits of the group of states regions over either the organic natural regions or a newly created series of sovereign regions. This latter will be discussed in Chapter X. We may now examine once more the conflict basis of the political rivalries that have grown up in the nation. Even in earliest days the New England colonies felt themselves to be different from those to the south; as they were. The poor rocky hillsides of New England could not support an agrarian culture such as that which became characteristic of the southern colonies. Industry and commerce were resorted to and differences in social organization and philosophy were emphasized. Regional consciousness appeared with the formation of the "United Colonies of New England," in 1643.

At the same time the pioneers along the western fringe of settlement felt themselves different from the established planters and commercial men of the tidewater areas; and the East-West dichotomy which has until recently been the most potent factor in developing our nation, perhaps, made its appearance. Time after time this feeling of conflicting interests has flared up dramatically—in Shays' Rebellion, in the Whisky Rebellion, in the threatened secession of the

New England States in the early years of the nineteenth century, and again when Texas was admitted to the Union; in the Jackson upheaval; in the Civil War; in sectional blocs in Congress and, most recently, in the riots and "quiet gatherings of interested neighbors" which effectively blocked the court officers from auctioning foreclosed lands during the presidential administration of Herbert Hoover.

With the exceptions of the secession movements mentioned, it seems only fair to say that these movements did not aim at the destruction of the Federal Government, but rather were attempts to gain recognition for and adjustment of problems which were not of fundamental national importance but were of vital significance to certain areas within the nation. Most such movements have attempted to establish what appeared to their leaders to be a more desirable equilibrium within the nation.

This idea of equilibrium between forces originating in different areas is the very fundament of the federal system of government. From the War of the Revolution, America has been dedicated to the proposition that the best government is that which most successfully combined the supervision of a central government with the initiative of local areas. The Articles of Confederation placed too much stress on the local areas and gave too little supervisory power to the central government. The result was near chaos. But when the central government was reconstructed in that time of disorder, the theory adopted was not that of a strongly centralized state, as was to have been expected, but that of a state in which the representatives of local feeling, the states, were jealously guarded in their rights. It was almost a century later that the fundamental issue of the locus of supreme sovereignty was decided on the battlefields. But following that decision students of politics began to point out that the states were becoming powerless and almost meaningless except in a traditional sense. That decline of the power of the states has proceeded until during the depression of the early 1930's the Federal Government went directly to the larger cities as the most efficient means of relieving the distress of the population. And the states encouraged such action. Thus it appears that the traditional guardian of local initiative in our governmental machinery has become impotent in at least some of its functions.

In this situation it is only natural that the proposal should be heard that the feeble state be replaced by a region large enough and

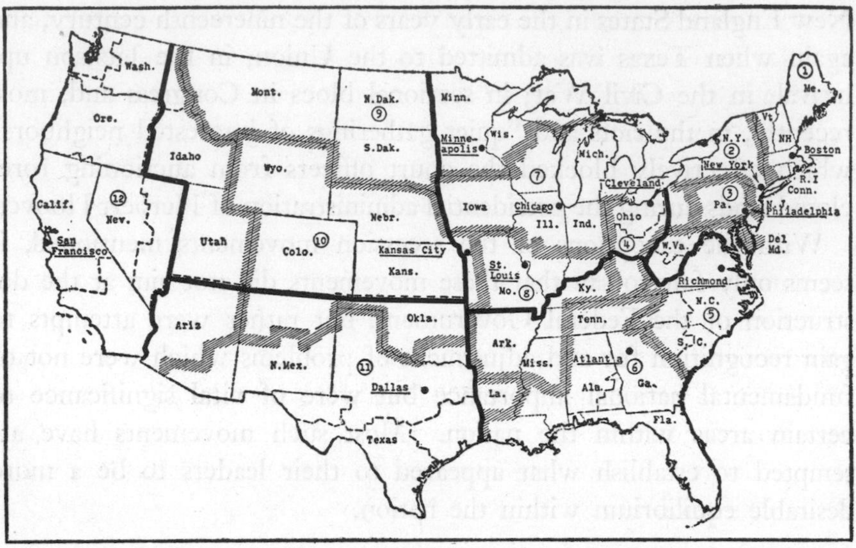

EXAMPLES OF VARIATION IN FEDERAL ADMINISTRATIVE DISTRICTS, IN WHICH STATE LINES ARE NOT FOLLOWED

Above: Federal Reserve Board Districts.

Below: National Labor Relations Board Regions. Adapted from *Regional Factors in National Planning and Development*, page 252.

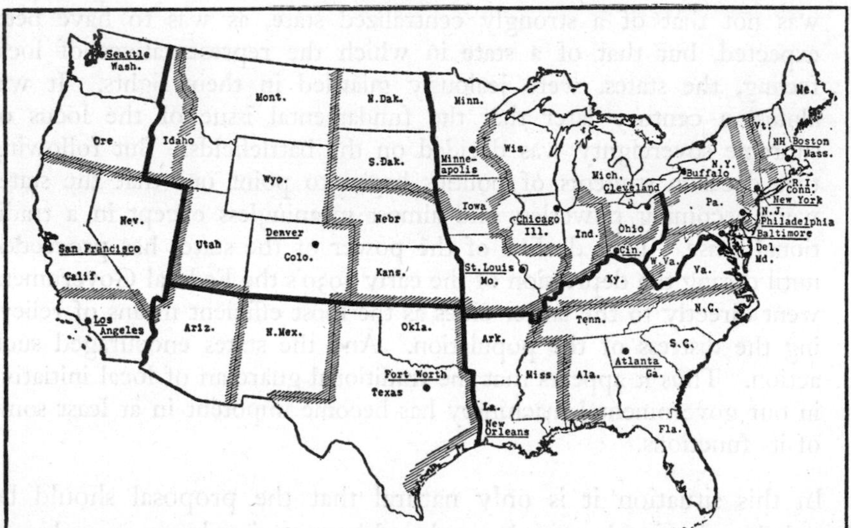

representative enough of a characteristic area of the nation to make its voice heard and its influence felt. Indeed, such action has arisen spontaneously, without benefit of sound theory which might have laid bare its implications. Since the formal organization of our government is based on the division of powers between one central and forty-eight state governments with no provision for any action on a level between with which to meet problems affecting areas not coterminous with lines or combinations of such artificial creations, both the administrative and legislative branches of our government have moved into this "No Man's Land" without warrant of specific authority. The results, viewed from the standpoint of the particular agency or bloc have often been gratifying; from the standpoint of the nation as a whole such action has led to redundance and lack of co-ordination in administration and to self-seeking sectionalism in legislation. Though the immediate function or section may have gained, the nation usually has lost.

Such action has, of course, often been termed the failure of the states to perform properly the function assigned them in our governmental system and has led many students to seek a better arrangement. In 1886, John W. Burgess remarked that the newer state constitutions showed a decrease in the power of the state and argued that ethnic and geographic unity must be the basis of what he called "nationality" feeling, the essential condition of political perpetuity. The states, he argued, had lost the power to encompass such areas of feeling, if they had ever possessed it, since they are too large for local feeling and too small for a feeling of nationality.[27]

> Four years later Simon N. Patten expressed much the same idea when he pointed out that the eastern areas of this nation were originally settled not by individuals, but by closely knit groups. However, the Western States were settled by individuals and families which lacked this cohesive tradition. This situation was then further complicated by grouping these people into political units bounded by artificial lines which cut across natural communities. The result has been, he says, that the legislature of the state of Illinois, for instance, could enact laws for the whole of the Upper Mississippi Valley as easily as for the area within its boundaries. At the same time local government was made impossible because of the union of differing small areas

[27] "The American Commonwealth," *Political Science Quarterly*, I, 9-35.

within the states. His proposed remedy might have been written by an advocate of sovereign regions today: "Instead of regarding the boundaries of our states as fixed and unchangeable, we should recognize that we are only beginning to get the data upon which to decide where the boundaries of states can be properly located. If our states are to be a vital part of our political system, each section of our land which has distinct physical, social or economic conditions should be carved out of existing states and given that independence needed to make its government reflect the sentiments of its inhabitants."[28]

Thus it would appear that the state has been impotent to a large degree for some decades at least, and that a part of its impotence is traceable to the manner in which the states were formed. Such a situation has inevitably resulted in duplication of legislation and administration on the one hand and in unresponsiveness to local needs and unwieldiness on the other. This was nicely illustrated by the predicament in which the "dry" states have found themselves since repeal of the national prohibition amendment to the Constitution—a situation in which local areas are forced to outlaw the sale of intoxicants, at least formally, and at the same time find themselves powerless to prevent citizens from securing such beverages from adjoining "wet" states.

If the states were natural social and economic units it is only logical to suppose consensus would be much more likely and problem solving would be much easier. As the situation now stands the states have the legal authority so that proposed solutions to regional problems must be approved by state legislatures representing areas which may be wholly or only to a small degree interested, whether such areas are of greater or lesser extent than the state. In some instances, even the Federal Government must secure state permission to initiate projects designed to meet problems.[29]

Problems of labor legislation illustrate this point nicely. Legislation affecting minimum wage, maximum hours or conditions of labor may cause a shift of industry from one region of the nation to another to the national detriment through depreciation of investment and at the

[28] "The Decay of State and Local Government," *Annals of the American Academy of Political and Social Science*, I, 40.

[29] See National Resources Committee, *Regional Factors in National Planning and Development*, December 1935.

same time create problems in the new, "cheaper" area which will tax local resources and lead to demands for interference by the Federal Government. The charge has been made that the shift of the textile industry from New England to the southern piedmont has had both effects. A series of articles by Thomas L. Stokes appearing in the Scripps-Howard newspapers during 1936 argues that the same thing has happened in other industries within the past few years.

The traditional southern defense of states' rights has promoted such situations. But it has also made it apparent that we cannot have a national policy based on state action, with the result that we have turned more and more to the Federal Government for control. The result has been a centralization and concentration of power in Washington which threatens not only the states but the larger, more natural, social and economic entities called regions.

One of the most important factors in the failure of the states has been the rise of the cities. When it is discovered that a list of the ten largest governmental units in the United States, including the Federal Government, as measured in money handled, includes New York City, Chicago, Los Angeles, Detroit and Philadelphia; that in 1930 the city of New York spent more on retirement pay of former city employees than the entire revenue of the state of Nevada, and spent more for police protection than the entire revenue of Missouri or Indiana or any of 35 other states,[30] it is all too evident that the city has become too large and too powerful to be ruled by the state as it is now organized.

The natural result has been that the cities have been given a large measure of autonomy. As this has worked out in practice it means that the cities have gathered into their confines many of the cultural institutions of the area of which, after all, they are only a part. This, in its turn, has been a powerful factor in the shift of population toward the cities. David Cushman Coyle estimates that in the cost of rearing migrants to the city, in inheritances, rents and interests the rural portions of the regions have paid tribute to the cities of the nation in ten years of some 36 billion dollars. From this he argues that subsidies for depressed rural areas should not be considered charity but return of excessive payments, like co-operative

[30] W. Brooke Graves, "The Future of the American State," *American Political Science Review*, XXX, 24-50.

society dividends.[31] The drain in vitality of the youthful migrants is not to be calculated.

Cities also cut across state lines in the problems they create in their immediate environs. New York problems cannot be confined to New York; no more can those centering about St. Louis, Philadelphia, Chicago, Kansas City, be confined to the states to which these cities are, legally, subordinate. The result has been that in each of these cases interstate metropolitan planning organizations have been put into operation. But if the city does not lie close to a state boundary, it is impossible to confine its problems to its corporate limits. Recreation, education, water supply, inspection of milk supplies, electric power service, transportation systems and other problems simply will not be so confined. This has forced the cities into extraterritorial activities. In one case a court ordered a city to sell water from its municipal plant to customers outside its jurisdiction.[32] Other cases have established the rights of cities to erect sewage disposal plants outside their corporate limits, to sell electricity to other cities, to police parks, and even to control subdivision of property within certain limits. But few rules have been worked out for competition between cities. The city seems to be the Topsy of our governmental units.

[31] "The South's Unbalanced Budget," *The Virginia Quarterly Review*, XIII, 192-208, especially pp. 194-196.

[32] Winston W. Crouch, "Extraterritorial Powers of Cities as Factors in California Metropolitan Government," *American Political Science Review*, XXXI, 289.

Chapter IX

SERVICE REGIONS: NON-GOVERNMENTAL

IN the utilization of practical, working regional divisions of national industrial and business concerns, the totality-unity aspect of regionalism is clearly evident. Manifestly, the regional divisions of a great chain store are not set up to enhance the interest of each separate unit, but to conserve and develop the whole. This is basic regionalism. On the other hand, regional centers serve as the basis for economy, efficiency, local good will, and other realistic considerations.

"Please order from the city nearest you." As one thumbs through the advertising pages of magazines, he is constantly struck by the above or similar words appearing at or near the bottom of appeals to buy radios, vacuum cleaners, typewriters, crackers, bird seed, matches, flowering bulbs, or this, that, or the other thing. Business men, like governmental bureaucrats and like heads of nationwide educational, philanthropic, and recreational organizations, have discovered through long years of experience that they can serve themselves and their customers better if they break the heterogeneous nation into more or less homogeneous regions.

Most big businesses have evolved regional schemes for the nation on the basis of expediency rather than in application of theory. In fact, as is pointed out elsewhere, economic theorists have been very slow to acknowledge that their rational explanations will not fit one region as well as another. As is so often the case, practice has outrun theory. Business men like governmental administrators divide the nation without being able to give adequate explanation in many cases. Nearly always this division is made in spite of the great desire of the corporation to sell exactly the same product in exactly the same manner throughout the country. Yet the regional and district divisions have grown logically out of practical experience and scientific management and conform to some extent to the theory of regional mercantilism, which assumes that the nation is too large and too complex to permit of effective administration through a single central station. The theoretical aspects of this regionalism will be treated in Chapter XV.

Here again some aspects of French and Polish economic regionalism will serve to illustrate both the basis and the practice of regions for service. Thus, it is pointed out that the division of France into sixteen, and then into twenty regions was inevitable, since the geography of France is such that concentration of economic forces at Paris would paralyze the rest of the nation. This was no sudden upheaval of existing conditions; it was a gradual development. There was already the tendency to develop regional centers of activity in the provincial cities. Therefore, when the system of economic regions was put in effect it meant simply the creating of regions around each of these cities as a nucleus. In a large measure, then, this form of regionalism may be directly traced back to the geographic principles of Vidal de la Blache, who was the first to envisage the provincial cities as "noeuds" of a geographic and, therefore, of an economic region. It must be observed, too, that such phases of regionalism in France as the sentimental or cultural, the literary, linguistic or academic are all intended to act as auxiliary forces in the advance of economic regionalism. M. Charles-Brun said, "Let us decentralize politically and economically. Literary decentralization may have been a stimulant; it should be a resultant. Autonomous regions will have their autonomous literature also."[1] Administrative regionalism itself has for its main objective the greater economic good of the country. So, too, the ideals set forth in Polish regionalism provide: "1. Each region of Poland should offer a distinct economic type, corresponding to the natural, demographic and cultural conditions of the territory it comprises. It is this harmonious coexistence of distinct economic regions, each with its own characteristic, but maintained at an approximately uniform level, which maintains the economic unity of the State. 2. Regionalism co-ordinates, awakens initiative, and penetrates public opinion with salutary ideas, thus stimulating:—(a) Scientific research and the establishment of individual economic programs suitable to the various regions; (b) work tending to raise the level of the individual charac-

[1] Quoted by R. K. Gooch, *Regionalism in France*, p. 99.

teristics of the separate economic regions. 3. Regionalism tends to realize these desirable objects by organizing local associations and by influencing the opinions and education of qualified persons whose work lies in the activities of autonomous institutions of either a general or a strictly economic character. This action might also extend its circle of influence to professional associations and the co-operative movement." [2]

One other example taken from German regionalism will suffice to illustrate the bases for the larger economic and industrial regionalism. In Germany, although to a less degree than in the United States, there have been experiments to divide the country into marketing areas with branches or regional offices in strategic points. The Rhineland-Westfalian Coal Syndicate is cited as the earliest to adopt this method of marketing. It is, however, not only the industrialists or merchants who are interested in the new regionalism, but scholars, governmental executives, social workers, and others have been exploring the possibilities of defining and of utilizing more effectively a larger number of regions.

Two things may be noted with regard to the German concept of regionalism as it has developed up to the present time. One is that attention is turned to the industrial area, rather than to the economic area, that is, to the producing unit rather than to the well-rounded economic region with its exchange distribution of goods and its consumption. Related to this rather one-sided emphasis is the fact that most studies deal with the area as a unit and in its relation to other districts rather than in detail with the economic structure within the unit itself. . . . If one considers regionalism as it has developed in Germany, one thinks first of all of the Rhineland-Westfalian district, or the Lower Rhine area. This is the most highly industrialized area in Germany, indeed, probably in the whole European continent. It is the leading German iron and steel district, far outranking Silesia, Siegerland, and the Saar areas. It has many other industrial interests as well, including among them the most important coal- and iron-mining, machinery, tools, cutlery, and other finishing industries, the chemical industry, and textiles. It extends, roughly speaking, from somewhat south of Cologne on the Rhine to the Dutch border, and from Holland on the west to a line running east of Dortmund, Iserlohn, and Lüdenscheid. This territory includes sixteen of the forty-six *Grossstädte* of

[2] Adapted from "Communications," *The Sociological Review*, XXIV, No. 2, pp. 197-199.

the empire and 20 percent of the population. It has a population density of 269 per square kilometer, as compared with an average of 133 for the empire. In it are employed 3,800,000 people, 20 percent of the total for the empire.[3]

More illustrative of the multiplicity of service regions in the United States are the scores of regional divisions of trade organizations, newspaper distribution, retail and wholesale trade, fraternal organizations, the American Library Association, educational associations, historical and learned societies. A sampling or two of these will serve to illustrate the case and to introduce a discussion of certain self-evident considerations which have resulted in the present regionalization of the country.

One interesting regional division was made the basis of the commercial survey of the United States Department of Commerce and the other was the United States Chamber of Commerce geographic regions. The former comprised nine regions as follows: New England, Central Atlantic, Southeast, Midwest, Central Northwest, West Mid-Continent, Gulf Southwest, Pacific Southwest, Pacific Northwest. The United States Chamber of Commerce division comprised only six divisions—the Northeastern, the Southeastern, the Southwestern, the Northern Central, the Northwestern, and the Western. Another similar illustration of regional America was Goode's political map of the nation, cutting across state lines and composed of nineteen regions. In general, the Northeast included three or four subregions; the Southeast about the same number; the Middle States four; the Southwest two; the Northwest and Far West combined in five. Another type of arrangement for a specific purpose was the Domestic Commerce Division of the United States Department of Commerce which listed 183 metropolitan and small city areas in the United States. These divisions, based upon indices of geographic territory, freight rates, zones of truck delivery, data from salesmen, and number of accounts in each county gathered from 2,303 cities, constituted an excellent basis for study of economic circulation, and, especially if done from decade to decade, would indicate changing areas. It was also of importance in showing a picture of intercorrelations with newspaper circulation and other items. As indicative of the possibilities of multiple subdivisions a somewhat similar map plotted by the J. Walter Thompson Company for retail shopping areas grouped 683 retail shopping zones about the

[3] Mildred Hartsough, "The Concept of Regionalism as Applied to Western Germany," *Publication of the American Sociological Society*, XXIV, No. 2, pp. 16-17.

same number of centers, to which were appended yet other 642 subcenters. A similar charting of metropolitan regions by Batten, Barton, Durstine, and Osborn divided the United States into 187 local area divisions comprising 745 subdivisions, in which the index used was the area covered by Sunday newspapers circulating out of major centers, and for subareas circulation of daily newspapers. In 1920 the Marketing Division of the International Magazine, Incorporated, attempted to simplify consumer selling from which maximum results might be secured. On the basis of studies of population, geographical characteristics, sources of wealth, trade outlets, and transportation, the boundaries of 632 trading centers were delimited.[4]

Obviously the need for regionalization varies greatly from business to business. New Englanders ride in almost exactly the same automobiles as do persons living along the shores of the Pacific. Almost but not quite. Even though the car is the same when it leaves the factory, regional variations in additions or replacements of various minor parts give the automobiles of each region easily recognizable differences. The tourist in the family car has undoubtedly had filling station and accessory store attendants point out various gadgets without which "you just can't drive a car in these parts." The heater of the north is replaced by the canvas water bag of the southwestern desert. Mountainous regions call for adjustment of carburetor and gear ratio; along the sandy coast huge air filters must protect the delicate moving parts of the motor from fine grit which otherwise would destroy the mechanism in a few weeks, and so on.

In such commodities as hats, clothing, foods, shoes, heating appliances, farm implements, used in every part of the nation, the widest regional variations may be observed. Even though the tightly fitting, hard bowler and the wide-brimmed, high-crowned, soft felt sombrero of the cowboy may both be manufactured in Philadelphia and although the trade mark may be the same, they are worn in different portions of the nation and by different types of persons. Even though style and design throughout the nation bear the stamp of Hollywood and New York, the materials in which they are executed will range from silks and woolens in one area of the nation to cotton and linen in another. This is true in spite of some few

[4] Adapted from Howard W. Odum, *Southern Regions of the United States*, pp. 265, 267, 269.

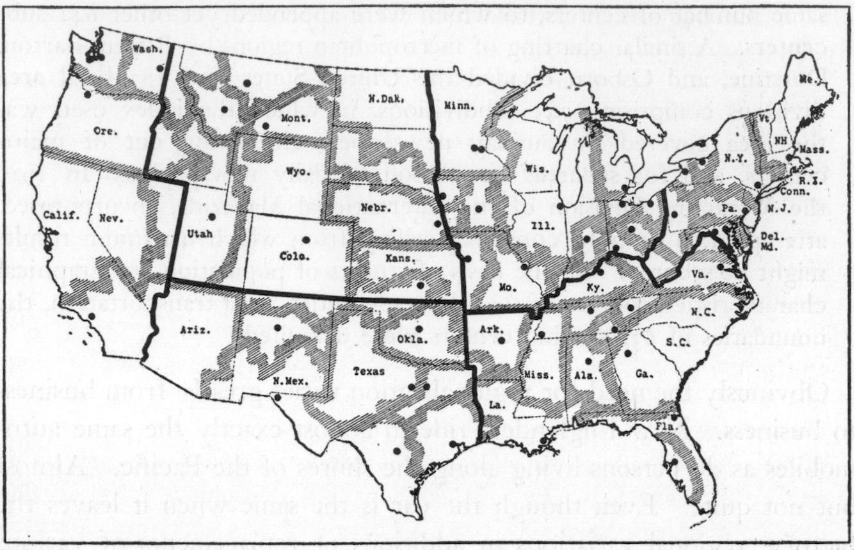

Above: Trade Areas adapted from *Market Data Handbook of the United States*, Domestic Commerce, Series No. 30, compared with,

Below: Metropolitan Regions of the United States as Defined by Daily Newspaper Circulation, 1920-1929. Adapted from McKenzie's *The Metropolitan Community*, page 107.

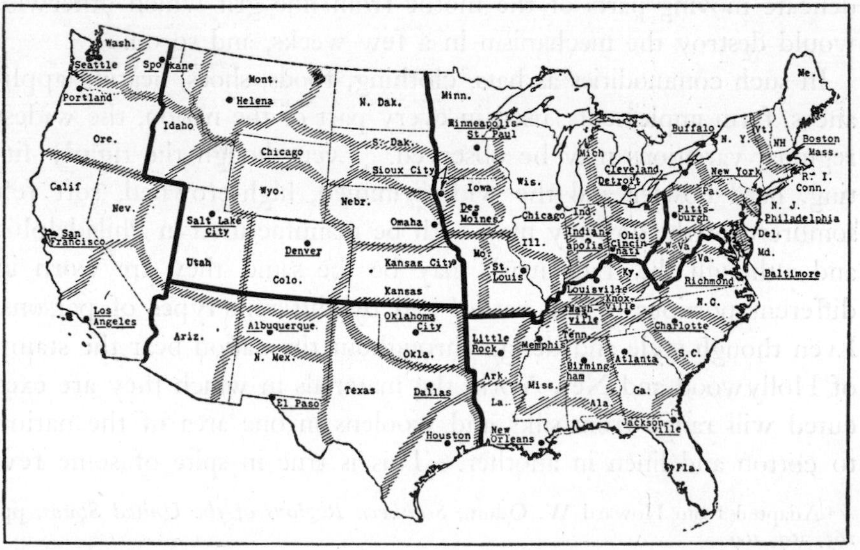

who make themselves intensely uncomfortable in a vain effort to subordinate climate to fashion.

The sales map of ten years ago should be thrown out of the window. The trading area is not determined by any map maker or any traffic manager or sales manager or marketing expert. Trading zones are demarked by people who live in the region. Trade follows people where they live and especially where they spend their money. The death knell of this type of map was rung when we began to make censuses of distribution, and in more recent years a score of traffic studies. The trading area based solely on population is a sad misconception. The reasons are obvious: different standards of living, the range of climates, average incomes, the inmixture of blood. . . . Uncle Sam has now spent millions in maps and in the several censuses of distribution and in the studying of wholesaling and the analysis of particular trades. In this manner we have constructed 750 or 800 local trading areas in the U. S. A. This number is being cut down to 50 major trading areas for use by the government for census taking and studies of marketing. . . . Classify your outlets under something of this sort: best, secondary, and small; then plan your selling so as to give attention to them in ratio to their importance, that is in relation to their potential value as outlets for your goods, and, finally, parallel local advertising investments to fit these same ratings.[5]

Every going concern should know the following basic facts about each and every one of its territories, or districts, before it distributes its annual quotas. Rate of growth; relative importance; price distribution of products; and monthly distribution of products. . . . It will be found that every section of the country has quite a different rate of growth for its population and for all the various commodities it consumes. Therefore, when establishing a sales quota for various territories, it is necessary to know how rapidly these districts grow. No amount of high pressure selling can materially change the buying standard of New England. . . .[6]

The following are factors on which thirty-four large manufacturing companies determine their regional division of the nation for sales purposes: 1. Topographical conditions. 2. Previous sales volume in the area. 3. Auto routes. 4. Railroad maps. 5. Number of customers in the area. 6. Market potential. 7. Sales management's index of spendable money in area. 8. Volume of business needed to be profit-

[5] H. A. Herring, quoted in a mimeographed sheet released by Association of National Advertisers, January 10, 1935, p. 594.

[6] Ray B. Prescott, "Scientific Sales Planning on a Territorial and Seasonal Basis," *Sales Management*, XVIII, No. 3, p. 633.

able. 9. Income tax returns, auto registrations, magazine circulations, and other indices. 10. Ease of office record keeping for mail order sales, etc. 11. Location of warehouse supplies and stocks. 12. Trading areas of wholesale distributors. 13. Area a man can work and live at home. 14. Area a man can work and be at home week-ends.[7]

Although the per capita distribution of each product is affected by regional factors and conditions peculiar to it, there are at least four main types of reasons for territorial sales variations: (a) The consumptive characteristics of the population in relation to each product, such as race, nationality, density, mobility, growth, buying power, and living conditions. (b) The competitive and merchandising conditions to be encountered. (c) The effort factors, including the quantity and quality of the selling effort put forth by salesmen, advertising, and other promotional methods. (d) The price charged for the product, whether uniform or not, for all areas in relation to the responsiveness of regional demand. . . .[8]

Perhaps the most important reason for the analysis of sales rates is the knowledge it gives sales executives of the relationship of his own products, marketing methods, efforts, and prices to the distributive agencies and consumer groups in the market. In fact, all of these phases of planning are regional market factors which influence sales rates and which at the same time are largely determined by the more or less conscious direction of the sales management. Each in itself is a complexity of economic tendencies requiring to be analyzed for intelligent planning.[9]

There are, of course, businesses of a nationwide scope whose product is exactly the same wherever found; who are called upon to make no variation in it in compliance to regional differences in taste. Publishing corporations are an example of such a business. The books read in the several regions of the country are manufactured in exactly the same manner. However, this does not mean that even in such a standardized business as this it has not been found advantageous to regionalize. Many large book publishing houses list their products as published at several different places. Others designate regional headquarters. The advantages of such a breakdown of the country are several. If copies of a given book as sold

[7] From "Operating Salesmen in the Field: Factors in Which 34 Companies Base Sales Territories," *Sales Management*, XXXVII, 439.

[8] Donald R. G. Cowan, "Sales Analysis from the Management Standpoint," *The Journal of Business*, IX, 54-55.

[9] *Ibid.*, X, 26.

in Florida and Idaho are identical, the number of copies or the number per thousand population of any book sold in the two states will be very different. Further, whether the book be sold in one type of store or another, the best type of advertising with which to secure sale, the credit terms as between the publisher and the retailer, the speed and cost of delivery—all these and other factors vary—and in varying make it essential for greatest efficiency that regional managers acutely familiar with these variations be given administrative latitude sufficient to take advantage of them. In those commodities in which the product itself varies or is varied to meet regional differences in needs or taste, this necessity is greatly accentuated. Modern business engineering uses such factors to turn probable losses into possible profits.

But there are many products whose uses are limited to particular areas and still others which are used in one way in one area and another way in another. One of the larger rubber companies of the United States has published a series of advertisements recently showing the adaptation of this commodity to the widest range of uses in mine, in factory, on farm, in home, in business. The manufacturer of a widely used plastic material has set up regional engineering offices where experts on the industries characteristic of such regions are constantly alert to find new uses for their products.

The largest of the mail order houses reports that "to a slight extent our catalogues differ in the different mail order regions because of varying local demands and differentials in transportation."[10] This corporation has divided the nation into ten areas for its mail order business and has located regional supervisors of retail stores in five cities, Philadelphia, Atlanta, Chicago, Dallas, Seattle. A map supplied by the company indicates a division between the territory in the eastern portion of the country to which "northern" and "southern" catalogues are to be distributed. Similar regional arrangements are utilized by many other concerns.

Economic standards vary widely from region to region and through their variation determine marketing practices and possibilities. Thus the United States Department of Commerce in its studies of uses of goods in various cities of the nation has uncovered very great differ-

[10] Letter, Sears, Roebuck Company to Harry Estill Moore, March 13, 1937.

ences. For instance, car ownership ranges from approximately 60 percent for cities in the western part of the nation to 35 percent in Wheeling, West Virginia. Ninety-six percent of the families in Baton Rouge, Louisiana, live in wooden houses, whereas only about 50 percent of the families of some other cities live in such dwellings.[11] Even more striking are the differences in amounts spent in various portions of the country in the so-called service industries—hotels, entertainment, etc. In the Pacific census division, such industries receive $35.54 per capita population per year while in the West South Central division as outlined by the same bureau this amount shrinks to $6.52. In Mississippi, the per capita expenditure in these industries amounts to only $4.55, whereas in the District of Columbia it rises to $65.41. On a resident population basis, this would seem to indicate, for a further detailed analysis, that Mississippians have an annual expenditure for amusements of seventy-three cents each whereas residents of the nation's capital find it necessary to spend $11.39 each to escape boredom.[12] These figures cannot be taken at face value, of course, since expenditure for such services rises with the number of visitors to a particular region. Studies of the distribution of family income in cities of the United States point also to important regional differences. For instance, one such study indicates that 11.6 percent of the families in Decatur, Illinois, had no income whatsoever at the time of the survey while 29.2 percent of the families of that city had incomes of less than $500 per year. In the same city this survey showed no income above $10,000. By way of contrast, in Greensboro, North Carolina, less than one percent of the families were without income. The modal group of 28.9 had incomes of between $500 and $1,000 per year and a little more than one-half of one percent of the families had incomes of more than $10,000 per year. In Sacramento, California, the modal income group was that having incomes between $1,000 and $1,500 per year.[13] Further, the rapidity with which various portions of the nation recovered from the depression of the early 1930's is an important factor in regional trade. A study by the Bureau of the Census in 1935 indicated that increase in wholesale sales, 1933-1935, was under 30 percent in Maine and Vermont, in Maryland and West Virginia, and in Louisiana and Mississippi. In contrast wholesale business had increased more than 50 percent in Virginia, Tennessee, and

[11] Ada Lillian Bush, *Consumer Use of Selected Goods and Services by Income Classes*, United States Department of Commerce, Bureau of Foreign and Domestic Commerce, Market Research Series, No. 5.12. September 1937.

[12] United States Department of Commerce, *Services, Amusements, and Hotels*, Census of American Business, 1933. May 1935.

[13] Bush, *op. cit.*

Arkansas, in Indiana and Michigan, in South Carolina and Florida, and in the area comprised of the states of Oregon, Idaho, Montana, Utah, Nevada, Arizona, and New Mexico.[14]

The size and shape of the regions used by various corporations will be determined in large part by the nature of the business. Corporations dealing with industrial manufacturing plants will, of course, concentrate most of their efforts on the area from Chicago eastward to the Atlantic. In this portion of the country regions used by such companies will be numerous, while vast stretches of the Middle States, Northwest, Southwest, Southeast, and Far West, or even all five divisions may be included in one grouping.

One corporation, which deals almost exclusively with industrial manufacturers, divides the nation into seven regions. One of these includes the traditional New England Group, plus a part of New York State. Another is composed of the greater portion of the State of New York and most of the State of Pennsylvania. A third region includes Long Island, the vicinity of the City of New York, New Jersey, a portion of Pennsylvania, Delaware, Maryland, and a part of Virginia. Ohio, Kentucky, most of Indiana, and Michigan constitute a fourth region. That part of Indiana near Chicago, Wisconsin, Minnesota, Illinois, Iowa, Missouri, and Kansas compose another. The Pacific Coast States are united in another, while the great crescent of territory from Virginia across the Gulf Coast and northward to the Canadian border is assigned to no regional headquarters, presumably because the market for this particular product is at a minimum in these states.[15] It is to be noted that in practically all places the regional schemes worked out by national corporations fail to follow state lines.

Assuming that the commodity dealt in finds a demand throughout the nation, the regions used by the distributor will vary roughly in proportion to population density. However, various other factors also enter in. Availability of the raw material of which the product is manufactured is a factor in that manufacturing and distributing facilities are often combined. Thus a railway equipment corporation says that its various plants are located primarily with respect to avail-

[14] United States Department of Commerce, Bureau of the Census, Wholesale Distribution, I, May 1935.

[15] Letter in files of Harry Estill Moore. This and many other corporations requested their names be not used.

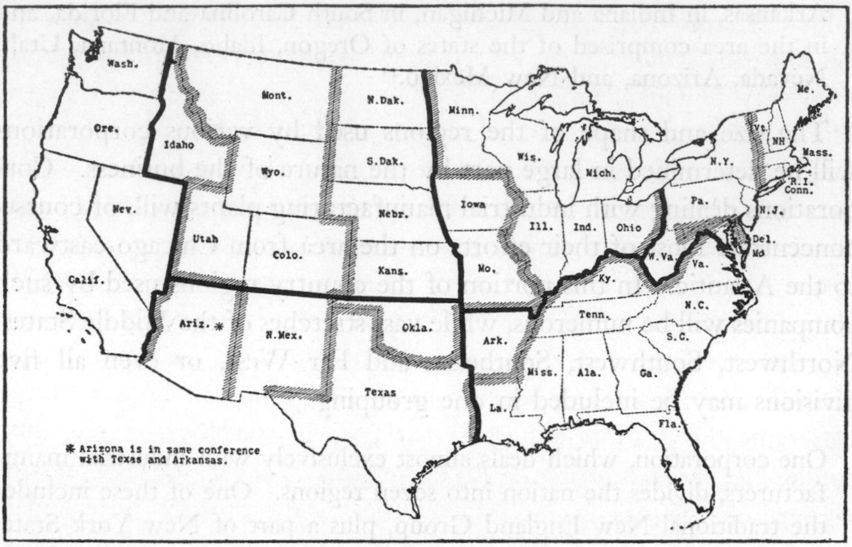

Above: Regional Divisions of the National Collegiate Athletic Association, from *Proceedings* of the 28th Annual Session, 1933.

Below: Major Athletic Conferences. Note Arkansas and Texas constitute a Southwest. With the exception of Arkansas, the Southeast coincides with the Southeast of *American Regionalism.* From the *Blue Book of College Athletics,* 1936-1937.

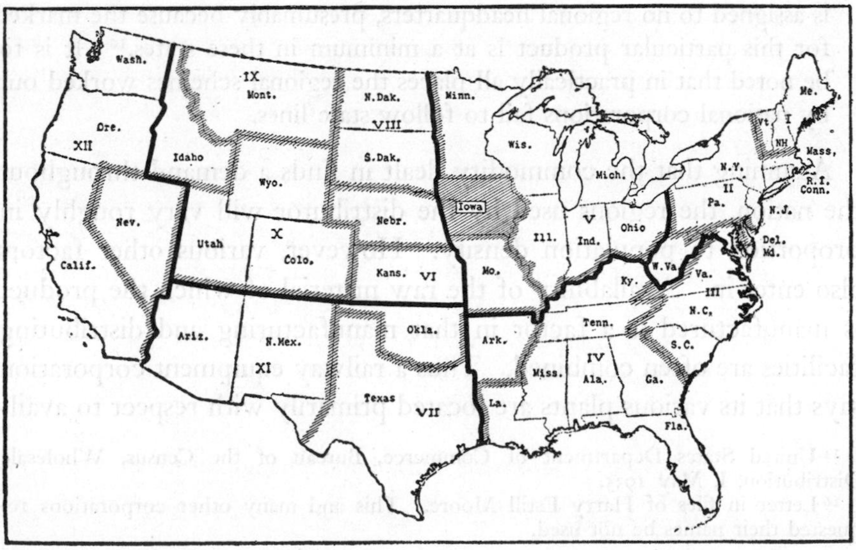

ability of steel though originally they were located with respect to the railroads which it was hoped they would serve.[16] Freight rates are a very powerful factor in determining size and shape of regions. The regional office will be placed in a city which has a favorable freight rate differential over a given area. The area over which such differential applies will usually be the territory assigned to such a branch office. However, rail connections and schedules may and sometimes do overcome the effect of such freight rate differentials where transportation facilities are meager. The growing importance of motor truck freight lines has, in recent years, also upset this type arrangement. The prevailing financial connections in an area partly determine the possible regions which may be developed. The city containing the dominant bank in an area will be selected as the regional distribution point other things being anyhere near equal. As is pointed out elsewhere in this study, some one city is commonly the center of banking, transportation, and communication facilities, and hence has achieved a position of regional dominance which makes it almost imperative that new businesses entering the area use such centers as regional headquarters.

However, there are certain other more intangible factors which are also powerful in determining regions. Business customs vary from area to area as regards length of credit, methods of salesmanship, seasons of greatest business activity, quality of merchandise desired, types of promotion which have proved efficient, and finally, those very intangible qualities referred to as *taste* and those others which reflect past experiences and are capitalized as *good will*. The importance of regional taste and custom is strikingly illustrated in the case of a common household commodity, which perhaps should remain nameless in this discussion. A vice-president of the corporation dominating this field says that the commodity sold by his company has become more and more standardized in the last twenty-five years or so, so that one traveling over the United States will secure practically the same article wherever it is bought, but adds, "It is still true that some markets prefer one brand to another, but they are all about the same kind, and while they may be under different brands and different-sized boxes, there is little or no variation."[17] Similarly a district manager for gasoline distribution explained a regional change in trade name by

[16] Letter in files of Harry Estill Moore.
[17] *Ibid.*

saying, "Of course the gasoline you get under this name is exactly the same as you got yesterday under the other name. But the folks in these parts are so used to this name that we wouldn't be able to sell them our gas if we called it anything else."

Good will often seems to be composed in part, at least, of an identity with the region. Doubtless a good part of this is due to the fact that regional concerns fit it with the customs, ideas, and ideals characteristic of the area. Also in part, it seems to rest upon more intangible sentiments of place, which are capitalized by alert corporation managers under such titles as "Northeastern," "Southern," "Pacific," or even "Gulf Coast," or "Carolinian," or "Texan." Purely local names are often similarly used. In such cases it matters little whether the corporation referred to be owned locally so that profits remain in the immediate vicinity of operation or whether such corporations be separate in name only, being in reality subsidiaries owned wholly outside the region. To the vast majority the name serves to identify the corporation with a region or locality whose name it bears, and thereby it profits from regional or local pride.

Thus the owning and managing corporation of a chain of twenty-five department stores reports that each store is operated as if it were owned locally; that policies are fixed, save in basic fundamentals, by the manager for each store.[18] Several large corporations selling highly standardized products have found it profitable to incorporate subsidiary entities for the various regions or even states.[19] The telephone corporation controlling most of the lines in the United States affords an excellent example of this practice. Incidentally they carry the regional name in their title in each of the incorporated areas, such as the Southern Bell Telephone Company.

Now come the newspapers announcing the formation of a radio broadcasting system consciously designed to meet the program taste of the Far Western Region. In the United States, at least, radio broadcasting, like newspaper publishing, is a distinctly commercial enterprise. Radio stations and newspapers often come to be considered representatives of, or at least dominant in, given areas. Such feeling is both recognized and fostered by the radio and newspapers.

[18] Letter in files of Harry Estill Moore.
[19] Cf. *Moody's Manual.*

Newspapers further such feelings by using and prominently displaying news meeting the peculiar interests of the area and in waging intensive circulation campaigns based on such news presentation. Radio stations have experimented successfully with electrical devices which direct their broadcast into certain areas while preventing it from entering other areas which normally would be within their circular range. The regional character of the broadcast is often indicated by the station identification such as that used by the *Atlanta Journal*, which "Covers Dixie Like the Dew."

It is because of these more intangible but nonetheless real feelings of regional pride, which business has capitalized upon, as well as the immediate practical benefits derived, that non-commercial, educational, religious, and recreational bodies have found it expedient to form themselves into regional units. In fact, such organization does make for greater efficiency in meeting needs more or less peculiar to such areas. Thus, the colleges have felt themselves and their problems separate enough that they have formed various associations of colleges and preparatory schools throughout the nation. Not only do such institutions themselves form regional associations, but their officers follow the same practice. This is also true of such semi-official organizations as alumni groups.

Typical of such regional associations are the following: Association of Colleges and Secondary Schools of the Middle States and Maryland, Association of Colleges and Secondary Schools of the Southern States, New England Association of Colleges and Secondary Schools, North Central Association of Colleges and Secondary Schools, Northwest Association of Secondary and Higher Schools, Classical Association of New England, Classical Association of the Atlantic States, Classical Association of the Middle West and South, Southern Branch of the Classical Association of the Middle West and South, Classical Association of the Pacific States, Eastern Arts Association, Middle West Society of Physical Education, Conference of Southern Mountain Workers, New England Home Economics Association, New England Modern Language Association, Private School Association of the Central States.

Academic societies composed almost exclusively of members of the instructional staffs of colleges and universities are finding it expedient to form regional units. The Pacific Coast section of the American Sociological Society has been in existence for some time and has recently been joined by the Southern, the Eastern, the Mid-West, the Ohio, and other Sociological Societies. These organizations hold themselves in a distinctly subordinate position to the nation-wide association of sociologists and find their reason for existence in the discussion of problems more or less peculiar to their areas. In fact, the main purposes are stated in terms of regional distances—a need for more people than can attend the national meetings to pursue the same purposes. Showing similar interest in regional problems are the Southern Economic Association, the Southern Political Science Association, and the Southwestern Social Science Association. Regional historical associations such as the Mississippi Valley Historical Society, and others of New England, of the South, and the Southwest also find obvious reasons for their existence. Not so closely connected to the culture of a given area and dominated more by regional sentiment of members than by regionality of subject matter are the multitude of organizations of teachers of Latin, geography, English and other modern languages, accounting, business subjects, physical education, education, elementary grades, secondary schools, private preparatory schools for boys or girls, junior colleges both private and public, military schools, mathematics, physics, chemistry, and geology.

Actual associations include the following:

Association of History Teachers of the Middle States and Maryland, Association of Modern Language Teachers of the Central West and South, Association of Modern Language Teachers of the Middle States and Maryland, Association of Teachers of Mathematics in the Middle States and Maryland, Association of Teachers of Mathematics in New England, Association of University and College Business Officers of the Eastern States, Central Association of Printing Teachers, Central Association of Science and Mathematics Teachers, College Conference on English in the Central Atlantic States, Conference of Deans of Men, Colleges of Western States, Eastern Association of Physics Teachers, Eastern Commercial Teachers Association, Eastern Music Supervisors' Conference, Mid-West Society of Directors of Physical Education for Women, New England Association of Chemistry Teachers, New England Association of College Teachers of Education,

New England Association of School Superintendents, New England Association of Teachers of English, New England High School Commercial Teachers Association, Northwestern Association of History, Government, and Economics Teachers, Private School Association of the Central States.[20]

From the point of view of the student, important regional schemes are those illustrated by the areas from which appointments to Rhodes Scholarships have been made for several years and the more recent scheme adopted by Cornell University whereby fellowships in various fields are awarded to students coming from a different set of regions. Also of student interest are the province-divisions of both social and scholastic fraternities.

The groupings of states into regions for the Rhodes Scholarships are: *Region I:* Maine, New Hampshire, Vermont, Massachusetts, Rhode Island, Connecticut. *Region II:* New York, New Jersey, Pennsylvania, Delaware, Maryland-District of Columbia, West Virginia. *Region III:* Virginia, North Carolina, South Carolina, Georgia, Florida, Tennessee. *Region IV:* Michigan, Wisconsin, Illinois, Indiana, Ohio, Kentucky. *Region V:* Minnesota, South Dakota, Nebraska, Iowa, Missouri, Kansas. *Region VI:* Alabama, Mississippi, Louisiana, Texas, Oklahoma, Arkansas. *Region VII:* California, Nevada, Utah, Arizona, Colorado, New Mexico. *Region VIII:* Washington, Oregon, Idaho, Montana, Wyoming, North Dakota.

A well-acknowledged historical background of the northern and southern branches of most Protestant denominations, which grew out of the animosity generated by the Civil War, is evidence of sectionalism in the nation in so far as these divisions have resisted reunion. Yet much of their separateness is still due to distinctions and differences in the religious thought and problems in the major areas in which they are found. However, fundamental religious divisions of the nation (which cut squarely across this division) may serve to illustrate cultural differences in the nation. The older more stable areas of the nation have consistently displayed a preference for the more formal, ceremonious types of worship, while the frontier regions have been characterized by an adherence to the dissenting

[20] *Educational Directory, 1927*, pp. 108-111, 113, 118-120.

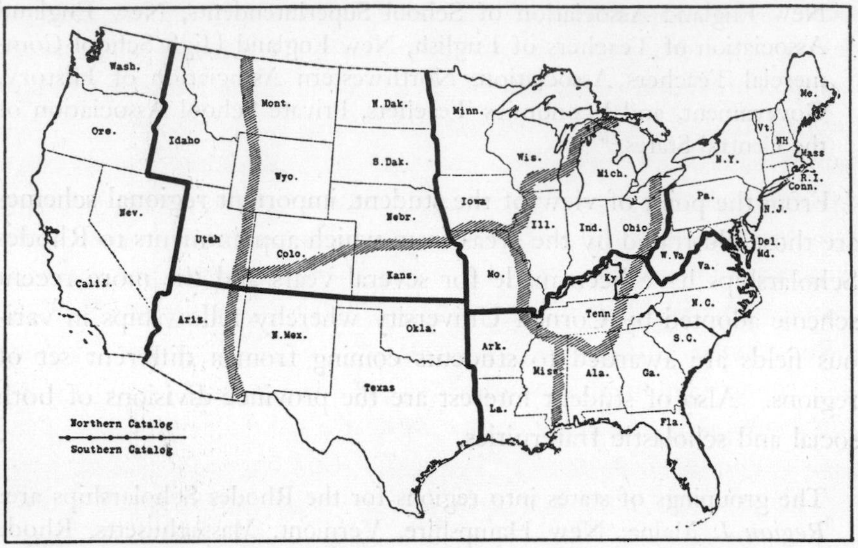

ILLUSTRATIONS OF SERVICE REGIONS IN THE BUSINESS AND COMMERCIAL FIELD

Above: Trade Divisions as Outlined by Montgomery Ward.

Below: Territorial Divisions of the Bell Telephone System. Adapted from maps provided by companies.

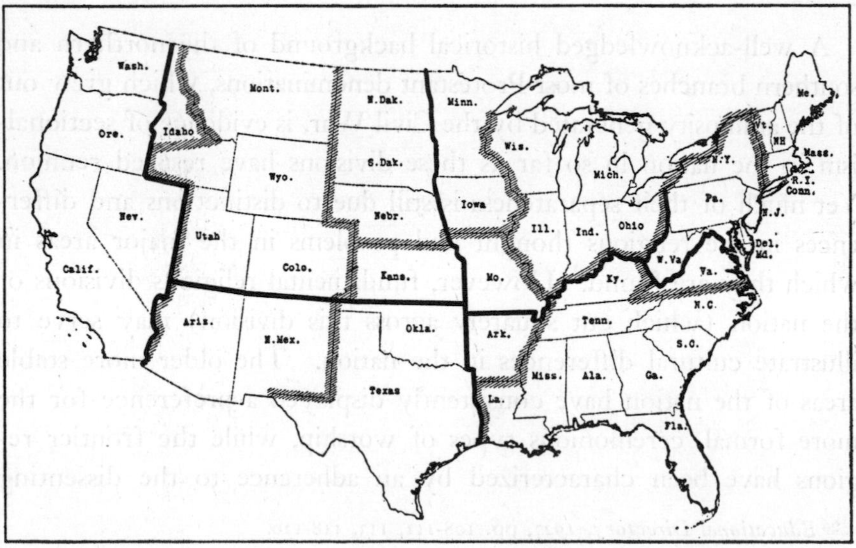

sects.[21] The appearance of the Disciples of Christ in the frontier region of western Pennsylvania soon after the beginning of the nineteenth century illustrates this more clearly but no more certainly than the preference of early Maine and Rhode Island for the tenets of the Baptist Church or the Great Valley of the Alleghenies for Presbyterianism. As the frontier has disappeared in America, there has been a noticeable tendency for these dissenting states to become more formalized and to take over many of the characteristics for the possession of which they inveighed so mightily against older churches.

Important also for purposes of this study are the regional divisions of religious denominations organized on the principle of congregational autonomy. These may be illustrated by the Southern Baptist Association, the Disciples of Christ, and the Congregational Church, in which the churches of a state or a group of states come together in a voluntary association for their various functions of wider-than-local nature. Other similar groups are the Northern Baptist Education Society; Southern Baptist Education Association; Presbyterian Education Association of the South.

The Young Men's Christian Association and the Young Women's Christian Association may be taken as types of organizations which combine religious, educational, and recreational functions, and which have also found it more feasible, if not necessary, to vary their approach and their plans of work from area to area. This is carried even to the point of regional conferences of the several working groups within the bodies, such as business men and women, industrial clubs, college students, and the high school group. Such conferences stress regional problems in their programs but emphasize the necessity for correlation with the broad aims of the national organization. Such handling of problems exemplifies the regional ideal of distinctive parts within a unified whole.

The Young Men's Christian Association has as its regional division a fourfold classification: Eastern, including Connecticut, Delaware, Maine, Maryland, Massachusetts, New Hampshire, New Jersey, New York, Pennsylvania, Rhode Island, Vermont, and West Virginia; Central, with Illinois, Indiana, Iowa, Michigan, Minnesota, North Dakota, Ohio, South Dakota, Wisconsin; Southern, embracing the states of

[21] J. M. Mecklin, *Story of American Dissent.*

Alabama, Florida, Georgia, Kentucky, Louisiana, Mississippi, North Carolina, South Carolina, Tennessee, and Virginia; and the Western, made up of Arkansas, Colorado, Kansas, Missouri, Montana, Nebraska, Oklahoma, Texas, and Wyoming.[22] As early as 1927 the Girl Scouts of America were recognizing the efficacy of regional interchange in the organizations' program. "The twelve regions, which are assuming more and more responsibility for their own affairs, are appointing regional education committees. . . . Regional Conferences and Training weeks are being held yearly, half-yearly, or more frequently in sectional forms to discuss matters of regional and national concern. . . . These regional meetings are bound to become increasingly important as the medium for national and local interchange of problems, experiences, and new ideas."[23]

Similar regional associations are those which may be called offspring of the American Library Association, in which the principal purpose is perhaps one of conference and education. The following illustrate present regional arrangements: *Middle Eastern Library Association:* includes Delaware, District of Columbia, Maryland, New Jersey, Pennsylvania, Virginia, and West Virginia. *Pacific Northwest Library Association:* includes British Columbia, Idaho, Montana, Oregon, Utah, and Washington. *Southeastern Library Association:* includes Alabama, Florida, Georgia, Kentucky, Mississippi, North Carolina, South Carolina, Tennessee, and Virginia. *Southwestern Library Association:* includes Arizona, Arkansas, Louisiana, New Mexico, Oklahoma, Texas, and Mexico.[24] Regional conferences on adult education have been explored and some regional meetings of authors and literary folk have been successful in the Far West and elsewhere.

Recreational aspects of these social institutions are standardized to a large extent, but even they are quick to capitalize upon opportunities or customs that are peculiar to the various portions of the country. Climate, of course, is an important factor in the distinctive recreational patterns of the regions. The winter sports program in the Northwest, Middle States, and Northeast in contrast to the emphasis on golf, swimming, tennis, and other year around outdoor sports of the Southeast, Southwest, and Far West illustrates this point. Although picnicking is a national custom, such outings are much more

[22] *Year Book and Official Roster, 1927, Young Men's Christian Association of Canada and the United States of America*, pp. 148-149.

[23] Elizabeth Kemper Adams and Eleanor Perry Wood, *A Five-Year Experiment in Training Volunteer Group Leaders*, pp. 9-10, 184-195.

[24] *Bulletin of the American Library Association*, 30, No. 11, pp. H-46–H-48.

numerous and much more continuous in the mild dry climates of the Southwest and the Far West than they are in the more humid areas of the nation. Migrants or visitors from these regions to other portions of the nation often comment on the infrequency of this form of recreation even in the beautifully wooded and streamed eastern portion of the country.

Hunting, another national sport, varies both in the frequency with which it can be indulged and in the nature of the game available in different parts of the country. The shooting of rabbits and other small game in the more densely populated areas is replaced by deer hunting, bear tracking, coyote running, or even the stalking of the large native American cats, such as panther and mountain lion in the West. Similarly, fishing is a gentleman's sport demanding expensive rod and reel, line, boot and basket, in the urbanized and industrialized areas where stream pollution has demanded private and public expenditures for stocking small lakes and streams; in many parts of the South as much aristocracy but much less pomp is attached to this same sport. Here the judge, the lawyers who practice in his court, the storekeeper, the plantation owner may be found in small boats, in wide streams or comfortably propped against the bole of a tree along narrow creeks, bamboo pole in hand and straw hat on head, fires of pipe and conversation burning lazily, enjoying a summer afternoon. Down the creek or in a shaded cove of a lake or even in the deeper roadside ditches along the highways may be observed tenant farmers, white or black, their children and their women, patiently squatted, dangling an earthworm from a small sapling, hoping for a nibble which will likely furnish the welcome substitution of a sun perch or catfish for "sow belly." Along the mountain creeks and stretches of the great rivers of the Far West fishing takes on still another aspect. Here the fisherman may have traveled hundreds or even thousands of miles to wet his lure and pit his strength and craftiness against that of the mountain trout or the leaping salmon.

Another form of sport which is nationwide but has also been regionalized is football. Scattered about the nation are the athletic conferences: The Big Six, the Big Ten, the Eastern, Southern, Southeastern, and Southwestern; the Gulf Coast, the Border, and the Pacific Coast, and the Rocky Mountain in between. Each has its rules of eligibility, its schedule, its attitude toward subsidization, its regulation of post-season games, its candidates for All-America in its "Snake Hip" Smith, "Bruiser" Brown, "Cannon Ball" Kelley, or "Slingin' Sam," but most important of all is its prerogative of placing a mythical crown upon the collective brow of its championship aggregation. The type of football played will vary also from region to region. In the Southwest they follow the example of the War Department in the same region and practice aerial maneuvers; in the more stable East and Middle States they keep their feet on the ground more often and depend upon power. Wet pigskins can be carried much better than they can be passed.

The actual athletic, regional divisions are: *Big Six* (Missouri Valley Intercollegiate Athletic Association): Iowa State College, University of Kansas, University of Missouri, University of Nebraska, University of Oklahoma. *Big Ten* (The Intercollegiate Conference): University of Chicago, University of Illinois, Indiana University, University of Iowa, University of Michigan, University of Minnesota, Northwestern University, Ohio State University, Purdue University, University of Wisconsin. *Border Intercollegiate Athletic Conference:* University of New Mexico, University of Arizona, Arizona State Teachers College at Flagstaff, Arizona State Teachers College at Tempe, Texas Tech, New Mexico State College of Agriculture and Mechanic Arts, Texas School of Mines. *Eastern Intercollegiate Association:* Pennsylvania, Columbia, Princeton, Dartmouth, Yale, Cornell, Harvard. *Gulf Coast Athletic Association:* New Orleans University, Xavier University, Southern University, Alcorn College, Leland University, Straight College. *New England College Conference:* University of Maine, Massachusetts State College, Rhode Island State College, Connecticut State College, University of New Hampshire, Northeastern University. *North Central Intercollegiate Conference:* North Dakota State College, North Dakota University, South Dakota State College, South Dakota University, Morningside College, Omaha University, Iowa State Teachers College. *Pacific Coast Intercollegiate Athletic Conference:* University of Oregon, Oregon State College, Washington State College, University of California, University of Washington, Stanford University, University of Montana, University of Idaho, University of California at Los Angeles, University of Southern California. *Rocky Mountain Faculty Athletic Conference:* Brigham Young University, Colorado Agricultural College, Colorado College, Colorado School of Mines, Colorado Teachers College, Montana State College, University of Colorado, University of Denver, University of Utah, University of Wyoming, Utah Agricultural College, Western State College. *Southern Conference:* Clemson College, Duke University, University of Maryland, North Carolina State College, University of North Carolina, University of South Carolina, University of Virginia, Virginia Military Institute, Virginia Polytechnic Institute, Washington and Lee University, Davidson, Furman, The Citadel, University of Richmond, Wake Forest. *Southeastern Conference:* University of Kentucky, University of Tennessee, Vanderbilt University, University of the South, Georgia School of Technology, University of Georgia, University of Florida, Mississippi University, Mississippi State College, University of Alabama, Tulane University, Louisiana State University, Alabama Polytechnic Institute. *Southern Intercollegiate Athletic Association:* Berea College, Centenary College, Centre College, College of Charleston, Eastern Kentucky Teachers College, Erskine College, Furman University, Georgetown College, Howard College, Kentucky Wesleyan College, Louisiana College, Louisiana Polytechnic Institute, Louisiana State Normal College, Loyola University (New Orleans), Mercer University, Millsaps College, Mississippi College, Mississippi State Teachers College, Middle Tennessee State Teachers College, Morehead State Teachers College, Murray State Teachers College, Newberry College, Presbyterian College, Rollins College, Southwestern, Southwestern Louisiana Institute, Stetson University, The Citadel, Transylvania College, Tennessee Polytechnic Institute, Union College, University of Louisville, University of Miami, Western Kentucky Teachers College, and Wofford College. *Southwest Athletic Conference:* Texas A. & M. College, Baylor University, The Rice Institute, University of Arkansas, University of Texas, Southern Methodist University, Texas Christian University.[25]

Climate also makes its influence felt in the type of sports in which regional representatives will excel in national competition. It is no mere accident that Southern California and Texas have produced many more than their proportionate share of top-flight tennis players, and very seldom have produced outstanding boxers or wrestlers. Budge, Wills, Jacobs, Mako, Allison, Bell, Barnes may owe as much of their fame to their opportunity to play outdoors throughout the year as they do to the coaches who instructed them. The same factors have enabled the University of North Carolina tennis team to dominate the eastern coast area from Boston to Miami. From

[25] Hugh A. McNeill, Jr. (editor), *The Blue Book of College Athletics, 1936-1937.*

Ty Cobb of Georgia and Tris Speaker of Texas to the Dean boys and Rowe of Arkansas, Hubbell of Oklahoma, Lefty Gomez and Joe Di Maggio of California, to mention only a few, baseball has drawn its heroes from the sandlots of the South and West. Even track takes on a regional flavor with emphasis on indoor in the Northeast, Middle States, and the Northwest, and on outdoor performance in the Southeast, Southwest, and Far West.

Thus in business, in education, in recreation samples chosen at random from the scores available point in one direction. Regional practice is a well-established principle of American social organization whether recognized under this name or not. Administrators, political and otherwise, have found their task simplified, their efficiency increased, the interest with the person with whom they work heightened, profit easier to secure, results simpler to attain, when they have broken a national organization into regional units whether on the basis of custom, tradition, climate, the findings of efficiency engineers, organization experts, or the empirical basis of trial and error. These regional divisions, as in the case of governmental-service areas, have usually followed state lines, or have been composed of districts and subareas marked off in accordance with states, counties, and subregional jurisdiction territories. We may next examine the basis upon which the states, subregions, and districts constitute the chief tools for regionalism.

Chapter X

TOOLS FOR REGIONALISM: STATES, SUBREGIONS, DISTRICTS

WE have already discussed briefly three major types of regions commonly advocated by specialists for functional and planning purposes. These are the natural regions, the urban-center regions, and the group-of-states regions. We have further proceeded upon the assumption that in the United States, for many reasons variously stated, the group-of-states regions can be utilized to the best advantage as major regions combining the largest degree of homogeneity in the largest number of indices for the largest number of purposes, both in historical and theoretical analysis, and in practical, workable planning. The natural regions will then constitute the fundamental subregions cutting across state boundaries and affording excellent opportunity for specialized efforts and unified attack through the co-operation of federal, state, and regional agencies and groups. We have also discussed the metropolitan area as a cultural region with its manifold implications as a tool for regional planning. We come now to examine somewhat more in detail the significance of the state in the delineation of major regions and of the national organic subregions comprehended in river valley, mountain, soil, crop, or special ecological regions.

There is no inclination here to underestimate the weakness of the states or the importance of natural regions which cut across state and county lines for specific purposes of planning or developing and conserving resources or preventing floods. There is no disposition to defend the narrow and selfish actions of the states nor to underestimate the difficulties involved in developing strong national unity through so many units as the 48 states. There appears to be no doubt whatever that in the case of the river valley area, such as the Tennessee River Valley, "nothing less than a single authority exercising at least some of the powers of government could develop and operate this unit" or that "the Federal Government, and the Federal Government alone, could operate the dams as co-ordinate units of river control." This seems a self-evident truth. The issue arises in relation to the fact that this river control is only a small part of the function of the sovereign Federal Government, organically constituted of states in the Federation.

The issue will appear by contrasting the TVA as a magnificent experiment in regional-national planning, in what is an almost perfect subregion within the greater Southeast, with the possible assumptions of the TVA as an administrative sovereign jurisdiction covering and transcending the seven states or those parts which are included within the drainage area. The issue would be made surprisingly vivid if the TVA should presume to be the major governmental region for administrative and juridical and legal functions, even for a single state, much more for the seven states. A similar illustration might be found in the case of the Dust Bowl, where manifestly remedial control can be effected only by one federal authority. Yet, historically, culturally, economically, and in many other ways it is manifest that this is only one function of the sovereign United States Government, in this particular case federated through eight or nine equally sovereign states having their own multiple other functions and jurisdictions. This, again, represents a subregional division for special purposes, in which, however, action, power to achieve results, and the democratic process must come through the major group-of-states region acting co-operatively and in advisory capacities to the end that the necessary legal provisions may be effected through the co-ordination of state, regional, and federal measures.

Manifestly, the key issue here is that of the states as units in the region or of some major regional entity which ignores, transcends, or eliminates the states from autonomy and control of many resources and activities. The emphasis, it must be repeated, is upon the states as *units* of definition or demarcation, and not on political entities as such. There is a second way in which political scientists have estimated new regional division of the nation would do away with the states. Something of this idea was presented in the previous chapter on service regions for governmental administration. It is important, however, to look further into some of the theories and postulates for the creation of governmental regions with definite boundaries, which have been advocated by writers and scholars within recent years.

Professor William B. Munro in *The Invisible Government* is a distinguished exponent of this premise. He introduces his argument by pointing out that "geography has made sectionalism inevitable in this leviathan commonwealth by differentiating the country into a corn belt, a wheat belt, a cotton belt, a desert area, a Great Lakes area, a Gulf area, and two ocean seaboards. Within their respective boundaries, their great natural regions have physical conditions which are measurably homogeneous, but the regions differ widely from one another in resources, in economic capacity, and hence in their political orientation. North Dakota and Louisiana, although under the same flag, are less alike in physical conditions than Denmark and Sicily. . . . As entities of government we accept the nation and the states, both artificial creations, and obtrusively decline to make full use of the natural divisions which the primal architect of the universe thrust in between. . . . The United States is a league of nations within a nation; it is a vast and varied union of unlike regions, each possessing a sense of distinction in interests and in point of view from all the rest. Our national future must be molded by this outstanding fact, whether we will it or no."[1] Two or three earlier popular advocates found a large and interested audience. One of these suggested the U.R.A., or the United Regions of America, in which eight regions would supplement the 48 states. These eight regions would be the New England Region, the Atlantic Seaboard Region, the Southeastern Region, the Middle Western Region, the Lower Mississippi Region, the Southwestern Region, the Colorado River Region, and the Pacific Seaboard Region. The author of this plan believes that the "present political boundaries can and must be dispensed with. Precedent and technique for such trenchant procedure are available. . . . Today most of us live and work together as units of a geographic region, and only secondarily as citizens of a state."[2] Two other illustrations of this new advocacy for sovereign regions may be cited. One is the suggestion of Professor Roy V. Peel of New York University, who recommends the

[1] William B. Munro, *The Invisible Government*, pp. 137, 151, 164.

[2] E. M. Barrows, "United Regions of America, A New American Nation," *New Outlook*, Vol. 161, pp. 17-21.

division of the country into nine regions, ignoring states in favor of reorganization by districts, industrial, economic, and metropolitan spheres of influence. His plan contemplates, therefore, a regional reorganization of the nation with regional representatives in the central body. A second recommendation is embodied in one of the "resolutions" in the chapter on "Democratic Government Today and Tomorrow" in *Democracy in Transition* by a Group of Social Scientists in Ohio State University, which is as follows:

"That an ideal solution of the problem of representation would involve the liquidation of the existing states and the substitution of regional areas more closely corresponding to actual economic and social interests."

As substantiating the plan of a slightly different nature from the group-of-states region, Burdette G. Lewis believes that "if we were starting from scratch, it would seem desirable that the country should be divided into natural rather than arbitrary and traditional areas. In other words, the country would be laid out in geographical units, each of which would comprise a section having common interests." "But," he adds, "we cannot ignore the state boundaries already existing and the fact that it would be almost impossible to persuade the states to surrender their sovereignty to the regional governments within whose geographical jurisdiction they happened to fall, even if it were proven that such action would be to the interest of the nation as a whole. The nearest approach to such an arrangement that we can reasonably look for, therefore, is the institution of organized co-operation between the states in these areas—or what is known as 'regionalism.' "

"The states of the United States," according to Mr. Lewis, "should be organized through the Compact Clause of our Federal Constitution into the following regions: (1) *The Northeastern Region,* made up of the New England and Middle Atlantic States; (2) *the Southeastern Region,* comprehending the states of the Old South and the border states, save Mississippi, Arkansas, and Missouri; (3) *the Middle South,* consisting of the states of Texas, Arkansas, Kansas, Louisiana, Mississippi, Missouri, and Oklahoma; (4) *the Middle West,* made up of the states of Nebraska, North and South Dakota, Minnesota, Wisconsin, Iowa, Illinois, Indiana, Michigan, and Ohio; (5) *the Northwestern Region,* comprehending the states of Oregon, Washington, Montana,

Idaho, and Wyoming; and (6) *the Southwestern Region*, consisting of California, Nevada, Colorado, New Mexico, Utah, and Arizona."[3]

Still another proposal for the reorganization of the Federal Government, through sovereign units different from the present 48 states, is the suggestion of Professor Charles E. Merriam and others that the American city-state may be the emerging solution for governing our great cities. This right-hand idea is in extraordinary conflict with the left-hand advocacy of fewer rather than more states and with the ideals of national unity through a harmonious co-operating federation of states. For there are even now no less than 90 metropolitan districts in which, with their surrounding areas, perhaps 50 percent of the people reside. The creation of a city-state in Illinois or New York or California might well multiply competitive regional centers and sovereign divisions of the country which would hardly harmonize with the ideals of efficiency and economy, on the one hand, or of American democracy, on the other. These suggestions are basic to the dictum of C. A. Dykstra that "If the City Fails, America Fails."[4] On the basis of conflicting sectionalism and of a conflict between the 155 American counties where 74 percent of America's industrial population live and the other 3,000 odd rural counties, the dictum might be reworded to read: "If the city succeeds, America fails."

In the further examination, therefore, of our major regional divisions, it is incumbent, first to show the exclusive place which the state holds as the key unit to regional divisions, with its corollary of district divisions and subdivisions within the state; second, to point up some of the other limitations of natural regions as administrative units; and, third, to point up the significance of subregions both for special functional analysis and planning and for providing additional tools for the major regional arrangements. Constant recapitulation is needed to sense the considerable number of vital considerations which contribute to the importance of the states in any realistic regional analysis and planning.

The first and simplest is, of course, the reality of the facts. The

[3] Burdette G. Lewis, "Regionalism, A Plan of Uniting the States More Effectively," *The Forum*, Volume 89, pp. 136, 138-139.

[4] *Survey Graphic*, XXVI, No. 12, p. 663.

states now exist and they represent also the historical unit-by-unit development of the nation from earlier seaboard to the western Pacific, through frontiers and ever changing sectional development. So, too, the states themselves utilize the subregional or district divisional approach to their own problems, and encourage the participation of thousands of citizens in their own study and planning. Thus, most states, working as totalities, seek to analyze their problems, administer their activities, and plan their development through a series of district or subregional divisions of the whole. As a matter of realistic facts, the states are experimenting today with more than four hundred such state-subdistrict units, determined on the basis of various indices of areal homogeneity, from the technical county line to the various physiographic traits. The aggregate of citizens, members of advisory and planning boards and of state departments at work would run into six figures and more. These are realistic factors which inhere in both the understanding of the nation and in the direction of its future course.

The elimination of the states would mean, of course, the junking of the great structure of American civilization as it has grown up to now, through a republican representation of federated states. This case was stated in *Southern Regions of the United States*, in which the states are represented as the warp and woof of the federal fabric. "They are the multiples of a cumulative nation. They are members of the families of historical sections and of current emerging regions. They are articulate individualists, jealous of their rights, prideful of their heritage, conscious of their autonomy. While this is especially true of the Southeast, it is likewise generally true of the nation. Yet the Federation of States, with its inevitable increasing range and power in an expanding and complex urban industrial America, we have equally and increasingly with us, constantly revivifying the problem of balance between central and local control in democratic society. It must be clear that the old state sufficiency and states' rights can no longer be effective; no more can the complete dominance of the central power. Hence, logically comes this buffer of regional arrangements to seek equilibrium between centralization of power and the doctrine and practice of states' rights, both of which still retain great vitality in the American order. If to the current national situation which also harks back to the unquestioned dominance of the states in the pre-constitutional days of the republic, we add 'the revivification of the states' rights pattern, through the Republican Party and many of the Democrats from the West and South,' it is easy to understand both the theoretical and practical significance of the state in the South in any realistic inventory of our regional status and problems. Dilemmas, however, are equally as realistic and as easy to understand. The states, too small, too historically incidental, too artificially set apart, manifestly are inadequate units for measurement or administration. Yet historically, legally, constitutionally, statistically, they are organic divisions which it is not possible to ignore as fundamental units of both appraisal and administration. The states, then, represent one horn of the national dilemma. The other extreme is the federal centralization of control, which is equally as realistic a trend as the states are historical fact. Not only, however, is the theory of the state and local control a part of the American system, but it inheres in the social objectives of democracy to develop, conserve, and give representation to each demotic unit of culture. It is a part of the doctrine of equality of opportunity which applies to local group units as well as to individuals. Thus, the revivification of states' rights and sectionalism is a logical outcome of the struggle to redefine this equilibrium between individuation and socialization. But it is more than that in that it challenges regional planning to the very practical task of achieving a more perfect union and reintegration of all parts of the nation without the old sectional conflict. The task is especially important in the light of the unevenness of our national development and of the opportunity to equalize more nearly wealth and standards of well-being in the different parts of the United States." [5]

As a matter of fact the existence and vitality of the states, as well as the natural loyalties which are part and parcel of the folk culture, illustrate the exceeding complexity of the nation and thereby the need for groupings of approximate homogeneity in terms of units that are measurable, authentic, and traditional. When we come to appraise any major region we immediately face the same problem of subregional divisions which we face in the total nation of states. And within each state there is the same problem of subdivisions; thus the need for subregional functional groupings both within the states and those which cut across state lines. Thus, the very persistence and vividness and stubbornness of state societies accentuate the need for other subregional divisions which, while recognizing the

[5] Adapted from Howard W. Odum, *Southern Regions of the United States*, pp. 533-534.

states, will transcend the states in particular and specialized economic and physiographic problems. We shall discuss the several aspects of subregional divisions subsequently. In the meantime, it is important to note the fact that the historical and cultural backgrounds of state loyalties is fundamental to all societies that have enduring stability.

Professor Giddings has illustrated the significance of these political areal units, loyalties, and adequacies in the case of the historical development of patriotism. Thus, he points out that "whether we like it or not, patriotism is a human fact. It is here, and here to stay. No fear of it, no propaganda, not even a religious drive against it, will rid us of it. But why? you ask, and I answer, Because all things in the universe, including ourselves, are made up of lesser things: they are aggregations. All living bodies, from infusoria to empires, are composite. They are not homogeneous and uniform masses of protoplasm, instincts and ideas. Our bodies are made up of organs, these of tissues. Tissues are made up of cells, cells of lesser bodies resolvable into molecules, molecules of atoms, and atoms of electrons. And in respect of such compositeness human society is no exception to the rule. There is no international society that is not made up of empires and nations. There is no nation that is not made up of federated states, as our own nation is, or of departments or provinces, as France is, or of remnants of old kingdoms, as Great Britain is; and there is no regional group that is not made up of cities, towns and hamlets. Naturally and inevitably it follows that there can be no such thing as a normal functioning of the great aggregations (with resulting happiness) unless the component groups of which they are made up are normally made up and are functioning rightly. . . ."[6]

That the states are functioning in the capacity of state planning seems apparent from the study of the recent trends in state planning and in the study of regional planning boards which utilize the states as units. It is noted also that the TVA, as well as the regional planning groups, apparently will continue to feature realistic, workable state, district, and county units.

The report of the Pacific Northwest regional planning group stresses the importance of regional planning which will conform to state and county units wherever possible. Thus, "In its definition of a region for governmental planning, the report follows the specifications which are set forth in the analysis of Regional Factors in National Planning,

[6] Franklin H. Giddings, *Patriotism*, Teachers College Bulletin, XXVI, No. 6, p. 449.

and puts a special emphasis upon the need, when considering the boundaries of regional areas, to provide for their coincidence wherever possible with whole counties and states. This emphasis is based upon the analysis of actual planning activities of the county, state, and regional planning commissions. These indicate the constant tendency of plans to require legislative and administrative action. The fruits of governmental planning, including regional planning, will not be garnered in most instances until they take the form of legislative policies and administrative behavior. On this account, it is concluded that it is easier to make certain compromises with the *ad hoc* character of problem areas than to run the danger of thwarting planning by cutting through states and counties when creating over-all state and county planning boards. It is a question of weighing the conflicting factors of functional wholeness and precision against the need for legislative and administrative action and the public's need for simplicity of structure." [7]

What these state and county lines mean in present reality may be seen from two inventories of state planning activities. One shows the subregional or district divisions of the states available for practical planning and work. The other gives a representative catalogue of the activities of state planning boards during recent years, this latter being treated in the next chapter. An approximation of representative state districts, as an index to the vitality and representative autonomy of the states, shows more than 400 districts as already being utilized.

The emphasis to be placed on these subdivisions or districts within the states is the fact that states can and do work together within their own borders, utilize local people and initiative which would be jeopardized by the elimination of the states and counties. Many typical state subregional studies and planning programs may be cited to illustrate further the significance of the states themselves in relation to the various proposed concepts which tend to ignore the states. Thus, in river valley regions themselves, nearly all of which overlap state lines, the states are of the greatest technical and practical importance. Take Kentucky, for instance, and note the studies by the University of Kentucky of natural resources and population trends of Kentucky river valleys. The viewpoint is expressed in the con-

[7] National Resources Committee, *Regional Planning, Part I—Pacific Northwest*, May 1936, pp. XI-XII.

clusion to the effect that "it may be seen that Kentucky's future is likely to be even more intimately connected with its water resources than its past. If national and regional plans are to be anything more than transitory dreams, Kentucky deserves to be in the forefront of such planning. Endowed with a fertile soil in many areas, much of it has been overworked and unwisely exploited so that the Bluegrass State will need to take more careful account of its mineral resources in the future. Especially will it need to develop a systematic program of utilization of its water and scenic resources, if the commonwealth hopes to hold its people in competition with the pulling power of industrial areas. Furthermore, the state needs to examine its hydroelectric resources with a view to enriching the rural life of the state. Farming as a way of life should be improved or else we will expect further migration of people from the state. The rural home will have to be brightened by something other than the famous Kentucky sunshine if the state is to maintain its proper place in the future of America."[8] The basis for this realistic appraisal is found in the study of seven river valleys which have great influence upon the life and labor of the people. These are the Ohio, the Tennessee, the Cumberland, the Kentucky, the Big Sandy, and the Green Valley.

Two other examples indicating the will and ability of the states to deal with river valley problems may be cited. One is that of an organization of the Ohio Valley Regional Planning Commission, which is composed of six members; the chairmen of the state planning boards of Pennsylvania, West Virginia, Ohio, Kentucky, and Indiana, and a sixth to be named by the National Resources Committee. "The Commission was formed to serve as a 'regional planning commission or board of the territory which constitutes the watershed or basin of the Ohio River.' Its functions will include the 'matter of comprehensive and directive planning' of this region, and will not include more detailed planes of planning which fall quite properly 'within the scope of administrative or operative planning, or the construction plans of specific public works or the more detailed planning of land uses which fall properly within the scope of administrative or operative planning, or the construction plans of specific public works, or the more detailed planning of land uses which fall more properly within the scope of county or city zoning.' In other words, the commission will offer

[8] J. B. Shannon, *A Survey of the Natural Resources and Population Trends of Kentucky River Valleys*. Studies in Regionalism in Kentucky, No. 1, pp. 27-28.

guidance 'toward a co-ordinated and adequate development of the region, including such matters as distribution of the uses of land for urbanization, trade, industry, habitation, recreation, agriculture, forestry or other purposes, and the efficient, adjusted and economic utilization and conservation of land, water and mineral resources.' "[9]

The second example is that of two interstate groups, reported by the South Dakota State Planning Board, in which "representatives of the State Planning Board of Minnesota, North Dakota, Montana, Wyoming, Nebraska, Iowa, and South Dakota met at Aberdeen, South Dakota, in April 1937, to consider organization of an interstate regional planning commission. Such a commission would have as its objective the co-ordination of activities bearing on common problems, especially those of an interstate nature–i.e., projects involving water rights on rivers crossing state boundaries. Whenever problems of an interstate nature arose, meetings of interested states would be called."[10] The other is the report of the same Planning Board, in November 1937, on the Red River Basin Commission. The report says, "Officials of Minnesota and the two Dakotas are planning for the development and use of water resources in this valley, which extends into three states. As an administrative unit to permit uniform planning and development, representatives of the three states have formed the Tri-State Waters Commission, through signing of a Tri-State Compact by governors of the three states. Under this compact, the three states have agreed to carry out a program for the full use and control of water in the valley, and subsequent research, study, and investigation has permitted formulation of a policy of planning that has received the approval of federal officials. Water conservation plans have been formulated for the area, including proposed projects ranging in size from small dams and lakes to relatively large reservoirs and municipal water works."[11]

It remains to point up briefly two other considerations: one, to re-emphasize the limitations of natural areas for administrative or social purposes, and the other to indicate something more of the importance of subregions to take care of areas and problems that overlap state and county boundaries. Perhaps brief and simple illustrations will suffice. To begin with an over-simplification, it would be clear that a chain store is not interested in river valley or dust

[9] "Ohio Valley Regional Planning Commission Is Formed," *Land Policy Circular*, June 1936, pp. 5-6.

[10] "Northern Great Plains Area Contemplates Regional Planning Commission," *Land Policy Circular*, June 1936, p. 7.

[11] South Dakota State Planning Board, *Progress Report*, Vol. 3, No. 18, pp. 1-2.

bowl, except in so far as the population concentration, purchasing power, and other socio-economic factors constitute the basis of its opportunity. Or, to take a larger illustration, the Appalachian Mountain Region comprehends, in New England, in New York, and in Pennsylvania many of the highest indices of civilization and wealth at the same time that the lower reaches include some of the most isolated and limited folk of the nation, to which factors are added great contrasts in climate, great distances in travel, great distinctions in culture and history, such that the test of homogeneity suggests the folly of making this an administrative and planning unit for human, cultural, political, and economic ends. The same type of illustration would be intensified if we recall that this region and other physiographic regions of America extend on up into Canada and down into Mexico, and that parallel regions are also found in Europe.

> The illustration sought may be made vivid by using Newbigin's major elements basic to her major regions. Thus, the map of North America, drawn to natural regions, gives little indication of any divisions between Canada and the United States or, in the extreme Southwest, between the United States and Mexico. Further than this, these four major elements show remarkable detailed resemblance to the major structural features of Europe, which have, of course, very little relation to political or cultural regions and administration. The four features of North America are: "the Canadian Shield, corresponding to the Baltic Shield of Europe; the Appalachian Highland, corresponding to the ancient fold mountains of Europe; the Interior Plains, corresponding to the Russian Plain and its westward continuation into East Anglia across North Germany; the Pacific Cordillera, corresponding to the young folded mountains of Europe." [12]

We have already called attention to the lack of economic or cultural homogeneity, suitable for reasonable administrative jurisdiction, in such a natural region as the Mississippi River Valley or the Ohio River Valley, in which Dayton, Ohio, and Dayton, Tennessee, for instance, would be co-ordinate units. We may cite finally a great geographer's regions of the United States, predicated upon the joint indices of people and resources. There are the 29 regions of J. Russell Smith in his *Men and Resources,* which is a study of North

[12] Marion I. Newbigin, *A New Regional Geography of the World,* p. 275.

America and its place in world geography. The limitations to any plan of making these natural areas basic to governmental administration appear, for instance, in *The Hudson Valley, Great Canal Belt*, running up and across New York, touching three or four other states and dividing completely the farthest Northeast from the rest of the country. It is a great natural belt, however, as a frame of reference for study and for commerce. Denoted by Professor Smith as "a thoroughfare and a string of towns," it would be manifestly absurd as an administrative entity in the present America. Or, we might cite a dozen others of those listed in Chapter IV to show the excellence of natural regions for special purposes and their limitation for composite cultural, economic, and political units in the present or future American civilization. Thus, the Appalachian Plateau and the Upper Ohio Valley are basic to "forest and fuel," but not much as administrative units; so, too, his southwestern intermountain areas are "great distances, few people"; his *Puget Sound and Willamette Valley* he terms an "American region with an English climate."

> Finally, as pointing up the limitations of the river valley regions for planning, the following opinion from *Regional Factors in National Planning and Development* is of significance: "that except for engineering works, the drainage basin is the poorest type of region to deal with. This is true (1) because of the extreme irregularity of drainage basins; (2) because they are topographical belts; (3) because the upper part of one drainage basin is likely to be more similar to the upper part of its neighbor across the divide than it is to the lower part of its own watershed. I am not in favor of using the watershed for any other type of planning than engineering plans dealing with power, navigation, and flood control, because this geographic peculiarity has not been as determinant of homogeneous areas as have soil, climate, and type of original settlement." [13]

As for making new city states to transcend present states in the interest of efficiency and harmony, it is of the greatest importance not only to know how many of the metropolitan areas would demand to be so constituted, but which ones, and what their relation would be to one another and to the nation. Thus, is Los Angeles or San Francisco so constituted? Or what must be the relation of the city

[13] National Resources Committee, *Regional Factors in National Planning and Development*, December 1935, p. 148.

states in a national political campaign for a Farmer-Labor Party? Or in conflict between city states and rural states, what of the strikes and sit-downs of the producers of foods and their delivery? It is understood of course that the city state is intended to integrate and develop the rural regions round about it; yet it is exactly this urban-regional dominance that regionalism seeks to counteract. If these seem over-simplified and elementary presumptions, they nevertheless reflect elemental factors in the structure of the nation and of enduring balance between opposing forces. What is needed, rather, is that which Mayor La Guardia, in December 1937 was advocating in the balancing of people and the adjustment of rural and city problems together. The city state apparently is not the answer.

Finally, we come to the point of appraising subregions as essential tools for planning. These are of two sorts. One is the major subregion of national import which cuts across state lines, but which comes within the general bounds of the major group-of-states regions. The second is the subdivision of states which we term districts for purposes of definition and administration. Of the major subregions, there are again two sorts, namely, the natural regions, such as river valley and land-use, and those other technically defined subregions according to economic, social, or other indices. We have already illustrated the natural regions, so that it remains only to illustrate further with subregions fabricated for special purposes of study and planning, where state lines need to be crossed in order to construct the complete homogeneities needed. We cite two examples, those of T. J. Woofter, Jr., for the Southeast, and those of Raymond D. Thomas for the Southwest.

The basis of adequate major subregions is well stated by Woofter. "Physiography has had much to do with regional differentiations, but physiographic peculiarities alone are not always sufficient to determine the boundaries. Soil and topography do not always coincide with belts of rainfall and temperature and all of these are often cross-sectioned by industrial belts or population classes. Therefore, while physical differences are the dominant factor underlying the subregional divisions of the South, other factors have been given weight in the final determination of the boundaries of these areas.

"The task of demarking and describing areas could of course be carried down to a very fine point, to such an extent that several hundred slightly differing localities could be distinguished. This, however, would eventually lead to the confusion of incidental with essential social differences. It was, therefore, decided to define only such subregions as would be large enough to constitute important socioeconomic entities and at the same time exhibit sufficiently different social characteristics from their neighboring regions to warrant the distinction between them. . . .

"To delineate a subregion geographically implies the ability to draw its boundaries upon a map. This is often as arbitrary a process as the fixing of the boundary between two states by the meandering of a river or the crest of a range of mountains. It was the objective of the method of the present study to fix the boundaries of the regions so that they would include as homogeneous a group of counties as was possible without reducing the number of counties too greatly.

"County lines themselves constitute arbitrary boundaries. True subregional boundaries would divide counties by soil or geographic areas regardless of the political boundary. . . .

"It was considered advisable to follow county lines in defining the larger subregions because the statistics which determine the basic indices of difference are compiled by counties, and it is difficult to secure definite enough information by lesser units to warrant the fixing of boundaries within counties.

"The counties at the core of each region are well differentiated from those at the core of the neighboring regions. The only difficulty in allocating counties arose in the fringe of counties between two cores, i.e., the difficult question was to decide which region should include these border line counties. The statistical procedure adopted was to allocate the counties along this border to the region in such a way that the variability of each region would remain at a minimum, i.e., the median was calculated for the core counties in respect to each of the fourteen indices of population, agriculture, trade, and industry."[14]

Although Woofter's subregions have been widely used and commended, no other major regions of the United States have as yet been so divided. The nearest approach appears to be an adaptation by Raymond Thomas of geographic-economic subregions of the Southwest and the agricultural regions of the nation previously described in the chapter on The Rural Nation. Two of the chief points of emphasis here are: First, there is a larger number of regions possible for special purpose under the plan of making subregions

[14] T. J. Woofter, Jr., "The Subregions of the Southeast," *Social Forces,* Vol. 13, pp. 44-45.

special units for special purposes. This is equally true of natural subregions and of socio-economic subregions. The second point is, of course, this very element of special objectives to be attained through a more specialized and differentiated technique than could be had in the case of major composite regions combining a very large degree of homogeneity in a very large number of indices susceptible of multiple utilization. Thus, the twin motivation of state function and subregional specialization proves to be effective in the largest number of instances commensurate with American conditions.

One of the best indices indicating the practicability of maintaining effectively the states and their autonomies is found in the actual working of those regional planning groups which so far have become articulate. We have cited certain interstate groups which are now on the eve of experimenting. We have pointed out the policy of the TVA, which has all along sought co-operation from all state and local agencies at the same time that it was a federal agency and was seeking its expert assistance wherever it could be found. Finally, the conclusion of the Pacific Northwest Regional Committee may well be cited as a sort of recapitulatory statement of a sound viewpoint and practice.

This statement, following the areal definitions involved in sections 1 and 2, continues: "3. That in the case of this region the Columbia River system is a tie of very great importance between the states which it drains and in particular that it is a close link between the parts of Oregon and Washington divided by the mountain mass of the Cascade range; 4. That flexibility of regional planning boundaries as well as flexibility of lesser planning area boundaries can and should be secured by interregional and inter-area co-ordinating devices without sacrificing the need for unity of regional, state, and county planning organizations; 5. That the greatest menace to effective regional action in the Pacific Northwest comes from tensions due to local rivalry which frequently have aligned one city against another, the small town against the metropolis and one irrigation district against its fellow." [15]

[15] National Resources Committee, *Regional Planning, Part I—Pacific Northwest*, May 1936, p. XI.

Chapter XI

TOOLS FOR REGIONALISM: REGIONAL PLANNING

WE have called attention to the prevailing tendency in the past for students and experts and the specially interested public to interpret regionalism as being synonymous with limited or special phases of the subject. Among these were metropolitan regionalism, literary regionalism, and sectionalism. We come now to a fourth concept which, in addition to a similar usage, may serve to recapitulate the characteristics and functions of regionalism. In addition to comprehending for many students the major fields and interests of regionalism, the rise and incidence of *regional planning* parallels that of metropolitan planning, such that even now regional planning more often than not connotes metropolitan planning.

Manifestly, urban planning is not the chief essence of the larger regional planning which after all must be envisaged in terms of the larger regional concept as opposed to metropolitan regionalism in its narrow historical sense. In the joint indices, therefore, of regionalism and regional planning we may point up a sort of recapitulation, without at the same time repeating too much of what has gone before. This recapitulation will be cumulative and inherent in the treatment of regional planning as the chief instrument of dynamic regionalism. It will suffice here, therefore, to cite a single authentic and comprehensive appraisal of regionalism in contrast to the specialized urban regional concept. Professor John Gaus' statement comprehends the whole picture when he says that regionalism is the basis for "the encouragement of a richer and more varied life for the Nation, whereby the peculiar characteristics, resources, and contributions of the major sections of the country can be protected from invasions, exploitation, and suppression by ill-considered and hasty national policies." [1]

> Manifestly, again, therefore, planning for such regional entities can "be successfully achieved only in relation to national integration and inter-regional adjustments. By the same token, national social planning must be based upon regional analysis and functioning, giving logical values to regional differentials and distributions. Realistic and stable results can be attained only through approximate delimitation and definition of the region on the basis of scientific and functional analysis, reclassifying border areas, and providing for adequate functional subregional divisions to meet the practical needs of overlapping areas and specialized activities. In this regional classification there is need for more approximate uniformity among the many national and local boards, agencies, and consultants, and less accidental and arbitrary allocation of areas and functions. The objectives of the new planning envisage no Utopias, yet they do look toward the rehabilitation of the people, toward the reconstruction of regional economy, toward increasing the region's revenue to the nation as well as its own wealth, and toward general regional, cultural adjustment. . . . Such emphasis ought to serve as a new regional motivation as well as to point the way to tangible, visible next steps." [2] In all this the several levels of regional planning subsequently catalogued, such as urban and rural, state and county, land and water, economic and cultural, and the others, will constitute their respective units in the whole, and the unit tools of states, cities, counties, districts, zones, and the like will be fully utilized.

It is necessary, however, before proceeding further to the discussion of regional planning to indicate clearly the nature and scope of the planning involved. Here, again, it is interesting to note that like regionalism, planning had its inception in city planning and has developed into a broader philosophy and political concept, as well as embodying techniques of physical designing of landscape and community. Thus, planning not only now connotes national planning, but social planning as a companion tool for machines and technology. Like regionalism, too, and even more so, the term planning, by its multiple usage, means many things. However, it is possible to indicate exactly what is meant by the term as it relates primarily to

[1] Quoted in *Planning for City, State, Region, and Nation*, p. 107.

[2] Adapted by G. T. Renner, "Regional Planning: Incentives and Objectives in Regional Planning," *Planning for City, State, Region, and Nation*, p. 108 from Howard W. Odum, *Southern Regions of the United States*, pp. 187, 189.

American regionalism as utilized in the present volume. In contrast to this meaning must be set up, of course, other usages for the purpose of classification and comparison.

Like regionalism, planning here connotes the composite and comprehensive rather than merely the specialized and technical. As such, therefore, it assumes a program which, on the one hand, approximates the largest number of technical, workable ways of attaining the largest number of desired ends commensurate with existing societal arrangements and in harmony with the largest number of groups and agencies in the service of the greatest good to the greatest number. By the same token it assumes flexible arrangements free from the largest possible number of contradictions and conflicts. This means, of course, that such a concept and practice provides for participation by governmental and civic agencies in the promotion of effective political, economic, and cultural arrangements for all sorts of planning—"economic," "social," and "physical" on the various levels of both natural and human resources. This means, again, that participation is assumed on the part of federal, regional, state, county, city governments as well as by federal, regional, state, and local public and voluntary planning boards or commissions, the nature of which will be described subsequently. The above is not a general designation, but, on the contrary, denotes a very specific characteristic of the planning concept. That is, *social planning, including national, regional, urban, state, community, on whatever levels of natural resources, connotes design, specific technical, workable ways of doing things set in priority schedules of time and spatial relationships, as opposed to the mere ideological, educational, exhortative general motivation inherent in metaphysical theories or philosophical "isms" and "systems."*

This is not to say that there are not many authentic, specialized concepts of planning which must be accepted as scientific within the framework of their premises and purposes. Of course, there is economic planning and the planned economic order in which inhere control by the government of economic processes and which subsume "collective control or suppression of private activities of production and exchange."[3] Of course there are other technical aspects such as

[3] Cf. Lionel Robbins, *Economic Planning and International Order*, p. 8.

planned money for the control of the capital market, and "planned society" for the direction and control of human migration as well as the use and movements of capital and materials. It is possible to accept the Lorwin definition of economic planning and yet point up the more comprehensive meaning of social planning as used in the present appraisal. "A planned economy," he says, "may [in general terms] be defined as a system of economic organization in which all individual and separate plants, enterprises, and industries are treated as co-ordinated units of a single whole for the purpose of utilizing all available resources to achieve the maximum satisfaction of the needs of a people within a given interval of time."[4] Still nearer to the composite planning for the region is Lewis Mumford's statement: "The main lines of economic regionalism are by now becoming pretty plain. Regionalism does not aim at the economic self-sufficiency of any region: that would be an absurdity in a civilization that is dependent upon such localized resources as rubber, iron, copper and petroleum. What it does aim at is a state of economic balance; a state in which the population of a region will be distributed with respect to its fundamental resources, in which agriculture, the extractive industries, manufacture and trade will be co-ordinated, in which the size of cities will be proportioned to open spaces and recreation areas and placed in sound working relation with the countryside itself."[5]

It is the assumption, furthermore, of this work that the question of whether we shall have planning or not is, on the one hand, an academic one or, on the other, an undebatable one. For, like regionalism, planning has long since become a reality in the American scene, now a popular terminology widely and variously used, now a term of opprobrium even more diversified in its usage. The realistic approach can neither attempt to capitalize planning as utopian flight from reality or make it synonymous with despotic government or "isms" subversive to American civilization.

Mr. David E. Lilienthal, director of the Tennessee Valley Authority, pointed up something of realistic planning in his address at the 1937 fall meeting of the American City Planning Institute. "There is," he said, "something about planning that is attractive to that type of person who has a yen to order the lives of other people. It has an attraction for persons of a vague and diffuse kind of mind given to grandiose

[4] Lewis L. Lorwin, *The Problem of Economic Planning*, p. 4.

[5] Lewis Mumford, "The Theory and Practice of Regionalism," *Sociological Review*, Vol. 20, pp. 25-26.

pictures not of this world. Planning is a subject that attracts those who are in a hurry, but are rather hazy as to where they want to go so rapidly, or whether people want to scurry along with them. But planning and those charged with responsibility for the formulation and execution of plans must, above all, be realistic and pragmatic. Effective planners understand and believe in people, in the average man. The average man is constantly in the mind of the effective planning technician. Planners, technicians and administrators alike, must recognize that they are not dealing with philosophical abstractions nor mere statistics or engineering data or legal principles. In the last analysis, in democratic planning it is human beings we are concerned with. Unless our plans show an understanding and recognition of the aspirations of men and women, we will fail. Those who lack human understanding and cannot share the emotions of the masses of men can hardly forward the objectives of realistic planning."

It is possible to set up a simple framework of features which characterize planning, in addition to those already cited. Perhaps we may emphasize four characteristics of planning which comprehend the principles and practices involved. The first of these may be denoted *specifications*. That is, there must be designation of particulars with written description of what we are seeking and they must be realistic and must be based on facts. They must involve standards and they must keep in mind not only the task to be done but the people and the means which we have with which to do it. Another way of emphasizing the significance of specifications is to say that mere generalities are not enough. The second characteristic of planning is that there must be *integration and co-ordination* of effort so that each part or department may work with every other unit or department. Planning sees the problem in terms of its units but with each unit properly related to every other unit and to the whole. Planning requires, in the third place, that we must have *skills and techniques* ample for the purpose in hand. Preachment is not enough, exhortation is not enough, and good will is not enough. There must be skilled and technical ways adequate for success. The fourth characteristic inherent in planning is that of a *long-time program and procedure* adapted to its setting. This setting, whether community, state, or nation, has itself grown up over a long period of years and must be understood in historical aspects as well as in terms of present dilemmas.

There is yet, however, one basic principle which underlies that sort of planning implied in the framework of American institutions. Like regionalism again, the key to planning is found in the need for balance and equilibrium. Whereas regionalism is a tool for attaining equilibrium in specialized ends, planning finds equilibrium and balance the basic principle upon which its major premises are based. Some of the points of imbalance or the need for balance appear self-evident. The first of the major foci of equilibrium, balance, and margins, around which cluster the critical problems of social emergency, may be stated as a new equilibrium between individuation and socialization, between individualism and co-operative effort, between variation and standardization. A second is the organic problem of balance between the stateways and the folkways, between legislation and education, between coercive procedures and voluntary co-operation. A third is equilibrium between the state and other social institutions of a free people. To what extent is the state, with its increasingly dominant role, to be supreme over industry, for instance? Other points of imbalance include balance and margin between nation and states, between federal aggregates and power and regional autonomies, between regional contribution to the nation and sectional advantage, in which are involved various aspects of regional resources and their use, equalization of opportunity, margins of abundance and scarcity, efficiency and deficiencies. There is new equilibrium between mass rule and representative government, between geographic and occupational representation, between minority propaganda and majority rights; and again between politician and expert, between ignorance and inefficiency over against training and economy. Also, there are the marginal measures of further centralization and decentralization in other aspects of American life: corporate control and individual rights, the limits to bigness and monopoly, big business and small industry. Then, there is the balance between resources and their exploitation, which challenges a new sort of planning, as do those balances between optimum programs of production and maximization of efforts, between production and distribution, and between abundance economy and scarcity economy. These balances, in turn, are interrelated with an equilibrium between technology and humanity, machines and men, science and common sense, artificial society and folk-capacity. These equilibriums, in turn, are inseparably related to the need for a new sort of balance between work and leisure. What sort of equilibrium can be worked out for an America, long conditioned to appraise work as the supreme virtue, now suddenly commanded to seek more leisure and less work? Other points of tension and imbalance include those between industry and agriculture, between agrarian culture and urban life, and between land

and people. Still other points of tension and imbalance are those between ownership and use of wealth, profits and price, money and credit, security and dependency, capitalistic economy and the socialistic order. In all of these are involved the orientation and constantly changing balance between the old and the new, transition and continuity, attitudes and values, science and morality, technology and tradition. Here, again, the attainment of equilibrium and balance is to be the test of reality over artificiality, of practical instrumentation over supertechnology.[6]

Within this general framework of American planning it is possible to distinguish two major types for the purposes of further definition. One is the general composite planning by state planning boards, of regional group-of-states planning groups, of national composite planning of the whole, such as Charles W. Eliot, II, executive officer of the National Resources Committee, characterized as "a peculiarly American custom based on an enthusiastic belief in the ability of democracy to utilize intelligence." For this type of planning, Frederick Delamo, sometime chairman of the National Resources Committee, has urged the need for "intelligent citizen understanding and support" and has characterized it as a clearing house for research which has national significance, but with the allied emphasis upon state and regional responsibility.

Mr. Eliot points up the same sort of emphasis when he says: "The National Resources Committee has always believed that the very nature of planning makes decentralization essential. We must have the participation and understanding of the people back home in planning to meet the problems of a democracy. Through its district chairman, through regional planning commissions, and with the co-operation of such agencies as the Council of State Governments, the Committee has aided interstate planning efforts in the Pacific Northwest, New England, the Ohio Valley, the Delaware Valley, the Upper Rio Grande Valley, the Red River of the North, the Central Northwest, and other areas."[7]

The second type of planning is more specific and comprehends definite plans and their execution for such definite areal problems as

[6] Adapted from Howard W. Odum, "A Sociological Approach to National Social Planning," *Sociology and Social Research*, XIX, No. 4, pp. 307-308.
[7] "What Is This Planning?" *New Horizons in Planning*, p. 41.

rivers and floods and power within river valley areas, forestry and conservation within park areas, soil conservation within the Dust Bowl, and other technical and engineering tasks for which specifications and provisions are concrete and for which special authorization is required. Even, here, however, the planning assumes no governmental fiat from central headquarters, but a co-operative arrangement provided through new legislation adapted to the states and regions with initiative and effort from within the region involved. Nevertheless, this sort of planning assumes more design and control of government than has hitherto been available and represents a departure from precedent and a different type of planning from that described above. This second type may, of course, be projected within and by the regional and state planning boards as a part of their general program and philosophy. The point is, however, that in neither case is there complete federal planned society or anything approaching the planned economy of the Communist or Fascist order.

> Illustrative of this sort of planning is the statement of the National Resources Committee: "The selection of the area and its planning center should be made with reference to the general coincidence of major planning problems, such as land use, water use, and public works, with the regional sentiment in a given area. Since these problems differ in the extent of the area which they affect, the boundaries of the area should be flexible rather than fixed, and the states with which co-operation must be sought will vary somewhat with the particular problem under discussion. The aim is always to interrelate the various federal agencies with state and other governments concerned with the planning problems of the given area, so that a comprehensive view of the operations of them all may be encouraged at the planning center most satisfactory to them all. It is impossible to predict how changes in such basic factors as population, the utilization of natural resources, transportation, industrial development will affect common regional problems and consciousness in the future. It is all the more important, therefore, that these changes be reflected as sensitively as may be necessary in the planning of national development, so that national policies will help and not impede the efforts of the states to carry out effective programs within their own regions. Frequently, the states may be acting through interstate agencies also." [8]

[8] National Resources Committee, *Regional Factors in National Planning and Development*, December 1935, pp. vii-viii.

From these characterizations of planning, we continue with some of the attributes of regional planning to be followed by a sort of preview of the different "levels" of planning from both the administrative and the physical-functional aspects, and subsequently by suggestions as to form and functions of national and regional planning boards. These, then, will be appraised, finally, in Chapter XXV, in which we discuss "problems and strategy." In all cases the purpose is to present, so far as possible, representative and comprehensive viewpoints in terms of authentic specialists alongside the sources from which the appraisals come.

Again, Lewis Mumford points up regionalism as the composite tool for the geographer, the economist, the sociologist, the citizen, and the planner. Instead of considering special phases or products or resources or disciplines he insists that "we think of the region as a whole, and we realize that in each geographic area a certain balance of natural resources and human insitutions is possible, for the finest development of the land and the people. . . . Industry, education, housing, culture, recreation, are not separable activities; they exist within a regional complex; and this complex changes, as the land itself changes from coastal plain to upland, from valley bottom to mountain top. To recognize these regional wholes is the business of the geographer and the sociologist; to plan for their development and better relationship is the task of the regional planner; to live in and through the region itself, to make the most of its possibilities and to bring it up to the highest pitch of appropriate culture—this is the effort of regionalism." [9]

The test of regionalism and of regional planning, both in its meanings and implications, can be found in illustrations that approximate reality. We have already referred often to the Tennessee Valley Authority as a combination of regionalism and regional planning, American style. The National Resources Committee in its excellent volume on *Regional Factors in National Planning and Development* has catalogued most of the current attempts toward various forms of regional planning, from which any study of regionalism must draw heavily. Perhaps a single example of the philosophy and procedures of a regional planning board will suffice to illustrate further the main thesis of the present work. Because the New England States

[9] Lewis Mumford, "Regionalism and Irregionalism," *Sociological Review*, Vol. 19, No. 4, p. 279.

approximate both a natural and historical homogeneity and because the New England Planning Board was a logical outgrowth of official state planners from six states getting together for co-ordinating and developing plans, this example is a good one to select.

James M. Langley, Chairman of the New Hampshire State Planning and Development Commission, has stated the basis and ideals upon which such a regional board rests. "This regional organization," he says, "violates no governmental bounds. It creates no new governmental units. It is suspended somewhere between local and federal arenas. It recognizes the joint sovereignty of the states and the federal establishment. It has no powers whatever. Its duties are whatever it may determine. Its authority is only that of persuasion.

"New England has always been considered a natural region, yet when its economy is studied it is found that regional and state bounds are violated by the bounds of watersheds and by the bounds of its agricultural, industrial, mineral, forestry and recreational areas. The arbitrary political bounds are no more confounding than the criss-crossing of the bounds of its economic areas.

"Practically there is no likelihood that state bounds will be altered, and despite the pronounced and continued trend towards vestment of all political authority in a central government abandonment of state bounds as limits of some sovereign jurisdiction remains a very remote possibility. So New England reasons that because planning must be made effective by governmental action the states should be recognized as proper planning areas and that interstate planning problems should be met by agreement or compact and through the promotion of better regional and interstate public relations, with federal participation kept at a minimum.

"New England has no illusions about discovery in this generation or any other of some profoundly simple solution to all the problems of mankind. It does not consider planning a final answer. It recognizes in the word two characteristics, principally—economy and co-ordination. The regional planning commission is essentially a means to better co-ordination. Economy depends upon the extent to which state and local legislatures and administrative agencies accept recommended plans, and the degree to which these plans can be said to be economical." [10]

The realistic meanings of regionalism are nowhere more clearly manifest than in the story of the rise and evolution of regional plan-

[10] James M. Langley, "Why Regional Planning?" *New Horizons in Planning*, pp. 150-151.

ning. Aside from the general historical and theoretical aspects treated in Part II of the present volume, the emergence of regional planning is reflected in a logical series of causes and effects, in addition to the special American historical episodes previously discussed as sectionalism and regionalism. George T. Renner discusses regionalism as a *motif* for planning, in which several "steps" seem to offer a logical sequence to the several incentives inherent in the present situation. Thus, he thinks the first step is to identify regionalism, the second is to demarcate the regional area, the third is to determine the needs of the area, and the fourth is to implement the plan in terms of state and federal sovereignties.[11]

> Renner sees six incentives to regional planning: The *first* is that "the constantly increasing complexity of society demands a constantly increasing service of government to the individual and to the group. . . . *Second*, large-scale physical development and conservation of resources are becoming increasingly urgent. . . . *Third*, it has been suggested that the planning and execution of programs of resource development and conservation be done by blocs of states actuated from a local center, such as Boston for the New England States or Atlanta for the Southern States. . . . This regional principle is also strengthened in reverse order by the fact that the Federal Government finds its bureau functions can be administered in the field more satisfactorily from subcenters than from Washington directly. . . . *Fourth*, economic planning, precipitated largely by the 'depression,' has also provided an urge toward the regional approach. . . . *Fifth*, the growing manifestation of the social phenomenon known as regionalism has also played a part. Regionalism arises out of a spontaneous loyalty to area. . . . The *sixth* and last incentive to regional planning is the deliberate encouragement and systematic stimulation by professional planners."[12]

In the way of substantiating this catalogue of incentives and also of illustrating the problems which have made regional planning vivid to the public we may catalogue the major "levels" of planning as they have recently been emerging in the nation, and then point up the regional aspects involved. It is possible to focus upon planning efforts on two types of levels. One might be called the specialized

[11] George T. Renner, "Regional Planning: Incentives and Objectives in Regional Planning," *Planning for City, State, Region, and Nation*, pp. 106-108.
[12] *Ibid.*, pp. 106-107.

functional level, such as land planning, water planning, planning and conservation of mineral resources, wild life, forestry; planning for communication and transportation; general economic planning and cultural and social planning. The other may be thought of as on an administrative-functional level, such as national planning, regional planning, state planning, and on down through the other administrative units, such as urban and metropolitan, county and rural, community and neighborhood. In all of these the nature and extent of planning, and especially the regional aspects, may be illustrated by the specific problems and areas of planning effort involved.

Illustrations are numerous enough to make adequate selections. *Water planning* comprehends *rivers, lakes, coast line, shores and harbors. Rivers and streams* comprehend: *Flood control* through various methods of large and small dams and reservoirs, reforestation and planting and the like. . . . *Irrigation* through dams and the planning for arid regions of fertile but dry land. . . . *Navigation* with the various elements involved, such as deepening and clearing of river beds, planning for river routes, freight rates, Lake to Gulf and multiple smaller routes. . . . *Power* through the construction of dams and distribution of electricity. . . . *Soil surface conservation*, such as erosion in the hills and sand in the bottom lands and river beds. . . . *Fish* through special stocking of streams, protection from pollution, recreation and game aspects. . . . *Water fowl* through special territorial and regional conservation and development. . . . *Water pollution* through planning in relation to industries and municipalities. . . . *The* two *other* major areas are those of providing adequate water supply for communities and recreation in parks, playgrounds, and in special areas. In addition to rivers and streams, water planning involves a possible recapitulation of many of the above points as they relate to *lakes and ocean fronts*, and especially with reference to recreation and fishing.

When we come to *land planning*, the catalogue of vital areas of planning reveals a similar large number, such as *land* use, which in turn applies to city and county, zoning and reallocation, marginal and submarginal lands and other aspects. So, too, *soil erosion* is a major problem alongside *soil improvement*, *forestry*, *parks*, all of these then being often closely related to minerals of coal, gas, oil, iron, bright metals and others dug from the land. Again, planning for *wild life*, flora and fauna, has become a major problem in modern America.

There are then the *technical* areas of planning, such as *communication* and *transportation*, highways, byways, railroads and freight rates, bus and truck, regulation and development, air routes, telephone and telegraph, regulation of public utilities and publishers and theater agreements and the like. On the larger level of economic planning there are a dozen major fields, such as planning for general property, equilibrium between industry and agriculture, crop control, distribution of wealth, modification of capitalistic competition, planned distribution and population, planned money, taxation and finance, regulation of hours and wages, adjustment procedures for capital and labor, regulation of working conditions.

So, too, in the area of social and cultural planning, there are public welfare and relief, social security, public health, public education, population planning, library and recreation, and the various problem areas, communities, and metropolitan areas.

It must be clear that in most of these areas of planning the territorial or regional aspects are fundamental both in the definition of the problem and in the administrative procedures necessary to successful planning. Illustrations are almost as numerous as cases. In Chapter IV, we have pointed out the regional significance and nature of water planning—floods in the Northeast and Middle States and Southeast; irrigation in the Northwest, Southwest, and Far West. Power and water supply, common problems to all, yet have regional aspects which determine the nature and outcome of planning programs. The New England lakes differ from the Great Lakes, the Florida Coast from New England, the eastern and southern mountains from the western. So, too, in planning for erosion control, for crop control, for parity programs for the farmer, the essence of planning is always the adaptation to the regional situation. Regional differentials also are fundamental factors in economic planning in industry and transportation and in the areas of interstate commerce.

The second *level* of planning is reflected in the administrative procedures required for the attainment of successful results. These levels may be envisaged in terms of planning boards set up for work in each of the respective levels from the top down to the smallest unit. These planning boards will be discussed at length subsequently, so that it will suffice here merely to look at the several levels of planning with a view to noting the relation of the several units to the whole fabric of American planning. Thus, the national planning board is set up as the major framework through which state planning boards and regional planning boards will function, with the regional planning boards being as numerous as are the major natural subregions set up or the major group-of-states regions. With the framework of the state planning boards would come county planning and special functional problem planning, while urban and metropolitan planning stand out as integral units in themselves within which community and neighborhood planning may be effected.

> The further illustration of this twofold range and "level" of planning may be seen from a summary of Charles W. Eliot, II, in *Planning Broadcasts* for July 1937, in which he points out the cumulative product of unit planning, which runs into the hundreds of cases. "From small beginnings—from experience in our own backyards—people have grown accustomed to the idea of arranging what we have for better use and more pleasure. We have found that our best use of our own 'backyard' depended on what our neighbors did with theirs, and so we got into planning groups of houses, subdivisions or neighborhoods. We found our neighborhoods were not the only ones in the city—we must have city planning. We found that the developments in one city affected its neighbor, and so, we have gone from linking the relationship between city and city, to county and county, from state to state, to region to region, and so to national planning. A recent check by the National Resources Committee shows that over 1,700 towns and cities have developed some form of planning or zoning to promote the 'good neighbor' policy within our cities and to protect investments in homes and business. Some 1,200 cities and towns have continuing planning boards for necessary adjustments in their zoning ordinances and to develop major thoroughfare plans, proposals for playgrounds and parks, to keep pushing for decent housing conditions, and to develop civic consciousness concerning all the problems of our physical environment. The growth of these local planning agencies has practically all come in the last twenty-five or thirty years; but city planning is not new—it is just renewed consciousness of the problems which we must solve if life in our cities is to be a true expression of our ideals for American civilization." [13]

Manifestly, the type of regional planning proposed presupposes the co-operation of states, subregions, and districts as previously implied. Subsequently, we shall illustrate with types of regional planning boards, in which both federal and state representatives combine to

[13] *Planning Broadcasts*, A Bulletin of the American Planning and Civic Association, July 1937, p. 20.

make the regional medium. This implies, further then, the effective working of state planning boards, from whose official members ex-officio representatives would participate in the regional planning. As a matter of fact, one of the distinctive records of the depression era has been the establishment and work of more than forty state planning boards. The nature of their work illustrates, again, the functional levels of planning, although for the most part "plans" more than planning predominate. Nevertheless, a glance at the nature and range of their "paper" plans and actual accomplishments will indicate both what is being done and what the problem is. In our previous chapter, we insisted that these achievements are enough to justify the encouragement and support of state planning boards in contradistinction to river valley regions as the unit of regional planning. The more than one thousand units bear witness to this.[14]

While the most notable result of the planning movement appears to be found in state planning, with no less than 46 states having some sort of arrangement, there are other measurable evidences of progress. One is the continuation of city planning with an estimated 1,700 cities with some sort of planning or zoning and some 1,200 cities or towns which have planning boards reported. In addition to these, there have been experiments in rural zoning and in subdistricts for state and rural planning. In addition, still further, to these units which may be used in the fabric of the total regional concept, there have been a number of realistic, regional approaches through actual boards. The National Resources Committee has issued several reports which illustrate the various types. The Pacific Northwest and the New England Planning Commission's reports represent the group-of-states regional boards. The St. Louis area and the Washington-Baltimore area represent types of metropolitan district planning. Others are reflected in the Columbia Basin Report, in the river valley studies and reports, and in the Tennessee Valley Authority as well as the proposed Seven River Valley Authorities proposed by the President for consideration in the extra session of 1936.

Manifestly, regional planning must be a complex affair, and by the same token a major tool for economic and social development of the nation. With reference to general purpose and motivation,

[14] Cf. special reports from state planning boards.

two chief functions appear: One is, of course, to see that the states broaden their concepts and policies beyond the narrow states' rights attitude into regional co-operation with each other and with the nation at large. This itself is ample purpose to justify the regional movement. The other is, contrariwise, to guarantee to the states and regions that measure of self-help, self-direction, and representation vouchsafed in the American system. This, too, is of sufficient importance to justify all that has been attempted in regional planning. Within each of these areas of purpose there are, of course, individuals who advocate extremes and some who appear to believe that the regional planning movement may be used subtly and subserviently in changing the American system. These are points to be watched.

> The two chief implications of regionalism with which we are concerned here are, first, a relative homogeneity of physical, economic and cultural factors within certain designated areas; and second, the minimizing of state boundaries. Such regionalism may be effective in two ways; the one as it affects the states themselves and the particular region of which they are a part. The other, as it affects federal centralization and national administration and policy. In each of these, again, there are two main aspects. With reference to the states, regionalism first of all affords an opportunity for more co-ordination, co-operation and mutual understanding of problems and work; for enlarging the total program through a planned framework prepared by the largest possible number of those interested; for conferences together on methods and skills, and for common utilization of results. This applies alike to research, extension and planning. It provides a medium for the minimizing of state jealousies and political handicaps and affords opportunity for the several states, working together, to devise more effective planning for the region. In much the same way, the regional approach is to be substituted for the older American historic sectionalism such as that portrayed by Frederick Jackson Turner and demonstrated so often in American history, a realistic regionalism, looking toward the integration of all sections into a greater national whole. This applies to the development of physical resources, the increase and distribution of wealth, and to politico-juristic affairs as well. In the same way that new times demand a strong American individualism to be merged into a stronger social minded co-operative endeavor, so also is demanded an enduring regionalism merged with a greater national-regional and regional-national co-operative arrangement for the "better ordering" of the whole. The implications of the

regional approach from the federal viewpoint are also two. First, with reference to the size of the job: The nation is too large, too characterized by complexity and heterogeneity, for any realistic commonsense planning and development except through the regional approach. It is not possible to understand the various parts of the country, to sense their culture and capacities without the regional approach. The vast ignorance and provincialism of the nation, one region of another, all regions of all; some of the extraordinarily ineffective methods and technics utilized by federal workers, and much of the conflict and confusion are bounded by misunderstanding and lack of co-operation which can be remedied only through the regional approach. Again, all cultures develop gradually through regional evolution; they can neither be understood nor redirected without reference to regional resources, history, institutions, folkways.

The second implication of regionalism in relation to the Federal Government has to do with the alternative policies of bureaucratic centralization and coercive federalism over against the traditional policy of geographic and cultural representation expressed through local responsibility and participation. Nearly all of our federal measures emphasize local responsibility and participation. Sometimes the local state or regional responsibility is characterized by the demand of the government to take over something which it started, the nature and principles of which the states or regions had little to do in the formative and determinative stages. Many of the minor administrative folk at Washington, most proclaimed as liberals and progressives, vie in their paternalistic attitude toward rural folk with the worst of their industrial paternalists whom they decry. Needless to say, these matters appear to be fundamental; lesser men so motivated and implemented may impede great programs conceived by men of greater stature.[15]

When it comes to the problem of determining the number and nature of planning boards, the regional economy, here as elsewhere, must be presented primarily as it envisages the maximum results of national planning through the regional approach. Thus, before we can discuss the nature and number of regional planning boards, we must first envisage the entire national framework of possible and feasible planning boards on the different administrative levels, and, to some extent, their functional nature.

[15] Adapted from Howard W. Odum, "The Human Aspects of Chemurgy," *Farm Chemurgic Journal*, I, No. 1, pp. 66, 68.

An adequate system of national and regional planning would envisage the types of planning boards of the number and nature as specified below. It is understood, of course, that these types are presented to illustrate the nature and function of regional planning, and that they are not exclusively "recommended." If it is objected that they "won't work" or that "it can't be done," the answer is "of course not"; neither does democracy, fascism, nor Christianity "work." The answer, like the concept of major regions, is found in the approximation of the largest number of purposes, with the smallest number of contradictions possible. The presumption is that within this broad premise it is possible to do something through regional planning, American style. With this general qualification in mind, there would be first the national planning board, second the state planning boards, and third, a series of major regional planning boards, working in group interrelationship and co-operation with special technical, subregional planning groups. These in turn would, of course, work with local planning boards such as city, county, and the subregional advisory boards within the several states.

For the national planning board, the following general specifications would seem to be appropriate within the American framework and system. Legislation creating the board as recommended by the President would be passed regularly by Congress, and hence would reflect a referendum to the people. The board would be entirely expert and advisory, with no executive or administrative power, and would report directly to the President. It might well consist of seven members, of whom three would be full-time, salaried experts chosen from the fields of social science, engineering, and public affairs, with salaries adequate to secure the ablest specialists in the field. The other four members would be selected from the nation at large in the general fields of politics, the press, agriculture, industry, and would receive only a *per diem.* An adequate staff would be provided, including executive assistants and associates, research specialists, draftsmen, and secretaries. The functions of such a board would in general be threefold. The first would be to act in the service of the President and of the Congress and provide information, facts, planning programs in special projects initiated by the President or Congress. The second function would be to carry on a continuous social inventory of the nation somewhat after the manner of *Recent Social Trends,* so that there would be an authentic research-planning group working all the time, not only in designing and planning research, but in utilization of the vast research agencies and statistics of the present federal organizations and departments. The third function would be to make contacts and co-operate with the regions and states, and to carry on adult education and promotion and continuous referendum and publicity to the people. Some members of the planning board would continuously be sensing the various situations in the different states and regions, as well as interpreting the nation to the President and Congress to the nation. It would be understood that research and plans would result in recommendation, action upon which would, however, always come through the regular administrative, judicial, or legislative function of government, and through the several regional and state agencies within which they were appropriate.

In this third function of promoting regional planning and for co-operating with state and regional agencies, the national planning board should have available a moderate amount of funds for allocation to the state and regional planning boards in accordance with definite and common sense co-operative arrangements within each of these. Although the suggestion is clearly "academic," such a planning board might well save the nation a great deal of money insofar as it would be competent to undertake the research and investigation now provided for in the scores and scores of congressional investigating committees and of isolated, overlapping and duplicating research agencies within the nation. Here would be opportunity better to implement the work and training of the expert in government without turning the government over to the scientists and students.

The second type of planning board in logical order is the state planning board, the general specifications and functions of which would in analogous measure tend to follow the general provisions set forth in the national planning board, except that all members of the state planning board would be voluntary and non-salaried. Each state planning board would, however, have in miniature an expert staff consisting of an executive official, research and planning associates and assistants, draftsmen, and secretarial staff. The state board would be official in the sense that it was constituted by an act of the Legislature, subject to the Governor's office, and with minimum appropriation for organization and for matching moneys with the national planning board. In general, the number of members should be the same as for the national, namely, seven, of whom not more than four should ever coincide with the official departmental heads of state government. The functions of the state planning board would again tend to be of the same threefold objectives as the national planning board; that is, its first function would be to assist the Governor in the work of planning and directing his state program. The second function would be to carry on a continuous program of study and planning for the state itself. The third would be to co-operate on the one hand with city and county planning boards within the state and regional and federal planning boards outside the state.

The third major type of planning board is the regional planning board, which should be less formal and less active than the national and state planning boards. In general, the desired objectives could be attained by the division of the nation into a minimum-maximum number of major regions which combine the largest possible degree of homogeneity measured by the largest possible number of economic, cultural, administrative, and functional indices, for the largest possible number of objectives. These areal divisions having been determined, the major regional planning boards might well be constituted as follows: one ex-officio member from each state planning board; one representative from the national planning board; two representatives from the region at large; and one ex-officio representative from each of the specialized, technical, subregional planning groups already at work in the region, such as, for instance, the TVA or special river-valley, or interstate compact groups.

Thus, to illustrate from three of the six divisions of the nation, utilized in this volume, the *Southeast Planning Board* would consist of eleven ex-officio members from the states, one member of the national planning board, two members at large, and one member ex-officio from the Tennessee Valley Authority, and if and when progress is made on other special subregional planning groups, such as the Lower Mississippi, an ex-officio member from this group. The *Northeastern Planning Board* would be chosen similarly with a special ex-officio member from the present New England Planning Board. The *Far Western* group would consist of four ex-officio members, two at large, one from the Federal Government, and one each probably from the Columbian Basin and Los Angeles County Planning Board, or other similar planning groups.

Such an arrangement would be flexible enough to allow adequate co-operation with the proposed seven river valley authorities and would not conflict with them. It would also give an adequate number of members to insure a satisfactory quorum, would give ample subgeographic representation, and would give adequate provisions for co-ordinating the work and keeping a clearinghouse of regional information. The function of the regional planning board would thus be even more advisory and general than the others, still following the general threefold objectives; that is, it would first of all focus upon its regional problems and planning, serving particularly as a buffer between the national planning board and the state planning board. In the second place, it would seek to keep continuously a preview of facts and situations and a preview of trends in the region with a view to co-ordinating the work of the states with that of the nation. In the third place, it would have the peculiar task of co-operating with state and subregional planning boards. For such a function, the staff of the regional planning board would be relatively small, including a permanent executive official and a minimum staff of research and planning associates. Such a planning board would be primarily one of co-ordination and would meet perhaps not more than twice a year. Under its auspices, however, might be held various regional conferences and subregional group conferences for co-ordination of the many state and national and district advisory efforts.

Although these three major planning boards constitute the backbone of the national-regional planning procedure, it is assumed that city, county, and districts within each individual state would provide for such planning boards and services as either the local, state, or regional associations might promote or encourage. The provisions of national and city planning boards are being more or less standardized, so that the best that can be done is to select continuously the most satisfactory type of board and procedure. The other two types of planning boards would naturally be combined; that is, instead of arbitrarily assuming and attempting to provide for a county planning board for each county, manifestly the most effective plan would be to set up a series of contiguous counties with which to comprehend the problems and programs of particular areas of the state and to join forces in a special program of research and planning over a period of six to twelve years. Such a program would comprehend the maximum advantages which co-ordination of federal, state, local, of official and voluntary educational planning programs will provide. Such a program would constitute experimentation and exploration from which ultimately the best results and plans for each county might be obtained. At the same time, it would pool resources to the best possible advantage.

We have assumed all along that the test of American regionalism will be found in the degree to which the concept becomes clear in acceptable terms and to the extent to which it can be implemented in terms of the reality of existing agencies and relationships. If federal equalization funds are needed, which is the best way to work out the problem of allocation and administration? If agricultural planning is needed, are there fundamental regional factors to be considered? If wages and labor, security and relief, conservation and development are involved, are there regional implications and resources through which effective results can be obtained? If there are conflicts between and among the states or regions or between the states and the federal authority, are the regional realities amenable to regional-national adjustment? If there is need for increasing wealth, for the redistribution of people and industry, does the regional approach have anything to offer which could not be had in the federal plan? If sectional conflict is to be minimized, can it be done through the integration of the regions into the national union? If overcentralization offers great danger to the nation, can it best be remedied through the regional economy? The consideration of these questions and others, however, will appear more logical in our last chapter on "Problems and Strategy of Regional Development Towards a National Reintegration."

Part II

HISTORICAL AND THEORETICAL ASPECTS OF REGIONALISM

Varying Concepts of Regionalism

At a period when the uniformities of the machine civilization were being overstressed, regionalism served to emphasize compensatory organic elements: above all, those differences that arise out of geographic, historic, and cultural peculiarities. In its recognition of the region as a basic configuration in human life; in its acceptance of natural diversities as well as natural associations and uniformities; in its recognition of the region as a permanent sphere of cultural influences and as a center of economic activities, as well as an implicit geographic fact—here lies the vital common element in the regionalist movement. So far from being archaic and reactionary, regionalism belongs to the future.[1]

When one searches for unity, the human race is obviously one. When one looks for differences one discovers not only national types and regional types, one discovers likewise important differences between a Florentine and a Neapolitan, between a Glasgow man and an Edinburgh man, even differences in language, accent, gesture, feeling between villages that are but a day's walk apart.[1]

Regionalism has been identified with sectionalism or separatism; and even the regionalists themselves have often laid too great stress upon the formation of fractional sovereign states, as if the evils of over-centralization and the superstitions of Austinian sovereignty were to be diminished by multiplying the opportunities for petty despotism. At the very beginning of the regionalist movement, intelligent observers like Auguste Comte and still later, Le Play, not merely observed that it was bound to take place, because it satisfied the ultimate conditions of political existence: but Comte indeed predicted that within a century or so there would be a hundred and sixty such regional entities in Europe.[1]

Regionalism, as one of the French observers of the movement has pointed out, tends to pass through a regular cycle. It begins with a revival of poetry and language: it ends with plans for the economic invigoration of regional agriculture and industry, with proposals for a more autonomous political life, with an effort to build up local centers of learning and culture.[1]

Regional planning is the conscious direction and collective integration of all those activities which rest upon the use of the earth as site, as resource, as structure, as theater. To the extent that such activities are focused within definite regions, consciously delimited and utilized, the opportunities for effective co-ordination are increased. Hence regional planning is a further stage in the more specialized or isolated processes of agriculture planning, industry planning, or city planning.[1]

The re-animation and re-building of regions, as deliberate works of collective art, is the grand task of politics for the opening generation. It raises anew, in a form that now has fuller human significance, the fundamental questions of human interrelationship across the ethnic, ideological, and cultural boundaries that have been carried over from the past. And as the new tasks of region-building imply shifts in the population, migration into more favored areas, and the building up or reconstruction of a multitude of new urban complexes, the politics of regional development become of critical importance.[1]

Regionalism must be distinguished from nationalism in that it recognizes a higher national unity and superior national interests transcending the attachment to the local region.[2]

It must be distinguished also from mere sectionalism in that it is not based exclusively on regional economic or class interests, but involves certain ethnic factors, such as cultural, traditional or linguistic peculiarities which provide a basis for what is often termed a subnationality.[2]

Regionalism is a clustering of geographic, economic, sociological, and governmental factors to such an extent that a distinct consciousness, the recognition of a separate identity within the whole and the desirability of autonomous planning, cultural peculiarities and administrative freedom are theoretically recognized and actually put into effect.[3]

Whether regionalism results from the growth of a sense of community, in turn dependent upon common traditions, interests and aspirations, or whether it results from man's rational analysis of economic and governmental problems needing solution, it is none the less regionalism.[3]

Regionalism strikes an effective and natural medium between uncontrolled individualism among the states and complete centralization of administration at Washington.[4]

Regionalism is the antithesis of false cosmopolitanism; the genius of the community symbolized by Patrick Geddes' trilogy of place, work, folk.[5]

Regionalism is the economic and cultural approach to the same set of facts which sectionalism approaches politically.[6]

. . . regionalism is the basis for the encouragement of a richer and more varied life for the Nation, whereby the peculiar characteristics, resources, and contributions of the major sections of the country can be protected from invasions, exploitation, and suppression by ill-considered and hasty national policies.[7]

Regionalism . . . stands somewhere between administrative decentralization and federalism. It touches on both; and if a more rigid logic envisages three schools of thought and three movements, a basic similarity none the less exists and a common principle underlies all three.[8]

Regionalism can therefore be defined as the study of the relation of man to geographic areas, and the potentialities which this relation represents in terms of human welfare and progress.[9]

The term "regionalism" is used in its broadest implications—namely, that of a geographic area or areas which a given civilization-standard of a people seems to require for the fulfillment of its aspirations through the material resources believed essential in attaining economic well-being.[9]

. . . regionalism and regional planning should embrace the study and development of all geographic entities, the nature of which would lend themselves to the best possible development along specific lines and does not necessarily imply any past settlements or exploitation.[9]

Fundamentally, the regionalism of the future must be evolved out of economic concepts in which the geographic environment would be capable of regional integration in terms of the most advanced application of modern technology within the limits of legal and administrative expediency.[9]

The above concepts indicate both diversity and a certain agreement with reference to the meanings of regionalism. The authors are: 1. Lewis Mumford, 2. Hedwig Hintze, 3. Marshall E. Dimock, 4. Burdette G. Lewis, 5. C. S. Ascher, 6. Donald Davidson, 7. American Society of Planning Officials, 8. R. K. Gooch, 9. Carol Aronovici.

Chapter XII

EXPLORING THE REGION: THE GEOGRAPHERS

IN Part I we have discussed the implications and meanings of regionalism, its rise on the American scene, something of its various forms and directions, and its possible bearings upon social planning and national development. Throughout the discussions we have assumed the solid background of historical authenticity and theoretical reality, pointing up from time to time instances and evidences appropriate to the topics discussed. We come now to the important task of presenting in more detail the historical and theoretical backgrounds of regionalism as found in the studies and researches of the social sciences, including the human geographers, with whose basic social science we begin.

Whatever else regionalism may or may not be, its first essence is to be found in the geographic factor. The mudsill of the idea of regionalism is that social phenomena may best be understood when considered in relation to the area in which they occur as a cultural frame of reference; that some consideration of the distribution of social elements over the face of the earth is either essential or beneficial to any further discussion of the characteristics they display.

To some regionalists this means that social phenomena are determined by the purely physical facts of nature such as geology, topography, climate; to others it means that physical environment and the expression of those physical facts in vegetation, animal life, changes of the face of nature affected by man, etc., make possible certain adaptations which man may or may not make in accordance with other factors such as culture; to still other scholars the map is merely a convenient means of expressing spatial relationships existing between social phenomena which have no more relation to the soil on which they exist than has the type of drama to the boards on which it is presented. But, to these latter, just as the stage offers the scene and limits the range of the action, so does the region illustrate the interconnections between the phenomena studied and the range of those relationships. Thus, these varied and often contradictory concepts of the region have at least one element in common, they agree that mankind must have some place on which to stand and to move as the eternal drama of humanity unfolds itself; that this action is not spread evenly over the surface of the earth but tends to cluster about certain spots and in certain areas, varying from one to another by greater or less degree so that it can be, or must be, segregated into regional parts for purposes of study.

> This idea that men in different, and differing, portions of the earth's surface behave in distinct manners is one of the oldest of man's notions. It is the basis of our perpetual interest in the tales of travellers, and early became the basis of literature as well as of philosophical speculation. In it, of course, lies the origin of geography. Now after some centuries of neglect and some salutary changes it is hailed as the culmination of that branch of human knowledge. Since some geographers appear to have been interested always in man's occupance of the globe, and since geography is the study which claims as its own exclusive field the investigation of the natural and physical features of the earth's surface, it seems inevitable that much of the impetus to regional study should have come from this discipline. Actually this is only partly true, but the geographers have made a series of contributions which demand attention.

There seems always to have been two schools of geographers, those who insist that the proper field of their discipline is the study of the physical aspects of the world as structure, geology, topography, configuration, rainfall, winds, ocean currents, temperatures, measurements of land forms, mapping, etc.; and another group who insist that such information is only the beginning of the study of geography, that the real aim must be to show how such factors affect human behavior, or at least who insist that the field of geography is the interrelationships between facts of physical nature and human behavior.

Traditions and folk tales of the ancients must have abounded in descriptions of "far" regions and the folk who lived in them; certainly the earliest extant literature has an abundance of such materials. Much of the interest in tales of Ulysses is inherent in his descriptions of the places he visited and the people with whom he came into contact. Just how much geographical knowledge is mixed into the purely fictional element is a fascinating problem which has intrigued historians and geographers for a long while. From an even earlier day, the poems of Hesiod are fairly inclusive pictures of the adjustments of a people to a region—one would guess of newcomers to the region since the mechanisms of adjustment were made the subject of a poem rather than appearing in proverbs, saws, etc. The tales of Herodotus are largely chorographical, in spite of his renown as a historian rather than as a geographer. Incidentally this ancient would find many modern geographers to compliment him on the insight he displayed in refusing to follow custom and make the Nile River divide Asia and Africa on the ground that a river inhabited on both sides by one people is not a proper boundary for a continent. So must have been the accounts of other early travelers who, lacking a concept of the world as a whole, probably described such portions of it as they had seen.

Apart from such materials, which seem to have been more for entertainment than for instruction, the ancient nations also endeavored to express on maps their knowledge of the regions they occupied. The Sumerians, for example, had a map of the military expeditions of their leader, Sargon.[1] This movement toward mapping received great impetus under the Roman Empire, in line with the practical nature of these people, who found military value in maps of routes through regions and in descriptions of the inhabitants. The opening lines of Caesar's treatise on the Gallic Wars, indelibly stamped on the minds of school children for generations, is an example of this type of description. But, of course, Strabo is the pre-eminent example of this sort of geographical work in that era. After a preliminary theoretical discussion, his seventeen volumes resolve themselves mostly into a description of regions known to the Romans, and particularly of those regions of political importance to the Roman Empire. These works attempt to give comprehensive descriptions of the physical nature of the inhabitants of the regions considered.[2] This work was followed

[1] R. E. Dickinson and J. R. Howarth, *The Making of Geography*, p. 4.
[2] *Ibid.*, pp. 28-29.

by that of Agartharchides of Cnidus who "was interested in the geographical environments of peoples" and who described regions about the Red Sea, the western portion of Asia, and what was then known of Europe.[3] By the fourth century there appears Ammianus Marcellinus who "recognized the value of geography in relation to history" and made free use of materials available.[4]

In this, he was largely following the reasoning of Aristotle, who some time before had considered the questions of size of territory, location of cities with reference to hinterland and outlet, climate and water supply in relation to public health, and even of city planning.[5] This philosophical trend was carried much farther by Polybius with his insistence on a naturalistic interpretation in which situation, soil, and climate are made to play an important part, thus foreshadowing the work of much later thinkers.[6]

Since such naturalistic explanations did not fit into the theology of a church relying on the principle of divine inspiration and explanation, it was not until St. Thomas Aquinas undertook the task of reconciling Christian theory with accumulated knowledge that such reasoning again appears in European writings. However, the Moslems, with access to the ancient treasures of knowledge in eastern libraries and spurred by visions of a world empire, did make notable contributions to the subject of environmental description and causation. Al-Masudi of Bagdad traveled extensively in the Caspian region, Africa, Madagascar, India, Ceylon, and probably visited China. As a result of his knowledge gained through travel, he was led to enunciate principles similar to those of Ammianus Marcellinus.[7] Ibn-Khaldun, the eminent Arabian philosopher, noticed differences between peoples in different regions and attempted to correlate such differences with environment. He arrived at the conclusion that nomadic life is associated with no high standards of culture, but inculcates bravery, loyalty to the tribe, and warlike propensities. He also postulated stages of social development, the nomadic preceding the agricultural. Finally, he worked out a sort of natural history for civilization, advancing the familiar argument that a settled civilized

[3] Dickinson and Howarth, *op. cit.*, p. 27.

[4] *Ibid.*, p. 43.

[5] Aristotle, *The Politics*, translation by Jowett, VII, *passim*.

[6] Cf. James P. Lichtenberger, *Development of Social Theory*, p. 64.

[7] Dickinson and Howarth, *op. cit.*, p. 52.

life is debilitating, so that highly cultured societies fall easy prey to primitive conquerors.[8]

The pious efforts of St. Thomas to reconcile theology and observed facts were followed by some geographic and regional speculation. Thus Dante and Machiavelli utter impassioned pleas for the resurrection of the Roman Empire, in both of which are to be found recognition of regional factors and regional consciousness. But the discoveries of new and strange lands, the access to the knowledge so long the exclusive possession of more Eastern peoples, and the general reawakening of European civilization are the more potent factors in resurrecting geography in general and chorography in particular. Travelers and missionaries, such as Marco Polo, had brought much information concerning more distant regions and had perpetuated it through the recently introduced art of printing.

With the discovery of the new world, interest in such reports was intensely stimulated. Accounts of distant places found ready market. Within a year of the return of Columbus to Europe from his successful voyage, printed accounts of his report to the Spanish king were circulated widely throughout Europe.[9] Richard Hakluyt, among others, collected, translated, and had published any and all accounts he could find of distant regions. Such diffusion of unreliable information brought a reaction from the more academic geographers of the time, as is illustrated by the distinction Peter Apian, German astronomer and cartographer of the early sixteenth century, made between geography and chorography. The latter, he says, "describes and considers places separately—without consideration or comparison between themselves, or with the world as a whole" with the aim "to paint and describe a particular place, as a painter would paint an eye or an ear or other parts of a human being" while geography studies the earth as a whole.[10] From his simile it would be easy to argue that he recognized an organic relationship between the places described in chorography and the remainder of the world.

Less than one hundred years later a scientific attempt at a regional survey was made by Sebastian Munster, German teacher, who used

[8] *Ibid.*, p. 54.
[9] Henry Harrisse, *Notes on Columbus*, p. 117.
[10] Dickinson and Howarth, *op. cit.*, p. 82.

the principle of triangulation to make a survey of the area about Heidelberg and divided Germany into regions to be surveyed similarly, though this plan was not carried into effect.

Mercator, whose name was Gerhard Kremer, prepared a regional map of Flanders, 1537-1540, which is commonly recognized as the first regional study, and which was followed by similar maps of France, Spain, and Bavaria by others evidently influenced by his work. Such work called for a distinction between general and regional, or special geography, as it was called at the time. Such a distinction was made by Varenius about the middle of the seventeenth century, and has been followed in principle since. Though one of the first works of this scholar is a geography of Japan followed almost immediately by a discussion of the religion of that region, he deprecates "special geography" because it was being taught at the expense of general consideration of the world. In his *Geographia Generalis*, 1650, he outlines special geography as being concerned with celestial properties, climate and appearance of the heavens; terrestrial properties, position, boundaries, shape and size, mountains, rivers, woods, deserts, fertility, minerals, animals; and human properties, under which he includes such cultural factors as arts, commerce, culture, language, government, religion, and famous men as well as a description of the inhabitants, their appearance, and famous cities and other sites. However, he feels that of the three divisions "though the last sort seem not so properly to belong to this science (of Social Geography), yet we are obliged to admit them for custom's sake and the information of the reader" and adds that in this branch of geography special features should be explained in terms of general laws.[11] Somewhat similar is the scheme for works in chorography presented by Cluverius, who was led into geography in search of materials which would aid in understanding history.

At a slightly earlier date Nathaniel Carpenter, of Exeter College, Oxford, in his work, *Geography Delineated Forth in Two Books*, discusses the description of regions in general terms. Towns, he argues, should be built on rivers whenever possible because rivers give ease of traffic, purge filth, yield fish for food, furnish water for fighting fire and "lastly, amongst other reasons we cannot forget the

[11] Dickinson and Howarth, *op. cit.*, pp. 100-102.

pleasantness of faire rivers." [12] He accepts the ancient generalizations concerning the effects of geographic factors on psychological elements of society, as that mountaineers are stout, warlike and generous, but not tractable, but seems to modify such generalizations when he observes that "Colonies transplanted from one region into another farre remote, retaine a long time their first disposition, though little and little they decline and suffer alteration." [13] That is, the psychological effects of physical environment are operative only over long periods of time.

The spirit of the modern human geographers is remarkably foreshadowed by Pinkerton in his *Modern Geography, 1807,* in which he advances the theory that the task of geography is to present the most recent available information concerning the nations into which the world is divided, giving much attention to the historical aspects of the nations, but including statistics. The study of the physical aspects of a region should *follow* instead of precede that of the cultural features, he argues, on the ground that the landscape is essentially a product of man's activity [14]—a point of view finding an echo recently.[15]

Alexander von Humboldt attacked the geographic problem from the point of view of the naturalist. Primarily interested in the relations between the earth and life, he went into the field for observations which might lead to generalizations. It was from this fieldwork, in South America and in Mexico, that the studies now recognized as the first great regional geographic work resulted. The theme of these works is that natural phenomena are essentially interrelated and have important effects on man.

> Thus "Whatever causes diversity of form or features on the surface of our planet-mountains, great lakes, grassy steppes, and even deserts surrounded by a coastlike margin of forest—impresses some peculiar mark or character on the social state of its inhabitants. Continuous ridges of lofty mountains with snow impede intercourse and traffic; but where lowlands are interspersed with discontinuous chains and

[12] Quoted in *ibid.*, p. 107.
[13] *Ibid.*, p. 107.
[14] *Ibid.*, pp. 121-123.
[15] Cf. discussion of R. B. Hall, "The Geographic Region: A Résumé," in *Annals of the Association of American Geographers*, XXV, 122-136.

with groups of more moderate elevation, such as are happily presented by the southwest of Europe, meteorological processes and vegetable products are multiplied and varied; and different kinds of cultivation even under the same latitude, give rise to different wants, which stimulate both the industry and the intercourse of its inhabitants."[16] That is, his study of the region went beyond a mere description of the land forms, vegetation, animals present, etc., and sought the relations of the region, direct and indirect, upon the whole life found therein. Carl Ritter, teacher and scholar, trained in the humanities, added to the investigations of Humboldt a philosophy of history. His thesis, as stated in his preface to a work on Europe, is "The earth and its inhabitants stand in the closest mutual relations and one element cannot be seen in all its phases without the others. On this account history and geography must always go hand in hand. The country works upon the people and the people upon the country."[17] He also praised the accomplishments of man in "conquering" nature by such means as irrigation, navigation, discovery of passes through mountain ranges, etc., and declared, "The changes which Art is yet to effect on our Globe are beyond all possible computation and it may be said beyond all possible exaggeration."[18] For purposes of this study his great contribution lies in the regional classification worked out by him on the basis of elevation and topography; highlands and plateaus, mountains, lowlands and the transitional regions between plain and mountain. On the basis of this system he worked out a regional division of Africa into four parts.

This line of reasoning was carried farther by another German, Friedrich Ratzel, 1844-1904, who entered geography by way of zoology, geology, and journalism. Here we find no shadow of a doubt as to the importance of the geographic factor.

"Man," said Ratzel, "is a product of the earth's surface. This means not merely that he is a child of the earth, dust of her dust; but that the earth has mothered him, fed him, set him tasks, directed his thoughts, confronted him with difficulties that have strengthened his body and sharpened his wits, given him problems of navigation or irrigation, and at the same time whispered hints for their solution. . . . Always the same, and always situated at the same point in space, the soil serves as a fixed support for the human and changing aspirations of men. . . . When they happen to forget the support, it makes them

[16] *Aspects of Nature*, Vol. I, quoted by Dickinson and Howarth, *op. cit.*, p. 149.
[17] Quoted in Dickinson and Howarth, *op. cit.*, p. 151.
[18] *Ibid.*, p. 156.

feel its power and reminds them by serious warnings that the whole life of the state has its roots in the soil. It governs the destinies of peoples with blind brutality. A people should live on the soil which fate has given it; it should die there, and submit to the law."[19]

Thus the fundamental concept of Ratzel and of his American disciple, Ellen Churchill Semple, is that man is a powerless puppet in the hands of physical nature, though the use of the verb "should" in preference to "must" in the above quotation might imply that even Ratzel had some small doubts. This appears again in the generalization that, as population density increases, the connection between land and man is of less force, or so it seems, but this is followed by the dictum that "A struggle for existence is a struggle for space" and that organized societies constantly tend to expand until they reach the limits set by nature, i.e., the physical boundaries of the region they occupy. So plains offer ample opportunity for such expansion and are the basis of great national life; small natural regions limit the civilization to be reached, though they may bring about a more rapid blossoming of that civilization. Isolated regions bring homogeneity and conservatism, but when communication is partly free, introduced traits can be well assimilated, since they come in small numbers, and a high civilization may result, as in Japan. But if the isolated region is too small, or too poor in resources, it must become a center of emigration or adopt such practices as cannibalism, infanticide, and polyandry.

Among regions, that embracing a watershed is of great importance and may serve to illustrate the manner in which physical geography is held to affect social organization; as witness the following quotations from Miss Semple's English presentation of Ratzel's principles, *Influences of Geographic Environment*.

"Owing to the strong pull exerted by a river's mouth upon all its basin, current, commerce and people alike tend to reach the ocean. For a nation holding the terrestrial course of a stream, the political fate of its tidal course or mouth must always be a matter of great concern. . . . The only satisfactory solution is undivided political ownership."[20] Similarly steppes dictate nomadic pastoralism as the way of life: "Des-

[19] Quoted by Lucien Febvre, *A Geographical Introduction to History*, p. 11.
[20] Ellen Churchill Semple, *Influences of Geographic Environment*, pp. 350-351.

erts and steppes lay an arresting hand on progress—their tribes do not develop; neither do they grow old. They are the perpetual children of the world. . . . Genuine nomadic peoples show no alteration in their manners, customs or mode of life from millennium to millennium. . . ." [21] Finally the importance of climate is indicated: "The North Temperate Zone is pre-eminently the culture zone of the earth. It is the seat of the most important, most steadily progressive civilizations, and the source of all the cultural stimuli which have given an upward start to civilization in other zones during the past three centuries. . . . As the Tropics have been the cradle of humanity, the Temperate Zone has been the cradle and school of civilization. Here Nature has given much by withholding much. Here man has found his birthright, the privilege of his struggle." [22]

One of the most interesting generalizations of the Le Play School, described more fully in relation to the sociologists, is that concerning the type of family growing up in differing geographic surroundings. Of these, that known as the "particularist" is the natural result of a geography which prevents settlement of children in the immediate vicinity of their parents, as in Norway and Sweden where bits of agricultural land are often so small as to necessitate the removal of the sons as they form new families. From this geographic fact grows democracy, independence, fierce love of individuality, and other similar characteristics which have been taken into England by early migrants from such regions and are held accountable for the world dominance of these people.[23] Due to differing geographic conditions other peoples could not hope to be so fortunate.

It is such works as these which prompted Lucien Febvre to write, "A well-meaning popularizer, with a very confident belief in his own capacity, shuts himself up in his own closet to reflect, as so many others had done, on the whole history of nations, and to discover the principle, the bond, and the explanation. By the side of M. de Tourville's *Nomenclature des faits sociaux* (we are dealing with an adept in *social science*), we imagine him putting on the table (presumably in order to support and at times excite the springs of his imagination) several good historical dictionaries, two or three recognized textbooks, and the *Geographie universelle* of Élisée Reclus, that Providence so

[21] Semple, *op. cit.*, pp. 510, 512-514.
[22] *Ibid.*, pp. 634-635.
[23] Cf. Edmond Demolins, *Anglo-Saxon Superiority: To What Is It Due?*, *passim*, but particularly introduction and conclusion.

often unacknowledged. . . . Then, starting with a brilliant idea, an ingenious hypothesis worthy of romantic fiction, he sets himself with a kind of mechanical fury to extract from it universal consequences and we have in twice five hundred pages *Comment la route crée le type social* by Edmond Demolins. . . . They stick to that geographical influence, at once powerful and obscure, multiform and complex, which is exerted, they tell us, both on man physical and moral and on man social and political—on the color of his skin, the shape of his body, the strength of his organism, his psychic qualities and defects, his judicial, economic and religious institutions—even the productions of his mind, the creations of art and genius. They state it as a fact. But they do not prove it."[24]

A somewhat different use of the central idea of Le Play was that made by Patrick Geddes and Victor Branford in England. Here the valley was taken as the unit and was looked at in profile, the general scheme of investigation worked out by Le Play being applied. Thus, it is said, a valley may be divided into several more or less distinct zones: the miner at the escarpment or in the highlands; the woodman on the high slopes, the hunter or shepherd below him, giving way in his turn to the small farmer in the piedmont section and the larger farms of the more level plains. At the mouth of the river is a central city, serving the zones upstream, while on the surface of the sea are the fisherfolk. This scheme has been followed in numerous local surveys in England and Scotland and has been made the basis of the geographical interpretation of the South by Rupert B. Vance.[25] In these works the physical geography is distinctly related to economic life and other phases of social organization, but is not made to determine them.

A reaction to the determinism of Ratzel and the too-enthusiastic applications of the principles enunciated by Le Play took place in France under the leadership of Paul Vidal de la Blache and Jean Brunhes, whose works are probably more widely accepted as expressing the present point of view than any others. Vidal begins from the assumption that the historical point of view must be followed even in geography; that present relationships between man and nature

[24] Febvre, *op. cit.*, pp. 15, 17.
[25] Victor Branford and Patrick Geddes, *The Coming Polity;* Rupert B. Vance, *Human Geography of the South.*

are a function of time as well as of place; thus physical environment is of great importance in holding together heterogeneous elements in a vital relationship. But in this relationship man is far from being the passive recipient of forces emanating from nature; he joins in nature's game and exerts an influence of his own. He has spread plants and animals friendly to him over regions they could never have entered without his help; nor would original conditions return if this aid were withdrawn. Nor does man always use the gifts of nature in the most obviously advantageous manner.

> As Vidal points out, the Chinese along the upper Hwang-ho and Yangtze, in Chihli and Shantung, Shansi and Honan, believe they came from the west, where irrigation is the basis of life, and loyally follow this method of agriculture, migrating long distances to find areas where their customary mode of life may be continued rather than to change techniques. Much the same thing appears in Japan, where only about 15 percent of the land is cultivated, for much the same reason, it seems. Little exploitation of the mountains is undertaken, in marked contrast to the nearby Philippine Islands. Similarly, in Polynesia, some tribes construct excellent boats and sail them most skillfully, while others in similar environments completely lack this art. In short, Vidal argues, nature makes possible certain modes of life, and prohibits others; but within this relatively wide range man is left to exert free choice.[26]

This theory has received the name of "Possibilism" from Febvre and is to be contrasted to the "determinism" of Ratzel and other early geographers. Here we find acknowledged the importance of historical stage, technological equipment, aptitude and racial factors. Such a writer lays stress upon the social heritage, but insists that geography is an essential approach to an understanding of human problems. That is, the emphasis is shifted from the physical facts of geography to man as the active agent who uses these facts, and is affected by them. As a safeguard against the universalistic tendency of the older geography, Vidal declares there can be no better antidote than the study of regions. In such studies the geographers will gather a large amount of data inductively, which later may be synthesized into general principles, if such are found to grow naturally.

[26] P. Vidal de la Blache, *Principles of Human Geography*, *passim;* especially ch. III.

Following this idea, Vidal made one such study himself, *La France l'Est,* and his followers made many others. The value of such studies is succinctly stated by Vidal thus: ". . . these researches result in an essentially geographic concept; that of the environment as composite, capable of grouping and of holding together heterogeneous beings in mutual vital relationships. This idea seems to be the law governing the geography of living creatures. Every region is a domain where many dissimilar beings, artificially brought together, have subsequently adapted themselves to a common existence."[27] The same idea is developed more fully in his essays on *Genres de vie,* and is also expressed by his disciple, Demangeon: "Every region has its unique character to which contribute the features of the soil, atmosphere, plants and man. The aim of all research consists in the analysis of these features. The aim of description is to synthesize them, and to show the interlocking of all the phenomena which comprise regional types."[28]

Jean Brunhes, another Vidal disciple, somewhat refines the concept by limiting the task of the human geographer to the description and analysis of the material works of man on the face of the earth, that is, the physical evidences of man's occupance of the earth, and through these into the more purely social phenomena, illustrating from the range of his "six essential facts." These "six essential facts" all have to do with man's effect upon the natural environment, it is to be noted. They are, first, facts of unproductive occupation of the soil; houses and roads. Second, facts of plant and animal conquest; cultivated fields and domestic animals. Third, facts of destructive occupation of the soil; exploitation of minerals and devastation of plant and animal life.

Here we find the geographer facing in almost the opposite direction to that taken by Ratzel, but not quite. All terrestrial forces are tied together into one interconnected whole and "Man does not escape the common law; his activities are included in the network of terrestrial phenomena. But, if human activity is thus circumscribed, it does not follow that it is fatally determined. Because of its connection with natural phenomena, it is, without question, included in geography in two ways: it responds to the influence of certain facts, and, on the other hand, it exercises its influence on other facts. . . . That is why we must add to the group of material forces, whose incessant interplay we have

27 *Ibid.*, p. 10.

28 Quoted, Dickinson and Howarth, *op. cit.*, pp. 234-235.

seen, this new force—human activity—which is not only a material thing but which also expresses itself through material effects. That is why, as geographers, we are led to study man's part in nature—without ever separating it from the study of physical geography." [29] Elsewhere he states the thesis even more emphatically: "The man is there, the flint is there, but it is the man who makes the spark fly," for "all the essential facts begin and end in facts of psychology." Further, "the outstanding psychological fact, then, is the antithesis of rigid, fatalistic determinism of human acts by climate and soil. It is this—that natural surroundings whether as a whole or in detail, react on us just so far, and just in such way, as we adopt them; in other words, according to our interpretation of them." [30] Hence, it is not so much the task of the geographer to determine what nature does to man as to discover what man does to nature. Generally, it seems fair to say, this is the point of view of the French human geographers since the teaching of Vidal.

The French school was led into regional geographic analysis because the region offered a unit small enough to be studied intensively and varied enough to afford many of the differences noted on a large scale elsewhere; not because of interest in the region *per se*. The English geographers on the other hand seem to have approached regionalism more inductively, that is, by building up small units into regions rather than by dividing larger units. This appears in a scheme advanced by H. R. Mill, during the last decade of the last century for the study of a small area in southwest Sussex, and in the teaching of Mackinder, at Oxford, who had students do several dissertations of this nature. Roxby applied the idea in an article, "Historical Geography of East Anglia," appearing in *The Geographical Teacher* for 1907-1908, in which he defined a region as "an area throughout which a particular set of physical conditions will lead to a particular type of economic life. A physical unit tends to become an economic unit," [31] and, thus, through economics, affects other forms of social behavior. However, prior to the publication of this article two other notable contributions had been made by Englishmen. In 1896, G. G. Chisholm had observed that culture was a potent factor in determining geographic data. He argued that "the

[29] Jean Brunhes, *Human Geography*, p. 27.
[30] Quoted by Dickinson and Howarth, *op. cit.*, p. 208.
[31] *Ibid.*, p. 236.

value of geographical advantages depends upon the state of the applied sciences" [32] and, furthermore, "The geography of a country gets altered by the interference of man, and in other ways. This has again and again been emphasized and abundantly exemplified." [33] He illustrates his thesis by recalling that England imported iron until fairly late in history; that the Roman boundary of England was in level country, but that later England and Scotland set the boundary in a region of sparse population; that it was only the growth of manufacturing which brought Liverpool into prominence.

A. J. Herbertson had approached a regional division of the earth in 1905 as a means of systematizing geography. Arguing that political divisions were unsatisfactory from the point of view of the geographer, he suggested a hierarchy of regions of the world analogous to genera and species in biology. In this scheme a region is a "complex of land, water, air, plant, animal and man regarded in their special relationship as together constituting a definite, characteristic portion of the Earth's surface." [34]

> Aside from the systematic and educational value of such a division, Herbertson saw the history of such regions as having value in the development of new regions of similar type: "The recognition of natural regions gives the historian a geographical foundation for his investigations. . . . By comparing the histories of the same race in two different regions, or of a succession of races in the same region, it should be possible to arrive at some knowledge of the invariable effect of a type of environment on its inhabitants, and permit some estimation of the non-environmental factors in human development. It would be difficult to exaggerate the importance of this investigation, which seems to me a fundamental one for all who have to deal with the study of man, or with his economic exploitation, or with his proper government." [35] In the discussion which followed the presentation of this idea, there was considerable objection raised on the ground that it would cut across various genera of phenomena, but the existence of regions such as visualized was generally admitted. The actual regional division of the earth's surface suggested by Herbertson and illustrated

[32] "On the Relativity of Geographical Advantages," in *Scottish Geographical Magazine*, XIII, 480.
[33] *Ibid.*, p. 476.
[34] "The Major Natural Regions: An Essay in Systematic Geography," *The Geographical Journal*, XXV, 300.
[35] *Ibid.*, p. 309.

in a series of maps drawn by him and his students is based largely upon temperature, elevation and rainfall, and seems to be based almost wholly upon factors of physical geography in contradistinction to the ideas expressed a short time before by Chisholm.

It has been noted that regional studies began in Germany at a relatively early date. A central committee for regional studies was organized in 1886 and there followed the publication of numerous monographs by such writers as Lehman, Kirkoff, Penck, Supan, Hahn, Hettner, and Fischer. It is from this work that the modern regional geographic movement in Germany springs. Penck, in his *Morphologie der Erdoberflache*, seems to have originated the expression "Landschaft" [36] now so widely used in that country and coming into wide acceptance in the United States as the "cultural landscape." Most of these works seem to be more descriptive than analytical, reflecting the general method of the German historical school. Hettner, in the *Geographische Zeitschrift*, 1906, presents a hierarchy of regions, but unlike Herbertson, begins with the major land forms and analyzes them into more and more minor divisions.

Since the publication of Hettner's articles, this idea of the region has been greatly refined by him, and by Passarge, Grano, Solch, and Braun. Topography and vegetation, that is, the visible aspect of the landscape, are made the basis of the minor divisions, the *Landschaftsteil* or *chore*, which may cover only a few square miles. These units combine into a *Landschaft*, in which the topography and vegetation are still the distinguishing feature, but need not be so homogeneous; and finally into *landesteil*, in which climate and relationships between the constituent parts are also criteria.[37] The later works of the German geographers insist upon the land area as the basis of consideration, but conceive it as the stage of man's action, taking as their task the tracing of the transformation of the natural region into the cultural landscape through the efforts of man. The regional concept has come more and more to dominate the thinking of geographers within the last two or three decades.

[36] Dickinson and Howarth, *op. cit.*, p. 235.

[37] *Ibid.*, pp. 243-244. For more detailed accounts of the German point of view, see J. F. Unstead, "The Regional Geography of Siegfried Passarge," *The Geographical Journal*, LXXXVIII, 164-166; Alfred H. Hettner, *Grundzüge der Länderkunde;* Siegfried Passarge, *Die Grundlagen der Landschaftskunde.*

The idea of cultural regionalism was given classic expression by J. F. Unstead, who developed the thesis that physical geography is important only because of its effects on man. Though the concept of natural regions has been of great value, other elements must enter in: "Indeed, it may be put forward as a general proposition that, in view of the essentially correlative nature of geographical science, the best method of discovering geographical regions is not to bring together on separate maps certain analyzed factors, such as relief, structure, temperature, rainfall, natural vegetation, etc., and to compare these elements, but to take their combined effects as they work themselves out, i.e., to take the actual complex of physical and human conditions, to regard this as a closely interrelated whole, to observe the predominant characteristics of this complex in different parts, and so, by a synthetic rather than an analytic method, to arrive at the determination of regions with common characteristics. After this survey the factors may be analyzed in order to describe the regions, and to explain their peculiarities." [38]

Much the same idea was expressed by H. J. Fleure, who entered geography from anthopology. Though "The results of human effort stand in close relation to the physical conditions of various regions," the most favorable regions may suffer from human mistakes and the growing complexity of civilization so that: "The early response which we have indicated as so characteristic of regions of increment has left complex legacies, and many parts are anything but regions of increment so far as the present is concerned." [39] But a note of skepticism as to the results of this increasing importance of man is struck: ". . . a region of specialization in large-scale industry is not only an irritant that troubles the world's life, it is almost certainly a pathological feature with the foreshadowing of decay written all over it," so that we should encourage co-operation of industry and agriculture and forestry "inspired by regional patriotism." [40]

This idea of the man dominating nature has been accepted through a process of infiltration. As has been pointed out, it has been foreshadowed throughout the history of geography, but has never been wholly accepted, unless, perhaps, by Hall, in 1935, in this country. However, in 1908, W. S. Tower injected a distinctly regional note in American geography through his "types of earth environment"

[38] "A Synthetic Method of Determining Geographical Regions," *The Geographical Journal*, XLVIII, 234-235.
[39] "Human Regions," *Scottish Geographical Magazine*, XXXV, 97.
[40] *Ibid.*, p. 100.

which would furnish "complete entities." He advanced the notion that regions are marked off by a peculiar combination of soil, topography, and climate, and applied his scheme to the study of the Great Plains region of the United States. It is to be noted that his criteria for the determination of regions are physiographic, but his thesis is that such physical factors make for particular human uses of such regions.[41] In this he was applying the idea expressed a short time before by W. M. Davis, who offered a definition of geography as the study of the relationship between the earth and all organisms, including man, upon it through the use of geologic and climatic conditions and their stages, by man.[42] However, as late as 1935 this idea had not won full acceptance, as is shown by J. Russell Smith's comment that "It was unfortunate that this new meaning had to be put into an old word. It is not yet clear in," in making the point that new terms are confusing.[43]

Much of this same insistence on physical geography has been retained in the thinking of American regional geographers. Wolfgang L. G. Joerg, who holds "recognition of regional geography as the ultimate and highest expression of geographic research" nevertheless offers this definition of the region: "A natural region may be defined as any portion of the earth's surface whose physical conditions are homogeneous." Such a region is determined by consideration of three factors only: structure, climate, and vegetation. Animals are excluded and vegetation is admitted as a criterion only because it is a very delicate index to climate. "Anthropogeographic factors are not suitable criteria." However, the human element is not ruled out entirely, since "it may be said that the recognition of the desirability of subdividing the earth's surface into natural regions is a direct consequence of the development of regional anthropogeography."[44]

In opposition to such a view, R. de C. Ward, and C. R. Dryer, some time before, had held that geographic facts are of importance

41 Cf. "The Human Side of Systematic Geography," *Bulletin of the American Geographical Society*, XL, 522-530.

42 *Physical Geography, passim.*

43 "Are We Free to Coin New Terms," *Annals of the Association of American Geographers*, XXV, 21.

44 "The Subdivision of North America into Natural Regions: A Preliminary Inquiry," *Ibid.*, IV, 55-83.

because of their relation to human activity. Dryer holds that the study of geographic regions is important as a means of presenting the relations existing between human activities and natural environment, since "in economic influence may be found a standard for estimating the relative value of the different factors which make up a composite region." These economic factors, he believes, will depend in turn upon climate and vegetation to a large extent.[45] In Ward's theory the geographic influence is no less potent, but more indirect, being based on climatic fluctuations.[46]

Mark Jefferson, in 1916, offered a discussion of geography in terms suggesting those of today when he stressed the idea of geography as the study of man using, and living upon, the earth; saw anthropogeography as a greatly neglected field and foreshadowed a concept popular within the last decade by stating that city and rural regions are unified by economic interests and that the city is the unit of modern civilization.[47] It was this growing tendency to define the region in terms of the adjustment made to it by man, and his effect upon it, which led to an abandonment of the older theory that natural physical regions could be delimited which would be found to be characterized by similar cultures.

R. H. Whitbeck, in 1924, pointed out that the existence of physically natural regions was somewhat questionable, since physiographic, climatic and mineral regions do not coincide, though all are of importance to humans: "These various natural regions cut across one another in every possible direction, and any effort to bring them all into harmony is impossible; it must result in ignoring, or largely ignoring, several considerations and considering only one or two of the possible eight or ten factors in the problem." [48] From this it follows that a map of a region is a particular view at a particular time. Thus the Appalachian Mountain system forms a physiographic region, but differs socially from one part to another as much as a particular part of it would differ from New Zealand or Australia. From this line of reasoning he is led to assert that the need is for many kinds of regional

45 "Natural Economic Regions," *Ibid.*, V, 121-125.

46 Robert de C. Ward, "The Weather Element in American Climates," *Ibid.*, IV, 53-54.

47 "Some Considerations on the Geographical Provinces of the United States," *Ibid.*, VII, 3 ff.

48 "Facts and Fiction in Geography by Natural Regions," *Journal of Geography*, XXII, 87.

maps on which no definite boundaries are to be marked but on which the region is distinguished by the use to which it is put by its occupants. Thus political considerations would enter and such regions may easily be recognized and mapped in terms of the dominant characteristics they display.[49]

Though couched in more deterministic language, this seems to be very much the idea expressed by Mabel C. Stark, who defines a geographic region as "those areas that show within their boundaries essential uniformity in dominant physical conditions and consequently in dominant life responses." Such a region is to be recognized by the human activity and the dominant physical influences making such activity possible.

The point of view received its classic expression by Harlan H. Barrows, in 1923; a view that is generally accepted at this time as the charter of the newer geography. Barrows argued that the task of geography is to examine, and explain in so far as may be possible, the relations of man to his physical environment rather than to attempt to ascertain geographic influence on man. In geography as envisioned by him, man is the central theme and the active agent; nature is more passive though not without power. But the action of geographic forces is important only in so far as it affects the organization of human activities.[50] This point of view, as indicated by the title of the article in which it appears, is borrowed from biology, where the actual study of plants and animals as they are found in the fields has been sought as a corrective to the artificial study of these forms of life in the laboratory. The common basis for such study is a geographic area, or region, and one of the essential elements of such study is the relation of the organisms to the physical environment, though the study cannot stop here; it must proceed to take into account the relationships between the various organisms occupying the region under consideration. This necessarily brings in a consideration of the time element, or historical factor; and it is here that attacks have been launched at Barrows and his idea.

Sir Halford Mackinder has expressed this fear: "There is a little danger that we should mix history and geography without seeing clearly what

[49] "Facts and Fiction in Geography by Natural Regions," *Journal of Geography*, XXII, 87.

[50] "Geography as Human Ecology," *Annals of the Association of American Geographers*, XIII, 1-14.

we are doing . . . geography proper is a description of things in the present. Geography should as I see it be a physiological and anatomical study rather than a study in development. As its name implies, it should be a description with causal relations in a dynamic rather than in a genetic sense." [51] Further, it is argued, the approach offered by Barrows stresses the adjustment of man to the environment, whereas the better point of emphasis is the adaptation of the environment through the activities of man; i.e., the creation of the "cultural landscape." P. W. Bryan has stated this idea clearly: ". . . in the main it would appear more and more clear that man has adapted nature rather than adjusted himself and his activities to nature. Hence it would appear to be desirable to lay the emphasis on the process of adaptation. . . . Fundamental to a clear concept of this view is the fact that all human activity takes place in response primarily to the demand for the satisfaction of human needs and desires, and not in response to the controlling influence of environment. . . . Unless human activity is considered first in this study we have no principle on which to base our selection of the facts of human activity. It is becoming increasingly clear that the geographer's approach to his subject through human activity is more fruitful than that through environment, since in the former case he has ready to hand a measuring rod wherewith to select for study the environmental facts which affect human activity." [52]

When the geographer approaches his task from the environmental side he is without such a yardstick and is forced to study all the facts of the environment. Further, in such study he runs grave danger of becoming a meteorologist, physiographer, or what not, and to study these facts *per se* rather than in their adaptability to the needs of man.

In the United States this idea has been expressed by Carl O. Sauer more emphatically, perhaps, than by anyone else. "The field of regional geography is not concerned with an encyclopedic compendium of facts that are bound together simply by their occurrence in a particular region. . . . The dominant theme is the expression of the individuality of the region as the site of a particular group of people and their work. To begin with there is the physical fact of the area characterized by a distinctive location, by a climate, and by a particular body of land. . . . This physical site has been occupied by a group

[51] *The Geographic Journal*, LXXVIII, 268.
[52] P. W. Bryan, *Man's Adaptation of Nature*, pp. 9-13.

of people or by successive groups. The occupation has led to a series of characteristic contacts with the area as cultural forms." [53] Elsewhere Sauer holds that adaptations, by which man derives from nature, perhaps through a partly unconscious imitative process, harmonies between his culture and the landscape, "are derived from the mind of man, not imposed by nature, and hence are cultural expressions." [54]

This functional view of the region has led to attempts to determine the region in statistical terms of the uses to which humans put the physical environment, to soil regions a decade or so ago, and to types of farming regions today, for example. Thus G. T. Renner would define the essential characteristics of the region as "an area within which certain types of socio-economic adjustments to the fundament have been made by man so generally as to constitute the real 'regionality' of the area, and therefore to provide the reason for separating that area from adjacent areas which are characterized by different types of adjustment to the fundament." [55] Though Renner here speaks of man's adjustment to the fundament, it appears that he is in essential agreement with Sauer; and it is also noticed that he makes different forms of adjustment to the fundament, rather than differences in the fundament, the basis of separation of one region from another; that is, the visible evidence of man's culture is the fundamental fact for the geographer. He further emphasizes this idea by his remark that the economic depression has forced the politician and economist to recognize what the geographer, sociologist, and historian already realized, that there are essential regional differences.[56] This theory is basic and is expressed explicitly or implicitly in numerous recent regional studies.

As samples of the application of this principle to a field in which data are more readily available than in others, T. J. Woofter, "Subregions of the Southeast," *Social Forces*, XIII, 43-50; O. E. Baker, "Agricultural Regions of the United States," *Economic Geography*, II; F. F. Elliott, "Use of Type of Farming Material of the 1930 Census," *Farm Economics*, XV; F. F. Elliott, *Types of Farming in the*

[53] Carl O. Sauer, *Geography of the Pennyroyal*, p. x.
[54] Carl O. Sauer, *The Morphology of Landscape*, pp. 46-47.
[55] "The Statistical Approach to Regions," *Annals of the Association of American Geographers*, XXV, 137.
[56] *Ibid.*, pp. 137-139.

United States; Natural Resources Committee, *Report on National Planning and Public Works;* Richard Hartshorne and Samuel N. Dickens, "A Classification of the Agricultural Regions of Europe and North America on a Uniform Statistical Basis," *Annals of the Association of American Geographers,* XXV, might well be cited.

A more generalized statement of the theory is that of Wellington D. Jones, who looks at the region from the point of view of "operation units" and offers a scheme of elements which should be included in any regional study. This list begins with the inherent traits of such operation units and proceeds to a study of them as shown in production, transportation, commerce, habitation, recreation, government, education, religion, construction and maintenance of such units, the disposal of their products, and, finally, a consideration of the phenomena accounting for the present situation, as inter-regional connections and relations.[57]

Finally, the idea of the cultural aspect of the region reaches its logical conclusion in the theory of R. B. Hall, who observes that the human, or cultural region does not coincide with the geographic or natural region since the same people react differently to the same or similar geographic influences at different cultural stages. Hence, he concludes, that though a survey of a region should include such factors as surface forms, vegetation, climate and the "six essential facts" of Brunhes, they should be studied on their local aspects and morphologically rather than geographically. Such importance does the cultural aspect of geography take that in his opinion, "Probably the greatest single need of the regionalist is a series of systematic studies of culture forms and complexes, *per se*. . . . One might hazard the opinion at this time that a great deal of value might come from approaching the region through the medium of culture rather than through the orthodox approach of surface configuration." [58]

By such a technique the geographer would arrive at a unitary conception of the region approaching the ideas of "total situation," "cultural determinism," and folk-regional societies as used by the sociologist, "sectionalism" of the historian, "culture area" of the anthropologist, "economic domain" or "regional mercantilism" of the

[57] "Procedure in Investigating Human Occupance of a Region," *Ibid.*, XXIV, 93 ff.
[58] "The Geographic Region: A Résumé," *Ibid.*, XXV, p. 129.

economist, or "biotic area" of the biologist. Such an approach would give further distinction of co-ordinate classes, furnish manageable divisions, serve as units of organization for welfare programs, and replace partial correlation by a "unity of the whole."

Following the presentation of this idea, George B. Cressey insisted on the addition of the time element to the factors mentioned by Hall, offering the following definition: "cultural landscape equals the fundament, plus the culture, plus the sequent occupance or succession" citing his work in the Orient as demonstrating the necessity for considering the time element.[59]

> Though there are minor differences of opinion as to the nature of the geographic approach to regionalism, perhaps the statement of Isaiah Bowman would meet with as general acceptance among geographers and other social scientists as any other: "Most branches of knowledge have to deal with *area.* From this simple fact and its multiplied bearings flows one of the most important values of geography in studies that deal with mankind. In going from the abstraction area to specific regions, geography provides: (1) a framework of physical facts, region by region, the world around; (2) unifying explanations of physical phenomena in terms of laws evolved through experimental methods or by elaborate testing of hypothesis following both inductive and deductive methods; (3) an identification of regional characteristics, physical and human, through detailed statistical methods and by field notation; (4) a comparison of regions with the object of widening the generalities of physiography and human experience that have their bases in local and detailed observation. . . . Related facts in great number are grouped around these primaries. They grow out of the complex conditions and relations of groups of men as affected by forces that at one end of the scale have to do with natural conditions and at the other end with the processes of civilization coming down from the past and modified by human choice and invention.[60]

In the foregoing analysis, attention has been restricted to those theories which were concerned primarily with the development of the regional concept. But, in addition to these, there are a host of geographers who have advanced ideas with an important bearing upon regionalism, though not directed specifically toward discussion

[59] "The Geographic Region: A Résumé," *Annals of the Association of American Geographers,* XXIV, p. 133.

[60] Isaiah Bowman, *Geography in Relation to the Social Sciences,* pp. 145-146.

or definition of the region. Indeed, all geographical work which seeks to account for human use of the earth falls within this broad category. Thus, there is a vast amount of material which seeks to correlate geographic factors with human efficiency, political organization, population distribution, vital indices, mental disturbances, art, literature, and religion. And so on. These ideas are all regional in that geographic factors may be used to delimit regions, and such factors certainly vary from region to region. The discussion of these theories, it seems, is more pertinent to the aspects of regionalism to which such factors are basic, hence consideration of them has been placed in chapters dealing with those factors rather than in the present chapter.

Though it is true, as R. B. Hall has said, that there are almost as many regional theories as regional theorists, it does not follow that this invalidates the underlying fundamental concept of the region. Indeed, such a divergence seems to be inherent in such a concept. The region will vary according to the approach taken by the student investigating it. Physiographic regions will not coincide with human use regions; nor will economic regions coincide with artistc or religious or political regions. But this is far from saying that there are no interrelations and mutual influences which stamp a region with a pattern which may be recognized even though it may not be susceptible of exact delimitation or analysis. One need look no further than his own community, or his own consciousness, to demonstrate this truth. In the United States there is a "cotton belt," a "midwest," a "Pacific slope," etc., which are and have been vital factors in the life of the nation, and appear to be destined to continue in that role. That they have not been analyzed and described as a chemical compound might be analyzed and described does not argue their nonexistence, though perhaps it does argue lack of technique for such social tasks.

The foregoing summary would seem to indicate a growing consensus as to the meaning of the regional concept among the geographers, the persons first most intimately concerned. From mere description of isolated areas, regional study has progressed through physiographic analysis, determinism by physical factors of social phenomena, the *possibilisme* of the French school, to an approach almost indistinguishable from that of the cultural anthropologist on the part of some of the present scholars. But also implicit in this evolution of the idea seems to be that of the region as a physical and social unity, a frame of reference for the study of societal phenomena.

Chapter XIII

EXPLORING THE REGION: THE ANTHROPOLOGISTS

THE anthropologists' postulate is that man's own activity is assuming more and more importance as a factor essential to any explanation of either his social organization or the environment in which he enacts his role in the social drama. Confined to the stage afforded by geographic conditions, he, nevertheless, exercises a wide range of freedom in selecting the properties he will utilize, and even in arranging the setting of the stage itself. While this has been recognized, even emphasized, by modern geographers, especially by the French school and the German cultural geographers, and while in this country, Hall and Sauer have called attention to the need of geographers to study culture, and have used emphatic language in doing so, the anthropologists have developed the idea further.

Beginning with the study of the customs and tools with which men have surrounded themselves, the anthropologists have gradually evolved theories of the regional distribution of man and his ways of living. In the concept of the culture area, he has reached a position which he is being asked to share with the geographer, the sociologist, and with nearly all other social scientists who seek a systematic explanation of man's activities. Approaching from different angles, many social thinkers are coming to believe that spatial relationships are a necessary part of such an explanation.

The culture area concept in its commonly accepted form had its genesis in the efforts of American anthropologists to classify the cultures of Indian tribes occupying the American continents before the coming of white men; the result of highly empirical investigations which were hindered by an almost complete lack of historical data from which explanations might have been derived. The idea was brought to popularity by Clark Wissler only after it had been the common property of anthropologists working in the field of the American Indian for a generation or more, as Wissler himself insists.[1]

> That is, anthropologists endeavoring to describe the culture traits observed in investigations of Indian life on this continent were struck by the regional or areal distribution revealed, and began, subconsciously, to refer to certain traits as belonging to certain regions. As Wissler says, "A general course of lectures upon the American Indians is almost certain to treat the tribes in groups, and though this grouping will differ slightly according to the individuality of the lecturer, the segregation of the tribes may be expected to follow, in the main, the accompanying schedule. . . . Such grouping is convenient and practical and is justifiable, even if not absolutely inclusive."[2]

This segregation of culture was first noted in the distribution of single traits or the complexes built up about some single element. A conspicuous example is that of the type house, the wigwam being characteristic of a large area in the wooded eastern portion of the continent, the tipi being the usual form of shelter on the western plains, the fishing tribes of the northwestern coast building and occupying large wooden homes, the tribes of the Southwest using pueblos of masonry, and so on. This naturally raised the question as to whether or not other traits would show a coincidence, whether culture formed a pattern which might be said to be characteristic of a given region. Wissler holds that there is such a cultural pattern: "If . . . we take all traits into simultaneous consideration and shift our point of view to the social, or tribal, units, we are able to form fairly definite groups. This will give us culture areas, or a classification of social groups according to their culture traits."[3]

In an area in which a characteristic form of dwelling, for example, is found, there would also be characteristic complexes describing clothing, food, and items of non-material culture, such as ceremonies. Wissler demonstrated the essential truth of this proposition in his work on the American Indians, cited above, and in subsequent works,

[1] Clark Wissler, *An Introduction to Social Anthropology*, p. 318.
[2] *Ibid.*, pp. 318-319.
[3] Wissler, *The American Indian*, p. 218.

by working out a division of indigenous North American culture into nine regional patterns, using a classification of nine categories which he says are universal, found in every large area. By the use of such methods, he concludes that "one can, as a mere matter of observation, convince himself that the geographical distribution of culture traits is regional. Anthropologists conceive, therefore, that tribal cultures are not solely the creation of a single tribe, but are units in a regional development." [4]

Nor is this distribution of culture into regional patterns fortuitous. The influences of the environment, the geographic factors, make themselves felt to a considerable extent, especially through their effects upon the economic portion of the culture pattern. "In each case," says Wissler, "the economic life of the tribe concerned is nicely adjusted to the principal food resource in its locality, and this type of adjustment extends as far as the particular resource is available and no farther." [5] Clothing and housing materials found within the region also dominate the forms these traits will assume, though there is some room for choice even in these matters.

> This influence of geographic factors, working through the economic organization, extends even further: "When we turn to other aspects of tribal life, social organization, ceremonial procedure, etc., in the pursuit of which many wish to believe the spirit of man free to do its will, there is also a large degree of regional uniformity. We have just called attention to the tendency of all traits of culture to manifest regional distribution, but further inspection of them will show that their distributions largely coincide with the economic type and so are restricted to the same region. It is this tendency of all tribal traits of culture to coincide with economic traits that gives a regional character to culture as a whole. However, this does not mean that every element of culture has the same regional distribution, for we have just listed a fair number of traits found elsewhere. Also there are traits of culture that seem to have a continental distribution, or at least, cover a large part of a continent. . . . However, when the details of such traits are closely scrutinized, they often reveal regional differences in procedure and in method. So, notwithstanding that all tribal cultures have something in common, the variations in procedure tend to conform to regional standards. Again, if we wholly ignore the tribe, and

[4] *Ibid.*, p. 325.
[5] *Ibid.*, p. 326.

consider the various culture traits separately, we find all but those having a range approaching universality to be spread out upon the earth in continuous distribution, or in that sense to be regional. In conclusion, we once more call attention to the concept of the geographical school that the tribal group is the first point of departure and that its total culture should be considered in its relation to the geographical region in which it is found. . . . In matters of observation and fact, the claim is made that we do not know a culture trait until we know its geographical distribution."[6]

This would seem to lead Wissler very close to geographic, or at least economic, determinism; and indeed he has been accused of carrying this tendency too far.[7] But it seems somewhat doubtful if Wissler himself intended to go so far. He points out that "A tribe may exploit some of the resources in the surrounding environment but it does not exploit all of them at the same time, but specializes in a few." In his discussion of regional culture types, Wissler pointed out the fact that "many successive culture types could find homes in the same geographical environment. Thus a hunting type of culture once prevailed in England, later an agricultural mode of life developed, and now the culture of England may be characterized as industrial, yet the environment is the same."

He continues, "It seems then, that the relation between culture and the environment is rather a dynamic one, in that a culture type is, in fact at least, an exploitation of the immediate geographical environment. A small tribe of a thousand adults or less—and we have seen that most tribes are small in number—cannot carry on a culture comparable in complexity and richness to that in modern England; such a small group must specialize narrowly, not only in food production and material matters, but in social and intellectual life as well. What the tribe exploits among the many material resources of the habitat may or may not represent the line of least resistance; no one has studied the subject from this point of view. . . . The environmental problem hinges upon the degree to which all the tribes in a region conform to one mode of life. The Eskimo, we are told, live only in Arctic lands; the Plains Indians lived on the open plains where the bison were found. Yet, as we have observed, the ceremonial practices and art of the

[6] Wissler, *The American Indian*, pp. 325-327.

[7] Cf. especially Leslie Spier, Review of Roland B. Dixon, *The Building of Cultures* in *American Anthropologist*, XXXI, 140-145; and the book under review.

Eskimo are not found beyond the limits of Arctic environment and such practices as the sun dance, age societies, etc., are found only in the plains, in the bison country. On the other hand, no one has been able to demonstrate a causal relation between the environment and such nonmaterial traits of culture. The environment really holds together the tribes occupying a region, and develops a community of interest and concentrates leadership within itself. The tendency for a bison-hunting tribe is, first, to confine its wanderings to the bison range; secondly, to observe and fraternize with other bison-hunting tribes. Under such circumstances, it seems inevitable that the tribes within a region should follow much the same round of life. The influence of the environment thus appears as a passive limiting agency rather than a causal factor in the development of tribal life." [8]

Wissler therefore seems to see the geographic environment exerting its influence largely by keeping tribes in contact with each other rather than by determining what their mode of life may or may not be. It is also to be noted that he clearly recognizes the dynamic relationship between geographic environment and a changing culture and the size and density of the population group. That is, he views the physical environment more as the stage upon which man operates than an active determinant in that action, reserving the latter role for social relationships.

This point is brought out even more clearly elsewhere by Wissler: "While it is clear that the geographical region has a powerful influence upon every type of primitive culture, it does not follow that future or past culture areas will have the same boundaries, even if there are no climatic changes. The economic basis to a culture area may change, as, a hunting culture may be displaced by agriculture. The boundaries and center of the former would depend upon the distribution of the chief game animals and the mode of hunting; whereas for the latter they would depend upon soil and climatic conditions. Even a change from one type of hunting to another might conceivably shift both the center and the boundaries. History and archaeology furnish sufficient evidence to justify these statements." [9] And almost the same point of view is stated by Lowie in his consideration of the geographic influence: "Geography, powerful in shutting out cultural developments, often fails to stimulate them." [10] Such considerations led Wissler to

[8] Wissler, *The American Indian*, pp. 338-339.
[9] *Ibid.*, pp. 348-349.
[10] R. H. Lowie, *An Introduction to Social Anthropology*, p. 214.

formulate definitions of the culture area as conceived by the anthropologists in general, though, of course, they are couched in his own terminology: "A culture area is delineated by listing the tribes with similar cultures and plotting their habitats upon a map. The geographical shapes of culture areas appear to vary according to the topography and other physical factors that enter into the environmental complex." [11]

It is evident, of course, that not all tribes in any given area have built up the same culture patterns. Even in highly homogeneous regions there will be culture complexes more or less widely varying from one another. Further, the break between culture areas is not sharp and distinct but gradual except in rare cases where geographic or other factors prevent communication. Observation of this fact led the anthropologists to develop the idea of the culture center as a modification of the culture area concept. Here again economic influence is often seen as the determining factor, with geography underlying and reinforcing its efficacy. Obviously fishing tribes will remain near waters plentifully supplied with fish, and may thereby be led to build relatively permanent settlements. Likewise, tribes whose economic basis is the bison, will live within the bison range, and will be unable to build a settled social organization since they must follow the herds. Where the culture is based upon agriculture, geographic conditions of soil and climate will set natural limits to the area in which the dominant crop may be grown with sufficient success. This consideration also applies to the range utilized by certain game animals upon which a primitive culture may rest. In each case, the disappearance of the basic commodity of subsistence will not occur suddenly, but it will become less and less plentiful or possible of successful cultivation.

If the assumption that the entire culture is a unit is correct, it follows that the culture characteristic of any of these economic modes of life will disappear with the attenuation of the resource. This, of course, is merely another way of saying that the culture will be most typical of the area where the subsistence element is most plentiful; but it also leads to the corollary that a given culture will tend to

[11] Wissler, *The American Indian,* p. 346.

extend itself to the limits of the area in which this economic base is to be found in sufficient quantity.

> The theoretical expectation is supported by the results of actual observations. The characteristic culture is usually found to be the possession of a few social units well within the limits of the culture area, though not necessarily occupying a position in the geographic center of the area. These tribes will display nearly all, if not all, of the trait-complexes unique in the region. But as one proceeds from this characteristic group outward in any direction it is observed that the variations in the culture become greater and greater until they begin to assume a new pattern, characteristic of a neighboring culture area. This phenomenon has led Wissler to generalize the situation. "A culture area will comprise a nucleus of two or more neighboring tribes around which the others range roughly according to their degrees of similarity to this central group."[12] That is, the tribes occupying the central cultural position may be taken as typical of the area, but it is not to be expected that the entire area will be homogeneous. On the contrary, groups farther away will be marginal and may show characteristics of two or more culture areas, as has been demonstrated in many studies.[13]

This, again, leads to the conclusion that boundaries for such areas cannot be marked upon the map as sharp thin lines, but must be considered as broad zones in most cases, sometimes so broad as to lead to consideration of the transition zone as a more or less separate culture area in itself. It also tends to fix attention on the culture center to the neglect of the culture area as a whole, a tendency especially notable in other disciplines, and not altogether lacking in anthropology, as is shown by Kroeber's study of the Indians of California. Here he shows that as one approaches the center of the region, the culture becomes more and more homogeneous.[14] Similarly M. J. Herskovits points out that though the tribes occupying the central portion of the American Great Plains Region possess most of the traits considered typical of that area, those on the eastern and

[12] *Ibid.*, p. 348.

[13] Cf. Leslie Spier, "Problems Arising from the Cultural Position of the Havasupai," *American Anthropologist*, XXXI, 213 ff., for an example of a tribe occupying a position on the margins of two culture areas.

[14] A. L. Kroeber, *Handbook of the Indians of California*, Bureau of American Ethnology, Bulletin No. 78.

western margins have certain traits typical of regions to the east and west of the region, respectively.[15]

This, of course, brings up the whole question of diffusion, since it assumes that the culture probably originates in the culture center and is diffused over the region from that small area. Under this assumption any factor which prevented free communication, whether it were of geographic or cultural nature, would form a barrier to the diffusion process, and hence set a limit to the region. Thus large bodies of water, deserts, mountain ranges and similar geographic elements would serve as boundaries of regions in many cases, as was pointed out by Miss Semple.[16]

> Further, diffusion would follow along the natural lines of communication, the river valleys, along mountain fronts, etc., where there is any serious handicap to travel and communication, rather than spreading in circular form as it might without such barriers. This process is illustrated by Miss Semple and Rupert B. Vance.[17] However, barriers in one culture may become highways in another; as rivers are barriers without a technique of boating, but become highways once the technique is attained. Similarly water isolation of the British Isles was changed into ease of communication when the cultural situation of Europe arrived at a commercial stage in which the use of sailing vessels was important. In more primitive cultures such factors exert greater influence and are more apparent in the case of the Indian cultures than in our modern civilization. But this is not to say that such considerations lose force in modern society. As Wissler says: ". . . we see that the basis for the diffusion of trait-complexes is environmental and, to a large degree, also economic, since, whether primitive or civilized, man preys upon the organic resources of his habitat. So the immediate factors in the determination of diffusion boundaries are the fauna and flora. . . . Were these uniformly distributed over the surface of the earth, there would be no such diffusion as now exists." [18]

Wissler's conclusion may be questioned on the basis of advantages of division of labor, so far as small areas are concerned, but would seem valid when speaking of areas as large as those he has in mind. Further, there are culture complexes which seem to have always a

[15] "The Cattle Complex in East Africa," *American Anthropologist,* XXVIII, 242.
[16] Ellen Churchill Semple, *Influences of Geographic Environment,* ch. I.
[17] *Ibid.;* also Rupert B. Vance, *Human Geography of the South,* ch. III.
[18] Clark Wissler, *Man and Culture,* pp. 138-139.

large degree of uniqueness within one single tribe; language is perhaps the most obvious example, according to Wissler,[19] although other complexes show the same characteristic in less degree. This means, of course, that no two tribes will possess identical culture, but it does not mean that no two tribes will have enough similarity of culture to allow the ethnologist to separate them from surrounding tribes. This is evident when the cultures are looked at as composite wholes, or when the individuals traits are separated and plotted on a map. What usually occurs is that the traits become more typical in some one small area, and thus indicate a culture center.

This leads Wissler to offer another definition of the culture area: "By the culture area is meant an aggregation of tribes conforming in whole or in part to a type of culture as defined in terms of specific traits. Culture centers are thus revealed. However, these centers not only influence the neighboring tribes but one another. The study of widely distributed traits does not reveal contradictions to the belief in culture centers, but, on the other hand, tends to reveal the leading centers of culture influence in the world." [20] While it is true that regional cultures thus tend to become homogeneous wholes as a result of this creative function of the center, it is equally true that differing cultures may occupy a geographic region at the same time. In such a case, however, Wissler argues that there is the greatest likelihood of borrowing and that the culture with the greatest vigor will tend to become dominant at the culture center. Such is shown to have occurred in the Southwestern Region, where different cultures are in contact, he claims.[21]

Such, in summary, is the culture area concept as developed by Wissler, who is usually given credit for its statement, though not for its origin. The idea is largely confined to American anthropologists, and undoubtedly arose because of the lack of historical materials by which the Indian culture of this continent could be explained. This, in turn, led to a view of the culture of a tribe as a whole, a functioning unit, rather than an attempt to break it into particular traits, the origin of which might have been traced historically. Because of this the American anthropologists have generally adopted the regional approach.

19 *Ibid.*, p. 140.
20 Clark Wissler, *An Introduction to Social Anthropology*, pp. 352-353.
21 *Ibid.*, p. 355.

Moreover, the culture area concept is held to be as applicable to modern civilized areas as to those occupied by primitives. Wissler cites the development of power resources in northeastern America and northwestern Europe as a basis of such modern culture areas. From these centers there is a distinctly noticeable spread of other, non-material culture traits associated with the general culture pattern of the areas; and a gradual fading of the elements of this culture as one proceeds away from the center, he observes.[22] Within the larger areas with their culture centers may also be located smaller areas, each with a center of its own. Thus the culture area concept would seem to hold out a research lead which may be of value in determining what is actually happening in any specific community, since the setting is fundamentally the same whether one studies primitive or civilized cultures.[23]

This assertion is based on the observations that "Culture in the concrete is found in patches, instead of scattered at random throughout the world's population" and "One cannot read anthropological discussions without becoming aware that the procedure is based on a belief in regional differences in social behavior and that social evolution itself is regional."[24] Further, the ethnological approach emphasizes the regional differences in culture, since specialization is usual in the study of a regional group, the investigator being led from one tribe to another similar one until the culture has changed sufficiently to be no longer homogeneous. This gives the investigator a dynamic, functional point of view, since the "primitive culture area . . . is not fixed, but a region in which culture changes are under way, a group of tribal communities differing more or less in culture, but continually adopting new traits, or variants of old ones, each at varying time intervals and not simultaneously."[25] Such an approach, he argues, gives the investigator of contemporary life the problem of accounting for responses to situations, and an escape from the deadness of statistical description. However, techniques for the

[22] Clark Wissler, *An Introduction to Social Anthropology*, p. 351.

[23] Clark Wissler, "The Culture Area Concept as a Research Lead," *American Journal of Sociology*, XXXIII, 894-900.

[24] Clark Wissler, "The Culture Area Concept in Social Anthropology," *ibid.*, XXXII, 882-885.

[25] Clark Wissler, "The Culture Area Concept as a Research Lead," *ibid.*, XXXIII, p. 898.

study of contemporary society by this method are yet to be worked out.

> Since Wissler wrote the above, the Lynds, with their studies of Middletown; and Redfield, with his studies of Tepotzlan and Chan Kom, have applied this idea to contemporary situations with marked success. Also Wissler feels that the same principle is of great utility to the archaeologist; that by its application ancient culture areas will be delineated. Historically Greece and Egypt may be considered such centers of areas. Thus, after asserting that community and certain types of response are universal, and that the procedure of science is to discover principles of wide validity, Wissler concludes: "The question now is whether the concept of the culture area has wide validity; our discussions of regional phenomena fully justify the expectation that it has. . . . In general, then, the culture area concept promises to be a lead in social science."[26]

Anthropologists are disagreed as to the correctness of that conclusion. For in spite of Wissler's insistence on the dynamic and functional nature of the culture area concept, it is objected by Bronislaw Malinowski, writing on cultural anthropology in the *Encyclopaedia Britannica*, that the idea of culture complexes takes a "lifeless and inorganic view," and treats culture as if it could be placed in cold storage for centuries, whereas the functional, and correct, view of the matter treats of relations of part to part and to the physical environment; that is, culture must be conceived as an organic whole which forms a milieu. However, it must be noted, Malinowski restricts this estimate to the term as used by Graebner and his followers, holding that the work of the American school in this respect constitutes "a valuable method of bringing out the influence of physical habitat as well as the possibilities of cultural transmission" and, as such, will have lasting value.

> More to the point is the illustration of Lowie of the occupancy of the same region by the Hopi and Navajo with distinct, if not wholly exclusive, cultures. "Though the same building material is available . . . the Hopi construct the well-known terraced sandstone houses with a rectangular cell as the architectural unit, while the Navajo dwell in conical earth-covered huts."[27] Of the same tenor is the

[26] Clark Wissler, *An Introduction to Social Anthropology*, p. 346.
[27] R. H. Lowie, *Culture and Ethnology*, pp. 49-65.

criticism of Leslie Spier, who remarks that the idea that the cultural and geographic areas are coterminous has become so well accepted that anthropologists have fallen into the habit of filling in unknown spaces on the maps on the basis of known cultures on either side. The Havasupai, a tribe in Arizona, disclose the danger of such procedure, since an investigation of their culture did not meet the expectations so raised, the cultural step-down being surprising. This tribe, occupying one of the few rich oases in that territory, has adopted an agriculture similar to that of the Pueblo Indians, though the remainder of its culture is of the Great Basin type. However, they display no traits not found in similar form in other tribes nearby, though the combination of these traits is unique.[28] Here, it would seem, we are dealing with a tribe on or near a cultural margin. Spier also points out that "Those who would derive the totality of a culture from its environment, as Wissler has of late been inclined, must reckon with the purely cultural facts that basic traits are by no means confined to a single culture area and that no culture area is uniform within itself." [29] Though Spier would seem to be greatly overstating Wissler's position, it is true that the lack of homogeneity of traits is a favorite point of attack on all regional theories. Dixon also attacks the idea of the regularity of culture areas: "We have seen that in the diffusion of trait-complexes within the area of their origin the erratic spread does indeed produce a roughly zoned distribution, but one which is far from symmetrically concentric. The nucleus is rarely central in location and there is no necessary relation between the distance from the trait nucleus and the extent to which the complex is developed. Nor is there any similar relation in time, i.e., we cannot say that because one tribe is nearer to the nucleus of the trait complex than another, therefore it will receive the complex sooner." [30]

Dixon also insists that cultural changes take place on the periphery of culture areas rather than at the culture centers as indicated by Wissler, but distinguishes two sorts of diffusion; primary, or that taking place within the area, and secondary, that taking place between two culture areas; and thereby accepts the general idea of the culture area and its center as a point of diffusion for that area, as pointed out by Redfield.[31]

[28] "Problems Arising from the Cultural Position of the Havasupai," *American Anthropologist*, XXXI, 213-220.

[29] Leslie Spier, Review of Roland B. Dixon, *The Building of Cultures* in *American Anthropologist*, XXXI, 140-145.

[30] Roland B. Dixon, *The Building of Cultures*, p. 179.

[31] Robert Redfield, Review of Roland B. Dixon, *The Building of Cultures* in *American Journal of Sociology*, XXXIV, 389.

Perhaps the most severe criticism of the concept is that voiced by Carter A. Woods, who recalls that the concept was originally used only with reference to material culture traits but that later Wissler "gratuitously expanded the culture content of his areas to give the impression that culture areas were regions with relative uniformity of total culture"—a procedure which Woods characterizes as "sketchy, loose-edged handling of data." [32] After distributing such non-material aspects of culture as social organization, political organization, sexual division of labor, war customs, marriage and family rites, criteria of prestige, means of self-gratification, and religion from the data on 118 tribes in Wissler's culture areas, he concludes that the Wissler scheme leaves too much margin and that the nuclear groups are too large, often covering almost the entire area. Clearly, he argues, it was erroneous to include the Pueblo Indians in the general Southwestern Region.

> Further, though it is possible to find nuclear groups: "These groups all show a relatively high homogeneity such as should be expected as a result of adaptation to common geographic conditions combined with the leveling effect of the diffusion process. They correspond roughly to Wissler's culture types, but they constitute only a portion (sometimes a minor portion) of the total number of tribes within the culture area. There is no reason why they should serve as the basis of generalization for the entire area. The regions are too widely drawn to possess a relatively uniform culture. . . . It is also apparent that certain culture areas appear to possess more homogeneous traits and complexes than other areas." [33] On a statistical basis, this writer argues that in the case of mutually exclusive traits one should expect to find homogeneity in at least two-thirds of the cases, whereas the actual situation is nearer one-half. Hence: "Even as a static approach, Wissler's culture areas leave much to be desired. Because there has been a tendency to draw them so carelessly and to interpret them so broadly, they have often failed to provide accurate information concerning the culture of specific tribes. . . . The failure of the distribution of non-material elements to coincide with the material culture areas does not, however, invalidate the regional approach. It is still possible to recognize the spatial distribution of culture elements and

[32] "A Criticism of Wissler's North American Culture Areas," *American Anthropologist*, XXXVI, 517.
[33] *Ibid.*, p. 521.

the significance of this circumstance."[34] T. T. Waterman makes much the same criticism, stressing the intangible nature of the boundaries and the great importance of the culture center, and adds that culture elements change radically in time. In the case of the pueblo culture this is especially true, he says, since these structures were used for only a short time, relatively speaking.[35]

Of a somewhat different nature is the criticism of Kroeber, who observes that the culture area concept is not concerned with the time element, except in the sense of the somewhat doubtful age-area concept. Further, anthropologists speak of culture areas when they are really interested in the content of such areas rather than the area itself. The concept was foreshadowed by Ratzel, and by Sophus Müller, who spoke of Europe as marginal to and to be explained only in terms of higher centers in the Orient; by Sapir, who discussed culture areas from the historical point of view as early as 1916. European anthropologists tend to reject the concept, partly because of their interest in the historical-diffusionist idea.

In spite of these criticisms, Kroeber holds that the concept "represents normally a synthesis useful in the organization of knowledge, tinged with a subjective element, and yet evidently resting on something objective because empirical opinion tends to be in essential concord in specific cases. In all these points the culture area is analogous to the faunal or the floral area. In other words, it aims at determining and defining a natural area. Adjacent areas normally intergrade, and progressive dissection can therefore always analyze them out of existence. . . . The core of the concept, in particular instances, is likely to be the culture center, as Wissler has recognized. This, however, is likely to be not only a 'crater' of diffusing productivity, as Wissler has in the main treated it, but also a 'focus' or gathering point."[36]

Further, the idea might be given a better application by using traits from several complexes and thereby delimiting a small "center." As developed by Wissler, the regions are unduly uniform in size, number

[34] "A Criticism of Wissler's North American Culture Area," *American Anthropologist*, XXXVI, 522-523. The exact percent of traits which must show homogeneity before cultures are to be described as similar offers abundant room for argument, it is to be observed. The lack of coincidence of material and non-material trait distribution is a more serious objection to the concept; but as this critic states, this non-coincidence is not great enough to invalidate the approach.

[35] "Culture Horizons in the Southwest," *American Anthropologist,* XXXI, 367-400.

[36] A. L. Kroeber, "The Culture-Area and Age-Area Concepts of Clark Wissler" *Methods in Social Science* (edited by Stuart A. Rice), p. 261.

of tribes included, and the implied uniform level of culture. The idea has been used for descriptive purposes, though it lends itself to historical uses, and has emphasized the stabilizing and binding function of the environment, though there is yet considerable developmental work to be done here.[37] Elsewhere the same writer has characterized the concept as "a non-philosophical, inductive, mainly unimpeachable organization of phenomena analogous to the 'natural' classification of animals and plants on which systematic biology rests."[38] (Thus the concept represents a consensus of opinion as to the classification of a mass of facts, slowly arrived at, contributed to by many workers, probably accepted in exact identity by no two of them, but in essential outlines by all.)

Herskovits adds that the concept has no time depth,[39] and Sapir remarks that it is primarily descriptive, not historical, in its implications.[40] Herskovits, however, also advances the idea that the cultural pattern enables the social scientist to lay open his problems much as the physiologist lays open the muscular system of the animal he is studying; that with history it enables the student to make an objective approach to his study of culture.[41]

Essentially, it would seem, the disagreement lies largely in the matter of viewpoint. To those students who insist upon a strictly scientific approach through analysis, the culture area concept seems vague and even mystical, while to those who wish to look at the culture of a region or a people as a whole, it offers a tool grown up from empirical and inductive work in the field and from the nature of the problems attacked and the data accumulated. Perhaps the vital question affecting the validity of the concept is the coincidence of material and non-material elements of culture in areas to a degree sufficient to make separation of such areas a practical as well as academic pursuit. Whether this can be done analytically or not remains to be seen; it is fairly certain that it *is* done empirically and by lay-

[37] *Ibid.*, pp. 249-265.

[38] Kroeber, *Anthropology*, p. 336.

[39] M. J. Herskovits, "A Preliminary Consideration of the Culture Areas of Africa," *American Anthropologist*, XXVI, 50-63.

[40] Edward Sapir, "Time Perspective in Aboriginal American Cultures," *Memoirs 90, Anthropological Series, No. 13*, Geological Survey, Canadian Department of Mines; quoted by Russell Gordon Smith, *Fugitive Papers*, p. 69.

[41] M. J. Herskovits, "Social Pattern: A Methodological Study," *Social Forces*, IV, 57-69.

men daily in their references to various regional divisions of the nation.

Redfield, as a result of his study of a Mexican village, Tepotzlan, raises certain objections. The culture area concept is qualified, he thinks, by the gradual change of the culture from one region to another, by the failure to give due attention to the effect one region may have on another while remaining relatively passive, and by a lack of due emphasis on the essential question of communication as the means by which culture is diffused. Among primitives this matter of communication is not so important since "A cultural variation among such peoples spreads from its innovator to the person standing at his elbow, so to speak, and from him to the next within easy speaking distance." [42] Hence the mode and character of communication should be the central point of attack in studies of culture distribution. Further, culture is essentially not the tool or form, but its *significance* to the user or performer, so that the culture area comes to be characterized as that area in which common things are given common meanings. This leads to doubt as to the validity of the concept under modern conditions of communication. Redfield illustrates his point by citing his finding in Tepotzlan that the central plaza with its immediately surrounding area is the locus of change in the culture of this village, and therefore, though centrally located, has become the cultural margin.

Certainly Redfield has pointed to limiting factors in the application of the culture area concept to modern cultures. These are supplemented by other criticisms of the sociologists. Whether their criticisms destroy its validity or not is another matter, of course. Empirically and impressionistically, it seems undeniable that, making all possible allowances for class differences, there are commonly recognized regions the essence of which is awareness by observers of the region as a whole of a general "spirit" or philosophy or *Weltanschauung*. This applies with equal force to the "personality" of various cities within this country.

Wilson D. Wallis agrees with the position that a unique reality comes into being whenever and wheresoever men live together and

[42] Robert Redfield, "The Regional Aspect of Culture," *Publications of the American Sociological Society*, XXIV, 37.

share a common heritage of thought, language, institutions, and technology. These entities may be plotted on a map, since every social phenomenon happens not only somewhen, but somewhere, and such plotting will facilitate the understanding of the geography of culture; but it is the relationship, the cultural pattern, rather than the area covered, which is important. As illustration, a radio, as a trait, has little significance, but when combined as an integral part of a culture pattern it creates new patterns and is itself changed into a new culture trait. That is, "Every new device calls for a psychological adjustment, which of course is a phase of adjustment within the culture."[43]

These psychological adjustments constitute what Ruth Benedict refers to as "configurations," and what Edward Sapir calls "genuine culture." Miss Benedict applies the philosophy of the German school represented by Dilthey and Spengler to American Indian tribes, and finds that the pueblo dwellers are characterized by an Apollonian culture, though they are surrounded by tribes best described as Dionysian and there are no geographic barriers to account for the differences. These pueblo tribes are wholly socialized; the group is paramount in their thinking and feeling. Rites and ceremonies are provided for almost every conceivable contingency, so that the individual has little opportunity for the expression of his own feelings or desires. The result is that the tribes are sober and serious-minded. On the other hand, the plains tribes express their emotions in wild behavior, such as scarification or mutilation at the death of a family member. Such traits are combined into configurations, or behavior patterns, which are characteristic of areas and "stand to the understanding of group behavior in the relation that personality types stand to understanding of individual behavior."[44]

> Over a period of many generations such configurations should produce harmony within the area, though they may not; nor is it proven that they are coterminous with traits of material culture, according to this writer. By "genuine culture" Sapir refers to: "Those general attitudes, views of life, and specific manifestations of civilization which give a particular people its distinctive place in the world. Emphasis is put

[43] Wilson D. Wallis, *Culture and Progress*, p. 31.

[44] Ruth Benedict, "Configurations of Culture in North America," *American Anthropologist*, XXXIV, 23.

not so much on what is done and believed by a people as on *how* what is done and believed functions in the whole life of that people, on what significance it has for them. . . . Culture thus becomes nearly synonymous with the 'spirit' or 'genius' of a people, yet not altogether, for whereas these loosely used terms refer rather to a psychological, or pseudo-psychological, background of national civilization, culture includes with this background a series of concrete manifestations which are believed to be peculiarly symptomatic of it. . . . Here, as so often, the precise knowledge of the scientist lags somewhat behind the more naïve but more powerful insights of non-professional experience and impression."[45]

Such culture is commonly found only within relatively small and autonomous groups, such as the Athenians of the time of Pericles, within which there can be found something like intensive spiritual contacts, and it is doubtful if it can spread over an area too wide for such contact, Sapir holds. This, moreover, is made almost impossible by our widespread political and economic organization and by our insistence upon standardization. The solution lies in the opportunity and desire to promote smaller cultural units, or regions, which should be largely non-comparable, or at least largely oblivious to each other.[46]

From the above survey of the concept of the culture region it would appear that the idea is empirical and inductive; that it almost literally forced itself upon field anthropologists in its original form, and thereby has the stamp of authenticity and usefulness. However, it has been charged that the concept has been taken out of its original setting and made to do duty for which it was not fitted, or for which its fitness is yet to be demonstrated. It seems certain that the concept lacks the qualities of definiteness demanded by many social scientists. The geographical connotation of the term "area" should be largely ignored. The boundaries of culture areas are vague zones, or if a definite limit is set by statistical methods there remains an indefiniteness indicated by lack of homogeneity of the traits used as criteria. The center also is often vague; indeed it is conceivable that different complexes within the same pattern might have different

[45] Edward Sapir, "Culture, Genuine and Spurious," *American Journal of Sociology*, XXIX, 405-406.

[46] *Ibid.*, pp. 401-429.

centers from which they are diffused. It has also been stated that the concept does not lend itself to historical treatment, that it is a cross section of culture in which the time element is missing or mixed, that it is merely a museum device. Here opinions differ, but it would seem that where and when historical data are available, the concept need not be applied, except in the sense in which it is used by Benedict and Sapir; that is, as having its essence in the relationships of the factors of the culture. Perhaps it is here that the greatest utility of the tool is to be found.

> This concept of the culture area has been given expression by Goldenweiser in terms as clear and precise as could be found: "A culture area is Bastian's geographical province raised from a state of vagueness and abstraction to one of concreteness and relative precision. A culture area is characterized by a catalogue of traits or features material, artistic, religious, ceremonial, social (so far like a Graebnerian culture), but also by the way in which such features are associated, interrelated, colored by one another (an outlook quite beyond Graebner's horizon). Such culture *complexes* show remarkable tenacity and chronological persistence. The further concept of a *culture center*, arising from the attempt to find the locus of greatest incandescence of the culture of an area with a concomitant attenuation toward the periphery, has proved less serviceable. While attractive, it is also dangerous and seems difficult of application. The facts may be too complex for so simple a formulation."[47] Goldenweiser also conceives the marginal areas as true culture areas in the psychological sense, and, like the writers quoted immediately above, lays particular stress on the psychological aspects of the entire concept—that is, the pattern or configuration of culture within the region. "An obvious homology to the culture pattern concept must be seen in Koffka's and Kohler's psychological theory of *Gestalt.* Similar categories are encountered in the study of organisms and of crystals. All these concepts are again related to the concepts of form and system in the plastic arts, music, and the abstract disciplines, such as mathematics and logic. Unless we are badly misguided, a concept of the general type of *pattern* or *Gestalt* may yet come to mark an epochal advance in our conceptual explorations."[48]

Here we find a concept of the culture area removed as far as may be from the narrow limits of geography within which Wissler is

[47] Alexander Goldenweiser, "Anthropology and Psychology," *The Social Sciences and Their Interrelations* (edited by W. F. Ogburn and Alexander Goldenweiser), p. 84.

[48] *Ibid.*, p. 85, note.

accused of confining the idea; finding its existence in the minds of men and connected with the earth only as men, by their specific gravity, are forced to remain on or near the surface of the earth and there construct their tools and their thoughts. But, it might be added, man's specific gravity is fairly stable, and it is very difficult to walk through clay without taking on some of its color, a fact fully recognized by Goldenweiser. It must also be kept in mind that the marginal lines between the sociologists and the anthropologists are scarcely distinguishable and that likewise the sociologists and human ecologists must work closely together in many phases of their study. We turn, therefore, next to the ecological approach.

Chapter XIV

EXPLORING THE REGION: THE ECOLOGISTS

IN his introductory statement to the members of the Conference on Regional Phenomena, held at Washington in April 1930, Professor E. B. Wilson, as Chairman of the Social Science Research Council, called attention to differences in point of view on the regional concept between the geographer and the anthropologist as reflected in discussion in previous conferences. This implication that the regional concept and the techniques for the further exploration of the region were limited primarily to these two disciplines was followed by the suggestion that since other fields "have also started to develop similar techniques," it was thought advisable to get representative investigators in different fields together for discussion. To this end, representatives of some ten disciplines registered as members, including the constituent members of the Social Science Research Council, in addition to representatives of the National Research Council, among whom were the Chairman of the Division of Biology and Agriculture and the Chairman of the Division of Geology and Geography, as well as representatives of the American Geographical Society and of the American Museum of Natural History.[1]

We continue in Part II the presentation of materials which indicate the contributions, techniques, and backgrounds of several of these sciences in relation to regionalism. The next viewpoint, following the discussions of the concepts of the geographers and anthropologists, is that of the ecologists. The ecological region is logically next in order for three reasons. One is because the ecological region and the geographical region are often used interchangeably within recent

[1] *Conference on Regional Phenomena, 1930*, p. 3.

years. Another is because the ecologists provide admirable techniques for defining the region and for setting up the frame of reference for analysis and classification. A third is because ecology affords an excellent borderline approach to the social sciences. Even as geography expands into human geography and anthropology into cultural anthropology, so ecology has rapidly extended its implications to human ecology. Although our first emphasis is upon the ecological regions of plant and animal life, nevertheless ecology affords an excellent example of a many-sided, yet scientific, delineation of elemental, organic regionalism.

This diversity of meaning is well illustrated by Warner P. Taylor in his question, "What Is Ecology and What Good Is It?" "One does not go far," he says, "in the study of definitions of ecology before he realizes that, as a rule, the content of the definition depends to a considerable extent on the field in which the writer is at work. According to a student of plants, ecology is perhaps very little more than a branch of botany. The zoologist is likely to think of ecology as animal ecology. Some of the physiologists have defined ecology as a part of general physiology, while others have regarded the two as identical. A forester is quite likely to think exclusively of forest ecology. One range ecologist defines it as the relation of invasion and succession to range management. Geography and ecology recently have been used as near synonyms. A number of workers regard ecology as the science of communities. There are other definitions: One writer thinks of ecology as the science of the repsonses of organisms to the factors in their environment. Still others, taking a cue from the Greek word from which the first part of the term is derived, define ecology as the study of the home life of organisms. . . . We can say that ecology is the science of relations of organisms to their environment. The field is so large that it is customary at present to break off the study of plant relations to their environment and call it a part of botany, also to put to one side the ecology of animals and call it a part of zoology, the ecology of human beings and call it a part of sociology."[2]

Returning to the Conference on Regional Phenomena, we find two of the best statements on the regional concept presented from the viewpoints of animal and plant ecology. In plant ecology, the phenomena of *distribution* is featured, including the study of geo-

[2] Warner P. Taylor, "What Is Ecology and What Good Is It?" *Ecology*, Vol. 17, No. 3, p. 333.

graphical distribution of individual species, genera, and families, the association of plants in "societies," the recognition of plant zones; the study of causes that have brought about changes in distribution, such as weather, growth, and interaction. Thus, the botanical concept of regions would include the major ideas of plant zones or life zone societies, and intermediate orders between these two dilimited by climate, topography, soil, and time factors and evolutionary processes.

The animal ecological region comprehends the following factors: "(a) Influence, or rather the interrelations of the physical environment on both plants and animals. This field is covered by ecological (plant and animal) geography and by phyto- and zoo-geography. . . . (b) Influence of these organisms on one another under different physical and ecological conditions. . . . (c) The productive or carrying capacity for plants and animals of different physical and ecological conditions. The capacity of given conditions to permit the production of plant and animal (floral and faunal) populations, and communities (ecological). . . . (d) The characteristic habits and behavior of plants and animals under internal and external environmental pressure. . . . There are numerous intensive local studies being made in various parts of the world on many aspects of the problem. These include descriptive aspects of regional studies, discussions of the faunas and floras and their distribution, as well as parallel studies of the ecological distribution of plants and animals. Considerable work is being done in America, in the British Empire, Denmark, Germany and other countries, while traveling naturalists cover immense areas. The Ecological Society of America, and the British Ecological Society are leading organizations in these studies of plants and animals."[3] Something more of the meaning, range, variety, of natural ecological regions may be inferred from representative concepts of plant and animal ecology. Thus, A. G. Tansley says that "In its widest meaning ecology is the study of plants and animals *as they exist in their natural homes.* . . . In a favorable climate and soil plants cover the ground more or less completely, thus *forming a natural framework or basis for the study of the living populations of the globe.*"[4] Royal N. Chapman treats of ecology as the "conception of a unit of association bound together by the interdependence of the organisms."[5] He also cites recent important books, such as Adams' *Guide to the Study of Animal Ecology*,

[3] *Conference on Regional Phenomena, 1930*, Appendix A, pp. 1-2.
[4] A. G. Tansley, *Practical Plant Ecology*, p. 15.
[5] Royal N. Chapman, *Animal Ecology*, p. 2.

1913; Shelford's *Animal Communities*, 1913; Borradaile's *The Animal and Its Environment*, 1923; Pearse's *Animal Ecology*, 1926, and Elton's *The Ecology of Animals*, 1927. In this connection he cites the foundation of the Ecological Society of America in 1916 and the beginning of their publication *Ecology* in 1920, while the British Ecological Society began the *Journal of Ecology* in 1913.[6] Pearse's ecology is "the branch of biological science which deals with the relations of organisms to their surroundings."[7] W. C. Allee stresses the association aspects in that "modern ecological work has shown that each different kind of a habitat contains a more or less characteristic set of animals which are not merely accidental assemblages but are interrelated communities."[8]

The ecologist, according to Eugene P. Odum,[9] characterizes his major divisions as "biotic formations" or "biomes," regions in which there is a uniform "climax," which is the highest type of vegetation possible in the region, and also in which the most important animals are similar. This idea of climaxes is fundamental in modern ecology, and it is believed that they represent climatic influences perhaps even more than soil. Another fundamental idea is succession, which represents, of course, the environmental and the time quality. Thus, if one lets a field in the southeastern deciduous forest area lie fallow, there are, first of all, grasses of various kinds, then pines, and finally if we wait long enough, the oak-hickory deciduous or hardwood forest, which is the climax for that area. The animals will also change with the plants. The grasses and pines are called "successional" or "sub-climax stages." The speed at which succession takes place and the types of successional stages depend on the soil, but the important thing is that eventually the sub-climax vegetation will be replaced by the climax, because the climate is a deciduous forest climate. The biome includes, therefore, not only climax vegetation and associated animals but the successional aggregations also. In the above pattern of development, the subregions of the ecologists, for example, would provide for the pine area of the South Atlantic and Gulf Coast which because of soil conditions and man's disturbance remains "sub-climax," the oak-pine of piedmont regions, the oak-hickory and beech-maple

[6] Chapman, *Animal Ecology*, pp. 2-3.
[7] A. S. Pearse, *Animal Ecology*, p. 1.
[8] W. C. Allee, *Animal Aggregations*, p. 8.
[9] The following summary is by Eugene P. Odum. Unpublished manuscript.

of the north and central states and other climaxes which make up the deciduous forest area. In so far as the major features of climate are concerned and the animals at large the major area is a definite unit.

These preliminary considerations will serve to give the basis for major ecological regions and to contrast them as a matter of classification and methodology with those of agricultural regions and soil regions. Such an ecological regionalism represents within the field of nature the equivalent of our total determinism in the sociological sense. The depiction of these major regions is also of great value in studying human ecology and, in particular, the larger human ecology of the United States.

In addition to possible other smaller biomes in the Far West, where the situation is complicated because of the great variety of climates, it is possible to characterize the nation in terms of ten major regions: [10] 1. The deciduous forest, including most of Eastern United States. Man is considered a deciduous forest animal since it is in these regions that he reaches highest development not only in North America but in Europe and Asia. The fact that he is such is shown when he takes trees with him when he settles the prairies. 2. The grasslands, the area generally known as the Great Plains. Here the climax is grass. This biome, like the deciduous forest, is subdivided into smaller associations as "tall grass prairie," "mixed prairie," "short grass prairie," and "Bunch grass prairie." This is the area which is now most disturbed by man by plowing and overgrazing with in some regions disastrous results. The study of ecology clearly shows that the short grass country should never have been plowed and should be only grazed sparingly. This is the basis for regional planning that needs to be done. 3. Northern Coniferous forest, including the Northern United States and Canada. This is "the north country" region of cold climate, evergreen spruces, pines, firs, etc., and heavy snowfall. 4. Montane or Mountain Coniferous forest of the high mountains of the West. 5. Coast Coniferous forest, a very humid region on the West Coast characterized by magnificent plant growth, such as the redwoods. 6. The tundra and alpine meadows, which include Arctic grasslands, northern Canada and Alaska, and tops of high mountains. 7. Pine-Juniper, low altitude forest area of Southwest. 8. Chaparral

[10] Regions after Weaver and Clement's "Plant Ecology," as modified by V. E. Shelford to include animal distribution also. From Eugene P. Odum's unpublished manuscript.

or region of winter rain in southern California. 9. Sage brush plains or cool desert in Nevada and adjacent states. 10. The desert, including southern Arizona and California. The desert plants of 9 and 10 have spread into much of the original grasslands because of overgrazing by cattle.

Two other major points of emphasis only need be noted here. The first has to do with the methodology and techniques through which the ecologist delimits his regions and the significance of this to larger problems of regional determination. The second is the measure of emphasis given to human ecology and the human region by the plant and animal ecologists. With reference to delineating regions, it would be possible to illustrate with a very large number, let us say, on the map of North America and then plot their relation to other natural regions. Some of these are indicated in the tall grass and short grass regions and the consequent habitat of certain animals, extending sometimes up into Canada, and sometimes of lesser extent. Animals studied might be the coyote, the "Jack Rabbit," or certain species of prairie hen or owl. The main point of emphasis, however, is that of the methodology and of the final product of delimitable regions, the techniques of which are important in the theoretical and scientific aspects of regionalism.

Thus Elton, after treating of animal interrelations, points up an important aspect of methodology in the characterization of regions or habitats. "In surveying the possible habitats available for animals, we are struck by the dominant influence of vegetation in creating large and comparatively uniform habitats all over the surface of the earth. Vegetation has two main effects (apart from food and shelter to animals). It modifies the natural climatic and soil conditions and to a certain extent smooths out their temporal fluctuations. At the same time the phenomenon of dominance, by which one or two species of plants dominate the rest in the competition for light and food, produces rather sharp boundaries between different plant associations. This produces comparatively sharp differences between the environmental conditions, e.g., of temperature and moisture in each habitat. Through the influence of vegetation most of the earth is divided up into a patchwork of habitats, each comparatively uniform in conditions and each rather abruptly separated from the next. This is usually what we mean when we speak of 'major habitats': the area covered by a particular vegetation type with its characteristic dominant species and corresponding association of other subordinate species. When we speak of vegetation making conditions uniform, it should not be forgotten that it also creates a variety of minor habitats, partly through the variety of plant species and partly through vertical layering, as in woods. It is the general climatic variations that are toned down. Another way in which vegetation affects animal habitats is through ecological succession. Ecological succession takes place also independently of vegetation, as when a river erodes its banks and lays down sediment elsewhere, or when a sand dune advances and replaces intertidal areas, or when the lime gets gradually leached out of soil. But these physical changes chiefly have the effect of creating new bare areas on which the development of vegetation takes place in a fairly orderly sequence which is characteristic for any particular climate and soil and geographical region."[11]

The final point to be noted here with reference to the ecologists is the almost universal tendency to extend ecology into the broader realm of human ecology. Thus, Bews says: "Since living organisms are either plants or animals, ecology can be divided into plant ecology and animal ecology. From the latter it is now proposed to separate human ecology."[12] So, too, Elton points up the socio-economic problems which come into the realm of ecology in several categories, namely, diseases of men and domestic animals, pests of agriculture, fisheries, conservation of wild life.[13] This latter is well illustrated in the United States by the conservation movement. Again, C. E. Allen, extending the preceding animal ecology to human ecology, includes the carrying capacity of human culture, involving wild environment, land, utilization of natural resources in its regional environmental aspects.[14] Allee features a borderline, using one of Professor Giddings' favorite terms, namely, aggregation. He says: "In the borderline field where general sociology meets and overlaps general physiology and ecology, the field which is being considered in the present discussion, it seems desirable to have a term which may be applied loosely, but not incorrectly, to any of the recognized units lying below the groups accepted as definitely social, just as the term 'community' is applied by the animal ecologists with equal propriety

[11] Charles Elton, *The Ecology of Animals*, pp. 36-37.
[12] J. W. Bews, *Human Ecology*, pp. 2-3.
[13] Elton, *op. cit.*, p. 78.
[14] *Conference on Regional Phenomena, 1930*, Appendix A, p. 2.

to strata, super-society, society, association, and what not. It is in this general sense, for this level of social or subsocial life, that I propose to use the term 'aggregation.'"[15]

The recent trend toward human ecology, outside of the American approach of the Chicago school, is illustrated by two new works. One is a forthcoming volume on human ecology by Professor R. Mukerjee, in which he apparently takes the position that man can achieve enduring civilization only if he lives in harmony with his natural heritage. The second volume, *Human Ecology*, was published in 1935 and is written by J. W. Bews, a South African botanist who magnifies human ecology as an integrating science which works with the truths discovered in the narrower specialties to create a balanced view of man in all his aspects. After stating the point of view of human ecology, he gives a brief outline of the contents of the new science. First comes a discussion of the physical environment and the non-human living environment and man's response to it as a living organism. Next comes a treatment of man himself and some of the obvious maladjustments to the above environments that result in disease. Since one of the most important aspects of man is his psychic life, a review of modern psychology precedes the section of man's control of his environment through his evolving culture. The greater part of the book concerns man's control of his environment seen through the function of getting food, which is the most basic function and thus serves well to illustrate an ecological approach. The ecology of ancient man is reconstructed from archaeological evidence, followed by the ecology of present-day food gatherers, of plant cultivators, of herdsmen and pastoral nomads, and of differentiated classes within cultures. In each type of culture the ecology of the individual is traced as well as that of the group. Finally, some recent studies that have been done from an ecological standpoint such as Jones' *Social Survey of Merseyside* and other co-operative research programs carried on by many specialists are cited to show the sort of thing that results when a problem is approached ecologically. Bews believes that, in addition to sound research, ecology makes a contribution to the quest for human happiness by showing that it results from harmonious adjustment of a functioning organism with its environment.[16]

Although the key relationship of human ecology to sociology will be presented in a later chapter, it is important here to feature the

[15] Allee, *op. cit.*, p. 9.
[16] Bews, *op. cit.*

contributions of the American human ecologists both in contrast to the natural ecologists and to the European scholars and in relation to the metropolitan region. Professor McKenzie has presented an excellent statement of the distinctions between human ecology and the regional concepts of geographers, demographers, and natural ecologists, from which also may be gathered the elements of human ecology.

"Human ecology," according to McKenzie, "differs from demography and human geography in that the main object of attention is neither the population aggregate nor the physical-cultural habitat, but rather the relations of man to man. The human ecologist, obtaining his point of view and some of his concepts from the plant and animal ecologists, concerns himself with the nexus of sustenance and place relations of the individuals and institutions which give the community its characteristic form and organization. Basic to the ecological idea is the concept of competition. The underlying assumption is that the fact of a struggle is associated with the function of order. Competition among human beings involves struggle for position—that is, for a sustenance niche and a spatial location in which the individual or institution may survive and function. The unit of ecological study is the communal organism, which is at once an aggregation of individual persons, a geographical and cultural habitat, and an interrelated and interdependent biosocial unity. The community thus conceived has many things in common with the plant and animal community. Its component units are bound together by the interdependence which arises out of specialization and division of labor. Its numbers are regulated in aggregate, and in each particular niche or occupation by competition. The characteristic form or spatial pattern of the community—the typical arrangement of population and institutions—is likewise conceived to be a function of competition and competitive co-operation. The relations of the associational units in the human as in the plant and animal community are dynamic, ever changing in response to environmental factors and ever tending toward an equilibrium or balance. Equilibrium in the modern human community is largely a function of mobility. The basic difference between human ecology and the ecologies of the lower organisms lies in the fact that man is capable of a higher level of behavior in his adaptation process. As a cultural animal man creates, within limitations, his own habitat. Symbiotic relations in human society represent adjustments to a cultural as well as to a biogeographic setting. And the fact that culture, or the superorganic, tends toward uniformity within the area of common dissemination of traits furnishes the basis for the similarity of spatial and symbiotic patterns found in widely separated human communities. The human ecologist attempts to discover, classify and explain these typical features of human association. In this respect he differs from the geographer who is concerned more with what is unique or different in the various areas of human habitation." [17]

It has been noted earlier that geographers have been willing, even anxious, to take part in this ecological movement. This desire has been manifested in the growing concern of the geographers with the purely human or cultural aspects of their field. This has led in several directions, it seems, but at least some of the notable geographers have seen the trend as toward human ecology. That is, the interest of geography has shifted from the physical to the human "until geographers in increasing numbers define their subject as dealing solely with the mutual relations between man and his natural environment." By natural environment "they of course mean the combined physical and biological environments. Thus defined, geography is the science of *human ecology*." [18]

Emphasis on change and relationship is also the characteristic of cultural geography, which finds an active exponent in this country in Carl O. Sauer. Factors of kind and position of geological materials, plus climate and the dependent vegetation, lead through time to characteristic land forms, or natural landscape. Then, "the cultural landscape is fashioned out of a natural landscape by a culture group; culture is the agent, the natural area the medium, the cultural landscape the result." [19] That is, the landscape changes through time under the influence of a given culture which, itself, is changing, though such a combination may reach a climax. But with the introduction of a new culture, the cultural landscape is rejuvenated, and begins another cycle. "This is the meaning of adaptation, through which, aided by those suggestions which man has derived from nature, perhaps by an imitative process, largely subconscious, we get the feeling of harmony between the human habitation and the landscape into which it so fittingly blends. But these too are derived from the mind of man, not imposed

[17] R. D. McKenzie in *The Fields and Methods of Sociology* (edited by L. L. Bernard), pp. 58-59. Copyright 1934. Reprinted by permission of the publishers, Farrar & Rinehart, Inc.

[18] Harlan H. Barrows, "Geography as Human Ecology," *Annals of the Association of American Geographers*, XIII, 3.

[19] Carl O. Sauer, *The Morphology of Landscape*, p. 46.

by nature, and hence are cultural expressions."[20] This concept of balance and equilibrium seems to distinguish the sociological view of ecology. Thus, Park and Burgess say that "The ecological conception of society is that of a society created by competitive co-operation."[21] McKenzie, of the same school of sociologists, says: "In the struggle for existence in human groups social organization accommodates itself to the spatial and sustenance relationships existing among the occupants of any geographical area. . . . In society physical structure and cultural characteristics are parts of one complex. The spatial and sustenance relations in which human beings are organized are ever in process of change in response to the operation of a complex of environmental and cultural forces. It is the task of the human ecologist to study these processes of change in order to ascertain their principles of operation and the nature of the forces producing them."[22]

"It has been claimed," Professor McKenzie points out, "that geography is human ecology. There are doubtless many points in common between the two disciplines; but geography is concerned with place; ecology, with process."[23] Thus, ecological distribution is spatial distribution which results in dynamic relationships between the units, individuals or institutions, comprising an aggregation in geographic space. A community becomes such an ecological distribution of people and services in which each is assigned a place by natural social processes and thereby forms a social unit. That is, there are always present in any social organization forces which tend to result in an orderly arrangement of the elements of such an organization, resulting in an ecological pattern. This, of course, results in a geographical distribution of relationships, but "Human ecology, as sociologists conceive it, seeks to emphasize not so much geography as space. In society we not only live together, but at the same time we live apart, and human relations can always be reckoned, with more or less accuracy, in terms of distance. In so far as social structure can be defined in terms of position, social changes may be described in terms of movement; and society exhibits, in one of its aspects,

[20] *Ibid.*, p. 47.
[21] Robert E. Park and Ernest W. Burgess, *Introduction to the Science of Sociology*, p. 559.
[22] R. D. McKenzie, "The Scope of Human Ecology," *The Urban Community* (edited by E. W. Burgess), p. 617.
[23] *Ibid.*

characters that can be measured and described in mathematical formulas." [24]

> Dawson and Gettys agree with McKenzie that "the idea of competition is basic in human ecology and the human ecologist proceeds to study the human community in the impersonal manner pursued by the plant ecologist. *Human ecology*, then, explains how human beings and their institutions assume their characteristic patterns of distribution in space at a given time. It pays particular attention also to the organic relations of the distributed units. The latter constitute a symbiotic unity based on mutual dependence, unintentional symbiotic relationships obtain between the various regional, institutional, and occupational divisions of labor in the human community. . . . To symbiotic dependence in human communities is added the interdependence which results from communication and mutual understanding. Furthermore, the ecological pattern in the human community is modified by the diffusion of knowledge in regard to community patterns which prevail in a given region. This accounts in part for the remarkable similarity in the physical structure of the towns in the Prairie Region of North America. Ecological units are communities, regions, and natural subdivisions of both." [25]

From the above it would appear that the social ecologist has taken over much of the biological point of view out of which the concept emerged, but always with the condition that man himself is a most active agent in arranging, maintaining and modifying that organization. With such restriction the conclusions of animal ecology may be applied to the study of human society in its ecological aspects. "It is clear from what has been said, that in order to understand the way in which any animal is affected in its numbers or distribution by the other animals living with it, it is necessary to study the *whole* animal community living in one habitat, and that it is useless to treat the animal as if it were completely isolated and acting as a separate unit." [26] That is, the ecologist is interested in the whole, in synthesis rather than in analysis, and in relationships and connections within that whole as an integrated unit rather than in a study of the parts

[24] Robert E. Park, "The Urban Community as a Spatial Pattern and a Moral Order," *The Urban Community* (edited by E. W. Burgess), p. 4.

[25] Carl A. Dawson and Warner E. Gettys, *Introduction to Sociology*, pp. 122-123 (1935 edition).

[26] Charles S. Elton, "Animal Ecology," *Encyclopaedia Britannica*, 14th edition, VII, 920.

of the organization. This necessarily leads to a dynamic conception of social organization in which forms and processes assume a dominant position, in contrast to the mechanistic conception of society of early thinkers. To the ecologist, it is this relationship which determines the region and which forms the object of study. The processes and factors in this organization of a regional culture occupy their attention to a large extent, though geographic factors are never ignored. However, transportation and communication are the two basic factors on which most stress is placed, while the city offers the most commonly accepted mechanism by which the pattern is integrated.

So fundamental is this relationship of the city to lines of contact that the ecological organization of the region about the city may fairly be said to depend upon it. Every school boy has been taught to talk glibly of the changes in the rise and dominance of cities as the result of the changes in trade routes; of how New York has risen to its present position because of the ease of access to the western regions through easy mountain passes and the construction of the Erie Canal; which as DeBow remarked with an astuteness not always applauded, made the Mississippi River flow uphill. But, as is apparent in the remark credited to DeBow, lines of communication not only fashion the pattern of social relationships, social relationships also fashion the communication net.

> This point was stressed by C. H. Cooley in his famous theory of transportation, though it is often overlooked in favor of his more obvious conclusions regarding the effect of natural factors in influencing the location of transportation lines, and thereby the location of cities. "The character of transportation as a whole and in detail, at any particular time and throughout its history, is altogether determined by its interrelations with physical and social forces and conditions. . . . The need of movement of things and persons underlies every sort of social organization, every institution whatever. . . . Precisely because transportation underlies social development, it is in turn determined by that development. It is the tool of the economic, the political, the military organizations; and the character of the tool varies with their needs. . . . Sociologically considered it is a means to the physical organization of society. Development or evolution, the organization of social forces implies unification of aim, specialization of activities in view of a common purpose, a growing interdependence among the parts of society.

Such organization, such extension of relations, involves a mechanism through which the relations can exist and make themselves felt. This mechanism is communication in the widest sense of the word; communication of ideas and of physical commodities, between one time and another and one place and another. These are the threads which hold society together; upon them all unity depends."[27]

Thus, though the major outlines of a transportation system may be set by geographic factors, social conditions also have a large part of the responsibility. Cooley advanced the idea that cities arise where a break in the transportation method was made. Such breaks may be of two sorts: physical transfer from one mode of transportation to another, as from ship to railway; or commercial, as in processing raw materials, change of ownership.[28] Thus, the railway has come to play much the role formerly occupied by the river or harbor, though it must be noted again that the location of cities exerts a great influence on the direction of railways, if the cities are present in the region, while the roads are powerful in locating the dominant centers of regions developed after the construction of the rail line. This latter function is abundantly illustrated in the history of the growth of the western portion of this country and has become the basis of a considerable literature.[29]

In the elaboration and extension of the Cooley theory, it is claimed that some advantage in transportation facility is almost the sole cause for the location of cities, or other distribution facilities. McKenzie points out that in our dynamic society many communities have rapidly passed through cycles of growth during the past fifty years, "the determining factors being changes in forms and routes of transportation and communication, and the rise of new industries."[30] He also quotes J. Russell Smith to the same effect: "In a level plain, a town will be near its center and a focus of railroads in such a plain,

[27] "The Theory of Transportation," *Publications of the American Economic Association*, IX, 40-42.

[28] *Ibid.*, p. 94.

[29] Cf. Glenn Chesney Quiett, *They Built the West*, as an example of the literature in which this thesis here expressed is developed.

[30] R. D. McKenzie, "The Ecological Approach to the Study of the Human Community," *The City* (edited by R. E. Park, E. W. Burgess, and R. D. McKenzie), p. 69.

fertile and populous, will almost surely make a city."[31] A. T. Hadley shows how this efficiency of transportation causes cities to rise at points dictated by transportation facilities rather than at points at which goods are most easily produced or raw materials are most abundant.[32]

The question of freight rate structure is one of the greatest importance to the concept of metropolitan integration, and to economic regionalism in general, but is too involved for more than a cursory consideration here. It appears to be certain that freight rate advantages have in the past, and still do, exert potent influences on the prosperity of regions and of cities serving these regions.

> Shaw points out that "freight rates go far to determine the habits of whole communities as regards to the things they eat, the houses they build, the fuel they consume, and the particular forms of employment they find profitable."[33] This fact has, of course, long been recognized and was the basis of the wave of legislation seeking to regulate railways which swept the nation during the last decades of the past century and which culminated in the formation of the Interstate Commerce Commission as a regulatory body. In 1922, Henry C. Wallace called attention to such effects in emphatic terms by showing what changes in rates meant to regions specializing in certain crops. "The increase in freight rates during the past four years imposes an additional charge per acre on lemons of $187.67; which capitalized at 7 percent would amount to $2,681; on oranges an additional acre tax of $192.39, which capitalized would amount to $2,748.28; on apples $160.87, which capitalized would amount to $2,298.14 . . . the increased rate tax per acre on corn, wheat and oats, and cotton is greater than was the net return per acre to the farmer during the pre-war period. . . ." In the same article this writer expressed the often-repeated charge that rates were set at the highest point the traffic would bear: " . . . rates on grain were fixed at a point which would not discourage the growing of grain, while rates on livestock were so adjusted as to come just within the point at which the stockman could better afford to ship them than to make his stock walk to market."[34]

[31] J. Russell Smith, *Industrial and Commercial Geography*, 1913 edition, p. 841.

[32] "Economic Results of Improvement in Means of Transportation," quoted by L. C. Marshall, *Business Administration*, p. 35.

[33] Albert Shaw, "How Railroads Adapt Themselves to National Conditions," *Proceedings of the Academy of Political Science*, X, 97.

[34] Henry C. Wallace, "The Farmer and the Railroads," *Proceedings of the Academy of Political Science*, X, 68-76, 65.

So important is this matter of freight rates to regional development that it has been made one of the primary factors in the delimitation of regions in the commercial surveys comprising the domestic commerce series of studies by the Bureau of Foreign and Domestic Commerce of the Department of Commerce. The effect is enhanced by the custom of rate-making bodies of dividing the country into large areas and "blanketing" charges for shipment to any point within such regions from other regions; such charges often bearing little discoverable relation to distance or cost of service rendered. This means that the relation of a given point of dominance depends more upon favorable freight rate structure than upon physical structure or other "natural" factors. Under the rate structure prevailing before 1925, for instance, it cost less to ship fruit to New York from California than from the Ozark fruit region, while the cost of fruit shipments from California was less than twice that applying from Florida, in spite of facilities for shipment by water in both the former cases.[35]

This matter of blanketing, or zoning, freight rates is of importance from the regional point of view from another angle. There seems good evidence to support the charge that the railways have deliberately set rates which would discourage the establishment of manufacturing enterprises in the western portion of the country. Wallace charges that "Efforts to establish industrial enterprises in the great surplus-producing states west of the Mississippi were systematically discouraged, even to the extent of making grossly discriminatory rates against such enterprises. . . . The railroad manager was a law unto himself, made rates according to his own sweet will, and made and unmade individuals and communities in his own interest and the interest of his own road. He conceived it to be to the advantage of the railroad to keep the farm and factory as far apart as possible in order that the railroad might haul their respective products the longest possible distances."[36]

But transportation lines and freight rate differentials are not the only means by which such regions may be delimited. Newspaper circulation has been used for such purposes for some time, following the suggestion of Robert E. Park. In summary, he says that cities

[35] W. P. Hedden, *How Great Cities Are Fed*, pp. 25-28.
[36] Wallace, *op. cit.*, p. 65.

have entered a stage of decentralization, whereby many of their functions are performed at some distance from the center. These subcenters are not urban, being dependent upon the central city, and this is demonstrated by their reliance upon the central city for news service. Newspaper circulation, thus, gives an excellent index to the zone of influence of a city. This is true because, in the last analysis, culture is based on communication, and because cultural, economic, and political organization tends to conform.[37]

This theory was tested by Park and Charles Newcomb in a study abridged in McKenzie's work on the metropolitan community.[38] This study shows that most American newspapers are local in their appeal because of the settlement of the country in more or less isolated areas and to the custom of emphasizing local news so as to supply advertisers with circulation composed largely of potential customers of the advertiser. That is, an advertiser is not interested in paying for circulation among people who have little opportunity of visiting his establishment, or otherwise coming into contact with his sales technique. And since newspaper circulation pays only a small part of the revenue of publishing, many newspapers have found it profitable to restrict their circulation to areas in which advertisers will pay for circulation. The size of the area thus defined depends upon the size of the city of publication and the proximity of other competing centers. Thus, it would appear that the circulation of a newspaper would furnish a fairly accurate guide to the sphere of influence of a center, of whatever size. This conclusion is borne out by a survey made in the Chicago area of passenger traffic on eleven railways. By locating points along these lines at which 50 percent of the passenger traffic moved toward Chicago, as against competing centers, an area was outlined which almost coincided with the area delimited by towns in which 50 percent of the metropolitan newspapers came from Chicago. From this and other considerations, it was concluded that "communication is fundamental to the existence of every form and type of society, and one form of communication, namely, the newspaper, has been found to circulate over the natural areas within which society is organized. Thus it may not seem unreasonable that the newspaper should be used as an index in outlining a number of metropolitan regions of the United States."[39]

37 Robert E. Park, "Urbanization as Measured by Newspaper Circulation," *American Journal of Sociology*, XXXV, 60-79.

38 R. D. McKenzie, *The Metropolitan Community*, ch. VIII.

39 *Ibid.*, pp. 100, 106.

On this conclusion and by this technique regions were outlined for the larger cities of the nation for 1920 and 1930. The resulting map is interesting for several reasons. It delimits a series of regions in terms of one factor in metropolitan integration; and shows, generally, an extension of the areas so defined surrounding the rapidly growing cities, with a consequent narrowing of the limits of cities now growing so rapidly. In the eastern portion of the nation, where metropolitan regions might be assumed to be well stabilized, few changes are noted. Perhaps most interesting is an area in northern Wyoming, southern Montana and western South Dakota, in which newspapers from Chicago have a higher circulation than those from any other metropolitan center. The authors accept the implication that this area is more closely tied up with Chicago than with the nearer cities, Denver, Omaha and Helena, and suggest it as a remnant of the old frontier served by Chicago mail-order houses.[40]

The study also shows numerous enclaves in which there is no sharp line between the dominance of the larger, more distant metropolis and the smaller, but more local, submetropolis, and where the newspaper from the larger center extends its circulation through and beyond that of the smaller. This leads to the conclusion that such smaller centers may be regarded as subcenters within a larger region, and leads to the conception of a hierarchical organization of the country.

The idea and technique are both stimulating and raise the question as to whether similar services might not be used. Rail traffic has been used in one instance by Park and Newcomb. Telephone toll service and home addresses of hospital patients are suggested as being almost equally reliable, and were used with what appears to be good results in a study of a Texas city. Movements of mail and of freight would serve as excellent indices, were figures available. Banking connections and wholesale distribution of commodities have been used by N. S. B. Gras and Mildred Hartsough in their studies of the Twin City Region. Any form of communication and transfer of goods that may be included as a form of communication, would serve, and all these together should give an excellent picture of the area tributary to a center.

40 McKenzie, *The Metropolitan Community*, 109.

Thus, organization seems to center around the communication and transportation agencies. Among these agencies there is a constant shift as to relative importance, the railway losing much of its dominance as other agencies come into wider use. But, because of its former greater importance, because statistics of its operation are available, while those of most other agencies are not, and because a large segment of such relationship is of an economic character, and economic relationships most often consist in the transfer of goods, credits, or other measurable things, the rail transportation system still furnishes the most practicable field in which to study spatial interconnections. Further, as Vance points out, the regulation of the rail system is one of the great economic complexes which will force—and have in the past forced—regionalism on the attention of the state.[41]

Such a network of transportation and communication results in a competitive process which tends to set cities and regions apart as competing units, but at the same time integrates them into an inseparable whole, bound together by railway, highway, airway, pipe line, press, telephone and telegraph, mails, radio—by all the facilities we have developed whereby the elements of our culture, material and immaterial, are disseminated. Thus, paradoxically, such agencies at one and the same time promote national and even international consciousness and provincialism,[42] a situation which comes close to the regional ideal. Further, as is true of most forms of social control, once such centers and regions are formed, they tend to become self-perpetuating. As McKenzie points out, once a metropolitan center is recognized, new business or service agencies entering the region are almost compelled to select such a center as their headquarters.[43]

Considerable space has been devoted to the organization of American society by the metropolitan center, because such a discussion seems to demonstrate the fundamental notion of ecology—that of organization and of interrelationships growing up through the operation of physical and social forces. Both geographical and cultural adaptation may be conceived as a continual adjustment to natural forces. The state of technology existent in any society determines

[41] Rupert B. Vance, *Human Geography of the South*, pp. 16-17.

[42] Malcolm M. Willey and Stuart A. Rice, *Communication Agencies and Social Life*, p. 213.

[43] *The Metropolitan Community*, p. 164.

to a large extent the uses to which so-called natural resources will be put. In turn, such gifts of nature exert a powerful influence on the culture exploiting them. The essential notion of ecology lies in the relationships growing out of this reciprocal set of influences and the resulting balance within a given area at a given time. The cultural order is woven within the ecological order; the interweaving of the two furnishes us with a web of life covering a region within which, in the absence of new elements, the trend is toward stability.[44] Such stability is not to be expressed in either geographic or cultural terms, but in a combination of the two.

Mukerjee defines the region as "an area where many dissimilar species of inhabitants adapt themselves to a common existence so that the ecological community as a whole keeps on."[45] Thus, through the processes of competition, invasion, and succession, spatial and symbiotic relations are established which are typical of the region. From this Mukerjee conceives the three tasks of social ecology to be the investigation of spatial and food relationships, the tracing of regional adaptation to nature, and the measurement of the balance found within the region as favorable or unfavorable from the point of view of man's occupance.

But this equilibrium, as implied above, is not stable; on the contrary it is easily upset by the injection of new elements into the social order existing within the region or even by the gradual changes in the earth-structure upon which the social organization rests. Variations in rainfall, exhaustion of soil fertility or mined products or exploited forests; changes in techniques of exploitation or of philosophies of use of land and mineral resources all bring about the necessity for a new social organization. The situation is further complicated by the fact that man has surrounded himself by artificially bred plants and animals which could not survive in a state of nature, "pampered monstrosities" which demand constant protection and which count for more in the regional economy than the native animals and vegetation, as Vance has pointed out.[46]

[44] Radhakamal Mukerjee, "The Ecological Outlook in Sociology," *American Journal of Sociology*, XXXVIII, 350.

[45] *Ibid.*, p. 349.

[46] Vance, *op. cit.*, p. 6.

This has placed man in a somewhat precarious position, as Mukerjee warns repeatedly. Man and his social organization is an integral part of the region, and man prospers or is doomed as the region as a whole prospers or is doomed. "Social ecology reveals how in crowded regions the unconscious or willful disregard of regional balance, the result of population pressure may ultimately lead both man and his habitat to a common doom." Man is largely unaware of his own role and often is guilty of actions which bring disharmonies which finally mean his own failure in that region.[47] Unfortunately, examples of the truth of his position are too numerous and too recent to require illustration. "Of all animals, man has not planned his effort and food supply as a species on a continuing basis, and the appellation *Homo Stultus* is nowhere more applicable than in rich regions laid waste after a few generations of his brilliant and wasteful achievement, Civilization."[48]

Man, in interfering with the natural balance, makes himself responsible for his own welfare and the welfare of future generations who must occupy the same space. He substitutes an active evolution for the passive one characteristic of other life forms, and attains Ward's goal of telesis with results not always to his credit. However, this is not the usual result: the competition for food and space commonly resulting in an optimum arrangement of the factors involved.

Mukerjee's dictum is that "as in the life-community, in a region there develops a complex interrelationship among the various organisms and a balance and rhythm of growth for all, so in the culture of a human community, which is woven within the framework of the ecological area, there is found a great complexity of interrelations among the social, economic, and other institutions and traditions, establishing some kind of equilibrium for the whole community or culture. Thus, like the ecological community, society or culture develops as a whole, maintaining a balance for its different institutions and traditions all interlaced with one another, as culture progresses, in finer and finer patterns of correlation and solidarity."[49]

From the above it is not to be concluded that the region must be homogeneous in any absolute sense. The ecological concept depends

[47] Mukerjee, "The Concepts of Distribution and Succession in Social Ecology," *Social Forces,* XI, 1-7.

[48] Mukerjee, "The Concepts of Balance and Organization in Social Ecology," *Sociology and Social Research,* XVI, 508-509.

[49] Mukerjee, "The Concepts of Distribution and Succession in Social Ecology," *Social Forces,* XI, 7.

largely upon the operation of the forces of competition and adjustment; forces absent in a highly homogeneous structure of any kind. Nor does it follow that the region thus described is self-sufficient. Indeed what has been said as to the necessity of balance and adjustment within the region might be repeated as to relationships between regions. The region may be self-sufficient in some respects, interdependent with other regions in others. This is one of the fundamental distinctions between the region and the section, as will appear more fully in the discussion of political regionalism. Reverting to the hierarchical nature of regions, it may be well to observe here that the region is made up of subunits and itself forms a subunit in an organization covering the world, or at least a "society" such as that usually referred to as "Occidental Civilization."

The ecological approach to the study of regions, the above indicates, offers many advantages. Mukerjee sees in it an opportunity to apply the fundamental logic of the physical sciences to the study of social relationships.[50] Whether or not this is literally true, as seems rather uncertain, ecology does give a tool by which the highly immaterial and intangible aspects of social organization may be manipulated with some degree of satisfaction. It stresses the form of social organization rather than the content, in line with the German sociological approach of Simmel and von Wiese, whereas the anthropological approach is more concerned with content. In the work of McKenzie and of Park it makes a close approach to measurable objectivity in some relations, at least. But this is not necessarily its greatest value. The insight afforded into the problem of social relations on the cultural level and as between man and nature may be most valuable, even when most intangible; and ecology does much to supply such values in its insistence upon the totality of culture and its stress upon the relationships and processes involved. It gives the student a comprehensive view of the region. "A good deal of the meaning of area lies beyond scientific regimentation. The best geography has never disregarded the aesthetic qualities of landscape, to which we know no approach other than the subjective. Humboldt's 'physiognomy,' Banse's 'soul,' Bolz' 'rhythm,' Gradman's 'harmony,' of landscape all lie beyond science. They seem to have discovered

[50] Mukerjee, "The Concepts of Distribution and Succession in Social Ecology," *Social Forces*, XI, 4.

a symphonic quality in the contemplation of the areal scene, proceeding from a full novitiate in scientific studies and yet apart therefrom. To some, whatever is mystical is an abomination. Yet it is significant that there are others, and among them some of the best, who believe that having observed widely and charted diligently, there yet remains a quality of understanding at a higher plane which may not be reduced to a formal process." [51]

[51] Sauer, *Morphology of Landscape*, p. 48.

Chapter XV

EXPLORING THE REGION: THE ECONOMISTS

IT is when the discussion of regionalism and regional theory enters the fields of history, economics, political science, literature, and the other more purely social and humanistic studies that the difficulty of anything like a monistic approach becomes more apparent. Having space or culture as their basic concept, the geographers, ecologists and anthropologists feel a freedom in discussing the various aspects of social organization which workers in at least some of the other fields deny themselves.

This separateness is, of course, in the best scientific tradition of the past few centuries and has great value for purposes of analysis. For instance, the Classical economic theorists gained an insight into the economic behavior of man which would have been totally impossible had they attempted to correlate such behavior with all the other factors entering into life patterns. They simplified their problem so that it could be much more easily grasped and so that they could invent tools which would fit, with some accuracy at least, these problems. At the same time, the restriction of the field in this manner is somewhat arbitrary, even if necessary, and has always been so recognized by economists. Such a technique of study has, in some cases, led to abstraction, to the ruling out of consideration factors of time and space; whereas the regional approach attempts to tie speculation to both by insisting that various earth areas have distinctive qualities and relationships which are worthy of and demand consideration.

If one theory could be made to fit exactly all conceivable areas and situations, there would be no reason, or excuse, for any theory of regionalism. This is not to argue that general abstract theory does not apply to regions or regionalism; it is meant to argue that regionalism sees the universe as composed of a fabric of areas between which there are certain differences of elements or patterns which make special application of generalized theories essential to the fullest understanding of such areas. Such differences are as important as the underlying similitudes; and their recognition is basic to any theory which is practically applicable. Actually, scholars in these various fields have always recognized the impossibility of complete separation and have called attention to influences of factors outside their limited fields, at the same time emphasizing their own particular approach. To revert to economics for illustration, this is especially apparent in the title under which the discipline operated for many decades and which is still often used, that of "political economy."

Application of the regional approach to economics affords an excellent case study because the economic theorists have practiced abstraction as much as those in any other field—unless it be that of philosophy. Although the economist deals constantly with man's efforts in producing and distributing wealth, the movement of goods, and other factors closely connected with the material aspects of human life, and although there is a wealth of material in economic discussions of interest and value to the regionalist, it is only recently that regional considerations, as such, have found their way into the more consciously theoretical works. Since land is one of the traditional three factors of production, it follows that geography often enters economic discussion; similarly exchange and transportation, resources and capital, demography and labor, location of industry and metropolitan regionalism are intimately connected, to say nothing of the interrelations between economics and politics, social patterns and various forms of economic organization, etc.

This necessarily intimate connection between physical geography and the efforts of man to convert natural elements into wealth has resulted in the growth of the borderline discipline of economic geography. Economic considerations have always been more or less present in geography, of course, but the movement now known as economic geography is said to have stemmed from Ritter's attempt to explain transmission of plants and animals.[1] Kohl discussed the geography of

[1] Karl Sapper, article on "Economic Geography," *Encyclopaedia of the Social Sciences*, VI, 626-628, from which most of the present discussion of economic geography derives its base.

commerce and of settlement; but it was not until 1882 that the term "economic geography" was introduced, by Gotz, who "assigned to economic geography . . . the scientific task of dealing with the nature of world areas in their direct influence upon the production of commodities and the movements of goods." [2] Since that time many others have added to the body of knowledge making up the field, Hettner, to mention only one, doing valuable work on the economic possibilities and relationships of countries and of localities.[3] Regional economic geography has concerned itself largely with problems of mobility of factors of production and location of industry, taking into consideration the physiographic, political, and other social factors; in Russia a vast amount of such work is reported as part of the efforts of the Russian government to build up an integrated economic life.

In this country, the familiar argument that available water power and good harbors resulted in the emergence of New England as a manufacturing region has been repeated by most of the writers who have touched on the subject. What is often overlooked is that "for nearly one hundred years the people [of New England] struggled along seemingly unable to discover that the greater part of the land was thoroughly unfit for agriculture; and during all this time crops of glacial boulders alternated with harvests of trouble." [4] Among others, Miss Semple stresses the influence of geographic factors in the form of harbors and water power in the destiny of New England, of the mountain barrier and consequent high freight rates in the location of the iron and steel industry near the headwaters of the Ohio River, and the rapid growth of Chicago because of its location, which gave easy access to regions of mining, farming, forestry, and ranching, and the interdependence of regions following such specialization.[5]

Buckle has pointed out the intimate relation between climate and soil and the accumulation of wealth, especially by the more primitive peoples.[6] Very recently Pomfret argues that "Economic planning in the United States will bear a very close relation to geography" since

[2] Karl Sapper, article on "Economic Geography," *Encyclopaedia of the Social Sciences*, VI, 627.

[3] Alfred Hettner, *Die Geographie; ihre Geschichte, ihr Wesen und ihre Methodie*, *passim.*

[4] Jacques W. Redway, "Effects of Topography on Economic Development," *Gunton's Magazine*, XIX, 136.

[5] Ellen Churchill Semple, *American History and Its Geographic Conditions*, pp. 252, *et. seq.*

[6] Henry T. Buckle, *Introduction to the History of Civilization of England*, pp. 24-28 (new, revised edition by J. W. Robertson).

industries depend on industrial crops, and food production on products of the soil, and laments the lack of attention given to economic balance within the nation. This writer also brings in with a vengeance the influence of social factors upon geography when he remarks that "Europe is regarded as a continent not because of any geographical individuality, for Europe is a peninsula of Eurasia, but because of its political, economic and commercial importance" enhanced by its location near the center of a "land hemisphere" without tropics or polar regions and with numerous indentions of seas, gulfs, bays and drowned rivers which result in climatic and commercial advantages.[7] J. Russell Smith "presents and describes the continent as a land for human use. Therefore, the units [he argues] need to have a unity that is based on human use; . . . [economic] regions whose boundaries result from the work of the forces that make climate, surface, soil, mineral deposits, land, lakes and sea."[8] Nor is this influence all expended upon the economic life of the people occupying the region, in the eyes of this scholar; religion reflects place and political geography, back of which lies economic geography as explanation, in large part, is fundamental to an understanding of what is happening in the world.[9]

From the ranks of the economists, distinctly geographically deterministic theories have been advanced by H. L. Moore, W. H. Beveridge, and others. Moore investigated the correlation between rainfall during the critical crop period in the Ohio River Valley and economic cycles by elaborate statistical devices.

Moore's conclusion is that "The weather conditions represented by the rainfall in the central part of the United States, and probably in other continental areas, pass through cycles of approximately thirty-three and eight years in duration, causing like cycles in the yield of the crops; these cycles of crops constitute the natural, material current which drags upon the surface the lagging, rhythmically changing values and prices with which the economist is more immediately concerned. . . . The rhythmically varying yield per acre of the crops is the cause of economic cycles; when the yield increases, the volume of trade, the activity of industry, and the amount of employment increase; the demand for producers' goods rises; with the ultimate result of a rise of general prices. The contrary changes would follow upon a fall in the yield per acre of the crops. . . . The fundamental persistent cause of

[7] John E. Pomfret, *The Geographic Pattern of Mankind*, pp. 308, 368.
[8] *North America: Its Peoples and the Resources, Development, and Prospects as an Agricultural, Industrial, and Commercial Area*, p. 33.
[9] *Ibid.*, p. 3, also *Geography, and Our Need of It*, p. 2.

cycles in the yield of crops is the cyclical movement in the weather conditions represented by the rhythmically changing amount of rainfall; the cyclical movement in the yield of the crops is the fundamental, persistent cause of economic cycles."[10] Likewise, Beveridge shows a correlation between wheat prices, and, through them, general prosperity, and weather cycles.[11] The importance of social and technological factors has also been recognized by O. E. Baker, as having effect on the use of geographic resources in agriculture. ". . . each advance in transportation facilities, in the technique of production, and in economic organization makes agriculture, at least, increasingly responsive to the conditions of temperature, moisture, topography, and soil. The control of the physical conditions over agricultural development, instead of being mitigated by the progress of science and invention, has been intensified and enforced. The commercialization of agriculture and the keen competition resulting between different regions make the production of a crop sensitive even to the minute geographic advantages or disadvantages of a district, and compel shifts in crop production or in use of the land to be made with an alacrity unknown in previous ages."[12]

What Baker is arguing here, it appears, is that economic organization and keen competition of commercial agriculture place the farmer on or near the economic "margin," where the difference between profit and loss is very slight and easily affected by differences of any sort. Such argument is sound, as is the more familiar argument that "dry-farming" techniques, better-adapted seeds, favorable markets, transportation, and such factors have made types of agriculture possible where they were formerly impossible.[13] However, this possibility is always strictly limited by factors geographic, economic, and social; and this would appear to be true of the entire relationship of geography to economic and social facts.

This intimate interrelationship between aspects of the physical environment and cultural facts has recently received classical expression at the hands of Erich W. Zimmermann: "The appraisal of regional resources, like that of private property values, must recognize the functional nature of wealth, its relativity, its dependence on the market. . . . By this time, nature and culture have become so intertwined that little can

[10] H. L. Moore, *Economic Cycles: Their Law and Cause*, p. 149.
[11] W. H. Beveridge, *Weather and Harvest Cycles*, *passim.*
[12] "Agricultural Regions of North America," *Economic Geography*, II, 465.
[13] Cf. Isaiah Bowman, *Geography in Relation to the Social Sciences*, p. 165.

be gained from an attempt to isolate the natural resources. Cultural and natural resources are inseparable and can only be considered together. . . . The study of resources must include as much an analysis of the cultural superstructure as of the underlying physical elements; it must include above all a critical search of social objectives. . . . We must know what kind of a society we want to see develop in this Southland before we can appraise its resources; for resources are the environment, natural and cultural, appraised as to its capacity to fulfill social objectives no less than to satisfy individual desires."[14] Thus, he argues, philosophy is an important element in determining the resources of a region; resources constantly change with philosophical and technological changes, so that no static, absolute analysis of resources is possible. Elsewhere he states, "Every change in human want patterns and in social objectives, every invention and increase in man's control over nature, constantly revises the criteria of availability and ordinarily tends to enlarge the aggregate of available resources. Man and his resources are functional reciprocals."[15] From the impact of such forces and interrelationships, emerge "resource patterns" characteristic of regional cultures, the two most widely divergent and therefore most easily recognized being the patterns built upon vegetable resources and exemplified in the monsoon areas of Asia, and those built upon the exploitation of inanimate energy and minerals as seen in northwestern Europe and northeastern America. "Resource patterns . . . are combinations of resources which function as systems. Such a combination may consist of coal, iron, electricity, scientific knowledge, mechanized agriculture and their corollaries. Culture patterns, in general, are adapted to resource patterns, but culture must also be viewed as a part of a resource pattern. Finally, economic systems are parts of culture patterns, namely, those parts which are specifically concerned with material civilization, particularly with making a living. Resource and culture patterns and economic systems together form the basis of human existence."[16]

Further, this patterning of resources leads to a resource hierarchy in which certain resource patterns have a dominant place, the coal-iron-electricity-science pattern being dominant at this time. Such dominance of resources arranges regions of the earth into a similar hierarchy, the relative position being determined by the possession

[14] "The Resources of the South," *South Atlantic Quarterly*, XXXII, 214-215.

[15] E. W. Zimmermann, "Natural Resources," *Encyclopaedia of the Social Sciences*, XI, 291.

[16] E. W. Zimmermann, *World Resources and Industries*, p. 139.

of these resource patterns; those with the dominant pattern being superordinate to those with other materials and philosophies: "The industrial powers fall heir to all the inherent advantages of 'pure industry,' of inanimate energy, of inorganic substance, of devitalized science, and of all the other paraphernalia of the raw arts. These powers are 'in'; the others are 'out,' dwelling in 'the provinces' economically tributary to the great metropolitan centers of industry. They are suffered as hewers of wood and drawers of water."[17] Thus the world is divided into economic regions on the basis of resource patterns, which, though they do not determine, reach into and affect the cultural superstructure of attitudes, folkways, mores, ethical standards, religious beliefs, etc.[18]

This position is very similar to that of the culture-area anthropologists, especially Miss Benedict, but with the emphasis on the physical environment and the material, economic factors of social organization. However, Zimmermann is careful to indicate the vast importance of technological changes for resource patterns, pointing out that the machine civilization has weakened regional independence and created interdependence, thereby becoming a carefully adjusted, complex mechanism of great efficiency but easily disturbed. Further, a culture based on inanimate energy tends to exhaust its fund of resources, whereas a vegetable culture practices a flow economy, although techniques and commercial devices, in effect, produce new resources through more efficient exploitation and through control of funds physically located in other regions, thereby counteracting the natural tendency of centers of culture to move to regions of greater natural advantages with the exhaustion of fuel and minerals.[19]

Thus, it appears, the economic region is a complex, composed of physiographic, technological, social, and philosophical factors, as are other types of regions. However, from the economic point of view, for purposes of clarity, those factors having most direct connection with acquisition of wealth are emphasized while other factors are either ignored or the consideration of them is minimized or post-

[17] E. W. Zimmermann, *World Resources and Industries*, p. 805.

[18] E. W. Zimmermann, Chapter on "Resources," *Economic Principles and Problems* (edited by Walter E. Spahr), I, 184.

[19] E. W. Zimmermann, "Natural Resources," *Encyclopaedia of the Social Sciences*, XI, 296.

poned. For practical purposes of theoretical examination, it is commonly assumed that all other factors will remain stable, and consideration is given the changes in purely economic aspects. This method is permissible, of course, if it is understood clearly that the other factors are present, though not taken into constant account. Thereby, it is possible to plot economic areas with a fair degree of definiteness on the basis of certain economic criteria. For instance, the Bureau of Foreign and Domestic Commerce of the United States Department of Commerce, in its regional marketing studies, plotted regional economic units on the basis of population, number of families, value added to products by manufacture, value of fishery and forestry products, bank deposits, income tax returns, status of home tenure, number of residence telephones, population to whom electricity was available, domestic electricity users, domestic gas users, sales per annum of new passenger automobiles, magazine circulation, wholesale and retail outlets.[20] This agency also found transportation facilities of great importance, particularly in the case of New England, a region dependent on other regions for both fuel and raw materials for much of its industry. Further, despite the use of such concrete indices, it was found that there was considerable overlapping of trade areas, one wholesale center often disputing four or five areas with other centers.

From the purely theoretical point of view, the economic region and interregional relations are discussed at great length by Bertil Ohlin in his work, *Interregional and International Trade*. Ohlin observes that economic theory generally has assumed a one-market form, in which the total supply of the factors of production, rather than their distribution in space, has been basic, when "As a matter of fact the geographical distribution of productive factors is important. Industrial activity must be adapted to the varying supply of such factors in different places; for only to a limited extent can the supply itself be adapted to the demands of various industries."[21]

Economic regions, he says, are to be distinguished by two criteria:

[20] Edward F. Gerish, *Market Data Handbook of New England*. Department of Commerce, Bureau of Domestic and Foreign Commerce, Domestic Commerce Series, No. 24, p. 4.

[21] Bertil Ohlin, *Interregional and International Trade*, p. 4.

They should be different from other regions from the point of view under consideration, and they should differ less as between parts than with other regions, i.e., they should have a relative uniformity. These differences are the basis of division and of advantages of specialization.[22]

Prices tend to vary from region to region in rough correspondence to costs of transfer, including tariffs; the regional proportionality of labor and capital has an important effect on the economic structure of the region, since a region with low capital supply but abundant labor will tend to specialize in handmade commodities while a region abundantly supplied with capital will tend to mass, machine production; the exports of a region will depend on distance and market relations, nearby regions exporting bulky, easily spoiled goods while those at a greater distance will specialize in those easily transported. Within the region the economic structure will be affected by transportation facilities, proportionality of factors of production, density of population, and tradition, since the conquest of new markets is expensive and increases, for a time at least, the costs of production.[23]

Of the three factors of production, natural resources—economic "land"—is largely immobile, while both labor and capital offer psychological resistance to movement on an interregional scale. However, the latter two do have supply prices and do migrate, their movements being complementary to commodity movement. Further, such movement may be of advantage to both regions concerned, as in the case of Europe and South America, where, in one region, diminishing returns have set in, and increasing returns are possible in the other through better proportionality.[24]

The industrial character of a region will depend upon the nature of the raw materials produced; if they lose great weight in processing, the processing will take place near the point of production. But when several factors enter into the manufacturing process, the industry will tend to locate at the point of minimum transportation cost, commodities being treated as if they were all consumed at one point in a region, that point being the regional distribution center. But

22 Ohlin, *Interregional and International Trade*, p. 9.
23 *Ibid.*, pp. 142-148, 162-164.
24 *Ibid.*, pp. 167-179.

transportation is to be conceived in terms of cost, and loading and unloading costs enter into the calculation. The nature of the raw material is also to be considered; for example, flour mills may serve vast areas, creameries must be located fairly close to the dairies. Those products capable of paying high rents will be produced near the cities, thereby modifying the older conclusion that products incurring heavy transportation costs would occupy such position.[25]

Regional income, and consuming power, is affected by the proportion of local or "foreign" ownership of resources, by income from outside the region, by savings inside the region; the type of industry of a region is affected by distribution of resources, transportability of goods, regional proportionality of factors of production, and distance-cost relations of the region to other natural resources and consumer markets. Real wages may vary greatly from region to region, though nominal wages are equal; further, the wage differentials are important since a situation in which wages are uniform in one region while varying greatly in another will have important effects on interregional trade. Thus, it is only when two regions are alike in internal structure as well as in total or average characteristics that they can be compared. The natural resources, supply of labor, type of industry, volume of saving, creditor or debtor relationship to other regions must all be equated in any adequate statement of interregional trade. That is, in Ohlin's words, "One fact has been abundantly described and illustrated in the preceding pages, namely, that everything depends upon everything else in economics."[26]

Such considerations lead Ohlin to criticize the classical theory of international (interregional) trade on the grounds of oversimplification. The classical theory, he argues, depends upon the assumption of an equal relation between capital and labor in all industries, an assumption "in striking contradiction to reality," but one whose abandonment forces the theorist to fall back on money or price, the position the theory was designed to avoid. Actually, interest rates have great effect on regions and on industries in correlation to the proportions of labor and capital used. Further, he argues, the classical reduction of all labor to an unskilled labor basis is misleading, since a nation with skilled labor will have high prices, while one

[25] *Ibid.*, pp. 184-192.
[26] *Ibid.*, pp. 194, 230-236; quotation from p. 230.

depending largely upon unskilled labor will maintain a low price level, with important implications for interregional trade. Mill's theory that the value of a product is to be calculated in terms of "real costs," i.e., days of labor, in the region in which it is produced, runs counter to the more modern theory of mutual interdependence, and the comparative cost theory is only an abbreviated statement of supply conditions, leaving out of account factors of demand and equilibrium. Finally, the classicists erred in assuming no mobility as between states, and perfect mobility within such units.[27]

The classicists endeavored to reduce cost of production to "real costs" measured in days of labor, or other units of "pain." But manifestly such a measurement cannot be used in international trade, so that they are forced into the position of saying that real costs approximate money costs—the calculus they seek to avoid—or of admitting that tariff barriers may be useful in adjusting real costs to money costs—in which case their argument for free trade is no longer tenable. Money costs per unit of production are so variable as between countries or regions—else there would be no interregional trade—that they give little idea of real costs. Here the theorist is forced to choose between the oversimplified but clear path of the price economist, or, dropping his cloak of theoretical objectivity, plunge into the wider field of social implications. Most writers have chosen the latter path; and not a few have followed it into the field of social objectives.

The works of List may be taken as an example of the latter approach. Though his intense nationalism vitiates much of his reasoning, there remains a core of regional discussion based on the coincidence of state and regional limits. His argument that there should be some unit between the economics of the individual and a universal economics, seems sound, based as it is on the assertion that nations, or regions, differ greatly in their economic possibilities and stages of development and that, therefore, a universal theory will not fit such differing conditions. His inclusion of immaterial as well as material factors in the productive forces is also a fruitful thought which is now being followed by many economists. In essence, it

27 Ohlin, *Interregional and International Trade*, Appendix III, *passim.*

seems that his contention is that each nation, or region, is sufficiently distinct to demand treatment as a separate entity.[28]

The matter of transportation facilities, already discussed in the previous chapter, is likewise so closely connected with that of regional economy that a discussion of one is utterly impossible without the other. Ohlin was led to declare that in a sense production is merely transportation; or that at least all production has the factor of transportation in it.[29] In fact, his theory of interregional trade is based largely on the difficulty of moving commodities or factors of production from one region to another. Obviously such relative immobility is the *sine qua non* of all interregional specialization and exchange.

The importance of this factor has been apparent for centuries, of course; it promoted the voyages resulting in the discovery of the western hemisphere, the purchase of the Louisiana territory by the United States, the digging of the Erie and other canals, and in the desperate fights of cities for rail connections and preferential freight rates. As a result of the increased importance of international trade, those cities having ocean navigation are tending to outstrip their less fortunate rivals, and there are appearing relatively "blighted" regions in the interior of the nation, accompanied by demands for possible or at least plausible solutions, such as the opening of the St. Lawrence-Great Lakes route to ocean traffic.[30] The construction of the Panama Canal has emphasized the disadvantage of such regions of the United States. This new route resulted in a change of freight rates which, in effect, moved Chicago $3.36 away from the Pacific Coast Region, while moving New York $2.25 closer, thereby doing much to reverse the trend of industry in the Chicago region.[31]

In a similar way electric transmission lines tie together the interests of a region and affect its economic and demographic structure. This factor is assuming greater importance with the increasing use of electricity for industrial and domestic purposes and the development of superior

[28] Friedrich List, *National System of Political Economy*, (translated by G. A. Matile), *passim;* S. H. Patterson, *Readings in the History of Economic Thought*, pp. 381-413.

[29] Bertil Ohlin, *Interregional and International Trade*, p. 231.

[30] *Ibid.*, p. 156.

[31] Hermann Schumacher, "Location of Industry," *Encyclopaedia of the Social Sciences*, IX, 589.

techniques of transmission of electrical energy. Bruere has coined a happy phrase to denote this importance in the title of his article, "Giant Power—Region Builder."[32] Lewis Mumford has referred to the age of electricity as the "neo-technic" era of civilization—an era to be characterized by diffusion of power and industry, better hygiene, advanced agriculture, higher status of women, balanced economic development, disappearance of the "mining" philosophy of economic activity and its replacement by true conservation. The dominance of the coal cities, he argues, has resulted in building national markets without regard to regional unities of energy, labor, or time, and "has created an elaborate mechanism for carrying coals to Newcastle."[33]

The distribution of industry within a region is a matter of great importance to the regional pattern. Perhaps the first attempt to work out a systematic description of such an economic pattern was that of Johann Heinrich von Thünen, who envisioned an entirely homogeneous plain with a city in its center and then proceeded to describe the pattern of agriculture surrounding such a city. Distance from market and resultant transportation costs, in equilibrium with ease of transportation and price at the market, would arrange agriculture into concentric circles, he argued. Though ideal conditions never exist in actual practice, and changes in transportation technique, including freight rates, distort the simple picture he drew, his principles are still held to be accurate.[34] As pointed out above, industry is commonly located because of advantages of minimum freight charges, or because of raw materials, labor, or consumption market, the importance of the three factors varying from industry to industry. However, the location of particular industries and the economic character of a region are often determined, in part at least, by political, military, or sentimental considerations, and, once established, an industry has a tendency to remain, and to attract to the same locality or region other industries which profit from the use of by-products, of labor supplies not used by the original industry, etc.[35] Thus, a region builds up its economic traditions which have considerable force.

[32] *The Survey Graphic*, LIV, 161 ff.

[33] "The Theory and Practice of Regionalism," *Sociological Review*, XX, 23.

[34] Edgar Salin, "Johann Heinrich von Thünen," *Encyclopaedia of the Social Sciences*, XIV, 627-628.

[35] Bertil Ohlin, *Interregional and International Trade*, pp. 239-240; Schumacher, "Location of Industry," *Encyclopaedia of the Social Sciences*, IX, 588.

Aided by efficient transportation devices, the city has come to be one of the greatest organizing forces in economic affairs. N. S. B. Gras and Mildred Hartsough have described the changes in economic life in terms of type of dominant center. "We may think of metropolitan economy as an organization of people having a large city as nucleus, . . . metropolitan economy is the organization of producers and consumers mutually dependent for goods and services, wherein their wants are supplied by a system of exchange concentrated in a large city which is the focus of local trade and the center through which normal economic relations with the outside are established and maintained."[36]

In such an economy towns exist, but in a subordinate role to the central city, many of them will specialize in some function, or functions, and hence require some superior organizing force. The metropolis furnishes this service by organizing the market, by developing industry both in the metropolis and hinterland and in co-ordinating the latter by becoming the center of a network of communication and transportation facilities, and, finally, by developing and organizing financial control. However, this organization is informal and largely uninstitutionalized—save for such elements as chambers of commerce, probably because it is a recent growth and has not yet seriously challenged the traditional political unit, the state.

Thus there is indicated a close correlation between the type of economic organization and the political forms, the clan being associated with the collectional economy and the imperial state with the metropolitan economy,[37] together with the possibility that the metropolis may become the basis of a new regional and international political control.[38] The central thought of the discussion, nevertheless, is the organization about the metropolis. This is so dominant that Miss Hartsough, a student under Gras, declares that "the growth of the center is so intimately connected with that of the area that the two cannot be isolated."[39] Cities themselves realize this as clearly as any economist, and through such organization as they possess fight desperately for acquisition and retention of areas of hinterland.

These metropolitan units in the world economy are not independent, nor of equal rank, with the result that an hierarchical tendency

[36] N. S. B. Gras, *An Introduction to Economic History*, p. 186.

[37] *Ibid.*, p. 317, *et. seq.*

[38] N. S. B. Gras, "The Rise of the Metropolitan Community," *The Urban Community* (edited by E. W. Burgess), p. 191.

[39] Mildred Hartsough, *The Development of the Twin Cities as a Metropolitan Market*, p. 168.

appears. At least until recently, it was generally admitted that London was the metropolis of the world; within the United States certainly New York is dominant, with other metropoli, towns, and villages arranging themselves into serried ranks. This means that some regions are still in the status of colonial economy. This is easily seen in the case of the political colonies, but is less apparent with states. However, the southern region has traditionally filled this role within the United States, and partly because of that fact, seems destined to continue doing so for some time.

This position goes back into the period of colonial history, when a mercantilist mother country made desperate efforts to promote an agriculture in the southern part of the American colonies which would supply cargoes for English ships on return trips across the seas. This attitude resulted in the attempts to establish various forms of agriculture in the colonies which were not suited to the soils nor climate,[40] and restrictions on trade finally led to the War of the Revolution.

Thus, the mere presence of resources—potential wealth—is not enough to assure prosperity for a region, as pointed out by Zimmermann above, who adds elsewhere, "Its assets the South shares with others; its liabilities are its own."[41]

> In striking language Peter Molyneaux never tires of insisting that the destiny of the South is tied up with the foreign markets and that any national action which limits such markets, as the tariff, is hurtful to such a region. "To say that the national welfare requires the maintenance of the high tariff policy is equivalent to saying that the national welfare requires the irreparable submission, economically and socially of the greater part of the population of a whole region of the country."[42] However, such complaints are heard not only in the South. The agrarian revolt in the Central West during the last year of the Hoover administration, the insurgent Republican movement in the Upper Mississippi Valley, as well as the persistent complaints from the western portion of the nation throughout its history, attest to the plight of colonial economy, that of sharing its wealth with other, better-established regions.

[40] Lyman Carrier, *Beginnings of Agriculture in America, passim,* but especially p. 231.

[41] E. W. Zimmermann, "The Resources of the South," *South Atlantic Quarterly,* XXXII, 220.

[42] Peter Molyneaux, *What Economic Nationalism Means to the South,* p. 24.

This is not to be construed as an argument in favor of regional economic independence, or a flat denial of the classical economic doctrine of comparative advantage. It is to argue that the region should form an integral part of the nation; that it does so in any case, and that the prosperity of the nation as a whole is inextricably tied up with the prosperity of each of the major regions.

The regionalist does not object to dependence of one region upon others; he does point out the imbalance of the economic, or other, development of a region; and, if he becomes a planner, he seeks ways of creating a harmony within the region which, at the same time, is harmonious with the general economic system. The South, for example, has a chronically adverse balance of trade based on excessive exports of raw materials which prevents the accumulation of capital needed for the better exploitation of its resources. Such capital is habitually supplied from other regions and nations, and the situation is thereby perpetuated.

Further, it appears that there is enormous waste incurred in extra-regional processing of materials produced and consumed in a region, unless the region has such a great comparative cost advantage as to outweigh this factor; a situation present in very few of the colonial regions. In the South, again, it seems that many industries might well be located within the region to the economic advantage of the entire nation, save, perhaps, a few manufacturers. Regionalism, however, would not demand the immediate relocation of such industries; it would ask consideration of the mutual advantages of such relocation as expansion and replacement occurs. The arguments for and against economic nationalism may be applied with equal force to economic self-sufficiency of regions. Somewhere along the scale between economic self-isolation and total dependence, there must be a point of optimum interdependence.[43] It is the task of the economic planner to discover, establish, and maintain this optimum relationship.

The necessity of integration of regional into national and international economy is even more apparent in Europe, where the very life of some nations depends upon the accessibility of certain products of regions from without the national state, either through colonial possession or through an economic system of relative freedom and

[43] Howard W. Odum, *Southern Regions of the United States*, p. 249.

stability, as was made abundantly apparent by Herbert von Beckerath in his consideration of international economic relationships at the University of North Carolina during the spring of 1936. Von Beckerath pointed out that the situation in this respect has changed drastically within the past century; before that time territorial changes made little difference to states, since each region was largely independent, but since that time an interdependence has grown up which makes the possession of regions containing certain resources a matter of gravest international concern.

> There is no conflict between regional and national and international economic organization. As Brocard says, the economic region is characterized by the fact that regional forces "have produced a solidarity within the region and the township, which is apparent from the fact that in each area all the industries, all the enterprises, all public service, and all social classes (despite the competition that exists between them) are dependent upon one another and are bound to one another by a common interest that is much stronger than any tie that exists between one region and another. . . . To an even greater extent than the nation as a whole, the regional economy depends for its complete development upon continuous contact with other regions, so that, by co-operating with them, it may facilitate the movement of commodities and men. It is necessary to combine with the complex economic development already discussed a certain geographical specialization of industry, by means of which the various communities may accentuate the prosperity of one another and of the whole nation." [44]

Before leaving the subject of economic regionalism some consideration must be given the close connection between that subject and political regionalism, though the latter will receive more attention later. The tariff, the traditional point of difference between the two major political parties in this country, has almost always been a regional, or better, sectional difference. During the past few years much has been written as to the effects of economic nationalism on the South, the contention being, basically, that the South as a region has economic interests which demand free international trade since its principal products enter into international trade. Turner's sectionalism in American history—to be distinguished from regionalism—

[44] Lucien Brocard, "Regional Economy and Economic Regionalism," *Annals of the American Academy of Political and Social Science*, CLXII, 84-85, 88.

is based largely on differences in economic structure and needs. The shift of industry from the Atlantic regions to the Middle States has been accompanied by a shift in political attitudes, and it is notable that the two southern states to break the "solid South" in the presidential election of 1928 were leaders in industrialization.

The interstate compact between the southwestern oil producing states has recently taken its place alongside the Port of New York Authority as an outstanding example of attempts to meet economic situations too large to be handled by any one state and yet not of national importance. Several writers have seen in the rise of the city to economic dominance the need for rearrangement of political structure to achieve more realistic political units. All of these matters form an essential part of the discussion of political regionalism.

Chapter XVI

EXPLORING THE REGION: THE POLITICAL SCIENTISTS

IT would be difficult to find a more trenchant dictum with which to introduce the regional aspects of political science and to tie in the present American situation with the classical political theory than the statement of Marshall E. Dimock that "Federalism remains the most difficult problem of the American constitutional system."[1] The special point which he is emphasizing here is that "in a country as vast and varied as ours, there is needed an intermediate level of administrative co-ordination and planning authority midway between the states and the Federal Government." This need has been accentuated, he thinks, by the growing fear that too much federal control would result in a paralyzing over-centralization and loss of democratic participation in government and that the remedy is to be found somewhere within the bounds of regional decentralization and planning. Yet this very timely characterization of current situations finds its theoretical background well integrated into the whole fabric of human society from the early tribal origins of the state on up to classical theories of sovereignty and its territorial aspects. Since this present treatise on regionalism seeks primarily to see the problem as a broad societal one, it will be well to point up the governmental aspects, first from early society, and, then, catalogue some of the concepts and theories of the political scientists.

Ralph Linton in *The Study of Man* points up the same issues of sovereignty in relation to regional groups in the states which evolved in the principles of confederation. If we substitute the term "states" for

[1] "Political and Administrative Aspects of Regional Planning," *Planning for City, State, Region, and Nation,* p. 111.

"tribes" we might well apply his text to the federalism of the United States. Thus, confederacies of tribes "owe their origin to a community of interest, even if this is of a very limited and specific sort. The function of the central authority is that of directing and co-ordinating the voluntary activities of the federated tribes. It derives its powers from the consent of the governed, and any attempt to coerce the tribes is promptly resented. However, the presence of common interests makes it possible for the central authority to perform its functions with a minimum of machinery and of delegated powers. Since the component tribes are always jealous of their rights, the government of a confederacy must be democratic in fact if not in theory." [2] Professor Linton does not hesitate to bring this problem of sovereignty up-to-date. He concludes his chapter on the "Tribe and State" by pointing out that "In spite of some 6,000 years of experimentation, the problems of organizing and governing states have never been perfectly solved. The modern world, with the whole experience of history to draw upon, still attacks these problems in many different ways and with indifferent success. One thing seems certain. The most successful states are those in which the attitudes of the individual toward the state most nearly approximate the attitudes of the uncivilized individual toward his tribe. If the members of a state have common interests and a common culture, with the unity of will which these give, almost any type of formal governmental organization will function efficiently. If the members lack this feeling of unity, no elaboration of formal governmental patterns or multiplication of laws will produce an efficient state or contented citizens. How such unity may be created and maintained in great populations and especially in fluid ones where the individual's close, personal contacts are reduced to a minimum is probably the most important problem which confronts us today." [3]

Before pointing out something of the place of regional factors in historical political theory it may be well to recall that historically the problem of local units versus centralization has a distinguished history in the United States as well as in the societal evolution of states. We have cited many times over the historical factors in the form of sectionalism and conflict between the several regions and especially Turner's treatises on the significance of sections in American history. A part of Turner's explanation was in terms of politics and political alignments and he was constantly warning of the dangers which

[2] Ralph Linton, *The Study of Man*, pp. 241-242.
[3] *Ibid.*, p. 252. (Quoted by permission of D. Appleton-Century Company).

might come from conflict between what might become sectional states in conflict with the nation. We have also pointed out the sectional emphasis by such historians as Beard, Adams, Schlesinger, Dodd, Buck, and others. It is, however, important to note the more nearly purely political aspects of these areal problems and there is no one perhaps who could symbolize both the problem and its contradictions better than Thomas Jefferson himself. For Jefferson even until his last days was deep in the contradictions of federal and state authorities. Before his tasks as President drew him into the difficulties of union, he was a strong states' rights advocate. So also he was until the end. In practice he was constantly on the verge of centralized federalism, either seeking through experiment to find equilibrium, or forced by exigency to go further in practice than his theories would justify. Then as now what to do and how to do it was the question.

> Wirth has pointed up the fear of overcentralization and the desire for liberty within sovereignty as the factor which led Jefferson to be overzealous to prevent the encroachment of a powerful centralized government upon the local units, the states. Distribution within consolidation or decentralization within federalism might be termed the Jeffersonian principle. Thus he wrote: "But it is not by the consolidation or concentration of powers, but by their distribution that good government is effected. Were not this great country already divided into states, that division must be made, that each might do for itself what concerns itself directly, and what it can so much better do than a distant authority. Every state again is divided into counties, each to take care of what lies within its local bounds; each county again into townships or wards, to manage minuter details; and every ward into farms, to be governed each by its individual proprietor. Were we directed from Washington when to sow, and when to reap, we should soon want bread. It is by this partition of cares, descending in gradation from general to particular, that the mass of human affairs may be best managed, for the good and prosperity of all."[4]

It would seem fairly easy to trace with considerable continuity this mooted problem from the present back through the nation's history and before that in the political theories which constitute the basis for

[4] Quoted by Louis Wirth, "Localism, Regionalism, and Centralization," *The American Journal of Sociology*, XLII, No. 4, p. 496.

sovereignty. Thus Merriam in his *History of Political Theories, Recent Times* interprets this relational factor of sovereignty as one of the chief subjects discussed since the turn of the century, from which point we may take the trail back through Dunning's earlier three volumes on the history of political theories. Up to the end of the first third of the twentieth century, however, Merriam finds no satisfying agreement among the political scientists. Thus his appraisal of recent theories seems to give the perfect background for such notable discussions as those of Gaus, Dimock, Renner and others in *Regional Factors in National Planning and Development.*

> Merriam's summary estimates that "One of the outstanding features of the time was the development of federalistic theories of the state. The political theory of federalism, based largely on geographical isolation, had developed in the earlier part of the nineteenth century, notably in the United States and in Germany, and had found expression in a definite form of political organization; but with the consolidation of such states, both the theory and the practice of federalism had tended to fall into a decline. Economic federalism, however, had also developed in the early part of the nineteenth century, notably in the theory of Proudhon. With the sharper division of classes on an industrial basis, and of professional and vocational groupings, attention was again directed toward the federalistic doctrine as a means of political association and organization. Again and again, especially toward the end of this period, recurred the problem of the organization of the state upon the basis of economic or professional groups rather than upon a geographic or an ethnical basis, or upon some combination of ethnogeographic factors."[5]

Continuing the Dunning historical thread, it is helpful to follow Dunning back to Bodin and Montesquieu. It is interesting to note the similarity between Giddings' theory of *causation* in which he related physical factors to psychic factors of state and the theories of Bodin in which he magnifies "the influence of the physical environment [which] makes the subject of a long and careful investigation in both the *Method* and the *Republic.*" Professor Dunning interprets Bodin to estimate "national characteristics" such that "northern peoples excel in bodily, physical strength, southern peoples

[5] C. E. Merriam and Harry Elmer Barnes, *A History of Political Theories, Recent Times,* I, 29-30. (Quoted by permission of The Macmillan Company.)

in craft and genius," while "the peoples between the extremes" are better adapted to "control politics and maintain justice."[6] So, too, Montesquieu features the influence of physical environment upon political institutions holding that "Institutions . . . vary . . . according to the characteristics of the people," which in turn are affected by "the energy and activity which are produced by the colder climates and the indolence produced by the warmer."[7]

> Professor Dunning thinks that "It is the relation between the climate and liberty that constitutes the most important feature of this whole subject for political philosophy proper. Summarily stated, [Montesquieu's] theory is that every species of liberty is favored by the colder climates, and slavery by the warmer. . . . Another influence that promotes the distinction between the two continents in respect to political liberty is the fact that in Asia the natural geographical divisions, as determined by river systems, mountain ranges, etc., are of vast extent, and, therefore, according to the principle already noted, promote despotism, while in Europe the natural divisions are small and therefore favor the compact communities to whom liberty is normal."[8] Professor Dunning says further, "The net result of all the speculation that has been noticed was that some relation between geography and the nation was recognized, but the character of the relation was not made at all definite. And such remained the situation throughout the fierce controversies of the mid-century over the rights and wrongs of nations and of nationalities. For none of the concrete problems as to boundaries could a scientific formula furnish an acceptable solution. The mountains, deserts, seas, rivers and other features of the earth's surface that had seemed to be natural marks of separation for communities of men either were lacking where need for them was greatest, or, when present, actually furnished additional incentives to strife in the rivalry for occupation and control of them. Nor could the limits indicated by geography be made to coincide with the limits indicated by language. A Germany that fulfilled the glowing demand of Arndt for unity *so weit die deutsche Zunge klingt* would outrage every canon of geographic theory, and would present many points where geography could find nothing whatever to offer as a boundary. And there in the heart of Europe lay the Swiss—a stout and respected nation, defying every rule of both language and geography in its national life.

[6] William Archibald Dunning, *A History of Political Theories from Luther to Montesquieu,* II, 113.
[7] *Ibid.*, p. 419.
[8] *Ibid.*, pp. 420-422.

"No more in the facts of physical environment than in those of blood and language, therefore, did the political theory of the early nineteenth century find an objective criterion of nationality that would suffice to still the insistent clamor of the democratic liberalism for recognition of the human will as the paramount factor. Through the growing precision of geographic science as wrought out by Humboldt and Ritter, and through the rise of ethnology and anthropology and comparative philology, the influence of heredity, environment and speech on the evolution of human societies was more justly apportioned and balanced, and political science defined the nation in terms that gave due weight to each, while assigning to the will and feeling of living men a part that was far from the least."[9]

Professor Dunning himself made one of his most distinctive contributions through his interpretation of the sectional conflict between the North and South. Epochal and pioneering were his treatments, through his graduate doctoral dissertations of reconstruction in the South, forerunner of later notable books such as Paul Buck's *The Road to Reunion*, Claude Bowers' *The Tragic Era*, W. E. B. Du Bois' *Black Reconstruction*, George Fort Milton's *The Age of Hate*, and a long list of critical treatises on the South, even prior to the popularity of books by and of southerners. These studies promoted by Professor Dunning must be accredited a big place in the literature of reintegration of an ostracized section needing to come fully into the greater union of states and regions. Professor Dunning's contributions, however, were not limited either to his history of theory or of the southern section. His keen and penetrating sense of political development led him like Turner to interpret the sectionalism of the country often in terms of delicate satire and humor. Thus describing the clamor of partisan strife between the Federalists and Republicans he pointed up a continuity of conflict in which "Then as now, the commercial and financial regions stood opposed to the agricultural; then as now, the regions where the Blacks were numerous stood opposed to those where they were few; and then as now—but even more than now—New England stood opposed to everything else—a thing *sui generis*."[10]

[9] William Archibald Dunning, *A History of Political Theories from Rousseau to Spencer*, III, 319-320. (Quoted by permission of The Macmillan Company.)
[10] William Archibald Dunning, *Truth in History and Other Essays*, p. 46.

Returning now to the concept of sovereignty and liberty with which we began this chapter it is interesting to trace the concept of areal or territorial relationships to government in the United States as expounded by American political scientists. Here again the earlier theories and the present dilemmas run, now side by side, and now in widely diverging streams. It is possible to take as text the orthodox theories of sovereignty and argue for the increasing functions of the central governments over the states and it is possible to see in the encroachment of Federal Government the nullification of local autonomy and liberty. So, too, it is possible to find in the *trends* of both theory and practice bases for arguments both ways. It is in the harmonizing of such apparently justifiable authentic differences of opinion and conflict that regionalism finds its chief service in government. For without doubt the principle of national sovereignty makes it possible to nullify much that has been traditionally the sphere of the state.

The key to this situation is that of sovereignty and the distinction which Willoughby makes between the real federation of states in the United States and the contrariwise confederation of states. Thus he thinks one of the most important points involved in the "nature and indivisibility of sovereignty is the distinction between what is known as a Federation or a Federal State, though this latter term is, as has been pointed out, an improper one, and a Confederation or, as the Germans express it, the distinction between a *Bundesstaat* and a *Staatenbund.* Both are made up of a grouping of large political units. In both the performance of the functions of the state is entrusted to two sets of governmental machinery, a general or central government which acts for all the units and a special government acting for each of the units independently of the others.

"Notwithstanding this similarity, the two are, from the political standpoint, fundamentally different. The former is a single State, the latter is composed of as many separate States as there are units composing the grouping. This difference arises wholly from the differences in respect to the location of sovereignty in the grouping. In the true Federation or *Bundesstaat*, sovereignty resides in the combined population of all the units. This population has, purely as a matter of practical expediency, decided to make use of two sets of governmental machinery for the performance of its functions: a central government to attend to matters which it is believed concern all, or should receive single generally-binding determination; and special machinery for each of the great geographical divisions into which the country, for historical or other reasons, is divided. Each of these governments is equally but the instrument through which the single State acts."[11]

John W. Burgess pointed out that a "State" such as one of the states in the United States Government is a kind of local government and under the federal system it is "a local self-government, under the supremacy of the Constitution of the United States, and of the laws and treaties of the central government made in accordance with that Constitution, republican as to form, and possessed of residuary powers—that is, of all powers not vested by the Constitution of the United States exclusively in the central government, or not denied by that Constitution to the 'State.' "[12] Yet this is only one form of local government and, as Merriam has pointed out so often, there is the emerging city-state local self-government and others, so that Burgess' further analysis of the subjectivity of the state to the federal Constitution has considerable bearing upon the increasingly complex problem of the United States, states' rights, constitutionality and regionalism.

Burgess continues, "Such being the nature of a 'State' of the Union and such the method of its creation, what reason is there for speaking of the 'States' in a system of federal government as indestructible? As they emerge from the status of Territories under the exclusive power of Congress, upon having attained certain conditions, why may they not revert to the status of Territories upon having lost these conditions of 'State' existence; nay, why may they not revert to the status of martial law by having lost all of the conditions of civil government? The dictum 'once a State always a State' in a system of federal government has no sound reason in it. Under the Constitution of the United States, every 'State' of the Union may through the process of amendment be made a province subject to the exclusive government of the central authorities. . ."[13]

Conflict and contradiction abound not only in political theories and in the practical implementation of these theories but in the

[11] W. F. Willoughby, *An Introduction to the Study of the Government of Modern States*, pp. 22-23. (Quoted by permission of Doubleday, Doran & Company, Inc.)

[12] John W. Burgess, *Reconstruction and the Constitution, 1866-1876*, p. 2.

[13] *Ibid.*, pp. 3-4.

historical development of the states and regions in the United States. Already we have pointed out many times the definitive contributions of Turner concerning the political sectionalism of the nation and we have noted something of the loyalties, priorities, and autonomies of the states, which themselves grew from a small number that were historically conditioned to a larger number which grew up through gradually shifting national frontiers. Yet it is important once again to have this politico-historical fact presented in the words of the political scientists. The conflict comes here between the principle of local government over against that of central sovereignty and between the historical traditional habits and patterns which grew up in each community and the encroaching technology and centralization tendencies.

> Willoughby reminds us that "The local-governing areas that exist within the states of the American Union were, in most instances, artificially marked out and created by the central authorities of those states, but in all cases this was done only after the principle had become well established in American political philosophy that, so far as practicable, each locality is entitled, as a moral right, to have its purely local interests determined by its own inhabitants, and satisfied according to the methods that they may think best. The result has been the carrying into practice in the American states of many of the same principles, and much of the same spirit, as are found in English local government bodies. . . . The only merits that the American system of administrative and local government control is supposed to have are that it prevents the growth of rigid bureaucracies which are out of touch with and often disregardful of the wishes and interests of the people, and that it tends to give to private individuals a reasonably secure protection against arbitrary and oppressive acts upon the part of their rulers. The first result is probably secured, although at the expense of considerable administrative inefficiency, but it is very doubtful indeed whether, in actual practice, private rights are any better secured in America than they are under the systems of administrative centralization and of administrative courts that exist in France and Prussia."[14]

The trend here, as in most of the ways of current civilization, is more and more away from the power and entity of the states toward

[14] W. W. Willoughby and Lindsay Rogers, *An Introduction to the Problem of Government*, pp. 448-449. (Quoted by permission of Doubleday, Doran & Company, Inc.)

federal centralization. All along the line—business, commerce, education, management—and in state governments themselves there is everywhere the strong tropism toward centralization. Here again the evolution of the conflict seems to be somewhere between the two extremes and in accord with such expediency and equilibrium as must generally characterize the practices and policies of modern administration. This trend has been admirably stated by the authors of *Regional Factors in National Planning and Development;* and their viewpoints will be presented at length. Yet it is important to note the earlier trends as background for their conclusions.

Merriam reviews the trend in the early twentieth century, "Both the institutional and the theoretical developments regarding the area or unit of government were notable. The general tendency was toward nationalism as against the state in accordance with the decision reached in the Civil War and with the economic and social tendencies of the time. Broader powers were conferred upon the nation by the Fourteenth Amendment to the Constitution, and these powers were often broadly construed by the courts, while the state lagged behind in ideals and organization. The state was no longer the rival of the nation, but tended toward the position of a subordinate though powerful agency. Powerful social and industrial forces constantly worked in the direction of the national unit as against the state. Commerce demanded a greater degree of uniformity in the commercial code, and a general sentiment urged the need of uniformity at many points. The theory of national supremacy was more sharply formulated than ever by Burgess and others who assailed the commonwealth as a unit of government. There were some *post-bellum* statements of the state sovereignty doctrines, but these were more in the nature of historic justifications of the 'lost cause' than serious advocacy of living principles of political action. The devotion to local self-government, notable in earlier years, declined during this period. It revived around the municipality, but even here the sentiment was by no means unanimous. Local self-government as a fundamental and necessary guarantee of liberty was not much in evidence, except for that development of the idea of local autonomy centering around the demand for broader powers of self-government for the city. Nor were these municipal powers asked as guarantees against some dangerous and centralized power, but as desirable means for the self-development and self-expression of communities with distinct local interests. Liberty was no longer regarded as primarily local in character, in danger of losing its soul if extended over too broad an area. Conceptions of liberty, justice, democracy were to a large extent interpreted in terms of the nation, rather than of the state of the city or the rural local government. . . ."[15]

There were abundant sources to support this theory of the trend away from states, in addition to the epochs of the Civil War and Reconstruction. Merriam quotes Goodnow and Burgess pointing to the *nation* as the road to advance. Goodnow thought that if we were framing a new nation we should undoubtedly give the national government greater powers than the present constitution allows. Colonel Roosevelt in his "New Nationalism" was cited as glorifying the nation as the chiefest instrument for social and political progress, and he expounded the doctrine of interstate relations by insisting that there must be no neutral ground "to serve as a refuge for law breakers."[16] Yet, once again it seemed possible to find distinguished authorities who saw in this trend great dangers. Even Professor Burgess himself, in later years, as interpreted by his friend and adviser, William R. Shepherd, complained of the process of deterioration which enabled the government more and more to encroach upon the legitimate domain of individual rights and wrote that "it is high time for us to call a halt in our present course of increasing the sphere of government and decreasing that of liberty."[17] Thus his doctrine of increasing sovereignty of the federal power over the states appears to lead directly to the thing he does not want to happen.

One other example may be cited to indicate perhaps the more favorable position taken by Woodrow Wilson in his view of the states. Says Merriam, "Possibly the best presentation of the importance of the state in our system of government was made by Wilson. He urged the importance of the state as an experiment station in which new plans might be tried. 'Every commonwealth,' he declared, 'has been a nursery of new strength; and out of these nurseries have come men and communities which no other process could have produced. Self-government has here had its richest harvest.' If our system of states had not come to us 'by historical necessity, I think it would have been worth while to invent it.' Local affairs are not uniform, and cannot be made so by compulsion of law. What we seek is co-operation, but not the

[15] C. E. Merriam, *American Political Ideas,* pp. 456-457. (Quoted by permission of The Macmillan Company.)

[16] Quoted by C. E. Merriam, *ibid.,* p. 236.

[17] Howard W. Odum (editor), *American Masters of Social Science,* p. 43.

strait jacket. Variety will not impair energy, if there is genuine co-operation.

"Our states have not been created: they have sprung up of themselves, irresponsible, 'self-originated, self-constituted, self-confident, self-sustaining, veritable communities demanding only recognition.' The remedy lies, not merely in changing the division of powers between state and nation, along lines of actual alteration of interest, but in reorganization of the state from within. Instead of upsetting an ancient system, we should 'revitalize it by reorganization.' 'Centralization is not vitalization,' said he, and the atrophy of the parts will result in the atrophy of the whole." [18]

Perhaps we have cited enough of the backgrounds within political theory to indicate the general consensus of opinion on many aspects of the relation of area to government in general and in the United States in particular. It seems clear that in both the organic relationships between governments and areas and between sovereignty of a centralized federation and the United States that while there are abundant theories and discussions there is as yet little agreement among scholars or administration. So, too, there appears to be a similar parallel in the case of the political geographers and students of government. Here again there is a great deal of evidence couched in plausible theories in many varying contributions, yet little of definitive agreement. As between Bowman's problem approach to political geography and Haushofer's functional-natural approach in Geopolitik there is a great chasm of difference. Yet in either case, whether in seeking harmony of international relations through the understanding of the habitats of men or seeking to find the nature and origin of nations through regional natural environments, the areal factors are fundamental. In the case of the problem approach the student is not worried about what has happened and why so much as he is interested in the next question as to what is to be done because of what. On the other hand the political geographer is more interested in trying to define the determinant effect of geography upon the nation and region so that if his premises are correct he will not only be able to explain states and nations but to advocate

[18] C. E. Merriam, *American Political Ideas*, pp. 239-240. (Quoted by permission of The Macmillan Company.)

new alignments in harmony with natural regions. Needless to say, there are great differences of opinion here.

The situation has been presented comprehensively and well by Professor Richard Hartshorne in a discussion of "Recent Developments in Political Geography" in the *American Political Science Review.* After first tracing the history and recent developments in the field he continues, "Whichever way the definition is stated, the field for political geography as part of the main field can easily be derived from it: the study of the relations between man's political activities and organizations (including the state, but also parties, etc.) and the natural environment or earth conditions, whether stated directly or conversely. . . . As Vallaux puts it, the essential problem of political geography is to determine whether 'the life of political societies is determined, in part at least, by the natural frame in which they develop; in what manner the soil, air, and waters . . . relate themselves to the collective action of men.' " He quotes Fawcett further as having as his main objective in a recent study: "to set out and examine those geographical facts which are of direct importance in their influence on the development and organization of the British Empire and its component parts"; and Haushofer the founder of Geopolitik in Germany: "Geopolitik is the study of the earth relations of political occurrences. . . . The character of the earth's surfaces . . . gives to Geopolitik its frame within which the course of political events *must* take place if they are to have permanent success."[19]

"Applying Hettner's definition of the general field," Hartshorne concludes, "the division, political geography, is a branch of systematic or general geography which concerns itself with those political phenomena of regions differing from place to place and bearing significant relations to other regional phenomena." After discussing a number of somewhat divergent definitions he sums up the definition as follows: "Political geography is the science of political areas, or more specifically, the study of the state as a characteristic of areas in relation to the other characteristics of areas."

More important and immediate are the distinctive contributions of the later current political scientists to the general concept, theory, and practice of regionalism or its related topics of sectionalism in politics, federalism and states, uniform state action, and regional administrative arrangements. We have already discussed in the pre-

[19] Vol. 29, pp. 785-803, 943-966.

vious chapters dealing with Governmental Service Regions and with States and Subregions as tools for regionalism something of the work of William B. Munro, W. Y. Elliott, Charles E. Merriam, John M. Gaus, Marshall E. Dimock, William Anderson, James Fesler. In particular we have studied Elliott's and Munro's suggestions for new sovereign regional arrangements, Merriam's proposal for the city-state as a form of regional entity, Holcombe's trend from sectional to class politics, and the special work of Gaus, Dimock, and Fesler in administrative regionalism. These concepts, however, have great theoretical importance to the whole question of regionalism, which, after all, is only partly political, partly of more specialized governmental concern, and partly within the still more specialized areas of public administration. They are, furthermore, not only illuminating but they represent the best of the current "evidence" on the subject. We shall, therefore, recall certain of these contributions to which, however, we shall add others to illustrate the points in question.

W. Y. Elliott writes that "The answer to the . . . question . . . of appropriate political machinery . . . assumes that the new role of the state requires, more than ever, an efficient administrative mechanism and a permanent non-political bureaucracy. . . . It is clear that so long as we duplicate bureaucracies by a federal centralization that overlaps the functions of the individual states, we have a wasteful system of government. A reduction of the number and functions of local (particularly county) government areas is certainly indicated. The same reasoning applies to the states. They should be supplanted, except as administrative areas or as convenient electoral districts, by geographically appropriate regions. As a suggestion I have termed these regions *commonwealths* and indicated an approximation of the present Federal Reserve districts, with perhaps one additional western commonwealth, as a more rational basis for our federal structure. . . . Federalism continues to exist in the United States only in the difficulty of formally amending the Constitution, in the extraordinary overrepresentation of small states in our powerful Senate, and in the unnecessary multiplication of jurisdictions and of bureaucracies. The domain of state control over finance, labor conditions, farming, manufacturing, mining, etc., has been almost obliterated by the avalanche of federal acts dealing with unemployment relief, national industrial recovery, agricultural adjustment, and codes and public-works programs. . . . The readjustment of economic life, particularly as international trade disappears through efforts at national self-sufficiency, demands co-ordina-

> tion by the state. That may mean as thoroughgoing a revision of our system as was Solon's for Athens. That means planning and, where necessary, coercion. . . . Planning of this drastic type is an executive function. . . ."[20]

Professor Elliott thinks that the states would have to be retained for some administrative units such as the English counties have, for centers of cultural differentiation, and for other purposes. His new regional commonwealths would become autonomous units for local functions but subject to one jurisdiction for courts. Quite a different viewpoint is that of Austin F. MacDonald who sees the solution more nearly in some adequate implementation of federal aid. This, of course, according to the broader premises of American regionalism, implies regional arrangements as minimum essentials.

> The right of the Federal Government to give to the states land from the federal domain and money from the federal treasury has never seriously been questioned. . . . But only within the last two decades has the Federal Government adopted the policy of purchasing with federal funds a considerable measure of supervision over numerous governmental activities not mentioned in the Constitution, and therefore presumably left in the hands of the states. Most of the money now appropriated by Congress for state use must be spent in a manner approved by the Federal Government. . . . For most purposes state boundaries have ceased to exist. But in the field of government state boundaries still play a very significant part. State railway commissions, industrial commissions, public utility commissions, insurance commissions, banking commissions, health commissions and a multitude of others are applying their local regulations to nation-wide enterprises with devastating results. The line of demarcation between national and state powers is very little different today than at the close of the Civil War. Forty-eight states are attempting to solve national problems in forty-eight different ways, most of them equally unsatisfactory. State constitutions, state laws and state judicial decisions have produced a bewildering patchwork of policies and counter-policies concerning matters of national importance. The demands for at least a measure of federal control have been insistent, and Congress has found a way to meet these demands in the newly developed system of federal subsidies. . . . Because it unites so skillfully the principles of local initiative and central supervision, federal aid is an important phase of American administration. The old line of division between state

[20] W. Y. Elliott, *The Need for Constitutional Reform*, pp. 9, 185, 186, 190-191.

> and national powers is manifestly unsuited to present-day conditions. Local authorities find themselves powerless to cope with problems that have become national in character. . . . But men are loath to sacrifice the autonomy of the states. They know the dangers of excessive centralization. They realize that central control of government activities means the crushing of all local initiative. The real need is for some device that will combine state control with national leadership. Federal aid meets that need. . . .[21]

In previous chapters and in subsequent discussions we have called attention to state compacts as a form of regional planning and administration. W. Brooke Graves suggests that uniform state action might be the "way out" of the dilemma of overcentralization. This he believes more feasible than new regional governmental units. He sees uniform state action as a means of securing uniformity in such matters as insurance, divorce, marriage, child labor, corporation charters, motor traffic regulations, etc., and also in "matters which are of common concern only to a particular region, such as river and harbor control, control over oil production, flood control, et cetera."[22] "All are agreed," he says, "that uniformity is urgently needed in many fields of state government activity, but many object to achieving it by federal action. The author wishes simply to make clear a point which has not heretofore been properly recognized—namely, that we have here a practical workable alternative if we desire to use it. . . ."[23]

Another important contribution is that of A. N. Holcombe in which he emphasizes the trend from *sectional politics* to *class politics*. Although recognizing the past America as one which featured the struggle between geographic sections he concludes that, due to urbanization and industrialization, this is now giving rise to class politics. His work here is also of considerable significance in the area of urban and rural culture.

> "American politics," he says, "was originally rustic politics. Its character was determined by the interests and attitudes of the rural population. In the field of national government the struggle for power took the form of a conflict between the geographic sections into which the

[21] Austin F. MacDonald, *Federal Aid*, pp. 1, 2, 4, 12.
[22] W. Brooke Graves, *Uniform State Action*, p. 9.
[23] *Ibid.*, Preface, vii-viii.

country was divided. The national parties were founded upon alliances between sectional interests, and the sectional interests were at first mostly agrarian interests. . . . The passing of the frontier and the growth of urban industry have shaken the foundations of the old party system in national politics. The old sectional interests are changing and the old sectional alliances are breaking down. . . . The character of the new party politics will be determined chiefly by the interests and attitudes of the urban population. . . . There will be less sectional politics and more class politics. . . . That rustic politics in the field of national government should have taken the form of sectional politics was also the necessary consequence of the original condition of the people. The essential fact was that 'the agricultural interest' was by no means uniform throughout the country. . . ." [24]

Professor John A. Fairlie's studies of administrative regionalism in Great Britain are of special timeliness in the American scene, as are also many informal inquiries into regional aspects of Russian administration and of Nazi reforms. Roger H. Wells writes of the "Liquidation of the German Länder" and Albert Lepawsky on "The Nazis Reform the Reich" and both study the internal balance of the new Germany and its relation to territorial reform and the unification.

Professor Fairlie's materials, however, are of more immediate relation to our own administrative regionalism. "In the administration of public affairs in Great Britain, several government departments have found it convenient to divide the country into varying numbers of regional districts, each covering a group of counties. These districts vary a good deal in number and in area for the different departments, though in some cases a similar area is used by more than one department. The largest area is Scotland, with an extensive organization of public administration under the Secretary of State for Scotland, and its own judicial system, while other departments also have branch headquarters for Scotland. Northern Ireland forms another important region, with a large degree of autonomy, under a separate parliament; while, as in the case of Scotland, several departments of the United Kingdom have branch headquarters in Belfast. Wales is also a distinct district for several departments.

"The number of such regional districts varies from four to twelve. The most clearly defined areas are Scotland, Northern Ireland, and Wales, though Scotland and Wales are sometimes divided. Other de-

[24] A. N. Holcombe, *The New Party Politics*, pp. 11, 13-14.

scriptive terms used by several departments are: Northern, Midlands, Eastern, the London metropolitan area, South Eastern, Southern, and Western. But the areas covered by these terms are not always the same; and in some of these cases there are subdivisions, such as North Eastern and North Western, East and West Midlands, and South-western."[25]

Such a brief review of the backgrounds of our present situation as has been presented seems to justify the conclusion that the authors of the notable work on *Regional Factors in National Planning and Development* have not only made a significant and comprehensive contribution to the new field but that their conclusions are based on an extraordinarily wide range of inquiries. We have already drawn heavily upon their findings but we know no better way of pointing up the situation than to introduce another of their conclusions and to follow this then with a brief restatement or recapitulation of the problem of regions and nation in terms of practical situations.

Thus they interpret the regional problem as it relates to federal activity in the United States as being twofold. "First, there are needed divisions of the country suitable for the carrying out, in the field, of administrative control from Washington. Second, subnational units of area are needed in order to accomplish actual decentralization of powers and activities of the federal agencies, particularly where planning and policy making are involved.

The first phase of the problem has been met by designing many different regional systems, wherein the individual regions are usually larger than a state and more nearly uniform in size than are the states. The second phase of the problem has been met, at least in a few instances, by devising systems of regions wherein each areal unit is more closely related to the function or object dealt with, than are the states or even the general run of federal administrative regions.

The bureaus of the federal departments have in most instances adopted regions simply to effect greater efficiency and convenience in administering their activities in the field. The significance of federal regions, however, transcends mere considerations of efficiency and economy in administration. The whole issue of regionalism is involved, or at least implied, and this is increasingly being raised by students of polity, geography, and social science. These students have demonstrated that most internal political boundaries exhibit slight con-

[25] John A. Fairlie, "Administrative Regions in Great Britain," *The American Political Science Review*, Vol. 31, pp. 937, 941.

formity to natural physical areas, or to the social, economic, and political problems which are closely related to such areas. They have demonstrated further that such things as literacy, crime, birth rates, urbanization of population, differentiation in agricultural production, problems of reclamation or reforestion (sic), are definitely regional in character and occurrence. It is fairly obvious, therefore, that these can be treated most effectively, not by direct handling from Washington, but by a regional approach."[26]

Outside of the historical and geographical incidence of regionalism it seems likely that the following considerations will suffice to restate the case for regions *vs.* nation. From the standpoint of utilization of natural resources, it is evident that major river systems are almost never confined to one state; yet such drainage areas furnish some of the most perplexing problems with which we must deal. Problems of flood control, hydroelectric development, domestic and industrial water supplies and stream pollution must all be approached from the point of view of an entire valley. Land utilization furnishes another excellent illustration of natural forces and areas cutting across state lines. The experiences of those hardy agriculturists who have pushed their way out onto the semi-arid Great Plains regions in accordance with one of the most prized of American traditions, only to find their farms literally disappearing from under their crops in great clouds of dust, give dramatic point to the arguments of those who have insisted upon a regional policy of land use. No less do the eroded fields of the Southeast and the barren cut-over lands of the former forest regions demand consideration.

Such regions are blighted areas which have given their resources to the nation as a whole and which now threaten to become a burden to the nation as a whole. In analogous manner the mineral areas of the nation have been exploited so that their natural wealth might be utilized by Americans everywhere; very little of the original wealth has remained in the regions of primary production. The prosperity and national defense of the nation are intimately tied up with petroleum production, with gold supplies, with sulphur mining, with the development of potential supplies of mineral fertilizers for agricul-

[26] Adapted from National Resources Committee, *Regional Factors in National Planning and Development*, December 1935, p. 31.

ture, such as phosphate, nitrate and potash, in spite of the fact that supplies of these modern essentials are found in only a few minor regions of the country. Yet it is highly unlikely that many voters in New England are even aware that huge deposits of potash, for example, are to be found in Texas, California, and New Mexico; they look to Germany and France as the source of supply.

In the field of commerce, trade currents and transportation lines cut across state boundaries, as we have been careful to insure they will by our prohibition of interstate tariffs. Our national economic structure is predicated upon the assumption that regions will more or less specialize in those industries for which they are best fitted by nature; that New England, for instance, will do much of the manufacturing for the nation while the South supplies cotton for her looms and the coal regions will supply fuel to drive those looms. The whole question of the economic desirability of keeping one region in the status of an economic colony to another immediately raises its head. Clearly such relationships transcend state lines.

In the field of social relationships the states are seen to be nearly as impotent. Throughout the history of the nation the piedmont sections have been in conflict with the tidewater areas. In the interior, streams of migration have swept in broad swaths across the map, leaving wide areas of tradition, religious prejudice and conviction, political adherence, familial patterns of organization which do not fit neatly into state boundary lines and which find their echoes in the unceasing wrangles on the floors of a score of state legislatures. Eastern Tennessee and eastern Kentucky form a social unit which finds little in common with the western portions of the states between which it is divided. Western Texas has sentimental and economic interests which combine it closely with New Mexico and Arizona, but which distinguish it from the pine-forested eastern portion of the state, at one with the old cotton belt stretching eastward across Louisiana, Mississippi, Alabama, Georgia, into the Carolinas. Most states contain more than one economic and social region; most regions contain more than one state.

The National Resources Committee notes that regional-political problems are forced on the attention of the nation by "The increasingly clear realization of the inadequacy of single states to carry out all planning programs necessary for conserving our national resources, both natural and human, as illustrated by the widespread efforts to negotiate interstate compacts dealing with watershed, oil conservation, labor standards, and crime prevention. . . . The development of an extensive interstate co-operation movement . . . The rise of interstate co-operation movement . . . The rise of interstate metropolitan planning . . . The emergence and activity of two groups-of-states planning regions . . . The establishment of more than 100 types of federal regional areas dealing with administration and departmental planning. The creation of the Tennessee Valley Authority and the proposals for the establishment of other like authorities. The pressure of economic distress and unbalance in various agricultural-industrial areas of the United States, and the corresponding necessity of establishing subnational administration in the areas served by the several economic groups . . ." [27]

Control of petroleum production and marketing, because of the spectacular nature of the problems involved, furnishes an example as enticing as it is pertinent to the discussion of the intimate relationships existing between the economic and the political region. Here is a giant industry, recognized as essential to the economic and military welfare of the nation, with social implication profound but as yet largely unanalyzed, and exerting strong influences on interregional as well as international politics. Oil production is highly speculative, and, in the past at least, has been very erratic. Within this nation for the past several years there has been at least one producing area which has had it within its power to flood the market and bring chaos to the entire industry. Within the framework of our prevailing economic and political philosophy, such a condition must inevitably ensue. Because of its fugitive nature, each producer of oil felt compelled to secure as much from as many wells as quickly as he might, for fear someone else would acquire the wealth he might have obtained. Conservation was invoked; but unfortunately for the oil producers, the boundaries of petroleum areas and state lines do not coincide; as is true for most economic areas. The matter was hardly one for national action, since the areas involved are relatively small and less than half the states were directly affected. Indeed it has been argued that the national interest was opposed to

[27] Adapted from National Resources Committee, *Regional Factors in National Planning and Development*, December 1935, p. v.

that of the petroleum regions in that flush production meant cheap gasoline for automobiles all over the country, while controlled production meant high profits for the oil producers who received permits to produce under such a system of control.

Faced with this problem, what actually happened was that exceptions to the prevailing philosophy were made; the producers, where their number was relatively small, entered into voluntary agreements to restrict production. The state governments, at the behest of the petroleum and conservation interests, enacted laws regulating production; the Federal Government set up organizations attempting to cope with the situation, and finally the states most immediately concerned established regional bodies with regulatory powers as great as it was thought the courts would uphold. However, these efforts were not wholly successful, and the Oil Conservation Board of the national government has advocated for several years the perfection of an interstate compact as the most feasible means of meeting those problems.[28]

Although an interstate compact designed to control petroleum production and marketing by means of an advisory commission was subscribed to by several of the states in 1935, it was not wholly successful. This compact relied upon the police power of the various states, aided by the national government operating under the interstate commerce authority to prevent the transportation of oil illegally produced from one state to another. The Supreme Court nullified the effort on the ground that the legislation did not set a standard for the guidance of the President,[29] as enforcement officer, but later still more restrictive legislation was passed.[30]

Though the details of this particular problem are interesting as well as instructive, the literature, legal and popular, concerning it is too voluminous for review here. Further, its significance for immediate purposes lies in its power of illustrating the lack of ability on the part of either the individual states or the national government to cope with a certain class of problems which are coming to have more and more importance as the nation becomes more and more closely welded into an organic whole, and presses more closely on its stock

28 Northcutt Ely, *Oil Conservation Through Interstate Agreement*, gives a summary of the steps taken looking toward control of petroleum production, the court decisions through which the rights of the State and Federal governments to control such production have been determined, and argues that an interstate compact is "the missing gear in the present machinery."

29 Panama Refining Company *vs.* Ryan, 55 Sup. Ct. 241, 1935.

30 Public Law No. 14, 74th Congress.

of natural resources. Similar instances might be drawn from the use of water facilities, the expedition of commerce, protection and taxation of property; or, in a field with greater social implications, the apprehension and prosecution of criminals. Indeed, in each of these fields, interstate agreements have been found useful.

Since natural regions do not coincide with states and since our government is based on a division of powers between one federal and forty-eight state governments, there is manifestly a no-man's land in which we have failed to provide machinery for action. However, this does not mean that regions have not made themselves felt in our governmental affairs. The United States has often been compared to a congress of nations, the emphasis being placed on the *States* rather than on the *United*, and the plural form of the national title stressed. This may lead to regionalism; in the past it has most often led to sectionalism. In fact, most of the discussions by historians and political writers of the past have stressed the separateness of the regions, or sections, rather than their integration into a national picture of distinctive but interdependent entities. Regionalism stresses integration, but not standardization.

We must repeat that this distinction between sectionalism and regionalism is of the utmost importance, but it is often ignored or not understood. Much of what has been written on sectionalism is regionalism, a considerable portion of what has been called regionalism is sectionalism. We have pointed out the fact that the fundamental distinction between the concepts is that sectionalism sees the nation from the point of view of the differing areas; regionalism sees the differing areas from the point of view of the nation. And it is important to re-emphasize the fact that the difference is not one of mere academic interest "but is of the greatest possible significance in the formation of new policies and in the probabilities of participation in new national and regional planning programs by any and all regions" in order to avoid "A revivification of the older sectionalism rationalized in terms of the 'new regionalism.'"[31]

This is exactly what Turner feared. He wrote, "I think it not too much to say that in party conventions as well as in Congress the out-

[31] Howard W. Odum, *Southern Regions of the United States*, p. 253.

> come of deliberations bears a striking resemblance to treaties between sections, suggestive of treaties between European nations in diplomatic congresses."[32] To this point of view, the regionalist would oppose facts and arguments to support the proposition that, though it is true that there has been sectionalism such as is here described and that such sectionalism may well continue, the emerging new regionalism offers a better, more workable solution of the problems arising from the complexity of American life. Recent efforts of the national government toward solution of such problems as those arising from farm tenancy, agricultural production control, population and income redistribution all have distinct regional applications and implications, but were approached from the point of view of national rather than sectional advantages.

The significance of economic interests is usually apparent in sectional political interests and is the basis of the need for regional realignment of areas. Plans for regional organization of districts served by power transmission lines, as the Tennessee Valley, to take the outstanding example, by rail systems, as illustrated in freight rate territories, by shipping facilities as demonstrated in the combination of ports into customs districts and the regulation of freight rates to these outlets, are obviously economic in their origin. No less so are the recurrent political movements, such as the opposition to the tariff by agrarian sections, demands for an inflated currency by debtor sections, interest in racial legislation by the South and the Pacific Coast regions, etc.; though the economic basis of the latter is often rationalized in purely political and social terminology. In a recent study of property ownership and political participation, including Georgia, Florida, Louisiana, North Carolina, Pennsylvania and Wisconsin, findings indicated that demagoguery flourishes in areas where the franchise is neglected and there is a high degree of propertylessness; that progressivism is characteristic of areas of high propertylessness and exercise of the franchise; and that conservatism is found in areas where the ballot is used extensively and there is a low degree of propertylessness; leading to a tentative conclusion that tenancy and non-participation in political affairs are related, and that the one-

[32] Frederick Jackson Turner, *The Significance of Sections in American History*, p. 41.

party system of the South is probably a result of the one-crop system characterizing the same region.[33]

But the central issue of political regionalism seems to be that of centralization versus some degree of decentralization. Under our working theory of division of power between state and federal governments, we are faced with the alternative of suffering existing evils or of transferring more and more power to the Federal Government. Usually we choose the latter alternative in our desire for relief, so that centralization constantly increases. But actually, we are faced with many problems, such as those centering about Boulder Dam, for example, which affect regions. "They are problems too big for any single state, yet not big enough for the nation as a whole. They should not be loaded upon an already overburdened Congress, yet they are obviously beyond the competence of any single state legislature. They belong by right to regional governments, if we had such things." [34]

Not only is some such arrangement needed to meet the actual problems of government which are rapidly multiplying, but also to develop vigorously regional distinctiveness as a counterpoise to mass action and mob psychology, the tendencies toward which are much stronger than the provincial spirit will ever be able to challenge.[35] Students are well agreed that it is neither possible nor desirable to establish absolute uniformity of governmental agencies over a nation of such differing regions as are found within the United States. They are equally agreed that there must be co-ordination and supervision to a measurable degree to maintain union. They are led thereby to a consideration of regional organization as a means of practical attainment of the end sought. Such organization is already under way in many of the governmental functions, and has been for decades, of course. Such a form of organization is "natural" in that it meets conditions growing up naturally as a result of geographic and social forces.

Such organization, at least in a modified, functional form, would have much to recommend it, according to one of the most recent students

[33] Mercer Evans, "Remarks on Professor Nixon's Paper," *Problems of the Cotton Economy*, pp. 76-78.

[34] W. B. Munro, *The Invisible Government*, pp. 153-154.

[35] *Ibid.*, pp. 159-164.

of the problem. "It is apparent that an attempt by the Federal Government to apply a rule of national uniformity to all phases of its administration would be productive of infinite harm and would, probably, result in the return of many powers to the states. If, on the other hand, the Federal Government acknowledges the differences which exist among the sections of this country, and provides for the recognition of these differences by regional administration, the principal vice of centralization, uniformity, will be avoided, and a return to the chaos of 48 independent jurisdictions will be unnecessary."[36] This writer sees ignorance and political maneuvering as the two greatest obstacles to putting such a plan into effect; ignorance because of the intricate political problems involved and politics because "it places personal and local advantages above the criteria of administrative efficiency and economy."[37]

The larger problem goes somewhat beyond the dichotomy of federalism-states' rights. It is estimated that there are some 175,000 governmental units within the United States; a multiplicity of units which inevitably makes for huge duplication of effort and confusion of function. "Our costly experience with devastating public confusion, with waste of all kinds, with projects inadequately investigated and planned—with political scandal, with inartistic outcomes . . . indicates the urgent need of prompt steps in the direction of more effective concert of action. Even the most rugged individualist cannot insist upon the general freedom of spending involved in such unlicensed liberty to build. There is nothing in the American situation, except inertia, to stand in the way of far closer relationships on the part of public works authorities. We may realize far-reaching advantages from the comprehensive view of the whole field, from the free interchange of information and experience, from the pooling of technical knowledge and facilities, from mutual consideration of credit situations, from such general advice and supervision as is not inconsistent with the requirements of vital self-government."[38]

Further, it is argued that such readjustment would be of the greatest benefit to those small governmental units and those poorer regions

[36] James W. Fesler, Federal Administrative Regions, with Special Reference to War Department Procurement Planning Activities, typewritten doctoral dissertation, Harvard University, 1935, p. 450.

[37] *Ibid.*, p. 417.

[38] National Resources Board, *Report on National Planning and Public Works in Relation to Natural Resources*, December 1934, p. 65.

which now are unable to secure adequate advice and supervision for the proper carrying out of their functions since they would be enabled to participate in general funds of knowledge and techniques. Thus, to them would be allocated functions and powers along with the ability to operate successfully, through relationships with other units.[39] Normally the initiative for such action would come from the locality, more keenly alive to its needs and opportunities than a central organization could be; the advantage coming from advice and co-ordination by the larger unit. "It is in a skilled balance between the overhead role of the Federal Government and the role of the localities and regions that wisdom lies. It cannot too often be reiterated that national planning does not involve or permit the centralization of all planning at the center, but presupposes a free flow of ideas, experiments, experiences from circumference to center and back again to the circumference." [40]

Actually, a system much like that described above is in actual operation in the case of the highway work of the national and state governments. Here the procedure is for the State Highway Commission to draw up plans and specifications for particular pieces of roadway construction and then to submit them to the *Federal Highway Bureau* for approval. By this system there is left a wide range for experimentation by the various states in efforts to meet local conditions and needs, while the wider experience of the Federal Bureau serves as a check upon local ideas and fits state plans into a national system. As Fesler shows in his study, the practice of dividing the country into administrative regions is already so well established that more than 80 percent of federal administrative employees are stationed outside the city of Washington.[41] However, as he and others show there is no unity in the regions chosen for administrative purposes. The National Resources Board in its work on regional aspects of administration maps more than 100 plans of division of the country into administrative units now in use by governmental agencies. In many cases it is apparent that differing functions of government would require differing regions for most efficient work; but in most cases it would appear that the divisions chosen are more or less arbitrary and might easily be combined or modified to fit into general regional outlines. Indeed, the National Resources Board remarks that "If co-ordinated planning

[39] National Resources Board, *Report on National Planning and Public Works in Relation to Natural Resources*, December 1934, p. 65.

[40] *Ibid.*, p. 87.

[41] Fesler, *op. cit.*, p. 405.

is to be successful, some degree of order must be brought out of the present chaos of regions and districts." [42]

While recognizing the region as the unit within the national picture, any administrative or planning activity is also compelled to take into account wide diversities within these major divisions. It is important that administration be unified for the entire region, so far as it is practicable, but it is equally essential to provide for subregional divisions of the regions in line with specialized problems affecting localities, as has been pointed out by Odum and by Fesler.[43] This point is also brought out by T. J. Woofter, Jr., in his observation that the work of agricultural experiment stations is commonly designed to fit into soil and crop regions which cut across state lines.[44]

Hope for progress toward regional organization is to be found in the activities of such semi-official regional organizations as the New England Regional Planning Commission, an outgrowth of the older New England Council; and the Pacific Northwest Planning Commission, operating in widely differing regions and under differing types of organization; the one based on historical sentiment and economic unity while the other is based on unity of a drainage system and the resultant economic and social problems. Neither has authority to enforce its recommendations, being forced to rely upon the voluntary action of the states concerned. The Tennessee Valley Authority, in contrast, has large measure of authority within its region as concerns the direct objective it seeks. This is due to its character as a corporation. Another type of regional authority which is gaining great vogue at this time is the interstate compact. Because its advocacy is more recent and because in some respects it holds out greater promise, a short discussion of this form of interstate co-operation is essential to any study of political regionalism.

The mere fact that during the period extending from the formation of the republic to 1918 the interstate compact was used only 24 times, while, during the period of 1918 to 1931, 31 such agreements were called into being, argues that there have been changes in our governmental problems demanding some authority between the levels

[42] National Resources Board, *Report on National Planning and Public Works in Relation to Natural Resources*, December 1934, p. 74.

[43] Howard W. Odum, *Southern Regions of the United States*, pp. 533-537; Fesler, *op. cit.*, pp. 473-476.

[44] "Subregions of the Southeast," *Social Forces*, Vol. 13, p. 47.

of the state and the federal governments. It is argued that bodies created by such means might receive public grants for public work construction, for soil erosion, reclamation, forestry, etc.[45] But it is objected that such a device lends itself to almost interminable delays; that the compacting states can usually refuse to follow their agreements with impunity; that action through such compacts may be taken without due regard to its incidence on the remainder of the nation; that the legal basis for such compacts views each state as a sovereign power equal in all respects to the other compacting states when actually such a condition almost never exists because of differences in resources, population, and similar factors; compact making is likely to become a matter of horse trading, in which each compacting state uses every device available to promote its own particular interests rather than those of the region or nation.[46]

On the other hand it is pointed out that such compacts have a real purpose to perform in many cases where the courts, because of range, intricacy, and technicality of the problems involved, are not adapted to cope with the situation. Such fields are to be found in boundary adjustments, navigation, uniformity of legislation, penal jurisdictions, interstate accounting, conservation of natural resources, utility regulation, flood control and protection of city water supplies, etc.[47] The Interstate Compact, in the opinion of Frankfurter and Landis, lends itself especially to problems of a continuing nature where adjustments must be made to changing conditions. "No one state can control the power to feed or starve, possessed by a river flowing through several states. . . . The whole economic region must be the unit of adjustment; continuity of supervision the technique. . . . The regional characteristic of electric power as a social and engineering fact must find a counterpart in the effort of law to deal with it. . . . The overwhelming difficulties confronting modern society must not be at the mercy of the false antithesis embodied in the shibboleths 'States' Rights' and 'National Supremacy.' . . . Our regions are realities. Political thinking must respond to those realities. Instead of leading to parochialism, it will bring a fresh ferment of political thought whereby

[45] National Resources Committee, *Regional Factors in National Planning and Development*, December 1935, p. 47.

[46] *Ibid.*, pp. 47-52.

[47] Felix Frankfurter and J. M. Landis, "The Compact Clause of the Constitution—A Study in Interstate Adjustments," *Yale Law Journal*, XXXIV, 685-758.

national aims may be achieved through various forms of political adjustment."[48]

Finally, we come again to the conclusion that none of the types of regional organization in common use has been found altogether satisfactory in all cases; the field is still one in which experimentation promises the evolution of theories of greater value in actual practice. It appears that differing regions and differing functions demand different types of organization, and will probably continue to do so. For the immediate present it seems wise to limit the statement of theory to the observation that the old state-federal conflict ignores the existence of many problems which are certainly neither intrastate nor national in character, and that, therefore, there is a real need for some political unit equipped with powers of initiative and administration on a level between the two. The exact form of such a unit can best be left, perhaps, until further experimentation and experience have somewhat clarified the problems.

[48] *Ibid.*, pp. 701, 717, 729.

Chapter XVII

EXPLORING THE REGION: THE SOCIOLOGISTS

BY way of recapitulation, we may introduce the sociological approach to regionalism by referring again to those studies of regionalism previously discussed in the chapters dealing with geography, anthropology, and ecology in particular, and to some extent with economics and political science. Such a review would not only indicate the basic need for sociological synthesis of materials and viewpoints on regionalism but would indicate sociology's late arrival into this major area of research and interpretation. For the most part sociology has not until very recently consciously explored the region as a major area of scientific study of society. In so far as sociologists have used the term regionalism they have followed largely the prevailing emphasis upon metropolitan regionalism and sectional provincialism, with certain exceptions which will be noted below.

As late as 1930 at the Conference on Regional Phenomena, held under the joint auspices of the Social Science Research Council and the National Research Council, the representative of sociology made the following general statement: ". . . It does not appear to me that the concept of the region has made very much of a dent as yet in the thinking of sociologists. It appears to me that interest has been devoted more particularly to problems of ethnic, class and similar groupings in society rather than to regional phenomena as such. The concept itself is, I am sure, lacking in clarity to most of us. I am not clear in my own mind, for example, to what extent the concept is based upon physiographic factors, and to what extent it is analogous to the notion of culture area. It seems to me to have a mixture of both. . . . I suppose there should be included in this, or possibly so, the 'ecological' studies which have been initiated at the University of Chicago.

You are no doubt taking account also of the regional planning studies of numerous cities (e.g., New York and Philadelphia) which might be construed as sociological. I have personally been interested in the possibilities of procuring quantitative indexes of social attitudes and public opinion, such as may be expressed in political behavior, and which point, according to some indications, to areal patterns. . . . My own mind as indicated above is still quite fluid upon the problem. It seems to me that the concept is likely to be more and more defined in economic and cultural terms. I suppose that the physiographic base, as conditioning the economic and the cultural, is still present." [1]

This test of contributions made by sociologists to regionalism may need checking with the views of the other scientists to see just what is understood by the concept. For the purpose of getting representatives of various sciences together and with a view to bringing about a possible correlation of the various ideas of regions a Conference on Regional Phenomena was held in Washington on April 11 and 12, 1930. This followed an earlier Conference on the Culture Area which had previously been held at Dartmouth and in which it was "evident that while several disciplines make use of the regional concept there is considerable diversity of points of view and methods of approach." It was suggested that with material from the several sciences it might be possible "to extend or reshape the concept of regional study so that data collected for some specific purpose may be useful and interesting to a larger number of investigators. The hope was also expressed that duplication would be avoided and cooperative studies promoted. Thirty-five members of the Conference attended, including representatives from the social sciences of geography, geology, biology, anthropology, sociology, economics, political science, history, psychology, statistics, agriculture. In preparation for the Conference four questions were sent to certain members to be answered and made the basis of discussion, one reply to which has been quoted above with reference to sociology. The questions were: "1. What regional phenomena do workers in your field recognize as so important as to necessitate separate study? 2. What specific investigations, with the regional point of view uppermost, are going forward at the present time? 3. What problems in your field

[1] Adapted from *Conference on Regional Phenomena, 1930*, Appendix A, p. 10.

seem to you to invite regional attack? 4. How on the basis of these questions do you formulate your concept of regions?"[2]

> Three objectives were stated as the desirable outcome of the Conference. "(1) The common recognition of some general regional concept as a useful tool in scientific investigation in a wide variety of sciences, natural or social. (2) Some better understanding by the students of each discipline of those problems of other disciplines which involve the regional viewpoint. (3) An appreciation of the fact that under the general regional concept each major problem, whether in a single discipline or common to a variety of disciplines, will presumably have to organize a body of viewpoints and definitions in no small measure especially suited to advance the analysis of that problem and in part particular to it."[3]

As a matter of fact it seems possible to point up a relatively large amount of material from the sociologists' workshop, focusing directly upon regions and regionalism and constituting the groundwork upon which to build an effective synthesis. Perhaps the best approach is through the citation of examples, illustrative of both actual regional studies and concepts and of work which contributes indirectly to the emerging premises of the new regionalism. These citations include the earlier and later contributions of Giddings, Ward, and Sumner, followed by Professor Mukerjee's *Regional Sociology* as a definite attempt to "present sociology on the basis of a scientific classification of types and regions." Alongside these might be cited the Regional Survey School in England which developed through the English group headed by Geddes in the implementation of the Le Play folk-work-place concept. There was, later, the new emphasis upon human ecology in the University of Chicago, in the work of Mukerjee and other human ecologists, and later in the re-emphasis upon human ecology by certain English authors. Next, "Cultural Sociology" reflected the sociological emphasis upon the culture area and the subsequent implementation by the sociologists of the culture emphasis as found in cultural anthropology and human geography. Later the *Publication* of the American Sociological Society and the annual programs featured regionalism and folk sociology. So, too,

[2] Adapted from *Conference on Regional Phenomena, 1930*, Appendix A, p. 1.
[3] *Ibid.*, pp. 3-4.

the effort of sociology to set up the sociological region and the sociological subregion for study and planning represents a step further in the implementation of the concept. There is, again, the emerging sociological synthesis of the studies of regionalism which attempts to present regionalism as societal determinism or as a *gestalt* in which the folk regional society becomes the elemental unit for the study of all society.

> Outside of his earlier zoogenic, anthropogenic and demogenic stages of cultural evolution, Professor Giddings' early direct approach to the study of society through the regional basis was found in his *Elements of Sociology* published in 1898. In this he frankly posited the study of aggregations of people through the regional areas. First, he divided North America into four major national areas which were the Grainless North, the Western Desert, the Region of Fertility, and the Pacific Regions. He then illustrated his premises further by setting up eight major subregions within the *Region of Fertility*. These eight regions with their characterization would do credit to current geographers and agricultural economists. The subdivisions were called respectively: *the Coast Swamps, the Atlantic Plain, the Piedmont Region, the Mountain Regions* or New England Hills, *the Great Plateau, the Interior Timbered, the Alluvial Region* of the Mississippi, and *the Prairie Region.*[4]

Giddings later based much of his social theory on the "sustentation field," which he defines as "a region or part of the earth's surface which sustains organisms and their functions, sustains life, including the lives of human beings; which provides, as we say in business, the upkeep of life." Following his usual emphasis upon resemblances and differences as basic to scientific study he points out that regions are different. "Some of them," he says, "are really fit to sustain abundant life and do it; others are not fit to sustain abundant life and they do not do it." Again he points out, "The sustentation field feeds us and furnishes us with our energies, but that is not all. The sustentation field stimulates us . . . finally, the sustentation field constrains us . . . and because it not only furnishes us with energies but also deprives us of energies, it depletes us. We have to consider in all our problems of human life the relation of the organism to food, to energy, to depletion, to stimulation, and to constraint, and any

[4] Franklin H. Giddings, *The Elements of Sociology*, pp. 15-18.

philosophy of society, or even of physiology, which deals with just one or two or a part of the effects of the sustentation field upon us will fall so far short of being adequate that it will really mislead us." [5]

> Among stimuli that all living bodies react to are phenomena of the surface of the earth, including its life-sustaining resources, and of the atmosphere, including variations of temperature and of precipitation. All these are unevenly distributed. Geography is a variegated thing. There are regions that forbid, repel, starve, and kill, and there are regions that nourish and attract. Therefore, the teeming life of the earth is apportioned and segregated, here in energetic aggregations, there in sporadic, ineffective examples according to the regional dispersion of environmental bounty and exaction, incitement and constraint.
>
> The distribution of inhabitable areas on the earth's surface is neither haphazard nor uniform. It is a grouping by coastal plains, river basins, and mountain systems, or in relation to them. The river deltas and the tide-water lowlands are relatively accessible. The bottom lands and lower levels of the watershed are abundantly productive of primary means of subsistence, the remoter plains and plateaus less so. Least bountiful in primary food products, least accessible, and, in general, least inhabitable are the high altitudes, in particular the continental divides, where river systems take their rise.
>
> The relative advantageousness of physical environments for sustaining, energizing, and stimulating pluralistic life is a factor of all social phenomena. It determines the density and the composition of every population. It provokes and limits collective effort. It fixes the possibilities of organization and of collective effectiveness. Directly, and indirectly through collective effort and effectiveness, it makes and limits the possibilities of well-being and of individuation." [6]

Professor Giddings goes further and traces the steps through which regional groups are formed after kinship no longer plays the most essential part. The modern states and empires are quite different from the little city-states of classical times. Thus Giddings might be said to draw a parallel then between the metropolitan region or city-state and the group-of-states regions that evolve over wider territory. Historically he cites the regional groups so formed in the eastern parts of the Mediterranean area, in Mesopotamia, in Persia,

[5] Franklin H. Giddings, *Civilization and Society*, pp. 3, 4.

[6] Franklin H. Giddings, *Studies in the Theory of Human Society*, pp. 253-254. (Quoted by permission of The Macmillan Company.)

and in Egypt long before the rise of the city-states. He calls attention to the fact, however, that regional factors of political organization did not then, or now, always "coincide with the great facts of geography and natural resources."

> The Giddings regional concept is that "The basis of organization of a great regional political group is usually a considerable population of one racial variety, with a common language and certain common traditions, and often-times regional groups without much evolution of town life; as, for example, the great tribal organizations that overran Gaul and Spain and Britain at the time of the so-called great migrations which resulted, in the course of time, in the formation of the modern nations. Take, for example, certain subdivisions of this large movement and subdivisions of population. There were in what was then known as Gaul, and now as France, the Burgundians and the Franks as the more powerful groups. For a long time they were separately organized; they were small nations after their settlement in various parts of Gaul. There were also the tribes that overran Britain and were for a long time consolidated in one kingdom. There were the people of Saxon origin quite different from the people who settled in the southeast of England, in places which are now known as the county of Kent, the county of Middlesex, the county of Sussex, the county of Suffolk; and people who settled along the eastern parts of Britain and farther north than the Saxons and the Kentish men; and presently people came over from Denmark and settled in what is now known as Derbyshire and the northwestern counties. So for a long time these regional groups which were developing into political life, survived as organizations having a good many of the characteristics of tribal society, although they had long ceased to have the organization of tribal society. And it was by the consolidation of such confederations of people, once tribal in organization, that the kingdoms, which played a part in ancient society, were presumably formed, just as it has played a part in the organization of those political entities which are the great modern national states." [7]

Professor Giddings also discussed the psychological effects of regionalism, advancing the hypothesis that the first social groups larger than the family were founded on like interests and occupations, tied to some place of intercourse. The most valid distinction between political and tribal organization, he held, was that between territorial

[7] Franklin H. Giddings, *Civilization and Society*, pp. 148-149.

and psychological unity. This psychological unity was also often the result of a common shrine, or of living within the same region.

In his distinctions between political regionalism which we have already discussed in Chapter XV, and social regionalism, Professor Giddings was constantly citing examples, also. His interest in social psychology led him to attempt to classify the various regions of the United States by psychological categories. He evolved four personality types which he found to predominate as follows: *forceful*, along the seaboards, Atlantic and Pacific, in the Ohio Valley and in the Great Plains Area; *convivial*, the southeastern portion of the nation; *austere*, along the New England Coast and westward just south of the Great Lakes into Iowa and Kansas; rationally conscientious type, confined to the large cities.[8]

The burden of criticism of sociology introduced by Professor Mukerjee's *Regional Sociology* was that no attempt has been made to classify social types which alone can be done through the study of what he termed harmony with physical environment or the regional balance of man. His appeal was for a broader sociology, which, while recognizing the geographers' and the anthropologists' several contributions, will attempt to correlate all the factors. Thus he points out that "in the same region, the stages of economic development govern the relation of man to land and natural resources and the possibilities of division and organization of labor, and hence different social types. Such a regional treatment of sociology will not only be a preliminary to the classification of social types by the selection of a natural entity as the unit of consideration; it will also emphasize the interweaving of the process of social adaptation and thus link together the now fragmentary studies of economic history, politics and ethnology in the central inquiry of the genesis and development of social types."[9]

Professor Mukerjee's premise for regional sociology may be gathered from two of his statements in his text and from numerous articles subsequently published. Thus "A great defect in logical analysis in sociology arises on account of the neglect of wider cultural groups or types which comprehend the entire life of races and regions other than the purely Euro-American and whose rich social and economic

[8] Franklin H. Giddings, *Inductive Sociology*, pp. 82-83.
[9] Radhakamal Mukerjee, *Regional Geography*, p. viii.

experiments have no less significance in the evolution of world life. The social sciences have not hitherto sufficiently taken into account the diversity of environment and the variety of life-schemes and values in different social and historic series. In biological studies, botany has developed towards ecological surveys and distributional inquiries. Zoology tends in the same direction, while anthropology, still more than either, seeks to learn from the study of a region the peculiarities of the life of man and his customs, though much error has resulted from an identification of political and administrative areas with the units of Anthropogeography."

The regional sociology of Mukerjee approximates, in his own words, and in his recent work on human ecology, the ecological-geographical approach to the study of society. Indeed Professor Mukerjee is now preparing a volume on human ecology which is the application of the biogeographical method to the study of society in which he features the role of man "on the surface of the earth placed in the organic setting of great harmonic vegetable or animal aggregations, which have arrived at a more or less stable equilibrium, and which impose on human society typical manners in which it adapts itself to the varied possibilities of the diverse regions." Thus, he continues, "already we are glimpsing a human ecology which seeks to provide us with the keys to the origin of diverse types, correlated with the plant and animal communities of a natural, easily distinguished region." [10]

Two other major contributions to human ecology by the sociologists may be found in the regional survey as developed in Great Britain and the human ecology studies and methodology developed by the University of Chicago group. C. A. Dawson discusses human ecology and regional sociology as being synonyms for the regional survey.[11] He calls attention to the fact that Patrick Geddes' leadership of the movement for the regional survey in the human field followed his earlier leadership in the development of plant ecology. This influence was later marked in both America and in France. Thus it was "in Great Britain rather than in America that the cross fertilization of sociology and plant ecology first took place."

[10] Radhakamal Mukerjee, unpublished manuscript.

[11] "The Sources and Methods of Human Ecology," from L. L. Bernard, *The Fields and Methods of Sociology*, p. 289. Copyright 1934. Reprinted by permission of the publishers, Farrar & Rinehart, Inc.

Dawson quotes from Fagg's "The History of the Regional Survey Movement": "The parallelism of the ecological movement with the modern regional survey movement is even more striking, for regional survey might very aptly be described as the study of human ecology, a conception, to be noted, that is far wider than the established science of economics. Just as Tamsley chose for the title of his early lectures on plant ecology 'The Plant and Its Environment' so 'Men and Their Environments' is the substance of human ecology or regional survey. The two developments have been contemporary and so far as Britain is concerned both have taken their main initiative from Professor Geddes. In the case of plant ecology he directed the energies of other botanists into the new field, but in the case of human ecology or regional sociology he has himself taken the leading part in the movement." Dawson notes further that "The regional survey in Great Britain has not developed along the lines of pure science. It has made its contribution to the scientific study of human regions, but, like the social survey in America, the reform interest, as applied to education, town planning, civic improvement, and good citizenship, has remained predominant. In all these precursory movements were sown the seeds of the more recently developed lively interest in the space, time, and sustenance relations of human beings. In fact, an interest in this phase of human existence reaches still farther back, and it is to be found in a far wider range of subjects than I have been able to mention. Human ecology, even though its present day purposes are more narrowly defined and its methods more carefully scrutinized than those of its forebears, is but a new name for a very ancient form of investigation." [12]

The American development of human ecology found its leadership in the University of Chicago School which was a composite of regional survey and ecological-geographic spatial concepts. On the basis of ecology as the study of "the correlations between all organisms living together in one and the same locality and their adaptation to their surroundings," [13] the analogy was to be applied to man and his environment. If we be permitted to include man in the term "organisms" and be further allowed to add some consideration of his adaptation of his environment to his needs, this definition expresses the idea of the subject held by present-day workers in the field. Thus

[12] "The Sources and Methods of Human Ecology," from L. L. Bernard, *The Fields and Methods of Sociology*, pp. 289-290. Copyright 1934. Reprinted by permission of the publishers, Farrar & Rinehart, Inc.

[13] Ernest Haeckel, *The History of Creation*, II, 354, quoted by Paul Vidal de la Blache in *Principles of Human Geography*, p. 9.

Roderick D. McKenzie, certainly one of the outstanding human ecologists, offered in 1925 the following: "In the absence of any precedent, let us tentatively define human ecology as a study of the spatial and temporal relations of human beings as affected by the selective, distributive and accommodative forces of the environment." [14]

> Later, writing in the *Encyclopaedia of the Social Sciences*, on "Human Ecology," he states that "Human ecology deals with the spatial aspects of the symbiotic relations of human beings and human institutions" and that it seeks to discover the principles underlying such relations. Such a study, he here argues, has little in common with plant and animal ecology, since interaction is fundamentally cultural rather than biologic and hence subject to more continuous and rapid change in form. Geographers, economists, and students of population problems have entered the field, but have usually delimited their areas by use of political boundaries rather than by the ecological method of using the area "which arises out of competitive co-operation." "In a word, the human community differs from the plant community in the two dominant characteristics of mobility and purpose, that is, in the power to select a habitat and in the ability to control or modify the conditions of the habitat." [15] The relationship with the forces of nature he finds in the economic organization of the life of the region.

Frank H. Hankins notes that the earth may be divided into regions along geographic lines, but that such regions are also characterized by differences in the type and numbers of plant and animal occupants which form themselves into an intricate web of relationships, maintaining a delicate balance with the seasonal and cyclical variations of the region. "Human life, especially primitive life, is an intimate part of this 'web of life.' " [16] Such statements would seem to imply almost an identification of social units with the biotic areas or ecological communities of the biologists.[17] L. L. Bernard is even more emphatic

[14] R. D. McKenzie, "The Ecological Approach to the Human Community," *The City* (edited by Robert E. Park, Ernest W. Burgess and Roderick D. McKenzie), p. 63.

[15] *Ibid.*, p. 64.

[16] *An Introduction to the Study of Society*, p. 193.

[17] Cf. L. R. Dice, "Biotic Areas and Ecological Habitats as Units for the Statement of Animal and Plant Distribution," *Science*, LV, 335-338; Merriam C. Hart, "Laws of Temperature Control of the Geographic Distribution of Terrestrial Animals and Plants," *National Geographic Magazine*, VI, 229-238; C. F. Marbut, "The Rise, Decline and Revival of Malthusianism in Relation to Geography and the Character of Soils," *Annals of the Association of American Geographers*, XV, 1-25.

in his insistence that human ecology must give attention to the facts of geographic environment. After heading into blind alleys, sociology has finally been brought back to a more realistic consideration of society through the subsistence ideas of Sumner and Giddings, the anthropological interests of Thomas, and the historical attitude of Turner, he thinks. "A theory of culture which begins in culture and ends in culture, which knows no geography and can bear no environment except that inherited from the past or from some other place—and smothers even this under the term culture—is the latest refuge of the thwarted neo-Hegelian ideologists." [18]

A special phase of the Chicago ecological study was that of its application to the city or urban community. McKenzie groups efforts in the ecology of the community into two categories: "(1) studies of the spatial distribution of biosocial phenomena within the urban area, and (2) studies pertaining to the determination of the natural—as opposed to political—boundaries of the local community organization." [19] Within this frame of reference many local studies have been made and Professor Burgess has set up a framework for analyzing the regional organization of the city in which he distinguishes four different types of areas, *the physical framework of the city*, *the economic structure of the city*, *the culture formation of the city*, and *the political organization of the city*.

> "The conception that the city should be studied in its regional aspects in sociology," Professor Burgess pointed out, "grew out of a few observations. One observation was that when any phenomenon like nationality of population or delinquency was plotted on a map the distribution was never evenly spread over the city, but there were always concentrations and scatterings. Another observation was that there were many different areas in the city with well-recognized character which was reflected in the names by which they were generally known, as the Gold Coast, Hobohemia, Little Sicily, the Ghetto, the artists' colony, the rooming-house area, the slum, apartment house areas. Still another observation was that these segregations in population appeared to correspond with the incidence of certain other factors; for example, the best residential sections in Chicago seemed to be

[18] L. L. Bernard, "Introductory Statement Regarding Human Ecology and Population," *Publications of the American Sociological Society*, XXIII, 33.
[19] McKenzie, *op. cit.*, p. 60.

along the Lake Front; in Chicago and other cities any elevation appeared to make for desirable places of residence, while the low lands were least desirable. Rooming-house areas and poverty areas went out from or encircled the central business district of the city. On the basis of these observations the conclusion was naturally derived that generalizations about the city as a whole or statistics for the entire city only concealed wide differences between its varying areas. Consequently, the assumption seemed indicated that any adequate understanding of the city must be arrived at by a study of its different regions."[20]

The sociologists along with other social scientists and students of civilization have, through thus focusing upon the city as *the society*, contributed no little to the doctrine that cities and progress, urbanism and maturity are synonymous. Since this urban emphasis constitutes a large part of the human ecological approach in sociology, since Spengler and many other observers take the contrary view, and since the problem of rural regions has been featured in the larger regional sociology of this volume, it seems important to review further something of the place of the city in this ecological-cultural appraisal as well as previous backgrounds upon which some of the conclusions rest. Thus Louis Wirth voices the idea, shared by many, that

> The city has come to be recognized as the center of culture. Innovations in social life and in ideas gravitate from the city to the country. Through its newspapers, theaters, schools, and museums, through its traveling salesmen and mail-order houses, through its representation in the legislatures, and through many other points of contact with the inhabitants of the rural periphery about it, the city diffuses its culture over a large area. The city is in this respect an important civilizing agent. . . . With the advent of modern methods of communication the whole world has been transformed into a single mechanism of which a country or a city is merely an integral part. . . . The city has become a highly sensitive unit in this complex mechanism, and in turn acts as a transmitter of such stimulation as it receives to a local area. This is as true of economic and political as it is of social and intellectual life.[21]

[20] *Conference on Regional Phenomena, 1930*, p. 36.

[21] "A Bibliography of the Urban Community," in *The City* (edited by Robert E. Park, E. W. Burgess, and Roderick D. McKenzie), pp. 182-186.

The city has always been the focus of social change, the hothouse of cultural mutation, because it has gathered ideas from a wider and wider region, synthesized them, and, after stamping them with its peculiarities, passed them on to the residents of the hinterland. Thereby the trademark of the metropolitan aggregation has more often than not become the brand of the region. It is on this assumption that it is claimed that the study of the city becomes applicable in its main outlines to the whole regional culture of which it is the center.

We have already emphasized the importance of the rural areas in the formation of regional culture and also have pointed out the oft-neglected fact that the character of the city is usually colored by its rural or industrial hinterland. Social ecological studies point out that, in view of the statistical fact that the city is composed largely of persons migrating there from rural districts, it is inevitable that the city bear more than a tinge of the culture indigenous to the surrounding territory. But just as the city synthesizes and transmutes the culture coming into the region from the outside, so does it perform similar functions for the region itself. The process is more easily observed in the city because there it takes place in much less time, due to the cross-fertilization of ideas and customs from a wider territory; the city becomes the center of mobility, vertical and horizontal, as Park expresses the idea in Sorokin's terminology.[22] Thereby the city becomes the organizing and dynamic force in the life of the metropolitan region. After observing that the city has always been the locus of the highest attainment in human mentality, initiative and achievement, Munro suggests that this is true because in the city man has had the advantages of a division of labor which has given him leisure, wealth, and education and that intellectual, artistic, and scientific development has been the result.[23]

> The higher efficiency of the city may be the result of the selective processes operating in the migration from country to city as well as of the greater stimulation offered by urban life. Both factors are advanced by J. M. Gillette, who believes that as a result of them "Our

[22] Robert E. Park, "Sociology," *Research in the Social Sciences* (edited by Wilson Gee), p. 26.

[23] Cf. W. B. Munro, *The Invisible Government.*

cities are the chief creators and the almost exclusive reservoirs and purveyors of the cultural surplus. It is inevitable, therefore, that the flow of cultural influences is from city to country and that there is a minimum of reverse current. The consequence is that the rural populations are being flooded and inundated not only by material commodities emanating from cities, but by ideas, actions and life-patterns, styles, fashions, modes of dress, of living, of eating and of drinking, of dancing and of courting, of bobbing hair and deforming the foot by wearing stilts for shoe heels, of automobiling, flying, sporting, dieing, and being buried." [24] From this it follows that the city dwellers have access to the entire regional culture, while the ruralites are largely denied such an advantage, and that the city with its superior organization and cultural reservoir is able to outwit and outvote the rural sections, even on matters primarily agricultural. The same authority declares that the public school curricula are designed in terms of urban, rather than rural, interests, thereby furthering the dominance of urban patterns in our society as it is now organized.[25]

It seems certain that the city cannot be too strictly limited in any sociological interpretation; that the city and its hinterland form a unit in our society, the parts of which may be separated for study, as is done in urban and rural sociology, but that when and if the mutual interdependence of these parts is forgotten or left out of consideration the whole picture loses its essential perspective. Granted that the city is the dominant factor in the ecological organization of our life, it is necessary merely to point out that dominance necessarily implies subordination, the two combining to form a whole. Historically this close relationship finds ample confirmation—in the dependence of Athens and Rome on colonies and other districts of the Mediterranean Region, in the plight of Constantinople during past centuries when cut off from its hinterland by Arabian conquest or the present-day dilemma of Vienna because of rearrangement of the political map and raising of tariff walls, of the rise of great cities in this country through the construction of transportation and communication lines—by which regions are bound together, literally, by bands of steel.

[24] "Urban Influence and Selection," *Publications of the American Sociological Society*, XXIII, 3.

[25] J. M. Gillette, "The Drift to the City in Relation to the Farm Problem," *American Journal of Sociology*, XVI, 645.

Another field of regional import in which sociologists have been much interested within recent years is that of the culture area concept. The viewpoints of a number of sociologists were presented in connection with those of the anthropologists in a previous chapter and it is necessary now only to point up the subject in relation to cultural sociology. Perhaps the most interesting of the anthropological approaches to sociological studies has been expressed by Clark Wissler in his introductory notes to two community studies. The first of these was *Middletown*, the introduction to which characterized the study as anthropological in the Wissler sense that the community was the areal unit basic to the proper study of society. The other book was Junek's *Isolated Communities* in which Wissler contrasts the newer social study with the older.

> "There is," Wissler points out, "another contribution of no mean significance. Thus while anthropological methods were developed for the study of primitive communities and though the dream of many has been that these methods could be turned upon communities in civilized areas, the outcome has been far from inspiring. In this volume, on the other hand, the author points the way to the anticipated goal. He shows that when an attempt is made to study a civilized community in an anthropological way, attention should be given to small units with rich folk backgrounds and persistent self-sufficient complexes of folkways, or culture. The approach may be easier if the unit chosen is marginal. The initial step is, then, to find this natural core of human social behavior which the author chooses to call culture. Once discovered, one may seek its position with respect to neighboring and distant communities and finally its place in the national framework. By such procedure the detailed descriptions of community life can be given meaning. Such, at least, the author finds in tiny but deeply human Blanc Sablon." [26]

Contributing largely to the sociologist's concept and techniques, as well as to the anthropologist's, Linton in his *The Study of Man* makes the regional concept articulate in his treatment of the local groups and in his study of the culture area. His interpretation of the culture area is that it is a technique of classification, the basis of which is the assumption of genetic relationships between the cultures of each area

[26] Clark Wissler, "Introduction," in Oscar Waldemar Junek, *Isolated Communities*, p. xvi. (Quoted by permission of The American Book Company.)

as a result of adaptations to local conditions which become increasingly complete and exact until the culture of each area diverges more and more from the cultures of tribes living in different geographic environments.[27] Linton thinks the significance of the local group has been underestimated by both anthropologists and sociologists and feels that in the folk-regional-culture approach will be found a promising field of scientific study.

> Concerning the local groups Linton expresses the opinion that "they are still the basis of our political organization though they are losing some of their former importance as functional units. Moreover, their qualities are so much the same everywhere in the world that these qualities can be studied almost as effectively fifty miles from any large city as in the wilds of Australia. While an understanding of the local group is vitally necessary to the understanding of any social system, the task of collecting the necessary information does not necessarily lead the student into romantic regions." Linton feels also that the folk-culture of the local group is of importance in the study of modern society as in all society. Thus "Although the disintegration of local groups in our society may progress even further than it has, the author is inclined to regard it as a transitory phenomenon. The sudden rise of the machine and of applied science has shattered Western civilization and reduced Western society to something approaching chaos. However, unless all past experience is at fault, the society will once more reduce itself to order. What the new order will be no one can forecast, but the potentialities of the local group both for the control of individuals and for the satisfaction of their psychological needs are so great that it seems unlikely that this unit will be dispensed with."[28]

This re-emphasis upon the anthropological approach to the culture area is featured here to point up an analogy between sociology and anthropology. Clark Wissler's critical note expresses the viewpoint better than any other we have found. Thus he insists that "the regional method of attack is basic in the study of all problems of culture. . . . No study which ignores the regional nature of cultural phenomena can be considered conclusive." And once again, "The errors made by the anthropologists of the evolutionary school were

[27] Ralph Linton, *The Study of Man*, p. 384.

[28] *Ibid.*, pp. 209-210, 230. (Quoted by permission of D. Appleton-Century Company, Inc.)

primarily due to the lack of regional studies."[29] The implication here is that sociology has made the same errors to the extent that it has ignored regional phenomena and regional groups as basic to societal analysis.

> The best sociological interpretation of the culture area concept that has appeared was that of Russell Gordon Smith in which he both traces the development of the concept and indicates its value as a technique or methodology for sociology. Thus he writes that "If one admits, as all scientifically minded persons must, that the classification of cultural data is prerequisite to valid factorization, two questions immediately present themselves: What is to be the unit of investigation? and What should be the basic principle of classification? Presumptive answers to these questions are quite worthless. Only by an empirical study of the artifacts, the symbols and the traditional procedures, which constitute objectively the cultures of various peoples, can the unit of investigation and the principle of classification be determined. The culture-area is an empirical grouping of cultural data in which the unit of investigation and the principle of classification have been derived from direct observation of the facts and of their temporal and spatial distributions. It is therefore receiving more and more attention from sociologists who are less interested in the chauvinistic defense of some sociological system than in a truly scientific analysis of collective human behavior." Malcolm M. Willey paraphrases an advertisement to read, "Tell me from which culture area you come, and I will tell you how you will behave," and adds: "This cannot, of course, be taken too literally. Individual differences are important. . . . But in a general way there is much truth contained in it. Knowing from what part of any culture area individuals come, it can be predicted within rather definite limits what reactions they will make in most of their life situations."[30]

Recently the annual meetings and *Publications* of the American Sociological Society have featured a number of studies and papers dealing with regional phenomena. Louis Wirth has made an excellent statement of the significance to sociology of the influence of area upon the concept and practice of liberty and sovereignty. He has also presented excellent studies of the Chicago Middle West

[29] *Conference on Regional Phenomena, 1930*, Appendix A, p. 3.

[30] Russell Gordon Smith, "The Concept of the Culture-Area," *Social Forces*, VII, 421; Malcolm M. Willey, "The Culture Area" in *An Introduction to Sociology*, by Jerome Davis and Harry Elmer Barnes, *et al.*, p. 550.

Region and other aspects of culture areas.[31] Niles Carpenter and Mildred Hartsough presented interpretations of the regionalist movement in France and Germany while Robert Redfield discussed "The Regional Aspect of Culture" [32] and Rupert B. Vance, the nature of the region and regional planning.

Still more recently Woofter and Lively have emphasized the importance of defining sociological subregions as fundamental to the study of regions and culture. Woofter's 27 subregions of the Southeast have already been described in a previous chapter on "States, Subregions, Districts." His work has been widely used and he is now attempting to define more definitely by more exact societal indices realistic sociological subregions comparable to the agricultural subregions so successfully projected a few years ago.[33]

> In much the same way C. E. Lively cites "the need for a genuine sociological analysis of rural life in the Corn Belt Area before any serious attempt at direct social planning is undertaken. Since complete sociological analysis of the region cannot be undertaken except as a long-time procedure, the program should begin with extensive and proceed to more intensive methods and should be so planned that each step will yield information of value for administrative purposes. It is my opinion that the first step is clearly indicated as a determination of the subregions and subregional characteristics of this area. The sociological subregion is the modern sociological counterpart of the social anthropologist's 'culture area' and the work of determining it is similar to that of the urban social ecologists in laying out the subareas of the metropolitan city. The subregion is important because it is essential (1) for the practical planning of social programs, and (2) as a unit for the control of representative sampling procedure in the study of regional characteristics.
>
> "The study of the sociological geography of a region is dependent, to a high degree, upon the availability of adequate indexes for measuring demographic and cultural factors. As you are well aware, many desirable indexes of this sort either have not yet been invented, or they have not yet been developed for local subdivisions. To substantiate this point I need only mention that we do not have, even on a county

[31] Louis Wirth, "Localism, Regionalism, and Centralization," *The American Journal of Sociology*, XLII, 493.

[32] *Publication of the American Sociological Society*, XXIV, No. 2, pp. 12-41; XXIX, No. 3, pp. 85-93.

[33] T. J. Woofter, Jr., "The Subregions of the Southeast," *Social Forces*, Vol. 13, pp. 43-50.

basis, satisfactory indexes of plane of living, agricultural income, natural increase of the population, mobility, and church conditions, to mention only a few. In the course of years, many indexes of economic and social factors have been developed. Some, such as the proportion of the sexes, are simple; others, such as expenditure per pupil for schooling and volume of retail sales per capita, are complex and represent a composite of variations not always evident. It is notable, however, that usable indexes of the more strictly economic factors are more numerous than indexes of factors more definitely social in nature. Certainly here is a field in which statistical-minded sociologists could be very useful." [34]

Still another area in which sociology has been exploring more and more of late is that of regional planning. Among the special contributions that appear pertinent to the present inquiry are E. W. Burgess' *Social Aspects of Planning*,[35] in which he has edited a number of papers prepared for the American Sociological Society; Rupert B. Vance's "Implications of the Concepts 'Region' and 'Regional Planning,' " [36] and *Regional Reconstruction: A Way Out for the South*; [37] T. J. Woofter, Jr.'s "Southern Population and Social Planning"; [38] Louis Wirth's "Localism, Regionalism, and Centralization," [39] and "The Prospects of Regional Research in Relation to Social Planning"; [40] Lewis L. Lorwin's "Social Aspects of the Planning State," [41] and "Planning in a Democracy"; [42] Robert E. Park's "Social Planning and Human Nature"; [43] E. W. Burgess' "Social Planning and the Mores"; [44] Howard W. Odum's "A Sociological Approach to National Social Planning," [45] "The Case for Regional National Social Planning," [46] "Orderly Transitional Democracy," [47] "Regionalism vs.

[34] C. E. Lively, "Social Planning and the Sociology of Subregions," *Rural Sociology*, II, No. 3, pp. 295-296.
[35] University of Chicago Press, 1936.
[36] *Publication of the American Sociological Society*, XXIX, No. 3, pp. 85-93.
[37] Foreign Policy Association and the University of North Carolina Press.
[38] *Social Forces*, Vol. 14, No. 1, pp. 16-22.
[39] *The American Journal of Sociology*, XLII, No. 4, pp. 493-509.
[40] *Publication of the American Sociological Society*, XXIX, No. 3, pp. 107-114.
[41] *The American Political Science Review*, XXVIII, No. 1, pp. 16-22.
[42] *Publication of the American Sociological Society*, XXIX, No. 3, pp. 41-48.
[43] *Ibid.*, pp. 19-28.
[44] *Ibid.*, pp. 1-18.
[45] *Sociology and Social Research*, XIX, No. 4, pp. 303-313.
[46] *Social Forces*, Vol. 13, No. 1, pp. 6-23.
[47] *The Annals of the American Academy of Political and Social Science*, CLXXX, pp. 31-39.

Sectionalism in the South's Place in the National Economy," [48] "Planning the Southeast" [49] (with Don Becker), and "Realistic Premises for Regional Planning Objectives." [50]

> The sociological approach to be implemented by regional applications may be summarized as follows: "1. The sociological approach must be an analysis of the problems involved. This is a problem in social analysis. . . . 2. It must be an integration of these problems in a coordinated, balanced picture. This is a problem in social synthesis. . . . 3. Equilibrium is the keynote to social planning. This is a problem of social balance. . . . 4. The transitional society between epochs or between crises or between changing cultures is the key problem to equilibrium. Mastery of the transitional society is a problem of social equilibration. . . . 5. Therefore, from the sociological viewpoint, the cultural, the folk, the regional, the national myth, the time-space relationships are fundamental elements transcending economic integration, which is the first essential of emergency reconstruction. . . . 6. The sociological approach is in contrast to that of political philosophy, exclusive economic planning, subjective ideologies, abstract utopias, the perfectionist's panaceas, and all of the specialized 'isms.' . . . 7. There must grow out of the sociological approach basic principles and framework upon which the administrators can build an enduring plan susceptible of flexibility and change. The sociologist does not perfect the plan, neither does he attempt to administer it. . . . 8. In America, social planning must be based upon American backgrounds, institutions, and conditioning which recognize a past as well as a present and a future. . . . 9. Social planning in America will, therefore, comprehend an extension and substantiation of the Constitution. It is a cultural extension of state planning, metropolitan planning, regional planning, and of such technologies as the reorganization of government and administrative procedures." [51]

All of this seems to lead naturally to the concept of the region as a *gestalt* in which the various factors find their meaning through their relationships to other factors; a complex of interrelationships. Within any given region the elements of society will arrange themselves into a pattern, a configuration, which is peculiar to that region and which gives it a character of uniqueness. This distinctive character is pro-

[48] *Social Forces,* XII, No. 3, pp. 338-354.

[49] *Plan Age,* II, No. 3, pp. 1-6.

[50] *Ibid.,* pp. 7-23.

[51] Howard W Odum, "A Sociological Approach to National Social Planning," *Sociology and Social Research,* XIX, No. 4, p. 306.

duced in part by the presence or absence of various elements of social organization, but in greater part by the pattern those elements which are present form through their interrelationships and through the peculiar interpretation given them by the folk occupying the particular region under study. The elements, therefore, can be understood only when conceived as parts of the whole social organization. In this sense, the region is a social gestalt.

This idea is, of course, an adaptation of gestalt psychology to sociology. The concept borrowed is that of the mutual dependence of the field and the figure, the insistence that form and relationship are as important as content, and give much of their meaning to the individual bits composing the whole; that the meaning of a line in a drawing, a note in a musical composition, or any other bit of sensory evidence depends in large part on associated sensory perceptions; for example, the remainder of the drawing or tune. This is tantamount to saying that all the factors are mutually conditioning, at once cause and effect. In still other words, regionalism points to cultural determinism in that the tools by which man has surrounded himself, both physical and mental, and by which he seeks his well-being, direct and affect his response to the physical area in which he finds himself. For both the individual and the social group, the pre-existing culture is largely determinative of the present organization. The older strata of this culture have become so customary that they seem to be "natural"; indeed make up the bulk of what is commonly referred to as "human nature." They form the valuable heritage of "the folk," and it is through the study of the folk that the significance of these elements becomes clear.

This leads logically to the next assumption of the present volume that regionalism approximates in itself a methodological approach to scientific social study. That is, it looks both to the explanation and direction of society; it is assuming a considerable body of knowledge accumulated through dependable techniques or methods. These techniques are found in several of the natural sciences and social sciences. There is, for instance, a region and a technique of study of the biologist, the geologist, the geographer, the anthropologist, the economist, the historian, the political scientist. The sociologist's region and regionalism must comprehend the nearest approximation to a synthesis of studies, methods, and concepts, to the end that regionalism may emerge as cultural determinism or "gestalt" on the one hand and a comprehensive methodological approach on the other.

In *An Introduction to Social Research*, published in 1929, Odum and Jocher held that the newer types of regional approach represented one of the best illustrations of the range and objectives of social research. "In the first place, the regional approach views a given society as a whole, and enables all of the social sciences to contribute. In the second place, it offers a concrete laboratory through which practically all of the present trends in social research may be applied. At the same time it provides for adequate delimitation of areas and scope and extends the range for quantitative effort to discover *new* facts. It is in accord with a considerable tendency to emphasize regions and community and with a number of the projects and programs of the Social Science Research Council. It is therefore concrete in the actual beginnings in a number of instances. The Southern Region is selected as an example for this volume because it is representative of a comprehensive social situation, because it lies within the field of attainable methods, and because concrete beginnings have been made. It must be clear, however, that one of the merits of this approach is that it may be applied to any other region, and that the tests of its validity and the expertness of the social science specialist will lie in the task of attacking, changing, and reworking to fit other areas. If the regional plan is not worked out in accordance with standard values, methods, and applications, it is not an effective illustration."[52]

So, too, the comprehensive approach of regionalism was stated by Harry E. Moore in his *What Is Regionalism?* "Such a view of regionalism takes it out of the province of any one field of thought and demands the co-ordination of all lines of approach. And it is just this correlating and co-ordinating of various factors which gives the regional approach its greatest value. It demands that the planner or investigator see the region as a whole. It is the interrelationships of the various factors in regional analysis which give to the region its distinctive character, its way of life. Environmental and cultural factors hunt in packs; as has been remarked, the phenomena which mark a region are not simply assorted, but are also associated; they exist in interrelationships. The region is a distinctive area whose uniqueness may come either from the particular forces present or the particular way in which those forces are interwoven. The pattern is as important

[52] Howard W. Odum and Katharine Jocher, *An Introduction to Social Research*, pp. 81-82.

as the material in the resulting fabric. But we have been so busy describing the material that we have largely overlooked the pattern."[53]

Furthermore, it seems possible that sociology can provide the framework and methods for combining the regional concept with the elemental factors of folk society in which inheres the nucleus of all society. The assumption here is that the folk-regional society is the definitive transitional society which if one understands, he understands all society. Thus is combined "regional sociology," "cultural sociology," and "folk sociology," the concepts of which, of course, still lack classification and unification in current sociology. The assumptions of the present volume go further and posit the idea of the fundamental importance of the folk, combined with the concept of the region, as the basis for an analysis and understanding of society elsewhere. In this concept of the folk, one looks askance at the reality of the collective mind assumed by Wundt, and would extend the meaning of folkways to include present-day directive processes of social change in the heart of New York City as well as in the most remote valley of the furtherest ridge of the southern Appalachians. Although "the folk" comprehends primitive and country people, the concept includes no less the cultivated and civilized. Thus Frederick P. Keppel characterizes modern advertising as a supreme example of folk art.[54]

Holding the folk as basic to society and social study, there is need to emphasize continually the theoretical significance of the folk and the region in the development of society, since there is an amazing ignorance of the various regions of the United States and their folk, even by well-informed persons. Hence, "It must be clear that it is not possible either to understand or direct any society without a knowledge of its folk-regional culture and backgrounds."[55]

In this position lies the implication that folk cultures differ from region to region and from time to time, a position which would easily lead to the tenets of the German philosophical school which holds that the

[53] Harry E. Moore, *What Is Regionalism?* p. 14.

[54] Frederick P. Keppel, "The Arts in Social Life," Chapter XIX in *Recent Social Trends*, II, 958-1008.

[55] Howard W. Odum, *Southern Regions of the United States*, pp. 251-253.

> study of civilization in the abstract is futile; that what one can do is to study particular cultures. However, without carrying the position to this point, it is insisted that one must know something of the unorganized culture of a people before that people can be understood. This position is stated by Marett: "The continuous life of the folk constitutes, as it were, the germ plasm of society. Unless the external conditions that so largely make up the apparatus of so-called civilization so act on the social body that their effects are transmitted to this germinal element and cause it to be transformed, then our cultural acquisitions are vain, because utterly transient, in the judgment of history. Why do survivals survive? It is this: that they survive because they are the constantly renewed symptoms of that life of the folk which alone has the inherent power of surviving in the long run." [56]

However, the primary significance of the folk lies in the fact that the ways of the folk are largely determinative in any society, since they tend to interpret actual situations in terms of the folk perspectives, of the mores. And, since folk cultures vary, the interpretations placed on facts will vary from region to region or culture to culture. The point is of particular interest to social planning agencies, since any plan which will succeed must fit into this pattern of folkways and mores, as E. W. Burgess argues in a recent appraisal of governmental planning activities in this country.[57] Burgess seems to imply that here in the folkways and mores and differing ways of interpretation of facts lies the *ethos*, or distinctive group character. Here also lies a possible line of reconciliation between the long line of "group mind" theorists and their opponents. At any rate in this idea of distinctive folk societies lies one of the bulwarks of regional theory in general. Regionalism, in one sense at least, is the identification of such societies with areas of territory: "The region as the hypothesis for special study is at once an extension and a subdivision of the folk society, characterized by the joint indexes of geography and culture and deriving its definitive traits through action and behavior processes rather than through technological functions or areas. For the purpose of this discussion 'region' is not an entirely separate concept but an extension and an attribute to the 'folk.' As contrasting it with

[56] R. R. Marett, *Psychology and Folk-Lore*, p. 26.

[57] "Social Planning and the Mores," *Publication of the American Sociological Society*, XXIX, No. 3, pp. 1-18.

the technological region it cannot be separated from the main discussion." [58]

There is yet one other larger implication of the folk-regional society in relation to modern civilization. This is the contrasting character of the natural folk-regional society set over against the bigness and artificiality of the complex, technological, and industrial urban society of the maturing nation. If the unit of sociological study is not the *socius* or the *family* or the mere *community* but the folk-regional society in which is involved the new science of the region, and, if the modern world reflects the technical and non-folk, there is the further implication that sociology must seek concepts and techniques for distinguishing between the two contrasting orders. Such a distinction is found in the *technicways* which tend to transcend the old folkways and supplant the old slow-moving mores, thus accelerating the rate of societal evolution. Sociology, therefore, through the basic medium of regionalism, may discover the way to explore the transitional modes of society in the modern world.

The premise of the folk regional society in relation to technical society is "found in the inquiries of folk sociology, a general sociology which is the study of the folk society as distinguished from the state society, the natural society as distinguished from the artificial or organizational. It is important, here, however, to point up certain theoretical and practical implications of such a sociology as may throw light on the role of the *technicways*. Thus, a theoretical implication is apparent in the attempt to discover fundamental or elemental factors in the imbalance between folk society and organizational society such as has been constant in the decline of great cultures in the past. The corresponding practical implication follows in the search for elemental factors of societal deterioration in technological or super-organizational society, on the one hand, and the elements of normal evolution and survival in the folk society, on the other. The implication is, of course, that the *technicways* might prove to be the key to substantiating the magnificent analogies of cultural senescence and decay of Spengler, Freud, and others or of proving them futile." [59] This is following the assumption that "in contemporary civilization, at least as it is found in Western culture, the *technicways*, transcending the folkways and supplanting

[58] Howard W. Odum, "Folk and Regional Conflict as a Field of Sociological Study," *Publication of the American Sociological Society*, XXV, No. 2, p. 9, and note.
[59] Howard W. Odum, "Notes on the Technicways in Contemporary Society," *American Sociological Review*, II, No. 3, p. 339.

> the *mores*, tend to so modify human behavior and institutions as to outmode the earlier, natural rate of societal evolution. In particular, the tendency is to accelerate the rate of change in behavior patterns as well as in technological process, and therefore the rate of cultural evolution. The tendency may be further to modify the whole behavior and character of the people. Thus in his *Revolt of the Masses*, Ortega complains of the immorality of European peoples who accept all from science, give nothing in return, demand more and more, thus surrendering the evolutionary processes of the folkways, mores, and character conditioning." [60]

The final point in this already long presentation has to do with the possible synthesis of regional studies and concepts through which sociology appears to find its greatest opportunities. In a word this may be illustrated by the present volume itself which points toward the sociological emphasis and methods of regionalism. The point may be illustrated further by hazarding something of a preview of next steps in American sociology. This is that, as a science, sociology will focus upon two major objectives. One is research in which the emphasis will be upon increasingly more vigorous scientific methods and analysis, and upon increasingly dynamic and realistic inquiries into the total societal area. The other will be a synthesis of this increasingly large and important body of knowledge with a view to the multiple tasks of social discovery, social interpretation, and social invention. The field of sociology, however, will not be limited to the formalized concept of society or human relationships or like-minded groups, but will comprehend the totality of the societal process which we call culture and the societal product which we call civilization with all the interrelationships of land and people, men and machines, time and change. In this approach regionalism offers an essential tool.

[60] *Ibid.*, p. 337.

Part III

THE REGIONAL DEVELOPMENT OF A CHANGING NATION

Per Capita Personal Income, by Regions and States, 1929

STATE AND REGION	Entire Population	Non-Farm Population	Farm Population
Southeast	*$365*	*$535*	*$183*
Virginia	431	594	182
North Carolina	317	472	167
South Carolina	261	412	129
Georgia	343	532	147
Florida	548	577	419
Kentucky	398	605	148
Tennessee	346	529	137
Alabama	331	527	141
Mississippi	287	530	173
Arkansas	311	503	185
Louisiana	438	603	186
Southwest	*564*	*683*	*366*
Oklahoma	503	699	243
Texas	531	690	298
New Mexico	476	549	354
Arizona	744	795	567
Northeast	*881*	*946*	*366*
Maine	645	689	474
New Hampshire	652	689	379
Vermont	633	761	351
Massachusetts	975	976	898
Rhode Island	881	881	859
Connecticut	1,008	1,028	630
New York	1,365	1,417	493
New Jersey	1,002	1,011	704
Delaware	1,315	1,550	368
Pennsylvania	815	865	305
Maryland	799	881	323
West Virginia	485	602	157

STATE AND REGION	Entire Population	Non-Farm Population	Farm Population
Middle States	*$715*	*$854*	*$262*
Ohio	795	893	255
Indiana	614	748	221
Illinois	987	1,091	299
Michigan	869	983	283
Wisconsin	682	807	389
Minnesota	610	802	248
Iowa	485	659	214
Missouri	675	851	189
Northwest	*590*	*703*	*426*
North Dakota	422	588	302
South Dakota	420	614	268
Nebraska	521	698	281
Kansas	569	686	376
Montana	698	856	435
Idaho	609	647	559
Wyoming	777	841	648
Colorado	690	772	470
Utah	600	629	496
Far West	*921*	*953*	*818*
Nevada	1,000	1,041	811
Washington	841	887	651
Oregon	757	817	563
California	1,085	1,066	1,246

Perhaps there are no more significant regional differentials than those indicated by income and wealth. Here are two excellent illustrations, adapted from Leven, Moulton, and Warburton's *America's Capacity to Consume*. Above, page 173, table 17; below, page 173, table 16.

Per Cent Regional Distribution of the Aggregate Personal Income of the Farm and Non-Farm Population, 1929

STATE AND REGION	Income of Entire Population	Income of Non-Farm Population	Income of Farm Population
Southeast	*10.00*	*8.60*	*24.30*
Virginia	1.14	1.04	2.12
North Carolina	1.09	0.88	3.21
South Carolina	0.50	0.40	1.44
Georgia	1.09	0.95	2.55
Florida	0.86	0.81	1.40
Kentucky	1.13	1.04	2.13
Tennessee	0.99	0.88	2.02
Alabama	0.95	0.82	2.29
Mississippi	0.63	0.41	2.82
Arkansas	0.63	0.44	2.51
Louisiana	1.00	0.92	1.85
Southwest	*5.20*	*4.40*	*12.70*
Oklahoma	1.31	1.14	3.00
Texas	3.34	2.83	8.44
New Mexico	0.22	0.17	0.68
Arizona	0.35	0.32	0.68
Northeast	*42.50*	*45.40*	*13.60*
Maine	0.56	0.53	0.93
New Hamphire	0.33	0.34	0.25
Vermont	0.25	0.23	0.49
Massachusetts	4.51	4.87	0.86
Rhode Island	0.66	0.71	0.11
Connecticut	1.76	1.87	0.62
New York	18.61	20.03	4.25
New Jersey	4.37	4.71	1.04
Delaware	0.34	0.36	0.21
Pennsylvania	8.56	9.09	3.15
Maryland	1.42	1.46	0.93
West Virginia	0.91	0.91	0.86

STATE AND REGION	Income of Entire Population	Income of Non-Farm Population	Income of Farm Population
Middle States	*28.50*	*29.00*	*23.40*
Ohio	5.74	6.00	3.13
Indiana	2.17	2.17	2.18
Illinois	8.17	8.62	3.62
Michigan	4.53	4.72	2.68
Wisconsin	2.18	1.99	4.13
Minnesota	1.71	1.61	2.66
Iowa	1.31	1.19	2.49
Missouri	2.57	2.57	2.56
Northwest	*4.60*	*3.70*	*13.00*
North Dakota	0.31	0.20	1.45
South Dakota	0.32	0.22	1.26
Nebraska	0.78	0.67	1.99
Kansas	1.17	0.97	3.21
Montana	0.41	0.35	1.09
Idaho	0.30	0.20	1.26
Wyoming	0.19	0.15	0.57
Colorado	0.78	0.70	1.58
Utah	0.33	0.30	0.65
Far West	*8.90*	*8.50*	*12.60*
Nevada	0.10	0.09	0.16
Washington	1.43	1.34	2.35
Oregon	0.78	0.71	1.50
California	6.56	6.35	8.64

Chapter XVIII

MEASURES OF AMERICAN REGIONALISM

NOW we come to test, through representative regions of the United States, the validity of our assumptions and the degree to which it is possible to approximate in actual life, the composite regions as described. For, after all, the United States, with its regions of historical and geographical units, is not an academic concept but a pressing reality to students, citizens, workers, statesmen, foreigners, Americans, all. The whole of a great nation, even as of other objects, is equal to the sum of its parts. "Every something," Professor Giddings was wont to emphasize, "is a number of somethings." Yet, in the case of a complex culture, such as the United States, it must be clear that the sum is much more than its parts, and that there is much more than mere addition and aggregates.

It is true that the unity of the nation is found in the integration of its diversities, but also the organic union of the nation is found in the continuing rediscovery and reintegration of its regions. Still more, each of the diversities or regions is fabricated of historical and cultural developments, of geographic and physiographic characteristics, and of the folk quality and culture of the people. Furthermore, there is such bigness and complexity and magnificence in the whole natural cultural and technological America that it is not possible either to understand it or to direct its continuing progress, except through the regional approach, analysis, and administration. The definitive analysis and utilization, therefore, of the major regions of the nation, the portraiture of their character and their culture, the inventory of their resources and their problems, and the regional interrelations of each, constitute not only a major problem of the present time, but also a test of American regionalism. It is the purpose of Part III of this volume to continue the exploration of regions through the application of the foregoing chapters to the United States in terms of the best possible regional delineations of the nation at the beginning of the second third of the twentieth century. Such a regional approach, in addition to being an exercise in classification, may possibly serve as an effective technique for the study of the nation as a whole and of the various parts of its culture and dilemmas.

For the key to this regional America will be found in its richness and reality whether it is reflected in the observations of our foreign visitors who marvel at its bigness, expanse, and complexity; or whether it is reflected in the enthusiastic admiration of each region by the vividly writing First Lady of the Land; or whether measured in terms of Babson's appraisal of prosperity and financial prospects; or reflected in the professor's or the administrator's verdict that the nation is too big for any single administrative unit to be successful; or in the enthusiastic but puzzled student of literature in search of the great American novel; or, as is everywhere in evidence in the quest of the traveler and the tourist and the searcher after new frontiers, for the enjoyment of a richer life in America.

Thus, Sir William Beveridge's "Six Americas in Search of a Faith" was one way of emphasizing diversity and dilemma. Another was the dictum of Count Keyserling that "First of all, America seems to be subdivided even now into large provinces of a comparatively unified character, provinces out of which there would undoubtedly have grown, in earlier days and under different conditions, separate cultures. There are New England, the East, the North, the Middle West, the South bordering the Middle West, the South in the real geographical sense, the Far West. But within these provinces almost every town has a spirit of its own, so that while traveling I constantly had in mind the dawn of European civilization, when the Teutonic nomads just began to settle down around centers such as Cologne, Worms, Nürnberg, Paris, Carcassonne." [1] Mrs. Roosevelt's dilemma arises because she likes so many parts of the country. "New England is a delightful part of the country. . . . When I am in the Southwest I think Texas is enchanting with its wide open spaces, and I know that I think Santa Fe is one of the most fascinating cities in the world. When I am on the West Coast, from San Diego to Seattle, I am enthralled by the life, the

[1] Hermann Keyserling, "Genius Loci," *Atlantic Monthly*, Vol. 144, p. 303.

climate, the variety of scenery and the way of living." About New England, she continues, "there is a sense of age and feeling that people have had time and leisure to beautify their own peculiar spot. You get it nowhere else in the country." [2] Mr. Babson must give his periodical reports in terms of regions. Thus, "The South is in good shape. Conditions in the farming regions have been ideal. . . . New England activity shows only a very modest gain over a year ago. . . . East of the Mississippi and north of the Ohio, business conditions—while slackening off—are relatively good. . . . West of the Mississippi, conditions are more spotty. . . . Business is really booming down in the Southwest. Lower cotton prices have taken some of the edge off Texas and Oklahoma's hilarity, but this section is still just like a 'boom-town.' . . . Business is also fine in the Rockies—from Pueblo to Spokane." [3] Representing another type of critique, Frederick Osborn reminds us that the United States "is marvelously favored in its human wealth," in that each separate state and region "can boast of special qualities in its people which are a proper ground for pride. There may be problems connected with so many cultural traditions and so many racial origins living together side by side, but their very variety gives hope for a rich flowering which would be impossible among a people less diverse in their qualities." [4]

This regional variety and dilemma have been emphasized of late not only in the numerous legislative issues at Washington and in widely distributed newspaper editorials, but have been well described in the last few years in a large number of excellent books on America and Americans. Perhaps a hundred volumes could be listed from which authentic pictures of America's diversified culture can be had. More than a thousand titles of fiction have attempted to picture the several regions, the land and people, their culture and folkways. So, too, more than a thousand authors have written in magazines and newspapers, in contests and in competition for the realistic portraiture of the living culture of these United States. Most of the books and articles reflect the nation as Americans see it; some reflect the observations of visitors; while most of them see the nation as a background of problems and dilemmas susceptible to regional approach. Foot-

[2] Mrs. Franklin D. Roosevelt, "My Day," *Raleigh News and Observer*, July 27, 1937.

[3] Roger W. Babson, "Business Spotty Throughout Nation," *The Greensboro Daily News*, October 10, 1937.

[4] Frederick Osborn, "The Human Wealth of the United States," *American Planning and Civic Annual* (edited by Harlean James), p. 31.

THE NAMES OF THE STATES, BY REGIONS

STATE AND REGION	1	2	3	4	5	6
Southeast						
Virginia	Ancient Dominion	Mother of Presidents	Mother of States	Mother of Statesmen	Cavalier State	Old Dominion
North Carolina	Land of the Sky	Old North State	Tarheel State	Rip Van Winkle State	Turpentine State	
South Carolina	Iodine State	Palmetto State	Rice State	Sand-lapper State	Swamp State	
Georgia	Buzzard State	Cracker State	Goober State	Empire State of the South	The Yankee Land of the South	
Florida	Alligator State (7) Gulf State	Everglade State	Flower State	Land of Flowers	Orange State	Peninsula State
Kentucky	Blue Grass State	Corn-cracker State	Dark and Bloody Ground State	Hemp State	Tobacco State	
Tennessee	Big Ben State	Lion's Den State	Hog and Hominy State	Mother of Southwestern Statesmen	Volunteer State	
Alabama	Cotton Plantation State	Cotton State	Lizard State	Yellowhammer State		
Mississippi	Bayou State	Border-eagle State	Eagle State	Ground-hog State	Magnolia State	Mud-wad-dler's State
Arkansas	Bear State	Böwie State	Hot Water State	Toothpick State	Wonder State	
Louisiana	Creole State	Pelican State	Sugar State			
Southwest						
Oklahoma	Boomers Paradise	Sooner State				
Texas	Lone Star State	Banner State	Beef State	Blizzard State	Jumbo State	
New Mexico	Cactus State (7) Sunshine State	Land of Cactus (8) Spanish State	Land of the Delight-makers	Land of Heart's Desire	Land of Opportunity	Land of Sunshine
Arizona	Apache State (7) Sunset Land	Aztec State (8) Valentine State	Baby State	Italy of America	Sand Hill State	Sunset State
Northeast						
Maine	Border State	Lumber State	Old Dirigo State	Pine Tree State	Polar Star State	Switzerland of America
New Hampshire	Granite State	Mother of Rivers	White Mountain State	Switzerland of America		
Vermont	Green Mountain State					
Massachusetts	Baked Bean State	Old Colony State	Old Bay State	Bay State	Puritan State	
Rhode Island	Plantation State	Little Rhody				
Connecticut	Nutmeg State	Constitution State	Blue Law State	Brownstone State	Freestone State	Land of Steady Habits
New York	Empire State	Excelsior State	Knickerbocker State			
New Jersey	Camden and Amboy State (7) New Spain	Clam State (8) State of Spain	Foreigner State (9) Switzerland of America	Garden State	Jersey Blue State	Mosquito State

Romance and History Abound in the Common Names of the States. Adapted from George E. Shankle, *State Names, Flags, Seals, Songs, Birds, Flowers, and Other Symbols.*

notes and bibliographies will give some idea of the range and quality of these contributions. Yet the case needs to be illustrated further with a sampling from our visitors' observations.

Thus Lucien Lehman writes: "In spite of himself a man's mind goes off into dreams. . . . Her lands are fertile in grains, rich in minerals, and endowed by Nature with all the attributes of charm and beauty. Her lakes, such as Michigan, Erie, Ontario, and Huron, are veritable inland seas; her rivers are of such majesty that our Seine and Rhone in comparison seem like negligible little streams. The Missouri River is 2,470 miles in length, the Mississippi 2,296, the Colorado 1,800, the Rio Grande 1,770, the Arkansas 1,487, the Columbia 1,200, the Ohio 1,086, etc. There are 82 great rivers, varying in length, but all magnificent and navigable, and in places of such width that the opposite shore is lost to view."[5] So M. J. Bonn: "The enormous territorial expansion of America . . . stretches from the Arctic Ocean of Canada to the Gulf of Mexico, from the gray coasts of New England to the laughing shores of California. It includes—and almost invariably on the largest scale—mountains and plains, prairies and forests, lakes and rivers, deserts and oases. It offers thousands and thousands of specimens of landscape, from the great rivers of the East which mirror the proud seats of an old aristocracy to the mud-walled ranch on the eastern slopes of the Rockies; from the plain of the Mississippi, with its rich black loam, and its almost suffocating productiveness, the land of Indian corn and the paradise of hogs, to the golden wheat-fields of the prairie provinces; from the neat orange groves of California to the porphyry gorge of the Saguenay."[6] Thus, also the urbane L. P. Jacks,[7] seeking to appraise the human resources of America, pronounced its physical backgrounds immense. The scene baffled all description . . . awful and bewildering grandeur . . . rivers thundering through hidden gorges or deep smooth-flowing through rich valleys, towering masses of rocks, untapped depths of minerals, a nation of many promised lands, in which, however, things are to be judged by the direction in which they are moving, and not by the point at which they have arrived.

The vividness of this regional character of the American United States has also been reflected of late in many regional celebrations, "world's fairs," historical collections, and especially in the Federal Writers' Project, through which for the first time there is being approached authentic guides to the nation's extraordinary range and

[5] Lucien Lehman, *The American Illusion*, pp. 30-31.
[6] M. J. Bonn, *The American Adventure*, pp. 20-21.
[7] L. P. Jacks, *My American Friends*, *passim*, especially pp. 7, 127, 128, 140.

THE NAMES OF THE STATES, Continued

STATE AND REGION	1	2	3	4	5	6
Delaware........	Blue Hen's Chickens State	Blue Hen State	Diamond State	Uncle Sam's Pocket Handkerchief	New Sweden	
Pennsylvania........	Coal State	Steel State	Oil State	Quaker State	Keystone State	
Maryland........	Cockade State	Monumental State	Old Line State	Oyster State	Queen State	
West Virginia........	Mountain State	Panhandle State	Panhandle of West Virginia	Switzerland of America		
Middle States						
Ohio........	Buckeye State	Modern Mother of Presidents	Yankee State			
Indiana........	Hoosier State	Hoosierdom				
Illinois........	Corn State	Egypt	Prairie State	Garden of the West	Sucker State	
Michigan........	Auto State	Lady of the Lakes	Lake State	Wolverine State		
Wisconsin........	Badger State	Copper State				
Minnesota........	Bread and Butter State	Gopher State	Lake State	New England of the West	North Star State	Wheat State
Iowa........	Hawkeye State	Land of the Rolling Prairie				
Missouri........	Bullion State (7) Show Me State	Iron Mountain State	Lead State	Ozark State	Pennsylvania of the West	Puke State
Northwest						
North Dakota........	Flickertail State	Great Central State	Sioux State	Land of the Dakotas		
South Dakota........	Artesian State	Blizzard State	Coyote State	Land of Plenty	Sunshine State	
Nebraska........	Antelope State	Black Water State	Bug-eating State	Tree Planters State	Corn Huskers State	
Kansas........	Central State (7) Sunflower State	Cyclone State (8) Squatter State	Garden State	Garden of the West	Grasshopper State	Jayhawker State
Montana........	Bonanza State	Stubtoe State	Treasure State			
Idaho........	Gem State	Gem of the Mountains	Little Ida			
Wyoming........	Equality State	Sagebrush State				
Colorado........	Buffalo Plains State	Centennial State	Lead State	Silver State	Switzerland of America	
Utah........	Bee Hive State	Desert State	Land of Mormons	Land of Saints	Mormon State	Salt Lake State
Far West						
Nevada........	Battle-born State	Mining State	Sage State	Sage-brush State	Sage-hen State	Silver State
Washington........	Chinook State	Evergreen State				
Oregon........	Beaver State	Hard-case State	Land of Hard-cases	Sunset State	Web-foot State	
California........	El Dorado State	Golden State	Grape State	Land of Gold	Eureka State	

Romance and History Abound in the Common Names of the States.

richness of scenic and cultural diversity. It so happens that the New England States have been pictured first and best, but the list also includes many others, featuring all the regions in varying degrees of thoroughness. Here again, however, the states and special subregions constitute important units in each regional fabric. Thus Maine is "A Guide Down East"; Vermont is "A Guide to the Green Mountain State"; Rhode Island is the "Smallest State"; and Massachusetts "A Guide to Its Places and People."

A current example of historical-regional representation is found in the forthcoming episode, in which six of our "Middle States," largely constituting the "Old Northwest," will be celebrating in 1937 the sesquicentennial of their Magna Charta. The news stories point out that "the 150th year of the ordinance of 1787 foundation of liberty and education for residents of Indiana, Ohio, Illinois, Michigan, Wisconsin and Minnesota, will bring, as the feature of the celebration, an ox-drawn pilgrimage over the route pioneers followed to new homes on the western frontier. A covered-wagon train, pulled by oxen, will leave Ipswich, Mass., December 13 on the way west. At West Newton, Pa., once 'Summerill's Ferry,' it will stop while the 1937 'pioneers' cut down trees and build rafts. These will carry the caravan—wagons, oxen and all—down the Youghiogheny, Monongahela and Ohio Rivers to Marietta, Ohio, first capital of the Northwest Territory. There, next summer, in a continuation of the celebration, a memorial will be dedicated. Then the wagon train will float on downstream to Madison, Ind., once the river gateway to Indiana. The ordinance which served as a constitution for the Northwest Territory, a 265,000-square mile area of former French, British and Indian land out of which the six states later were carved, was adopted by the Continental Congress July 13, 1787. The Territory included all land bounded by the western Pennsylvania border, the Ohio River, the Great Lakes and the Mississippi River."[8]

There was an early day when Thomas Jefferson, surveying the American prospect, pointed to it as perhaps one of the most stupendous in all nature. Even so, his picture was but a fraction of the spectacle of the United States in the 1930's, with its 1,900,000,000 of acres of land and its more than 122,000,000 people. There was another day, following long planning and negotiating for an ex-

[8] "Midwestern States Having Celebration," *The Greensboro Daily News,* October 17, 1937.

anded domain upon which could be built a great agrarian culture, when for the bargain price of $15,000,000 the Louisiana Purchase was added to his picture. Even so, again, this great acquisition was a relatively small part of the total domain which was to constitute the United States of America. But, although this great purchase was but the beginning of American expansion, its development had been such that in the 1930's its people, its land, and its wealth exceeded by far the total of the early Jeffersonian America. Twenty-five million people, owning billions of dollars in invested capital and in land, had developed a new empire from Louisiana on up—Arkansas, Missouri, Iowa, Minnesota, North Dakota, South Dakota, Nebraska, Kansas, Oklahoma, and parts of Montana, Wyoming, and Colorado. No prophet appeared to point to the stupendous developments from this purchase of fifteen million dollars' worth of land and river, forests and stone, which was to be the forerunner of the great American bargain counter and of the institution of land development and land booms. Land and still more land was to feature the crowning domain of Jefferson's American democracy but playing different roles and even more significant and complicated parts in the drama than he foresaw.

There was another day more than a half century later when Herbert Spencer looked at first hand for the only time in his life upon the evolving American picture and pronounced it good. The American people, he reported, had come into possession of an unparalleled fortune in mineral wealth and vast tracts of virgin land. They had inherited all the arts, appliances, and methods which had been developed by old societies. Inventiveness had been widely fostered, vast bodies of immigrants of various bloods had been incorporated, and an immense plexus of railways and telegraphs had consolidated the aggregates of states as had never before been done. Yet it is not recorded that Herbert Spencer ever envisioned a nation with technology playing upon its regional resources such that, having only a fraction of the world's areas and a twentieth of its population, it would produce half of the work of the world, half of the world's energy from coal, most of its energy from oil, and wrap itself in copper wire enough to make twenty thousand crossings of the continent. Here was to be a new picture, beyond dreams, of this same nation producing a third of the world's iron, half of its copper and zinc, half of its steel mills, three-fourths of the world's corn. Measured in the 1930's there were to be more than twenty-five million automobiles, fifteen million radios, fifty thousand miles of natural gas lines, more than a hundred thousand miles of oil pipe lines, nearly a million miles of surfaced highways, and nearly a quarter million miles of railroads. It is not recorded that either Jefferson or Spencer saw the future picture of America as one in which by a single day's travel by air one could see practically every variety of topography, climate, soil, crops, minerals, and activities in the world. Regions undreamed of, frontier on frontier, with unfolding opportunity and resources; such as the founding fathers could not have foretold.

The *New York Times* makes an editorial page feature of a story powerfully suggestive of some magic world in which the Far West has been transformed into an epochal region typifying the greatest variety and highest standard of living in the known world. The *Times* recalls that "Some three-quarters of a century ago a little girl was helping to tend sheep on her father's ranch on the rolling hills, very green after the Winter rains, golden brown during the dry season, near the shores of the Pacific Ocean and not far from the old Pueblo de la Reina de los Angeles. At the age of 2, as she was later to tell, she had come across the plains with her parents in a caravan which was guided over the latter section of its route by Kit Carson. When Mrs. Carolina Foote Griffin died in Los Angeles the other day, at the age of 82, the old sheep ranch had taken on the name of Hollywood. . . . It is true stories like this that make one rub one's eyes and ask whether one has not wandered by mistake into *The Arabian Nights* or *Alice in Wonderland*, or into some set in modern Hollywood that will soon be folded up and put away. Sheep one can understand. As far back as one can remember there have been sheep. They are in Homer, in the Bible and in still older writings. . . . All this is natural. It fits into the legends of the race and somchow connects today's suit of clothes with the glory that was Greece, and with Ulysses, and with Abraham of Ur. What is difficult to grasp is that a certain tract of ground should be in one woman's lifetime first a lonesome ranch and then Hollywood; that during that brief period Kit Carson and all the wild, strange existence for which he stood should become not only a memory but a memory artificially kept alive in one of the very areas where he may have camped, by the most gigantic amusement enterprise in history." [9]

[9] "Story of a Sheep Ranch," *New York Times*, August 4, 1937.

Perhaps these illustrations are not needed to supplement the previous chapters, or to give emphasis and vividness to the quest for regional reality in America. The historical, cultural, theoretical, and practical applications leave little doubt as to the necessity for satisfactory composite regional divisions of the nation for the purposes described. These reasons will be further reflected in our final chapter on "Problems and Strategy of Regional Development towards National Reintegration." There is, however, one major area of interest and usefulness which needs to be emphasized further before presenting samplings of the detailed basis for the delineation of the six composite cultural regions and of the prevailing characteristics of each region. This is the importance of the region as a frame of reference for research and study, on the one hand, and for literary portraiture on the other. This, of course, has often been emphasized by the geographers as a prime basis of regional classifications. It is of even greater importance in social research and especially where the social and physical sciences join hands in the newer approaches to research and the implementation of their findings in actual situations. So also in many ways regionalism as a frame of reference for research and a framework for social inventory and planning serves to recapitulate the basic importance of regions in the nation. Whether it is to study and understand the nation, to enjoy its richness and variety, to travel over its vast domains, to administer its governmental and business agencies and organizations, to build its future, or to "save the nation," the minimum first steps must comprehend the regional approach and methodology. Or to look at it in another way, if science is the observation and recording of likenesses and differences, the scientific inventory of the United States must be found, not in its universal averages, but in its incomparable variety and richness where similarities and dissimilarities are symbolic of the nation and its democratic foundations, philosophy, and government.

The other side of the interpretation picture, namely, that of the literary artist and poet, has been well presented in the prospectus of one of the publishers announcing a series of volumes on American rivers. Upon the authors, it is insisted "now in America, as in all lands and times, rests the real responsibility of interpretation. If the average American is less informed about his country than any other national, knows and cares less about its past and about its present in all sections but the one where he resides and does business, it is because the books prepared for his instruction were not written by artists. Few artists have displayed to him the colors and textures of the original stuff of American life; or made him a comrade of the folk who came from the crowded civilizations of the old world and entered the vast wilderness of the new by all its shining rivers; or thrust him, as one of them, into the clash of spirit with circumstance, under the green arches of beauty, from which emerged the democratic ideal and American individuality —'rugged' truly, in its loyal strength, sacrifice and self-dependence. He has not been led to feel himself a neighbor and brother in the foreign groups which developed into separate Little Americas; evolving their own lore by blending old memories with fancies kindled by the new experience and, as the groups enlarged and mingled and occupied wide sections of river-pathed territory, spreading their imaginative compound of pioneer and Indian folkways, stories, songs and myths like a rich loam over all the seeding-ground of this present nation.

"The average American has been prevented from a profound self-knowledge, as a descendant and a citizen, and deprived as an individual of the thrill and inspiration of a dramatic experience, because the epic material of America has been formulated by the scholastics instead of by the artists. This is said with full realization that we can hardly give adequate thanks for the patient researches of the scholars, and may properly say a word in censure of those budding writers who went to colleges and drowsed through the history hours without hearing even a few phrases of the great rhythm pulsing under the berceuse." [10]

What then are adequate regions, acceptable as frames of reference for research and portraiture, as basic divisions for administration and planning, and as fundamental, yet flexible, units in the totality and union of the states and regions? What is the nature and size of those regions best suited to the largest number of purposes and how may they be determined? What are the limitations of regions too small and too numerous or too large and too few? What are the limitations of the incidental regions chosen for convenience or for political ends? What, further, are the limitations of regions which rest primarily upon physiographic character and ignore the units of states as legally constituted administrative and fiscal entities? These are some of the realistic questions, the answers to which, or the unsatisfactory answers to which, have tended to retard regional realism in

[10] Constance Lindsay Skinner, *Rivers and American Folk*, pp. 3-4.

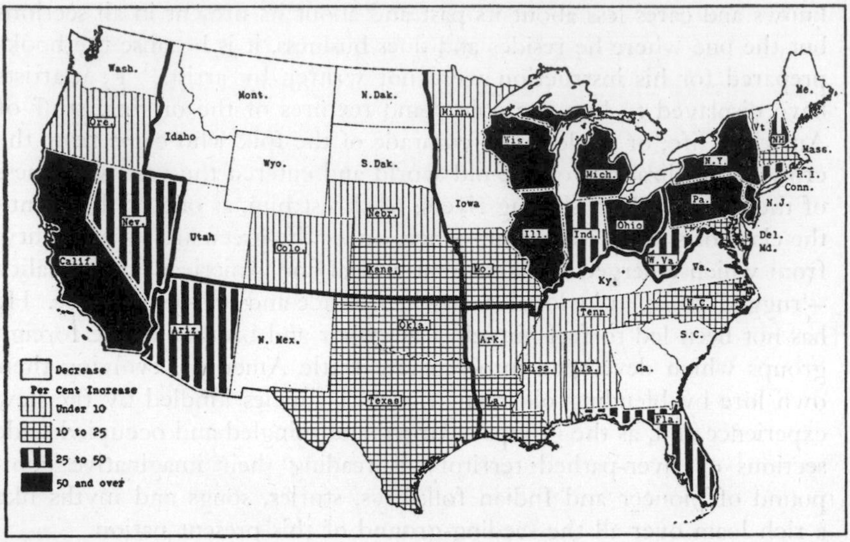

Above: Percentage of Gain or Loss in Negro Population, 1920-1930, compared with,
Below: Percentage of Negroes in Total Population.

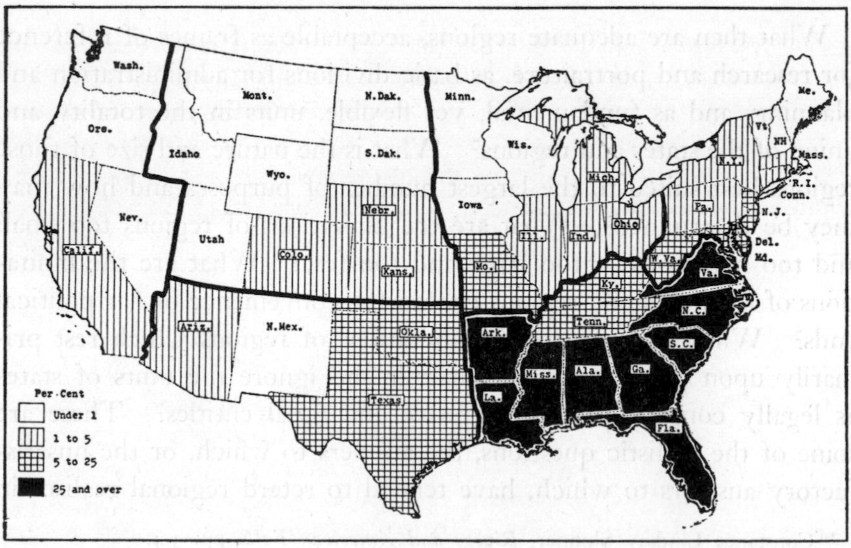

America and elsewhere. From the viewpoint of academic interest, most of these questions have been answered in Parts I and II. It remains now to indicate further the basis upon which the present six-fold division of the nation approximates an adequate regional characterization and, for further comparative purposes, the most effective division possible at the present time.

By way of recapitulation it should be recalled that the case for major regional divisions has been made already through the catalogue of actual experience and multiple regions. In one sense these experimental regions constitute sufficient data to point up the most useful classification by merely delineating regions which combine the largest number of advantages of the largest number of regions already tried out. By way of further recapitulation it is recalled that the term region is used in the sense of a composite major societal region of the nation. Such a region, to be definitive, must approximate the largest degree of homogeneity, measured by the largest number and variety of indices or units of homogeneity for the largest number of purposes. Such major regions are generally considered under two categories. One is the group-of-states region such as constitutes the foundation for the present work. The second is the organic physiographic region, such as the river valley regions proposed by President Roosevelt for seven regional planning areas. In the present work the physiographic regions are rejected for two reasons. While such regions, for limited purposes, are desirable and fundamental, affording many special advantages over the group-of-states region, they are not practically realistic because their range of climate, topography, historical diversity and other features militate against their use as cultural composite regions and because they cannot approximate adequacy without ignoring the technical legal and administrative foundations of the nation. They cannot, therefore, qualify according to our definition of the major region. On the other hand, provisions are made for the utilization of such areas which overlap state boundaries through subregional classifications for special purposes.

Of course the perfect region would have the natural area coincide with the cultural and administrative. Since this is never possible we must approximate the combination as best we can, allowing within the major regions ample opportunity for delimiting and using major subregions of geographic areas and of socio-economic subregions which cut across state lines. On this basis the six major regions of the United States have been characterized as the *Northeast* and the *Southeast*, the *Northwest* and the *Southwest*, the *Middle States* and the *Far West*. This is the classification set forth in *Southern Regions of the United*

States in which the grouping was first described. From the study of various regions as found in the many map pictures available and by combining a wide range of factors, based upon general historical, cultural, and several hundred statistical indices, it is possible to construct a regional picture adequate for comparative purposes. For the purposes of measurement and for other purposes already stated, it was necessary to designate each region in terms of a number of states, with the subregions taking care of cultural and economic factors which transcend state boundaries. On such a basis these six major regions approximate the largest degree of homogeneity measured by the largest number of criteria for the largest number of purposes. They are, moreover, regions not too large for measurement and distinctive characterization, not so small and numerous as to complicate the picture. The *Northeastern Region* is practically synonymous with Frederick Jackson Turner's greater New England and includes twelve states: Maine, Vermont, New Hampshire, Massachusetts, Rhode Island, Connecticut, New Jersey, New York, Pennsylvania, Delaware, Maryland, West Virginia, and the District of Columbia. The *Southeastern Region* includes eleven states, approximating the "Old South": Virginia, North Carolina, South Carolina, Georgia, Florida, Alabama, Mississippi, Louisiana, Arkansas, Tennessee, and Kentucky. The *Southwestern Region* represents a new cultural region long since differentiated from "the South" and nearer West than South, including the four states of Texas, Oklahoma, New Mexico, and Arizona. The *Middle States,* largely what was long known as the Middle West, include eight states: Ohio, Indiana, Illinois, Michigan, Wisconsin, Minnesota, Iowa, and Missouri. The new *Northwest,* comprising much of what was called the Mountain States, includes nine states: North Dakota, South Dakota, Nebraska, Kansas, Montana, Idaho, Wyoming, Colorado, Utah. Finally, the *Far Western* picture holding to the concept of the Pacific West includes the four states: Washington, Oregon, California, and Nevada.

If it were not necessary to adhere to state lines, the same general sixfold division could be made still more nearly to approximate a cultural division combining nearly all of the desired indices. Thus the eastern border of the Great Plains would represent the western boundary of both the Middle States and of the Southeast, adding to the Middle States a part of the Dakotas, Nebraska, and Kansas, while to the Southeast would go a small part of Oklahoma and Texas. So too the borders of the Northeast would change to acquire a small part of Ohio, Kentucky, and Virginia, and to give up a part of West Virginia to the Southeast. The border of the Far West, too, would shift to leave parts of Oregon and Washington to the Northwest. It would be possible, too, that the Southwest would annex a part of California's "Southland," while other shiftings would conform to specialized indices or functional analysis in accordance with the nature of the classification wanted or the focusing of indices.[11]

It must be emphasized again and again that there is no "perfect" region nor is it possible to designate major regions which will be satisfactory to even a majority of students and workers. To say the region cannot be set up as a working premise because it is not satisfactory is, of course, to beg the question. There must be regions, there are regions, and it is possible to describe some regions which combine a larger number of desirable qualities than others. The further basis upon which the present sixfold regional division has been made will appear from the characterization of each region in the unfolding picture of the nation and from an examination of typical steps in the process of delineation. Yet it is necessary here to indicate the types of indices which have been used. In general, the criteria are of three sorts. The first is found in the arbitrary standards prescribed for the region as already described and in the irreducible specifications that the *number of regions must not be too large for practical purposes and the regions themselves must be large enough* to comprehend the largest number of values specified for applying both to the present and to future trends, and for comprehending realistic subregions and districts. The second of the general criteria is found in the measures of physiographic homogeneities, historical development, folk culture and institutions, the origin and character of its people, and of special features commonly accepted as characteristic. The third type of criteria consists in statistical indices of a socio-economic nature compiled from an inventory of physical, technological, economic, and social facts.

The historical basis of regionalism has been presented in Chapters I and II, while in Chapter VII there were presented representative literary and historical characterizations of the people and their culture in the several regions. So, too, in each region there will be cited adequate evidence of the historical and cultural data. Manifestly, the first historical divisions were in the way of "naturals" in the sense that there was a North and a South and then subsequently a West.

[11] Adapted from Howard W. Odum, *Southern Regions of the United States*, pp. 269, 271.

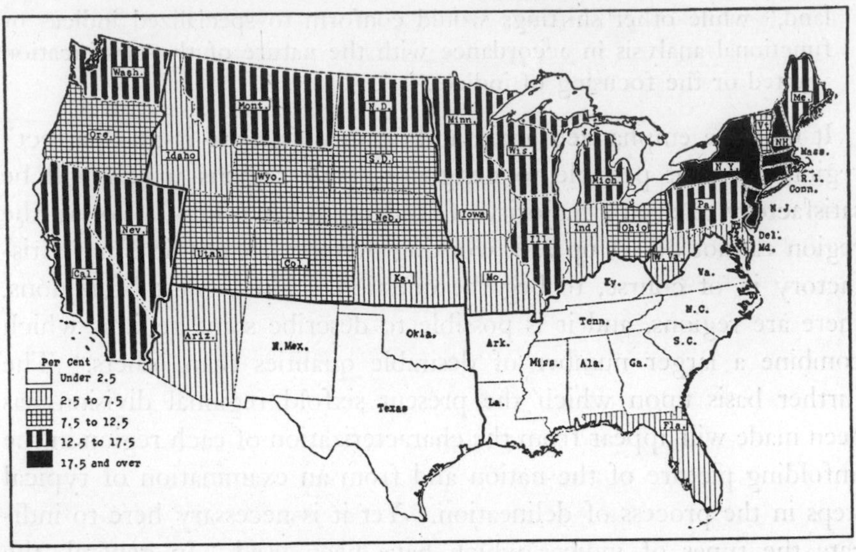

Above: Percent of Foreign-born Population in the Total Population of the United States.

Below: Distribution of the Negro Population in 1930 and Cities Outside the South with More than 50,000 Negro Population.

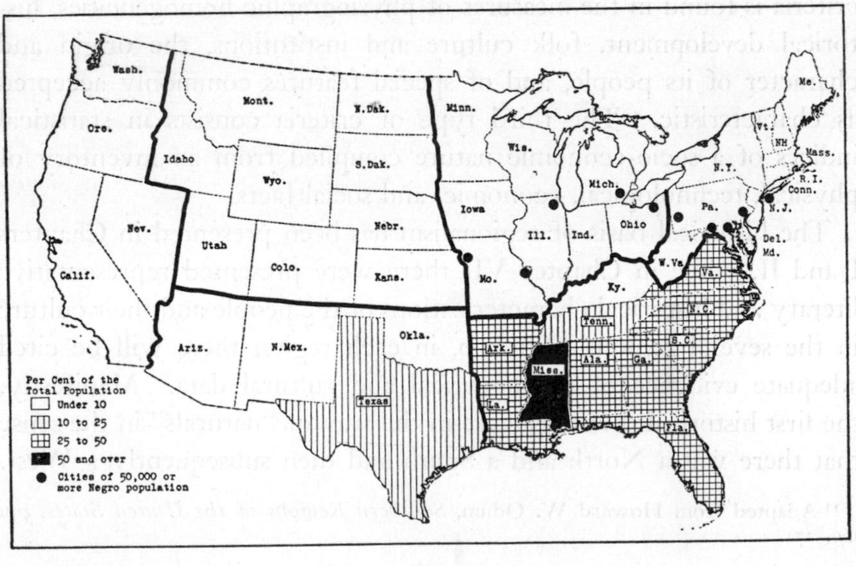

This later became an East and a West over against a South. The historians agree on this, each describing the development and process in his own way. Thus, Charles A. Beard features the three great sections characterized by the capitalists in the East, the landed aristocracy in the South, and the farmers in the West. The basis for the dividing of each of these into two current major regions will easily be found in the gradual unfolding of the nation into more and more wests until the West became a Southwest, a Northwest, and a Far West, leaving the earlier wests far back in the Southeast and the Middle States. Two Norths, two Souths, two Wests, are symbolic of the changing nation and of the need for adequate reclassification.

That this threefold terminology is still very much in use may be seen from two recent examples. No less important a report than that of the Report of the President's Committee on Farm Tenancy in 1937 let creep into its tabular classification, among one of several different regional divisions for the same purpose of study, Table I which divided the nation into three divisions. The *Northern States* included 21 states going so far west as to include the Dakotas and Nebraska and Kansas. The *Southern States* comprehended 17 states, including Delaware, Washington, D. C., West Virginia, Texas and Oklahoma. The *Western States* reserved only eleven states including the southwestern states of New Mexico and Arizona.[12] So, too, Walter Prescott Webb, he of the *Great Plains*, insists that the nation is a threefold compound of North, South, and West. Thus he writes in his 1937 *Divided We Stand*, "Aside from class distinctions, divergent views on social and political questions, and other minor differences, there are certain definite 'fault lines,' as the geologist would say, which divide the nation into distinct economic and social sections. These dividing lines so nearly follow the country's social, economic, and political history and its climatic and topographic lines that, when viewed from the future, I believe it will be clear that there have been developed in this country three fairly distinct cultures–ways of life. Each of these can with reasonable accuracy be marked off geographically and adequately described. For the purposes of this study it will be convenient to call these divisions of the country 'sections' or 'regions'; and, at times, to think of them as three distinct nations, or at least as a 'confederation' of three geographical and cultural units held together by a central government, a common language that can be fairly well understood throughout, and by highly developed systems of transportation and

[12] *Farm Tenancy*, Report of the President's Committee, 1937, p. 89.

communication. But despite these bonds, each section has its own mores, ways of life, and culture complexes, which have thus far refused to be obliterated. These sections are designated as the North, the South, and the West. Each will be shown to have a history of its own, a distinct way of life determined by the character both of its inhabitants and of its physical environment, and a fundamental economic structure, which the political, economic, and financial expansion of this country has tended to accentuate."[13]

Webb's "North" includes, with the exception of West Virginia, the exact states which constitute the Northeast and the Middle States of this volume, his dividing line between the North and the West sloping with the Dakotas, Nebraska, and Kansas. That is, that which was originally the great Middle West and that area which appears to be the most American of all the regions is characterized as the same North as New England and New York. This is manifestly an area too large and too wide and divergent in its historical, cultural, physiographic and economic character for either scientific analysis or for social planning. This point may be made clear at the same time that the general criteria of delineation of the region may be illustrated if we look at the great "North" in terms of our twofold division of Northeast and Middle States.

Thus for the Northeast here are dependable general criteria for distinguishing it from the Middle States but also for pointing up its realistic homogeneities. First of all the traditional bitterness between "the East" and "the West" was that of New England against those crude frontiersmen of "the West," which of course was Ohio, Illinois, Indiana, Minnesota, Michigan, Wisconsin, and the others. This was *the East* against *the West* and was therefore the essence of Americanism of that day. In the next place "the East" and "the South" were historically separated from the Middle States in terms of the chronology of the 13 colonies. They belonged to a different historical level. In the third place, the Northeast coincides with the "Greater New England" of Frederick Jackson Turner, the greatest of the historical sectional classificationists.

Another illustration is found in the regional classification of Secre-

[13] Walter Prescott Webb, *Divided We Stand,* pp. 3-4. (Quoted by permission of Farrar & Rinehart, Inc.)

tary Wallace, himself a lifelong product of the Middle States, in which when emergency demanded a regional conference on agriculture included exactly these northeastern states. It would scarcely occur to him to join the two regions together in agricultural homogeneity. Once again the Northeastern Region symbolizes the great metropolitan-industrial-philanthropical-financial and organizational America, *sui generis,* and boasts the *loci* of nearly all of those sixty families reported to "rule America." So, too, the Northeast is peculiarly susceptible to distinctive characterization in its educational institutions, in many of its industrial and economic factors, and in its availability for subregional classification in terms of New England States, river valley subregions, metropolitan New York and Philadelphia.

These are authentic general criteria which not only justify the separation from the Middle States but make such a major region absolutely necessary for research and administrative purposes. By the same token when we turn to the Middle States we are faced with many character traits as nearly opposite as possible—the first breaking away from the English culture, the essential frontier nature of men and institutions, an agrarian culture and the richest farming area in the nation, a great industrial center of small businesses and factories as well as large, a folk spirit and culture emphasis characterized by literary folk and historians as different from the East. These traits will, of course, appear in the subsequent chapters. Suffice it to point out here that the distinctiveness of the Middle States appears to be such as to justify the assumption in this volume that of all the major regions the Middle States is the most "American." In making the distinctions between Southeast and Southwest, exclusive of the hundreds of socio-economic indices available and subsequently indicated, we may point up a similar historical-cultural parallel to the contrasts between "East" and "West," and likewise we shall be able to indicate differences in terms of borderline studies about which something will be said subsequently.

In the meantime, however, keeping in mind the "East" and "West" and "South" and especially the distinctions between the East and the Middle States, we may illustrate other general cultural criteria with a phase of the national picture which has been at times well-nigh universally neglected. This is the story of the ethnic groups and their contributions to the regions and nation, worthy of an Epic Hall of

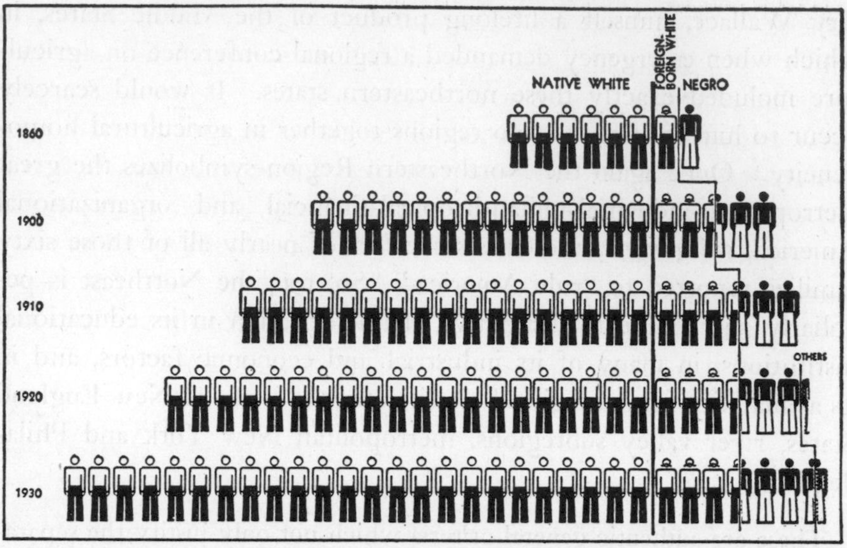

THE GROWTH AND DISTRIBUTION OF POPULATION NOW PROVIDES ONE OF THE CHIEF PROBLEM-INDICES OF THE NATION

Above: Native White, Foreign Born and Negro Increases from 1860 to 1930.

Below: Dark symbols show increase by migration and light symbols decrease, each symbol representing 300,000 population. From Educational Policies Commission's *Effect of Population Changes on American Education*, page 16.

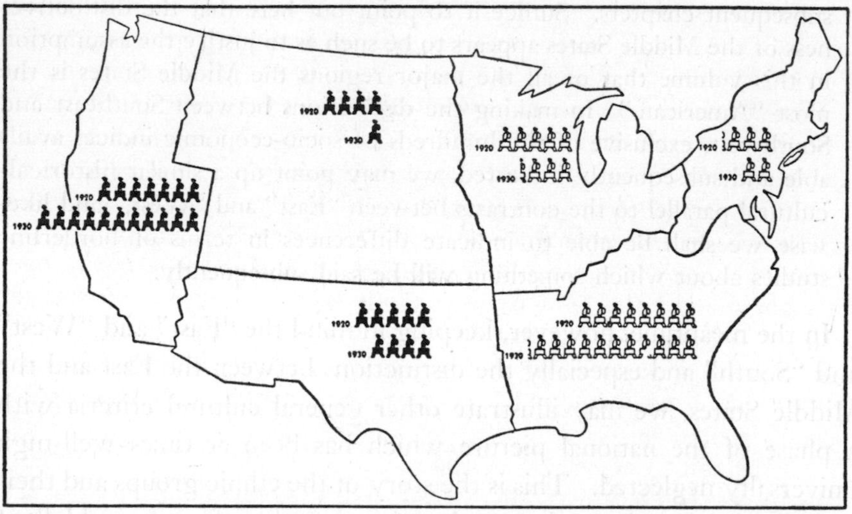

America. Here again this cultural index affords an excellent opportunity for delineating important subregions of the nation in which state lines are less important than clustering of peoples. Tested by these criteria the six regions qualify for both major regional homogeneities and for subregional specialization. It still remains true that the character of each of the regions has been greatly conditioned by the types of its earlier settlers and of its later migrants. Here is a picture which needs to be presented through the new population studies and through the regional analysis of problems and units of American democracy.

Since we have characterized the Middle States as the basic region around which to radiate our general portraiture, we may illustrate how the clustering of facts about the population gives us a regional homogeneity measure worthy of recording. Thus Avery Craven writes: "After early French and English days and up to 1860, three main streams of population entered this Middle West. From the upland South came the first settlers to occupy the Ohio River Valley, where the abundance of wood and water satisfied their requirements. Largely English, Scotch-Irish, and German in blood, but well mixed by years of moving and toiling in the Piedmont Region, they blended without discord with the steady flow which soon set in from the lower Middle States. Sallow, lean woodsmen they were as a rule, with homely vices and virtues and with more than their share of half-starved emotions—men who without show or complaint set about reproducing the life they had known in such varied places as tidewater Virginia, back Pennsylvania, and the upper Carolinas. In spite of substantial islands of New England and foreign settlement, they gave flavor to the entire region until the middle of the 1830's and brought it to a stage which men in upper Illinois of that day called 'finished.'

"The second stream of population, caught and held for a time in upper New York, swept along the lakes and into the northern hardwood and prairie sections in the decades after 1830. They were New England and New York born, carrying with them the economic and social patterns of those regions. They broke the prairie soils, added a bit more of professional service than was common to their neighbors, and soon began exploiting the northern forests as they had already done their own.

"The third element came from abroad. Englishmen and Germans had early entered the Ohio Valley, but in the '40's and after, a new flow set in from Germany, Ireland, and Canada to give a decidedly foreign tinge to portions of the Lake Prairie Region and to deepen the flavor in Cincinnati and eastern Missouri. By 1850 there were over 640,000 foreign-born in the North Central Region. Coming into a land where institutions, habits, and values were as yet unfixed, they found it much more a 'mixing bowl' than a 'melting pot,'—a place where divergent elements could adjust themselves by compromises into a comfortable civilization. The Irishman, toiling on canal or railroad at first, ultimately found a place in the rising towns or on farms along the transportation lines he had helped to build. The plain German took up the poorer lands, often in heavily wooded corners, or accepted the opportunities afforded in the towns to become butcher, baker, or candlestick maker." [14]

In these threefold criteria of physiography, population, and cultural history are thus seen abundant evidences for pointing up the homogeneities of the several regions. They must, of course, be liberally supplemented with socio-economic measures, but this should in no way minimize their importance. For here again it is the fundamental fact of the cultural product of people and their work playing upon the soil and its resources which gives us the only ultimate measure of the region. This is illustrated by James Truslow Adams' characterization of the merging of southern and northern peoples to make "the West" and by Avery Craven's historical-geographical build-up of the region of the Middle States.

James Truslow Adams sees in his *Epic of America* the growing cultural homogeneity which distinguished the region. Says he, "However different the northern and southern sections of the West might be growing from each other, the West as a whole was a unit as compared with North and South in the East. In twenty years two million people had shared the experience of pioneering. That in itself was a bond as strong as it was subtle. The Connecticut Yankee might talk with a nasal twang and the neighbor who had trekked over the mountains from the upland of Carolina might talk with a drawl, but between them was a common bond of great experience and of the acceptance of a mode of life. Debt, hardship, independence, a dozen things bound them together and made them brothers when contrasted with the northern merchant or southern planter 'back East.' And the Mississippi, 'the River,' 'Ol' Man River,' bound them again. Back East a

[14] Avery Craven, "The Advance of Civilization into the Middle West in the Period of Settlement," in Dixon Ryan Fox, *Sources of Culture in the Middle West*, pp. 44-46. (Quoted by permission of D. Appleton-Century Company, Inc.)

Yankee farmer never went visiting to a Georgia patch up on the mountain side, but up and down 'the River' people traveled and met and mingled." [15]

Professor Craven shows the historical homogeneity which grew up through the subregions. "In the Ohio Valley, embracing portions of Pennsylvania, Ohio, and Kentucky, as well as a long, narrow wedge running across southern Indiana and Illinois into Missouri, we have something of a unit which constituted the first Middle West. Beyond it and above it, ever a stage behind in development to 1860, lay a second region, embracing the remainder of the Old Northwest and parts of Iowa and Minnesota. Together they formed a giant section equal in area to the original thirteen states or to pre-war Germany and Austria-Hungary combined. Its geographic form was relatively simple, but varied enough to present three distinct zones. To the south, the lands along both sides of the Ohio River, covered with hardwoods and partly untouched by the later glaciers, formed something of a unit. To the north, the Great Lakes Basin, with its dense pine forests shading southward into hardwoods and oak clearings, constituted a second zone. Between them, and blending into each, the prairies widened and swept off to the west." [16]

One other reference to the people as indices of regional distinctiveness may be found in the study of the human wealth of the nation made by a special committee of the National Resources Committee, which follows the sixfold regional division of the nation in the present volume. To cite one approach this Committee has utilized the work of Carter Goodrich in his *Migration and Economic Opportunity*, and has pointed up a considerable number of gross differences in material of the several regions. These indices when charted and mapped do two things: They characterize the regions and they test the validity of the sixfold division into Northeast and Southeast, Northwest and Southwest, Middle States and Far West. Thus, the belt representing the highest plane of living if drawn on a map would extend from southern New England through New York south of the Great Lakes and up to the borders of Nebraska and Kansas of our Northwestern Region. That is, as will be pointed out, the high plane of living in the Middle States tends to approximate that of the Northeast and,

[15] James Truslow Adams, *The Epic of America*, pp. 153-154.

[16] Avery Craven, "The Advance of Civilization into the Middle West in the Period of Settlement," pp. 43-44 of Dixon Ryan Fox, *Sources of Culture in the Middle West*. (Quoted by permission of D. Appleton-Century Company, Inc.)

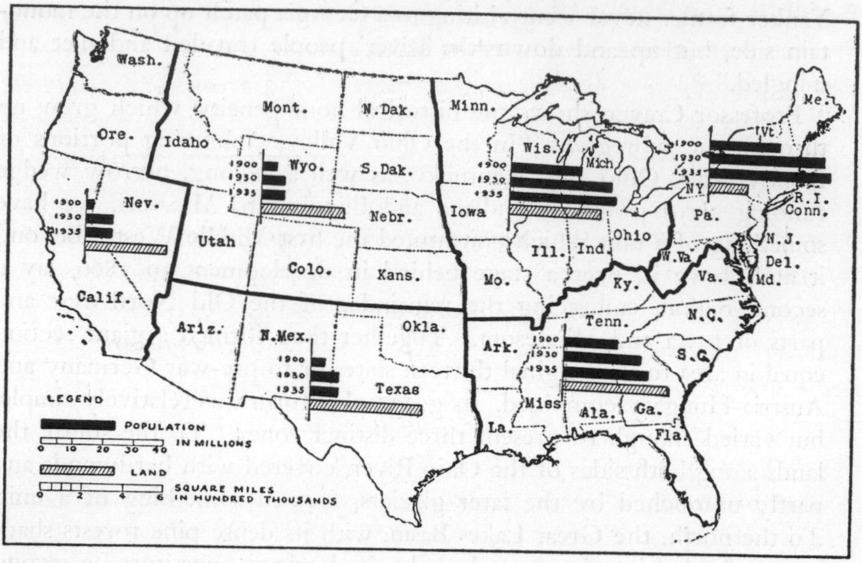

Above: Regional Distribution of Total Population in 1900, 1930, and 1935 in Relation to Total Land Area.

Below: Regional Proportion of the 1930 Population and the Proportion of the Annual Natural Increase, 1930-1934. Both from *National Population Problems*, Chapters II, page 4a and IV, page 3a.

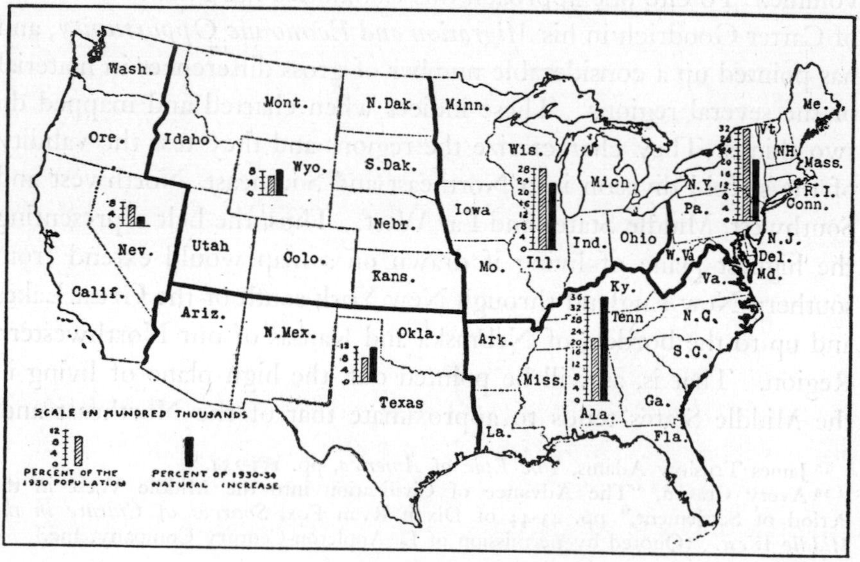

as will be shown later, of the Far West, as contrasted with the Southeast and parts of the Southwest in particular.

It is pointed out, however, that most of the areas of the highest plane of living are urban and industrial, or else they contain special technical concerns, such as universities, governmental agencies, and resources. That is, when we come to compare the Middle States with the Northeast, the Southeast, the Southwest and Northwest, for instance, we must keep in mind differences between the rural and urban culture, between agricultural and industrial, between the momentum and incidence of cumulative capital and concentrated population over against isolation and financial handicaps. In other words, the mere grouping together of facts and indices of differences does not give us an organic regional entity, but simply gives us a description, an inventory of what has happened and what *is* under the given forces, which, of course, must be duly analyzed. This is of the greatest importance in the study of the American regions, particularly with reference to trends, planning, and the development of resources together with distribution of people in relation to natural wealth. It is with such points of major consideration in mind that we divide the nation into relatively large areas, allowing thereby for the interpretation of historical and cultural forces and for flexibility and the selection of subregions for intensive study and for the projection of trends in the borderlands.

These general criteria are adequate to indicate the reliability of our classifications; yet the most commonly utilized criteria are those of socio-economic data. However, when we came to the next consideration of the more specific indices through which the sixfold regional grouping has been presented as the most satisfactory division that now seems available for the largest number of purposes, in general, a twofold approach was necessary. The first was the grouping and clustering of socio-economic data so that the extent and nature of homogeneity would appear by states or by districts, counties and subregional divisions when the pattern is so clear that regional delineation is relatively simple. The second approach was through special exploration of regional borderlands or border lines with a view again to allying each borderland with that region with which it is most harmonious and with a view to permitting of flexibility of several regional borders susceptible of indicating trends. In both of these approaches the fact must be re-emphasized that they are approximations, but approximations that utilize the largest number of data yet available and provide actual premises which give usable units and can be tried out successfully.

The indices utilized were more numerous than those of Carter Goodrich in his studies of migration and planes of living. Yet his regions with a bare half dozen indices approximate in many instances the sixfold division of the present work which leads one to agree with Woofter that after 29 or 30 indices have been found to give clusterings of homogeneities, one need go no farther. However, in view of the composite nature of the desired regions and of the claims made for those regions as well as for eliminating error so far as possible, the Southern Regional Study explored a much larger number for possible intensive methodological study and for actual use in these preliminary classifications. These included the following major groupings: land and farms, production and distribution of commodities, finances and taxation, income and wealth, industry and labor, potential and developed water power, natural resources, population traits and distribution, education and cultural factors, political and governmental data. From these it was possible to find as many as 700 detailed indices from which to chart the major regions and subregions. The limitations of such indices were emphasized. In the first place, "Special limitations of such comparative indices are apparent. In the first place, comparisons in terms of census data and other measures are not always in terms of homogeneous figures, in the sense that data gathered by southern enumerators may not be gathered under the same conditions as in some other regions; in the sense that regional estimates of values are often conditioned by other cultural factors and are stated in terms of averages based on unequal quantities and distribution; that various contributing factors to standards, income, wealth, and general culture are often not included; and that many of the cultural factors, such as personality, folkways, motivation, handicaps, are not measurable in terms of our present objective methods. Yet, in spite of these limitations, the picture of the region for the purposes in hand, due to the large number of varying indices susceptible to checking and cross checking, is relatively authentic and complete." [17]

To the criticism of the statistician, that the indices are not sufficiently defined or scientifically correlated, there are several adequate replies. One is that no statistician or other social scientist has been found who was willing or able to present any complete and satisfying methodology. A second is that this book is not a work on statistics as methodology. A third is that beyond the peradventure of a doubt we do have abundant indices, and more, to set the frame of classification of the regions which we have delineated and the subregions which we have assumed. Furthermore, the validity of an arrangement is measured in terms of what it is intended to do or be, and in the present case the sixfold regional division meets the test of its stated objectives.

The general method and procedure of delineating the several regions may appear more clearly if we recall that the sixfold division comprehends two subdivisions of each of the older historical areas. That is, there are two Souths, the Southeast and the Southwest; there are two Norths, the Northeast and the Middle States; and there are two Wests, namely, the Far West and the Northwest. The classification involves also especially the breaking down of two great traditional concepts, namely, "The Middle West" and "The South." The approach by which each of these older Norths, Souths, and Wests were subdivided will give the general basis for the final sixfold division.

Since the first steps were taken in the attempt to redefine the South we begin by indicating something of the method described in *Southern Regions of the United States* by which the Southwest was differentiated from the Southeast and the Southeast then redefined to exclude Maryland and Missouri. Our first task was manifestly "to appraise the traditional 'South' as a premise for such analysis. This broad grouping generally comprised seventeen or eighteen states, including from the Northeast, Maryland, West Virginia, the District of Columbia, and sometimes Delaware; from the Middle States, Missouri; and in the Southwest, Oklahoma and Texas. The first task in the examination of this older and larger regional hypothesis was to seek measures of

[17] Howard W. Odum, *Southern Regions of the United States*, p. 4.

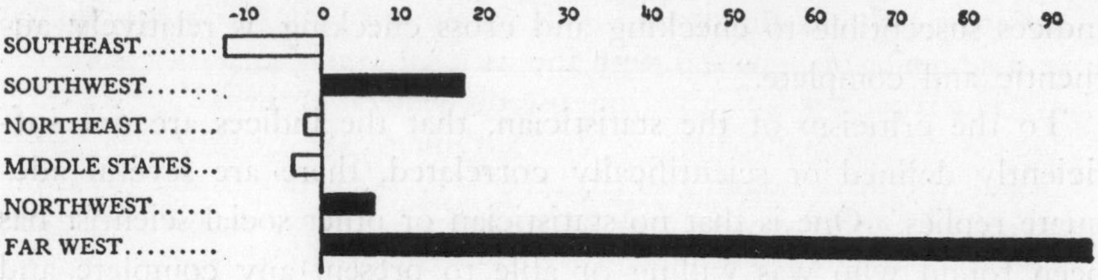

NET GAIN OR LOSS BY INTERREGIONAL MIGRATION, 1930

SOUTHEAST...............	— 3,412,150
SOUTHWEST...............	+ 1,281,007
NORTHEAST...............	— 632,452
MIDDLE STATES............	— 1,072,376
NORTHWEST...............	+ 394,542
FAR WEST.................	+ 3,263,866

Percentage Which Net Gain or Loss by Interregional Migration Forms of Population in Region, 1930. Adapted from T. J. Woofter, Jr.

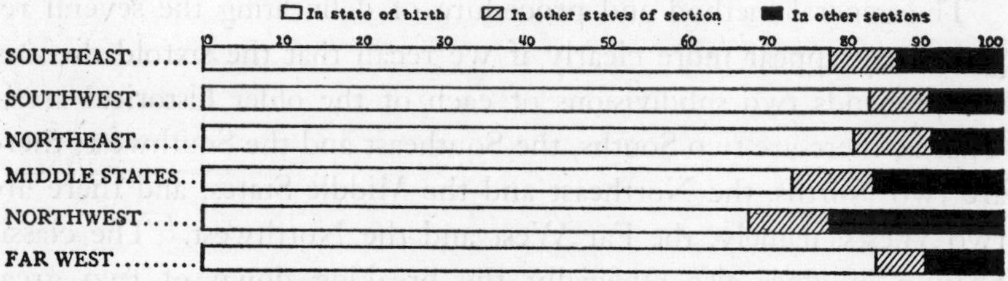

Population Born in Each Region by Place of Residence, 1920

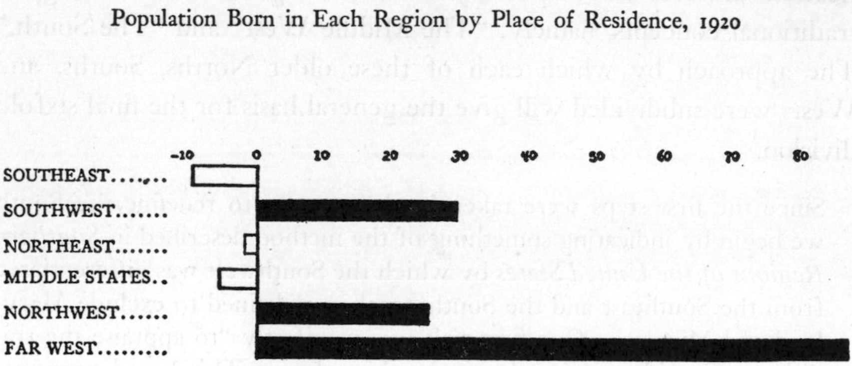

NET GAIN OR LOSS BY INTERREGIONAL MIGRATION, 1920

SOUTHEAST...............	— 2,378,639
SOUTHWEST...............	+ 1,502,362
NORTHEAST...............	— 1,036,253
MIDDLE STATES............	— 1,514,788
NORTHWEST...............	+ 1,200,911
FAR WEST.................	+ 2,060,142

Percentage Which Net Gain or Loss by Interregional Migration Forms of Number Born in Each Region, 1920

homogeneity and differentials when compared with the 'border' states and adjoining regions and with the national averages.

"The second task was to appraise the general historical and cultural factors which might apply to such groupings and to gauge the practicability of encompassing so large a part of the nation in any workable techniques either of study or of planning. Tested by both of these criteria it was clear that so large and traditional a 'South' was no longer a reality either in the spirit or the measure of the regions. First of all, Maryland qualified as 'South' in a very small number in a field of more than 500 indices. By way of illustration, to attempt to characterize or plan for Maryland as a region of farm tenancy or of Negro-white population or of illiteracy or of agrarian culture or of children per 1,000 women or of wealth and income or bank resources and savings or value of land and buildings or land use and industrial indices, and a hundred other socio-economic factors, basic to needs and planning, was at once to invalidate the scientific validity of regional analysis. On the other hand, to add Maryland's aggregate to the Southeast in the effort to bolster up its claims and ratings would defeat the object of seeking workable differentials upon which to reach accurate diagnosis. Having rejected Maryland as a southern state, Delaware, being beyond and to the northeast, was no longer considered hypothetically within the South. The District of Columbia obviously belongs to no region. Missouri, following much the same process, showed only a score more indices of homogeneity with the South than Maryland. By the same token, it was overwhelmingly not 'southern,' except in certain parts of the state and in certain historical, legislative, and institutional affiliations, all of which, however, no longer appear valid as definitive characterizations. When we come to consider West Virginia the task is more difficult. Manifestly it is not southern except in the prevailing quality of its economic per capita indices and a few others relating to people. And it could qualify also for either the Northeast or the Middle States.

"Turning next to the western border states, Texas and Oklahoma qualify as 'southern' in less than a third of the indices selected. As measured, therefore, both by a predominance of the selected indices and by general geographical, industrial, and cultural conditions, these states do not belong in the 'South' of the Southeastern States. Having characterized Texas and Oklahoma as belonging to the Southwestern States, there remained the problem of classifying Louisiana and Arkansas, both west of the Mississippi, and often characterized as Southwest. Tested by the criteria, on the one hand, of the Southeast and, on the other, of Texas and Oklahoma, they qualify overwhelmingly with the Southeast and are differentiated from the emerging greater Southwest

> in a plurality of indices. In addition to this, they fall within the geographic bounds of practical homogeneity of culture and function. Thus the Southeastern Region of eleven states conforms to a dominance of characteristics which indicate a quite satisfactory general southern homogeneity."[18]

The fixing of the border where the South ended on its western boundaries was to fix the border of the Southwest, and on its northern border, of the Northeast. In the case of the Northeast, we have already pointed out the historical cultural differentiation between that region and what was the Middle West. The problem most debated was whether to make of the traditional New England a separate major region and if not where should the line between these and the Middle States be drawn. In this case relatively arbitrary criteria seemed more satisfactory than the detailed economic indices, although the case can be made almost equally with such indices. The final result was to combine three or four criteria, such as prevailing economic indices of wealth, industry, labor and the like, to take into consideration the historical boundaries of the regional colonies, to respect the traditional concept of "the East," to accept the Turner grouping of greater New England, and certain other similar classifications which approximate the greatest homogeneity. Finally the major natural regions which Newbigin in her *New Regional Geography of the World* calls "The New England" and "The Middle Appalachian States with a continuation along the highland," will coincide almost entirely with this region. On these bases the line between Pennsylvania and Ohio was manifestly logical and West Virginia ranks better with Pennsylvania than with Ohio or the Middle States. The special exercises in the study of borderlands apparently support this demarcation.

The subdivision of the "West" into two major regions was of course a more difficult task. First of all there was the old Middle West, now no longer "West," to be disposed of before the new western regions could be designated. Here again, if we use state lines as boundaries, "North Dakota, South Dakota, Kansas, and Nebraska rank with the Northwest of the present regional classification, rather than with the Middle States, as indicated by a hundred or more in-

[18] Odum, *op. cit.*, pp. 7, 9.

dices. . . . In fifty or more these states might as well rank with the Middle States; Minnesota, Iowa, and Missouri might lean toward the further western group.

"If state lines are omitted, then the regional division will be easily defined. Thus, the eastern portion of the Dakotas and Kansas and Nebraska is clearly homogeneous with the Middle States in soil regions, forestry belt, precipitation, land use, agricultural provinces, types of farming regions, natural vegetation, quality of land, submarginal land, as classified by the National Resources Board. Here also county medians indicate other indices which would give similar results." [19]

The importance of flexible subregions is indicated in the further study of these borderlands between the regions. There are, also, certain states which it is not possible to classify exclusively with any region according to present status and indices. West Virginia has been mentioned. Arizona and New Mexico are others and perhaps Nevada. This, however, but accentuates the need for continuing efforts to so classify and for a definite policy of setting up subregions for exploratory purposes. A good statement of this problem is that of Dr. Willis H. Miller,[20] namely, that it is not possible to agree upon group-of-states regions which will satisfy all ultimate purposes. His reference to certain of the states illustrates this point as well as that of the needed borderland study and flexible subregions. He points out that "Missouri, Illinois, and Indiana might be grouped with their northern neighbors to form a North Central Region. This would result from considering the characteristics of the northern portions of these three states. But if attention be focused upon the characteristics of the southern parts of Missouri, Illinois, and Indiana, one can make just as valid a claim for grouping these states with their neighbors on the south. There is no known or possible grouping of states which would provide for Texas, which lies partly on the Great Plains and partly in the Cotton Belt, and both western and southern in its characteristics. The same may be said regarding Missouri, of which part is southern and part is midwestern; part is forest and part

[19] *Ibid.*, p. 272.

[20] Quoted in *Regional Factors in National Planning and Development*, December 1935, p. 163.

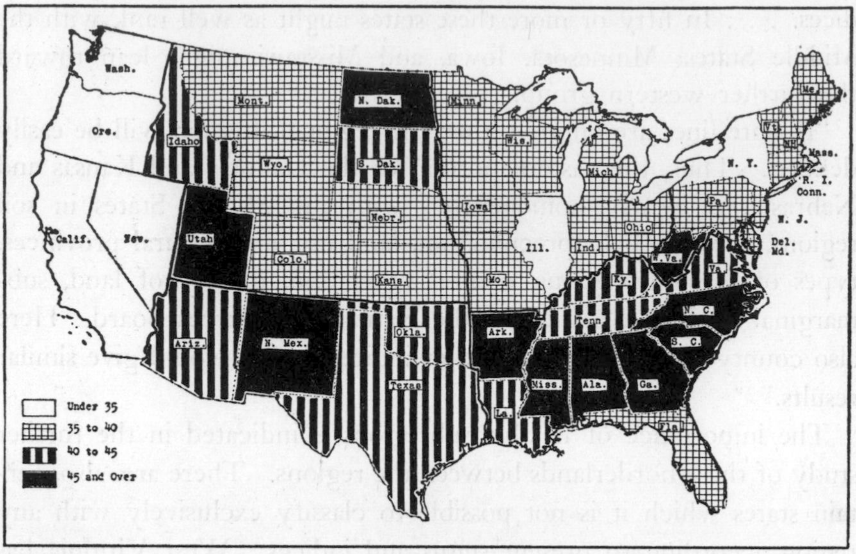

PERCENTAGE DISTRIBUTION OF TOTAL POPULATION, 1930

STATE AND REGION	Under 20	20 to 55	55 and Over
Southeast			
Virginia	44.4	44.6	11.0
North Carolina	49.3	42.2	8.5
South Carolina	50.6	41.5	7.9
Georgia	46.3	44.6	9.1
Florida	39.2	49.6	11.2
Kentucky	43.9	44.0	12.1
Tennessee	43.8	45.6	10.6
Alabama	47.0	44.3	8.7
Mississippi	46.6	44.4	9.0
Arkansas	45.8	44.6	9.6
Louisiana	44.0	47.2	8.8
Southwest			
Oklahoma	44.2	45.8	10.0
Texas	42.6	48.0	9.4
New Mexico	46.8	43.6	9.6
Arizona	42.1	48.9	9.0
Northeast			
Maine	37.3	44.9	17.8
New Hampshire	35.2	46.2	18.6
Vermont	37.0	45.2	17.8
Massachusetts	35.1	50.0	14.9
Rhode Island	37.0	49.1	13.9
Connecticut	37.0	49.5	13.5
New York	33.6	53.8	12.6
New Jersey	36.1	50.9	13.0
Delaware	35.9	49.3	14.8
Pennsylvania	39.4	48.2	12.4
Maryland	37.2	49.7	13.1
West Virginia	46.1	44.3	9.6
Middle States			
Ohio	36.1	50.1	13.8
Indiana	36.5	48.1	15.4
Illinois	34.9	52.4	12.7
Michigan	37.7	50.5	11.6
Wisconsin	38.0	48.0	14.0
Minnesota	38.3	48.1	13.6
Iowa	37.2	47.1	10.7
Missouri	35.7	49.5	14.8
Northwest			
North Dakota	45.4	44.3	10.3
South Dakota	42.5	47.9	1.6
Nebraska	39.3	47.7	13.0
Kansas	38.1	47.3	14.6
Montana	39.0	48.8	12.0
Idaho	42.8	45.5	11.7
Wyoming	39.2	51.2	9.6
Colorado	38.0	49.5	12.5
Utah	46.1	44.1	9.8
Far West			
Nevada	31.8	54.9	13.3
Washington	33.7	51.5	14.8
Oregon	33.1	51.3	15.6
California	30.4	54.8	14.8

PER CENT OF POPULATION UNDER 20 YEARS OF AGE, 1930

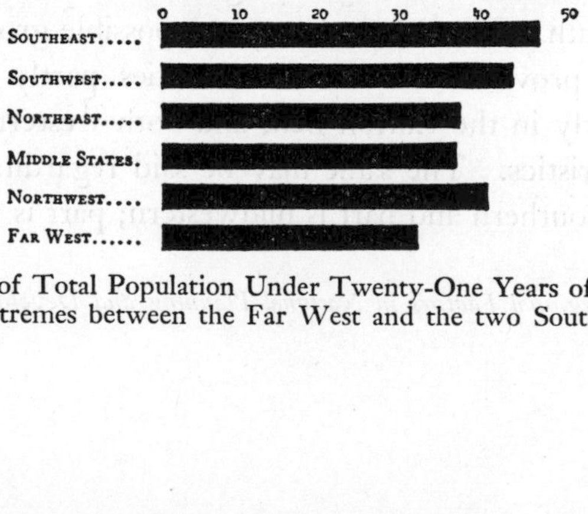

Map: Percentage of Total Population Under Twenty-One Years of Age, 1930. Note extremes between the Far West and the two Souths.

is prairie; part is plain and part is Ozark; part is Corn Belt, and part is general farming."[21]

Further criteria of the several regional classifications will appear in the characterization of the regions themselves and in particular the Far Western Region which joins California with Oregon and Washington on the primary basis of the Pacific West and of climatic and other physiographic coast character. Nevada groups with the Far West, in addition to its high indices of per capita status, in that it comprehends most of Russell Smith's Great Basin as the gateway out and into California and because of its urban character and folkways and of dominating Reno, again, a gateway.

It is, however, important now, before turning to the regions themselves, to indicate further the extent to which these borderlands of regional boundaries or no-man's lands exist and to note something further about possible methods of studying them as subregions cutting across state lines and affording always opportunity for supplementing and qualifying the data of the several regions. The maps in Chapter IV give a very general idea of marginal lines between regions. Yet in most cases large portions of the states must be studied with a view to correcting the alignment. We have already referred to the states between the Southeast and Southwest and between the Middle States and the Northwest. Another series is found in the marginal points between the Southeast and the Middle States as also parts of Virginia from the South and Ohio from the Middle States tending to the Northeast. W. G. Piersel, experimenting with one of these borderlands, selected southern Illinois. He thinks the chief influences that determine the border lines are "(1) contiguity, (2) population movements, (3) physiographic features, (4) natural resources, and (5) indeterminateness of culture domination. Accordingly, there are five index groups which will aid in classifying our data. These can be called the physical, production, ethnic, industrial, and cultural. The influences and index groups do not exactly correspond, because we have not, as yet, reached the stage of being able to measure accurately all influences. Our measures are sometimes concerned with more than one group. This overlapping is inescapable, and must be endured.

"Two criteria for selecting indices are acceptable: dependability and differentiation. Dependability includes not only accuracy, sheer correctness of figures, validity and reliability of data, proper sampling, but also the proper labeling. Differentiation is a prime requisite of indices, since if they do not show differences, there is no reason to use more than one index in the group."

[21] Quoted from Howard W. Odum, *Southern Regions of the United States*, p. 274.

As an exercise in testing border lines Piersel "used the following indices, which were found to be selective and available, in attempting to ascertain the borderland area in southern Illinois. Following this sixfold regional division of the country one finds that the division between the Middle States and the Southeastern States is the Ohio River, from southeastern Ohio to the river's confluence with the Mississippi at Cairo, Illinois. The borderland will extend some distance on each side of the line. An arbitrary line was drawn across the state, beginning north of Adams County (Quincy) and extending eastward so that the area to the south included Sangamon and Macon Counties (Springfield and Decatur), but excluding Champaign and Vermilion Counties (Champaign-Urbana and Danville). The physical group comprises physiographic, meteorological, land, and fauna and flora data. The land and water area, land elevation and contour, concern us. Many climatic indices, such as precipitation in both rain and snow, winds, sunshine, and length of the growing season, give clearly differentiated sections. All of these taken together cut across the state just north of the seven southernmost counties, never more than twenty miles apart. Land study includes the types, prairie, hilly, woodland, swamp, and the characteristics of soils and man-made alterations. The hilly land, an extension of the Ozark Ridge, pasture and forest, and serious erosion land, is practically of the same extent. . . . A line along the southern edge of Sangamon County (Springfield) shows approximately the division of Illinois farms into two groups on the bases of value of farm land and buildings, size of farms, gross income per farm, corn acreage, and oats acreage; the northern part in every case being considerably higher than the southern. On the basis of a triple division of the state into northern, central, and southern districts, the products found in the north and central are not found in the south, and vice versa." Other indices were from trends, ethnic factors, industrial data, social and cultural conditions, such as education, schools. On the basis of these indices "one is able to draw a line of demarcation between the borderland and the North Central Region. This line starts north of Gallatin, sweeps over White and Hamilton, curves down and forks on Saline, unites north of Johnson, swings northwest across Jackson, and comes to the river about half way up Randolph. The reason for the forking at Saline is that half of the indices include it and the other half do not. Thus is drawn the limit of the borderland in southern Illinois." [22]

[22] W. G. Piersel, Notes on the Study of Regional Borderlands, unpublished manuscript.

In the chapters which follow the six major regions are presented in a general outline framework only. The chapters are not intended as treatises on the several regions, which, of course, would require many volumes. The American Guide Series, under the auspices of the Federal Writers' Project, in its effort to present to the American people a portrait of America, has already published more than one hundred books, and another hundred are scheduled for publication in the near future. Here are thousands of pages which still fall short of an adequate picture; 1,500 pages for Washington and its capital, 2,000 for New York, 700 for Massachusetts, reduced from 2,000 pages with such conflict and tension over the elimination of desired features as to endanger the whole project. It must be clear that in every state and region are scores and scores of vivid pictures, rich sources, valuable materials, all ready for the gathering and interpreting.

One interpretation of this sixfold general outline of the major regions is, of course, a challenge to the further study and picturization of them all. Since certain experiments in this regional methodology have been undertaken in the South, the framework of such study as projected there may be given as an illustration of a type that might well be applied to the other five regions.

"1. The First Objective of the Southern Regional Study is to present an adequate picture, partial but representative, of the southern regions of the United States in fair perspective to time-quality, to geographic factors, and to the cultural equipment and behavior of the people.

"2. It is desired further to present this picture in such ways as to indicate the place of these regions in the nation and to explain something of the dramatic struggle of a large and powerful segment of the American people for mastery over an environment capable of producing a superior civilization, yet so conditioned by complexity of culture and cumulative handicaps as to make the nature of future development problematical.

"3. Over and above any conventional social inventory, it is important to point toward greater realization of the inherent capacities of the southern regions; and to indicate ways and means of bridging the chasm between the superabundance of physical and human resources as potentialities and the actualities of technical deficiencies in their development and waste in their use.

"4. It is equally important to point toward a continuously more ef-

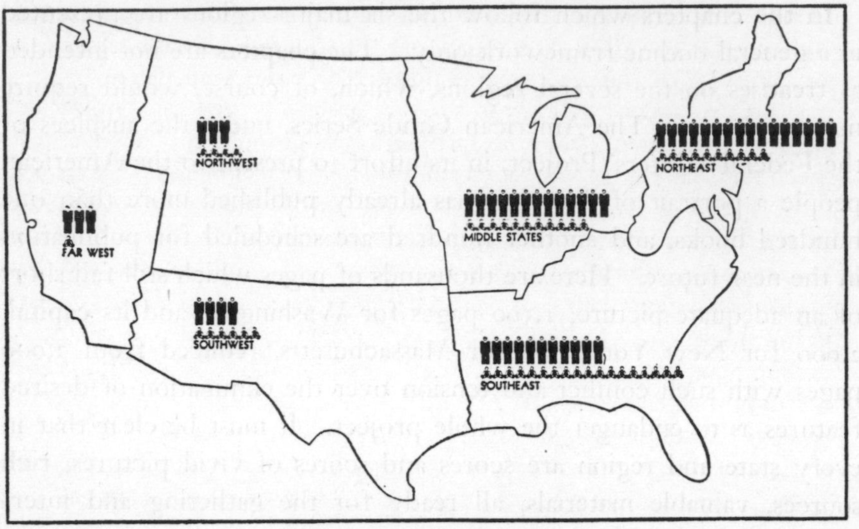

Above: Proportion of Total Population in Each Region, top, and Total Natural Increase, Children, bottom, 1936.

Below: Percent of Nation's Children, top, and Percent of Nation's Income, bottom, 1935-1936. Educational Policies Commission, *The Effect of Population Changes on American Education*, pages 10, 29.

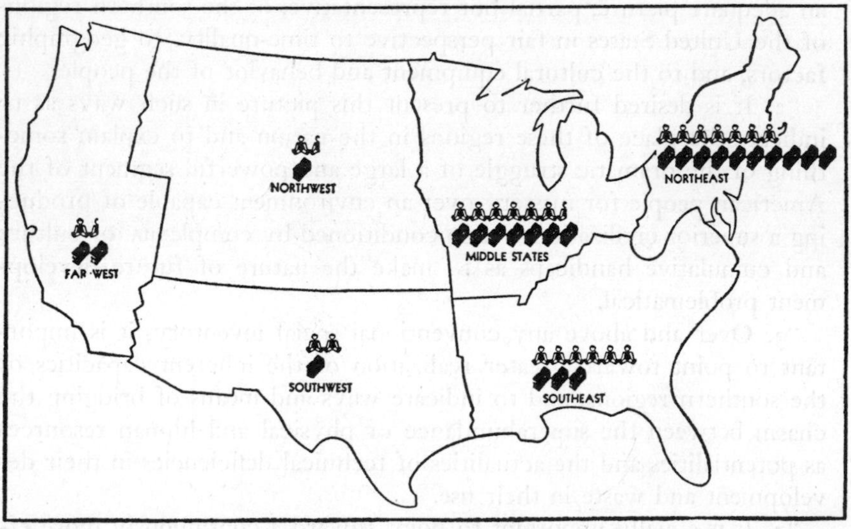

fective reintegration of the southern regions into the national picture and thereby toward a larger regional contribution to national culture and unity. To this end, it is important to make available and to reinterpret to special groups and to the public in general, within and without the regions, and in as many ways as possible, the facts basic to the understanding of the situation and to the planning of next steps.

"5. Partly as purpose and method and partly due to the recognition of the extraordinary difficulty and importance of these tasks, it was desired to project the study upon a theoretical framework which would insure measurable reality in research and attainability in whatever programs might emerge. Such reality was, of course, manifold. It would comprehend not only measurement, but perspective and interpretation; not only the general picture of aggregates and averages, but the specific facts of distribution and such detailed analysis as would focus upon critical problems toward which continued research might be directed.

"6. Basic to such a framework was a clear recognition of the historical and theoretical significance of the region and of the power of the folk-regional society in modern culture, as well as the very practical problem in the United States of what divisions of the nation might meet the largest number of requirements for general regional analysis and planning and what other special regions and subregions might be effective for more specific purposes.

"7. More specifically, such a theoretical framework must give reality to the southern picture. This reality, again, is of many kinds. A part is the facing of absolute facts rather than substituting rationalizations which grow out of irrelevant comparisons or defense explanations of how things have come to be as they are. Yet another form of reality must be found in the measurement of conditions in terms of comparison with certain selected standards and with regional and national variations. Yet, still again, a part of the reality must be found in the clear recognition that mere comparisons with national averages or aggregates are valid only within the bounds of their particular limitations and definitions, the problem and methodology of evaluating such comparisons and differentials being a part of the task. Furthermore, the greatest measure of reality can be found in the balanced picture of basic facts rather than in, and largely exclusive of, vivid extremes.

"8. Again, such a theoretical framework must be practically comprehensive enough to insure a fair picture of the major resources and forces which have determined and will determine the capacity of the southern regions. In terms of 'wealth,' they are natural wealth, technological wealth, artificial wealth, human wealth, and institutional wealth. In terms of a larger twofold measure, there would be, first, an inventory of natural resources together with the visible ends of technological mastery in human use aspects and in the resulting artificial wealth of the regions; and, second, an appraisal of human resources together with the visualized ends of social achievement in the development of a richer culture and social well-being.

"9. One of the special premises of the study is reflected in the past constricting power of sectionalism in contrast to the current motivation of substituting the new regionalism for the old sectionalism in American life. Since sectional conditioning appears more marked in the Southeast than elsewhere, the study was, therefore, projected to feature the regional-national as opposed to the local-sectional emphasis. Such a regional premise manifestly would avoid any hypotheses of a self-contained or self-sufficing South and would stimulate a greater degree of federal interest and participation on the part of the South.

"10. It was understood that many of the dominant forces of the regions, such as tradition, opinion, conflict, arrangements of local stateways and folkways, which constitute a part of the picture, are not measurable in terms of units that can be counted. On this assumption a part of the reality of the picture is inherent in the need and capacity for such authentic interpretation of the South's background as will give 'the dignity of cultural history' to its chronological lag, its retarded frontier dominance, its agrarian culture, its youthful and immature population, its lusty vitality, its unevenness of life, and its marginal struggle for survival.

"11. The study sought, further, to explore the southern regions as a laboratory for regional research and for experimentation in social planning. Of special importance might be the regional testing field for adjustment between industry and agriculture as the basic economic goal of government, and for the more general objective of reintegrating agrarian culture in the national picture. Again, the study was projected as a regional approach to the new demography which in both method and content may contribute largely to the revitalized study of the people and their institutions. Such a study of contemporary civilization would recognize certain values inherent in logical differentials which abound in the regions. Manifestly, such a theoretical framework must assume a less provincial and a more objective, long-time view of the South than has commonly obtained, and a more generous patience with the realities of societal evolution on the part of all those who seek reform and reconstruction." [23]

In general, it is desired, in the impressionistic outline of the several regions, to recapitulate a number of concepts and principles which

[23] Howard W. Odum, *Southern Regions of the United States*, pp. 1-3.

have been set forth. That is, it is desired that the region be seen as a whole, but essentially also as a constituent part of the national unity. This regional whole represents a composite major region, combining the largest possible degree of homogeneity as measured by the largest possible number of indices for the largest possible number of purposes, and very specifically featuring major natural subregions, minor subregions, districts, and divisions adequate to analyze the whole through the pluralism of its parts. It is intended also that each region shall appear in relation to both its historical sectionalism and to the hazards of sectionalism which might come through any new organization for regional government which would give too large an area and too much power to any major division of the nation. So, also, the region is to be envisaged as much with a view to its present trends and emerging prospects, whenever possible, as of its historical and geographic incidence. Finally, the regions are presented with a view to the sympathetic understanding of historical and cultural backgrounds and enthusiastic appraisal of problems and planning for next periods of development.

Chapter XIX

THE MIDDLE STATES AND THEIR "MIDDLE WEST"

OF these "six Americas in search of a faith," the great region which we have called the Middle States may be characterized as the most American of them all. This is not to say that there will not be found in each of the other regions special character traits easily identified as extremely "American" but that this region combines a larger number than any other region and therefore approximates the first place in any picture of the nation to be envisaged through its major regions. By "America" we mean this particular geographic area—map of the United States—which is the nation. It is an actual physical part of the world, different from the rest of it, and sufficiently isolated boldly to try its own experiments. It is that separate reality characterized by these authentic, historical episodes and developments, which through the nurture of established institutions, in the framework of capitalistic democracy, has set the nation apart. Of realistic "Americanisms" there are two major sorts: one the earlier, authentic, historical, and the other the later, composite technological.

The basis for the characterization of the Middle States will appear with the gradual unfolding of our brief outlines for the appraisal of each of the several regions. Yet before proceeding to the consideration of the areal boundaries of our Middle States it may be well to indicate some of the region's many "American" traits which symbolize the drama and struggle of the American people. The very names which have characterized the region are eloquent of the frontier nation in the making, as distinctive from the earlier historical seaboard nation, the offshoot and expansion of European cultures. For here are symbol and reality of "West" and "The Great Northwest";

"Middle West" and "Middle America"; "Midlands" and "The Middle Border"; "Midwest" and "Midwestern Empire" and all that "West," the supreme symbol so bitterly attacked by "The East" in the earlier frontier reconstruction of the nation. Here, too, was the great valley of the Upper Mississippi Basin comprehending most of the area between the Missouri and the Ohio and typified by the Mississippi River, "The most eloquent symbol of space and unity in America." Here, again, are symbol and reality not only of Frederick Jackson Turner's frontier America, but of the living land and people, of the man himself, bred and born in and of it. Here were epitomized the two great motivations of the nation—migration and westward movement, where first Europeans became in reality Americans rather than Europeans transplanted. Here were symbol and reality of rivers and forests, of land and prairies, of plain people and democratic patterns, symbols of the American dream. In the quality and number of its people, the nature and number of its occupations, its small industries and great agriculture, in the best examples of balanced industry and agriculture, are typified the heart of America and the backbone of its national framework. And here are American manners and morals, folkways and customs, religion and politics. Finally, here too are emerging industrial and metropolitan regions challenging the East, set in the midst of a vast wealth of natural resources, with all that train of social and economic problems which follow so naturally in the wake of a complex of technology, industrialization, and urbanism built upon an agrarian nation. Here, then, are at once symbol and reality, test and promise of American regionalism in all its manifestations and implications.

We must proceed, however, more immediately now to the task of outlining briefly some of the prevailing characterizations of the great Middle States. This will be followed, as also in the chapters on other regions, with brief outlines of historical development, cultural traits, economic and social indices suggestive of further study, and special regional factors basic to realistic action. Manifestly, an outline must not be interpreted as a complete exposition of so great a theme, which, as must be self-evident, would require volumes for treatment.

In this major eight-states region described as the *Middle States* are included Minnesota, Michigan, Wisconsin, Ohio, Indiana, Illinois, Iowa, and Missouri. In terms of the United States Census classification the region comprehends all of the states of the East North Central Division together with Minnesota, Iowa, and Missouri of the West North Central Division. Its metropolitan regions, in addition to Chicago, include the St. Louis area, the Twin Cities area, together with the Detroit, Cleveland, Cincinnati, Indianapolis, and many lesser urban areas later catalogued. As a natural physiographic major region it coincides fairly well with the framework of what Marion I. Newbigin, in her *New Regional Geography of the World*, terms the "Central Lowlands," and describes as follows:

> "This region may be defined as extending westwards from the slope of the Cumberland-Alleghany Plateau till, round about longitude 100°, the climate becomes too arid for cultivation without irrigation, and the surface rises to the Great Plains, the beginning of which in the Dakotas is indicated by the scarp of the Missouri Plateau. Northwards the region extends to the international boundary, and if it is difficult in the South to draw a sharp line of demarcation from the Gulf Plains, the presence of the Ozark Mountains in southern Missouri and northern Arkansas affords at least a convenient landmark. This great area may be said to possess as its main feature the fact that it contains large tracts admirably fitted for temperate crops, but that upon its agriculture has been superimposed, especially in the Northeast, a certain amount of industry as a result of the mineral wealth. . . ."[1]

Within this major natural region are numerous subregions. Of these, important for the present purpose, are three groups, namely, those designated by J. Russell Smith in relation to "men and resources," the river valley regions, and the agricultural subregions. Of Professor Smith's 29 subregions the Middle States comprehend all of one and nearly all of three others. These are the *North Central Dairy Region*, the *Lake Region*, the *Corn Belt*, and the *Lower Valley of the Ohio*. Of the *River Valley Areas*, the region includes most of the *Great Lakes-St. Lawrence Group*, exclusive of Ontario and parts of Huron; the *Wabash* and parts of the *Lower Ohio;* nearly all of the *Upper Mississippi-Red River of the North.*[2]

The Middle States are especially adaptable to analysis in terms of agricultural regions, industrial and trade areas, and communities of

[1] Marion I. Newbigin, *A New Regional Geography of the World*, p. 330.

[2] National Resources Committee, *Drainage Basin Problems and Programs*, December 1936, *passim;* and also J. Russell Smith, *Men and Resources*, *passim.*

ethnic groups of people. Most of the state planning boards have made excellent subregional analyses of land, resources, people, and communication agencies. Of special significance are the reports of the Minnesota, Michigan, and Wisconsin planning boards showing the Great Lakes Region as the focus of a great mineral distribution throughout the northern and eastern part of the nation, and pointing up ways and means of developing natural resources. In addition to the major agricultural regions, there are within its borders approximately 138 sub-farming areas designated in the national map.[3]

The subregions of agricultural or farming areas so listed, exclusive of smaller subdivisions of the same areas, include the following: Northwest Minnesota, West central Minnesota, Southwest Minnesota, North central Iowa, Southern Iowa, Northern Missouri, Iowa, West central Missouri, Kansas, Ozark border, Southeast Kansas, Missouri, Western Missouri, Minnesota, East central Minnesota, Southeast Minnesota, Twin Cities, Central Wisconsin, Langlade, Wisconsin central sand plains, Eastern Wisconsin, Northeast Iowa, Vernon County, Dane County, Wisconsin-northeast Illinois, Milwaukee-Chicago metropolitan area, West Illinois-east Iowa, Northwest Illinois, East central Illinois-Indiana, Calhoun County, Morgan-Scott-Macoupin, Eastern Illinois, Southwest Illinois, Centralia, Southern Illinois, Southeast Missouri, Black and Cache Rivers bottoms and terraces, Northeast Michigan, Lake Michigan, West Michigan sandy area, Central Michigan, North central Michigan sandy area, Saginaw Valley, Thumb Area, Oakland Lapeer, Grand Rapids Ottawa, South central Michigan, Detroit, Southern Michigan, Southeast Michigan-North Ohio, Kankakee Basin, Northern Indiana, East central Indiana-Ohio, Central Indiana, Owen Clay, Southwestern Indiana, Ohio-Wabash-White Rivers bottoms, Southern Indiana, East south central Indiana, Southeast Indiana, East central Ohio, Tuscarawas-Carroll, Miami Valley, Fayette-Champaign, Columbia, Zanesville-Cambridge, Cincinnati, Southeastern Ohio, Parkersburg-Marietta-Athens.

The Middle States Region ranks second only to the Northeast in the number of its metropolitan areas, or districts, as designated by the United States Bureau of the Census. On the basis of McKenzie's thesis that population movements tend toward deep water centers, the Middle States will afford in the Great Lakes concentration a

[3] Types of Farming Areas in the United States, 1930. Division of Commerce, Bureau of the Census.

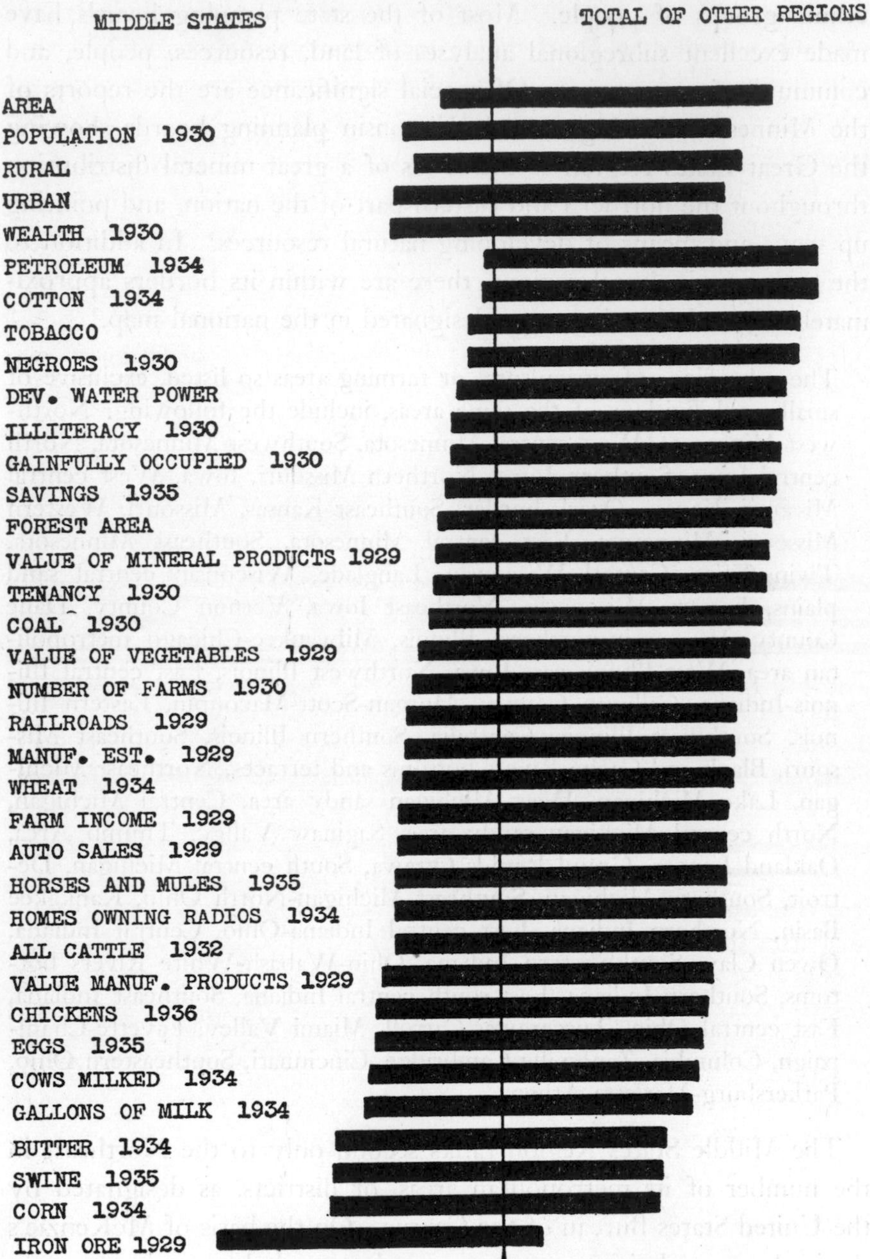

Regional Ratios to the National Total. Random Miscellaneous Indices: The Middle States

major area for the testing of such a hypothesis. The whole region contains no less than 23 of the 93 metropolitan districts, each with a population of 100,000 or over. These centers are in the order of size: Chicago, Detroit, Cleveland, St. Louis, Milwaukee, Minneapolis, Cincinnati, Kansas City (Missouri), Indianapolis, Toledo, Columbus, St. Paul, Akron, Dayton, Youngstown, Grand Rapids, Flint, Des Moines, Peoria, South Bend, Evansville, Duluth, Gary.[4]

W. F. Ogburn has made special studies of the character of cities and finds regional variations enough to note. Of the cities of the Middle States he says: "The traits of the middle western cities lie in the middle, between those of the South and those of the Northeast in many cases. Hence in only a few cases do they rank highest or lowest. In general the middle western cities are closer to those of the Northeast than to those of the South.

"The cities of the Middle West have higher wages than do cities of the Northeast and, of course, than of the South. Western cities, being new, may have developed a practice of higher wages. The middle western cities also have the largest number of home owners. The cities are more recent in origin and perhaps more rapidly growing, in which case home ownership is associated with the expected financial reward of the unearned increment from increasing land values. Not only are the wages highest, but more members of the family earn a money income than is the case in the other two regions. This employment, however, is not based on the employment of children, since the cities of the Middle West have the lowest amount of child labor. Correlated with the scarcity of child labor is the largest percentage of children in school. These middle western cities spend slightly more also on their libraries. In the occupations there are few marked distinctions. The percentage of the working population engaged in the clerical occupations and in the professions is high. So also is the percentage in industry. The proportion in architecture is high. There seems to be also a slightly larger proportion engaged as musicians, partly a function of the school system, though the tradition of music is quite strong in some of these cities, particularly where the German element is large."[5]

With reference to the people, the Middle States rank high in "American" quality, both in the earlier historical and in the later

[4] R. D. McKenzie, *The Metropolitan Community*, pp. 336-338.
[5] William F. Ogburn, *Social Characteristics of Cities*, pp. 30-31. (Quoted by permission of the International City Managers' Association.)

stages. With reference to the present population and its reproductive character, the Middle States approach the great American mode. There is an approximate balance between land in farms and farm population. The Region supplies a considerable proportion of the total annual natural increase, and in several states the last two decades showed an increase in the ratio of children under five to *native* white urban women of child-bearing age. In the counties with a high plane of living, however, there is an actual deficit in children needed to replace the population. Other population facts show that, in proportion to the 1930 population, this Region stands second only to the Northeast; in proportion to the average annual natural increase (1930-1934) it stands second only to the Southeast; in percentage deficit of children under five relative to the number needed to maintain population permanently in counties having a high plane of living, it is exceeded only by the Far West, and ranks about the same as the Northeast and the Northwest.

With reference to the region's early settlement, its people were of, for, and by the settlers from the East and South; and of, for, and by the immigrants of northern Europe; while in later years Chicago, Cincinnati, Cleveland, Detroit and others of the urban centers have gathered abundantly of the melting pot of the great flood tide of the early twentieth century. We have called attention to the drama of the traders and hunters and explorers where frontier roadways were for the most part rivers. It is, accordingly, important to recall that the earliest white men to settle there were the French traders, but their number was never very large; and when the Anglo-Saxons began to seek homes in this section of the country during the early part of the nineteenth century, the French either left or were completely outnumbered by the new arrivals. These new arrivals in the old Northwest Territory were the Ulster Scots (Scotch-Irish) and the Germans from the piedmont section of the South and they met those of Puritan descent who had come by way of the Erie Canal to Albany. These two groups, one from the north, the other from the south, co-operated in the early conditioning of the great "Middle West."

These native pioneers were soon joined by the immigrants from across the sea who hastened to this country when they heard of the opening of the Northwest Territory. They came in the main from northwest Europe, and the larger number of them were British, German, Scandinavian (Norwegians, Swedes, and Danes). Although the Irish clung to the Northeast more tenaciously than any other of the group, still a considerable number of them were scattered through the Middle States Region in Indiana, Illinois, and Michigan. Of lesser numerical importance were the Welsh who settled primarily in Ohio, while the Dutch concentrated in Iowa and Michigan, and the Finns preferred the rural sections of the Middle States. So long as there was free land, this region was the favorite destination for the immigrants coming to this country, especially for those interested in agriculture. Thus, even of the Second Immigration group, many Poles and Bohemians became farmers in the Middle States. But, after most of the free land was filled up, the urban centers, such as Chicago and Cleveland, were second only to the cities of the Northeast in offering inducements to the immigrants, who began to come from southeastern Europe, often with little money, education, or cultural background. First, there were the Italians from southern Italy, then the Slavs from Austria-Hungary and Russia, the Lithuanians, the Magyars, the Greeks, the Persians, the Syrians, the Jews, and many other races of the motley group found in southeastern Europe. In fact, they were the same people, that is, the same races and classes, who crowded into the urban centers of the Northeast.

Of the total of nearly twelve million foreign-born population of the United States in 1930, the Middle States had a little more than three and a half millions, the Northeast a little more than six and a quarter millions, and the Far West a little more than a million. Of these, there were in the Middle States nearly 700,000 Germans and about 300,000 Swedes, yet also more than 400,000 from Poland, and more than 200,000 each from Russia, Czechoslovakia, and Italy.

One other regional factor should be noted in that the larger percentage of the immigrants of the "Old Immigration" settled in the rural sections of the Middle and the Northwest Regions. Thus, they played an important part in developing the territory between the Appalachian and the Pacific. Further, from a racial and cultural standpoint, they were little different from the original settlers of the country. They could thus be easily assimilated and in fact have been to a surprising degree. On the other hand, the immigrants of the "New Immigration" have settled primarily in the industrial and mining centers, most of which are in the Middle States and the North-

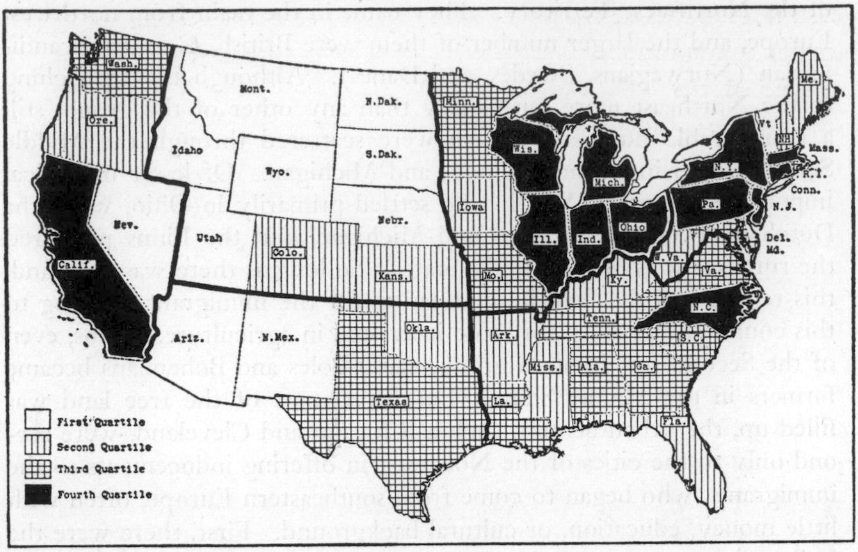

Above: Regional Distribution of Industry and Wage Earners Showing the Predominance of the Industrial Belt Comprising Parts of the Northeast and the Middle States.

Below: The Statistical Distribution as Shown from Census Figures of Manufactures.

NUMBER AND PROPORTION OF WAGE EARNERS IN MANUFACTURING, BY STATES AND REGIONS, 1929

STATE	Number of Wage Earners	Per Cent of Total Wage Earners in U. S.	Per Cent of Total Population
Southeast	1,165,092	13.23	20.8
Virginia	118,399	1.34	2.0
North Carolina	208,068	2.36	2.6
South Carolina	108,600	1.23	1.4
Georgia	158,280	1.80	2.4
Florida	64,936	.74	1.2
Kentucky	76,201	.87	2.1
Tennessee	126,921	1.44	2.1
Alabama	120,064	1.36	2.2
Mississippi	52,039	.6	1.6
Arkansas	44,073	.5	1.5
Louisiana	87,511	.99	1.7
Southwest	177,772	2.02	7.4
Oklahoma	31,279	.36	2.0
Texas	131,503	1.49	4.7
New Mexico	4,490	.05	.3
Arizona	10,500	.12	.4
Northeast	3,903,994	44.32	31.4
Maine	69,593	.79	.6
New Hampshire	65,119	.74	.4
Vermont	27,582	.31	.3
Massachusetts	559,443	6.35	3.5
Rhode Island	124,838	1.42	.6
Connecticut	253,468	2.88	1.3
New York	1,106,976	12.57	10.3
New Jersey	441,105	5.01	3.3
Pennsylvania	1,006,946	11.43	7.8
Delaware	23,382	.26	.2
Maryland	131,399	1.49	1.3
Dist. of Columbia	9,683	.11	.4
West Virginia	84,460	.96	1.4

STATE	Number of Wage Earners	Per Cent of Total Wage Earners in U. S.	Per Cent of Total Population
Middle States	2,917,985	33.11	27.6
Ohio	737,469	8.37	5.4
Indiana	313,829	3.56	2.6
Illinois	687,917	7.8	6.2
Michigan	528,512	6.0	3.9
Wisconsin	264,061	3.0	2.4
Minnesota	102,408	1.16	2.1
Iowa	82,615	.94	2.0
Missouri	201,174	2.28	3.0
Northwest	169,678	1.93	6.0
North Dakota	4,033	.05	.6
South Dakota	6,518	.07	.6
Nebraska	28,219	.32	1.1
Kansas	46,906	.53	1.5
Montana	13,673	.16	.4
Idaho	15,656	.18	.4
Wyoming	6,288	.07	.2
Colorado	32,735	.37	.8
Utah	15,650	.18	.4
Far West	473,015	5.39	6.8
Washington	114,591	1.32	1.3
Oregon	65,521	.74	.8
California	290,702	3.30	4.6
Nevada	2,201	.03	.1
United States	8,807,536	100.00	100.0

east Region. Racially and culturally they are far different from the earlier immigrants and they have not been easily assimilated.[6]

One of the basic features of regionalism is found in its emphasis upon the realism of the people, both creators and creatures of the changing nation. Nowhere perhaps is this more true than in the great "middle empire," the story of whose development and the character of whose civilization can almost be epitomized in the coming of its people. Here indeed is America *de luxe*, the expansion of the nation symbolic of the metamorphosis of its people. New Englanders there were, and Puritans in abundance, influencing the fabric of the new nation but somehow transformed into the new democratic pattern. Germans and Swedes and Norwegians there were but loving the flat lands of the new world more than the mountains of the old. And everywhere the tempo of the pioneer and the pattern of the democrat, strong builders, sturdy fighters, dominant explorers, common men pointing to the aristocracy of achievement and worth. Here soil and climate, forests and rivers, transform men of all ranks and origins into the citizens of Middle America through which and from which would flow other men and resources and forces to perpetuate that union which comes through the unity of diversities.

> Beverley W. Bond, Jr.'s characterization of the region as of the earlier historical epoch is good. Says he, "Late in 1787 an emigrant wagon left New England with the legend, 'For the Ohio,' painted in large white letters on its black canvas cover. This wagon was the vanguard of a migrating host which was eventually to take possession of some 248,000 square miles that lay roughly between the Ohio, the Mississippi, and the Great Lakes. The Old Northwest, as this region came to be called, had been ideally fashioned by Nature to become the home of a thriving population. A gently rolling country for the most part, it had few elevations that even approximated 1,500 feet. The eastern section and the northern tips extending along the Great Lakes were heavily forested. In what is now northern Indiana, however, in southern Michigan, and to the south in the main body of the land there were broad stretches of prairie that broadened out toward the West until they finally covered the landscape, except for a few trees along the watercourses. Usually the soil of the Old Northwest was

[6] This summary is largely that of Martha Edwards.

exceedingly fertile. South of the Lakes stretched the great Corn Belt where the glaciers, as they receded, had left behind deep deposits of rich earth that was almost entirely free from stones, and once the trees had been cleared away, or the tough prairie sod had been broken up, this fertile stretch was easily cultivated by the primitive tools of the settler. Both in soil and climate this area between the Great Lakes and the Ohio was peculiarly suited to settlers from the original states. Here the Georgian or the South Carolinian, as well as the New Englander, would find a climate that was neither so warm as that of the South, nor so cold as that of the North, and a soil that in general was well adapted to the varied grain and stock agriculture of the Middle States and Maryland." [7]

Professor L. M. Larson thinks that the three outstanding elements that went into the molding of American life represented in this vast expanse of forest and prairie, a thousand miles wide and a thousand miles deep and comprising the most richly endowed region of large dimensions in the world, were the Puritan of New England, the cavalier of the South, and the Scotch-Irish of the frontier. Each of these, of course, had important contributions to make and made them. There were, later, the contributions of the many other foreign ethnic groups but these were primarily symbolized in the culture of the great cities.

Arthur Train recalls a popular estimate that 70 percent of the people of the United States have a strain of Puritan inheritance evolved through 250 years of emigration from the Northeast which has disseminated both Puritan blood and Puritan traditions. He points out the fact that "As the frontier was pushed back from the seaboard, the frontier Puritans—as differentiated from the coast Puritans, who had developed an aristocratic leisure class—went with it. These frontiersmen, trekkers on wheels and runners, sweeping across Lake Champlain, over the Hudson to the Susquehanna, and up the Mohawk to Genesee and Buffalo, carried New England with them and planted it along Lake Erie, in the 'Western Reserve,' in Indiana and Illinois, so that today the Middle West is more like old New England than New England itself. . . ." And "finally the tide swept over Wisconsin, which from the very first until today has been dominated in its history and institutions by persons of Puritan descent. . . ." [8]

[7] Beverley W. Bond, Jr., *The Civilization of the Old Northwest: A Study of Political, Social, and Economic Development, 1788-1812*, pp. 1-2. (Quoted by permission of The Macmillan Company.)

[8] Arthur Train, *Puritan Progress*, p. 177.

Bond reminds us that similarly the settlers from the South introduced a "southern element that was in strong contrast to the Puritans of the Ohio Purchase and to the Middle States settlers of the Miami Purchase. Strongly Republican in their politics, and ardent followers of Thomas Jefferson, they had the Southerner's talent for politics, and they quickly assumed the leadership in local affairs. The many native Virginians among them came chiefly from the Piedmont yeomanry rather than from the landed aristocracy of the Tidewater, an origin that easily explains their intense democracy and their religious affiliations, which were chiefly Methodist and Presbyterian." [9]

The cumulative product of all this was "American" and democratic. Professor Ernest R. Groves in tracing woman's influence in the nation emphasizes the trend on the frontier toward the democratic attitude, as contrasted with the New England and the southern tendency toward class distinctions. Then in the Middle States frontier men and women were expected to stand on their own achievements rather than those of their ancestors. Furthermore, "There was more than an indifference to eastern ways. On the part of many who went into the frontier there was a positive antagonism. They wanted to be rid of traditions that had irritated them back in the old settlements. It would be misinterpretation to insist that the frontiersmen maintained social equality. It is rather that they refused to accept artificial or vicarious distinctions. It was obvious that there were genuine differences between people and there was a disposition to credit individuals with their superior merits, but the basis for determining character traits rested upon personal behavior. The methods for giving or denying prestige were distinctly frontier measurements. The Westerners were willing to follow leadership, but only as it was supported by qualities that they approved and admired." [10]

Professor Larson generalizes the westward movement in terms of Americanism, democracy and protestantism, the latter two qualities being symbols of the earlier authentic historical Americanism. "The movement," says Professor Larson, "was American not only because the pioneers were commonly of native birth, but also because they usually had no interests beyond their own country. . . . It was a

[9] Bond, *op. cit.*, p. 13.
[10] Ernest R. Groves, *The American Woman*, p. 83.

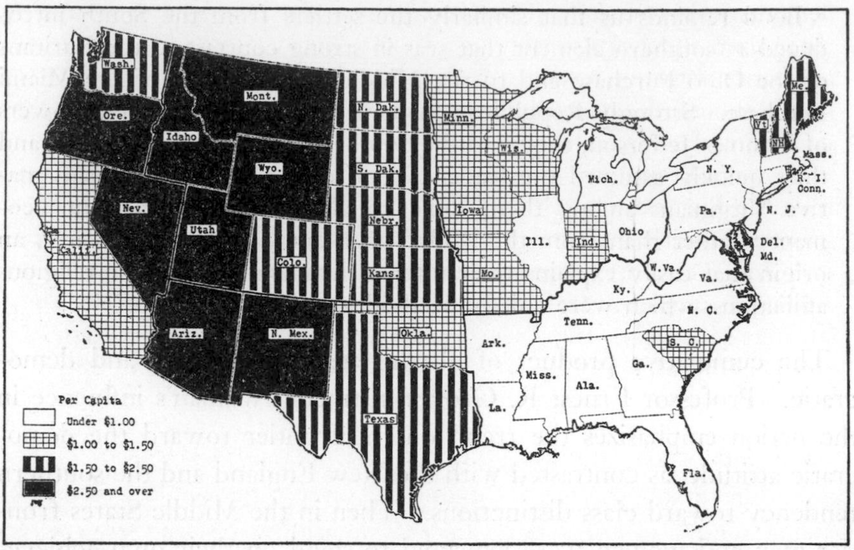

Above: Per Capita Total Federal Aid to States, 1930.

Below: Net Indebtedness of State Governments Per Capita of Total Population, 1930.

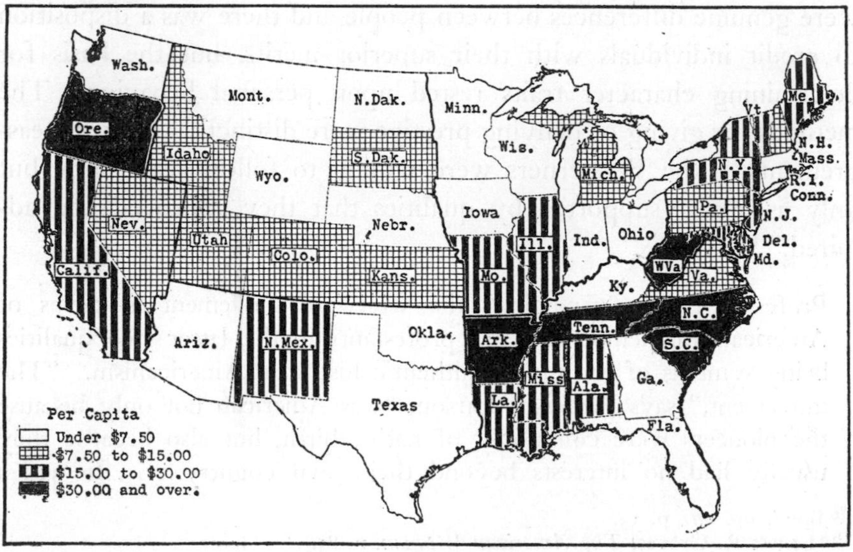

democratic movement. The pioneer host was unique in this, that it recognized equality not only as a theory but as a fact. In the strenuous battle with untamed nature, a battle that raged on a front of more than a thousand miles, privilege could not flourish and there could be no leisure class. . . .

"It was a Protestant movement. Far to the front on the skirmish line rode the Methodist preacher and the Presbyterian elder, industriously gathering their adherents into societies and churches. The Baptist minister and the Congregational missionary were not far behind, the one finding an unusually fertile field in the South, the other achieving a greater success in the North. The Lutheran, the Anglican, the Quaker, the Mennonite, and the Catholic, with many other types of believers, were all represented in the new settlements."[11]

So abundant are the testimonies to the distinctive development of the Middle States that it is difficult to omit many of the historical passages which so aptly describe the situation. At least two other types of cultures and influences must be presented before turning to the measures of social economic factors which characterize the present region. The first of these is the subregional ethnic-group culture to which reference has been made and the second is the urban movement, which in this case must be typified by Chicago, itself symbolic of the old Middle West. For the illustration of the early ethnic-group subregion we select the Norwegian element as described by Professor Larson in the new volume on *The Changing West*.

Beginning in 1833 "about 60 miles southwest of a little forlorn village called Chicago" there was formed in the half century following "a geographical unit which has sometimes been called the 'New Norway.' This area extends from Lake Michigan westward into the Dakotas and well on toward the Missouri River, or to the margin of the land with insufficient rainfall. A somewhat irregular line drawn westward from Chicago to Sioux City will approximately mark the southern boundary. The area thus delimited will include half a dozen counties in northeastern Illinois, a dozen counties in northern and central Iowa, nearly all of Wisconsin and Minnesota, and the eastern parts of the two Dakotas, approximately one-third in either case. Within these boundaries 80 percent, and possibly more, of all the Norwegians who have come to the United States have found their homes. To a great extent their descendants still have their homes in this region. Their

[11] Laurence M. Larson, *The Changing West*, pp. 6-7.

number is variously given, but a million and a quarter, or possibly a million and a half, seems to be a conservative estimate.

"The Norwegian immigrant came with a strong attachment to the soil. He hungered for land; he felt the need of a home. A home, however, could not be a mere abiding place: home, as he saw it, was something to which one has the title of ownership. In his attitude toward society he was often stubbornly individualistic. It was his great pride that he came from a land of democratic freedom. In his quiet, somewhat unemotional way he was deeply religious. In the Lutheran faith he had found a religion that brought responses from his inner being; he was a strenuous defender of the traditional faith. In the homeland he had frequently acted in opposition to his superiors; but he usually believed in yielding obedience to law. Finally, like most aliens, he suffered from a troublesome suspicion of inferiority, and to disguise this he spoke freely and sometimes boastfully of his fatherland and of its glorious past." [12]

Finally, there is the great capital of the Middle States, Chicago, candidate for Professor Merriam's first American city-state, distinctively American in all that sense in which the Middle West is American. Louis Wirth has described the whole Middle West as Chicago's hinterland and he makes a good case of it. The social-ecological studies of the University of Chicago have pictured its ethnic groups and their culture as well as the structure of the great metropolis. Merriam and White and others have depicted its government and politics while the world at home and abroad has characterized its erstwhile Mayor Thompson, the 102 percent American, and its racketeering patterns as the new urban America so much feared by Thomas Jefferson. Its universities and its center of public administration and public welfare study and education have stamped it again the symbol of America's progress. As for this center and symbol of the Middle States and the other metropolitan regions, McKenzie and others have provided materials for their adequate appraisal. These constitute a separate episode.

Perhaps it is permissible, however, to present one more composite picture of the region in terms of the Chicago center of it—even if Count Keyserling thought it was *not* American. "Surely," writes Waldo Frank, "no other American city lives so close to its earth. You must

[12] Larson, *op. cit.*, pp. 71-73.

think of prairie. Beyond the flatness of Lake Michigan another flatness. A thousand miles of it, rising with incalculable leisure to the sudden climax of the Rocky Mountains. This is the prairie. Rich black earth spread like the sky. The Mississippi and his legion of waters make it fecund.

"The train flows over the flatland. Green farms, the warm, brown lurch of country roads wither away. Here is a sooty sky hanging forever lower. The sun is a red ball retreating. The heave of the prairie lies palpably still to the grimed horizons. But on it, a thick deposit: gray, drab, dry—litter of broken steel, clutter of timber, heapings of brick. The sky is a stain: the air is streaked with runnings of grease and smoke. Blanketing the prairie, this fall of filth, like snow—a storm that does not stop. . . . The train glides farther in toward the storm's center. Chimneys stand over the world, and blackness upon it. There is no sky now. Above the bosom of the prairie, the spread of iron and wooden refuse takes on form. It huddles into rows: it rises and stampedes and points like a lay of metal splinters over a magnet. This chaos is polarized. Energy makes it rigid and direct. Behold the roads without eyes wrench into line: straighten and parallel. The endless litter of wood is standing up into wooden shanties. The endless shanties of wood assemble to streets. Iron and smoke and brick converge and are mills and yards. The shallow streets mount like long waves into a sea of habitations. And all this tide is thick above the prairie. Dirt, drab houses, dominant chimneys. A sky of soot under the earth of flaming ovens. Rising into a black crescendo as the train cuts underneath high buildings, shrieking freight-cars, to a halt. But on all sides still, with vast flanks spreading and breathing and inviting, the unburied prairie. . . ."[13]

Rich sources of recent appraisals of the culture of the Middle States, in addition to other appropriate documentation by authors already cited, constitute a small library in themselves. Dixon Ryan Fox's *Sources of Culture in the Middle West* is indispensable for its critique of the Turner Frontier Theory, *pros* and *cons*, and for brilliant description of the region by Avery Craven and others. James Truslow Adams' *Provincial Society, 1690-1763*, as well as his *The Epic of America*, *America's Tragedy*, and *The March of Democracy*, all provide comprehensive historical backgrounds for the regions of the nation and convincing specific illustrations. Arthur M. Schles-

[13] Waldo Frank, "Our America," Lucy Lockwood, *In Search of America*, pp. 462-464.

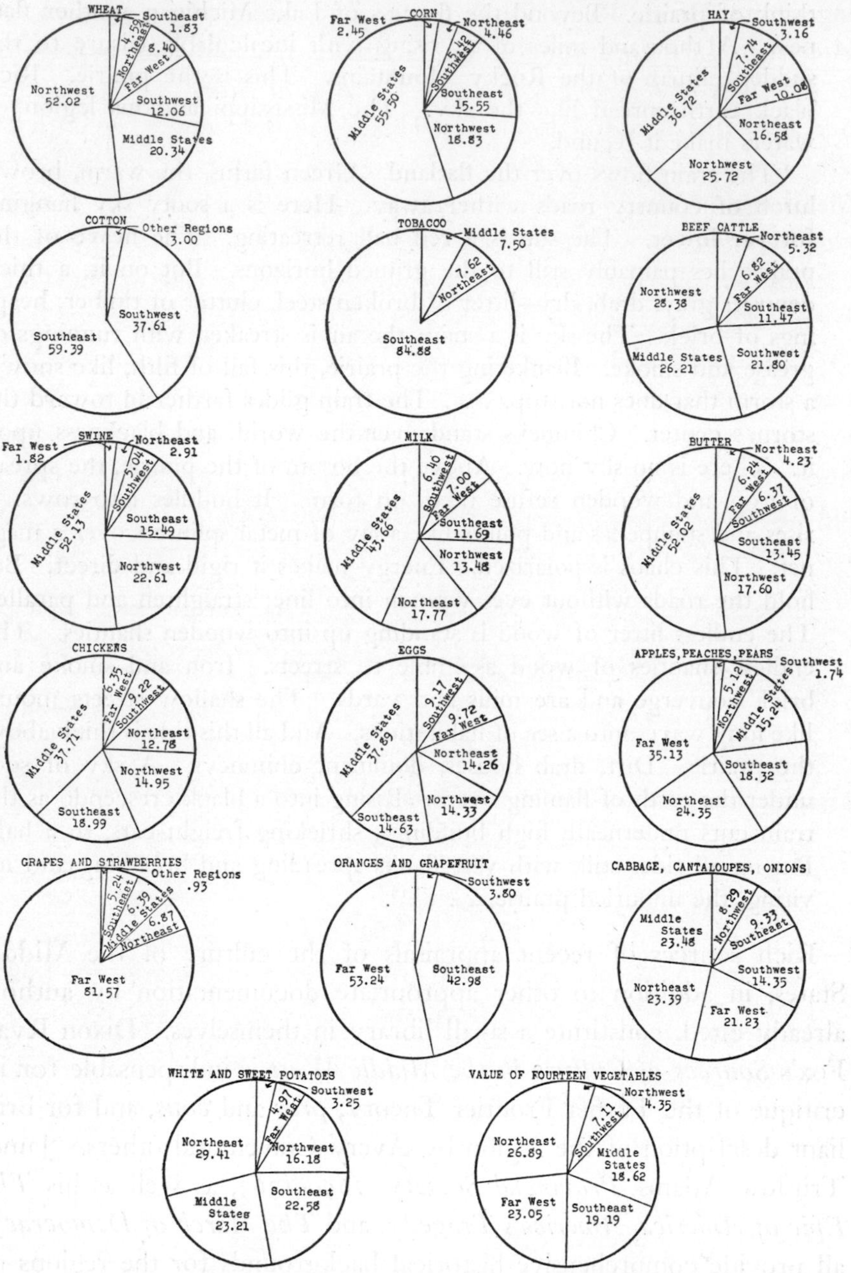

The above graphic illustration shows the general regional distribution of commodity production at a glance.

inger and Dixon Ryan Fox's series of volumes in *A History of American Life* constitute almost complete source books, especially in *The Rise of the American Man*, *The Rise of Cities*, *The Quest for Social Justice*. So, too, Louis M. Hacker and Benjamin B. Kendrick's *The United States since 1865*, and two new volumes of Samuel Eliot Morison and Henry Steele Commager, *The Growth of the American Republic*, as well as the standard, Beards' *The Rise of American Civilization* scarcely need supplementing except for the newness and freshness of specific sources and appraisals. Then there are the hundred or more popular volumes, impressions and observations in abundance, which have come in recent years as a fresh stream of regional interpretation. The newest, *Upper Mississippi* by Walter Havighurst, is one; *Earth Horizons* by Mary Austin is another peculiarly appropriate to the "wests," while Mark Sullivan's *The Turn of the Century* and other volumes are eloquent with descriptive writing.

These sources must be consulted to appreciate the richness of their supporting evidence of the great regional range and variety of the nation. Perhaps a final sample or two must suffice. Of the "culture" of the region, John D. Hicks, in his chapter on "The Development of Civilization in the Middle West" in *Sources of Culture in the Middle West*, stresses several qualities of the region's culture. He says, "The Middle West takes on a personality of its own, in part by picking up from here and there the ideas it likes, in part by independent experiences and experiments from which it acquires something to hand back to the older centers of civilization in return for what it has received. . . . In this respect the Middle West kept well abreast of the East, maintained close contact with Europe, and blazed some new trails. Thanks to the terms of the Northwest Ordinance the urge for a free public school system was a birthright in every western state; and in no other section of the nation was faith in general education as a remedy for the ills that afflicted mankind more pronounced. On this point the foreign element, especially the Germans and the Scandinavians, who had been used to liberal educational opportunities in their homelands, agreed heartily with the native Americans. Democracy in education may not have been the panacea that our forefathers believed it to be, but the fact remains that by the end of the century the states of the Middle West had achieved a higher percentage of literates among their people than most of the states of the East. . . . One more illustration of the western contribution to civilization must suffice. Creative writing, to borrow a none too lovely term from our departments of literature, seems to be somehow associated with the highest good, and by the last half of the nineteenth century Middle Westerners had reached even this coveted goal. Now the birth of a literary genius is not a matter of transit across the Atlantic or across the Appalachians, nor of the advance of civilization from one place to another. It may happen any time, anywhere. Possibly genius may be suppressed by unfavorable surroundings, and conditions of life in the early Middle West may so have operated. Abraham Lincoln, however, grew out of these primitive conditions, and only a few critics would deny him a place among the masters of English prose. Two decades after Lincoln assumed the presidency, Englishmen were according recognition to another western writer, Mark Twain, and a little later even New Englanders conceded with some reluctance that at last books worth reading were being written by a man who came out of the West. It is indeed hard to see how a writer could have been more closely associated with his environment than the author of *Life on the Mississippi* and the *Innocents*. Mark Twain was educated, as were so many other Middle Westerners of his time, primarily in the school of experience, he wrote of the life which surrounded him, and yet few, if any, American writers of his generation deserve to be set above him. From his time foward the West continued to produce writers of merit. William Dean Howells, whose Ohio birth and training he at least did not forget, stood far more consciously than Mark Twain, and perhaps with greater sophistication, for the same sort of realism, the same insistence on truth in fiction. Hamlin Garland, too, came out of the West, and although he, like Howells, owed much to the East as well as to the West, his youthful experiences gave him the materials with which to work, and possibly the inspiration to write." [14]

Turning now to the sampling of regional character as measured by socio-economic indices, we may begin with some of the larger measures of agricultural, industrial and general cultural facts. Subsequently other detailed indices may illustrate further the range and richness of such data both for more inclusive study and for incorporation of any special interpretations desired. First of all the Middle States comprise the greatest agricultural-industrial group of states [15]

[14] John D. Hicks, "The Development of Civilization in the Middle West, 1860-1900," in Dixon Ryan Fox, *Sources of Culture in the Middle West*, pp. 85, 90, 93-94. (Quoted by permission of D. Appleton-Century Company, Inc.)

[15] This is the substance of an unpublished appraisal on "Characteristics of the Middle States," by Dwight P. Flanders.

in any region in the United States. Their lands have not been long tilled and their industries are yet young; the region has still the prime vigor of youth. Once called the "granary of the East," these states have rich, heavy soils that yield bountiful corn crops, accounting for 55.5 percent of the nation's yield. In turn this helps produce 52.1 percent of the swine raised in the United States. Close to 10,000,000 milk cows and heifers graze on the lush pastures, and double that number of cattle and calves are kept for milk. In both classifications, the value of this livestock is the greatest in any region. Our Middle States have approximately twice the number of purebred, registered cattle than has any other group of states. This explains the production of 52 percent of the butter and 43.7 percent of the milk in our country. Eighty-eight percent of the cows of the region are milked. So, too, the region leads the rest of the regions with nearly 5,000,000 horses and colts, and in the carrying capacity of the pastures and rangeland. They also lead the whole nation with 37.7 percent of the chickens, 37.9 percent of the eggs, and 36.7 percent of the hay. As an incidental, in the classification of cabbages, cantaloupes, and onions, they are again first with 23.4 percent of the total.

For each index cited above, the Middle States are undisputed leaders in the field. There are many other agricultural products in which they are ranked as second, but are still one of the leading producers. They rank next to the Southeast in the number of farms and next to the Northeast in the largest number of acres in farmland. Second only to the Northwest are the Middle States in the production of wheat, in cereals in general, and in raising of beef cattle. They contribute about one-fifth of the wheat and over one-fourth of the cereals and beef cattle. The Northeast leads this region by a small percent in the raising of white and sweet potatoes, and the Middle States are next to the Far West in the percentage that cooperative farm sales formed of the total cash farm income. In this same area there is owned on farms, the greatest number of passenger cars and trucks, about a million and a half passenger cars and 287,000 trucks. These states are spending more than any other region for the support of their State Agricultural Stations, in amount nearly $4,000,000 a year. A trifle over one-third of the total country

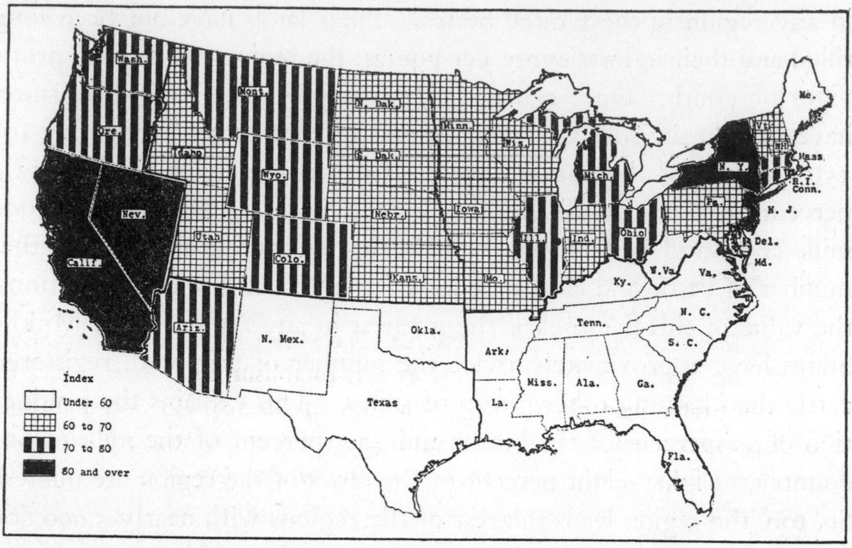

RANK OF STATES IN PUBLIC EDUCATION: 1930

INDEX NUMBER

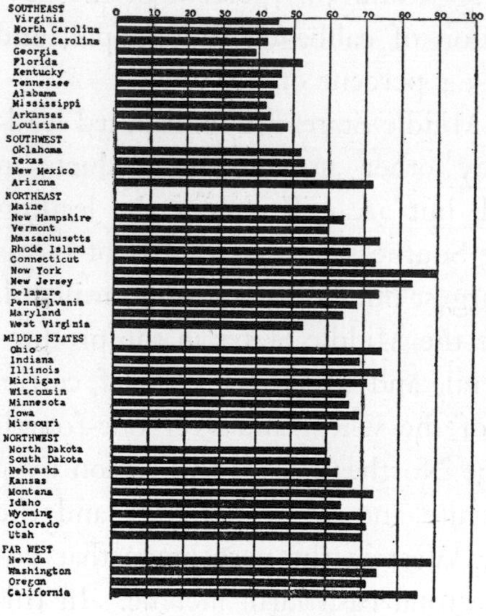

SCHOOL DEBT OUTSTANDING PER PUPIL IN AVERAGE DAILY ATTENDANCE: 1930

DOLLARS

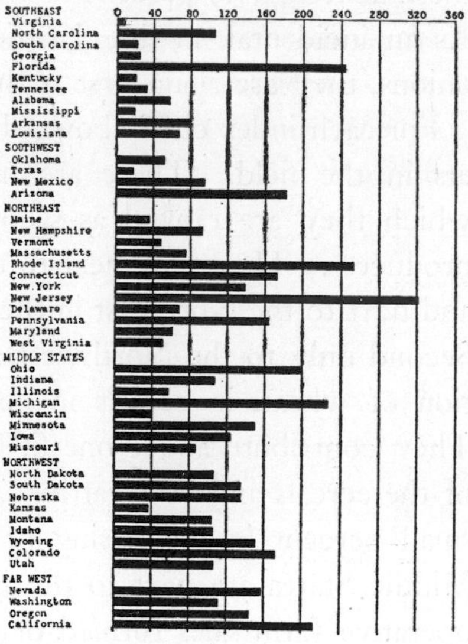

Rank of States in Public Education, 1930

weekly newspaper circulation is within the Middle States. They also lead in the percentage of farms having telephones.

From this brief description it might erroneously be assumed that the region is devoted solely to agriculture. This is far from the truth, however, since the center of industry has been constantly shifting westward until it is now in eastern Indiana. While it is common knowledge that the center of the nation's agricultural commodity markets are in this region, it is likewise common knowledge that the industrial tide has far from completely ebbed from the Northeast. These highly industrialized states lead the nation in most of the manufacturing indices. In the number of establishments, however, the Middle States lead all in the production of machinery, not including transportation equipment, with 40.1 percent of the total number of establishments. They are first, too, in the production of transportation equipment, land and water, with well over a third of the total, and have 34.5 percent of the railroad repair shops. There is laid in this region close to 50,000 miles of railroad, excluding switching and terminal companies; this mileage is 28 percent of the total in the United States. The largest number of trucks is possessed in the Middle States. These together with the railroads form a highly efficient web of transportation knitting the region together. Such miscellaneous industries as broom making, dairying, poultry raising, creamery and factory supplies, and roofing, have more establishments in the Middle States than in any other region. The disparity between the Northeast and the Middle States is very small in most of the indices in which the former is superior. One-third of the total number of wage earners are in this region. The wages paid were approximately four and a quarter billion dollars and the value of the manufactured product about twenty-five and a half billion dollars. The Middle States lead, however, in the average wage per wage earner. They are second to the Northeast in the amount of horsepower, having 32.9 percent of the nation's total.

Considering now the number of establishments as the index for industry, the Middle States are second to other regions with 12.9 percent of the textiles, 28.6 percent of the paper and allied products, 32.1 percent of the printing, publishing, and allied products, 27.3 percent of the products of coal and petroleum, 19.9 percent of leather and its manufactures, 32.2 percent of stone, clay and glass products, 38.2 percent of iron and steel and their products, not including machinery, 31.1 percent of the nonferrous metals and their products, and 27.4 percent of miscellaneous industries not included in the above classifications. The Middle States have a little over one-fourth of all the manufacturing establishments in the country. They are well supplied with the basic raw materials to industry: coal and iron.

Thus, in the combination of both agricultural and industrial indices the Middle States are unsurpassed by any other combinations of states which form a homogeneous region. The vigor of their industry, the close association with the soil and the tillers thereof, have had their effects on the life of the people. What we have discussed thus far are the material aspects of the culture; now let us turn to the more immaterial aspects. With almost a third of the material wealth of our land concentrated in these eight states, the people possess a considerable stream of income with which to purchase the material comforts and leisure to develop the arts. Significant of the democratic atmosphere is the predominance of coeducational institutions. This region has the greatest number of such accredited and unaccredited institutions of higher learning. There exists among the young men and young women a great demand for business training; consequently there is found the largest number of collegiate schools and departments of commerce and business. Also, there is the greatest number of member schools of the National Association of Accredited Commercial Schools.

The greatest number of motor vehicles, one-third of the total in the United States, are centered in this region. There are over seven and a half million registered, which is an easy explanation of the $140,000,000 of receipts collected from the gasoline tax. From these taxes and for these cars and trucks, the greatest mileage of high-type surfaced highways are in this region. Approximately one-third of the nation's total miles of high-type surface are in the Middle States. Ninety-four and five-tenths percent of the state highways are surfaced and over half of these have a high type of surface, which is the finest record of any group of states. A survival of the days when every man not only owned but had to build his home is the fondness for home owning, since the Middle States rank first in the number of homes occupied by home owners.

Some of the absolute figures may be tempered a little when it is known that over one-fourth of the population lives in this region. Furthermore, there are some distinctly undesirable qualities which the Middle States have in abundance. These include the second lowest per capita farm income, a high degree of mortgaged indebtedness on farms operated by their owners, while the region is the recipient of the second largest amount of relief funds. The loss by interregional migration is over one million a year, being second to the Southeast in net loss. The Middle States have had the lowest increase in percentage of high school graduates of any region.

However nearly we may approximate a composite region, flexibility is of the essence of regionalism; and, however closely knit a region may be, there are intra-regional differences and subregions that illustrate such flexibility and variety. On the basis of growing season and soil there are agricultural belts across the Middle States. Chief among these is the corn-hog belt, stretching from Ohio across Indiana and Illinois to Missouri and Iowa. South of this in these same states, excluding Iowa, is the winter wheat belt, and north of the corn-hog belt is the spring wheat belt. These belts are intermingled as they approach each other, but the clustering is strong along the line of their focal points. The north-central hay and dairy region, which replaced the lumber and later the wheat region, includes Minnesota, Wisconsin, Michigan, and parts of Illinois, Indiana, and Ohio. The focal point of this subregion is Wisconsin. The wooded and plains areas are also subregions.

The industries have a decided pattern with Ohio, Michigan, and Illinois having the largest part. The net income from corporations, the percentage of population that is urban, the wages paid, and the value of the manufactured product may all be used to set apart this industrial belt. It is contiguous with the industrial belt of the Northeast. The lumbering industry has moved from Michigan across Wisconsin into Minnesota, leaving behind a vast cut-over region of the Great Lakes. Copper and iron center about the upper lakes, with 80 percent of the pig iron from these great ranges. Coal underlies the Ohio Valley, Illinois, Iowa, and Michigan.

These large subregions might be broken down into still smaller subregions that spread across and ignore man-made political boundaries. These in turn have their focal points from which the homogeneities are gradually diffused. Minneapolis is the center of the milling business, Chicago the center of the meat industry, and Detroit the center of the automotive industry. This might easily be carried

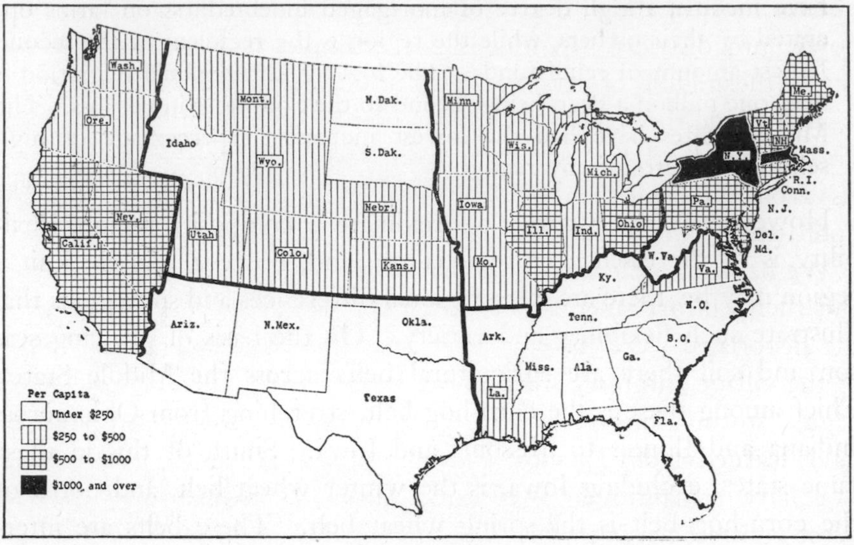

ILLUSTRATIONS OF THE GREAT DIFFERENTIALS IN WEALTH AND CAPACITY TO SUPPORT INSTITUTIONS

Above: Per Capita Bank Resources, 1930.

Below: Per Capita Savings Deposits, 1930.

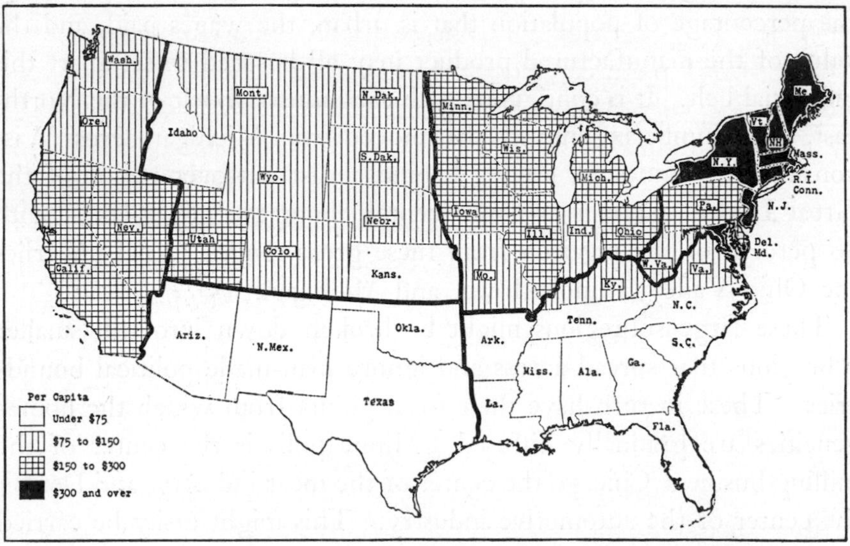

out for most of the different industries. Each state might be broken down into districts. In Illinois, for example, if a line were drawn across the middle of the state, with the exception of one county, it would divide the state into counties that receive more from the state distributive fund for education from those counties which receive less from the fund than they put in. The southern counties depend upon the northern counties to help them with their education.

We have, to some extent, found the general character of the people and their culture summarized in some of the descriptive passages of the historians. We have assumed the *Main Street* characterization of the village and town life. We have enjoyed Carl Sandburg's Chicago, "stormy, husky, brawly, city of the big shoulders," and we have learned from London all about the criminals and racketeers. We have romanticized two world fairs and have pointed out the great contrast between the cultural contribution of the first World's Fair to architecture with the Chautauqua-esteeming people of those days. We have watched a picturesque Bryan swing the "West" into a populist tempo and have watched the conflict between urban and rural counties. We have rejoiced when our European visitors marveled at the great plains of corn and wheat and railroad tracks bedecked with grain elevators and miniature stock yards for loading millions of livestock. We have echoed "American," "American," "Middle West," "Middle West." And perhaps we have yet to seek the perfect "American" portraiture in the agrarian people of the Middle States, pictured through their socio-economic folkways–folkways of the individual, of the family, of the community, of politics, of "Americanisms."

Here are genuine regional Americanisms as estimated by a group of eager students seeking to characterize the Middle States, and summarized by Eugene Link. First, individualistic folkways: Individual competition, or rugged individualism. . . . A real sense of what is "mine." The farmers, still vestige from the pioneer, are individualists. . . . It is "my farm, I run it." Willing to co-operate, even join co-operatives, providing it is beneficial and does not talk of group management. Will fight "be gorry" to maintain their own and their neighbors' individual rights. So the industrial magnate fights the closed shop, too. . . . Get ahead in life, improve oneself. . . . Rise from farm-boy to President of the country. . . . Thrift and hard work the roads to success. Anybody can succeed if he follows this formula. "Hoe your own row," and it is your own fault if you turn up in your old age a dependent. . . . Man gets out of life exactly what he deserves. . . . Doles are immoral. They make the working man dependent, he won't "get down and dig." . . . We need the money incentive to make us work. . . . Therefore, we look up to the rich man as smarter and a better man than the poor. He got what he rightly deserved, too. . . . "Keep a stiff upper lip." Adversities are bound to come, good days with evil, drought, flood, dust, cyclone. Take it. Adjust yourself and try again. Look at Grant Wood's pictures of the faces of the farmers. Written all over them is hardship and grim determination to live despite it all.

The family-economic folkways of the Middle States are, again, American *de luxe*. For instance, a strong sense of family, harking back to the essential familism of frontier days. "Tsch, tsch, those people have been divorced. Shameless." Divorced men and women are wicked. Even though father and mother are completely incompatible, unhappy, they continue on each doing an expected task in silence. . . . Family status is measured by wealth. A fine family is one "with some means." Each family has arrived when a new car is purchased; they have securely arrived when they own property. . . . Father is the "good provider." He supplies the raw materials. Mother is the fabricator; she "puts up" some peaches, apple-butter, corn, beans. The children do the "chores," with each one an after-school assignment daily. Fathers don't retire so often as in other regions; they "die with their boots on." Mothers can products even though they no longer need to, for after all at Thanksgiving "how can you be thankful out of a tin-can?" . . . Men dress in shirtsleeves, rolled above the wrist or elbow; or overalls, or odd pairs of pants. In the Winter the suit is worn only for warmth, baggy, shiny, wrinkled, and then many times only on Sunday. Women dress in calico; they wear stockings not rolled below the knees. In general the family front is carried around by the women; they dress a little better than the men, for "by their wives ye shall know them."

Again, here are community folkways, early American vintage. A community spirit. Even though you may have the old division between the haves and have-nots, Pepville vs. Stringtown, as William Allen White calls the division, still the community has a oneness. No native is allowed to starve; therefore they believe that "during a depression nobody actually goes without food." . . . The civic clubs where oil station attendants sit down with bankers is typical. "They profit most who serve best," say the Rotarians. So they all sing about serving together, go through the motions at church and civic club, and the rest of the time count the profits. . . . Community friendliness. A democratic spirit. You speak to strangers more often on the street. "High hat" does not go. How the West dislikes the snob, the one who "puts on airs." The young Lochinvar who goes East for an education and returns "needs to be taken down a notch or two." The minister always gets an invitation, or more often several, to Sunday dinner; it would be an insult for him to eat in a restaurant were he visiting for a Sunday. . . . The community leader is the community booster. He talks of white-ways, memorial drives, new school houses. He is a simple, "hail fellow, well met" sort. He knows lots of people, and has probably been mayor two or three times. . . . "The Spit and Argy Club" meet around the courthouse, discuss the weather, politics, and "conditions." Every smart lawyer or business man must take time at least once a day to fraternize with the boys, otherwise he is "stuck up." These groups spread the economic folkways of the Middle States. . . . "Buy at home" and beware of the chain stores. Patronize your own community; be a community booster. The chain stores have gotten such a bad name for running out the solid citizen of Main Street that they now hire a community booster to head the store, and keep the fact that it is a chain absolutely silent. Poor "Piggly-Wiggly" couldn't overcome the folkways of the Middle West! . . . A rigid cultural pattern. If you do things differently you are a little "cracked." If your tastes are not the community's tastes, if your ethics are a bit off color, if you stay up after 11:00 o'clock, if you don't go to church, if you don't have children, if when you do you dare to be frank and not hypocritical with them, you are sure to set in motion a babble of tongues second to no other on the globe. . . . These folks look askance at change. "Give me the old-time religion; it's good enough for me." They fear change and want to whip the changer into line by social ostracism. Radicals are feared and unwelcomed in the community. They are "ferriners and outside agitators." The word "communist" is synonymous with blood, a sort of superbeast. Any talk of a new social order is at once considered un-American. Try to bust Main Street, and Main Street will bust you.

And here are several socio-economic folkways: Hard times and prosperity are often caused directly by politicians. "Dirty, rotten politics" is responsible for our ailments, while "Teddy and his Big Stick" clean things up and bring good times. . . . The East is crooked and the West is honest. It is the "Wall Street gamblers" or the "international bankers" that are wrecking the country. Father Coughlin and the people never get any more specific than that. "Down with the banks" is popular, and that is about as far as a criticism of the economic system goes. . . . "Good times" and "bad times," prosperity and depression, are entirely natural and to be expected. You can't change the laws of God's universe and His will by any man-made regulations. You must learn to accept hardships as inevitable, whether flood or fifteen cent wheat. . . . Closed shops are un-American. Unions are a foreign product and break up the partnership between capital and labor. Only troublemakers come in and cause dissatisfaction and strikes. "Wages are low because industry can't help it"; hard times hit them, too; we just have to grin and bear it.". . . Capital is to be thought of as the accumulated savings of a thrifty, industrious individual. He has a complete right "to what is his own." Even then, American business is the best in the world, making the best products, under the best conditions, for a better America. . . . Vote Republican and keep up the tariff which protects American business, which prospers, which benefits the farmer secondarily. Let the "smart," the "cautious," the "thrifty," the man from log-cabin to white house run the country. . . . Foreigners are inferior to American stock. More, they are not to be trusted, they may stick a knife into you. The Mexican laying the Santa Fe road-bed never fraternizes with the natives. Most of them never even learn to speak English. . . . The ideal is a city of small business men, each working hard to live and let live. Classes are not rigid. The Middle West is still largely classless and democratic. All men are equal (except the Mexican, Negro) economically and socially. Hence out of these states come the protests against trusts and monopolies, the plea for a reformistic return to economic equality.

This is the great Middle States agrarian American, "backbone of the nation," for whom the Harvard economist prescribed a formula that unless he could show, even in the depression, a profit on his farm by standard accounting methods, he should be deprived of his land and put on the dole. This is the Middle America of geography and of history, heart of the nation's bigness and complexity. This is the America against whom urban consumers protest. This is the land of "the sons of the wild jackasses" as seen by the Northeast and its New England, to which we now turn as the next "most American" of the regions.

Chapter XX

THE NORTHEAST AND ITS NEW ENGLAND

THE Northeast of our six major regions is, in terms of Turner, Dodd, Beard, Adams, and all those historians who have interpreted so brilliantly the sectional development of America, "The East" and "The North," thus coming logically and literally to be the Northeast of history, geography, and culture. To "The West" it was East and to "The South" it was very much North. Thus, at least in priority of development, the claim of the Northeastern Region of the United States that it, rather than the Middle States, is the most "American" of all the regions finds without doubt much to substantiate it. For if ever there was a more "American" region than the Middle States, it would appear to be the great Northeast commonly assumed to be the America of the Americas, prideful of its historical, cultural, and economic priority, and jealous of its dominant place in the nation.

This regional claim for American priority is not only based upon New England, the historical cradle of the nation, with its distinctive culture of the newest new world; with its plurality of the thirteen colonies; or metropolitan New York, often informally designated as America and dominating the financial and organizational nation; or Pennsylvania with its Cradle of Liberty and the City of Brotherly Love, center and symbol of Benjamin Franklin, forerunner of our technology; and also its Pennsylvania Dutch and Friends; or its coal and iron resources, basic power of American dominance in the world; or Maryland and its Baltimore metropolitan area, borderland between North and South; or Washington and the District of Columbia, center and symbol of the earlier planned historical nation, as well as of a new nation in travail. It is all of these and more—wealth of capital and wealth of people, wealth of schools and wealth of philanthropy, wealth of industry and wealth of technology, cradle of the Yankee, cradle of the immigrant, cradle of the Jews, cradle of industry, gateway to Europe. And the region is American of the Americans in so far as it claims most of the wealth of the wealthiest nation and nearly all of the three-score vaunted families that "Rule America."

The Northeastern Region comprises the twelve states of Maine, New Hampshire, Vermont, Massachusetts, Rhode Island, Connecticut, New York, New Jersey, Delaware, Pennsylvania, Maryland, and West Virginia. In area this is the smallest of the major regions with about 8 percent of the nation's territory, but in population it is the largest with more than 30 percent, followed closely, however, by the Middle States. This is in almost exact contrast with the Northwest, with nearly 30 percent of the nation's land and less than 8 percent of its people. The Northeast not only has the largest total population, but the largest non-farm population with the smallest amount of land in farms.

In terms of the United States Census classification the region comprehends all of the divisions of the *New England States* and the *Middle Atlantic States*, together with Maryland, West Virginia, and Delaware of the *South Atlantic States*. Its metropolitan areas include some 31 of the total 93 metropolitan districts classified by the Census. These are New York, Philadelphia, Baltimore, Boston, Pittsburgh, Buffalo, Washington, Jersey City, Syracuse, Worcester, Hartford, New Haven, Bridgeport, Scranton, Paterson, Yonkers, Albany, Trenton, Camden, Erie, Fall River, Elizabeth, Cambridge, New Bedford, Reading, Wilmington, Lynn, Utica, and Lowell.[1]

> Among Newbigin's major natural regions, the Northeast includes all of her New England and most of her Middle Appalachian. In her brief description she says that "the six states of Maine, New Hampshire, Vermont, Massachusetts, Connecticut and Rhode Island constitute a very well-defined unit. The Appalachian Highland here is represented by two parallel ridges, the White Mountains of New Hampshire, atttaining in Mount Washington (6,300 feet) the highest point of the Northern Appalachians, and the Taconic and Green Mountains,

[1] R. D. McKenzie, *The Metropolitan Community*, pp. 336-338.

which separate the Hudson and Connecticut Rivers. . . . The Middle Appalachian States, strictly speaking, should be regarded as including only the three states of New York, Pennsylvania and New Jersey, with their great mineral wealth, particularly the coal of Pennsylvania, and their associated enormous development of manufactures. We shall, however, include here also the southern prolongation of the industrial area. It should be realized that New York and Pennsylvania extend over the Highland to the shores of the nearer Great Lakes (Erie and Ontario), and that the Pennsylvania coalfields extend into the state of Ohio, as well as into those of West Virginia and Maryland."[2]

The J. Russell Smith subregions charted on the basis of men and resources include perhaps the largest number of any other region. These are the New England-Canadian Maritime Region, the Northeastern Highlands, Metropolitan New York, the Hudson Valley, the Erie Canal Belt and Buffalo, the North Atlantic Coastal Plain, the Northern Piedmont, and parts of the Appalachian Ridge and Valley Region, the Appalachian Plateau and the Upper Ohio Valley, and a little of the Lake Region.[3]

Of the River Valley Regions, the Northeast comprehends all the rivers of the New England drainage basin—the Maine, Merrimack, the Thames, Blackstone, Taunton, the Connecticut; those of the North Atlantic drainage basins, namely, the Hudson, Delaware, Susquehanna, and parts of the Upper Chesapeake and the Potomac.[4]

In his Northeastern Regional Conference on Agriculture, November 8 to 10, 1935, in New York, Secretary Wallace pointed up the unity of so large a region's agriculture in and among its own states and in particular in relation to the nation at large. The contrast between Northeastern and Middle States agriculture is typified in the technical problems involved in the great milk sheds and in problems relating to the production of fruits, vegetables, potatoes, and to their processing and marketing. In the midst of a great industrial region in which there are nearly 40 percent of the industrial workers and less than 15 percent of the farmers, the type of farming is essentially specialized.[5]

[2] Marion I. Newbigin, *A New Regional Geography of the World*, pp. 325-326, 327. (Quoted by permission of Harcourt, Brace & Company, Inc.)

[3] J. Russell Smith, *Men and Resources*, pp. x-xii.

[4] National Resources Committee, *Drainage Basin Problems and Programs*, December 1936, pp. 103-104.

[5] *Proceedings of the Northeastern Conference on Agriculture*, held in New York, November 8-10, 1935.

Even though farming is among the smallest of industries, there are high values of land and stock and great strides in both technical farming and marketing. Different from all the other regions, the Northeast is yet typical of modern American agriculture in the midst of industry. Something of the nature and scope of this can be seen from an examination of the farming regions listed for the Northeast and shown on the great map, Types of Farming Areas in the United States: 1930, prepared by the Division of Commerce, Bureau of the Census. Considerable emphasis is placed upon these farming areas because they are recognized by such geographers as J. Russell Smith and Ellsworth Huntington as the best definitive subregions of most of the major American regions.

Exclusive of the smaller subregions of the same main subregions the following include most of the 122 farming areas listed: West Virginia-east Ohio, Charleston, Alleghany County, Clarksburg, Connellsville-Uniontown-Morgantown, Pittsburgh-Wheeling, Northeast Ohio, Lake Erie, Pittsburgh, Johnstown, Shenandoah-Cumberland, Alleghany Plateau, Blue Ridge Valleys, Appalachian Valley, Eastern Shore, Southern Maryland, Washington, Dover, South New Jersey pine barrens and coastal plain, South central New Jersey, Central New Jersey, New Jersey potato area, Monmouth County, Raritan Bay, Long Island, Metropolitan-semiurban area, North New Jersey uplands, Appalachian valley and uplands, Penns Manor, Limestone Valley, Lehigh County, Pocono highlands, Philadelphia-Wilmington-Baltimore, York County, Lake Ontario, Western New York, Finger Lakes, Onondaga, Tug Hill Plateau, Saint Lawrence Lowlands, Lake Champlain, Mohawk Valley, Central New York, Catskill-Pocono highlands, Ulster County, East Hudson Valley, Western Vermont, Green Mountains-Berkshire Hills, Aroostook, White Mountains-Maine woods, Eastport, Washington County, Bangor, South central Maine, Kennebec, Penobscot Bay-Portland, Merrimack-Nashua Rivers valley, Housatonic-Naugatuck valleys, Central upland-Blackstone River Valley, Connecticut Valley, Farmington-Quinnipiac, Upper Thames Basin-western Rhode Island, Narragansett Bay, Cape Cod, South of Boston-Buzzard Bay, Hudson River Valley, Eastern Vermont, Springfield-Holyoke, Portsmouth-Newburyport-Gloucester, Lancaster County, Chester County, Middlesex, Baltimore-Anne Arundel, New Haven.[6]

Of the metropolitan districts, we have already discussed in Part I of this volume the greater New York and its environs and the emerging Washington-Baltimore metropolitan area described in one of the

[6] Adapted from the map, Types of Farming Areas in the United States: 1930, Division of Commerce, Bureau of the Census.

special reports of the National Resources Committee. It is important here, however, to note the very large ratio of the nation's urban population and the plurality of its cities which are found in the Northeast. Thus the New York district contains approximately 10,-000,000 people. Five of the ten largest metropolitan areas are found in the Northeast while *all of the first ten* urban areas in density of population are in this region. So, too, the Northeast exceeds all the regions on the ratio of its people who live both in urban areas and in metropolitan districts. In all urban areas in 1930 were 74.4 and in metropolitan districts 70.2 percent of its people. This was in contrast to the next highest, namely, the Far West with 67.2 and 61.5 percent respectively, and with the lowest of the regions, the Northwest, with all urban at 35.6 and all metropolitan at 14.3 percent. Other characteristics will appear in the socio-economic indices cited subsequently.

As would be expected, the Northeastern Region has a large ratio of the trading areas mapped by the Department of Commerce and delineated by trading era outlines around major city centers of trading territory. These should be studied in relation to the metropolitan districts. Whereas the Northeast has one-third of the 93 metropolitan districts, its 37 trading areas are scarcely more than its pro rata share of the total 183 for the nation. These trade centers, overlapping state borders in many cases, include, in addition to the metropolitan districts, such cities as Manchester, Keene, Utica, Binghamton, Wilkes-Barre, Du Bois, Altoona, Johnstown, Cumberland, Clarksburg, Parkersburg.[7]

In the meantime, Ogburn's characterization of the region's cities will indicate certain measures of homogeneity and contrast with cities of other regions. "The outstanding population characteristic of the cities of the Northeast is the large percentage of the foreign-born, due in part to proximity to the gateway to Europe. In regard to age, the ratio of young persons to the middle-aged is somewhat large as compared with the other regions, perhaps because of the presence of immigrants with the Roman Catholic religion. The proportion of elders in the eastern cities is large, doubtless attributable to the influence of New England and the migration of the younger adults westward. In

[7] *Market Data Handbook of the United States*, Domestic Commerce Series, No. 36.

these cities is found the largest percentage paying income taxes and also the highest average value of owned homes.

"Among the occupations, these cities have a large percentage of their working population in manufacturing and a low percentage in trade and transportation. The percentage in personal and domestic service is low also. It is surprising to find in these cities of the Northeast the low percentages of lawyers, musicians, writers, and actors. The proportion of the clergy is small, but the church membership is highest. The high church membership may be due to the large numbers of Roman Catholics that report children as church members without their having had to make specific confession of faith, as is the case in most Protestant churches. In the northeastern cities are found the fewest small families, the most large families, and the fewest families with lodgers. Here there are the largest numbers of single men and single women and also the smallest percentages of the population married. The sales in restaurants are low. Government costs the most in these cities of the Northeast, more is spent for health, charities, and correction; and these cities have the largest number of police per unit of population. The large expenditures by government are accompanied by high taxes. In concluding the presentation of data for cities of the Northeast, many of the distinguishing characteristics are accounted for in part by manufacturing, the wealth that goes with it, and by the presence of immigrants with their religion." [8]

Measured by the people, the Northeast again ranks high in "American" qualities, whether in terms of the early historical Americans, or whether we consider the later complex of all the elements of the melting pot. Its mixed population gives it many paradoxical traits. In most respects the Northeast is similar to the Middle States, yet in proportion of the average annual natural increase (1930-1934) it stands below the Southeast and the Middle States, but above all the others. It was the first region to show a steadily declining fertility rate. According to Goodrich's data, it has next to the highest percentage excess of children under 5 years, relative to the number needed to maintain population permanently in counties with a low plane of living. In percentage deficit of children under 5 relative to the number needed to maintain population permanently for counties having a high plane of living, it is exceeded only by the Far West and ranks about the same as the Northwest and the Middle States.

[8] William F. Ogburn, *Social Characteristics of Cities*, pp. 29-30. (Quoted by permission of The International City Managers' Association.)

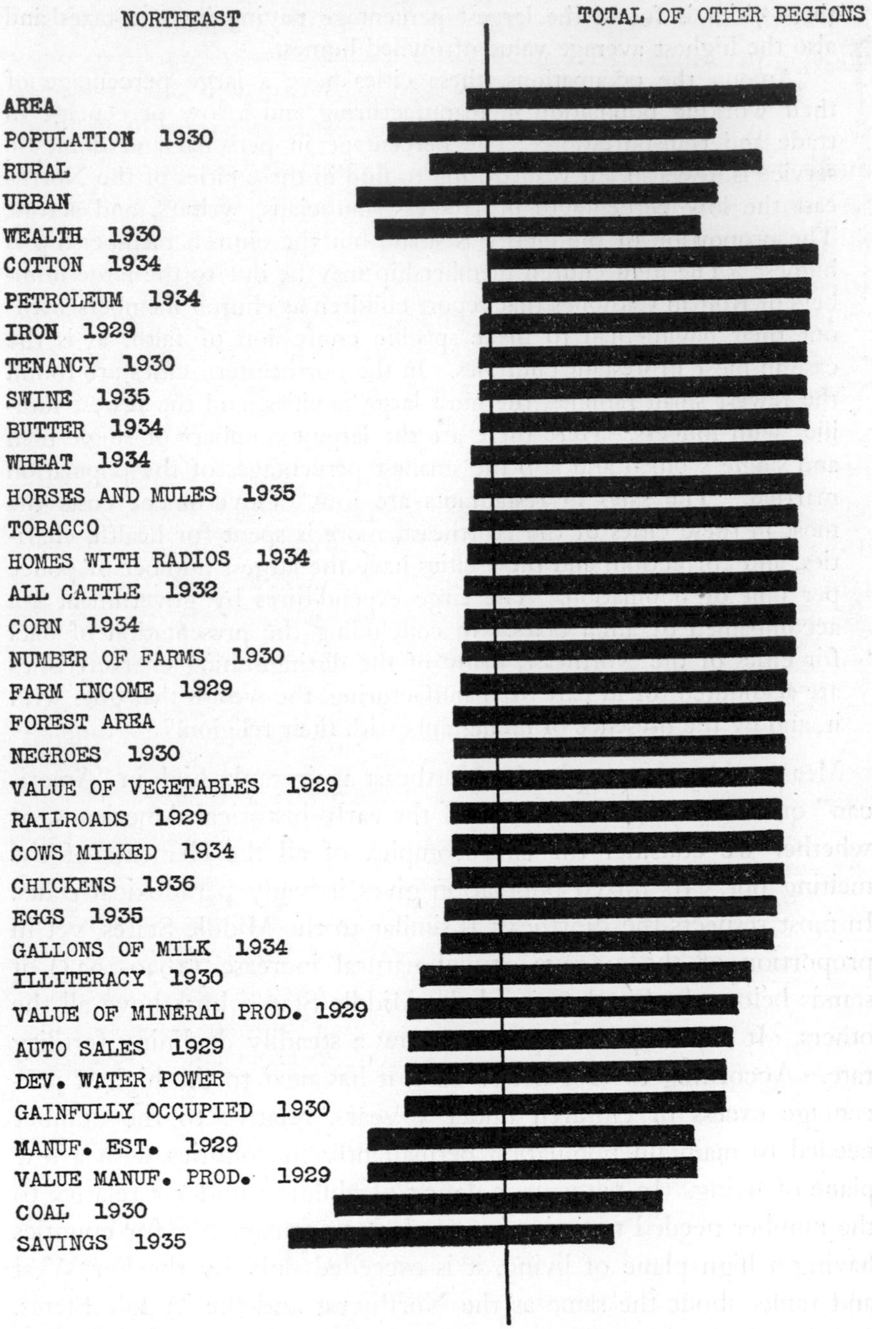

Regional Ratios to the National Total. Random Miscellaneous Indices: The Northeast

It was the only region to show an increase in the ratio of children under 5 per 1,000 native white rural women aged 20-44, 1910-1930. The Northeast, the Middle States, and the Northwest were the only regions to show in several states an increase in the ratio of children under 5 per 1,000 *native* white urban women, aged 20-44, 1910-1930. So, too, it was the only region showing an increase in several states in the ratio of children under 5 per 1,000 white women, aged 20-44, 1910-1930.

The Northeast is the most "American" of all the regions in the sense of the melting pot, and even its New England fringe vies with New York and Pennsylvania in the complexity of its ethnic composition. Of the nation's nearly twelve million foreign-born people, the Northeast has over half, with more than six and a quarter millions and nearly twice as many as has the great Middle States. In the order of numbers there are more than a million and a quarter from Italy, a little more than three-quarters of a million each from Russia and Poland, more than six hundred thousand each from Ireland and Germany, and more than two hundred thousand each from Austria and Czechoslovakia.

The story of the region is in many respects the story of how its people come to be what they are. To begin with New England, of course, the original white settlers were called Puritans. When they had gone west, they influenced that land but they left the habitats of the Puritan or at least lost them in a single generation. Their leaders were of the English gentry or wealthy well-to-do mercantile class; but by far the greater number of these people were the small farmers, the mechanics, and the laborers. Their religious exclusiveness tended to preserve the section as "Anglo-Saxon" until late into the nineteenth century. On the other hand, the southern section of the Northeast Region has been quite cosmopolitan from colonial days. Indeed, Governor Horatio Seymour was able to say that nine men prominent during the early period of New York represented just as many races: English, German, Dutch, Swedish, Scotch, Irish, West Indian, French, and Prussian. So, too, Pennsylvania, originally settled by Quakers from England, soon welcomed people of every creed, belief, or religion. Through her ports during the eighteenth century passed especially large numbers of Ulster Scots (Scotch-

Irish) and Germans, and, though many later migrated to other regions, a goodly number remained in Pennsylvania. Although a considerable number of migrants from Northwest Europe remained in the Middle Atlantic States of the Northeast Region, including especially the Irish, and a substantial contribution from the British and the Germans, the racial complexion of New England itself was little changed. By the end of the first four decades of the nineteenth century, the peak of the emigration from Northwestern Europe had been reached and passed, and most of the free land of the Middle States had been taken up, and still the immigrants poured into the United States. But now they were coming largely from Southeastern Europe and Asia, and they were stopping, for the most part, in the large urban centers of the Northeast. It was during this period, that is, largely since 1890, that the racial make-up of the whole Northeast underwent a change, but nowhere quite so rapidly and so radically as in Puritan New England.

> The first of the foreigners of any numerical importance to enter New England emigrated from Canada. They were the French-Canadians who came to work in the mills in the industrial centers of New England. Then came the Italians, mostly from southern Italy, the Slavs, including the highly artistic Bohemians, the land-loving Poles, the illiterate Slovaks and the Slovenians, the Roumanians, claiming descent from the imperial Romans, the Bulgarians, the Magyars of unknown origin. Next were the Asiatics, including Persians and Syrians, usually represented by unattached males who had left their native land because of religious persecution. There came, too, the Greeks, inclined to be gregarious and to live in colonies in the large cities. But of all the newcomers, none stuck to the urban centers with quite the tenacity of the Jews, who mostly emigrated from the old Austro-Hungarian Empire, Russia, and Poland Germany (Poland). (Suddenly New England, which only yesterday had boasted of her native-born American stock, awoke to the realization that today she was European.) Thus, New England became "Northeast" in fellowship, through the same class of immigrants who had filled the urban sections of New York, Pennsylvania, and all the industrial centers of the Northeast.[9]

No other region can boast of so complete an inventory of all the peoples of the nation as the Northeast, for (it literally shelters every

[9] Martha Edwards, adapted from unpublished manuscript on Summary of the Racial Composition of the Six Regions of the United States.

type and ethnic group. In this respect the supreme melting pot, it is essentially "America." Yet its diversity of peoples must be pictured both as a whole, a region, and yet also in subgroups. Such a picture is in itself a subject for many volumes. For the purpose of the present outline, however, the people may be viewed from perhaps a half dozen viewpoints: First, the earlier settlements which in turn are those of New England and of the lower Middle Atlantic States; second, the later immigrants from lower Europe who remained for the most part in the metropolitan areas; third, the people who came to the Northeast from the other provinces, especially from the Southeast; fourth, the special migration of Negroes from the South; and finally, there is in contrast to the earlier New England, New York, and Philadelphia culture, the newer intelligentsia of the mixed vintage of European influence transplanted upon American youth and the emerging labor class and mass population. Somewhere in the margins and framework of this mixture will be found the regional character of the great Northeast.

We have already called attention to the sudden transformation of New England through the infiltration of hordes of foreign elements. Massachusetts and Boston typify both the old and the new at its maximum gauge. But we must remember that New York and Pennsylvania had a rich and varied heritage of earlier settlers. Thus in contrast to New England's earlier religious exclusiveness which preserved the English in New England as a peculiar people until well into the nineteenth century, the races admitted to New York, as already shown, have always been representative of diverse cultures, even during the earlier period. It will be recalled that the Swedes first established themselves in the Hudson Valley, but the more aggressive Dutch drove them out. But, though the Dutch called the section New Amsterdam and were quite prosperous farmers, the territory was taken over by the English and renamed New York in honor of the King's brother. However, the Dutch settlers were allowed to remain, and many influential families of New York, among them that of President Roosevelt, trace their ancestry to these ancient Dutch settlers of the seventeenth century.

Another colony to which all races and nationalities were admitted and sometimes welcomed was Pennsylvania. Twenty years after the

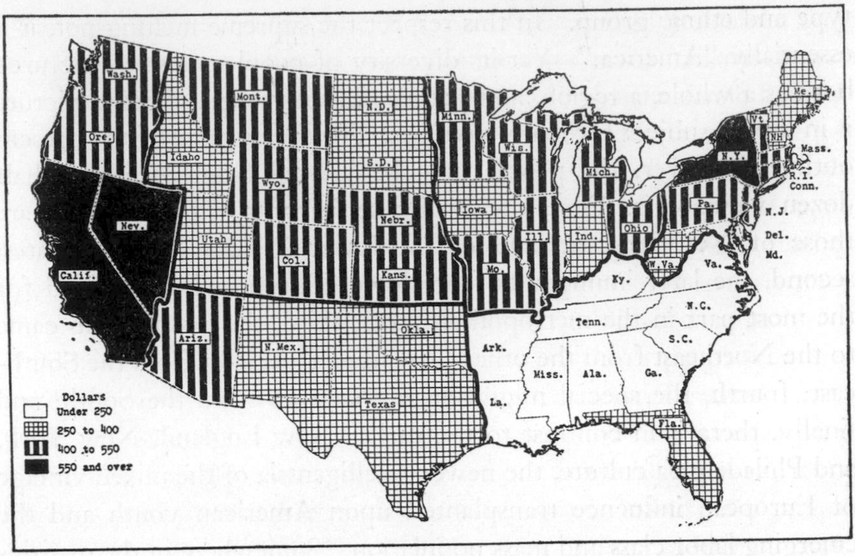

Above: Retail Sales Per Capita in the United States in 1929, compared with,
Below: Wholesale and Retail Trade in the United States. Compare these with the standard of living studies of Carter Goodrich and others in relation to migration.

STATE	Wholesale Trade Per Capita 1929	Retail Sales Per Store 1929	Retail Stores Per 1,000 Population 1930
Southeast			
Virginia	$270.97	$22,759	10.8
North Carolina	227.15	25,697	9.1
South Carolina	191.79	19,827	8.7
Georgia	349.87	21,466	9.9
Florida	317.69	22,203	15.3
Kentucky	204.31	21,712	10.4
Tennessee	411.82	27,656	9.0
Alabama	216.98	24,471	8.6
Mississippi	191,65	23,880	8.1
Arkansas	201.22	22,810	9.7
Louisiana	405.86	20,082	11.1
Southwest			
Oklahoma	324.24	28,878	11.5
Texas	481.46	30,839	11.5
New Mexico	126.58	28,748	9.9
Arizona	228.87	38,148	11.6
Northeast			
Maine	238.36	27,932	14.0
New Hampshire	132.81	27,867	14.0
Vermont	159.42	29,420	14.4
Massachusetts	727.48	38,230	12.7
Rhode Island	437.68	33,366	13.8
Connecticut	322.06	34,651	13.7
New York	1,403.28	38,119	15.1
New Jersey	251.04	30,753	14.9
Delaware	991.87	27,378	15.2
Pennsylvania	494.42	29,590	14.2
Maryland	454.44	29,051	13.0
Dist. of Columbia	720.23	56,088	12.1
West Virginia	200.60	25,581	10.0

STATE	Wholesale Trade Per Capita 1929	Retail Sales Per Store 1929	Retail Stores Per 1,000 Population 1930
Middle States			
Ohio	$465.54	$36,372	12.6
Indiana	284.60	29,412	12.9
Illinois	899.79	37,985	12.7
Michigan	449.03	39,715	11.6
Wisconsin	333.20	31,110	13.5
Minnesota	669.61	31,027	12.1
Iowa	427.76	32,991	13.4
Missouri	926.34	31,560	13.0
Northwest			
North Dakota	385.40	28,632	11.9
South Dakota	341.25	29,160	13.0
Nebraska	764.86	32,677	13.3
Kansas	542.62	30,691	13.8
Montana	294.69	34,317	13.0
Idaho	272.34	34,257	11.1
Wyoming	153.36	34,315	13.1
Colorado	521.62	35,402	13.6
Utah	355.56	37,808	10.4
Far West			
Nevada	150.75	38,177	14.4
Washington	733.88	34,866	14.2
Oregon	489.35	31,432	15.3
California	732.60	37,995	15.1
United States	567.12	32,297	12.6

first settlement by English Quakers nearly one-half of the population was German. Over one-half of the Ulster Scots who came to the United States settled in Pennsylvania. For the most part, they entered by the way of Philadelphia and Baltimore and went from there into the interior of Pennsylvania. Pennsylvania was the only colony except Maryland that tolerated the Roman Catholics. Thus, with "all phases of the Christian religion, and all branches of the Teutonic and Celtic races, Pennsylvania set the original type to which all America has conformed; that of race inter-mixture on the basis of religious and political equality." The Middle Atlantic States, that is, New York, New Jersey, Pennsylvania, and Delaware, became quite cosmopolitan, especially New York and Pennsylvania. To a greater extent than New England to the north and the Southeastern regions to the south, these States of the Middle Atlantic group welcomed people of various nations, creeds, and beliefs.

As indicating the regional background of the present Northeast it is important to note that, although the Germans took a prominent part in the development of the Middle States, as we have pointed out, almost 50 percent of them remained in the urban centers in the Northeast Region. For instance, one-fourth of all the German immigrants are found in New York. Forty percent of them are in New York, Chicago, Philadelphia, and Brooklyn. The Irish immigrants, who are exceeded only by the Germans in number, have clung largely to the Northeast. They are concentrated especially in Connecticut, Massachusetts, Rhode Island, New York, and New Jersey. The city of New York contains a large Irish population, while one-sixth of the population of Boston is foreign, the larger portion being Irish. This tendency to settle in urban centers may be noted from the fact that over 45 percent of the Irish in the United States in 1880 were in New York, Philadelphia, Brooklyn, and Boston.

> In order to understand fully the "American" character and power of the people of the Northeast, it is necessary to recall the fact that there is a later "American" type of people who now give authenticity to the Northeastern Region. This second movement, or New Immigration, was largely in its inception, at least, a movement of laboring men who came in anticipation of returning to their native lands. More often than not they came in response to a call for industrial workers in the Northeast and Middle regions. There were times when they were

welcomed; there have been others when their presence has been greatly resented. The main contributors of these people, who threatened the very racial unity of the United States, in the order of importance were Italy, Austria-Hungary, and the Russian Empire, yet there were millions of others contributing to the complex fabric which is the Northeast.

Italy leads in sending more immigrants to the United States than any other of the Second Immigration groups, and is second only to the Germans of the non-English speaking people. The Italians, who have come to the number of four and a half millions (most of them since 1890) are concentrated in the Northeast Region. However, both the Middle States and the Far West regions include Italians among their foreign population. Louisiana is a favorite southern center, and a few Italians, engaged in the cigar-manufacturing establishments, are at Tampa, Florida. About four-fifths of these Italians should be classed as urban, a much higher proportion than that for the country's population as a whole. In New York, no foreign people save only the Russian (including the Jews) are so strongly represented. In New Orleans, the Italians exceed all other foreigners. Philadelphia, Chicago, Boston, Pittsburgh, Jersey City, Buffalo, Cleveland, St. Louis, and Baltimore all have Italian settlements.

Next to Italians, the Slavs, who have come in varying numbers, and are usually found in the great industrial centers of the Northeast and the Middle regions, are among the most numerous. In fact, it may be said that the textile manufacturing centers of the Northeast—such as Fall River, Lowell, New Bedford, Massachusetts; Manchester, New Hampshire; Providence, Rhode Island; Wilmington, Delaware; Utica, New York; Newark, New Jersey—all these and many more have colonies or sections populated with recent immigrants, many of whom are Slavic. The same condition of affairs is found in the iron, steel, and other older manufacturing cities and towns of New York and Pennsylvania. A second type of immigrant community is that found in connection with the coal and mining industries in Pennsylvania and West Virginia.

In these industrial centers, the foreigners of every race and nationality may be found. The majority of them reached the country with few funds. They were consequently willing to work for little. These facts give rise to the common impression that these communities are often more like those of a foreign country than American.[10]

In any thorough inventory of the people of the Northeast, of course, it would be necessary to make discriminating distinctions

[10] Martha Edwards, adapted from unpublished manuscript on Summary of the Racial Composition of the Six Regions of the United States.

between and among the several groups; yet the total picture is as presented, with the outline providing for adequate study of the Bohemians, the Slovaks, the Polish, the Finns, the Roumanians, the Magyars, the Bulgarians, the Lithuanians, the Turks, and the others. All of this would again be basic to a consideration of that other great group which has come through Russia, Austria, and Poland, namely, the Jewish people now comprehending a larger number than all the people of Thomas Jefferson's early America. To indicate the essential "Americanism" of the Northeast as typified by these ethnic elements we need only return to such episodes as Mayor La Guardia, representative of great Italian folk, prospective candidate for President of the United States, in his popular role of attacking the German Nazi on behalf of America's millions of Jewish people, or Governor Lehman of New York, or the intellectuals who contribute to the American science of society, or the leaders of finance, theaters, moving picture industries, great merchants, and others. This is indeed America, yet regionally homogeneous in a different way from most of the other great American regions.

It is important to note also the increasing ratio and number of Negroes in the Northeast which by 1930 could show nearly a million and three-quarters Negro population, which is a little more than 14 percent of the total Negroes in the nation. At least seven of the Northeastern States now have considerable Negro population. The facts are shown in the statistical tables; yet it is important to note that New York and Pennsylvania each have over 400,000 Negroes and that the largest Negro cities in the nation are not in the South but are, respectively, New York, Chicago, Philadelphia, Baltimore, and Washington. In many Northeastern and Middle Western industrial communities the Negro population has increased in the decade from 1920 to 1930 by from 100 to 400 percent. This, again, reflects an aspect of the Northeast's "Americanism" in that it is largely from this region that the leadership for giving the Negro a greater part in the political, economic, and social opportunity in the nation emanates. It is from this region largely that Negro educational leadership for the South has been recruited, with, of course, the Middle States contributing a fair share and the Southeast itself greatly increasing its contribution. The Northeast represents also in this respect

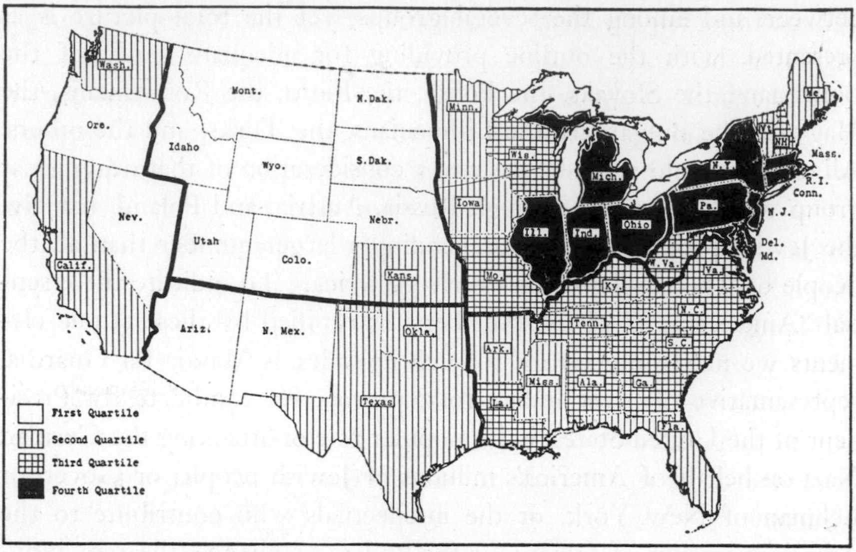

REGIONAL CONCENTRATION OF POPULATION AND FOREIGN-BORN WHITE POPULATION CORRESPOND IN GENERAL TO THE CONCENTRATION OF INDUSTRY

Above: Population Per Square Mile.

Below: Percentage of Foreign Born in the Total White Population, 1930.

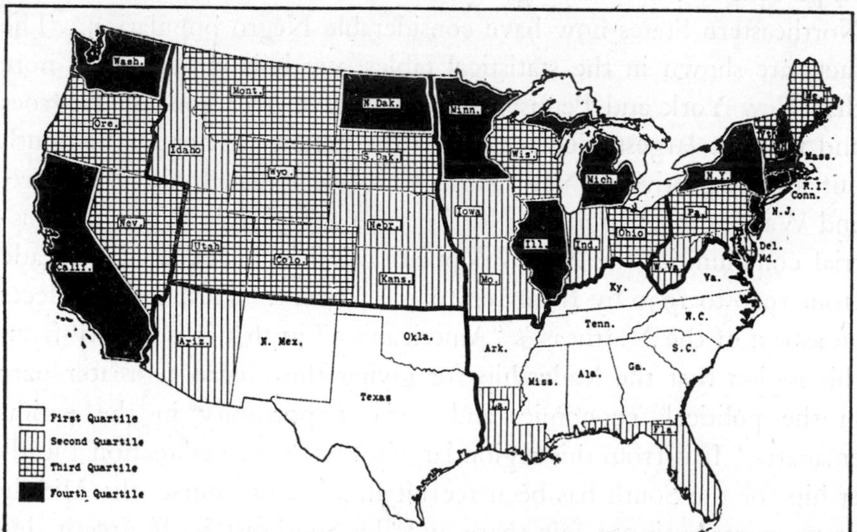

the metropolitan problem of adjustment, for the Negro is an urban people in the North.

In the final characterization of the Northeast as a major region, we recall again the earlier concept of "The North" and "The East" as used by "The West," the financial domination of the nation by "The East," as well as the urban industrial predominance of this region. This unifying factor of "The Commercialization of the North" plays an important role in the development of the nation, and appears as a constantly recurring motif in James Truslow Adams' *History of American Life*. Yet both historically and structurally there must be the threefold approach, one for New England, one for New York, and one for Pennsylvania and the lower states, all of which make up the mosaic of the region's fine subregional constituency.

This pluralism of the Northeast is especially in evidence in the major project of the WPA providing an American Guide Series of volumes which feature first and foremost six beautiful volumes on the New England States and the two volumes of the *Almanac for New Yorkers*. Something of the range and richness of the material may be suggested in the Massachusetts volume of approximately 700 pages which represented such great elimination of valuable data as to endanger the project. Thus the State Director writes, "Out of several millions of words there slowly grew a book—nay, a BOOK some 650,000 words long. The editors, abandoning a momentarily considered idea of publishing a volume of 2,000 pages mounted on wheels with a trailer attachment, sharpened a gross of blue pencils and attacked the typescript to condense it to a portable size. Chapters became pages, pages became paragraphs, paragraphs became sentences. Tempers wore thin as cherished passages were cruelly blue-penciled, and editorial conferences developed into pitched battles. But out of it all, writers of varied ability and training and of widely differing temperament, thrown together on the common basis of need, shared a new experience—an adventure in co-operation."[11] Titles for other beautiful books of the series indicate the enormous task of characterizing any such section, much less the major area of the Northeast. These titles are: *Maine: A Guide "Down East," Rhode Island: A Guide to the Smallest State, Vermont: A Guide to the Green Mountain State.*

[11] Ray Allen Billington, "One Moment Please!" *Massachusetts: A Guide to Its Places and People*, pp. ix-x.

In our chapter on the Middle States we pointed up much that was characteristic of the New England heritage and its influence upon the rest of the nation. Most of this, as well as most of the other characterizations which we might present, take on the nature of commonplace Americanisms, yet they bear repeating often in so far as they are elemental factors in our regional outlines. And there is no more logical authentic interpreter of New England or the nation than James Truslow Adams, long nurtured and working in, of, and for the region.

Whether commonplace or not, New England's character is still powerfully integrated in the realism of the nation. The historian illustrates well the viewpoint of cultural determinism of our regional and subregional approach by pointing up "the diversity and the homogeneity of New England." "As contrasted with the rest of America, even in colonial times, New England became a section clearly differentiated from the others socially, economically, and psychologically. The obviousness of this broad differentiation, however, should not lead us to overlook the marked local differences existing within the New England section itself. . . . In part these heterogeneous interests derive from obvious factors of location. A fishing community will be found on the coast, whereas a manufacturing city may develop about a water power on an interior river, and not vice versa. What I wish to point out is that there are also marked distinctions in character and outlook betweeen some of the subsections that can be derived only remotely, when at all, from their geography. For example, whereas the early settlers of Boston and Newport took advantage of geographical circumstances to develop these towns into the most important ports of the entire section, geography was not at all responsible for the fact that under their several early leaderships Massachusetts should have developed a harsh, dogmatic, persecuting spirit, while Rhode Island should have been our first colony to insist on complete toleration, with all that later stemmed from these contrasting attitudes. When the banished Roger Williams tramped in the winter snow from Boston to establish a new settlement devoted to freedom of spirit, he did not choose Rhode Island with the slightest thought of the type of economic state that might there arise. He went solely because he knew an Indian there. Nor had the divergent physical aspects of Massachusetts Bay and Narragansett Bay anything to do with the vastly different intellectual outlooks, in respect to toleration, of the communities that grew up on their separate shores. Again, Vermont, owing more to the character of its settlers and the accidents of history than to anything inherent in its landscape and position, became a state so much apart that for a while, during the American Revolution, it set up as an independent one internationally and for some time after remained uncertain as to whether it would even enter the American Union. On the other hand, the inhabitants of all six New England states resemble one another fundamentally much more than they do those of any other section, and we must here concern ourselves with these broad resemblances and not with the minor differences." [12]

Of the traditional backgrounds, in addition to the people themselves, Adams features first the Puritan tradition. The New Englanders' belief that they were a people set apart by destiny as a chosen people gave rise to unyielding dogmatism in other matters as well as religion. Thus dogmatism became, because of the close-knit communities, a group unity more than merely individual character. So arose work and thrift and snobbishness as New England traits, and these were greatly accentuated by the physiographic nature of the region which was a hard taskmaster, in agriculture, hunting, fishing, forestry, and communication.

A citation from Adams, supplemented by two or three others, will be adequate to make the case. "In New England, balked by soil, topography, climate, and the comparatively stationary population, the people had to turn to other means for the accumulation of capital. Work and thrift were not only virtues but economic necessities. In the absence of large enterprises, of any labor to be exploited, and of new immigration, the New Englander if he wanted to 'get ahead' by his own exertions had to make one penny do the work of three as contrasted with his fellow American in more favored sections. All factors—the frontier, religion, land, and climate—thus combined to make the New Englander think long and carefully over the advisability of the least expenditure. Such necessity produces a certain type of character. If it may easily descend to the vice of miserliness, it also makes for self-restraint, strength of will, and extreme conservatism. This conservatism, once thoroughly instilled, comes to operate on everything, from the spending of money on the gewgaws of fashion to the accepting of new-fangled ideas in business or government." [13] On the other hand, Count Keyserling sees the basic New

[12] James Truslow Adams, "The Historical Background," *New England's Prospect: 1933* (edited by J. T. Adams, H. S. Graves, *et al.*), pp. 1-2. (Quoted by permission of Little, Brown, & Company.)

[13] *Ibid.*, pp. 5-6.

COUNTIES IN THE UNITED STATES HAVING MORE THAN 100,000 COTTON SPINDLES EACH, 1929

County	State	Spindles (number)
Bristol	Massachusetts	6,144,328
Providence	Rhode Island	1,525,952
Gaston	North Carolina	1,184,298
Spartanburg	South Carolina	975,608
Hillsborough	New Hampshire	879,836
Greenville	South Carolina	766,316
Anderson	South Carolina	647,024
Windham	Connecticut	592,456
Hampden	Massachusetts	486,948
Berkshire	Massachusetts	477,684
New London	Connecticut	473,772
Worcester	Massachusetts	472,152
Pittsylvania	Virginia	467,440
Cabarrus	North Carolina	454,208
Kent	Rhode Island	444,920
Muskogee	Georgia	444,106
Androscoggin	Maine	427,212
Essex	Massachusetts	412,252
Middlesex	Massachusetts	348,534
Union	South Carolina	347,100
York	Maine	332,984
Madison	Alabama	314,716
Strafford	New Hampshire	307,180
Guilford	North Carolina	305,548
Oneida	New York	302,796
Mecklenburg	North Carolina	294,324
Greenwood	South Carolina	289,116
York	South Carolina	270,434
Richmond	North Carolina	267,816
Laurens	South Carolina	264,616
Pickens	South Carolina	254,732
Richland	South Carolina	252,792
Cherokee	South Carolina	233,764
Albany	New York	229,960
Hudson	New Jersey	222,080
Rowan	North Carolina	220,440
Bristol	Rhode Island	217,900
Rutherford	North Carolina	209,380
Fulton	Georgia	207,850
Rockingham	North Carolina	202,852
Chambers	Alabama	199,178
Cleveland	North Carolina	195,854
Troup	Georgia	195,192
Newberry	South Carolina	194,232
Richmond	Georgia	191,720
Aiken	South Carolina	189,948
Knox	Tennessee	187,236
Tallapoosa	Alabama	184,456
Stanly	North Carolina	180,248
Calhoun	Alabama	175,602
Durham	North Carolina	174,928
Talladega	Alabama	170,574
Lancaster	South Carolina	163,928
Floyd	Georgia	162,188
Kennebec	Maine	160,704
Alamance	North Carolina	160,500
Chester	South Carolina	148,648
Halifax	North Carolina	147,080
Hall	Georgia	146,520
Spalding	Georgia	143,344
Cumberland	Maine	138,400
Hampshire	Massachusetts	137,906
Upson	Georgia	134,256
Catawba	North Carolina	130,848
Davidson	North Carolina	130,656
Lincoln	North Carolina	128,936
Iredell	North Carolina	127,160
Caldwell	North Carolina	118,444
Chattooga	Georgia	117,648
Hamilton	Tennessee	116,264
McDowell	North Carolina	115,474
Coweta	Georgia	113,240
Robeson	North Carolina	109,856
Oconee	South Carolina	106,828
Polk	Georgia	106,454
Merrimack	New Hampshire	105,404
Newton	Georgia	104,568
Essex	New Jersey	104,348
Vance	North Carolina	101,184

Source: Census Bulletin 166.

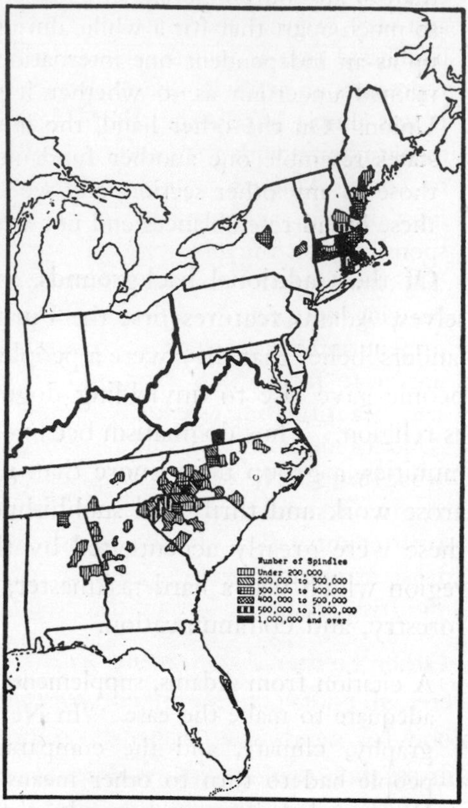

REGIONAL DISTRIBUTION OF PRODUCING SPINDLES

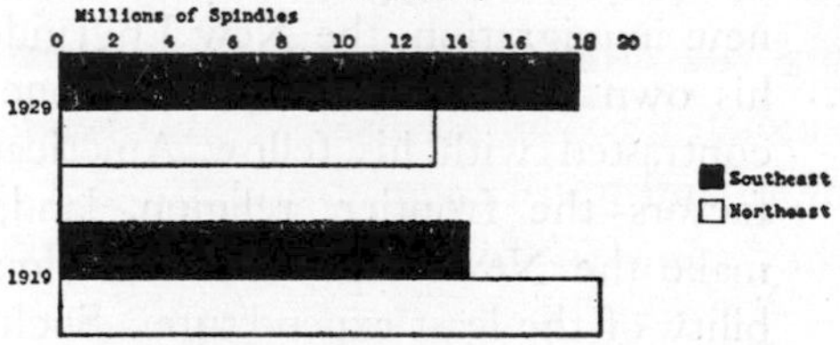

PRODUCING SPINDLES, ACTIVE AT SOME TIME DURING THE YEAR

	1929	Per Cent	1919	Per Cent
United States	31,583,588	100	33,718,953	100
Cotton Growing States	18,318,642	58.1	14,568,272	43.2
Northeast	13,264,946	41.9	19,150,681	56.8

Source: Census of Manufactures, 1930.

The above figures and map illumine the interregional problem of cotton textile competition in the United States.

England quality of another origin. Says he, "New England's great and very original charm is, alas, that of a dying culture. There is little likelihood that it will survive even for a century; all the less so as it represents an artificial civilization from the point of view of the earth. It was almost purely spirit-born; only a certain ethereal lyricism seems to harmonize with the peculiar hazy beauty of the land. In centuries to come, America will probably see New England's main, because most lasting, achievement in the fact that its sons are chiefly responsible for the colonization of the South and the Middle West. The lines of development American historians are in the habit of drawing between New England's past cultural achievements and the present and future state of America are, in my opinion, all of them untrue to fact. New England's culture was an exclusive thing in itself, beautiful but essentially sterile, and even today what is vital in America derives little more from Boston than it does from Athens; what seems to be of New England origin is really of generally Puritan origin. I should not wonder if New England ended as an essentially Irish country—less because of the growing percentage of residents of Irish extraction than because of a pre-established harmony between the Irish temperament and the New England landscape." [14]

Other factors contributing to the Americanism of New England were, of course, numerous. One was the long lack of infusion of blood for nearly two centuries which contributed to inbreeding of culture such that Adams wonders whether Harvard College "was not detrimental to the intellectual life of New England" because it kept its students from better training abroad. So through lack of training and ethnic contacts there was "less healthy stirring of the provincial life than almost anywhere else in America. New Englanders more and more came to think of themselves as a race apart, and . . . they came to think of themselves and their ways as superior." [15]

Thus, "New England had always liked to consider itself the driver of the American coach, and the old die-hard Federalists there fought tooth and nail against the upbuilding of a new section which might threaten its dying influence. Through their mouthpiece in Congress, Josiah Quincy, they had thundered against the addition of French Louisiana and the creation of new states. 'You have no authority,' Quincy told the members of Congress, 'to throw the rights and property of this people into the "hotch-potch" with the wild men on the

[14] Hermann Keyserling, "Genius Loci," *Atlantic Monthly*, Vol. 144, p. 304.
[15] James Truslow Adams, *The Epic of America, passim.*

Missouri, nor with the mixed, though more respectable race of Anglo-Hispan-Gallo-Americans who bask on the sands in the mouth of the Mississippi. . . . Do you suppose the people of the Northern and Atlantic States will, or ought to, look on with patience and see Representatives and Senators from the Red River and Missouri, pouring themselves upon this and the other floor, managing the concerns of a seaboard fifteen hundred miles, at least, from their residence?' "[16]

Yet with all its pride and priority, New England is a relatively minority portion of the great Northeast, boasting first in people, first in wealth, first in industry, first in philanthropy, first in universities, first in national organizations and agencies—all these larger in those areas of the Region below New England. The metamorphosis of New England from agrarian and fisherman's land of first Americans to urban and industrial stronghold of later Americans has been told. While this transformation was taking place, the definitive America of "The East" was being molded in a similar process with New York as the center and with the major force being what Adams calls "The Commercialization of the North," to which we have called attention in Chapter II, which contrasts sectionalism and regionalism. Next to the frontier and westward movements, all of this sure but subtle evolving and emerging Northeast appears to be the most organic Americanism as measured by the inventory of the nation at the end of the first third of the twentieth century. To know America and to envisage its trends, it is necessary to understand such fundamental forces and developments as made the Northeast the ruler of the nation.

James Truslow Adams points up significantly the change. "As in the South, so in the North, the growing wealth of the few was utilized in a more luxurious mode of living and in the erection of commodious mansions which mark a great advance upon the preceding period, the introduction of the Georgian style everywhere modifying the earlier type of house. Dignified dwellings, of wood in New England, and of brick in New York, New Jersey and Pennsylvania, replaced the simple homes of the close of the preceding century. As contrasted with the South, however, these were for the most part town houses and must be looked for in Portsmouth, Boston, Newport, New York, Philadelphia or other towns and their near neighborhoods. . . . This divorce

16 James Truslow Adams, *The Epic of America*, pp. 147-148.

from the soil and from agricultural interests of the main body of the wealthy and aristocratic class in the North, and their gathering into towns, were to have marked political and social effects, but before touching upon those we must turn to the country districts and to a very different economic class to see what their condition was in the new period. The situation varied in the several northern colonies, which from the standpoint of the agrarian question may be divided into three groups—New England, New York, and the two colonies of Pennsylvania and New Jersey." [17]

Writing in that illuminating symposium by twenty-seven authors on *New England's Prospect: 1933*, R. J. McFall shows through a statistical comparison the relative place which New England holds in the total of the Northeast. Entirely independent of the regional division utilized in the present volume, McFall delineated his Northeast to include the identical states of the present arrangement with the exception of West Virginia. That is, Washington, D. C., and Maryland were included along with New Jersey, Delaware, Pennsylvania, and the others. In his comparison of the New England States with the total region he also gives an excellent statistical picture of the whole. Enough of his comparisons are given to illustrate the case.

> The land area of all these northeastern states is 5.8 percent of the total land area of the United States, while that of New England alone is 2.1 percent; thus the area of the whole section is about two and three-quarters times that of New England. A much smaller proportion of the national population, however, is found in the six New England states, New England's population accounting for only 6.7 percent of the 30 percent contributed by the entire Northeastern area; thus the density of population is much smaller. The density of the population of the whole region is well over two hundred to the square mile, while that of New England alone is only five-eighths as great. Thirty percent of the national population lives in these Northeastern states on less than 6 percent of our land area. From the standpoint of congestion of population it may readily be concluded that the region as a whole is much more specialized in industry and commerce, much more one-sided, than is its easterly portion.

[17] "The Commercialization of the North, 1713-1745," James Truslow Adams, *Provincial Society, 1690-1763*, pp. 236-237. (Quoted by permission of The Macmillan Company.)

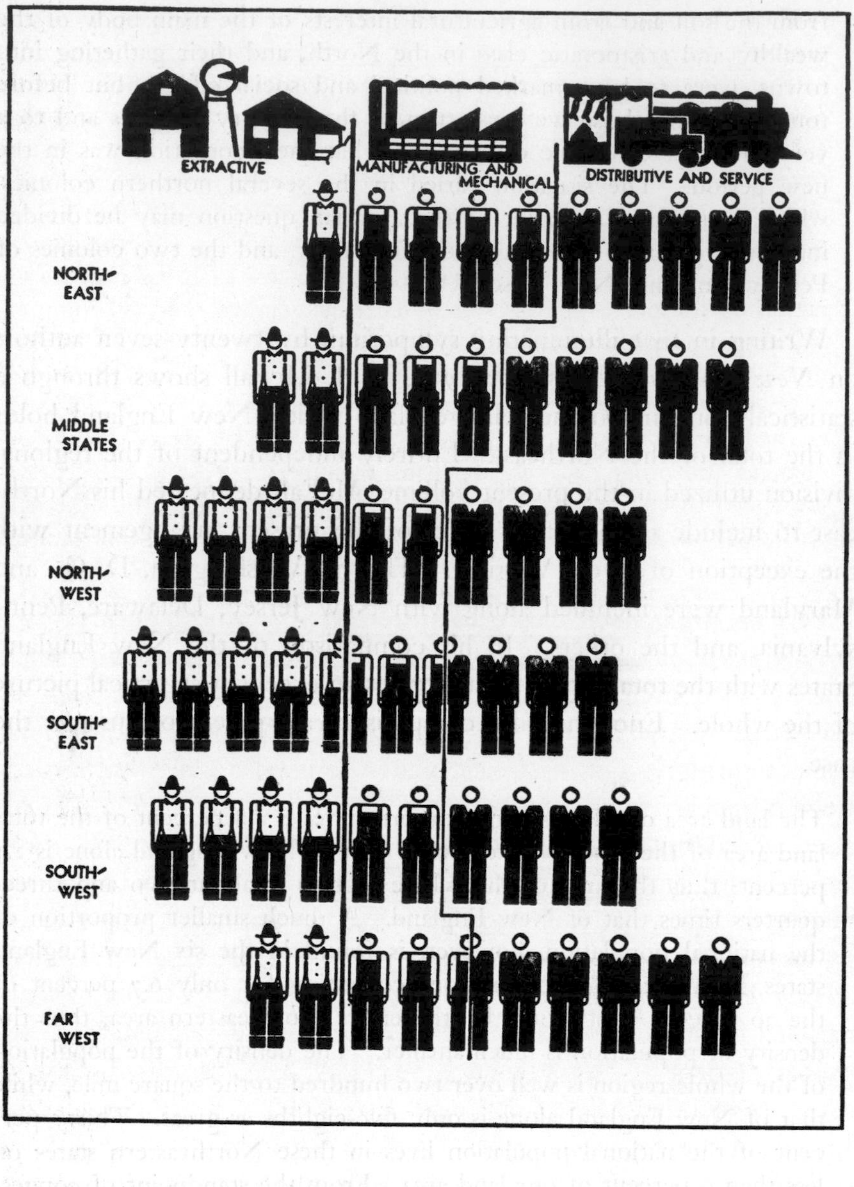

Regional Ratios of Occupational Services. Note the three great agricultural regions—the Southeast, the Southwest, and the Northwest. Adapted from Educational Policies Commission, *The Effect of Population Changes on American Education.*

> With the concentration of human beings in this region goes a still greater concentration of income. It is estimated that just over one-half of the total income accruing to individuals in the whole United States appears in this small area of less than 6 percent of the national area. The income of our corporations is even slightly more concentrated. New England, however, is not so richly endowed; its individual income is less than 10 percent of the national total, and its corporate income only a little more than 6 percent of it. In the case of corporate income, New England has slightly less than its share in the nation on the per capita basis. . . . If it be assumed that the commercial activity registered by total check payments is an index of the economic status of a region, New England takes a small place, but the area as a whole takes an overwhelmingly large place in the nation. Thanks to the business activity centering in New York, with its speculative exchanges and other great financial institutions, the Northeastern States show over three-quarters of the monetary activity of the nation through check payments. New England has less than 5 percent of this national business. . . .[18]

Perhaps the general characterizations of the region already given are adequate for the outline of further treatment. Yet in two general aspects, so dominant is the region, it seems important to point up further distinctive claims. These are financial resources and national manufacturing. The financial predominance of the Northeastern Region appears in the statement of the distribution of the national assets or liabilities, and of banking deposits, among the regions. The latter figure includes both public and private funds in banks, and interbank deposits as well, and hence does not stand as a clear measure of the private commercial financial resource. The Far West alone among the remaining regions has a disproportionate share of the national financial resource as measured by this index. The trade and export centers of San Francisco and Los Angeles and the export activities of other West Coast cities may absorb a very considerable amount of this apparent surplus. It is clear that the great agricultural regions cannot operate upon an adequate financial base without importing both short-term and long-term credit from other regions. The inference that, directly or indirectly, this credit deficit is made up in the eastern money markets cannot be tested by exact measure-

[18] R. J. McFall, "New England and the Northeast: A Statistical Comparison," *New England's Prospect: 1933* (edited by J. T. Adams, H. S. Graves, *et al.*), pp. 96-97. (Quoted by permission of American Geographical Society.)

ment. However, in view of the emphatic surplus of Northeastern bank assets and the equally emphatic deficit in the Northwest, the Southwest, and the Southeast, the assumption is justified.

The Northeast stands out as the dominant region not only in the indices of finance and banking but also in all manufacturing industries, with nearly a third of the total population accounting for virtually 40 percent of both the national income and the national manufacture. The Middle States are not far less important, especially in the field of manufacture, where their pro rata activity (i.e., volume of manufacture divided by proportion of population) is greater than that of the Northeast. Together these two regions have 58.4 percent of the total population, 68.2 percent of the total income, and 76.8 percent of the manufactured product. Forty-one and two-tenths percent of the population in other states receive only 31.8 percent of the national income and produce only 23.2 percent of the national manufacture. In view of these regional comparisons already cited it is not surprising to find a tendency for bank assets and liabilities to concentrate in the Northeast and the Middle States. Thus of the total assets of all active banks in 1935, the Northeast reports 61.5 percent and the Middle States 19.4;[19] of the total assets in Federal Deposit Insurance Corporation Banks, the Northeast has 52.1 and the Middle States 24.2 percent, with about the same ratios for total deposits.[20] It is manifest that the Northeast has a sufficient supply of bank resource not only to supply its own needs, but to make up the deficiencies of the other regions. The data above, moreover, must be regarded as a minimum statement of the relative importance of Northeastern finance in the national economy. The extent to which banking institutions and non-banking financial agencies in other regions are only technically resident in the latter areas cannot be estimated, but must be assumed to be large. The importance of the Northeast may correspondingly be assumed to be even greater than the apparent measure.

John Maclachlan has summarized the general data indicating the "regional profile" of the national manufacturing plant in 1935. Since the place of the Northeast can best be told in comparison with the other

[19] John Maclachlan, unpublished manuscript.
[20] *Ibid.*

regions, the comparative figures will be given in the present chapter rather than in the several chapters dealing with each region. In general, the Northeast remains somewhat more important than the Middle States as a manufacturing area, having a slightly larger share of both the national gross manufacture and of the value added by manufacture. However, the production of the Middle States, carried out by 47,825 plants as compared to 73,485 plants in the Northeast, is characteristically done by considerably larger manufacturing units than in any other region. The Northeast, nearest to the Middle States in this datum, shows a 46 percent smaller gross output per plant operating. The manufacturing processes of the Southwest and the Northwest are characteristic in a much higher value of product per wage earner. This figure for the Northwest in 1935 was nearly twice the national average, and two-and-a-half times the Southeastern figure. The contrast is consistent whether the value of raw materials, etc., or the value added by manufacture, or both these items, is being considered. The nature of the manufactures conducted in these regions, following upon the extractive industries, is clearly indicated.

The three westerly regions (the Northwest, the Far West, and the Southwest) show a significantly higher ratio of value added to wages paid than do the easterly regions and the Middle States. This tendency might be attributed to a complex causation, but in any event appears to suggest that wages constitute a smaller proportion of total costs, despite the fact that in the Northwest and the Far West the wage rates appear to be significantly higher than in the Southeast and slightly higher than in the Northeast. The Northwest, accounting for 3.0 percent of the national manufacturing output through the employment of 1.6 percent of the total number of wage earners and the payment of 1.7 percent of the wage bill, with a gross value of output per wage earner of $11,216 and a value added by manufacture per wage earner of $3,083, presents the most distinctive regional manufacturing pattern. This must be traced, of course, to the nature of the industries which deal with the natural resources of the area, but since the wage earner of the Northwest is second only to his contemporary in the Middle States in terms of annual wages paid, the pattern is, through 1935, one of very considerable vitality.[21]

It is, of course, not possible to characterize the folkways and folk culture of so large and complicated a region as the Northeast. Nowhere perhaps is the pluralism of America more marked. Alongside a sort of supreme composite unity in a dozen urban centers can be

[21] *Ibid.*

found almost everything comprehended in the modern industrial technological trend of America. Of Pittsburgh a recent study says: "Its scope and its outlook are national; its financial interests are at least country-wide; and the forces that control its destinies, which are basically economic, are forces that move with the large strides of national progress and regression."[22] Baltimore is the great border-line city. Washington, D. C., comprehends all that we have been saying about the nation and apparently everything else which could be said but which cannot be encompassed in a reasonable general appraisal. West Virginia is North, East, South, and Middle States all in one. And New York is again "America."

The irrepressible Count Keyserling, in his article in the *Atlantic Monthly*, "Genius Loci," gives one view of the great city. "Every intelligent American will tell every intelligent European he meets that New York is not America. . . . Yet New York belongs to America, as a part of the planet, as necessarily as any other city. It is America's clearing house. Surely, it harbors more foreigners than natives. Surely, there is no unified atmosphere at all. Surely, life is feverish there; this typical quality of every business center of the Wall Street type is enhanced by the truly horrible climate of New York. . . . But . . . it means to America exactly what St. Petersburg used to mean to Russia, and Vienna to the Near East: it is America's window opening on Europe. Here American and European influence meet. Here one of the great brains of mankind is developing. And accordingly the best minds of America crowd together in New York and will continue to do so for a long time to come."[23]

In the Northeast, too, are more than two-thirds of the great national agencies and organizations looking toward the reform and relief of the nation's ills. Here are nearly all of the great publishing houses with their magnificent lists and creations. Here are the great centers of art, literature, drama, theater. Here are the cradles of the intelligentsia of the new megapolitan provincials. Here strangely enough are the cradles of reform and radicalism and the bulwarks of conservatism. And call the roll of *America's 60 Families*.[24] Among

[22] Margaret F. Byington, "Pittsburgh Studies Itself," *The Survey Graphic*, XXVII, No. 2, p. 75.
[23] Keyserling, *op. cit.*, pp. 310-311.
[24] Cf. Ferdinand Lundberg, *America's 60 Families*.

those present in the Northeast are the houses of Rockefeller, Morgan, Stotesbury, Steele, Lamont, Lloyd, Cochran, Whitney, Leffingwell, Bartow, Anderson, Davison, Newhall, Hopkinson, Gilbert, Dickey, Harkness, Mellon, Vanderbilt, Bedford, Du Pont, Baber, Fisher, Guggenheim, Fields, Curtis-Bok, Berwind, Lehman, Widener, Astor, Winthrop, Stillman, Timken, Pitcairn, Warburg, Metcalf, Clark, Kahn, Patterson, De Forest, Gould, Hill, Drexel, James, Schiff, Weber, Blumenthal, McLean, Higgins, Storrow, Baruch.

Paradoxically, again the Northeast as the North is so fabricated of people from the other regions that it vies with the Far West as the melting pot of older Americans, and New York City has sometimes been termed the home of Southerners. Dominating the scene, overlooking the nation, controlling its credit, the great Northeast is nevertheless "looked down upon" by the provinces of the West and the South, partly in reality and partly through defense mechanism. A well-known and recognized national-regionalist, William Allen White, has sometime put into words the sentiment of the Westerners who ". . . have got to hating the feisty patronage of a lot of these intellectual city slickers. I mean the way they take the world's heroes and God himself on their knee and patronize them and tell them the facts of life. . . ."[25] Yet, all in all, the Northeast is perhaps the least "regional" and "sectional" of all the great areas. And, finally, if, as many students point out, the primary issues of the next period of development are found in the question of whether government or business shall dominate, there is possibility on the one hand of more dominance and, on the other, of a greater regional diffusion of power and wealth through the new regional economy.

[25] William Allen White, Review of Frazier Hunt, *One American and His Attempt at Education*, *Saturday Review of Literature*, XVII, No. 14, p. 5.

Chapter XXI

THE SOUTHEAST AND ITS "OLD SOUTH"

IN addition to the usual multiple claims for the "most American" of the major regions of the nation, the Southeast qualifies admirably as an example of Frederick Jackson Turner's sectionalism and of his historical frontier Americanism. That is, the Old South, itself an administrative confederacy, has commonly been considered as not only typifying, but as embodying the essential episodes of sectionalism. This, as will be seen subsequently, offers an excellent opportunity to illustrate essential differences between the section and the region. Likewise, in so far as the South was the gateway to the first "Wests" and "Southwests" and "Northwests" through Tennessee and Kentucky, then Alabama and Mississippi, it was essentially a continuing frontier, and its society is even now often characterized by the appellation of the arrested frontier.

As a matter of common characterization within the region itself, the Southeast is usually and unqualifiedly called the most American part of the nation. By this is meant, of course, that part of the nation which, holding on to its historical priority of the 13 original colonies and the traditions of the early settlers, still retains, since the turn of the twentieth century, more of the early "Americanisms" than any other region. These "Americanisms" are usually interpreted to mean the largest ratio of native whites of native parents from original upper European stocks, small foreign population, the largest ratio of Protestants in religion, agrarian in culture, simple in living in rural isolated life, and retarded in certain aspects of culture so as to rank along where most of the nation ranked before the turn of the century. The fact that there is so much evidence which can be used to support this rationalization is eloquent testimony to the great American unity in diversity, both in the segments of historical sequence and of regional variation.

For without doubt the Old South provided much of the ideology, leadership, and statesmen who gave form and content to the political philosophy and practice of the nation, such as Washington, Jefferson, Madison, Monroe, and Calhoun; and of later popular democratic types, such as Andrew Johnson and Andrew Jackson. Jefferson was and is American in both the realistic and symbolic sense that he held every important political office in the gift of his own state, penned the Declaration of Independence, outlined the American land system and, to a great extent, organized the Democratic Party, set up new standards of liberalism and freedom from church domination, formulated the doctrine of agrarian democracy, set up the foundations for a great state university, negotiated the Louisiana Purchase, experimented widely in scientific agriculture and architecture. Surely, the Old South was American what time it provided a dozen presidents of the United States, more than 50 cabinet members. And of 41 political scientists, important in domestic affairs before the Civil War, deemed worthy of a place in the annals of American scholarship, only 14 were not of the South, while of those sketched as important for the development of political theory, the Southeast recorded more than all the other states.

The Southeast was essentially an "American" region in the range and abundance of its flora and fauna, of its land and forests, of its mountains and rivers, of its minerals and climate, and withal in its prevailing tempo and pattern of ruthless exploitation of resources, natural and human. Its people were symbolic, too, of all those who came down from the Northeast and from the upper European borders, adventurers, free and debtors, noble and common. Yet it is a long way from the pioneer days to the glory that was the Old South and a long way back again, through the scarred battle fields of sectionalism to a broken and charred region, humiliated with slaves turned rulers. Yet, all of this was of the essence of sectional America and of its paradoxes and contrasts, fact and symbol of the evolution of America.

In particular here was a large segment of "America's Tragedy" with its harvest of later conflict and confusion, born of undesigned and un-

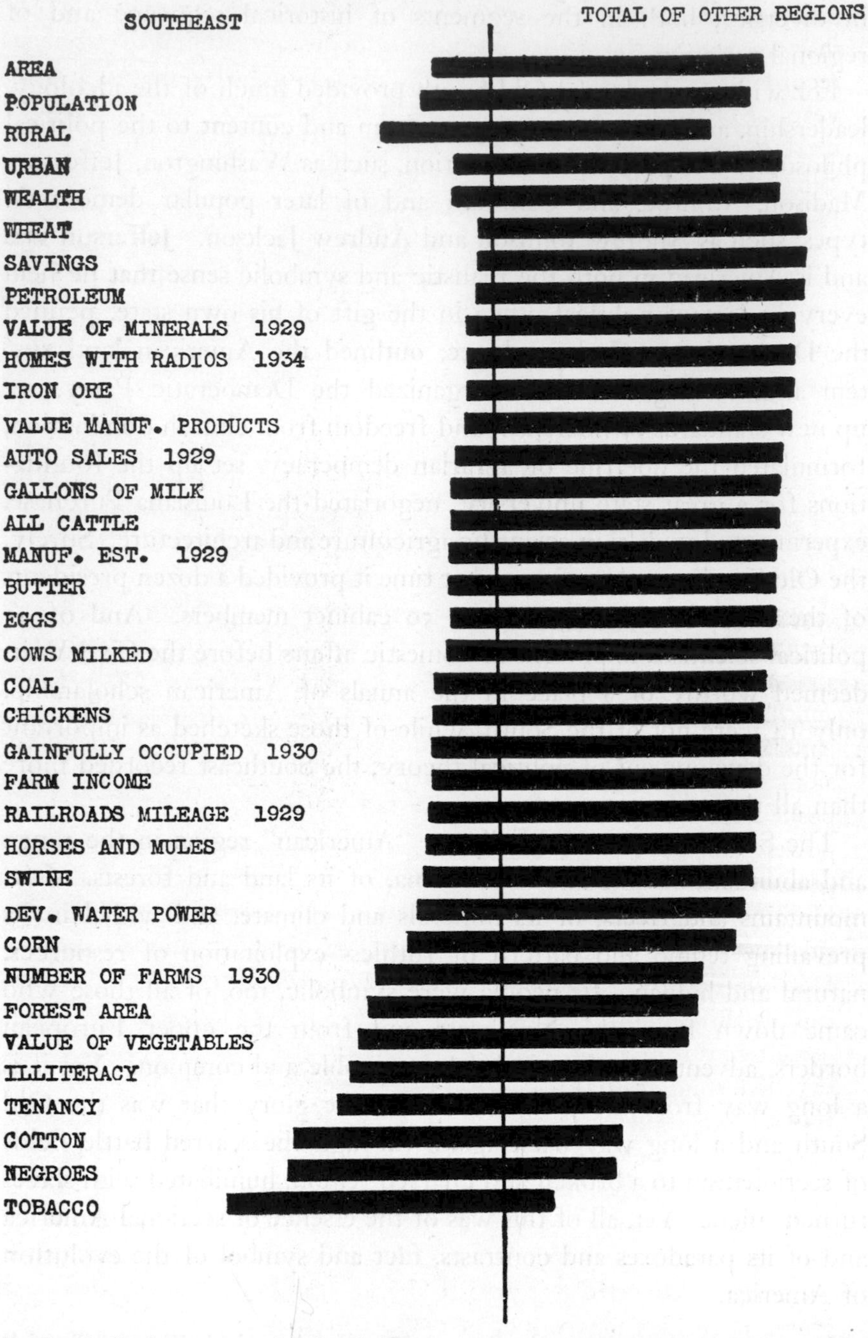

Regional Ratios to the National Total. Random Miscellaneous Indices: The Southeast

balanced programs of reconstruction. So came an American epoch that was the South. Old golden pages of history, shining parchment records of culture, then yellow and faded, scorched and seared with years of embattled conflict, and epic struggle. . . . Gallant figures on black horses and white . . . and crude, simple folk, sore with the footfall of time, passing across an epoch which was to be destroyed by physical and cultural conflagration and to rise up again in another American epoch strangely different and vivid and powerful. Cultures in the making, social processes at work, portraiture descriptive of how civilizations grow. All the South's yesterdays, with their brilliant episodes and with their sordid pictures receding, giving way to the South's tomorrows, through a sweeping American development reminiscent of universal culture. Thus, there are many Souths yet *the* South. It is pre-eminently national in backgrounds, yet provincial in its processes. There are remnants of European culture framed in intolerant Americanism. There are romance, beauty, glamor, gaiety, comedy, gentleness, and there are sordidness, ugliness, dullness, sorrow, tragedy, cruelty. There are wealth, culture, education, generosity, chivalry, manners, courage, nobility, and there are poverty, crudeness, ignorance, narrowness, brutality, cowardice, depravity. The South is American and un-American, Christian and barbaric. It is strong and weak, white and black, rich and poor. There are great white mansions on hilltops among the trees, and there are unpainted houses perched on pillars along hillside gullies or lowland marshes. Yet, here is reflected a composite region-in-the-making, descriptive of American reality, rich in power, range, and contrast, shaped and proportioned by strong backgrounds whose unfolding episodes were vivid with the quiver of life. Here are epic and romantic materials of history and literature alongside measurable elements for the scientific study of human society. Here are illuminating materials for the better understanding of American life through the study of regional situations and folk society. Their consistency is often in their contradictions, their unity in their diversity, like some masterpiece of orchestral harmony. Or, like some unfolding evolution of social culture or some masterpiece of narrative, charm and power are revealed only through dramatic unfolding, episode upon episode, year upon year. Here is a civilization slowly gathering together its processes and patterns until the magnitude of the whole has been fashioned, nevertheless, whose power and brilliance are cumulative, residing unescapably in separate units, yet also, and more, in the high potentiality of the final unity.[1]

[1] Adapted from Howard W. Odum, *An American Epoch*, pp. 329-330.

The "Old South," of the seceding states, bound together by common cause and isolated from the nation in a Confederacy of States, and later through reconstruction tragedy, constituted the section *de luxe* in all the meanings which we have ascribed to sectionalism. Here were 15 slave states, of which 11 finally seceded and in which all, including the later Oklahoma, were unified through the problems of Negro and white, slave and free. These states included Texas and the border states of Missouri, Maryland, and West Virginia, and they found their homogeneities largely in terms of beliefs and customs, laws and regulations dealing with Negroes. Even the churches became northern and southern. These states, so bound together, looking to their own priorities rather than the nation's welfare or unity, constituted "the South," which was the supreme "section" of the nation. To perpetuate this sectional unity as a region whose homogeneities are measured more by indices of traditional, religious, and ideological factors than by organic, socio-economic, or administrative, would be to multiply the hazards of disunity rather than to plan for greater unity and strength through the better integration of the nation's major regions.

With this in view, the delineation of the Southeast which would comprehend the greatest degree of homogeneity, measured by the largest number of indices for the largest number of purposes, was undertaken with the results described in Chapter XVIII. The Southeast comprehends the 11 states of Virginia, the two Carolinas, Georgia and Florida, Alabama and Mississippi, Arkansas and Louisiana, Tennessee and Kentucky. In this region will be found a little more than a fifth of the people in the nation and a little less than a fifth of its area, thus striking a good balance as compared to the Northeast with its smallest area and largest population and the Northwest with its largest area and smallest population. All of these except Kentucky were states of the Confederacy, as was also Texas, for reasons already pointed out, now the key state to the great Southwest. In terms of the Census classification, the region includes all of the *South Atlantic States*, except Delaware and Maryland, all of the *East South Central States*. Of the 93 metropolitan districts with a population of 100,000 or more, as potential metropolitan regions, the Southeast has 13, including, in the order of population, New Orleans, Louisville,

Atlanta, Birmingham, Memphis, Richmond, Nashville, Norfolk, Jacksonville, Chattanooga, Miami, Knoxville, Tampa. The Southeast's ratio of people that live in all urban areas is 29.2 percent and of those who live in metropolitan districts only 14.6, in striking contrast to the Northeast where the percentage of all urban is 74.4 and of metropolitan districts, 70.2 percent.

In terms of major natural regions and subregions, the Southeast is both more difficult and more easy to classify. That is, if we follow Newbigin's major regions, we find she has shifted from topography and resources primarily to land and crops, so that she makes both her Southern and Southeastern Lowlands largely coincide with the Cotton South, extending into Texas, and subsequently describes the southeastern part largely in terms of crops. On the other hand, this gives a fine unity for the region from which to chart the fringes of its borderlands and within which to plot its natural and socio-economic subregions.

Woofter's subregional analysis of the Southeast represents the most successful attempt to study a group-of-states major region through the delineation of its subregions which cut across state lines. Thus, he points out that "physiography has had much to do with regional differentiations, but physiographic peculiarities alone are not always sufficient to determine the boundaries. Soil and topography do not always coincide with belts of rainfall and temperature and all of these are often cross-sectioned by industrial belts or population classes. Therefore, while physical differences are the dominant factor underlying the subregional divisions of the South, other factors have been given weight in the final determination of the boundaries of these areas." He continues, "The task of demarking and describing areas could of course be carried down to a very fine point, to such an extent that several hundred slightly differing localities could be distinguished. This, however, would eventually lead to the confusion of incidental with essential social differences. It was, therefore, decided in this project to recognize only such subregions as would be large enough to constitute important socio-economic entities and at the same time exhibit sufficiently different social characteristics from their neighboring regions to warrant the distinction between them. In general the geological belts of the South extend north and south, while the climate zones extend east and west. The Coast Plains parallel the Atlantic, bending westward along the Gulf. Above these the Piedmont, the

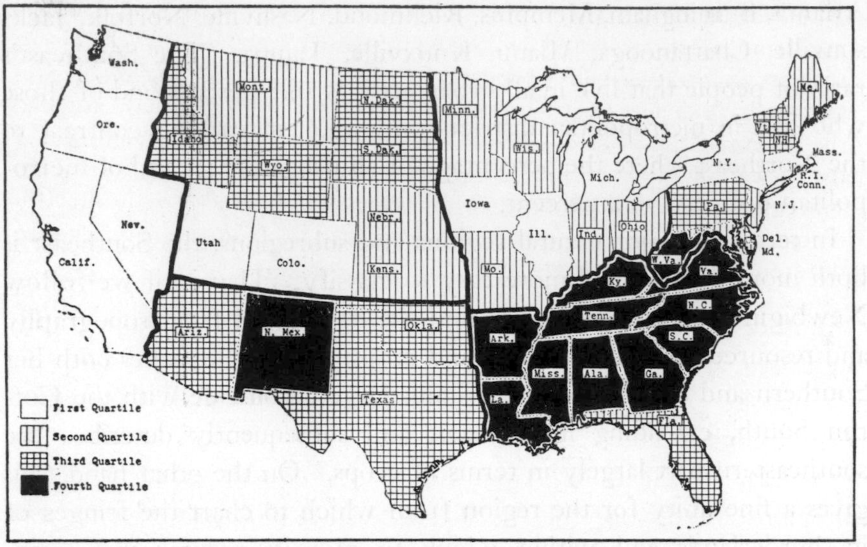

TRENDS TOWARD THE INCREASE OF FEDERAL EQUALIZATION FUNDS ARE BASED UPON REALISTIC REGIONAL DIFFERENTIALS

Above: A General Composite Index of the Relative Standing of the States in Wealth.

Below: The Same for Education. Based upon Census data and tabulated for several standard indices.

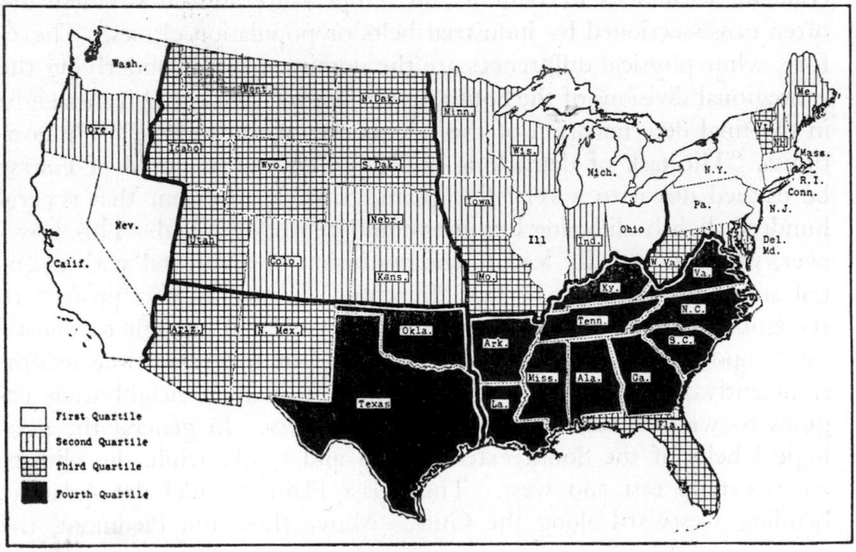

Appalachian ranges, the valley, and the Mississippi bluffs and delta all run from north to south, but the temperature zones extend from east to west and rainfall belts cross-section these. These blends of soil and climate have dictated certain crop practices, which in time have formed the habits of the people. The combinations of these have determined the extent of some of the subregions. By this process twenty-seven subregions were delineated. As has been said, they are usually locally recognized as different from each other and they show up markedly different in regional, social, and economic averages."[2]

Another excellent contribution to the subregional division of the Southeast may be found in Vance's *Human Geography of the South*, in which he gives an adequate framework for the study of people, work, and place, to refer again to the Le Play-Geddes formula. As in the case of the other regions, J. Russell Smith's men-resources subregions and the agricultural subregions are important elements in the understanding and planning for the major Southeastern Region. The catalogue of various subregional divisions by Smith, Bennett, Woofter, and Vance will illustrate more specifically.

The Smith subregions include all of the Blue Ridge and Carolina Mountains, the Cotton Belt, the Gulf Coast and the Florida Peninsula, together with parts of the Appalachian Ridge and Valley Region, the Appalachian Plateau, and of the Lower Valley of the Ohio. Hugh H. Bennett has mapped the large-scale subregions of the Southeast on the basis of soils and agriculture into the following: Coastal and Interior Flatwoods, Middle Interior and Upper Coastal Plains, Sand Hills, Piedmont, Appalachians, Clay Hills, Bluffs, Silt Loam Uplands, Black Prairies, and River Bottoms. Rupert B. Vance's subregional economy and patterns are reflected in some 15 zones as follows: Fishing and Trucking Fringes; the Rice and Sugar Bowls; the Piney Woods and Cut Over areas; the Southern Highlands of Appalachians and Ozarks; Tobacco Zones; the Piedmont Industrial Crescent of minerals, water power, textiles, tobacco, and furniture manufacturing; and the Great Cotton Belt. The Cotton Belt splits into Atlantic, Gulf, Delta, and Southwestern areas. The Southwest includes a Ranching Zone, a Cotton Empire, an Oil Region, with special Sulphur, Gulf Ports, and Rio Grande Valley areas. The emphasis in this analysis is found in the attempt to present the patterns of regional housekeeping rather than in the exact delimitation of the various areas.[3] Woofter's 27 regions

[2] Quoted from *Southern Regions of the United States*, p. 571.
[3] *Ibid.*, p. 159.

are differentiated by indices of physical, demographic, agricultural, trade, and industrial character, recognizing, however, only those subregions which are large enough to constitute important socio-economic entities, yet which exhibit sufficient distinctive characteristics to warrant differentiation from neighboring regions. The regions thus approximating homogeneity are Cotton Piedmont, Shenandoah Valley, Tennessee Valley, Atlantic Tidewater, Northern Piedmont, Tobacco Piedmont, Blue Ridge Mountains, Cumberland Mountains, Blue Grass, Tobacco-Cattle, Muscle Shoals-Nashville Basin, Bluffs, Northern Cotton and Tobacco, Southern Cotton and Tobacco, Black Belt, Citrus-Vegetable, Vegetable-Citrus, Semi-Tropical, Gulf Coast Plain, Mining, Gulf Tidewater, Interior Ridge, Delta, Ozarks, Interior Plain, Red River Bottoms, Rice-Cane.[4]

It might very well be assumed that the subregional divisions already cited would be adequate, yet two or three others are perhaps necessary to illustrate fully. These are the sub-subregional divisions cited for all the river regions and from the exhaustive analysis presented in the map of Types of Farming Areas in the United States previously cited. These are important for the Southeast, in order to facilitate the further specific studies. Thus, in *Southern Regions of the United States*, this has been illustrated by the distribution of cropland acreage devoted to various crops in which such wide range is illustrated in the following: in cotton, from no cotton grown in four of the subregions, or less than 1 percent in three others, up to 67 percent in the Delta and the Red River Bottoms, over 50 percent in the Interior Plain, and over 40 percent in the Cotton Piedmont, the Interior Ridge, the Bluffs. Likewise, the whole tobacco economy is one of subregional base, while important planning for corn, hay, oats, orchards, vegetables, and dairy products can be effective only through some such subregional approach. The same is true of the tenant farmer and his problem where there is a variation in the percentage of tenancy from more than 90 percent in the Delta to less than 10 percent in the Citrus-Vegetable, with subregions in between of 80, 73, 63, 60, 58 on down to 15, 16, 8.6 percent. So also the percentage of land in farms ranges as low as 3.1 to as high as 88, while the value of land and buildings per acre varies from as low as

[4] Quoted from *Southern Regions of the United States*, pp. 159-161.

$19 to as high as $205, and the value of land and buildings per farm from $1,300 to $14,000.[5]

> The hundred and fifty or more types of farming areas, exclusive of overlappings, include: Southwest Arkansas, Southern Arkansas-Sand Hills-Ouachita River Valley, Red River Delta, Southwest Louisiana-Texas, Louisiana sugar-cane area, Central Louisiana, Gulf Coast, Louisiana strawberry area, Ozark, Arkansas River Valley and uplands, Hill cotton area, Grand Prairie, Arkansas, Mississippi Delta, Lower Mississippi and Arkansas Delta, Texas-Mississippi Delta, Copiah County, Longleaf pine cut-over area, Lower coastal plain, Clay Hills, Mississippi-Alabama Black Belt, Upper coastal plain, Appalachian Plateaus, mineral region, Tennessee Valley, South Tennessee, western highland rim, West Tennessee-North Mississippi silt and sandy loam area, Perry-Humphrey, Central Basin, Eastern highland rim, Sequatchie Valley, Great Smoky Mountains, Blue Ridge Mountains, Asheville, Roanoke, Shenandoah Valley, Albemarle, Washington, Northern Virginia, Piedmont, Tidewater, Richmond, Virginia peanut area, Norfolk, Lower Piedmont, Flatwoods, Limestone valleys, Coastal Plains, Georgia peach area, Rabun-Habersham, Atlanta, Eastern Gulf Coast flatwoods, Black and Cache Rivers bottoms and terraces, Brown loam area, Purchase, Paducah, Union County, Henderson, Owensboro, Hardin-Larue, Louisville, Outer Blue Grass, Maysville-West Union, Lawrence County, Ashland, Inner Blue Grass, Glasgow-Campbellsville-Lebanon, Cumberland Mountains and plateaus, Cumberland Valley, West Kentucky, Clarksville-Hopkinsville, Bowling Green, Central Florida uplands, Florida flatwoods, Lake Okeechobee, West central Florida flatwoods, Everglades, Key Largo, Sanford-Oviedo.[6]

Again, the Southeast is rich in river valleys, and, as a group-of-states major region, it is well adapted to co-operative arrangements with the planning of river valley subregional development. Of the 17 major drainage basins described by the Water Resources Committee of the National Resources Committee, the Southeastern Region comprehends all of the Southeast Drainage Basins, the Tennessee Valley, and the Lower Mississippi Drainage Basin, and the greater part of the Middle Atlantic Drainage Basins, with parts of the Ohio and of the Southwest Mississippi River Basins. All these comprehend more than thirty subregional river valleys, including the Lower

[5] *Ibid.*, p. 161.
[6] Adapted from the map, Types of Farming Areas in the United States: 1930. Division of Commerce, Bureau of the Census.

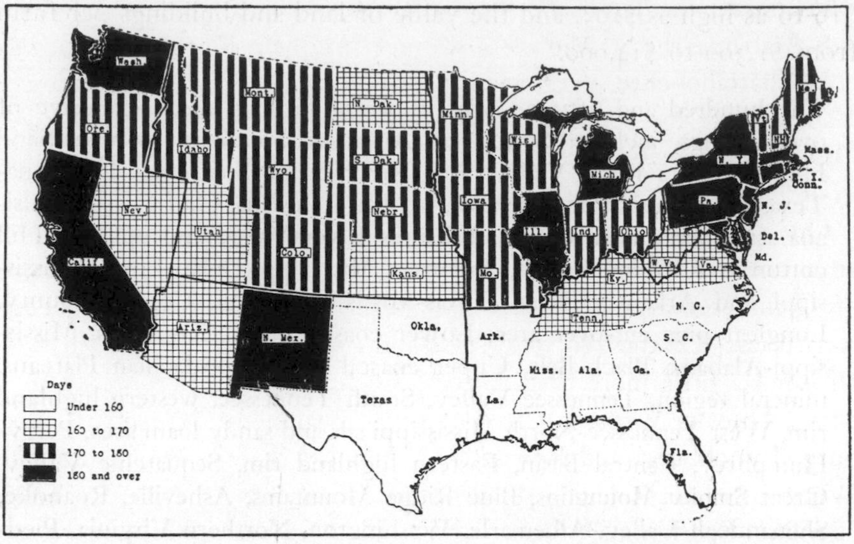

Above: Average Length of School Term in Days, 1927-1928.

Below: Average Length of School Term in Days, 1927-1928. | Average Number of Days Attended by Each Pupil Enrolled in 1920 and 1930.

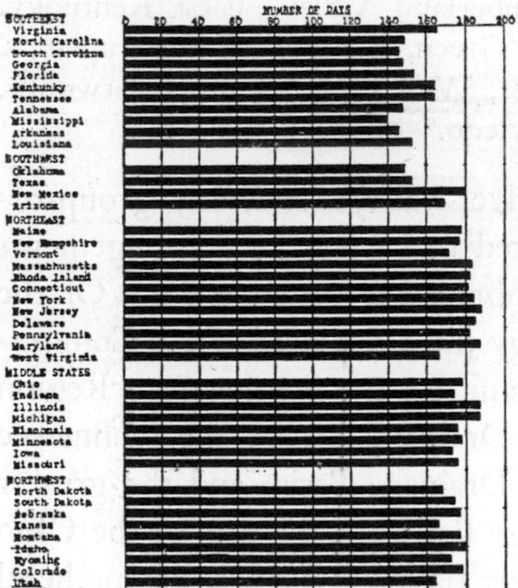

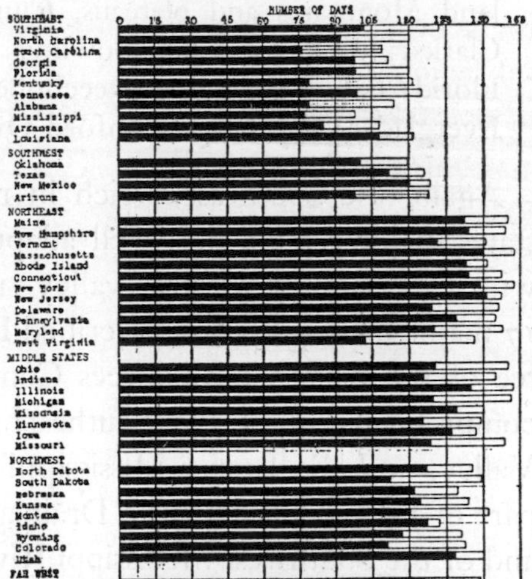

Regional comparison of educational data is of great importance in the consideration of the proposed Federal equalization funds for education.

Chesapeake, the James, the Chowan, the Carolina Coast, the Savannah-Alabama, the St. Mary's-Suwannee, Southern Florida, Appalachicola-Chattahoochee, the Eastern Gulf and the Mobile, the Tennessee Valley, the Ohio Southern tributaries, five subdivisions of the Lower Mississippi, namely, Cairo-Memphis, Lower Mississippi, Yazoo-Black, Pontchartrain, Pearl-Pascogoula.

One other arrangement for working with subareas which will give an entirely different analysis is that of the United States Department of Commerce arranged according to urban and wholesale grocery territories. Of the 180 total such areas in the nation, the Southeast afforded a little more than thirty. Each subarea was centered in a city. Thus, in Virginia—Charlottesville, Richmond, Norfolk, Petersburg, Lynchburg, and Roanoke; in North Carolina, the regions are Winston-Salem, Raleigh, Wilmington, Charlotte, Asheville; in South Carolina—Spartanburg, Greenville, Columbia, Charleston; in Georgia —Atlanta, Augusta, Macon, Columbus, Albany, Savannah; in Florida —Miami, Tampa, Orlando, Jacksonville, Pensacola; in Alabama—Birmingham, Selma, Mobile; in Mississippi—Jackson, Vicksburg, Meridian, Natchez; in Arkansas—Fort Smith, Little Rock, Pine Bluff, Texarkana; in Louisiana—Shreveport, Alexandria, Lake Charles, New Orleans; in Tennessee—Memphis, Nashville, Chattanooga, Knoxville; in Kentucky—Paducah, Louisville, Lexington. The significance of subregions, however, is emphasized by the overlapping of state lines of many of these regions. Thus, the Memphis region includes about 30 counties comprehending all of the north of Mississippi, as well as about 20 counties in northeast Arkansas. The Chattanooga area includes counties in both Georgia and Alabama. The Norfolk region includes a large part of the northeastern area of North Carolina. A part of Kentucky is included in the Evansville, Illinois, subregion.[7]

> This brings us to the Ogburn characterization of southern cities as compared with eastern and western cities, with his classification also applying to cities of the Southwest. "In population characteristics the cities of the South have the lowest percentage of immigrants of any of the regions, as is generally known. There is also the lowest percentage of men—probably because the South is a region of emigration, since men migrate in larger numbers than women. The death rate is

[7] *Southern Regions of the United States*, p. 157.

higher, and so is the birth rate, but only slightly higher in these southern cities. Wages, both in manufacturing establishments and in retail stores, are the lowest of the three regions, but so is the monthly rent. The percentage of the adult population paying an income tax is low also. Practically all of these indices quoted mean less satisfactory economic conditions for the average inhabitant, as is also shown by the smallest percentage of radio owners.

"In occupation, the South has the smallest percent of its working population in manufacturing industries and the largest percentage engaged in trade and transportation. This fact does not mean that other regions may not have more transportation and trade, but rather that the proportion of their population engaged in these occupations is smaller than is the similar proportion in the South. Southern cities have also the smallest proportion of their working population engaged in the higher services known as the professions. This small proportion is probably due to low incomes and to fewer school teachers, who comprise a large part of the professions, for in both law and medicine the southern cities have the largest percentages as compared with the other regions. Also the clergymen as a class constitute a larger percent of the southern population than they do in other regions.

"In regard to family life the records for cities do not bring out many outstanding characteristics for the cities of this region. There is a large percentage of widowed in the South, which may be due in part to the presence of the Negro, among whom widowhood is known to be common. The racial influence probably also accounts for the very large percentage of women employed, the large number of domestic servants, and perhaps the lowest percentage of home owners. It is not clear why the southern cities should have the largest percentages of families with lodgers nor the largest proportion of hotelkeepers among their working population.

"In the matter of cost of government, southern cities rank low. This means low taxes, but also less governmental expenditure for health, for public recreation, for libraries, and for schools. The number of social workers is also low. On the other hand the debt of southern cities is high.

"In conclusion, it may be said by way of interpretation that the presence of Negroes, with a racial history of slavery, enters into all these calculations since they are a part of the population. Low incomes are also a basis for many of these distinguishing traits." [8]

[8] William F. Ogburn, *Social Characteristics of Cities*, p. 29. (Quoted by permission of The International City Managers' Association.)

The South is generally considered to have the most "American" population since its percentage of foreign-born is insignificant. Yet, if one looks at statistics and forgets the details, he will be surprised to find that, of the total population, the Southeast has the smallest ratio of native white of any of the regions. That is, in order of the lowest to highest the Southeast has 68.6, the Northeast 73, the Southwest 74.8, the Middle States 75, the Far West 77, and the Northwest 87 percent. This is all due, of course, to the large percentage of Negro population.

If we compare the region with other regions in both the total number and relative ratio of foreign-born people, the South's reputation for "one hundred percent American" holds good. For, of the nearly twelve million foreign-born population the Southeast has only about 175,000 which fits in with the traditional "less than one-tenth of one percent" boast. And of these foreign-born, Germany and Italy lead with thirty thousand each while England supplies the next largest number—twenty thousand. Its twenty thousand from Russia and Poland and its eight thousand from Greece indicate the other variations. If we look at the ratios for the several states the same general picture emerges. "Thus all of the Southeastern States, except Virginia, Louisiana, and Florida, still show less than 1 percent foreign-born population. This is in contrast to such states as New York with 26.3 percent; Rhode Island with 25.3; Massachusetts, 25.1; Connecticut, 24.3; New Jersey, 22. During the last decade there was a decrease in foreign-born population in the following states: Virginia, 5.8 percent; South Carolina, 8.2; Georgia, 13.9; Kentucky, 28.9; Tennessee, 15.4; Alabama, 10.8; Missouri, 11.1; Arkansas, 26.2. Of this white population, further, at least 4,000,000 abide in the hill country of the Southern Appalachians; 4,900,000 in all the Southern Appalachians including West Virginia and the western fringe. These millions represent the original gateway to the West; they continue a gateway between the past and the future; and they constitute one of several blocks of the population of the Southeast, which afford abundant evidence to support the conclusion that, just as there is no longer a 'South,' so any blanket classification, 'southern people,' no longer constitutes an authentic characterization. Even within the restricted Southern Appalachian Region of some 200 counties in six states with an area of a half hundred million acres, there is considerable diversity of people and culture. . . .

"The white population of the Southeast tends to reproduce at a higher rate and has a larger ratio of children and young people than

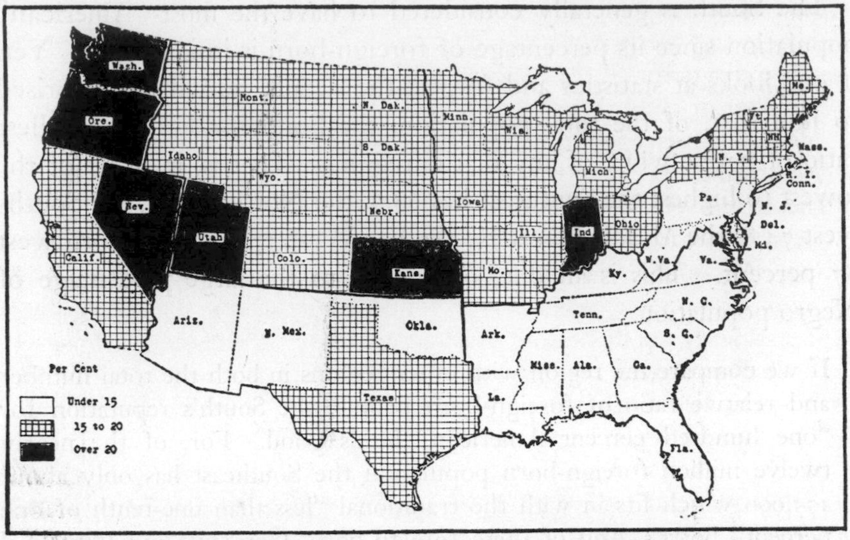

HIGH SCHOOL STUDENTS*

	Per Cent Total Enrollment in High Schools	Total Number of Graduates 1928	Per Cent Increase in Graduates 1911–1928
Southeast			
Virginia	10.2	5,877	463
North Carolina	12.1	9,533	980
South Carolina	11.3	3,363	284
Georgia	10.2	5,000	247
Florida	11.3	3,660	1,212
Kentucky	9.5	7,172	601
Tennessee	9.7	6,108	687
Alabama	8.6	5,113	650
Mississippi	8.3	3,191	303
Arkansas	8.1	3,250	384
Louisiana	11.5	4,379	511
Southwest			
Oklahoma	13.5	9,848	1,045
Texas	17.5	16,254	382
New Mexico	10.4	1,071	743
Arizona	13.5	1,523	864
Northeast			
Maine	18.7	3,683	127
New Hampshire	17.9	2,099	135
Vermont	17.1	1,367	88
Massachusetts	19.9	20,641	156
Rhode Island	14.3	2,096	248
Connecticut	14.8	6,056	220
New York	17.4	37,908	291
New Jersey	14.0	12,432	366
Delaware	15.5	704	263
Pennsylvania	13.9	35,976	232
Maryland	13.4	4,245	283
West Virginia	11.0	5,212	940
Middle States			
Ohio	18.7	31,010	220
Indiana	20.1	18,339	178
Illinois	19.5	32,444	308
Michigan	15.5	17,711	210
Wisconsin	17.8	14,490	213
Minnesota	16.2	14.411	302
Iowa	19.9	18,427	217
Missouri	18.4	13,723	205
Northwest			
North Dakota	15.5	3,505	429
South Dakota	17.0	4,275	368
Nebraska	20.0	10,987	261
Kansas	20.4	15,041	339
Montana	18.8	3,389	933
Idaho	19.7	3,267	703
Wyoming	20.0	1,279	948
Colorado	18.5	5,660	258
Utah	20.5	2,799	610
Far West			
Nevada	23.9	488	495
Washington	23.1	10,667	414
Oregon	22.6	5,875	496
California	19.8	27,293	534

**Statistics of State School Systems*, Bulletin, 1930. No. 5. p. 49.

PER CENT OF PUBLIC SCHOOL ENROLLMENT IN HIGH SCHOOLS

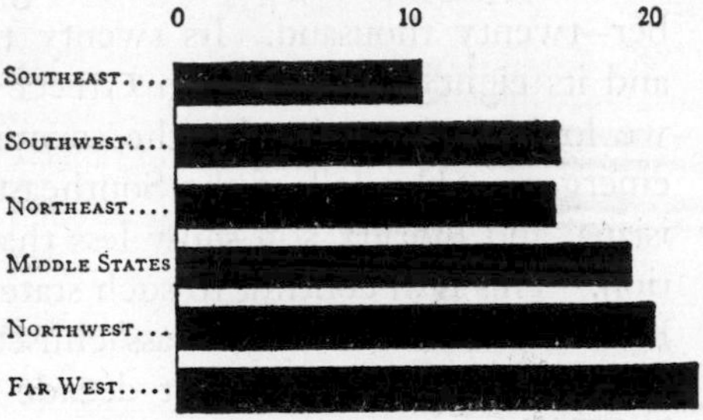

PER CENT INCREASE IN GRADUATES, 1911-1928

Regional Variations in High School Enrollment

any other region. The ratio is much larger than for the nation as a whole and nearly twice as high as for a number of states. For instance, the average for all the Southeastern States shows more than double the number of children under five years of age, with native white mothers per 1,000 native white women 20-44 years, as for the State of California. California's 341 stands in stark contrast to North Carolina's 827. Connecticut's 371, Rhode Island's 363, New York's 362, and Massachusett's 359 are more than doubled by Alabama's 786, South Carolina's 777, Mississippi's 740, and Arkansas's 798. Or to cite an index of net reproduction per generation in which 100 represents the trend toward a stationary population, all the Southeastern States, except Florida, show an index of over 130, with four states over 150 as compared to all of the Far Western States, six of the Northeastern States, and Illinois in the Middle States, below the 100 index."[9]

The question has often been raised as to what the nature of the southern civilization would have been had it been populated by German and Scandinavian folk. Be that as it may, the facts are that, disregarding the outlying regions of Florida and the Lower Mississippi, which were settled by the Spaniards and the French respectively, the earliest permanent white settlers of the Southeastern Region of the United States were predominantly Scotch and English, with the English concentrated along the Atlantic Coast, and the Scotch more in the interior. Prominent, of course, as minorities were the Germans who were early settlers of the Piedmont Section of the Southern States along the Atlantic Seaboard. Of all the states in the Southeast Region, only Louisiana contained an heterogeneous group which was not completely submerged by the Anglo-Saxons. For in Louisiana there was a large number of Creoles, in its broadest sense meaning all of Spanish or French descent as well as those of mixed blood. Holding on to their racial integrity, they today still remain as testimony of the French and Spanish regime in America and give folk character to that part of the region. Likewise during more recent periods, only Louisiana and New Orleans have received a sufficient number of foreign immigrants to affect materially their racial make-up. New Orleans has particularly appealed to the Italians, and there are today over 50,000 of Italian descent in the city. But mention should be made of the fact that Eastern Europeans (Italians, Slavs, Magyars,

[9] *Southern Regions of the United States*, pp. 91, 93.

Bulgarians, etc.) have attached themselves to the iron- and steel-producing communities of the Birmingham District in Alabama, and the bituminous coal mining territories of Virginia, Alabama, and Arkansas. Cubans and Spaniards have entered the cigar manufacturing establishments of Tampa and Key West, Florida, and have built up colonies in these cities. Nevertheless, generally speaking the white racial complexion of the Southeast has remained largely what it was in 1800, so that the South still boasts of its distinctly Nordic and Anglo-Saxon folks and of its "less than 1 percent foreign-born."

The story of its people is in many ways the story of the Southeast, reminiscent of its history and struggles and symbolic of its present troubled years with farm tenancy and wasted lands. Again the realism of the people! Something of the rise of the southern people has been pictured in *An American Epoch* as "On the shores of the River James there had been early first American settlers, and from them were descended much of the 'royal' blood of Virginia. Here was the 'general assembly' covenanting a year earlier than even the Mayflower Compact of 1620. Later settlements and counter-invasions from northern states added numbers and variety for many generations. . . . There were 'Friends' and German sectarians, crowded out of Pennsylvania and Maryland, moving down to the Piedmont of Virginia and the Carolinas to meet the other streams from Delaware. There were Moravians and Mennonites and Presbyterians to mix with Quakers, Anglicans, Methodists and Baptists. Thence these spread in all directions south and then across the Cumberland Gap with its varied romance and adventure as represented by the blazing of trails by George Rogers Clark, Daniel Boone, and hosts of hunters looking for the new promised land. . . . Then there were other migrations to the lower South differing from the earlier ones in Virginia and Kentucky, where people were impelled from their first settlements by lack of land or hard times. Here were new caravans of people merely desiring to get on in the world. From the vantage point of New Jersey, Rhode Island, and other New England States, the Lower South looked like a land in which great wealth might be developed. Then the slave owners of Kentucky and Virginia and the would-be slave owners from Indiana and Illinois, or from the East, looked longingly to broad acres and white-columned houses deep in the Lower South where adventure and wealth were theirs for the possessing. . . . There were many pictures of sub-settlements and migrations within the various states. In Mississippi and Louisiana, besides many others, from New Orleans to

Natchez there were early Tories migrating from South Carolina and Georgia westward, to be joined by similar folks from northern states. These, well fortified with rich alluvial lands of the river bottoms, were met by other groups and settlers coming by boats from Virginia, Kentucky, Tennessee, and from northern states. Or again by still others coming from Georgia and the Carolinas to merge in a regional group expanding somewhat to the east until stopped perhaps by still another group which represented the overflow of those who had failed, or were too restless to succeed, in the sandhills or seacoast range of the more easterly Southern States. . . . There were other streams of settlers—Welsh, Quakers, Scotch-Irish—moving, one branch from Pennsylvania and westward, then south through the Shenandoah Valley into the Carolinas to be joined by similar groups who had landed in Charleston and had extended their wanderings wherever adventure led. These pioneers, 'hardy, proud, land-hungry,' had in them the making not only of the traditional Southerners but of the sundry borderland Southerners who extended themselves north, south, east, and west. From these came not only Indian fighters and continuous pioneers but a later brood of southern leaders like Calhoun, Quitman, Prentiss, Yancey, Davis, new Southerners in the vanguard of that great tragic region of the United States. To these, and many more like them, were added others, French, Spanish, German, San Domingans, Italians, Minorcans, Choctaws, Cherokees, Creeks, and Seminoles, and the hosts of Negro slaves from many sources whose stocks multiplied and mixed with many strains. The one-third of a million slaves who had been imported had multiplied until by 1850 there were three million, most of whom were in these Southern States."[10]

That which has probably characterized the Southeast more than any other factor except the cultural conditioning of slavery and the Civil War with its aftermath was its large ratio of Negro population. Of the "southern people," nearly 8,000,000 or 30 percent, are Negroes. No southeastern state, except Kentucky and Tennessee, has fewer than a fourth of its population Negroes, while Mississippi has half, and four other states, Alabama, Louisiana, Georgia, and South Carolina, have more than a third. There are, however, yet other four million Negroes in the nation outside of the Southeast, or approximately as many as were all the people of the nation in Jefferson's day. Of these a million are in the Southwest, a million and a half in the Northeast, a little more than a million in the Middle

[10] Howard W. Odum, *An American Epoch*, pp. 19-22.

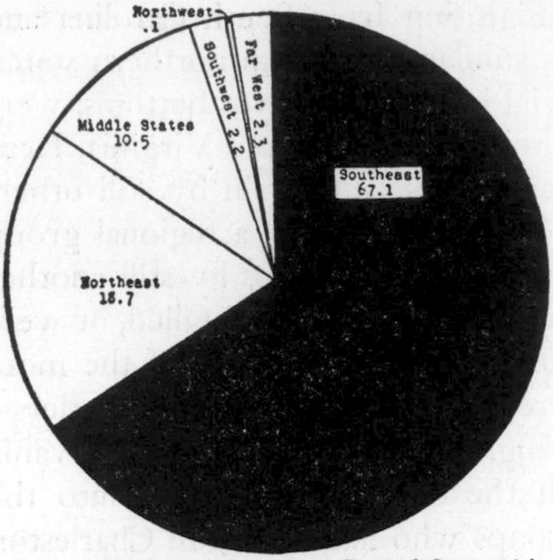

Regional Distribution of the Total Tons of Commercial Fertilizer Bought in the United States During the Crop Year of 1929

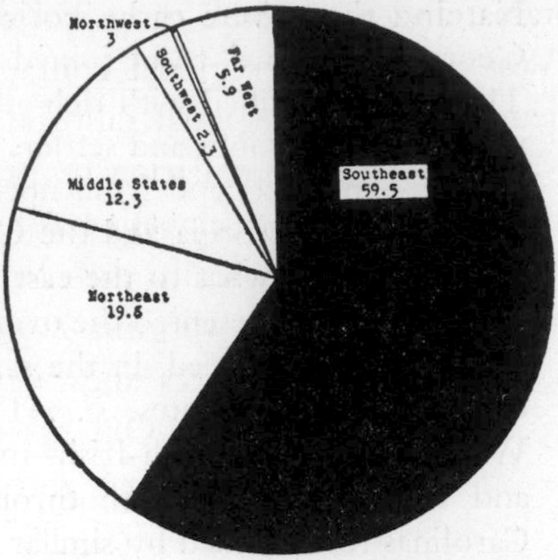

Regional Distribution of the Total Expenditure by United States Farmers for All Types of Bought Fertilizers During the Crop Year of 1929

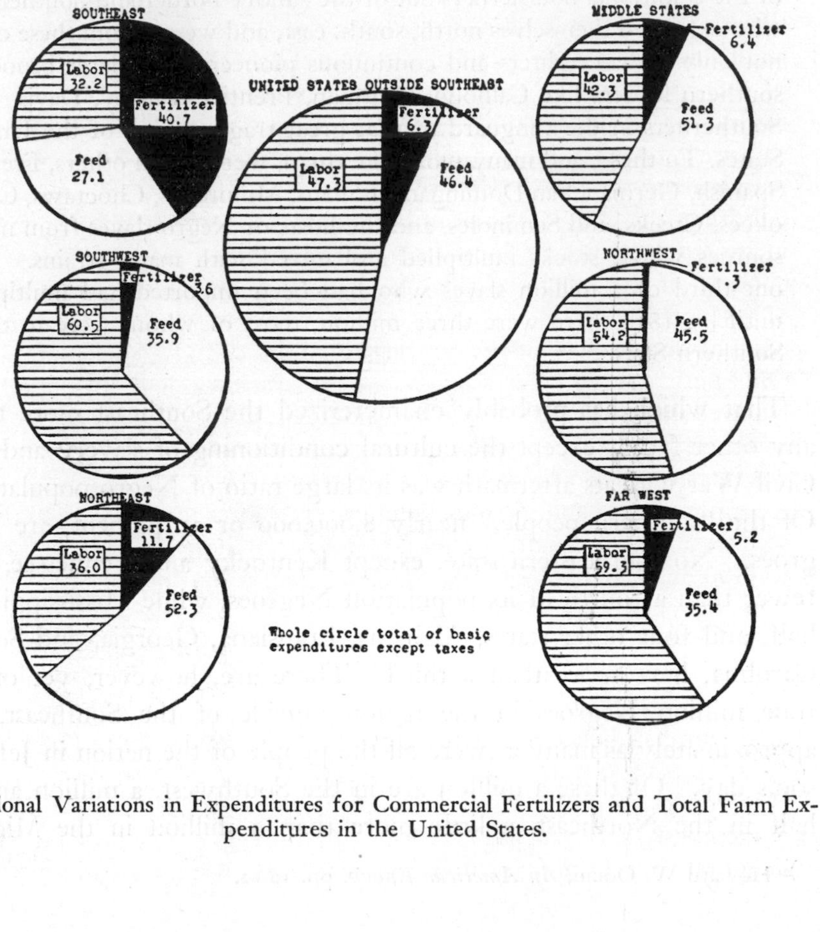

Regional Variations in Expenditures for Commercial Fertilizers and Total Farm Expenditures in the United States.

States, and a hundred thousand each in the Northwest and the Far West. This interregional contact of races is one of the important elements in the regional cultural landscape. Likewise the ratio of Negro to white population constitutes one of the indices by which the border states are classified as Southeast or otherwise and by which the Southeast is logically differentiated from the Southwest. Thus, Missouri and West Virginia each has only about 6 percent Negro population, while Texas and Maryland show respectively less than 15 and 17 percent, with Oklahoma barely 7 percent. Whatever else may be said about the South and its Negro population, there has not been dissent from the premise that the South's whole cultural landscape has been largely conditioned by its biracial civilization.

The realistic picture of the people of the Southeast is in contradistinction to the too-often dramatized stories of the aristocracy, on the one hand, and of the "poor whites," on the other. Here, again, is a picture of the common man from *An American Epoch*, reminiscent of that reality which was "'too completely tragic to furnish material for theatrical tragedy, far too high in spirit for written romance which crawls along the beaten paths of life, too stark for poetry.' Indeed the culture of the Old South and of the New was found exclusively neither in the romanticism of its aristocratic gentry nor the tragedy and comedy of the much-described poor whites, but in the living drama of its common folks. . . . Pictures of Lee's army, the best fighting units of the whole Confederacy, reflected the complex structure of the Old South. Scions of aristocratic houses marching alongside conscripts from countryside, backwoods and mountain coves, fighting a common battle, reflected much of the glory of the common man, 'their beards unkempt, their uniforms torn and patched with clumsy hands, their feet upon the ground, devoted men, ironsides after the fashion of Cromwell's army two hundred years before, their commander second only to God himself.' So they marched and fought during the war; so also they marched sadly back—common men but with heroism a sort of commonplace virtue within them . . . armless sleeves, . . . crutches, ragged, gray uniforms, in battered hats and caps, . . . remnants of flags, . . . relics of a brave army, . . . wrecks of men, . . . common men who had borne the physical burden of a nation for its error slavery, . . . plain countrymen . . . blameless victims of a sectional wrath. Nevertheless, a part of their story was found in the fact that they 'had miraculously survived and crawled to barren homes from the clash and slaughter and from starvation and such deadly vain endeavor as no other men have ever known and lived. . . .' The mosaic of the Old South was made up of non-slaveholders and the small slaveholders scattered everywhere, as well as of the larger owners. At least three-fourths of the white population had no proprietary interest in the Negro. . . . Other pictures of the mountain comman man abounded in the southern highlands . . . Blue Ridge Hills . . . ridge country of Virginia . . . Eastern Kentucky . . . Eastern Tennessee . . . Western North Carolina . . . Northwestern South Carolina . . . North Georgia . . . Northeastern Alabama . . . a hundred and twelve thousand square miles . . . New York and New England combined, or . . . England, Ireland, Scotland, and Wales put into one . . . young life in its prime . . . energy and daring . . . leaping from childhood into manhood . . . gambling squarely upon the benevolence of soil, growth and weather . . . planting crops, hunting game, catching fish, harvesting fruits and berries . . . self-sufficiency. The wife cooking, churning, making the clothes, keeping the home, and picking the geese for feather beds . . . midwives, herb doctors, basketmakers, carders, millers . . . water mills, farm boys with bags of shelled corn swung over their horses' withers . . . shirts open, lips pursed for whistling, bodies asway to the leisurely, plodding gaits of their mounts . . . surprisingly free from awkwardness and uncouthness . . . an unpresuming dignity, a quiet courtliness, unspoiled by the conventional forms of etiquette and politeness . . . a genuine, unhurried serenity . . . old-time, homely ambitions . . . folk romancers and romantic rascals . . . moonshiners . . . Robin Hoods . . . Friar Tucks . . . Maid Marians . . . Little Johns . . . Greenwood revels . . . sheriffs . . . Saturday night gambles and gambols . . . handcuffs, jail houses, penitentiaries, and buryin' grounds . . . the Land of the Sky . . . azure walls of the Blue Ridge . . . the cool spicy breath of shady glens . . . swift streams . . . overhanging masses of mountain laurel and rhododendron . . . the banjo . . . Monkey Simon with his tambourine . . . the master instrument of music, the fiddle . . . uncramped by books and black notes of the masters . . . sentimental songs . . . sung by lovely women and gallant men . . . intricate circles of the country dance, weaving and swinging in graceful winding figures through the trampled stubble of the darkening field . . . The voice of the caller . . . borne far into the evening air . . . The 'old-time fiddler' an institution." [11]

This is not to say that the culture of the Old South was not a genuine and realistic culture of great distinction. It is rather to point up the fact that there were, after all, in the South, as in other regions,

[11] Odum, *op. cit.*, pp. 53-54, 60-61.

many subdivisions of its culture as well as of its geography. Since the romance and glamour of the southern aristocracy has been featured so often, it should constitute in any general outline appraisal of the Region only its pro rata part. This does not mean, again, that we need dissent from many enthusiastic estimates that have been published in literature and even in historical studies. What it does mean is that these must have their true perspective. There can be no doubt about the glory that was Charleston or the grandeur that was envisaged in the great colonial homes. There can be no doubt as to the distinction of Richmond and of New Orleans, of Savannah and Vicksburg, of Old Hickory and the Hermitage. Nor need there be any debate as to the regionality of Virginia, mother of presidents, or Louisiana and Florida with their natural charm of live oaks, hung with moss, subtropical flora, blue waters and soft air. In the case of Louisiana, there is the culture of its old French civilization and architecture, and in Florida the magic upbuilding of tropical playgrounds.

> If perhaps Count Keyserling, writing profusely on "Genius Loci" in the *Atlantic Monthly*, has thought that perhaps only in Virginia and New Orleans could he find a satisfying culture, this ought to be recorded in the picture alongside the observations of other visitors to these shores. Thus, "Nowhere did the absolute superiority of real culture strike me so forcibly as there [New Orleans]. The percentage of Frenchmen who live in that city today is infinitesimal. Yet it is imbued with the tradition of the eighteenth century; it still owes all its charm to Old France. . . . It is the one place in America with a tradition of good cooking; and this is being kept up by the French element, whose beneficial influence does not end here. Owing to that tradition even Americanism acquires a halo of beauty in New Orleans. I spent a night walking through those docks and market places where vegetables and fruits are being loaded in and out and sold by wholesale and retail in overwhelming, truly American quantities. But the exquisite sense of beauty of the French has conquered and now rules even this extravagent accumulation of material. The millions of radishes, beans, bananas, oranges, and so forth, look, in their arrangement, like so many artistic nosegays; a walk through the market halls of New Orleans at night is probably the most remarkable sight of culture-born beauty one can find in the United States." [12]

[12] Hermann Keyserling, "Genius Loci," *Atlantic Monthly*, Vol. 144, pp. 307-308.

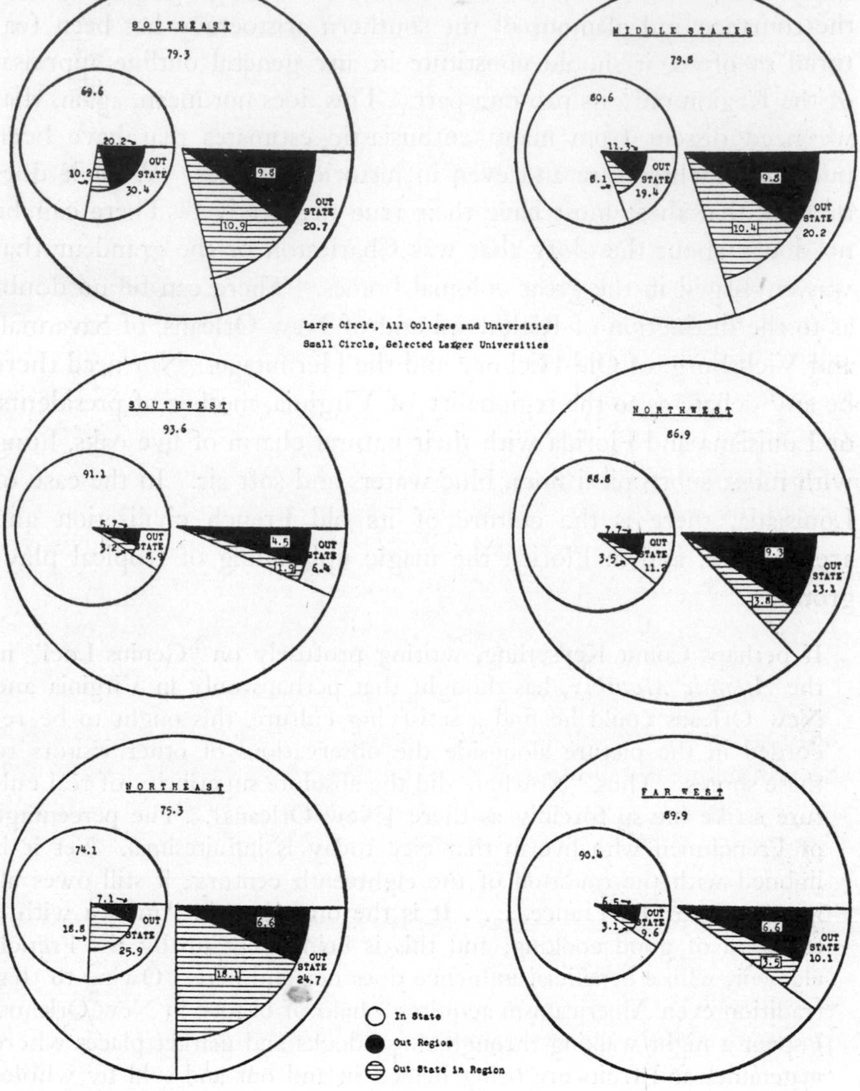

ONE OF THE "CULTURAL REVOLUTIONS" GOING ON IN THE NATION IS THE INCREASINGLY LARGE NUMBER OF STUDENTS FROM OTHER REGIONS ATTENDING UNIVERSITIES OF THE SOUTH

Above: Three Indices of Residence of Students.

All of these aspects of culture are important in the total perspective of the region's multiple indices: historical, geographic, general cultural, economic, and social. They should be presented and interpreted in relation to all those statistical indices which place the states of the Southeast nearly always in the lowest quartile of the 48 states. The rural South should be taken into consideration in the measurement of many of the standards of living, of housing, and of attitudes, since many of the indices used to rank the region are merely indices of measurement for technology and urbanism. Here, as in other regions, the historical factors of settlement, of slavery, of Negro and white, and the traditions of exploitation of soil and forest must become a part of the larger picture as well as the handicaps, cultural complexes, and lack of capital which have dominated the region.

We have already, in our chapter on the rural nation, called attention to the fact that the South, after all, is a rural region as compared with the Northeast. We need here, then, only call attention to a few of the indices by which the rural South is characterized. Sufficient for illustration are these: It has the largest number of farms and the smallest acreage per farm of any region in the nation. By the same token, it has the largest number of farmers and the smallest-scale farming, alongside its contrasting plantations. It ranks highest of all the regions in the number and proportion of its farm tenants and in the low income and standards of expenditures of its farm people. It buys two-thirds of the commercial fertilizer of the nation. It has a low ratio of pasture land, a low average annual per capita income for both farm and non-farm people, a low value of farm land per capita, of land per farm, average farm income, average net value of farm products per agricultural worker, and many others such as will appear presently in a more general appraisal.

Our outline appraisal of each of the regions is essentially a multiple one. There is, of course, the historical-cultural approach closely linked with that of the people, such as we have indicated in each of the regions. There is, then, a catalogue of the abundance of resources and of potentialities which then must be followed by a similar inventory of deficiencies, waste, and limitations. From these, of course, emerge the totality of the region with respect to its science, skills, and technology, its wealth and its institutions, and especially its "problems." In all of these aspects there is usually in every region a large clustering of indices which make a fine and plausible homogeneity for the ultimate appraisal of the region. It has often been stated, in particular by L. R. Wilson, professor of Library Administration and dean of the Graduate Library School of the University of Chicago, that the Southeast has been more completely documented than any other region of the nation. For this reason and because southern regional studies for the last decade have attempted continuing inventories, the findings of *Southern Regions of the United States* will be utilized more than any other sources.

"Inventory of the natural 'wealth' of the Southeast, if adequate, must be in terms of enormous aggregates as it relates to range and quantity and in terms of superlatives as it relates to quality and possibilities. There is not only no objection to presenting such a picture in authentic glowing terms but such full appraisal is fundamental to competent regional analysis provided the picture is also interpreted in relation to capacity for utilization and actualities of waste and in some comparative relation to other regions.

"This superabundance of well-nigh limitless sources of natural wealth is measured also by great range and variety: rainfall and rivers; climate and growing seasons; land and forests; minerals and mines, coal and iron and phosphate and hundreds of other minerals from the land undug; sticks and stones of fabulous quality and quantity for the fabrication of great buildings and for the construction of roads and bridges; energy and power, dominant or surging from oil and gas and electricity; sea water minerals and tidal power; iodine and phosphorus and nitrogen wealth; chemical resources from pine and vegetable, cotton and corn; parks and playgrounds, mountain and seashore, summer and winter resorts, play places of a nation; Nature reserves and sanctuaries for wild life; flora extraordinary, grasses and cultivated plants to feed man and animal and land; fauna of the woods and fields, millions of game, for commerce and recreation; domesticated animals on farm and grazing lands, race horses and work mules, makers of a culture; and many other tangibles and intangibles of geography's situation, relief, and area.

"If the enumeration of the superabundance of natural resources begin with oceans and rivers and rainfall, and if to abundant waters be added long, frostless growing seasons and soil of variety and richness, there will be projected boldly the basic vein of natural resources stretching across and throughout this Southeastern Region of eleven states no one of which is outside the range of superior advantage. In the measure of its rainfall, the whole of the Southeast lies within the bounds of that magic area which measures more than forty inches' average annual precipitation. Of the 27 percent of the nation's total land area with a precipitation of forty or more inches, the Southeast's own part is nearly two-thirds. Again, of the 55 percent of the nation's area in which a frostless growing season of six months or more is available, the Southeast itself has nearly a third, while the Southeast and the Southwest together aggregate more than two-thirds of the total."[13]

"Yet the first of all American resources is that of land, the source and power of all the Jeffersonian dream of the greater domain and democracy. This has been especially true of the southern agrarian culture. The heart of the Southerner has been in his land, the early richness of which, like the prodigality of his rainfall and climate, he has nonchalantly taken for granted. This measure of land resources in the Southeast is reflected in its nearly 325,000,000 acres of the nation's 1,900,000,000; such southern land expanse alone comprehending an area many times greater than all of Jefferson's early America. In other measures of general land area the Southeast constitutes in itself an empire of more than 500,000 square miles or slightly more than 17 percent of the nation's total, as compared with the Southwest's slightly more than 19 percent, the two southern regions aggregating more than a third of America's vast domain. Or, another indication of this superabundance of land resources in the Southeast may be indicated by the fact that this region alone might easily add forty million acres, the commonly quoted post-war surplus of harvested crop lands in the nation, to its present area; or just as easily take out of cultivation that amount and still, through better utilization and management, enrich its agricultural capacity and output.

"Another way of envisaging the nature and use of the region's land resources is to appraise its farm ratios and classification of land uses. Of the more than 6,250,000 farms in the United States in 1930 the Southeast had a little more than 2,380,000 or nearly 40 percent. Its acres in farms is of a lesser ratio with 170,507,839 of which the total crop land was a little more than 70,000,000; the total pasture land nearly 45,000,000; woodland not used as pasture 41,000,000;

[13] *Southern Regions of the United States*, pp. 27, 29.

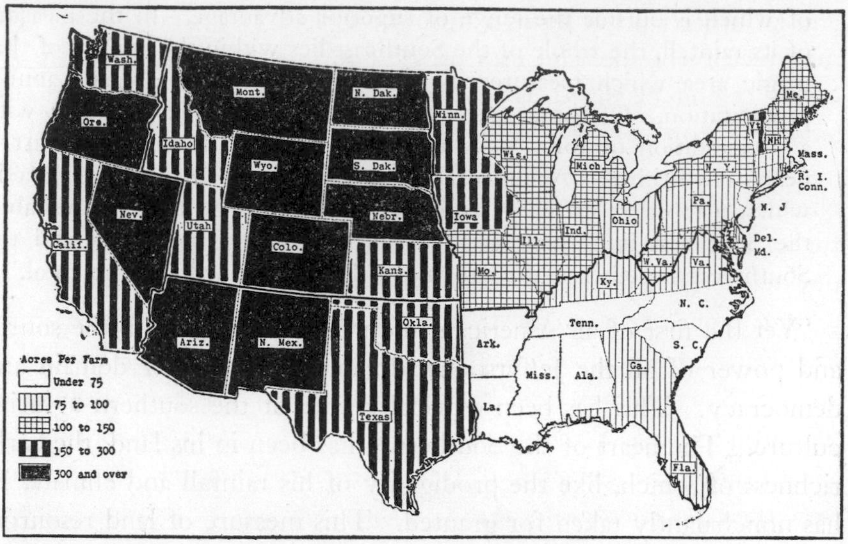

LAND IN FARMS, 1930

REGIONS	Number Farms 1930	Total Acres in Farms	Average Acreage Per Farm
Southeast	2,388,806	170,507,839	71.4
Virginia	170,610	16,728,620	98.1
North Carolina	279,708	18,055,103	64.5
South Carolina	157,931	10,393,113	65.8
Georgia	255,598	22,078,630	86.4
Florida	58,966	5,026,617	85.2
Kentucky	246,499	19,927,286	80.8
Tennessee	245,657	18,003,241	73.3
Alabama	257,395	17,554,635	68.2
Mississippi	312,663	17,332,195	53.4
Arkansas	242,334	16,052,962	66.2
Louisiana	161,445	9,355,437	57.9
Southwest	744,932	199,846,608	268 3
Oklahoma	203,866	33,790,817	165.8
Texas	495,489	124,707,130	251.7
New Mexico	31,404	30,822,034	981.5
Arizona	14,173	10,526,627	742.7
Northeast	618,079	63,407,903	102.6
Maine	39,006	4,639,938	119.0
New Hampshire	14,906	1,960,061	131.5
Vermont	24,898	3,896,097	156.5
Massachusetts	25,598	2,005,461	78.3
Rhode Island	3,322	279,361	84.1
Connecticut	17,195	1,502,279	87.4
New York	159,806	17,979,633	112.5
New Jersey	25,378	1,758,027	69.3
Delaware	9,707	900,815	92.8
Pennsylvania	172,419	15,309,485	88.8
Maryland	43,203	4,374,398	101.3
West Virginia	82,641	8,802,348	106.5
Middle States	1,622,625	209,566,897	123.0
Ohio	219,296	21,514,059	98.1
Indiana	181,570	19,688,675	108 4
Illinois	214,497	30,695,339	143 1
Michigan	169,372	17,118,951	101 1
Wisconsin	181,767	21,874,155	120.3
Minnesota	185,255	30,913,367	166.9
Iowa	214,928	34,019,332	158 3
Missouri	255,940	33,743,019	131 8
Northwest	648,927	278,832,755	429 7
North Dakota	77,975	38,657,894	495.8
South Dakota	83,157	36,470,083	438.6
Nebraska	129,458	44,708,565	345.4
Kansas	166,042	46,975,647	282.9
Montana	47,495	44,659,152	940.3
Idaho	41,674	9,346,908	224 3
Wyoming	16,011	23,525,234	1,469 3
Colorado	59,956	28,876,171	481.6
Utah	27,159	5,613,101	206.7
Far West	265,175	64,605,943	243.6
Nevada	3,442	4,080,906	1,185.6
Washington	70,904	13,533,778	190.9
Oregon	55,153	16,548,678	300.1
California	135,676	30,442,581	224.4

AVERAGE ACRES PER FARM, 1930

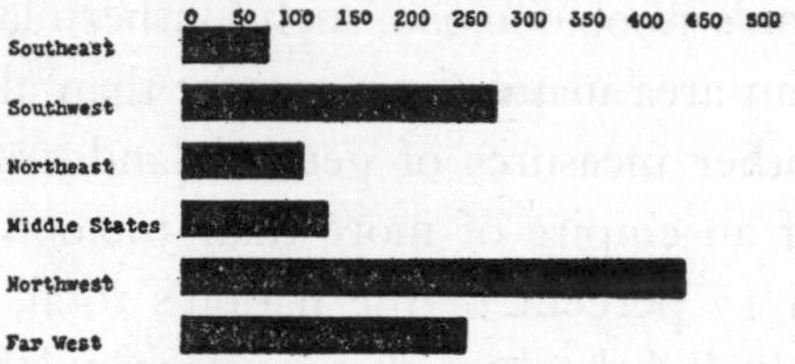

LAND IN FARMS, 1930

Average *Total* Acreage Per Farm in 1930.

and all other land in farms a little more than 11,500,000 acres. The map picture of the land uses of the Southeast shows practically the entire region classified as featuring the highest multiple land use; namely, 'crop land, grazing-hay land, forest.'"[14]

Among the other resources of the Southeast are its climate and climatic zones for not only the widest possible range of its flora but for an almost unlimited development of recreation, leisure-time activities with parks and playgrounds, bird sanctuaries, gardening and garden movements, scenic beauty, hunting and fishing. Of special importance, even as in New England, the Southwest, the Far West, and the Northwest, are its outer branches of seaboard and Gulf Coast playground areas, the Carolinas, Georgia, east and west Florida, the great Gulf Coast playground from Florida to Louisiana. All of these have their possibilities measured only by capacity to develop and use.

Coupled with all these are the mineral resources, elemental needs for any rich civilization. To describe these, of course, would require, even as in the other regions, statistical volumes of many pages. The next point of emphasis in the appraisal of the Southeast, however, is its deficiency in skill and technology through which to translate all of these resources into capital wealth and cultural endowment. There is waste of land and water and forests. There are deficiencies in equipment and technology and training. There are almost immeasurable deficiencies in farm homes and buildings, farm equipment, and farm management. There are yet other deficiencies in income and wages and in industrial capital, as well as in organization and personnel, alongside great deficiencies in human waste. These deficiencies reflect a long catalogue of problems and crises which have faced the South.

> It has already been pointed out that "the cultural equipment of the Southeast is not only powerfully conditioned by its geographic factors but can be understood only through a knowledge of historical backgrounds and regional incidence which have played an extraordinarily dominant role in the development of the civilization of the South. The visible ends of this historical influence are manifest in a folk-regional culture of distinctive features, including many special 'problems,' a long catalogue of crises, handicaps, and deficiencies, and a number of quality

[14] *Southern Regions of the United States*, pp. 29, 31.

characterizations commonly assumed to be superior. The special problems and deficiencies constitute a separate category as do also the cultural distinctions of the past. The 'crises' which have faced the region have been almost continuous and more numerous than is commonly understood. Some have been dramatic, some more subtle but not less powerful in their hidden influences upon the culture and economy of the South. These crises have been of several sorts. The most dramatic and tragic group of crises is that centering around secession and war. Following in the wake of the earlier secession crisis, the later secession and war, were the tragedies of reconstruction, of race conflict, of Negro-white and white-Negro domination, of turbulent politics, and multiple minor crises within the several states and institutions. Sectionalism itself has constituted a continuous major crisis. Powerful in the development of all the nation, it became in the South 'America's Tragedy,' being the final arbiter of economic and cultural fortunes and conditioning the South to isolation, individualism, ingrowing patriotism, cultural inbreeding, civic immaturity, and social inadequacy.

"A special group of related crises centered around cotton and its evolving economy. One was the early crisis of the South's expectation that Europe was dependent upon its cotton for industrial adequacy. Earlier, slavery with its economic, philosophical, and political influences was background and motivation for colonial policy, low labor and living standards, the 'Negro question,' the tenant system, the one-crop economy. Early soil leaching and erosion, waste of land and forests, hard labor of the people, were followed by later and greater soil waste, heavy fertilizer drain of cash value of cotton, the boll weevil, the westward expansion of cotton culture, the cotton crashes of 1914, of 1920, of 1929, the loss of exports and the bankruptcy crises of the early 1930's. Further impending crises may take form from constricting tariffs, from cotton belt competitors in other parts of the world, from economic nationalism, and from the substitution of new materials and processes for cotton. The early emergencies due to the wearing out of lands and the consequent migrations to other and richer lands were not the only crises of physical environment. Rice culture on the coast, indigo and sugar, the prevalence of the cattle tick and 'Texas fever,' and earlier malarial conditions were dominant influences in shaping and reshaping the southern economy. Deserted lumber towns, the exhaustion of forest and naval stores reserves, the shifting fortunes of fruit grower, Florida freezes and fruit fly, were handicaps alongside crises of Ku Klux and demagoguery, populism and prohibition, lynching and mobs."[15]

[15] *Southern Regions of the United States*, pp. 11-13.

Of the general culture and folkways of the South so much has been written in song and story, in caricature and stage portraiture, in romance and realism, that the region is presumably an area of both interest and geography to stimulate best sellers and to stimulate controversy and conflict still among the peoples of the different regions. And even in the late 1930's the old sectional question of the Negro disturbs the Senate and filibusters that august body into impatience and inaction. "Perhaps the nation's most critical problem yet" is a verdict still heard in the halls of learning and politics. "Essentially the supreme test of American regionalism" is another. It's a long way from Erskine Caldwell's *Tobacco Road* to Stephen Vincent Benét's, *John Brown's Body*—

> But something so dim that it must be holy.
> A voice, a fragrance, a taste of wine,
> A face half-seen in old candleshine,
> A yellow river, a blowing dust,
> Something beyond you that you must trust,
> Something so shrouded it must be great,
> The dead men building the living State
> From 'simmon-seed on a sandy bottom,
> The woman South in her rivers laving
> That body whiter than new-blown cotton
> And savage and sweet as wild-orange-blossom,
> The dark hair streams on the barbarous bosom,
> If there ever has been a land worth saving—
> *In Dixie land, I'll take my stand,*
> *And live and die for Dixie! . . .*[16]

[16] Stephen Vincent Benét, *John Brown's Body*, p. 77.

Chapter XXII

THE FAR WEST AND ITS CALIFORNIA

"IF," said one of America's most eminent statesmen, "we include the totality of the great Pacific West, extending somewhat up into Canadian territory, we have a region which reflects the highest standard of living in the world." It is always a startling revelation to "the East," as well as to the Middle States, to learn that the Far West, all of a sudden, as it were, has outstripped these two great and wealthy regions in the mode or average of most of the usual standard economic indices of material and cultural progress. But such is the case and it is reminiscent of those other earlier days when Oregon and California skipped over, as it were, the great way places of mountain and plain and desert to establish another "West" on the outmost borders of the continent.

We move then next, not to the last "West" chronologically, but to the Far West, driving through, as did the pioneers, this later West of the plains and mountains to that Pacific West, which must remain an indescribable American empire of contrasts and paradoxes, of miraculous transformations, and of a new composite America. This great West, new melting pot, cradle of the rebounding frontier, represents perhaps the greatest "unity in diversity" of all the regions, and one of the best epitomes of pluralistic America.

> Illimitable veldts tremble under a blasting summer heat; there are vast terrains of lava and scoriae; steaming deltas where the Oriental farmer is fief to the conquering anopheles; regions as tawny and stone-girt as in Spain; tundras, Nile banks, thousands of square miles of desert, deep in alkali, with mountains of harsh, virile contours, so spectral that they recall delirium or the moon. In the north are magisterial forests, blankets of fog, much winter green, seacrags under dripping rain, and

around Carmel a grandeur verging dangerously on the aniline charms of the Riviera.[1]

We have called attention to the fact that our six-fold regional division of the nation reflects a natural expansion of two Norths, two Souths, and two Wests. That is, the historical "North" was undoubtedly fabricated from the "East," our Northeast, and of the Middle West or the "Old Northwest," which is the Middle States of the present. The "South" has clearly evolved into a Southeast and a Southwest, with the latter more "West" than "South." Clearly, too, the Far West or Pacific West is fabricated of a western culture distinctive from that of our new Northwest of the Great Plains.

More literally from the historical viewpoint, however, there is one North and East, one South, and four Wests within the framework of our six Americas. This is another way of emphasizing the multiplicity of "Wests," of which in all there could be counted a good baker's dozen, if we recall that the "first Wests" comprehended northern and southern poles of the frontier conflict between the Tidewater East and the emerging Mountain Frontier West. Between these and the Far West were as many minor Wests as historian or regionalist is minded to characterize until we come finally to the "Last West," which is substantially our Northwest, the last major frontier attacked from East and Far West in the continued westward march of the nation and its rebound to new mines and borderlands.

When we come to our "next West," namely, the Far West, it is clear that once again we have two more new Wests, characterized at first only by the great Pacific Coast line and later by this great gateway to the Orient. These Wests were the two branches of the great westward trek of the forties, the one the Oregon Trail and the other the Gold Rush to California. Because of these great historical trails and of what followed, we are calling this Pacific West our next "most American" major region. First of all, the Far West antedates in historical perspective both the Southwest and the Northwest in so far as these regions represent present composite major regions of the United States. It happens, therefore, that the regionality of the culture of the Far West, long separated from the East

[1] Idwal Jones, "Letters on the Pacific Rim," *Saturday Review of Literature*, Vol. 15, No. 14, pp. 4, 15.

and the Eastern Wests, was being developed for some time before the maturing of these two later Wests.

Morison and Commager, in their chapter on "The Passing of the Frontier," call attention to the fact that by the 1840's the westward moving frontier "had reached the edge of the Plains. Then, instead of moving progressively westward as it had always heretofore done, the frontier leaped fifteen hundred miles to the Pacific Coast. For thirty years the intervening territory was practically uninhabited except by Mormons; not until the decade of the seventies did permanent settlers begin to close in on the Plains and Mountain regions; then the process went on with unprecedented rapidity until by 1890 it was complete and the frontier had disappeared.

"The Plains Region had long been known as 'the Great American Desert'; it was not, of course, a desert, but the designation was not without justification. For over two hundred years the American pioneer had moved westward from one woodland frontier to another, and in all that time it had never been necessary for him to make any radical readjustment to forest and prairie and stream. But when the pioneer came to the edge of the Great Plains he found an environment fundamentally different from that to which he was accustomed."[2] So, too, Hacker and Kendrick interpret the Far West as constituting one of the earlier Wests, but also as introducing that possible culture influence which has later characterized the Pacific West, namely, the influence of the Pacific Ocean and oriental culture. "It had become apparent, however, by the seventies and eighties, that American life revolved on two axes, an Eastern and a Western one. To the opening of California and the whole Pacific Coast, the life of the nation turned about the East. The Middle West was, in large part, a New England colony. As far west as the Great Plains, the people of the country looked to the eastern seaboard for their inspiration. But with the acquisition of Oregon (1846) and California (1848) there began to develop a life on the Pacific which became more or less self-centered. More than two decades elapsed before Far West and East were united by the iron bands of the transcontinental railways; another two decades were to round their course before West and East became integral parts of the same whole, through the disappearance of the frontier. In those forty years it was inevitable that Far West and East should have developed different interests and attitudes that did not originate from the same sources or indeed contemplate the same ends.

[2] Samuel Eliot Morison and Henry Steele Commager, *The Growth of the American Republic, 1865-1937*, II, 79-80. (Quoted by permission of the Oxford University Press, New York.)

The Far West had its eyes turned west over the wide expanses of the Pacific Ocean, just as the Atlantic seaboard and the Middle West looked across the Atlantic to Europe." [3]

Another reason for advancing the Far West to a priority before the Northwest and the Southwest is found in the fact that the eastern parts of these regions were for a long time the western fringes of the Southeast and Middle States and as such were gradually extending their reach as far as expedient into the farther Wests. Thus, Texas was of the South in its people, its cotton and slaves, and in its allegiance to the Southern Confederacy. So, too, the eastern parts of the Dakotas and of Kansas and Nebraska were fringes of Minnesota, Iowa, and Missouri, especially in the settlement previously described as the new Norway and of that expansion of the great land and agrarian domain of the nation which has usually been included in the historical "Middle West." There are still two other reasons for characterizing these two major regions subsequently to the Far West. One is the fact that much of their later development, and consequently present characteristics, were conditioned by the rebound from the Far West, and the other is that much of their present status is due to the products of later technology as it has developed oil and commerce in the Southwest and mines and machine farming in the Northwest.

We may, therefore, leave these two major regions to their development and to the play of time and technology upon their destinies. But with one exception, namely, that we cannot jump over the great desert and plains to the Far West without first recording something of the great American character of the covered-wagon-pioneer-frontier West and its people. For these not only made possible the settling of the Far West, but gave character to it in terms, again, of the "American" West. Thus, R. L. Duffus points out that these great western prairies and their episodes "will remain forever, in their loneliness and silences, a dramatic contrast to our crowded and hurrying cities. And, so remaining, they will contribute an element to our national psychology which must not be overlooked by anyone who is trying to understand us. . . . Those vast mountaintops that will forever look down on solitude . . . are . . . a symbol. We turn to them, in the flesh or in

[3] Louis M. Hacker and Benjamin B. Kendrick, *The United States Since 1865*, pp. 117-118. (Quoted by permission of F. S. Crofts & Co.)

imagination, to refresh our memory of the brave days of our national youth. We turn to them, from our crowded streets, our skyscrapers, our mighty machines, in a kind of nostalgia. Sometimes we do this in a mood of imbecilic sentimentality. Hence the mawkish 'Westerns' of our motion pictures, our cheap fiction and our wood pulp magazines. In revulsion, many of our more sophisticated citizens dismiss everything west of the Mississippi with a gesture of amused contempt. But there is sincerely in the hearts of our people a love of the large-scale western scene—of its long-dead heroes, its humor, as gargantuan as its mountains and plains, its adventurousness. It is this that the automobile tourist seeks to rediscover as he heads westward over the prairies. To the casual observer he may be a vulgar Babbitt, defacing the landscape with his very presence. But to himself, unconfessed, he is Daniel Boone, he is Kit Carson, he is Frémont, hunting for the road to India.

"Where the pioneers struggled forward with lolling tongues are now hard-surfaced roads, filling stations, hot-dog stands, even at times a traffic problem. But on either hand is the unconquerable West. Here, forever, is the primitive, the sun, the winds, the blizzard and the thunderstorm. Here there is room, remote from cities and from salesmanship, for a national soul to grow." [4]

This Far West is in many respects both the most "un-American" and American of the great regions, testimony again to the sweep and unity of the nation. It is un-American in so far as its exotic culture contrasts with the earlier historical nation and in so far as its oriental character contrasts it with the Eastern United States. It is un-American in so far as "there is none like it"; that is, it is a different world from "the East," or "the Middle West," or "the Great Plains," or "the South." It is un-American in its lower borders in so far as the Spanish influence represents the pre-national pattern and in the northern part in so far as its earlier pre-national culture or later "northwestern" culture prevails. Thus, A. L. Kroeber writes of the Northwest Coast that "it lacks regularly the generic American elements that were developed on American soil and became diffused; and that what is specific in it is either a direct outgrowth on the spot from the relatively undifferentiated primitive American culture or the result of later Old World influences. . . . In short, the outstand-

[4] R. L. Duffus, "The Open Spaces and the American Myth," Fred J. Ringel, *America As Americans See It*, pp. 2-4. (Quoted by permission of Harcourt, Brace and Company, Inc.)

ing characteristic of Northwest Coast culture is its seeming comparative aloofness from both Asia and America." [5]

> Yet, both the upper and lower Pacific west are often characterized as American phenomena, Oregon for its early development of a great agriculture and forestry and for the large-scale capacity of its land and forests and streams; the California west because of the composite character of its people from all the states in the Union and the multiple complex nature of its culture and credos. Thus, Idwal Jones writes of California as the microcosm of the United States. "Let anything happen," he says, "in the rest of the country, in Arkansas or Maine, and there is instant repercussion inside its borders. It has absorbed the frontier; it has become the national hot-bed and testing-ground. Hardly anyone has described this aspect of California so well as Farnsworth Crowder in 'Westways' did the other month: 'Here American institutions sharpen into focus so startling as to give the effect, sometimes, of caricature. Here the socio-economic class conflict is vividly posed in burning silhouettes against the walls of the factory and the hinterland. Here American scholarship and research are at their best, American cults and quasi-religions at their shabby and shallow worst; here America's indignant soap-boxers and pamphleteers, her bigots self-surrendered to some oversimplified ideal, its scared reactionaries and its grim standpatters; its baronial aristocracy, its patient poor and its sober, good-natured, self-centered middle class; its promoters, racketeers, opportunists, and politicians; its fagged-out oldsters and its brash, raw youths. . . . What America is, California is, with accents, in italics.' " [6]

Of particular emphasis at this point is the essential "American" nature of the Far West as pertains to its regional character and implications. It is a major part of the nation, boasting the highest standard of living in the nation or, for that matter, in the world, yet it is so far removed from the New York center of finance and of national organizations and the Washington center of government that it is necessary to operate through regional divisions, through telegraph and telephone communication, and through other techniques which must somehow transcend the distance and time elements involved in travel and personal contact. Certainly, the Far West would afford an excellent example of the dangers of sectionalism if

[5] A. L. Kroeber, "American Culture and the Northwest Coast," *American Anthropologist*, Vol. 25, No. 1, pp. 7, 8, 20.

[6] Jones, *op. cit.*, p. 3.

too large a number of states should be merged into the proposed regional government of Munro and others. Be this as it may, the Far Western Region is perhaps the most difficult of all to classify and characterize with satisfactory finality. Admitting its complications and the difficulties of finding approximate homogeneities, we must nevertheless proceed to the further exploration of its present reality and future possibilities for rearrangement. It is not likely, however, that with the increasing international relations with the Far East that the significance of the Pacific Ocean will be minimized or that the need for unitary regional co-ordination will be decreased. Here, as in the Northeast with its New England, diversity must be provided for in the major subregions, of which the Far West affords almost perfect examples.

Perhaps the best way to introduce the Far West, as here delineated, is forthwith to call it the Pacific Coast Region, since it comprises the Census classification of Pacific States—namely, California, Washington, and Oregon—to which we have joined Nevada, gateway in and out, marginal and connecting land of the Great Basin, marginal trade areas for California, and again cradle of other connecting links, namely, Lake Tahoe and the City of Reno.

This Far Western Region has a little less than 15 percent of the total area and about 8 percent of the people of the nation. Its metropolitan regions comprise eight of the total 93 urban districts with 100,000 or more population in 1930. These are, in the order of size, Los Angeles, San Francisco, Seattle, Portland, Oakland, San Diego, Long Beach, Tacoma, of which it is noted five are in the California area. The Far West is below only the Northeast in the ratio of its urban population with a percentage of 67.2 for its all urban and 61.5 for its metropolitan districts, as compared with the Northeast with 74.4 and 70.2 percent respectively and followed by the Middle States with 61.5 and 46.6 percent respectively.

In terms of the Newbigin major natural region, the Far West coincides largely with her *Pacific Coastal Area*, which derives its chief importance because of "the presence of the Great Pacific Valley, bounded on the west by the Coast Ranges and on the east by the Cascades, with their continuation the Sierra Nevada . . . ; the significance of the region is greatly increased by the breaches in its western wall, which permit of the rise of the great ports. A mountain knoll in the region of the Klamath River divides the valley into a northern section lying within the States of Oregon and Washington, and a southern one included in California. The boundary between Oregon and California, in latitude 42°, marks the division line between the two sections."[7] Within the major natural region are, of course, many subregions, the two chief ones being the North and the South, as indicated above. J. Russell Smith's *Men and Resources* subregions include a relatively large number, showing the availability of the *Far West* for subregional analysis without sacrificing the Pacific West unity. It comprehends all of four subregions, namely, Southern California, Central California, the Puget Sound and Willamette Valley, and the North Pacific Coast and Mountains, while it also includes parts of the Great American Desert, the Great Basin, and the Columbia-Fraser Basin. Its river valley regions include some fifteen of the subregional valleys; nearly all of the *Great Basin* with its Central Great Basin, Northern Great Basin, the Sierra Nevada, the Humboldt and Eastern Nevada, the *California Drainage Basins,* with Northern California, the Central Valley, the Central California Coast, the Southern California Coast; the Pacific Northwest, with its upper and middle and lower Columbia, Puget Sound, Oregon Coast and Washington Coast.[8]

Again, the types of farming areas are significant in the appraisal of the region through various subregional units. It is recalled that both J. Russell Smith and Ellsworth Huntington suggest that the nearest approach to scientifically delineated subregions, such as Woofter's 27 subregions of the Southeast, are those found in the map on Types of Farming Areas in the United States, previously referred to. This is particularly important in the Far Western Region, where land and water must be combined in usable proportions and where a new epoch in small farming and large-scale commercial farming have both been reflected in the Far West.

The areas, exclusive of duplications, include the following: Imperial Valley, Yuma, Palo Verde, Thermal, San Diego, Pacific Coast ranges and valleys, San Jacinto, Riverside-Pomona-Santa Ana, Long Beach, Ventura, Los Angeles, Dry Lake area, San Luis Obispo, Lower San Joaquin Valley, San Joaquin Valley, Salinas River Valley, Santa Cruz, Santa Clara Valley, San Francisco, Oakland-Berkeley, Antioch, Brack,

[7] Marion I. Newbigin, *A New Regional Geography of the World,* p. 335.
[8] J. Russell Smith, *Men and Resources, passim.*

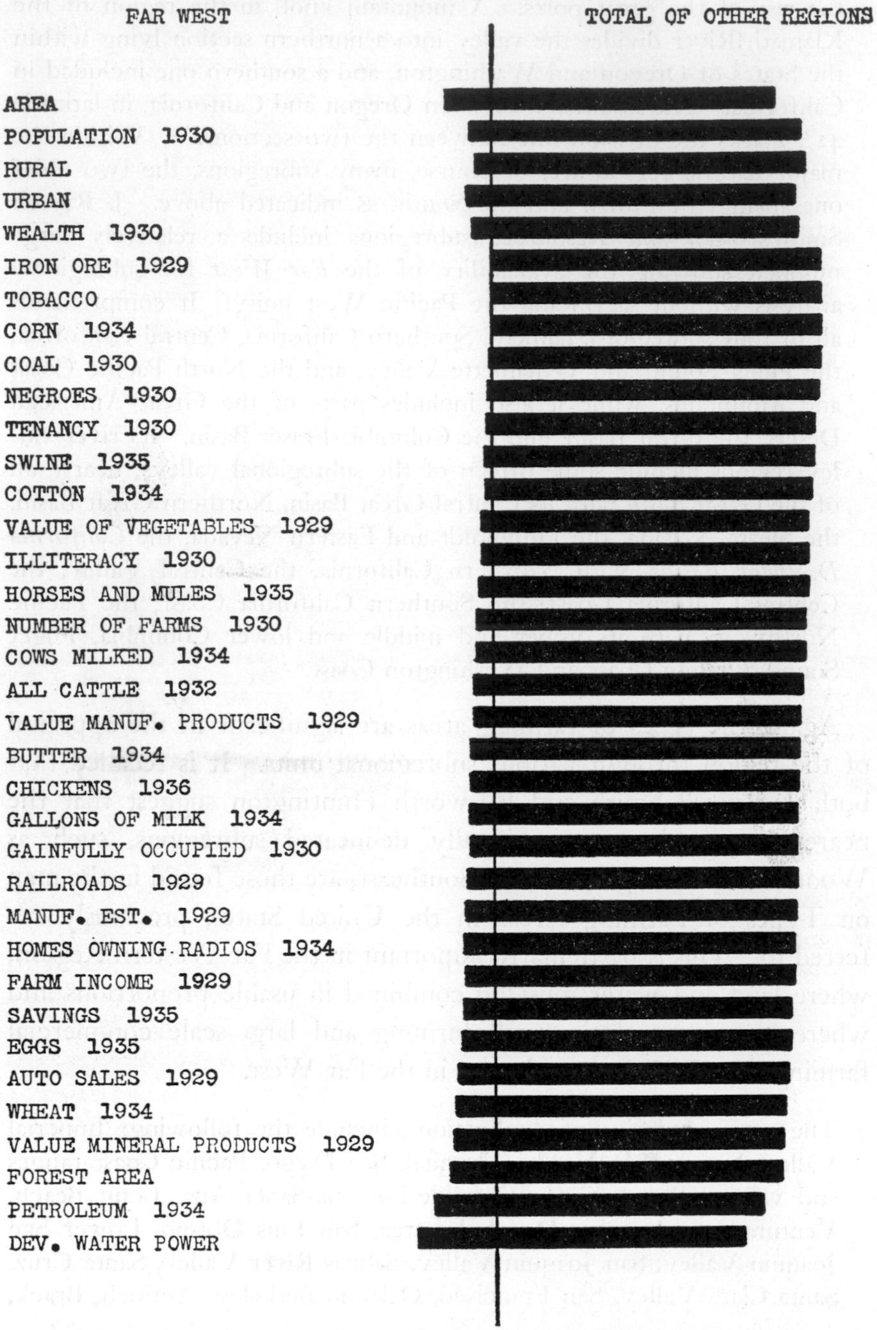

Regional Ratios to the National Total. Random Miscellaneous Indices: The Far West

Great Valley, Sierra Nevada Mountains, Great Basin: mountains and valleys, Great Basin semideserts, Klamath-Pit Plateau, Harney Basin-Broken Lava Plateau, Mohave-Colorado Rivers deserts, Las Vegas, Virgin Valley, Southern Idaho highlands, Shasta, Humboldt, Alkali deserts, Honey Lake area, Lovelock Valley, Truckee River Valley, Lahontan Valley, Carson River Valley, Walker River Valley, Upper Sacramento Valley, Sierra Nevada foothills, Sacramento Valley, St. Helena, Marin County, Petaluma, Klamath Basin, Rogue River Valley, North Pacific Tillamook, South Oregon coast, Umpqua Valley, Willamette-Cowlitz Valleys, Chehalis, Puget Sound Valley, Okanogan, Sanpoil Valley, Upper Columbia, Colville Valley, Pend Oreille Valley, Northwestern Rocky Mountains, Spokane-Coeur d'Alene, Big Bend, Palouse, Walla Walla-Pendleton, La Grande-Wallowa Valleys, La Grande Valley, Moro, Walla Walla, Umatilla Project, Blue Mountains and valleys, Deschutes, Baker Valley, Boise-Payette-Weiser, Moses and Soap Lakes, Okanogan highlands, Methow River Valley, Wenatchee, Ellensburg, Yakima Valley, Goldendale, Hood River-The Dalles-White Salmon.[9]

Of the 183 areas based upon wholesale grocery-urban territory and prepared by the United States Department of Commerce and bounded by trading area outlines, the Far West apparently had but eight or nine, with the following cities as major centers of trading areas: San Diego, Los Angeles, Fresno, San Francisco, Sacramento, Portland, Spokane, Seattle, and Tacoma. It is interesting to note the fact that nearly all of the Nevada territory is served by the Los Angeles and Sacramento areas, there being no major trade area outlined with a Nevada center. These, of course, like the drainage areas of the Great Basin are important criteria for including Nevada with California in the Far West.

Again, the Ogburn *Social Characteristics of Cities* gives us some indices of regional homogeneity. Thus, "the number of cities in the states of the Pacific Coast is small compared to the numbers in the other sections, hence it did not seem desirable to include these Pacific cities in the detailed comparisons by classes with the more numerous cities of the other regions. However, the Pacific Coast is far away from the other regions, and it comes to possess a number of distinct characteristics.

[9] Adapted from the map, Types of Farming Areas in the United States: 1930. Division of Commerce, Bureau of the Census.

"Quite distinct is the small number of children, which affects the size of family, schools, income, and many other activities of life. There is consequently a large proportion of adults, which means more of the ages that earn an income. Sales in restaurants are large on the Pacific Coast, and the number of electricians is greater than in the cities of other regions, all perhaps features of the excess of adults. Curiously, the proportion of elders is great, though no greater than in the Northeast, yet notable in a region in which there is a large proportion of immigrants. Generally the old people are not ready immigrants. Wages are high in the Pacific region, as are the proportion paying income taxes and the number having radios.

"As to occupational activities the cities of the Pacific Coast are in the main trading centers with, however, a quite large sprinkling of the professions, especially teachers, musicians, writers, and artists. Church membership is low. Many who migrate do not transfer their church membership. The support of schools and libraries is liberal.

"It may be observed that most of the characteristics in which the Pacific Coast cities outrank those of the other regions flow from the large percentage of adults and amount of wealth." [10]

When it comes to the task of characterizing the region through whatever indices of population may be chosen, the Far West will show a fourfold classification. That is, in addition to the Orientals and the Mexicans, there were the earlier settlers and the later migrants who had poured into the West from all parts of the nation. It is important to recall again the fact that the Far West is older in terms of its present population of "Americans" than the Southwest or the present Northwest, for both California and the Oregon Trail antedate many of the states of the Southwest and the Northwest. Thus, California, the earliest settled and the most populous of the Far West States, now containing a white population representative of every state in the union, is likely to forget its old days of the Gold Coast and after. The discovery of gold in California naturally precipitated the settlements of the Far West and accounts for the variety and number of sections represented in her early population. In the most northerly of the states of this region, there are large numbers of British and French-Canadians. A large percentage of the native-born American settlers are either of southern or New England stock.

[10] William F. Ogburn, *Social Characteristics of Cities*, p. 31. (Quoted by permission of The International City Managers' Association.)

Some Germans and Scandinavians have also ventured as far as the Far West, particularly in Washington. Nevada, like California, represents a composite of the Northwest and of special folk from all the states. Of the Mexicans, who are found in fairly large numbers in Southern California, more will be said subsequently. But, of the more recent immigrants to the United States, only the Orientals, the Chinese and the Japanese, have entered in sufficient numbers to be noted before the Great War. Since the War, the entry of Filipino young men has become a disturbing element.

Like the Northeast, which must be envisaged in terms of its New England and its later expanding Middle Atlantic States, and the Middle States, which must first be seen in terms of the historic Middle West, the Far West must be appraised in terms of two major sections, the Oregon-Washington North and the California South. This is especially true with respect to the people. Covered wagons to Oregon and Gold Rush to California are equally historic backgrounds for this great unmeasured region of the nation. Here, again, as in the case of the Northeast, where the common tradition is to see New England primarily, so in the Far West, California is commonly assumed to be *the* region. It is in respect to this aspect that the redefinition of the region may be of the greatest importance.

Nevertheless, California is of the Pacific Coast West, again both symbol and reality. Popular characterizations of the people may well be utilized to introduce the more academic outlines for appraisal. And few such pictures can be found better than that of the redoubtable L. P. Jacks, who, happily arrived in California, finds it difficult to find Californians. "Not," says he, "that I found the country uninhabited; Los Angeles alone, my first stopping-place, having a population of a million and a half. But the people I met and conversed with were immigrants and from other states, differing widely in antecedents and outlook, to say nothing of the Chinese, Japanese, Filipinos, Mexicans and Negroes who swarmed in certain streets. Here, thought I, is a new kind of 'melting-pot' where the ingredients are of Uncle Sam's own making, an interesting variation of the grand melting-pot 'problem' which contains ingredients much more refractory and forms the staple of discourse whenever the future of America is under consideration. My first impression, gained from delightful people living in delightful places, was such as one might receive on arriving at a City of Refuge, or alternatively on entering the atmosphere of a religious retreat. Here, it seems, is the place where harassed Americans come to recover the joy and serenity which their manner of life denies them elsewhere, the place, in short, to study America in flight from herself; and even now, when my first impressions have been radically corrected, I feel that this was not wholly wrong . . . in general California is a magnet; the farmer from Iowa, tired of plowing and reaping the level earth; the cultured Bostonian, tired of the Lowells and Cabots; the tired meat-packer from Kansas City; the stockbroker from New York, the banker from Philadelphia, the newspaper magnate from Chicago, the steel magnate from Pittsburgh, the oil magnate from Oklahoma, a host of magnates, and sub-magnates of every known variety; seekers of health, sunshine, change, pleasure, beauty, rest; shunners of toil, care, routine and tumult; haters of closed walls and lovers of the open air; some fleeing the killing cold of the Boston winter, others the killing heat of the New Orleans summer; some the monotony of plains, great lakes and sluggish rivers; others the more dismal monotonies of fashionable life; some thinking of themselves, others of their children."[11]

The earlier American quality of California was found in the essential frontier nature of its people. In addition to the Spanish and Indian influences which are still reflected in many of the culture patterns, there were the early dominating pioneers who were even in those days advocates of "America for Americans," "California for Americans." The drama of the Gold Rush is exceeded only by the drama of the building of the state and its glamorous cities by these pioneers.

B. Schrieke describes these earlier days with the view of characterizing the region's foreign peoples. "California," he reminds us, "was ceded to the United States by Mexico on February 2, 1848, by the treaty of Guadalupe Hidalgo. Gold had been discovered in California during the preceding month, but it was not until Autumn that the news became generally known. The gold craze swept from the United States to all corners of the globe. Drawn by the lure of the precious metal, men hastened towards California: rowdy adventurers, speculators of every class and nationality—a restless, lawless, reckless crowd of men, jealous and greedy, determined to make no less than a fortune as easily and as quickly as possible. They had left behind all claims to social recognition based on family, social ties, or previous attainments. In the rough life of the early California mining camp, distinction was

[11] L. P. Jacks, *My American Friends*, pp. 97-99. (Quoted by permission of The Macmillan Company.)

commanded solely by vigor and personal courage. It is estimated that by the summer of 1849 there were at least 20,000 men at work in the diggings and that 77,000 persons entered California in 1849; 82,000, in 1850. Among the first to go to the mining districts were many American soldiers who had served in the Mexican War. Naturally, they did not take too kindly to the presence in the camps of Spaniards and Mexicans, many of whom were skilled miners able to locate the more valuable claims and to work them to better advantage. Their 'greasy,' 'swarthy' appearance inspired disgust. As the Americans, who had been in the minority, increased in numbers, they began with the cry of 'California for Americans!' "[12]

Yet early Oregon, too, was so supremely American that it would be difficult to find a better example. The Oregon Trail, of all the covered wagon traditions, is perhaps the most dramatic and representative. The Oregon land and trees and water offered everything the American farmers dreamed of and to this day produce superlatives in fruits and trees and production of dairy cattle. And it was especially characteristic of the expanding America in so far as it was a territory of international conflict. Like Louisiana and Texas and California and Florida, the Oregon-Washington Northwest was a part of the diplomatic battle of the expanding frontier. Perhaps there was fear that Russia and the illiberal nations of Europe would hem the nation, or England claim it because of Cook's 1778 exploration. Yet the United States claimed it, too, because of the Gray expedition in 1792 and that of Lewis and Clark in 1805. Be that as it may, the United States as usual took it into the great American domain, and presently with the addition from the war with Mexico of California and that other great Southwest Region, the bounds of the nation were ended with the Pacific. The Pacific West, then, it was and is.

Although this Oregon-California trek, the Oregon trailers and the Forty-niners constitute about the most romantic of the great western movement, the story is in historical perspective, shorn of its five months' trail of drama and struggle, a relatively simple one. But it stamps the Far West as of the most distinguished of all American regions. Turner's statement gives the essential facts. "Thus, the Eng-

[12] B. Schrieke, *Alien Americans*, pp. 3-4. (Copyright 1936 by The Viking Press, Inc., New York.)

lish frontier and the American frontier were meeting in a region disputed between the two nations. The Snake River Brigade had enabled the British fur traders, under the leadership of Dr. John McLoughlin, to widen their field, and P. S. Ogden, one of their agents, had reached the area of Great Salt Lake. In 1832 the silk hat had begun to replace that made of beaver, so that the price of the fur of this animal, as well as the supply, had steadily declined. The era of the fur trade had passed its height; but the problem of occupation of the contested territory became serious at the very time that the vanguard of American fur traders was approaching the Columbia Valley; and hard on their heels came an active movement of American settlement of the lands in controversy, stimulated in part by the missionaries and in part by New Englanders like Hall J. Kelley and the more practical Nathaniel J. Wyeth.

"Hoping to engage a profitable trade in the Far Northwest, Wyeth had organized a company of New Englanders, who left Missouri in 1832 with a trapping party. Repeating the journey in 1834, he allowed a Methodist missionary, the Reverend Jason Lee, and others, to go with him, and established Fort Hall, in Idaho. Here he met the opposition of the Hudson's Bay Company, under the control of McLoughlin, whose generosity toward American explorers and settlers was noteworthy, though he was loyal to his company and, in accordance with its policy, had discouraged settlement north of the Columbia. Moreover, the Hudson's Bay Company now built Fort Boise in order to intercept the Indian trade from Fort Hall, and, shortly after, Wyeth was obliged to sell that station to his British rivals.

"By this time, therefore, the traders had outlined the course of the Oregon Trail, which ran from Independence, Missouri, along the old Santa Fe Trail into Kansas, where it crossed the Kansas River to the Platte and followed the latter to its forks, and then, by way of the North Platte, proceeded to Fort Laramie (begun in 1834), in Wyoming. Reaching the Sweetwater River, the trail led to South Pass, and thence, by several routes, to Soda Springs, and, by way of Fort Hall, to the Snake River. From there it continued to Fort Boise and Walla Walla, and down the Columbia, by boat, until later migrations, when a wagon road was established."[13]

Turner records the first great dust-covered caravan of 1843 as comprising something like a thousand people with fifteen hundred oxen and cattle and a hundred and twenty wagons, as a real coloni-

[13] Frederick Jackson Turner, *The United States, 1830-1850, the Nation and Its Sections*, pp. 361-363.

zation from the Middle West. He estimated that 1844 witnessed a similar expedition, with perhaps 3,000 in 1845 and 1,350 in 1846 and between four and five thousand in 1847.[14]

> The census of 1850 showed that Oregon had a population of over 13,000, of which natives of the North Central States aggregated slightly more than 5,000 (including 2,200 furnished by Missouri alone). The number born in the South Central States was about 1,200; in the South Atlantic, somewhat in excess of 800; in the Middle Atlantic, around 1,000; and in New England, less than 600. Taking into consideration the origins of the Missouri element and of that in the zone to the north of the Ohio, the people of southern stock in Oregon far outnumbered those of northern birth; but the preponderance of natives of the North Central section was unmistakable. The territory itself had given birth to more than 3,000; and the foreign-born (largely former British subjects) numbered 1,150. The oxcart migrations bore a natural relation to Missouri's leadership in the raising of oxen; and the caravans organized on the Oregon Trail resembled interestingly those that had formed long ago on the Santa Fe trail.[15]

Strangely enough this Far West is a melting pot both of native Americans from the states of the Union and also of many peoples of other nations. Next to the Northeast and the Middle States, it has the largest number of foreign-born people, its more than a million aggregating more than all those in the Northwest, the Southwest, and the Southeast, if Mexicans are not included. Yet with the exception of its sixty thousand Japanese and its twenty-three thousand Chinese, its foreign-born population is extraordinarily well distributed. If it has nearly a hundred thousand Orientals, it likewise has little more than that many from Switzerland and Sweden. Its Italian and its German people are nearly the same in number, with more than a hundred thousand each. And it has more than fifty thousand from Ireland and from Norway and from Russia. It has from twenty to twenty-five thousand each from France, Finland and Portugal, from ten to fifteen thousand each from Spain, the Netherlands, Greece, Czechoslovakia, and Austria. And it has more than five thousand each from Turkey, Roumania, Hungary, Belgium, and

[14] *Ibid.*, pp. 366-367.
[15] *Ibid.*, p. 368.

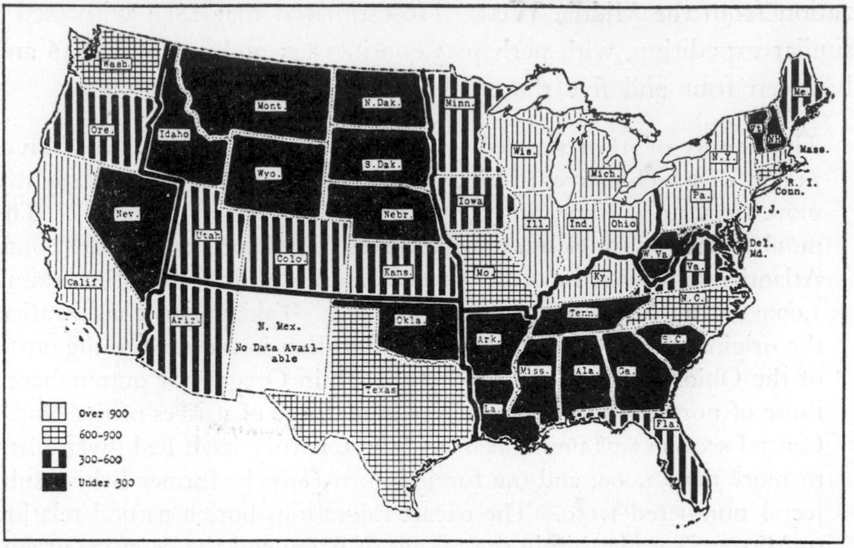

VARIOUS INDICES ARE USED TO INDICATE REGIONAL DIFFERENTIALS IN VARIOUS CULTURAL AND ECONOMIC ASPECTS OF LIFE

Above: Total Sales at Sporting Goods Stores in 1935, in Thousands of Dollars.
Below: Per Capita Expenditures for Appliances and Radios in 1935. Adapted from *Chicago Tribune,* February 9, 1937.

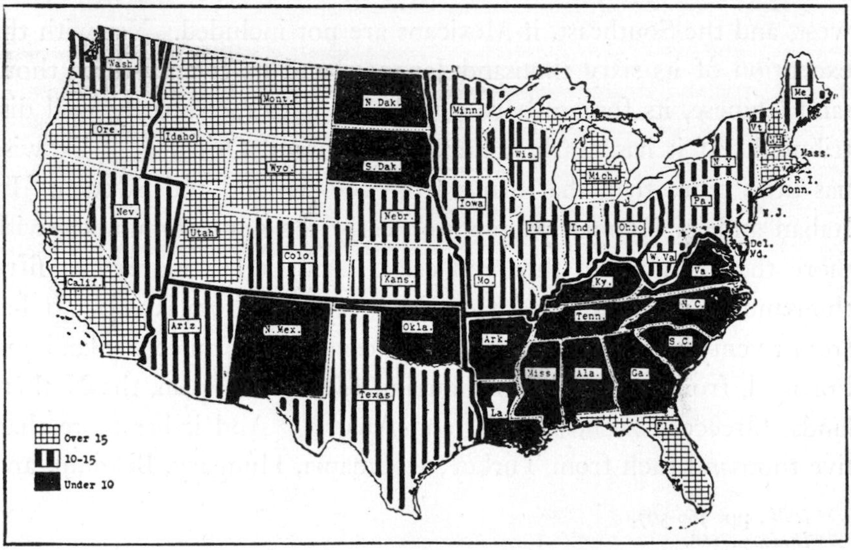

Australia. And it has a great migratory Mexican and American labor population.

Yet the people of the Far West are pre-eminently "American." "They did not have to invent or to learn 'Americanism.' . . . Their fathers and grandfathers had done that for them. . . . The Far West is a beautiful laboratory for the citizen who is truly interested in American tendencies and characteristics," thus wrote Katharine Fullerton Gerould.[16] This, of course, is similarly true of California with its melting pot of old Americans.

With reference to the Old Oregon Trail, Howard R. Driggs asked and answered the question of the people and their origin. "Whence came the folk that enacted this epic drama? A revealing answer to this question was once given by George Himes, a pioneer of Oregon. Guiding a visitor through the historical museum at Portland, the veteran paused to say: 'Here is a special collection of relics that represent every state east of the Mississippi. This clock, for instance, once ticked time in Vermont; this old Franklin stove was brought from Pennsylvania; this scythe has mowed bluegrass in Kentucky; and in this cradle an Indiana baby was rocked while the oxen plodded westward.' Far more than old relics lay back of that exhibit. The pioneers came carrying not only their household necessities and the basic tools for subduing the soil; they bore also the essentials of American civilization. They came to build homes, to found schools, to erect churches, to establish self-governing communities and states based on our constitution. In the hearts of these nation-builders was the inner spirit of America."[17]

This Pacific West, in addition to claiming the highest standard of living of all the regions and an essentially "American" stock, may claim many other distinctions almost unbelievable to those who have not seen it. Thus both California and the southern part of Oregon and Washington of the north, strangely enough offer great opportunity for tropical sports and for winter sports at the same time. "Sundown Seaboard" and the Far West is land of perpetual bloom and golden points. All this; yet, too, it is Death Valley and desert and mountain crags and snow and blizzards, sand and floods.

[16] Katharine Fullerton Gerould, "Our Northwestern States," *Harper's Magazine*, Vol. 150, p. 414.

[17] Howard R. Driggs, "The Old Oregon Trail," *The Journal of the National Education Association*, Vol. 25, p. 176.

"Neither Europe nor Asia nor South America," wrote Viscount Bryce, "has a prospect in which sea and wood and snow and mountains are so united in a landscape." [18]

The common picture of California is of the blue waters of the Pacific, the balmy tropical scene, while the Oregon country connotes big trees, big fruits, big rivers. Yet the scene which the United States Department of the Interior features in the new recreation is the winter snow and sports. Here is one picture: "Winter sports enthusiasts are waxing up their skis, snow trains will soon be off to the races, and Switzerland and the Alps are forgotten in the glories of the mountains, valleys and winter beauties of the United States. . . . Mt. Rainier National Park, Washington, will launch its formal season on the day after Christmas with slalom races for men and women. General Grant National Park will celebrate Yuletide as usual at the foot of the ancient and gigantic General Grant Tree, known as the Nation's Christmas Tree. In Lassen Volcanic National Park, California, winter sports were in full sway early in December on solidly packed snow, three feet deep. . . . Mt. Rainier National Park, only a few hours from the wild Puget Sound country, has a carnival of winter sports covering a season beginning this year on December 26 and extending through May 1. Last year it drew 65,936 winter sports enthusiasts during its winter season. Paradise Valley, with snowy expanse of unobstructed hills and vales and steep inclines, is an ideal terrain for skiing and has been the scene of national championship and Olympic trials. It is a picturesque setting for the world-famed Paradise Inn. Surrounded by alpine meadows covered with more than 25 feet of snow, the roof and high dormer windows peek invitingly above the snow, and huge fireplaces in the lobby, as well as the less charming but more practical steam heat throughout, are tempting and welcome. The Silver Ski course here extends from Camp Muir at the 10,000 foot level on the mountain slopes to the Valley, and involves almost five miles of skiing and turning and a vertical drop of a mile. The Silver Skis Race will be held this year on April 17.

"Other major events of the Rainier season, already announced, are the Tacoma Winter Sports Carnival, sponsored by the Tacoma Chamber of Commerce on January 30, opening with a carnival dance the night before; the Pacific Coast Conference Ski Tournament on February 25 and 26, with all universities and colleges affiliated with this conference competing in downhill, slalom and cross-country ski races; the Washington Ski Club Downhill and Slalom on April 3, the Rainier

[18] *The New York Times*, April 25, 1937, Section 11, p. 1–xx.

National Park Slalom Championships on April 10, the Rainier National Park Novice Slalom Championships on April 24, and the Sitzmark Carnival Slalom on May 1. . . ." [19]

"Out of the barren desert of central Washington," begins a news story widely published. It refers to the "greatest engineering project ever undertaken by man"—the *Grand Coulee Dam* which in its unfinished state is already larger than the next largest structure, namely, Boulder Dam. Something of the problem of water distribution in the Far West has already been described in our previous chapter on River Valleys. Yet here is description that belongs to a region —not just to the valley.

The story continues, "When completed, in 1942, the dam will stand 550 feet above bedrock, 4,300 feet long, 500 feet thick at the base and 30 on top. It will contain enough concrete to build a standard highway from New York to Los Angeles and back.

"In the center, a waterfall more than twice as high as Niagara will hurtle over the spillway. At flood stage, a million cubic feet of water will pass over the dam each second.

"Flanking the dam will be two powerhouses, each containing nine huge generators. These will produce electric energy almost twice the present total production of Washington, northern Oregon, northern Idaho and western Montana.

"Above the dam the Columbia River will form an artificial lake 151 miles long, averaging more than a mile in width. From storage reservoirs, powerful pumps will divert excess water to the farms of an arid area larger than the state of Delaware." [20]

This Washington-North of the Pacific West is not to be outdone by its California colleague of this great region. For is not Washington State "the doorway, and the only doorway to more than one-sixth of the population of the United States"? [21] And the doorway to Asia as well? Climate, health, agriculture, industry—all these and more stamp the region as worthy of its high appraisal.

Washington State is the Columbia River and Puget Sound combined. The one is the greatest river, the other the most remarkable inland sea

[19] United States Department of the Interior, News Release, January 2, 1938.

[20] *Durham Morning Herald*, February 3, 1938, Part I, p. 7.

[21] Robert Whitaker, "Washington: The Dawn of a Tomorrow," *These United States, A Symposium* (edited by Ernest Gruening), p. 235.

on the Pacific side of the Americas. Together they constitute a length and breadth and volume of water surface, closely interwoven with narrowly separated shores, such as no other state of our Union, and no other country on the two continents can quite match. . . .[22]

More comprehensive, and not less enthusiastic, is the testimony of one of our own American writers, Dr. Woods Hutchinson, in his "Conquest of Consumption": "When once we cross the summit of the Cascades we enter a totally different climate, an air which is mild, gentle, and moist, but never depressing; a country of green mountains, dazzling snow-tipped peaks, of grass, of moss and fern, which knows neither the barrenness of Winter nor the brownness of Summer, a land which has all the best and most invigorating qualities of the cradle of our Teutonic race, with none of its extremes. From one end to the other it is the land of tall trees and tall men, of the apple, the peach, the prune, and the pine; the land of the green valley and the rushing river. The rosy pink of its orchards every Spring is equaled only by the sunset glow upon its peaks of eternal snow. It is the charmed land of the American continent, where a temperate sun, a mild climate, and a fertile soil give man the stimulus of the green and rain-swept North, with the luxurious returns for moderate effort of the teeming tropics. . . . If you have never seen Oregon, Washington, or British Columbia in Summer, you lack important qualifications for imagining what the climate of heaven may be like." [23]

So much labor trouble has lately dominated the agriculture and commerce of the Far West that the nature of their output has been largely overlooked. California has been described more often, yet Oregon and Washington are epochal in themselves in their output. High producing farms, irrigated and non-irrigated; record-making Jerseys and Holsteins, "beating-the-world" dairying and poultry in the grand manner. "Agriculture in the Pacific Northwest runs the whole length of its possibilities from sea level to the high mountain valleys. Almost every type of farming is practiced and the methods for the same type may be vastly different on the opposite sides of a mountain range. In the Pacific Northwest a farmer may find his choice of a farming industry under almost any climatic conditions he prefers." [24]

[22] Robert Whitaker, "Washington: The Dawn of a Tomorrow," *These United States, A Symposium*, p. 237.

[23] *Ibid.*, p. 239.

[24] *The Land of Better Farms: The Pacific Northwest*, p. 15.

> As for Oregon, what better source of enthusiasm than *The Journal of the National Education Association* inviting its members to see ". . . a vast empire of natural wealth and beauty. . . . In Oregon Nature strewed her treasures with a lavish hand. One half of the valuable timber of the Pacific Coast stands in Oregon. Gold is dredged from its streams. Its mineral-bearing rocks yield silver and copper and lead. On its grazing lands roam thousands of cattle. Its rolling hills are covered with yellow waves of grain as far as the eye can see. Its fertile valleys produce a goodly share of the nation's most delicious fruits. From its swift rivers come the world's most valuable fish, of which the Royal Chinook Salmon is king. . . . Vacationists who seek the solitude of primitive forest; the majesty of snow-capped mountains; the music of falling waters; wild animals; the picturesque abodes and dress of the disappearing Redmen—will find them on the ranges, along the well-paved highways, in the national forests and the Indian reservations of Oregon." [25]

There is something to think about and to inquire into in the oft-heard assertion in the Far West that the great culture of the future will be evolved here. This is not only California or southern California with its look to the Orient and its premises of combining not only eastern America with western America, but contrariwise the evolution of a culture in which Western civilization represented by America and Eastern civilization, represented by the Orient, will constitute the new fabric. It is also Oregon and Washington and the Puget Sound, double gateway to Asia and New York, from Northwest America to Alaska, to Canada and south and east again into all America. This is a prospect at least representative of the need for more inquiry and more portraiture than we now have of the Far West and of its culture, in contrast to our New Northwest, called by some historians "The Last West" to which we now turn in the next chapter.

[25] Belmont Farley, "The Land of the Royal Chinook," *The Journal of the National Education Association*, Vol. 25, pp. 130-131.

Chapter XXIII

THE NORTHWEST AND ITS GREAT PLAINS

"TAKE this town here. It's built from grass. Wool built this town. Wool keeps it going. And grass makes the wool. Nine-tenths of the good towns in all the West are grass towns. Out here grass raises our buildings, pays our peace officers, puts fat on our politicians. They forget it, though, damn 'em, they soon forget."[1] Thus a man of the grass lands hammering away to remind the world of "an enduring American countryside, its roots spear deep into American earth," which will eternally fight the prospect of its desertion or of its being permanently tagged as problem area to be dominated by an American problem administration, APA. And, again, "In case you don't know it, this here is buffalo grass, real honest-to-God buffalo grass. It's been here for centuries. It'll stay for more centuries. It builds cow brutes—bones, meat, taller and hide all at once. It builds the finest beef on earth. It never dwindles. It stands and grows forever. When you and me are rotted to dust, when all these damned cities are sunk to ashes and rust, this grass will still grow, finer than ever."[2]

Yet some of the traditional opinion of this great Northwest must still prevail. Hear Will James describe it: "And to me the West is, as I look at my spurs now, a country where you can still ride a whole lot and can throw your rope without having it caught in a fence-post. The countries I mean, besides where the dude ranches are running, are countries where dudes would never go, with all my due compliments to them. There is countries where you can still ride one hundred miles without striking a fence nor seeing a house, and you'd be lucky if you found water in them countries. Them is the countries

[1] Charles Morrow Wilson, *Roots of America*, p. 246.
[2] *Ibid.*, p. 257.

I know well. I'd like to say that in them countries, which takes in a good third of the United States, there's many wild horses, many wild cattle yet, the long-horned breed from old Mexico, and today, of course, these long-horns have been bred up into the heavy market stuff. Even at that, them bred-up cattle are near as wild and near as hard to handle as the old long-horn. There is cow outfits today in the West that is running up to as high as one hundred thousand head of cattle and with them there must have to be some cowboys because who else is going to handle them? You can't handle them cattle over that rough country in a car. So as I said before, even though there might not be any Indians to fight much, there is still lots of cattle, lots of rough horses in our country and the cowboys are still the same today as they was in the seventies. It took two generations to make a cowboy and it will take five to unmake him."[3]

So we come to "the last West," which is what some of the historians have called our New Northwest of the Great Plains and Mountains. Once again our region bids high for the appellation of the "most American" region, if we accept the R. L. Duffus dictum that "The open spaces in America are the symbol of our myth," or the frontier as the index of national character, or a group of new states "with a taste for social and political experiments," or the Great Plains as elemental fabric of the continent, or the clash of upper and lower wests of Far West and East, miners and adventurers, cattle men and sheepherders, land lovers and adventure hunters, patriots and boosters, Federalists and states-righters. "Every nation," writes Duffus, "has a national myth without which it would be not a nation but a mob." And even though "the great open spaces of the American West ceased about 1890 to be determining economic factors in the growth of the nation, they remain, and always must remain, an important psychological factor."[4]

We approach the general outline-characterization of our New Northwest more from the psychological viewpoint perhaps than was the case in any of the other regions. This seems logical for several reasons, but particularly in view of the prominence which the region has played in the public eye during the last few years of growth and

[3] Will James, "Cowboy and Dude Ranches," Fred J. Ringel, *America As Americans See It*, pp. 62, 64. (Quoted by permission of Harcourt, Brace and Company, Inc.)

[4] R. L. Duffus in Fred J. Ringel, *America As Americans See It*, p. 2.

the evolution of the Dust Bowl concept and the various proposals to move the people away from such areas which are again to be turned into parks and grazing areas for the nation. Pertinent, too, is the contrariwise trend to build dams, expand irrigation, and afford both opportunity and motivation for richer cultures within the bounds of the barren lands. This feature, namely, of developing and continuing folk-regional cultures to be launched by national planning, is of the greatest significance in the whole concept and practice of American regionalism. In the two great regions of the Northwest and the Southwest these factors assume almost priority proportions over most other considerations.

It seems permissible, therefore, to begin our outline of this great empire of the New Northwest, the greatest of any in area, with the characteristic American note of patriotism or love of locality, which, contrary to unthinking assumptions, does abide and abound. In her *Pathfinders of the West*, A. C. Laut describes the great Canadian Northwest, which may well symbolize the American frontier strength and hardihood.

I love thee, O thou great, wild, rugged land
Of fenceless field and snowy mountain height, . . .
Yes, man must sink or fight, be strong or die!
That is thy law, O great, free, strenuous West!
The weak thou wilt make strong till he defy
Thy buffetings; but spacious prairie breast
Will never nourish weakling as its guest!
He must grow strong or die! Thou givest all
An equal chance—to work, to do their best—
Free land, free land—thy son must work or fall,
Grow strong or die! That message shrieks the storm-wind's call!
And so I love thee, great, free, rugged land
Of cloudless summer days, with west-wind croon,
And prairie flowers all dewy-diademed,
And twilights long, with blood-red, low-hung moon
And mountain peaks that glisten white each noon
Through purple haze that veils the western sky—
And well I know the meadow-lark's far tune
As up and down he lilts and circles high
And sings sheer joy—be strong, be free; be strong or die! [5]

[5] Adapted from A. C. Laut, *Pathfinders of the West*, pp. vii-viii.

Thus a poet of the past apostrophizes this fascinating land of "roaring tempests," "storm-swept plain," "hissing snowdrifts," "land of mountains, of fruitful valleys, and wide open spaces." "This land of bread and meat, or better, iron ore and wheels," has to varying degrees been included in the familiar terms of the Northwest, the Old Northwest, the Great Northwest, the Pacific Northwest, the Middle West, the Great Plains, the Western States, the Land of the Dakotas, and the Dust Bowl. Only those who know the Great Plains and love the land of mountains and wide open spaces can see the beauty and splendor in contrast to dust and drouth and storm. Thus there are two extreme symbols, the one "Nothing could make me live in such a country" and the other "Nothing could make me leave." In between these, of course, are the great hosts of tourists, American seekers after beauty and change and excitement, and that other sizeable group of folk who seek to appraise a region by scientific study and intelligent planning.

> Annie Pike Greenwood writes of Idaho, "I loved the fabulous sunsets, lakes of gold, and the dreamy purple mountains that appeared in the sky along their rims; and when these gradually dimmed and vanished, a million stars in the dark-blue sky—a million stars, seen at a breath. . . . It was not all beautiful. Idaho's wild winds raged for days at a time, lifting the earth in great clouds of dust. Fields were literally transferred by the power of those winds, some of the land having to be sown over again. On everything within the house lay a thick gray powder, like that on a moth's wings exaggerated ten thousand times. Hair was transformed to dun color, eyebrows shelved with it, skin thickly coated, eyes red and smarting, teeth gritty. . . ." Yet again, "Perfume of the hay-fields, and the way they rolled up and then down, toward the Sawtooth Mountains, toward the black volcanic cone. Valley to the south, beginning to have little farms where was wilderness when I had come. And the blue, the serenely blue Minidokas. Skies, skies of every kind: the beauty of piled-up clouds, rippling clouds; sunsets over the black buttes, which lie prone, as though they were sleeping mourners, their cloaks drawn over them; sunsets seen through delicately penciled trees that ran a single lovely line, like a Japanese print, on the boundary of Endicott's far eastern field. And the swelling roar, always the swelling roar of the great, gorgeous Jerome Canal, a man-made river which steals the children of man and laughs at his grief. . . ." And still again, "Never a day passed that I

was not thrilled with the changing beauty of the vast cloud-filled skies, the purple and gold sunsets, the blue and white mountains, our gray and green valley, our own lovely, undulating farm, with its ivory wheatfields, its green beet-fields, its purple-blooming alfalfa. I loved to go to sleep to the chorus of the crickets in the grass just outside my window, with its thorough-bass of the frogs down along the canal. The cool, delightful summer nights; the limitless stretches of clean, white winter snow . . ."[6]

The Northwest is characteristically "American," of course, in its historical development, its states representing the later cluster of stars to be added to the flag, alongside those of the Southwest, New Mexico, Arizona, and Oklahoma. If we keep in mind our marginal areas of the eastern bounds of the Dakotas, Kansas, and Nebraska, and the western bounds of Idaho, and the southern bounds of Colorado and Utah, we have here the great final overflow reservoir for the nation following the rebound from the farthest Pacific western frontier, and shading off in the east from the Great Middle States. The explanation of this great unsettled no-man's land is easy to find in the fact that without science and invention the frontiersman could not cope with this harsh environment which gave him too little water, provided no fences, and no transportation that was dependable for quantity production. As Walter P. Webb puts it, " 'the attempt of a migrating people to cross this line of the 96th or 98th meridian resulted in social chaos and economic ruin which continued through invention and much experiment, new weapons were adopted, new implements invented, new methods devised for getting water, making fences, and farming, until new institutions were evolved or old ones modified to meet the needs of a country that was level, devoid of timber, and deficient in rainfall; until a plainscraft took the place of woodcraft.' "[7]

Yet the character of the region in so far as it was "West" was fixed to some extent during this period of transition. "In the course of this long and arduous struggle with the Plains environment, the miner, the cattleman, and the farmer evolved social and economic institutions that

[6] Annie Pike Greenwood, *We Sagebrush Folks*, pp. 26, 141-142, 170-171. (Quoted by permission of D. Appleton-Century Company.)

[7] From Samuel Eliot Morison and Henry Steele Commager, *The Growth of the American Republic, 1865-1937*, II, 80.

differed markedly from those which had obtained in the woodlands of the East. The Plains environment necessitated a modification not only of the tools and methods of farming but of social attitudes, economic concepts, political and legal institutions as well. 'The physical conditions which exist in that land,' as Major Powell said, 'and which inexorably control the operations of men, are such that the industries of the West are necessarily unlike those of the East and their institutions must be adapted to their industrial wants. It is thus that a new phase of Aryan civilization is being developed in the western half of America.'

"Thus there emerged in this last American West a regional consciousness as distinct and characteristic as that of the Old South; a common feeling that expressed itself not only in politics and economics, but in social attitudes, legal institutions, art and literature. This sectionalism of the last West, rooted in geography, was cultivated by the impact of the industrial revolution on the process of settlement, and by the manner in which the various stages of economic development—mining, cattle-raising, and farming—all came to be controlled by outside interests. This interplay of basic local forces with absentee political and economic interests in the creation of this last West makes a fascinating study in the history of sectionalism."[8]

All the states of this New Northwest were admitted to the union long after the Civil War, Utah as late as 1896, Wyoming and Idaho in 1890, the Dakotas and Montana in 1889, and only Colorado in 1876. In territory this region is the largest of all the regions with nearly a third of the nation, justifying again its appellation of the great open spaces, while its ratio of the population is smallest, with about 6 percent of the people. In terms of the United States Census, this region comprehends all of the mountain division except Nevada, which we have allocated with the Far West, and Arizona and New Mexico, which of course are southern, and hence align with the Southwest. In addition, the region includes four states of the West North Central Division, namely, the two Dakotas, Kansas, and Nebraska. Of the 93 metropolitan districts of the United States, this region has only Denver, Omaha, Salt Lake City, and Wichita. On the other hand, because of its great distances, it has a relatively large number of trade areas with small urban centers. Such as they

[8] *Ibid.*, pp. 80-81. (Quoted by permission of the Oxford University Press, New York.)

are, they radiate around towns other than the four metropolitan centers as follows: Butte, Boise, Pocatello, Helena, Great Falls, Havre, Billings, Miles City, Minot, Grand Forks, Fargo, Mandan-Bismarck, Aberdeen, Casper, Grand Junction. Pueblo, Hutchinson, Salina, Topeka, Lincoln.

Strangely Newbigin classifies the Great Plains and Mountain Belt as two regions which "may be considered together as being of minor importance." [9] This is an excellent illustration of the fallacy of evaluation by natural regions alone. The region fares better in J. Russell Smith's *Men and Resources* [10] in which are found a half dozen varied subregions, including all of the Winter Wheat Region, the Spring Wheat Region, the Rocky Mountains, nearly all of the Dry West and Great Plains, the Southeastern Intermountain Plateaus, and a part of the Great Basin. Likewise it is rich in the plant and animal ecology regions showing the original potentialities of grasses in relation to maximum capacities or climaxes of flora. There are the great tall grass and short grass regions, which have made the Great Plains famous as the land of buffalo and cattle and home of the American cowboy. Strangely enough, the region fares well in the number and importance of its river valley subregions, especially in the light of what modern technology is doing to the new Northwest and its problems. Of the river valleys it comprehends most of the Missouri Basin, with the Missouri Headwaters, Western Tributaries, Yellowstone, Cheyenne, White Niobrara, Platte, and Kansas. It embraces the upper part of the Colorado Basin, a small part of the Great Basin, and the Snake River Valley of the Pacific Northwest, a small portion of the Upper Rio Grande, and a small portion of the Upper Mississippi-Red River of the North.

Of special distinctiveness is the relation of river valleys and water to the farming areas in which again the region shows a remarkable variety and richness according to the scientifically delineated subareas shown on our great farming area map previously described.[11] Thus, the Water Resources Committee points up the importance of water for irrigation in the great arid portions of the region. Adjustment of water and land thus became a key problem affording unexcelled opportunities for the new frontier conquests of the Plains. Accord-

[9] Marion I. Newbigin, *A New Regional Geography of the World*, p. 334.
[10] J. Russell Smith, *Men and Resources*, *passim.*
[11] Adapted from the map, Types of Farming Areas in the United States: 1930, Division of Commerce, Bureau of the Census.

ingly, five types of measures for the improvement of the Great Plains are suggested, namely: "1. Small dams may be constructed in certain areas devoted to grazing in order to make water available for stock on range lands that otherwise could not be grazed, or to reduce the distance which livestock must be trailed to water. 2. Springs may be improved, shallow wells may be dug, and deep wells may be drilled to supply water for livestock in favorable areas. . . . 3. In grazing areas having adequate supplies of stock water, unappropriated water may, where topographic and soil conditions permit, be stored and used for the irrigation of forage crops, thus building up feed reserves for dry years. . . . 4. In areas to be devoted mainly to dry farming, there are opportunities to irrigate scattered tracts of small size, in most cases, from reservoirs or by pumping. . . . 5. Construction of reservoirs for recreational use and for wild-life conservation and provision of wells for domestic use would measurably increase the comfort of Great Plains occupance. . . ." [12]

The number and variety of farming areas is surprisingly great and provides an excellent index of the subregionality of the great frontier empire. Exclusive of overlappings, the 163 areas include the following: Kootenai River Valley, Priest Lake, Pend Oreille Lake, Lewiston, Nez Percé, Seven Devils-Craig Mountains, Big Camas prairie, Twin Falls-Jerome, Gooding-Shoshone, Rupert-Burley, Snake River Plains, Southeastern Idaho, Gallatin Valley, Anaconda, Butte, Helena-Boulder, Townsend, Intermountain, Bitterroot Valley, Kalispell, Flathead Valley, Blackfoot-Piedmont, Teton Plains, Triangle Plains, Great Falls, Judith Basin, Intermountains and foothills, Milk River plains, Missouri-Musselshell plains, Broadview, Billings-Red Lodge, Hardin-Sheridan, Northern Great Plains, Golden Valley, North Dakota Bad Lands, Missouri-Yellowstone Plains, Scobey-Plentywood-North Dakota, North Dakota Black Prairies, Souris Sandy Lands, Red River Valley, Missouri Plateau, Stark-Hettinger, Southeast North Dakota-South Dakota, Brookings, Iowa-Nebraska-South Dakota, Missouri River bottoms, Nebraska Plains, Northeast Kansas-Nebraska-Missouri, Kansas City-Saint Joseph, Southeast-Kansas-Missouri, Flint Hills, Wichita Prairies, Great Bend plains and sandy lands, Smoky Hills, Republican Dissected Plains, Nebraska plains, Central Nebraska, Loess hills-Holt sandy plain, South Dakota Black prairies, Pierre plains, Northern Great Plains

[12] National Resources Committee, *Drainage Basin Problems and Programs,* December 1936, p. 59.

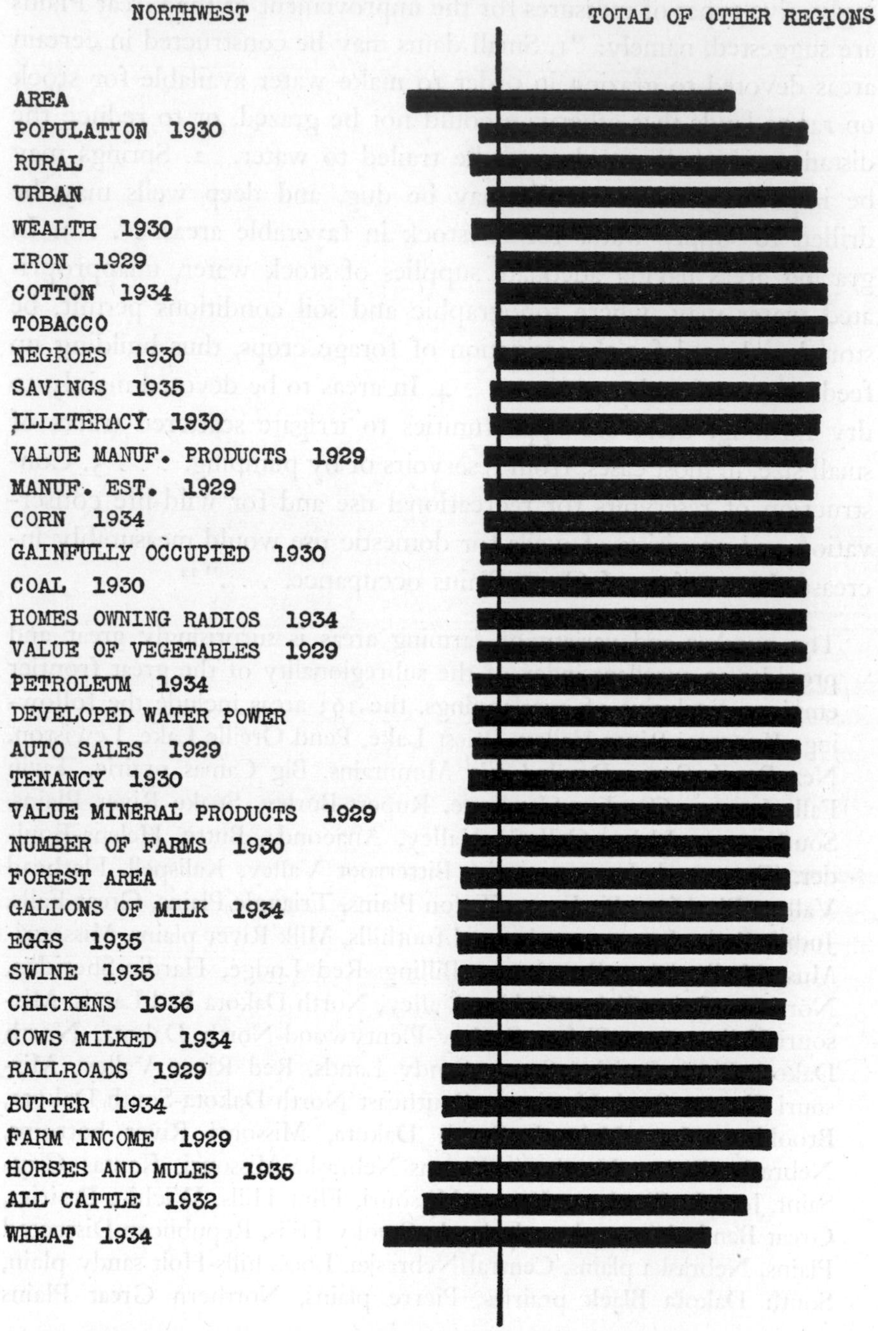

Regional Ratios to the National Total. Random Miscellaneous Indices: The Northwest

roughlands, Jones-Lyman, Rosebud Plains, Great Plains sand hills, Alliance, Platte plains, Platte-Republican high plains, Canadian-Cimarron high plains, High plains, Sand hills, Platte high plains, Scotts Bluff Basin, Niobrara plains, Rocky Mountain foothills, Arkansas Valley, Platte Piedmont, Southern Rocky Mountains, Routt-Moffat Plateau, Red Desert, Wyoming Basin, Fort Bridger, Big Horn Basin, Driggs, Salt River Valley, Wyoming, Alkali deserts, Forested Plateaus, Rabbit Valley, Bear River Valley, Cache Valley, Uinta-Wasatch Mountains, Castle Valley, Emery-Castledale, Colorado River Plateau, Beaver, Intermountain woodlands and grasslands, East Millard, West Millard, Sevier-Sanpete Valleys, Dog Valley, Utah Valley, Salt Lake Valley, Weber River Valley, Bear River Valley, Ogden River Valley.[13]

Like the other major regions, the Northwest shows distinctiveness in the number and character of its people. Here, again, both vertically and horizontally, the inventory reflects several areas of development. There were, of course, the several groups which represented the expansion of the great "Middle West," especially the Norwegian Americans, as already described. There was then the fringe of expansion from Texas and New Mexico as well as the early backwash of Oregon and California. And, of course, more specifically there were the great Mormon American pioneers who constitute a separate subregional episode of their own. We must keep recalling the fact that after the Middle States and, to a lesser extent the Far West, were filled up, including, of course, Oregon, which was the earliest of the Far West, the surplus population from these regions began to overflow into what we term the Northwest. This means that the native Americans are the same stock which contributed so materially to the building up of the Middle States, that is, the Ulster Scots (Scotch-Irish) from the Piedmont section of the South and the New England pioneers. Some of these states, as Idaho, contain an unusual proportion of men of southeastern or southwestern ancestry. In Utah are concentrated the Mormons, largely from New England and New York. Of the nineteenth-century immigrants, the British were the first to settle in this section. Later the Germans and the Scandinavians, especially, expanded from the Middle Region, the Dakotas and Nebraska having a large number of these immigrants.

[13] Adapted from the map, Types of Farming Areas in the United States: 1930, Division of Commerce, Bureau of the Census.

Of the immigrants of the Second or the New Immigration, the Poles are to be noted as settling in the Northwest Region and in particular to having preferred the Dakotas.

Concerning the early settlement of the region, Taeuber and Taylor in their *People of the Drought States*, one of three monographs prepared under the direction of T. J. Woofter, Jr., Coordinator of Rural Research in the Works Progress Administration, call attention to the fact that "rarely, if ever, has so large an area been occupied and brought under cultivation in so short a time. Rarely, if ever, have so many persons attempted settlement under conditions with which they were so wholly unfamiliar. As a large-scale experiment, the conquest of the plains has few or no parallels."[14] Although they include parts of Minnesota, Wisconsin, Oklahoma, Texas, and New Mexico in the drought area, thus confusing the picture from the viewponit of social-economic regional homogeneity, nevertheless their characterization of the people and their settlement is effective. Thus, they remind us that "Once the conquest of the prairie was possible, people from the Eastern States and from European countries flocked into this region in large numbers. The development of the railroads which brought the farmer nearer his market, the development of the barbed-wire fence which enabled the small homesteader to guard his plantings from the ranger's cattle, and the development of the windmill which raised the much-needed water to the surface—all contributed to the settlement of the Great Plains States. A large army of restive settlers flocked into the area, laying claim to more and more of the land. The demand for homesteads and the desire to bring each homestead under the plow were so insistent that no thought was given to those factors which might limit agricultural activities. And when conditions seemed unfavorable, an unstable population, avoiding rather than solving its problems, simply moved on. But after the first wave of settlement had subsided, a much slower process of adjustment began; villages and cities developed and, in many parts, farms too small for efficient operation were abandoned or combined with others.

"From the time of earliest settlement, the population of the Great Plains has been a youthful one. Large families have been the rule, and long before wheat seemed necessary to win the World War, the area was producing a human 'export crop.' Every year has found numbers of young people moving to other farms, to near-by villages and cities, or to other states. . . . Like the whole body of westward migrants during this period, the early populations of the region were

[14] Conrad Taeuber and Carl C. Taylor, *The People of the Drought States*, p. 13.

cosmopolitan. The population of Kansas in 1860, for instance, included persons who were born in every state and in 28 foreign countries. Nevertheless, the Great Plains area was for the most part originally settled by persons who came from Iowa, Missouri, and states immediately east of them. While 90 percent of the 107,000 persons in Kansas in 1860 had been born in other states or in foreign countries, almost 12 percent were natives of Missouri and more than 50 percent were born no farther east than Ohio. Many of those who were not born in Missouri had lived in that state immediately preceding their move directly across the border into Kansas. . . ." [15]

We must not, however, overlook the great Mormon thread in the fabric of this vast region. For here was a pioneer movement and distinctive institution comparable to the Gold Rush and the Oregon Trail in many respects and representing the dramatic episode of the winning of the West as vividly as any other. Here is a subregional culture certainly distinctive from the East or from the Kansas borders of this West, and certainly distinctive from its near neighbor, Reno. How this epoch of the region developed is a major part of the story.

Frederick Jackson Turner has described how the movement which had deeply affected the Mississippi Valley by the middle forties was basic to the Mormon settlements. "The next great migration was to lodge a center of expansion in the vast arid country that extended from Great Salt Lake as a nucleus. A new and characteristic phase of the religious emotionalism of the period; the creation of a church hierarchy capable of dealing with the problem of irrigation in this great region; the spread of the New England type of community, modified by the conditions of the desert; and the inhospitable reception of this religion, and its Yankee followers, in the parts of the North Central States that had been occupied by the southern stock, with its conservatism and religious prejudices—these were involved in this migration. Suddenly, there were opened, in the Far West, conditions differing radically from those in the areas to which other colonization had gone, as well as a society entirely unlike that of the settlers on the Pacific Coast." [16]

In 1930, the Northwest's people numbered a little more than seven and a quarter million folk or about 6 percent of the nation's total.

[15] *Ibid.*, pp. 3, 14.

[16] Frederick Jackson Turner, *The United States, 1830-1850, the Nation and Its Sections*, pp. 368-369.

These constituted the smallest number of any region, situated in the largest region—hence the least dense of any region. Of the total number, only 269,766 are of races other than the white, the Negroes in Colorado, Kansas, and Nebraska, and the Mexicans in the southern part of Colorado being the largest of the groups. There are Indians in the northern part of the region, Japanese in Wyoming, Utah, Montana, Idaho, and a few Chinese in Montana, Idaho, and Utah. Of the total of nearly twelve million foreign-born population, exclusive of Mexicans, in the nation, the Northwest has scarcely more than a half million, ranking, however, considerably above the Southeast and the Southwest. Of these, in order, there are nearly a hundred thousand from Germany, 70,000 from Russia, 60,000 each from Norway and Sweden, 40,000 from England, 30,000 from Denmark, with 20,000 or more from Italy, Czechoslovakia, and Ireland.

Population increased in the decade 1920-1930 less than in any other region—with even a decrease noted in Montana—in spite of the fact that the 8.9 percent excess of births over deaths and the 19.1 percent birth rate is exceeded only by the Southeast, and that the infant mortality rate per thousand births is only slightly higher than that of the Far West or the Middle States. Of the total population, 35.6 percent is urban; 39.6 percent is rural-farm; and 24.8 percent is rural non-farm. The Northwest has the lowest population of all the regions in metropolitan districts, namely, 14.3 percent, although its 35.6 percent in all urban areas is a little larger than the 29.8 percent of the Southeastern Region. Nevertheless, some parts of the great Northwest are characterized by an urban population, similar to Nevada of the Far West with its Reno urban plurality of people, although abounding in great isolated land areas.

We have already called attention to the fact that the Northwest has always been and is now above all an inland, rural region. Climate is the chief determining factor, being largely arid in the western portion and semi-arid in the central and most of the eastern part. It is what Mr. Webb terms treeless in all excepting the area in the Rocky Mountain Region, and part of that extends upward above timberline. Beginning with the Dakotas we find stretching westward before us the Great Plains, the flatness broken only by the Black Hills, like an oyster uplifted suddenly in the heart of the plain, until we come to the foothills of the Rocky Mountains, extending south from the western third of Montana to the southern part of Colorado and spreading over into part of Utah. The eastern fringe of the Dakotas lies within the spring wheat belt, while the eastern half of Kansas demarks the western portion of the corn and winter wheat belt. Straw stacks and silos might almost be considered cultural indices here. A hard winter wheat belt, 300 square miles located largely in Kansas and eastern Colorado, is a transitional area from the east to west leading us into the Great Plains, a zone transitional between desert and fertile plainland.

The Northwest, with an area of 818,508 square miles, is not only by far the largest of the regions but it has a larger percentage of the nation's total area in farms than any other region, namely, 27,833,000 acres, or 23.8 percent, and derives a greater proportion of its total income from agriculture than any other, all of the states having a percentage of 30 and more, with the exception of Utah and Colorado. Furthermore, though it ranks only fourth in the total number of farms, it has the largest percentage of the large farms in the country, over half of the farms exceeding 500 acres as compared with the 17.5 percent of the Southwest, the next in rank, or the 2.6 percent of the Northeast. Correspondingly, it has the least percentage of small farms with its 3.6 percent, since only one-fifth of its farms are under 100 acres. It comes second among the regions with its 43.1 percent total crop land and third in the total pasture land.

When we consider the products from these farms we find wheat to be the unquestionable leader in 1930, over half the wheat of the entire nation having been produced here. In the production of corn and hay it is second only to the Middle States. More alfalfa is cut for hay than anywhere else. In livestock production, the Northwest leads the nation in beef cattle, which yields 13.5 percent of the gross income of the region, and in the number of sheep and lambs; and it is second only to the Middle States in swine, the number of all cattle and calves, horses and horse colts. It is third in the number of milk cows and heifers. However, the percentage of cash farm income from this livestock is a different story, since the Middle States and the Far West far outrank the Northwest here. The cows of three other regions yield more milk per animal, and are worth more per

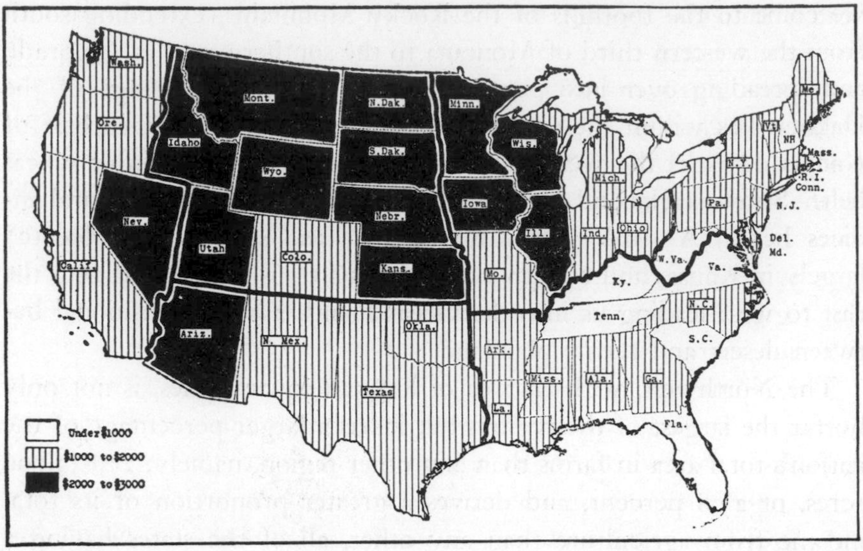

Above: Average Agricultural Production Per Full Time Worker, 1924-1928.
Below: Horsepower Available Per Worker, 1924. Adapted from O. E. Baker.

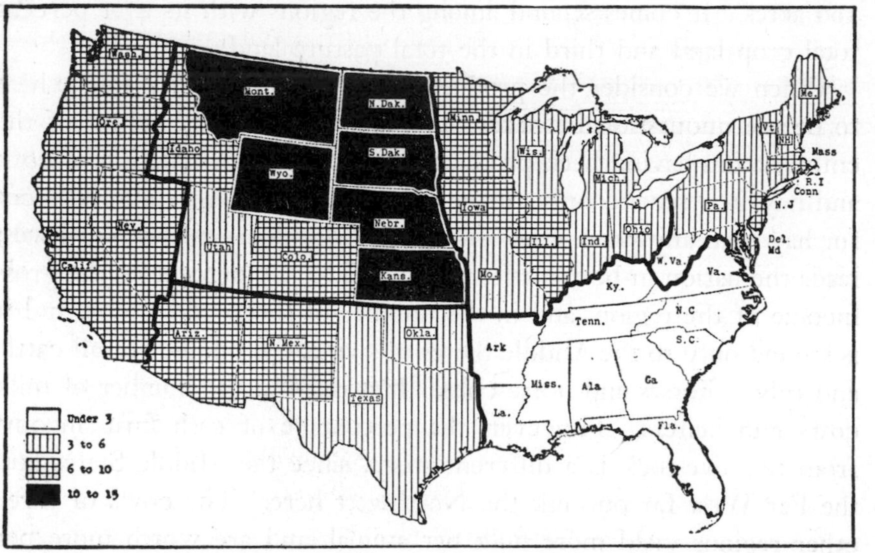

head. Similarly, though the Northwest is second in the number of horses and horse colts, and fourth in the production of mules and mule colts, it is fifth in the value per head. It takes third place in the number of chickens, but excels only the Southwest in its value per chicken of 57 cents, half of what they are valued at in the Northeast. In the matter of products such as fruits and vegetables, it almost invariably comes lowest or next to lowest in rank. Vegetables are only 3.34 percent of the gross value of the total. Nevertheless, we find this region excelling all others in average agricultural production per full-time worker.

Manufacturing and industry—in the commercial sense of the term, not in the sense of the industry of the various individuals—are conspicuous in the Northwest by absence. The Northwest is lower than other regions in almost any index, coming ahead of the Southwest only in a few cases, such as that of the percentage of total income from manufacturing. Colorado is the only state of the region with more than 10 percent of its income from this source. Compare the 4 percent value of manufactured products of the Northwest with the somewhat over 40 percent of the Northeast. The manufacturing enterprises and industries found there are largely based on the products of the different areas and in most cases are only for local consumption. Thus, we have flour and grist mills and dairy products in almost every state, unless Utah be an exception, but they are the leading manufactures only in North and South Dakota. Slaughtering and meat packing lead in Kansas and Nebraska. Smelting and refining of copper are the leading manufactures in Utah and Montana, constituting two-thirds of the total manufactures in the latter. Idaho is more concerned with working of timber and lumber, while foundries and machine shops, beet sugar refineries, smelters, canning factories, all get attention in Colorado. Wyoming's industry is almost exclusively for home consumption, including establishments for petroleum refining, railway car construction, slaughtering and meat packing. The estimated potential water power of the mountain portion of this region is far more than that of the rest of the nation in aggregate, but so far little has been done to make use of it. While some individual states rank favorably with those in other regions, the region as a whole has next to the least per capita value of mineral products, and rises only a bit above the Southeast in the percentage of the nation's total.

The Northwest is now traversed by main lines of the Northern Pacific, the Burlington, the Union Pacific and the A. T. and S. F. railroad lines, together with minor branches of these and other lines. Some excellent transcontinental highways, such as the Yellowstone Trail, Pikes Peak Ocean to Ocean Highway, and the Lincoln Highway, generally running from east to west, make this region more available.

A region which includes Yellowstone National Park, Grand Teton National Park, Glacier National Park, Rocky Mountain National Park, and the Black Hills affords marvelous scenery and recreational playgrounds for the tourist, the nature lover, and those in need of recuperation from an overdose of urban life. There are several Indian reservation scattered in the northern portion of the region, the last stand of the tribes who used to roam freely over this land.

Not only has this region been the home of such prehistoric dinosaurs as Triceratops, Titanothen, Hesperornis, and Pteranodon, but it is also the present habitat of a variety of wild life, including the coyote, the prairie chicken, the prairie dog, the jackrabbit, the rattlesnake, catfish and mountain trout, the chipmunk, the antelope, mountain sheep and goats, deer, puma, elk, moose, bison, and the famed grizzly bear.

In commonly accepted socio-economic indices the Northwest is most often to be found in the lower quartile of the nation, though it sometimes is third or even first in rank. Such is the case with illiteracy. It stands well again in the percentage of the total families in each state receiving unemployment relief from public funds in which it ranked better than at least four other regions. On the other hand, it leads the regions in the number of the states out of the whole which received federal aid and the Northwest always ranks high in federal aid to parks, forests, and playgrounds. It ranks quite favorably in the per capita governmental outlay for education, hospitals, roads, etc., and in 1930 was second (sic) in home ownership though that might not be true today. It is second in the percentage of public school enrollment in high schools and in that of total population enrolled in public schools. On the other hand, it pays its teachers about as low salaries as any region and ranks only above the Southeast and the Southwest in the per capita expenditure for public libraries. It takes third place when measured by the percentage of farms having telephones and radios per family. The Southeast and the Middle States were the only ones having more railroad mileage in 1933.[17]

It ranks well in quite a few other "averages" and per capita or per farm or industry indices. Thus in the value of farm buildings, in the value of farm implements and machinery, in its total farm lands, in the size of the farms, in total pasture land, in the average net value of farm products per farm worker and in the percentage of farms which produce more than six hundred dollars gross per farm, the region ranks well up toward the top. So, too, although its manufacturing is small, its value of products per wage earner and per horsepower and value added by manufacture rank high among all the regions. So, too, like Nevada and the Far West, its per capita wealth and its taxable wealth will be found up and around the top of the table. Yet the region also ranks high, perhaps first, in the percentage of farms mortgaged and in some other negative aspects which will be noted subsequently.

Yet we must not depend too much upon these "averages." The per farm value of buildings which appears so much larger than that of the Southeast may reflect a bigger barn than residence, and a great mountain of alfalfa hay as big as a building. So, too, with the largest-sized farms and fewest workers, the average net value of farm products per worker would naturally be large. So, too, the first place in the number of acres in total pasture land must be compared with other regions. Thus the Senate Report on *The Western Range* points out that its lands and pastures are "largely open and unfenced, with control of stock by herding; where fenced, relatively large units are enclosed. It supports with few exceptions only native grasses and other forage plants, is never fertilized or cultivated, and can in the main be restored and maintained only through control of grazing. It consists almost exclusively of lands which, because of relatively meager precipitation or other adverse climatic conditions, or rough topography, or the lack of water for irrigation, cannot successfully be used for any other form of agriculture. In contrast, the improved pastures of the East and

[17] Much of this description follows the manuscript of Ella Courter.

Middle West receive an abundant precipitation, are ordinarily fenced, utilize introduced forage species, follow cultivation for other crops, are often fertilized to increase productivity, and are renewed following deterioration." [18]

It remains to provide in our outlines for regional appraisal an important place for the understanding of the scores of distinctive communities, achievements, and qualities of this great Northwest. It must be clear that in every state there are factors which in themselves constitute distinction and in which inhere symbols of the whole civilization as it has grown and as it now is. The Guide Book Series of the nation illustrates this well; yet other hundreds of stories of communities, each of which claims exclusive distinction in many points of interest, might well be outlined.

Here is, for instance, *Pierre*, South Dakota, on two national and one state highway, and with six passenger trains a day, four bus lines, and a government-approved airport, and "the only city on the Missouri River owning its entire stretch of water front. Riverside drives through several miles of city parks afford a closeup of the Missouri River, as well as scenic and historic spots along its banks. Benches are available under the highway bridge and along the drives; a municipal tourist camp, picnic grounds and free swimming pool are near the hospital." [19] And here is indeed the "colorful capital of South Dakota located at the approximate geographical center of the state and North America, and stands where the East-river farming section merges with the West-river ranching country.

"To the east gentle rolling fields of grain swell to the rich farming region and to the west a long, flat prairie stretches for miles into the cowboy realm. The West-river rancher with his typical broad-brimmed hat, dark shirt and high-heeled boots rubs elbows with the East-river farmer, the businessman and the government official. At this natural and geographical 'transitionary' point between the two sections lies Pierre, neither eastern nor western, but cosmopolitan." [20]

Or here is Watertown, "Summer Playground of the Dakotas, where recreation and industry meet." Or, again, here are the surpassingly colorful "Towns of Eastern Idaho" into the indescribable Yellowstone, Idaho Falls, Pocatello, Butte and Dubois, Blackfort and Orco, and the craters of the Moon National Monument.

[18] *The Western Range.* Senate Document No. 199. 74th Congress, 2nd Session, p. 2.
[19] *Guide to Pierre, South Dakota, and Vicinity*, p. 4.
[20] *Ibid.*, p. 2.

Of the great recreational possibilities of the Northwest it is only necessary to catalogue its parks and playgrounds, its natural forests and reserves and to note its great national highways and its local highways to sense the outline of its development. Thus, of the country's 26 national parks, all but three are open the year round. In the Northwest there are not only the hundreds of thousands of summer visitors who come to know America but also in the Winter "snow fans will soon be off to the races and Switzerland and the Alps are forgotten in the glories of the mountains, valleys, and Winter beauties of the United States." More of this feature of the "Last West" will be discussed in relation to the Southwest.

If we follow the framework of our park and playground recreation facilities, we come at once to a recognition of the extraordinary resources which the Northwest and the Southwest afford, perhaps approximating the Far West in this respect. Thus, we check state by state, the following major land units capable of utilization: *Recreation Communities.* Many cities exist primarily because of their recreation attractions. *Seasonal Colonies,* such as are found in the cabin-site areas of National Forests, along the shores of lakes, on the borders of streams and in remote mountain and forest regions. *Camping Centers* where tourists stop. These range from small roadside rest spots to large, well-equipped areas in public forests. *Hunting and Fishing Grounds,* where natural conditions clearly call for reservations, either public or private, serving the sportsman. *Scenic Areas and Regions,* embracing natural landscape features of notable quality. The National Forests abound in scenic values. *Parks* in which vegetation and landscape effects, either natural or created, form a dominant background of uses and constitute the primary attraction of the area. *Historic and Scientific Areas* which deserve preservation and improvement because of their cultural value. In this class would come ruins of the Missions, the Indian village sites. *Special Purpose Areas,* such as beaches, shores, lakes, rivers, canals, unique wild-life centers, bird and game refuges, primitive areas, sites for winter sports and the like. *Pleasure ways.* The demands of the pleasure-seeking motorists are to be satisfied by distinctive types of scenic and pleasure highways.[21]

And, of course, there is no other Salt Lake City in the world, no Denver anywhere else, not another Emporia, not another like breed

[21] Adapted from L. Deeming Tilton, "State Park Planning: Recreation Facilities in the State Plan," *American Planning and Civic Annual* (edited by Harlean James), p. 234.

of "common clod-hopping, sod-busting, pumpkin-husking, hay-mowing," weather-gambling men "that make a stock speculator or a crap shooter look like a Christian soldier." Yet Salt Lake City, and its tradition and irrigation, and Denver, with its mountain urbanism, are still symbols of what must be done for much of the region.

For the great Northwest there is still the problem of harnessing technology to build its agricultural, recreational, and industrial structures. There must still be mastery of the physical environment and in particular the conservation and utilization of water and of land. These are the principal tangible dilemmas. Yet, as is the case in the nation, twin problem with the development and conservation of natural resources is the problem of the people and their liberty which, in the case of the Northwest, keeps the region in healthy ferment. Again the picture is one of the new realism of the people, the folk-regional society struggling for mastery in the new frontier. So, we return to the "democratic" and "American" aspects of the New Northwest.

Thus, Rupert N. Richardson writes that "The Plainsman is likely to be enthusiastic; indeed he must be so if he is to succeed, for his country offers many disappointments, and it takes courage and zeal to overcome them. Also his is a land of magnificent distances, and he thinks and talks in terms of great dimensions, using many superlatives. Like the inhabitants of all new countries the people of the Plains resented criticism of their country, especially by an outsider. Because its characteristics stood out in bold contrast to those of other regions it was often maligned, thought the Plainsmen, by persons who did not appreciate its advantages and were jealous of its rapid growth. Hence to sing its praise was not only profitable but was a bounden duty." [22] So, too, writes Julian Ralph, "With surprise we find the New England leadership missing. Here is a great corner of America where the list of the *Mayflower's* passengers is not folded into the family Bibles! . . . The new Northwest is peopled by men who followed the Missouri and its tributaries from Kentucky, Indiana, Iowa, Arkansas and Missouri. . . . They are not like the thrifty, argumentative, and earnest New Englander, or the phlegmatic Dutch and hard-headed English of the Middle States. These new Americans are tall, big-

[22] Rupert N. Richardson, "Some Historical Factors Contributing to the Problems of the Great Plains, "*The Southwestern Social Science Quarterly*, XVIII, No. 1, p. 10.

boned, stalwart folks, very self-assertive, very nervous, very quick in action, and quicker still in forming resolutions. If it would be fair to treat of them in a sentence, it could be said that they act before they think, and when they think, it is mainly of themselves. Their European origin is so far behind them that they know nothing of it. Their grandfathers had forgotten it. They talk of Uter, Coloraydo, Illinoise, Missourer, Nevadder, Ioway, Arkansaw, and Wyoming. The last two names are by them pronounced more correctly than by us. In a word, they are distinctly, decidedly, pugnaciously, and absolutely American." [23]

[23] Julian Ralph, *Our Great West*, p. 142.

Chapter XXIV

THE SOUTHWEST AND ITS TEXAS

IN the great emerging region which we call the Southwest, potential empire in itself under the old sectional economy, we have left perhaps our best for the last. And strangely enough, and grudgingly, too, perhaps we must characterize the Southwest as the least American of all the regions, if we must choose one for this designation. Such is the extraordinary diversity throughout the nation, yet homogeneity in the continental meaning of what is known as "American," that we must score this Southwest frontier, with its abundance of Americanisms, below all the others. It's a long way from New England to Texas and from Texas to Oregon, with all in between a vast subregional wealth of Americanisms to choose from. Surely this great empire is American in size and open spaces, with its symbol and reality of "the West," its cradle of cowboy lore, its allegiance to the Old South, its Spanish origins and its historical romance with Mexico, its heroic military traditions and episodes, its great Indian territory and traditions, and its quick-growing cities and "bigger and better" motivations, of oil derricks and cattle ranges, cotton fields and turkey ranches. American, too, it is in the pre-civilization sense that it comprehends the basic examples of early American culture and of the anthropologist's "culture area."

Because "American" culture is so new in this vast region, and because Latin and Indian culture was so well embedded there before the dominant group entered, there still remain more vestiges of the "foreign" civilization than in any other portion of the nation. This situation has been perpetuated to some extent by the presence of vast numbers of "Mexicans" in the present population—people of whom many have lived within the region for many generations, who speak the Spanish language and hold dear many of the Spanish culture traits so painstakingly taught them by patient Catholic padres, but who also retain many of the deeper feelings and more unobtrusive folkways of the Indians who have bequeathed them a high percentage of the blood which courses through their veins. Dominant though the "American" now is, his daily contact with a Latinized culture has had its inevitable effect in his speech, his manners, his ways of doing business, as well as in the names he gives the streets of his towns and his children.

Here two great culture systems have met and clashed and fused and are still in process of clashing and fusing. Here the elements in that typically American situation described as the "melting pot" are clearly drawn because of the relatively small numbers of culture systems involved and because of the distinct nature of those systems. Here, in a truly cultural sense, is found and may be observed the last frontier. In these elements the Southwest is American; in the further sense of bringing into contact the two culture systems which dominate the western hemisphere and affording a testing ground and experimental field, here is an opportunity for the "America" of the north, the giant of the western political world, to observe and select cultural elements and traits which will bring this nation into closer understanding and sympathy with that older "America" of the south, Latin-America, which the circumstances of geography and politics have decreed must be our closest neighbor of the future, with all the implications of that fact. Here we have a blending of the two Americas, a circumstance which makes the region less "American" in the sense of the United States than any other, but from the point of view of the hemisphere, the most truly American of all possible regions.

It is perhaps in this pluralism of the region together with the dominance and self-sufficiency of the great State of Texas, the exotic symbolic culture of Arizona and New Mexico, and the newness of the three states other than Texas, defying, for the present, classification or integration, that makes it less possible to picture the region as one approximating a large degree of homogeneity in the sense that some of the other major regions have. Yet this need and opportunity for integration in the great American process of frontier growth, especially in the newer developments of the nation, is of the essence of American regionalism and in particular of this Southwestern area. More of this will appear in the outlining of the region's cultural and physical profile, yet it is well to introduce here a vivid picture of this new Southwest as presented in 1938 by the United States Department of the Interior.

> This Southwest is a land of color, of amazing distance, of the romance of vanished civilizations, and of living cultures closely related to prehistory and vastly differing from the habits and mode of life of the Anglo-Saxon and of the white man generally. Young in years, young in settlement by English-speaking peoples, the Southwest has the oldest definite records of human occupancy in the United States; and it was explored and to a certain extent settled by Spanish adventurers and missionaries long before English occupation of the eastern seaboard.
>
> The Southwest is a land of contradictions—of high mountains, tremendous canyons, and flat deserts; of little moisture and yet of torrential downpours that leave broad rivers which for a few days usurp old roadbeds; of abandoned prehistoric ruins hundreds of years old and of modern motor camps; of lands that lie parched for rain, yet "bloom like the rose" given a little water; of primitive Indian travel afoot and on horse, yet crossed by transcontinental highways, railways, and airway routes, the latter with huge beacons that intrigue the imagination; of enormous, rainbow-hued bridges built by nature, and of man's great engineering feats in bridge building and in conquering the mighty rivers that were Nature's tools in her bridge and canyon building.
>
> In all, it is a land of fascination, with its scenery, its traditions, and its relics of the past. Enchanted it has been called; mysterious, gorgeous, multicolored, primitive, romantic, artistic, vibrant—then adjectives fail, and the writer confesses that words cannot convey to the uninitiated the glory that is the Southwest.[1]

Whatever else may be true, here is the living reality of the four great states of Texas, Oklahoma, New Mexico, and Arizona comprising nearly one-fifth of the total area of the nation with about 7 percent of its people. The region is the youngest of all the regions, only Texas having been admitted to the Union before the turn of the century, with Oklahoma in 1908, and New Mexico and Arizona

[1] *Southwestern National Monuments.* Headquarters at Casa Grande National Monument. United States Department of the Interior.

as late as 1912. Yet in the "pre-American" sense, it is so old that the culture of the "Old South" or of New England reflects only yesterdays.

In terms of the United States Census it comprises two states each of the West South Central and of the Mountain States. Here is represented a large section of that American anomaly whereby the Mountain States are classified as plains, and desert states as grazing lands. Although it is, in contrast to the Northeast, a great rural country, as compared with the Northwest above, it reflects much of the urban trend in both the growth of cities and in metropolitan areas. For Phoenix and Santa Fe and Albuquerque reflect much of the metropolitan pattern of culture and of the recreational mood of city folks. Of the 93 metropolitan districts having a population of 100,000 or more, the Southwest has only seven, namely, Houston, Dallas, San Antonio, Oklahoma City, Fort Worth, Tulsa, and El Paso. Of the subregional trade centers delineated by the wholesale trade-urban indices, the region has about twenty-five, including, besides the metropolitan districts already cited, Flagstaff, Globe, Phoenix, Tucson, Douglas, Albuquerque, Amarillo, Abilene, Brownwood, Corpus Christi, Austin, Waco, Galveston, Beaumont, Tyler, Corsicana, Paris, Muskogee, McAlister. Its urban trend is reflected in the 38.2 percent of its population being all urban and 17.7 in metropolitan districts, which is greater than that of either the Southeast or the Northwest.

Raymond D. Thomas interprets these features of the region as follows: "The urban centers of the Southwest are quite distinctly regional in their foundations and development. Like the general region from which they draw their strength, they are comparatively new. The urban area along the Texas Gulf Coast, the Houston-Galveston-Beaumont districts, has had a phenomenal growth during the past quarter of a century. The principal economic bases of this district are petroleum production and refining, cotton compresses, and foreign shipping. On the southern fringe of the Texas Black Belt, the San Antonio-Austin area is growing to an important position as a distributing point and resort center. The Dallas-Fort Worth district in the northern Black Belt is a strong urban center with meat packing, general merchandise distribution, and manufacturing as the principal sources of economic support. El Paso on the Mexican border in west Texas is a distribution point for a broad area and an important center of contact for over-land trade with Mexico across the Rio Grande. The urban life of Oklahoma is concentrating in Tulsa, the 'Oil Capital of the World,' and in Oklahoma City, the state capital and a rapidly growing center of manufacturing and wholesale distribution. In New Mexico the flow is toward the Albuquerque-Santa Fe district, and in Arizona principally toward Phoenix. . . . The Southwest is rapidly developing its own ports. The rise to first rank importance of Beaumont, Port Arthur, Houston, Galveston, and Texas City as shipping ports is one of the interesting new aspects of the developing foreign trade of the Southwest. These ports are among the nation's chief outlets for the shipping of cotton, grains, and petroleum. The traffic through the Houston harbor alone amounted in 1930 to more than five hundred million dollars." [2]

In major natural regions the Southwest must classify largely with the Northwest north of it with the predominating grasslands and steppe and bush steppe belts. Of J. Russell Smith's subregions of men and resources the Southwest comprehends all of the Lower Rio Grande Valley, and parts of the Dry West and the Great Plains, the Southwestern Intermountain Plateaus, and the Great American Desert. Of the river valleys it comprehends all of the Upper Rio Grande, the Western Gulf with its Lower Rio Grande Pecos, the Brazos-Colorado, the Guadalupe, the Nueces, most of the Colorado Basin, and part of the Central Great Basin. Raymond D. Thomas has suggested the following subregional divisions of the Southwest, somewhat after the manner of Woofter's 27 Southeastern subregions, but less accurately defined in terms of socio-economic indices. "The Northern Ozarks, the Arkansas Valley and Eastern Plains, the Southern Ozarks, the Northeast Texas Piney Flatwoods, the Southeast Texas Piney Flatwoods, the Gulf Coast Area, the Oklahoma Sand Hills, the Central Oklahoma Prairies, the Black Belt and Timber Borders, East Wheat-Grain Sorghum Region, East Cotton-Wheat-Grain Sorghum Region, West Texas Cross Timbers, the Edwards Plateau and Borders, South Texas Fruit and Vegetable Region, West Wheat-Grain Sorghum Section, West Cotton-Wheat-Grain Sorghum Region, West Texas-New Mexico Mountain Irrigated Valley Section, the Colorado Plateau, Arizona Mountain-Irrigated Valley Section, the Sonora Desert." [3]

The richness and variety of the agricultural Southwest is indicated by both the catalogue of its products and the classification of its special areas. So also the variety of temperature and rainfall, to-

[2] From Howard W. Odum, *Southern Regions of the United States,* pp. 183-185.
[3] *Ibid.,* p. 186.

gether with topography and soil, gives opportunity for small-scale self-sufficiency farming, mixed farming, large-scale cotton farming, hard winter wheat farming, cattle and sheep ranching, irrigation farming for fruits and vegetables, for specialized farming with such drought-resisting crops as sorghum and kaffir, and for special vegetable crops, such as white potatoes, watermelons, and a county that boasts of growing more spinach than any similar area in the world.

Agriculturally, the most important single crop of the region is cotton, the production of which, in Texas and Oklahoma reaches 38 percent of the nation's total. Aside from cotton, the varieties of soil and climatic differences lead to a great number of variations in agricultural pursuits. In the Ozarks of Oklahoma small self-sufficient farms are common while large-scale cotton and winter wheat production have developed in parts of Texas and Oklahoma. Irrigation for the production of fruit, vegetables, and small grains is common in the Rio Grande Valley of Texas and in various valleys of New Mexico and Arizona. Dry farming around the 100th meridian region has made some success with drought-resisting crops, as kaffir and grain sorghums.

There are quite a number of specialized areas of crop production. White potatoes are produced commercially in the Arkansas River Valley near Muskogee in Oklahoma. Broom corn yields abundantly in Garvin, Grady, McClain counties in southwestern Oklahoma, also in smaller districts in northwest Oklahoma, and in the tier of counties in New Mexico along the northern half of the eastern boundary of that state and in Bee County in southern Texas. In Wilson and Atascosa counties in southern Texas, in Parker and Wise counties in north-central Texas, in Grady County in Oklahoma, and in Willacy County on the lower Texas Gulf coast are important commercial watermelon districts. Other small crop areas include pecans in Bryan County in the lower Oklahoma Red River Valley and in Comanche and Eastland counties in central Texas; blackberries in Tarrant County in north-central Texas; strawberries in the northern Ozark district in Oklahoma, in Atascosa County in southern Texas, and in the Houston district on the Gulf coast. Tomatoes are produced commercially near Tyler; 50 percent of the world's pecan tonnage comes from Texas, while in another region near Tyler almost one-third of the world's commercial roses are grown. An important strawberry and spinach region occurs in the Rio Grande Valley. The cattle industry is still of importance. New Mexico, ranking first among the states in this respect, derives 30.5 percent of its gross income from beef cattle; Arizona, ranking fifth, derives 16 percent of its income from beef cattle; while Texas and Oklahoma derive 7.0 and 8.0 percent respectively of their gross incomes from cattle.[4]

Once again the farming areas are catalogued. Exclusive of overlappings, there are some 88 plotted on the map, Types of Farming Areas in the United States: 1930: Virgin River, Parker, Yuma, Gila Valley, Casa Grande, Tucson, Safford, Upper Gila Valley, Forested Plateaus, Colorado plateau and mountains, Nogales, Bisbee, Mimbres Valley, Rincon Valley, Mesilla Valley, El Paso Valley, Semidesert, Brewster-Presidio, Espanola Valley, Mora, Harding County, High plains, Foothills, Hondo Valley, Tularosa basin, Fort Sumner, Pecos-Estancia high plains, Roosevelt County, Rosewell, Hope, Carlsbad, Pecos, Dalhart, North Texas-Oklahoma Panhandle, Red Hills, Enid, Canadian River, Roger Mills-Wheeler, Southwest Oklahoma-Texas, Southwest Oklahoma, Wichita Mountains, Low rolling plains, North central Texas, Western Cross Timbers, Edwards plateau, Winter Garden,. San Antonio, Rio Grande plains, Corpus Christi, Northeast Oklahoma, Eastern Oklahoma, South central Oklahoma, Southern Oklahoma, Grand Prairie, Texas, Black Prairie, Postoak Strip, Upper coast prairie, Piney Woods, Piney woods lumbering area, Coast prairie, Houston-Galveston, Lower Rio Grande Valley.[5]

The settling of the Southwest, like that of the Far West and the Northwest, reflects two or more stories. There was first that of Texas and the gradual extension upward toward Santa Fe and to the Northeast. Later there was the development of "Indian Territory" and the rush of Southerners and Easterners to the new land of Oklahoma, and still later the inhabitants already referred to as inhabiting the barren lands of Arizona and New Mexico.

Frederick Jackson Turner long ago stressed the *western* as opposed to the southern character of Texas. Thus he says, "The conquest and occupation of this extensive empire, and especially Texas, has too often been dealt with by historians who were under the spell of the slavery issue or swayed by the divisions between Whigs and Democrats. In fact, in our period, the movement was at first primarily the continuation of an old process of western advance. By 1830, probably hardly

[4] Adapted from "Wealth and Variety of Scenic Beauty Awaits Visitors," *Southwest Business*, March 1936, p. 98, in unpublished manuscript by H. E. Brogden.

[5] Adapted from the map, Types of Farming Areas in the United States: 1930, Department of Commerce, Bureau of the Census.

more than 16,000 Americans and 3,000 or 4,000 Mexicans lived in Texas; scarcely an American and only a few British subjects, in Oregon; and in California, but a few hundred Americans in a total white population of about 4,000, mostly Mexicans. Some 40,000 Mexicans lived in New Mexico, and around 2,000 in Arizona. . . . The occupation of Texas had fairly begun by 1830. Geographically, this region is a portion of the coast and back country of the Gulf of Mexico and consequently, in common with Florida, it holds a commanding position with respect to the outlet of the Mississippi Valley. The curving shore of the Gulf, like the jeweled scimitar of Kipling's *Naulahka*, seemed to have a fatal influence upon its possessors. Along its warm waters, revolution seemed to breed spontaneously; and a special form of society developed from the meeting of the Spanish and American frontiers and the different habits, institutions, and purposes of the two peoples.

"Fundamentally, the colonization of Texas resulted from the same advance of the southern stock, particularly from the South Central States, of which we have already taken notice; but all sections shared in the movement. It was as inevitable as any part of the western advance, but, because it involved the spread of cotton culture along the Gulf Basin, carrying with it some of the slavery that existed in the South Central States, and because at the beginning the movement was into territory outside the limits of the United States, it came to have, as we shall see later, a special bearing upon the sectional antagonisms of the period. Particularly to the North, it has been too often interpreted as merely an attempt of the so-called 'slavocracy' to extend their power and political influence into new areas." [6]

The settlement of Oklahoma by pioneer homeseekers constitutes one of the most romantic episodes of all the frontier experiences of America. It was, however, different in many respects from most of the other "rushes" to new territory in that it represented a formal "opening" of federal territory and was attacked from north and south by armies of prospective settlers already encamped. It was a great American scene oft and vividly described. A single sample from S. J. Buck must suffice.

Word had gone forth throughout the United States that Oklahoma was at last to be opened to the homeseeker, and long before the opening day her future population began to gather on the borders. Those

[6] Frederick Jackson Turner, *The United States, 1830-1850, the Nation and Its Sootions*, pp. 353, 354-355.

on the north stopped at Arkansas City or Caldwell or camped along the border. Each of these places had its population increased many fold by this great influx of transients, while on the southern border a veritable metropolis sprang up where before was nothing but a railroad station and a water tank. This was at Purcell in the Chickasaw district, just across the Canadian River from Oklahoma. A week before the opening there were about fifteen hundred prospective settlers at each of the northern cities, and the number grew at a rapidly increasing rate as the time drew near. Together with those at smaller camps and on the southern line, there were on the twenty-second of April at least twenty thousand people waiting for the sound of the bugle which should let them into the coveted territory.

As those on the north would otherwise have been at a serious disadvantage compared to their southern rivals, the authorities decided to permit them to cross the Cherokee strip after the eighteenth. Consequently most of the outfits moved down from the cities to the line on the seventeenth to get an early start the next day. At a signal blast from a bugle in the morning, the procession started across the strip. Before noon five hundred wagons had crossed the border of the extemporized road near Arkansas City, and more were on the way, and still the city was overflowing. Trains came rolling in every hour filled with prospective settlers from all parts of the Union, and on the morning of the twenty-second most of these gathered around the depot and the five trains drawn up on adjacent tracks ready to make the run, and speculated as to which train would start first. But so great was the crowd that those were lucky who got a place on any of the trains. The platforms were overflowing, some clambered up on top of the coaches, and a few even rode on the car trucks in their anxiety to get there in good season. As the trains moved slowly across the strip, the passengers could see the endless procession of wagons still winding on toward the goal. When the Oklahoma border was reached, the "boomers" were found drawn up in a line awaiting the sound of the bugle which would give them permission to cross the imaginary line protected by the troops. In the front rank were the best riders of each outfit mounted on their fleetest steeds, and behind were the "prairie schooners" and mule teams with the families and outfits driven by the "boomers'" wives.

At exactly twelve the blast from the bugle rent the air, an exultant shout came forth from the throats of the waiting "boomers," the quivering steeds sprang over the line, and the race for homes was on. One by one the reckless riders disappeared over the crest of a hill, closely followed by buggies and buckboards with the rear brought up by heavy wagons and outfits, so that the spot where thousands had been camped during the forenoon was practically deserted within half an hour after the first man crossed the line.[7]

Of the nine million people in the Southwest, a little more than a million are Mexican and Indian, this region having a majority of both Mexicans and Indians. Texas alone has more than 680,000 Mexicans. Oklahoma still has nearly a hundred thousand Indians, while New Mexico and Arizona have approximately thirty thousand and forty thousand each. Negroes constitute another million of the population of the Southwest. Yet the Southwest has the smallest number of foreign-born European people of any of the regions, the total being scarcely more than 130,000, with 34,000 of these being from Germany. The region still has, therefore, about 75 percent of its people native white.

We have already pointed out many of the indices by which the Southwest was differentiated from the Southeast. Thomas reminds us that the historical uniformities of the Gulf Southwest go back to a very old Indian civilization in the broad southwestern country. Certainly, too, the old and romantic Spanish heritage is everywhere abounding in New Mexico. Yet in spite of this distinctive ancient heritage, which distinguishes the region from the Southeast, it is paradoxically distinctive again because of its cultural infancy, since the region was a wild and western country long after the culture of the Old South had matured. There is, also, historical documentary agreement with this classification of the Greater Southwest, and a considerable new emphasis upon the better delineation of the emerging Southwest of the present and future. The Texas Centennial Exposition featured the great Southwest in which Fort Worth and Dallas were the gateways, no longer answering to the roll call of "The South."

Thus Paul Horgan gives an earlier concept of the greater Southwest. "A French map in the year 1679 showed the new land explored as far as the *terra incognita* of present-time Utah. The groaning wagons and horses had tried the terrain of Nueva Granada, that embraced everything we know now as New Mexico, Texas, Arizona, and part of Oklahoma. . . . His [the cartographer] chart of what he found

[7] Solon J. Buck, "The Settlement of Oklahoma," Wisconsin Academy of Sciences, Arts, and Letters: *Transactions,* 15, Pt. 2, 1907, pp. 344-346.

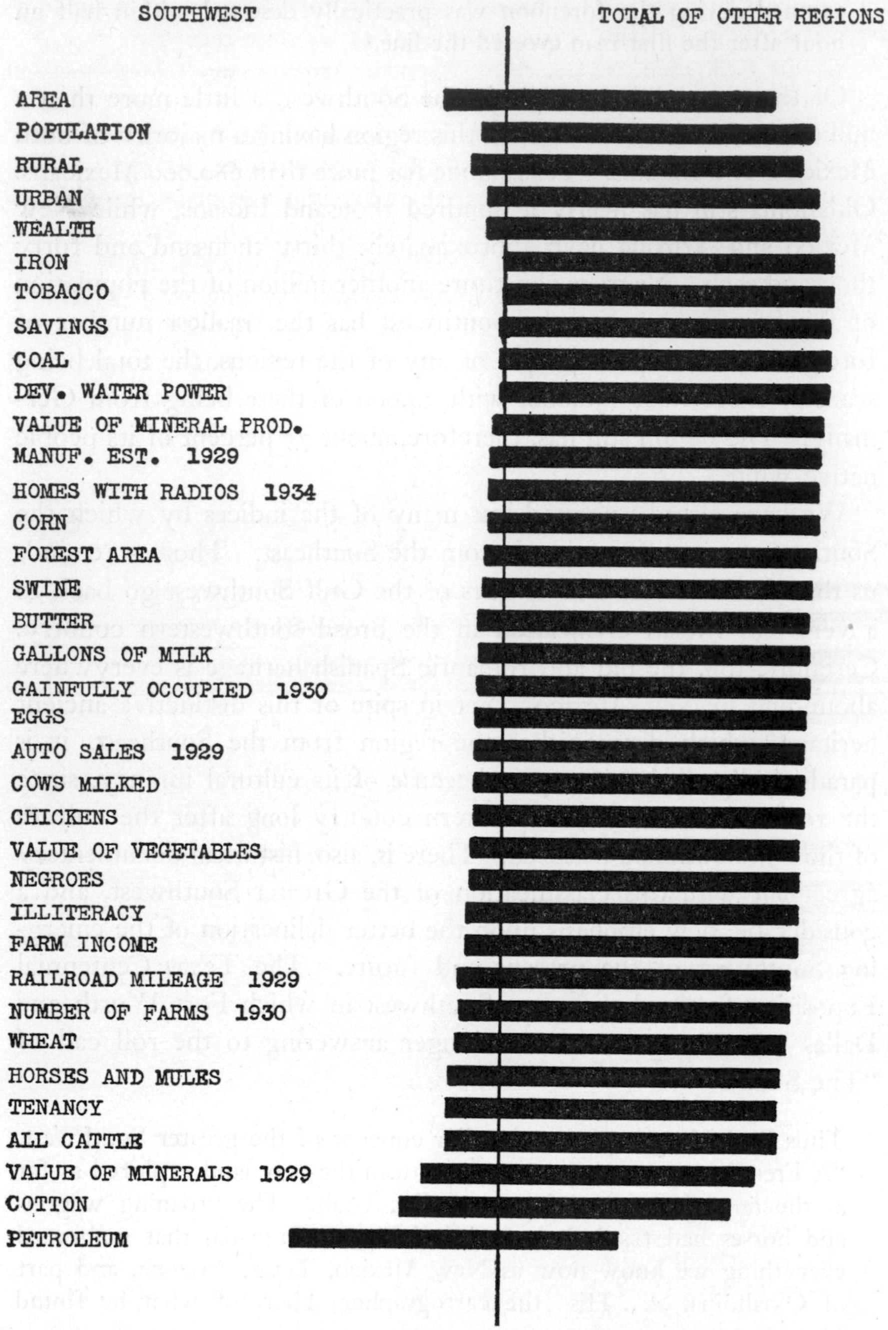

Regional Ratios to the National Total. Random Miscellaneous Indices: The Southwest suggests that we use his name for the territory, since it so easily indicates the boundaries of the Southwest as we now regard it.

"In area, then, Texas, New Mexico, Arizona, and Oklahoma will constitute the Southwest of our time. . . .

"The Southwest is large enough to include the widest varieties of terrain, and thus of weather and of human pursuits. It is a country of one of two characters: either there are immense plains flat alike to the tempest and the endless days of sunlight, or there are mountains that challenge the zenith with the power of a legend. Only in the littlest local sense are there pastoral regions, with bounding green hills and sustained valleys. This meant that, looking for natural securities and havens, the early people found none; and the resultant exercise of human ingenuity and faith produced that crew of pioneers whose philosophy so often seemed almost geological in its simplicity and its strength. The great river, Rio Grande, went slowly and widely down to the Gulf of Mexico, hardly oozing enough water in Summer to slake a traveled animal train, going brown and reedy in the Winter under its red banks, tearing away from the course of mountains in the Spring, and changing the face of the deserts through which it went with the high breast of flood. So, either sleepy and endlessly peaceful, or sudden and terrible with storm and change, the life in the valley of the Rio Grande affords an easy figure for the life of the entire region." [8]

The settlement of the Southwest, like that of the Northwest, was, first of all, an extension of the Southeast through a rapid populating of Texas from which later the western character gradually evolved. This was somewhat parallel to the earlier growth of Kansas and Nebraska before the other Northwestern States. Oklahoma is also a separate story, while the Spanish and Indian thread in the fabric of New Mexico and Arizona, as well as in Oklahoma, gives them distinctive character. Nearly a million Mexicans add to the pluralism of the region and its total structure, which defies standardization or approximate characterization in terms of a single or even a few indices of homogeneity.

Yet again, the earlier trend toward such a region was unmistakable and perhaps inevitable, even as was that of the Great Northwest above it. Thus Thomas points up a number of foci. "Decades before the South-

[8] Paul Horgan, "About the Southwest. A Panorama of Nueva Granada," *Southwest Review,* XVIII, No. 4, pp. 329-330.

west area arrived at the status of political partnership as sister states in the Federal Union, the flow of economic and cultural life in the surrounding area had marked out fairly definite channels. The 'economic nerves' of Louisiana and Arkansas centered along the Mississippi River, converging on New Orleans. Up in Missouri and Kansas, transportation and financial connections were established with Kansas City and St. Louis toward the east and northeast. In the mountain states of Colorado and Utah, Denver and Salt Lake City were the points of cultural concentration. The desert region west of the Colorado River formed a natural barrier to cultural relations between southern California and Arizona. Accordingly, the cultural life of southern California centered along the Pacific Coast.

"Conditions within the Southwest draw the cultural currents toward points of concentration within the region. The transportation routes —railways and highways—head at the Gulf ports in Texas, which are the gateways leading from the Southwest into the Gulf and Latin-American commercial areas. El Paso is an important connecting point between the Southwest and Mexico. The valleys of the Rio Grande and of the Pecos River lead southward from the high plateaus of northern New Mexico. These rivers with important railways tend to turn the flow of economic intercourse to the east and Southeast into the Texas and Oklahoma region. The cities of Tulsa, Oklahoma City, Dallas, and Fort Worth draw the currents of trade southward and southwestward from the northern and eastern borders of the Southwest Region." [9]

No less focal and perhaps inevitable was the later great development approximating boom proportions. First, there was Texas, and then Oklahoma, and subsequently the sure emergence of the urban-west centers of Santa Fe, Phoenix, and scores of way places where urban-eastern folk might work and play, rest and recuperate, seek adventure and surcease from boredom. This great development has comprehended the growth of cities, the development of subtropical fruit and vegetable areas, the irrigation of land for cotton cultivation in New Mexico and Arizona, the great ranches for cattle and turkeys, and later the "American" rush for "black gold" to Texas and Oklahoma, where white men and Indians sometimes grew rich overnight.

Thus Richardson and Rister describe this period as a great boom era in which the boom spirit took hold of the people. "The surprising ex-

[9] From Howard W. Odum, *Southern Regions of the United States*, p. 182.

uberance of the town-builder of the semi-arid prairies or the desert regions can be explained in no other way. To have builded great cities with their highly complex industrial and social relations in such areas as these would have seemed impossible achievements to their forefathers. But to the new citizens of the Southwest nothing of this character was impossible if the leadership of the community were optimistic and progressive. That they succeeded, again and again, speaks well for their faith; but that they also failed, time after time, and still remained cheerful and hopeful, is far more complimentary. As the Southwesterner saw his problems, it was optimism and success, or pessimism and failure. As a consequence, he schooled himself to be optimistic. This was hard to do when the black-leg killed his cattle, the grasshoppers ate his growing crop, or the death of boom-towns blighted his hopes; but he knew at the same time that pessimism would bring his defeat all the more surely and quickly. Then, too, the country was new and undoubtedly its youth was reflected in the life of its people.

"During the frontier period the southwestern citizen was, and still is, permeated with the idea of democracy. It is reasonable to maintain that this spirit was in part a consequence of the free and open life of the country. Land was cheap, restrictions of movement were few, and activities in general were seldom circumscribed by conventionalities and laws of the states and territories. So raw and unsettled were conditions throughout the entire region that it was difficult for the forces of law and order to hold the inhabitants within reasonable bounds of propriety. 'I am a free American citizen,' was often bluntly asserted by him who felt the restrictions of reproof; and liberty was sometimes taken to mean license. The pastime of the cowboy in shooting up a peaceful town, the promiscuous use of a rope by the vigilantes in bringing to an abrupt and disastrous end the career of an overly ambitious horse-thief, the violent action of fence cutters—all were evidences of this tendency to misconstrue the meaning of liberty of action. He demanded that he be given the right of settling his problems in his own way, and thought little about how such a course of procedure would affect the nation as a whole. Although he made mistakes which have bordered on both comedy and tragedy in adhering to this principle, his aggressiveness in maintaining his ideals under conditions which were unsettled, had worked for the benefit of the Southwest." [10]

[10] "Reprinted by permission of the publishers, The Arthur H. Clark Company, from Richardson (Rupert N.) and Carl C. Rister's "The Greater Southwest," pp. 481-482.

What the ultimate measure of the region's wealth may be is unpredictable. A part of this inheres in the problem of regional-national planning. In addition to its possibilities for increased exports, there is always the immense field of chemurgy and the development of great wealth through the manufacture of alcohol from sorghums, the growth of tung trees for oil now imported, and the possibilities of great development in the field of small industries and processing plants. Texas alone claims the capacity to grow enough cotton for the world, which again answers the nature of a problem more than a prospect. There is, however, finally, the incontrovertible fact of its minerals and especially of its oil, new key to a power-driven civilization.

Raymond D. Thomas summarizes this phase of the great Southwest. "The Southwestern Region is a rich empire of natural resources. The heart of the mid-continent oil and gas fields is within the area. In 1930 the United States produced about two-thirds of the world's output of crude petroleum, and nearly two-thirds of this total of 898 million barrels produced by the United States came from the fields of Texas and Oklahoma. At the present time the major portion of the world's production of commercially used natural gas comes from the Texas-Oklahoma fields. The story of the Mineral Empire of the Southwest can perhaps best be told in figures. Take Texas as the chief example. The total value of the mineral production in Texas in 1929 amounted to close to a half billion dollars, which was approximately 10 percent of the total mineral wealth production of the nation in that year. This vast Texas production came from the following principal sources: petroleum, $322,520,000; natural gas, $67,474,000; sulphur, $43,811,000; natural gasoline, $26,561,000. Other minerals of importance in Texas are cement, clay products, sand and gravel, gypsum, and stone. The total mineral production, measured in dollars for Oklahoma for 1929, went slightly beyond a half billion dollars, or 10 percent of the total for the nation—petroleum, $364,650,000; natural gasoline, $42,766,000; zinc, $25,349,544; coal, $11,481,000; lead, $5,860,638; gypsum, $2,255,374; with lesser amounts from clay products, sand and gravel and asphalt."[11]

There are so many possible developments and so many varied and attractive subregional objectives that it is easy to grow over-enthusiastic about this great southwestern empire. Keeping in mind

[11] From Howard W. Odum, *Southern Regions of the United States*, p. 184.

our earlier premises that one of the special values of regionalism lies in its decentralization of congested areas and of urban tensions and that another is found in the enrichment of increasingly large numbers of folk-regional cultures and communities throughout the nation, thus pointing toward a quality civilization in a quantity world, the possibilities of the great Southwest are almost unlimited. Accordingly, it is possible to develop, as does young H. E. Brogden,[12] the thesis that notwithstanding the rapid growth of the oil industries in east Texas and Oklahoma, the fruit region of the Rio Grande, the cotton of Texas and Oklahoma, and the cattle and sheep industries of the western portion, the Southwest presents its most beautiful possibilities as a national recreational center. Excluding for the moment east Texas and Oklahoma, the Southwest presents a panorama of broad plateaus, mountains, deserts, and semi-arid plains which seem to offer few possibilities in the way of agricultural or industrial development on a large scale. Long hours of sunshine, with a low humidity to remove the sting of the sun and insure cool evenings, and Winters permitting year-round sports activities, provide an excellent climate. Golf and tennis have grown tremendously; swimming is possible six months of the year, while the hunting and fishing in New Mexico and Arizona are the best to be found. Scenic possibilities are endless. The Grand Canyon, the Painted Desert, the Carlsbad Cavern and the Moon Craters of Arizona are all well-known. One can wander through New Mexico's mountains and mesas, still partially in the cowboy and ranch stage, with its old Spanish missions and customs, with countless dwellings and buried cities of a race existing thousands of years back. These small stone homes under the ledges of nearly any New Mexico mesa, of the circular cities or pueblos in valley after valley, or possibly perched on the top of inaccessible mesas, added to the natural beauty of the country and picturesqueness of its present ethnic groups and their customs, give almost unique possibilities for national tourists' use such as was indicated for the great Northwest.

In developing the possibilities of the region as a recreational and tourist center, Brogden points out that one of the first factors for considera-

12 The following summary is adapted from an unpublished manuscript by H. E. B. ogden.

tion is the climate. From tables giving the number of clear, partly cloudy, cloudy, and rainy days, the Southwest rather plainly leads all of the regions in the ratio of clear and partly cloudy days to the cloudy and rainy days. Mapping of the annual precipitation shows that with the exception of east Texas and Oklahoma, the region is very dry. While in the southern part of Texas, the warmth is sufficient for tropical growth of all sorts, the increasing altitude of the plateaus and mountains of New Mexico gives the sparkling dry days and the cool nights which the inhabitants are so proud of. The shortness of the winters is brought out when we consider that a third of the national area with a frostless growing season of six months or more is included in the region.

Sports are developing rapidly in the Southwest. A review of recent tennis and golf champions, both of which sports are possible the year round in most of the Southwest, is rather on this point. Much of the Southwest is still in the ranch and cowboy stage, so that those wanting riding or any of the activities of the dude ranches will find them in New Mexico or Arizona. Large forests in the mountains and other areas have possibly the best hunting of deer or other game to be found. In the Sacramento mountains the deer were so thick they were tending to destroy their food supply, and although a special open season killed hundreds of them, it was estimated that a thousand would have to be removed from sixty square miles to reduce the figure to normal. Trout streams are to be found all through the mountains, many of which are practically untouched. Any novice can catch the limit in a day's outing.

It is rather a difficult task to give a picture of the beauty of the cities and country, and the unique picturesqueness of the mixture of the cowboy, the pueblos, the Apache Indians, and the old Spanish with the modern America. A city such as Dallas, new and wealthy, with an immense amount of money spent on imposing residences, landscape gardening, is as beautiful as any in the country. Since natural gas is used in heating, and few industries are located there, the cities are all remarkably clean. On the other hand, San Antonio and Santa Fe possess all of the glamour and beauty of the Spanish influence and history. Here, too, many wealthy Americans have spent small fortunes, usually adapting their architecture to that of the past.

Of the natural scenes, the Grand Canyon has many smaller rivals all through the mountain and plateau country of Arizona and New

Mexico; there are the Carlsbad Caverns, the largest of their kind in the world; the Petrified Forest, with few standing timber of ten feet in height, but with petrified trunks of seventy-five or a hundred feet. Beyond these, an immense variety waits the tourist. In Texas, as a chamber of commerce article has said, there are mountain ranges containing the tallest peaks east of the Rockies, picturesque ranch country with great herds of cattle grazing over lush prairies, impressive tablelands of the Panhandle Plain country, giant pines and oaks embracing forests hundreds of miles in extent, sub-tropical flowers and plants in the Rio Grande Valley, sea sports and fishing off the long white beaches of the Gulf Coast country, rodeos and cowboy sports, the deep gorges of the Rio Grande in the pictorial Big Bend country, and all the background of history and glamour in the Spanish-named cities.

Possibly one of the big assets of New Mexico is the wealth of ruins found there. Studded over a large part of this state, nearly every valley or mesa is apt to have ruins of pueblos and dwellings centuries or even a thousand years of age. In the heart of the Navajo country in northwestern New Mexico, Chaco Canyon contains two of these pueblos, which are being studied by archaeologists. With no forewarning, a drop of two hundred feet or so, seemingly cut directly from the level plateau, leads down a wash to the floor of the canyon, where one reaches a small group of buildings, housing the scientists, and the huge and silent ruins of a forgotten age. The ruins, shut in by the narrow canyons, give a feeling of unimaginable quiet, and give a strong stimulus to stifled imaginations. The spirits of thousands of peoples seem to slip softly around into the scores of doors and over the terraced floors. The building is superior to the house construction in Greece and Rome—made of thin sheets of laminated sandstone done by master masons, bands of thicker stone are worked in to break the monotony and give a characteristic beauty not found elsewhere in the world. One of the pueblos might have contained 1,500 persons while the other would probably contain twice that many. Pottery, cylindrical jars of new and strange design, and inlaid turquoise and jade give evidence of the skill of their workmen. Archaeologists estimate that they lived there from about 900 A.D. until 350 years later.

New Mexico has been described as a land of fertile valleys, mighty mountains, fantastic deserts, enormous forests, bottomless lakes, extinct volcanoes, and caverns so huge that the whole population of Detroit could easily find standing room in one of its compartments.

Besides the better-known sights there are the craters of the moon near Mt. Taylor with their huge lava beds; the canyon of the Red River second only to the Grand Canyon; Cimarron Canyon with palisades comparable to those of the Hudson; acres and acres of yucca in bloom, with their great spikes of white waxen bells; the Enchanted Mesa and Acoma, the city of the sky, with its old mission once carried up the precipitous cliff piece by piece; Inscription Rock with its carved messages of 300 years ago; the beauties of the mountain region in the Black Range Country; the Pueblo dances with their infectious rhythm, cadence, color and mystery; the beautiful Taos Canyon; the famous Corn Dance at Santo Domingo; the Valle Grande, said to be the largest extinct volcano crater in the world, with a huge bog in the center, supposed to be the grave of thousands of prehistoric animals; and all of the natural beauty of the mountains, mesas, and valleys.

Arizona is an extension of New Mexico so far as tourist possibilities are concerned. In the south, the deserts and the Indians; north of the Grand Canyon huge forests spread out; and steep-sided Canyon de Chilly, home of ancient cliff dwellers and the present-day Navajoes; snow-capped peaks of the Qunicha Range; the bad lands of the Painted Desert, looking like so many little piles of color thrown in a huge sandbox; the huge reservoir behind the Roosevelt Dam; the Navajo National Monument, with three well-known cliff dwellings built, used and abandoned long before the discovery of America; and Montezuma Castle, built in the side of a huge cliff and said to be the best-preserved cliff dwelling in America today. While this rather sketchy review may seem unsystematic and inadequate, it should bring out its attractiveness to tourists which should be second to none other in America today.

It would be easier to treat of Arizona as Dominion than as one of these United States. Not that there is any question about the swift and whole-hearted allegiance of Arizona, but there are distinctions. Her territory is about equal in map miles to the combined areas of New York, New Jersey, Delaware, Pennsylvania, and Maryland, which means, taking the mountainous nature of the country into account, that there are about as many more miles standing straight in the air, lying at the bottom of deep canyons or doubling in immeasurable folds of crumpled rock. To this dramatic variety of contour is added color and a play of light and atmospheric effect which for pure splendor and subtlety is not elsewhere matched. This superlative intention exhibited in the topography is reflected in the history of Arizona to an extent that makes it obligatory to add -est to every adjective that describes it. Not only is its Grand Canyon the grandest and its cotton staple the longest in the world, but it is the newest state and the seat of the oldest civilization within the territory of what is now the United States. In Arizona one finds the scale of amazing things running from petrified forests to common weeds that produce rubber in what promises to be commercial quantity.[13]

And of Oklahoma the cataloguers have found a worthy task in listing its "firsts" and its "onliests," in contrasting its present and its past. Oklahoma, like many another subregional unit of the nation, is still little known by other regions. There was, for instance, a distinguished Harvard professor who had lived much in Europe and also much in the Far West and the Middle States who exclaimed upon the beauty of the University and its young women students, the cleanness of the Oklahoma cities and "all that" in contrast to what he frankly expected, namely, deserts and cattle, cowboys and Indians, oil and dirt.

Listen, however, for a while, to the enthusiasts: " . . . And what a difference these forty years have made. Then, millions of undeveloped acres—grass and birds and wild game; Indians, herds of cattle and buffalo, and jack-rabbits. Now: population of 2,500,000 creating annually approximately $1,500,000,000 in new wealth, almost equally divided between agriculture, mineral and forest products, and manufactured products. . . . Two cities with more than a hundred and fifty thousand population each, and numbers of cities with from six to forty thousand . . . 29 railroads . . . 6,000 miles of electric power transmission lines . . . 162,000 miles of telephone wires . . . Five state-owned and -financed universities and colleges . . . Numbers of private schools and colleges . . . Millions of dollars invested in oil pipe lines, oil machinery, and refining plants . . . Creameries, condensaries, airplane factories, stock yards, packing plants, flour mills, and numbers of other industrial plants . . . Scores of cities with modern buildings, strong banks, palatial hotels.

"Such is Oklahoma today. Millionaires have replaced the jack-rabbit and the buffalo; airplanes are almost as numerous as the cow pony of 1900, and the ten-gallon hat has disappeared. Indians are still here, but

[13] Mary Austin, "The Land of the Joyous Adventure," *These United States, A Symposium* (edited by Ernest Gruening), p. 326.

they ride in Cadillac cars. Without doubt the mental attitude of the people has undergone greater change than the physical appearance of the state. Back in the 90's no thought was given to building a state. Oklahoma then was sought for agricultural purposes only. Today the businessmen are thinking in terms of hundred million dollar banks, and gigantic manufacturing plants, small industries, and a thousand head of poultry for each oil well. . . . Although one naturally thinks of Oklahoma in terms of oil, 70 percent of the population is rural. Farm products last year were worth $541,236,000. . . . Rural life borders on the ideal. Preparation of land is easy, climate is pleasing, rainfall sufficient. Many farms have their own generating plants, but more than 700 farm plants were connected with utility high tension lines supplying the state last year. Principal crops of the farm are wheat, corn, oats, rye, grain, sorghum, broomcorn, barley, cotton, Irish potatoes, sweet potatoes, tame hay, wild hay, peanuts, and sorghum syrup. The state ranks first in broomcorn production. Dairying in a few years will be one of the best-paying industries. . . . Little effort has been made to present Oklahoma to the world as a place of scenic beauty. . . . However, the hills and streams of eastern Oklahoma, the Arbuckle Mountains in the west, the inspiring rolling plains, and the timbered lands of the southeast combine to make as scenic a trip as may be found anywhere. Nor can one discount the inspiration of the oil fields in their course of development, the tank farms and the ever thrilling ring of the drill as it winds its way into the rock formations that incase pools of 'black gold.' What is more pleasing to the eye of the traveler than miles and miles of waving wheat—of threshing machines at work, and of skyscraping flour mills. . . . Most interesting are the people. Truly this is the melting pot. . . . Oklahoma is composite America."[14]

Yet not all of the Southwest is physical, either in commodities or in scenery. Here are great places for the implementing of the dynamic art of a quality civilization in a quantity world. Old Spanish and Indian and Mexican heritage vie with the glamour of nature and the new geographic patterns of mankind in search for new frontiers. Here the application of modern technology to living arrangements will do for this area of intellectual activity what it does to agriculture in the great Northwest. New frontiers indeed.

Thus Norman Macleod writes, "As I sit here in the front of a small adobe house (once a part of a big hacienda but which, due to the

[14] Bryan Mack, "Oklahoma—Forty Years Young," *The Review of Reviews,* Vol. 80, pp. 134-140.

Spanish custom of willing separate rooms to offspring, has been broken off from what was at one time a building covering two blocks with a large patio in the center), listening to some modern caballeros singing a Spanish song in a Mexican bootlegger's joint next door, I realize once again what I felt and knew the first time I walked across the outer fringes of the Southwest ten years ago: the poetry, drama, lore and legend still bearing the mark of regional authenticity in a land which has integrated and synthesized (as far as this ever occurs) the cultural traditions of at least three civilizations. This land is young and old at the same time. Only the occasional outposts of eastern industrialism have struck a false note (in this country as yet unready to be oriented to a modern industrialism), and they are far and few between. Several years ago artists and writers discovered in this region what was not so obviously apparent at that time in other sections of the country. Indeed in many parts, the traces of the region, its tradition and color, had been obliterated. All that remained was the chaos: and the result: the poets of sincere frustration, baffled and confused, heartsick and weary with the modern panorama gutted with industrialism, webbed with capitalistic lines of community. . . . But in the Southwest the problem has not been so exigent. The modern consciousness is aware and the international influence is to be discerned, but yet there is still room for spiritual quietude and calm. . . . That is why the region looms so large in the creative consciousness. There is order. There is meaning. There is a wealth of detail and possibilities of culture."[15]

Like the great Northwest or any of the regions, there are, clustering here and there, cultural groups or isolated communities which defy classification and description. They reflect the extraordinary richness which comes from such an adventure as the Federal Writers' Project to present *to the American people a portrait of America*—its history, folklore, scenery, cultural backgrounds, social and economic trends, racial factors. Such an example is that of certain groups of the Santa Cruz Valley in which both the romantic and realistic side of some 800 families is discovered to be "American" and "un-American." Such is the calendar of annual events in New Mexico with more than a hundred days in the year with particular celebrations or ceremonies. Such are the special industrial groups,

[15] Norman Macleod, "Notes on Regionalism," *Sewanee Review*, Vol. 39, pp. 456-459.

agricultural groups, religious groups from the corners of Texas to the borders of California.

So, too, no portrait of the Southwest could be presented without the cultural values of the romantic cities, old and new. These are epitomes of southwestern culture and of the conflict of civilizations and of new melting pots in Santa Fe, in Albuquerque, in Phoenix, in San Antonio.

San Antonio has been there a long time, and has seen enough to be no longer easily perturbed by anything. Though now but third in population in Texas, San Antonio was a flourishing city when Bryan built the first log cabin on the Trinity and when, a few years earlier, Houston and Galveston were a-borning. Spiritually, it is a brother of Santa Fe, and only a little younger. Though it is so far outstripped in size by the cities of the East, San Antonio has a history going back almost as far as that of Philadelphia or Boston.

But the town is not remarkable for its antiquity alone, which, after all, is not so great. What is most important is that San Antonio, having seen a variety of civilizations, is hardly to be compared with any of the cities mentioned. Along the banks of San Pedro Creek and the San Antonio River have flourished three major civilizations—Indian, Spanish, and American; and the Americans themselves have been responsible for at least three different and important styles of living—the life-pattern of the frontier, that of the ranch, and that of the blueprint. In addition, San Antonio has been influenced to some degree by German immigration, by the large numbers of tuberculous patients who have come there seeking health, by the soldiers who have been stationed at this important army post, and by the winter vacationists of recent years. . . .

Things were still in their primeval state when the written history of the San Antonio region begins. Texas itself was an unknown land, about the borders of which there had clustered on the south a few settlements of daring and ambitious Spaniards or Spanish-Mexicans, and on the east a few French outposts for trading and exploration. Beyond the Great Plains on the west lay the present New Mexican region already partly brought under the dominion of the Spanish Crown and the Catholic Cross. In all the vast region of Texas proper, however, there were only Indians.

It is with the activities of the French and Spanish adventurers, reckless men, eager to earn a title and a fortune, that subsequent history is concerned. Neither nationality knew anything about what lay in the interior, but each was eager to lay claim to it as soon as the other had

> shown that its subjugation might prove profitable. There was, however, a striking difference between the two types of men. The French were out only to trade and barter; but with the Spanish explorers and soldiers at their outposts were Franciscan friars from the colleges of Zacatecas and Querétaro. Upon this difference depends the story of San Antonio. . . .[16]

In the distinctive "urbane" and cultural frontier, balance and equilibrium between the rural and urban, between nature and wealth, between leisure and work may emerge as one of the great prospects of the New Southwest. Driving across the great farm areas of Oklahoma or Texas or the great desert areas of New Mexico and Arizona, the sudden looming of a sky-scraping building, set in the long distance, appears first as one of those beautiful mirages of this West and of the Northwest. Yet it is new reality. For the ratio of urban growth in the Southwest has been larger than that of the other regions, and the extraordinary vigor and cleanness of many of these new "cities" mark the region as "different." No, the Southwest is not North, not South, not East, not West. It is superlatively *Southwest.*

[16] John Chapman, "San Antonio," *Southwest Review,* XXII, No. 1, pp. 16, 17.

Chapter XXV

PROBLEMS AND STRATEGY OF REGIONAL DEVELOPMENT TOWARDS NATIONAL REINTEGRATION

WE return now to our earliest assumption, in Chapter I, that the real theme of American regionalism is essentially that of a great nation in whose continuity and unity of development, through a fine balance of historical, cultural, and geographic factors, must be found the hope of American democracy and, according to many observers, of Western civilization. We have pointed up something of the range and meaning of this regionalism in both its theoretical and historical aspects and in its practical implementation in the American scene. We have illustrated some of these applications through the sixfold division of the United States into major regions which without doubt qualify as composite societal regions in which may be found for our purposes, the largest possible degree of homogeneity, measured by the largest number of indices available for the largest number of practicable purposes. Or to state the case differently, these composite six major American regions comprise a larger degree of homogeneity measured by a larger number of indices for a larger number of purposes than can be found in any other classification available. They further are susceptible of combining within their frame of reference a large number of the multiple regional classifications and arrangements now being used or proposed.

Now regionalism in itself needs no apology. By and within itself it merits continuing study, more adequate definition, more comprehensive presentation, and more critical analysis than it has had. Its historical and scientific heritage as well as its increasing importance justify whatever of co-operative study and analysis may be devoted to it. Yet it still remains to explore its place in the total perspective of a changing nation to see to what extent, as motivation, concept, and tool, it may contribute, on the one hand, to better analysis and understanding of the scene and, on the other, to a more realistic reintegration of national diversities. On this assumption, we still have to envisage the nation in terms of its present dilemmas, set in the framework of its past heritage and performance and of its present struggles and confusion. We need to question the extent to which we may need to "retrace our steps, and, region by region, learn to do intelligently and co-operatively. The grasp of the region as a dynamic social reality is a first step."

There appear to be two major areas of inquiry, and each reflects the cumulative product of past heritage. Each holds something of the puzzle of how the nation has come to its present dilemmas. The one is the American background with its extraordinarily undesigned mastery of the continent and its pluralisms in time, geography, and culture. The other is the impact of modern civilization itself upon the changing nation. Nor should the desire to present the picture as objectively as possible obscure the dramatic proportions of the American struggle or the range and depth of national crisis. For undoubtedly there is being enacted the most momentous drama of survival-struggle that has yet tested the enduring qualities of American civilization.

It is scarcely necessary to remind ourselves that there is need for a dynamic and realistic defining of the concept of Americanism to take it out of any possible shallow connotation of reaction or conservative implication. Classifying people and policics as "American" or "un-American" is a poor substitute for reality in a day when the nation needs to go on as a nation, set in the American scene. The facts are that the reality of the nation is found, first of all, in its geographic situation, and secondly in the peculiar culture, people, and institutions which make America what it is.

> There are authentic historical Americanisms and there are realistic current changing Americanisms. Earlier Americanisms which have molded the nation include high motivation and purpose, idealism and optimism, religious motivation and character, the passion for liberty and freedom, a capitalistic social order, "the American Dream" of op-

portunity for all, in which the emphasis was on the common man, a nation of realized "opportunity," a rural and agrarian culture, a pioneer and frontier economy, ruthless exploitation of resources, homogeneity of northern European stocks, homogeneity of Protestant religions, autonomy of local government, a nation of states' rights and of sections, a nation in which politics was the key to public policy. Over against these are the ways of a changing nation in a world of urban and industrial emphasis and of technological dominance in which co-operative endeavor and regional arrangements must needs supplant the extreme individualism and sectionalism of the small frontier, rural nation.

In much the same way it is important to dissipate the shallow notion that regionalism connotes primarily localism and provincialism. For whatever America is, in addition to its major continental position, it is a fabric woven of regional patterns and forces. By the same token, the future must be American, in fact, and the sooner realities may be substituted for superficialities the more effective and co-ordinated will efforts become.

Lewis Mumford's interpretation of the organic nature of regionalism illustrates the point of view. Behind the great regionalist movements are certain common ideas. "At a period when the uniformities of the machine civilization were being overstressed, regionalism served to emphasize compensatory organic elements: above all, those differences that arise out of geographic, historic, and cultural peculiarities. In its recognition of the region as a basic configuration in human life; in its acceptance of natural diversities as well as natural associations and uniformities; in its recognition of the region as a permanent sphere of cultural influences and as a center of economic activities, as well as an implicit geographic fact—here lies the vital common element in the regionalist movement. So far from being archaic and reactionary, regionalism belongs to the future."[1]

In the American background, as it has been responsible for the present American scene, there appear to be a number of basic characterizations which justify the conclusion that the nation has reached its present crises at the crest of unprecedented achievements wrought more through undesigned development and exploitation of resources and regions, of land and men, than through well-planned arrange-

[1] Lewis Mumford, *The Culture of Cities*. Quoted, by permission, from proof sheets.

ments, through which equilibrium of all parts of the nation would be maintained with equity to all. This, of course, was but natural in a frontier civilization, but it does not change the fact.

Because the people of the nation had succeeded far beyond their expectations in developing their great resources—physical resources, technological power, artificial wealth, human resources, institutional modes of life; and because the nation had grown and sprawled this way and that throughout the uneven development of states and regions, often featuring sectional advantage and conflict, America had come in the late 1930's to the top of a new hill from which the people faced a frontier of social action and difficulties predicated upon super-achievements in nearly all aspects of life and culture. From this hilltop, to look back only, there could be little doubt of the extraordinary progress which had been made. To ask whether the nation had developed the great natural resources of the continent and mastered its physical forces was itself to answer the question in the affirmative. To review the sweep and power of recent scientific discoveries and mechanical inventions was to present a picture in which technical progress in a phenomenal and unbelievable number of fields and extraordinary ways had been everywhere apparent. And the assumption and claim in this country and abroad that America was the wealthiest nation in the world undoubtedly had ample support. Likewise, the picture showed great progress in the development of human wealth, in the strengthening of the people, in child welfare and public health, in the better ordering of human relationships in their physical aspects; and unbelievable progress in the development of education and educational institutions, in the expansion and efficiency of industry, in the expansion and sweep of government, in the vast domain of community organization, in communication and transportation, in the changing quality of religion, in the more earnest examination and qualitative development of the home and family relationships and in many attitudes and activities relating to children, to women, to races. And, specifically, the picture showed a nation that had won its wars; led the nations in many achievements; attained the much-sought leisure, luxury, and power; and made an American standard of living.

Yet something was radically wrong; the nation had made its mistakes as well as its successes. What was the nature and measure of its errors? What to do with these designless and unco-ordinated gains, now reflected in multiplied lack of equilibrium and balance—these were questions to be answered only through an understanding of the actualities in terms of something to be done about it. For no less than the

> greatness of American achievement, American tragedies are of the essence of the American fabric; exploitation of human and physical resources, tragedy of the Indian, tragedy of the Negro, the immigrant, the tenant; the crushing power of master builders in ruthless competition; sectional conflict and war of brothers stranger than fiction.[2]

It was nowhere difficult to portray the state of the nation in the early 1930's. The picture was everywhere eloquent, not of a wealthy nation so much as of the plight of a wealthy nation bordering dangerously near disintegration and chaos. One half of its more than thirty times the people of Jefferson's America was living on such meager subsistence as to make joking stock of the boasted American standard of living. Rich America was not providing for the basic necessities of its citizens. Yet in the picture somewhere were still billions of wealth, millions of units of subsistence and comfort and abundance. More than a fourth of the nation's total number of normally gainfully occupied workers were without work. Yet somewhere in the picture were nearly a million establishments equipped to employ millions while still other millions of unemployed awaited the call of great fields of occupations now woefully depleted. One-fourth of the nation's citizens were to all practical intents and purposes on "charity." Yet somewhere in the picture were billions of dollars of uncirculated money, billions of dollars of surplus wealth in the control of an extraordinarily small number of individuals and corporations in turn, in the current picture, impotent to use it or to let others use it. Nearly one-half of the farms of the nation, fruits of life-time work, were ready for the auction hammer, yet somewhere in the nation were millions of people needing the buyable products of the farm and millions of capital available, under a different picture, for needed credit.

The engineers, the economists, and the technicians all assured the public that the nation's industries and machines, power and energy were capable of producing three times the maximum output at the crest of the 1920's, ample for not only necessities but for comfort and convenience and leisure for a new American standard. Yet, not somewhere but everywhere, there was breakdown in distribution and

[2] Howard W. Odum, "The Case for Regional National Social Planning," *Social Forces*, Vol. 13, No. 1, pp. 13-14.

consumption processes and standards. This was a motif that kept recurring again and again. Wasn't it possible, somehow, some way, sometime; anyhow, anyway, anytime, to break this tragic deadlock between the giant forces of abundance and the insatiable demon of want? Millions of the nation's best citizens, broken from the unequal struggle, had laid down the burden of living in one way or another, many in "the only way out," in mournful numbers uncounted by any man. Millions of children, born and unborn, like the countless victims of war, awaited the crippling aftermath of this devastating peacetime crisis. Yet somewhere, everywhere, in the nation there had seemed to be new gains and new hopes for the vitality of the American people, promise of new highs in human wealth. And everywhere, anywhere, the nation seemed impotent, *was* impotent at least for the time being, to do aught save stand by and look helplessly on.

If it may be said the nation came to its dilemmas through logical sequence of cause and effect and especially through imbalance and unevenness in its regional developments and integration, it seems equally apparent also that a large part of the situation is part and parcel, creator and creature of the modern technological and urban civilization. Here, then, is challenge to show cause why there should not be, on the one hand, abandonment of those procedures which appear to lead in the wrong direction, and, on the other, the setting up of new designs for new order. If the causes of catastrophe are apparent in major trends, then the remedy will be sought in some counteracting force. Is it possible, therefore, to focus upon a number of explanations of the tragic crises in which the nation found itself and in which the civilized world now finds itself, and at the same time to find some constant factors in them all, susceptible of isolation and utilization?

A part of the glamour and adventure of this fascinating and tragic picture of the 1930's was found in the sheer chasm of contrast between the swift-moving drama of current Western civilization and the slow journeying of mankind toward his earlier cultures. There was the spectacle of civilization moving faster and going further in multiples of technological achievement in one short third of a century than in all the long centuries before. Incredible, breath-taking; yet stark reality it was with everywhere all the time the clamor for faster, faster, further, further, more, more, new, new, now, now. It was as if the acres of yesterday, with all their harvests of achievements and failures, were suddenly receding before the limitless reach of todays and tomorrows, with their rapidly changing and adventurous social frontiers. The drama of such change was found not so much in the contrasts between the pictures of the present and those of the earliest cultures, or of slow-forming boundaries from the Near East to Western Europe and thence to all the Western World, as it was in the flashing movement of this particular nation at this particular time in contrast with an already forgotten era so recent even as that of Thomas Jefferson, apostle and progenitor of the earlier American democracy. This statesman, farmer, scientist, dreamer, planner, with all his skill and mastery, had he been walking at Washington in the 1930's, or speeding the long roads across the continent, or sojourning in the great cities and industrial places, must needs have the help of many interpreters, turning slowly the pages of pictures, to comprehend so stupendous a transformation in so extraordinarily brief a span of national life. Such was the unprecedented growth and change that every part of the American picture indicated that Jefferson's democracy would have been hopelessly inadequate and that he himself would have failed miserably had he been called upon to direct the nation in its latest emergency. This bridging of the chasm, therefore, between the earlier Jeffersonian democracy of the simple government and agrarian culture and the new greater democracy of the designed and controlled complex social order, must appear as an exciting and recurring motif in this continuing American drama.

There was the Jeffersonian picture of the nation in which the farmer was the main bulwark of democracy, and there was the 1930 picture of agriculture providing less than 13 percent of the nation's income. There was Thomas Jefferson proclaiming that "the mob of great cities add just so much to the support of pure government, as sores do to the strength of the human body," and there was the 1930 picture of America with more than 60 percent of its people living in cities or in the metropolitan-village fringe, and 93 metropolitan districts each with over one hundred thousand population ranging up to ten million people, with a single city area housing twice as many people as all of Jefferson's beloved America. There was Thomas Jefferson admonishing to "let our workshops remain in Europe" and there was the American picture of the early 1930's with more than 37,000,000 or 76.2 percent of all the nation's working folks occupied in manufacturing, mechanical, distributive, and social services, leaving only 23.8 percent for all of agriculture, mining, lumbering, fishing, and allied branches of the early primary extractive occupations. There was Jefferson idealizing that government as best which governed least and there was the picture of the NRA of America, approximating social control of individuals and groups in the heroic effort to start the nation on its new era of salvaging what it could of the Jeffersonian democracy of the simple rural nation and of building a still greater democracy for the bigger and bigger complex urban and industrial America. Jefferson's constitution and government constituted a great experiment; but the America of the 1930's was continuing in a still greater experiment. It was to be both a stupendous picture and a gigantic struggle.[3]

Still more of adventure was found in the sheer mass spectacle of this American picture set in the modern world of nations. A spectacle of civilization grown immeasurably big and powerful, yet paradoxically being transformed through science and technology into an ever smaller and smaller universe, and still again being threatened with impotency or self-destruction, constituted a dramatic picture of exciting proportions. For such was one picture that was being constantly thrown across the screen to portray the extreme movements possible for an American civilization, reaping where all history had sown, gathering where had been strewn the factors of Western life which have given new design to all our culture, and flowering into a gigantic struggle between the powerful onrush of science and the decay of tradition.

Bigness, complexity, science, technology, speed and change were the new masters, dominating the American picture as they had never done before. Masters they were of the whole incredible, and as yet uninventoried, sweep and drive of the modern age—science, invention, management, machines, cities, industry and business, education and government, communication and world community relations, social organization on a scale never yet attempted in the history of man. Early modest millions in wealth multiplied to nearly four hundred billions of dollars with nearly one hundred billions of in-

[3] Adapted from "The Case for Regional National Social Planning," *Social Forces*, Vol. 13, No. 1, p. 13.

come. Picture extraordinary of a federal loan increase of 2,000 percent in the short span of a few years. Jefferson's Louisiana purchase price, multiplied five hundred and sixty and more times in the single item of mortgage debts on farm lands and buildings in the United States. The same purchase price multiplied many times over in appropriation for flood control and drainage work on the bounds of Old Man River alone. A million inventions in electricity, chemistry, physics, biology, metals, construction, transportation, transforming the whole national life—comforts, recreation, education, leisure, social legislation.

In this pageant of super-achievement strange and mighty doings were on parade. A nation now working mightily; now appearing as children playing in the dark with toys of production; now venturing new reaches in distribution, magnifying the people as consumers of goods, experimenting with science and technology and all the while terribly in earnest. Kaleidoscopic pageant of the past; some whom the gods made; some whom they destroyed. Following the World War's reshaping the destinies of America, involving the whole fabric of civilization and changing the tempo of living, unprecedented changes were wrought through the vast sweep and power of this new science and technology. Great cities were built and over-built, fabricated through a new metropolitan architecture and planning. Industries, old and new, grew up and waxed powerful. Incredible highways and airways and lines of communication were built tending to make the ways of the nation the ways of the city and connecting the nation with the world. An energetic people created bursting bubbles and booms, went up hills and down again, conquered frontiers and came back for more. They multiplied and concentrated wealth, increased philanthropy, developed resources, and destroyed them. They printed millions of books, reached new highs in the circulation of newspapers and magazines, developed new social welfare programs, created new standards of living and of comfort, made comfort and culture perilously near the same thing. They multiplied the power and costs of government tenfold. There were panics and depressions, political battles and struggles, the rise and recession of organized labor, the emancipation of woman, the prohibition amendment, the rise and fall of Kukluxism, and the battles of fundamentalism, humanism, technocracy, and beer. And there were still other mighty pageants and parades, a nation colorful and rich in organizations and slogans, reformers and patriots, forbidders and saviors of other people's destinies.

Another basic element of dramatic interest in the American picture was the newness of the world which this extraordinary transformation of technology had wrought with such breath-taking swiftness. A new world, a new epoch, a new deal—new ways, new morals, new manners, new tempo and new prospects and new dangers—so ran the catalogue of characterization of a nation dominated by speed and change, breath-taking and devastating. President Roosevelt, in a few hours, could traverse more miles than Thomas Jefferson moved in a lifetime; contact in a few brief moments more European situations than were encompassed in all of Jefferson's gracious diplomatic experience. There was the new world of communication, operating to modify the whole environment, creating new problems of adjustment, transforming the world of nations into accessible community. Elimination of time and space and distance—telephone and telegraph, radio and television; transportation systems and the new mobility, highway and airway, trucks and trains, interacting units transforming individuals and communities, remaking areas of land and units of government. New pictures of two-miles-a-minute trains, network of roadways and waterways, pipe lines of energy, transmission streams of power. New machines of production outmoded before installation was completed; new fashions of architecture proclaiming archaic great structures yet in process of construction; new models today, old models tomorrow, fashions today out of fashion tomorrow. Pictures, therefore, of alarming unevenness and lack of equilibrium in the rates of change in many parts of society; pictures of herculean tasks of readjustment and adaptation; new types of education, new modes of leadership, new tempo of action.

Chiefest among the elemental dilemmas was the ever resurgence of the common man. For, in this transition to a new stage of civilization, the mass-man, the whole, real people approximated an accession to social power such as has hitherto not been recorded. Now the American ideal had always insisted that it was through the vigor and freshness of a strong and virile people and through the orderly development of a natural folk society that we must attain stable and permanent social development. As between the too artificial and too technical specialist and the native wisdom and strength of the well-bred and -nurtured common man, the American picture had always featured the latter as superior in his capacity to carry on. There was Woodrow Wilson's picture: "The great voice of America does not come from seats of learning. It comes in a murmur from the hills and woods and the farms and factories and the mills rolling on and gaining volume until it comes to us from the homes of common men—" Nevertheless, the phenomenon of the dominance and revolt of the masses, in a quick-changing mass emotional process beyond reasonable capacity for quick adjustment must surely appear as a new frontier of civilization. It was surely in contrast to the Jeffersonian ideal of democracy ruled by the few chosen representatives, chosen for skill, training, experience, and devotion to the public weal. The great forces of technology, speed, change had contributed largely to this phenomenon as to others. This was true whether it applied to the people and politicians of the United States or to the new Russian, German, Italian, or Spanish reconstruction, or to revolution in the orient or elsewhere, or whether it was reflected through the general effects of mass communication, increasing the range and possibilities of education, information, and propaganda.

This phenomenon of the folk mass power was reflected in the picture in many divergent ways. If it was a sort of constant in a world of great variables, constituting the basic assets of new cultures, it also afforded a great variable in the contrary threats of reaction or revolution. And since the sweep and speed of technology had exceeded the capacity and development of even the most highly educated and widely experienced leaders, it was not surprising that the processes of education and cultural experience had conditioned the common folks still less for intelligent social understanding and action. There was another dramatic aspect of the picture in the modern folkways and mass emotional reaction of the urban intellectuals. Not all of mass reaction was of and by the "masses." The episodes of the technocrats, of the humanists, of the EPICS, of the Townsendites, of the young Hitlerites, and of many of the liberal-radicals in a sort of blind allegiance to artificial formulae as the indices of progress, the trends toward dictatorship on the part of minorities—these and other manifestations were evidences of mass-mindedness which was to add to the later confusion of the scene.

For these and other reasons the chasm of distance between modern artificial society and supertechnology, on the one hand, and the facility and capacity of the people and of their institutions, on the other, appeared much greater than ever before in the history of human culture. Pictures of many cultures reflected the axiom of social theory that when the demands and sweep of artificial society and of supertechnological processes exceed the natural capacity of the people or of a living culture to absorb and adjust, and when there are inadequate media of integration and leadership, there must inevitably be crisis, maladjustment; and if the process goes on long enough, disintegration. This implied no value or moral judgment of what might be desirable or what might be the standard of the future, but reflected purely and simply impressions of the picture. How much could the people stand? How much would their institutions bear? How much ahead of the people were the thought, ideologies, and technologies of the leaders? If there was not a natural capacity for adjustment, on the one hand, or a directed guidance, on the other, survival was not likely. Here were new dilemmas of artificial society and supertechnology which the nation had not yet faced.

Still other important elements which added zest and fascination to the picture were the widespread confusion approximating despair, the resistless onrush of action, the dangers and hazards in prospect, the catastrophe of every man's own personal fortunes, the crises of emotions and tensions, and the quick sweeping away of standards and belongings dear to the race. With confusion abounded conflict; mighty struggle of capital, mighty struggle of race, conflict of individual, conflict of group, old ways and new ways—which would survive? "Will our civilization survive?" "Which road shall we take?" "Who shall lead the way?" The scene of the New Deal, therefore, reflected a dramatic crisis which demanded heroic men and measures without which must come greater chaos. The drama was swift-moving, threatening mass tragedy. The new epoch was fascinating alike in its dangers and its opportunities.

Confusion was, of course, a perfectly logical and natural product of these bewildering developments. The citizen was confused. The leader was confused. The scientist and the specialists were confused. No one, for once, boasted of knowing the way out. Some of the evidences of this product of our onrushing civilization were: a sort of mass panic among the intellectuals as well as the common man; a sort of blind movement to turn back the clock and undo quickly what had taken so long to accomplish; a too easily accepted verdict that "the end was in sight"; an all-sweeping emotional factor with reference to finances and money, characterizing the nations of Europe as well as America; an apparent unanimous appraisal that finances and budgets were the supreme value of the day; the seeming low repute of things intellectual and artistic; an apparent Samsonian effort of many of the best people to threaten the structure of our culture in a leveling process; and a flood of contradictory advices from many reputable sources.

But whatever else might be true, one thing was everywhere clear in the picture, and that was the fact of the dilemma of bigness and technology and the consequent stark reality of crisis. The magnitude of this problem of adaptation was such as to lead many observers to conclude that the chief dilemma of the time was that of society's ability to accommodate its natural capacities and institutions to the artificial demands of bigness, speed, technology, change. This was not only a supreme test of survival in the crisis of the 1930's, a very practical and imminent test, but it was of great theoretical significance in the future planning of American civilization.

Stated in simple terms, the problem was one of marginal capacity. In proportion as the demands of artificial society or bigness or rapidity of social change or technology exceeded the capacity of the people, or their institutions, to that extent not only prosperity and happiness but also survival was being endangered. This demand of artificial society or bigness might be for super-achievement in some gigantic emergency or for sudden adaptation to new conditions. It might be the ever-broadening power of centralization over local groups. Such demands might constitute sheer quantitative tests of magnitude and speed, or they might be qualitative tests of artificiality over against what was "natural" or possible or attainable without wrecking the social or human organism. Or, again, the demands might be the fabrications of idealists or theorizers, based upon subjective rationalizations unsupported by fact or experience, suddenly thrust upon the people for absorption.

The significance of regional structure and arrangement may be envisaged further in the reflection of a certain artificial society which grows up and divides the people wherever concentration of politics or wealth or professions or science or expertness had separated the politician or the specialist or the individualist from the mass of people. There is not only the fact of their flight from reality but of the imposition of the will and patterns of the few, often untested and unsound, upon the many. There is the danger of the rule of the self-appointed intellectuals whose arbitrary, isolated, and specialized training is often mistaken for comprehensive education. There is also the danger of the pure scientist or the experimentalist confusing his learning or his ability to discover facts with similar ability to enact practical programs of policy. Thus, it is that there is the same general danger of the learned individual, isolated from the people, developing the same provincial autocracy as the politician, the dictator, the wealthy individual, the labor agitator, the propagandist, the aristocrat.

So, too, the primary weakness of the more than one hundred new political groupings and creeds, of the more than a thousand "plans" proposed for superimposition upon the American people, of the dogmatizing of enthusiastic liberals and propagandists lies in the essential artificiality of most of the proposals. Many of their tenets are so artificially designed as to be impracticable; so specialized as to be incomplete; or so technical as to preclude enactment. They do not come to grips with the complicated social problem involved; they stress action and audacity where also are needed science, intellectual design, and social equilibrium. In so far as they constitute a literature of escape or the essence of romance, they cannot meet the new demands for social achievement.

> There were two fundamental aspects of the question. First, how much could the people and their institutions do? How much would the people stand? How much *could* they stand? What was the limit of their present capacities? How fast could they go without wrecking the men and institutions? How far could the "new" always be substituted for the old in quick succession without having the people prepared? To what extent and how rapidly could the capacities of the people and their institutions be increased, and what were the ways of increasing them? How, therefore, should the demands of new technology and change be so graduated as to insure reasonable attainment for given periods of time, for given regions, for specified institutions, for varied objectives, and for social organization in general? On the other hand, there was a second fundamental dilemma. How many and

of what sort were the supertechnical demands which ran counter to "nature" and the normal capacities of mankind? Which ones would retard human development and welfare, and therefore were of themselves detrimental to civilization or to the things of the spirit or intellect as opposed to that which was primarily material or mechanical or physical? How many and of what sort, therefore, were the demands of artificial society and of supertechnology to which society could never adapt itself and in the midst of which would not survive?

These were questions which were rarely ever asked and more rarely answered. And because they were neither asked nor answered, the prevailing tendency was to set up unrealistic schemes and plans and "isms" magnifying monistic forces out of perspective in the composite scheme of things. We have recounted at length all of these contributing factors which assume the proportions of major structural and organic features, in order to point up the fallacy of attempting to rebuild society through quick-moving schemes of reconstruction or through technological transformation of materials. Concepts, even if valid and in adequate perspective, cannot take the place of realistic implementation through the equilibrium of time and place and people. Even so, the concepts of redistribution of wealth, of class against class, of the capitalistic or non-capitalistic system, of planned money, of collectivism, and/or of the other scores of remedies urged upon a troubled nation are no substitute for actual, realistic growth, through orderly processes of the people and their institutions within the living geography of their regions and in harmony with their natural heritage. Even so, again, if they were valid, the sudden imposition of multiple schemes under the enthusiasm and high pressure of individuals temporarily in the service of philanthropy or of the government, but soon to depart leaving their unfinished and unrelated work, cannot be a substitute for sound theoretical and administrative measures safeguarded by constitutional arrangements within the framework of democracy. Perhaps there is no better way to make this point clear than to illustrate with samplings of the extraordinarily varied and numerous volumes, discussions, and plans which have been so abundant during the 1930's.

It was a perfect setting for everybody's prophecy and promise. For the professional critic, for the eager reformer, for the breathless propagandist, for the lovers of confusion, turmoil and strife, here was a nation eloquent with impending crisis, with unprecedented disaster in sight, and with such glorious threatening doom as the tongue and pen of man had not yet had the opportunity to portray. For the historian here was surely the ending of a phase of civilization. For those who gloried in the cyclical order of civilizations, the rise and fall, the ebb and flow of cultures through some great universal and inevitable rhythmic sequence, here was analogy extraordinary with the most optimistic prospect that this nation, through its disintegration and decay, had made the greatest of all contributions to the next great civilization which would rise from its ashes. For those who saw a new middle or dark ages, there was abundant prophecy that it would be "impossible to maintain unimpaired the heritage of civilization." On the other hand, for those who foresaw more concretely and hopefully into the ways and centuries ahead, this nation was paving the way toward that world economy in which all paths would be paths of peace, in which intellect and emotion, iron might and tender loving, science and philosophy, men and technology, would attain the perfect balance in a new world of social equilibrium. And to all and sundry leaders and thinkers, liberals and intellectuals, students and planners, pioneers in experimentation, patriots and philanthropists, artists and literateurs, here was the perfect problem setting, the perfect social laboratory, the perfect theme, with abundance of material for achieving master work.

Inventory the long roll of those who saw in the American picture the ways of general economic theory or of single unit theories of cause and cure. There was no gainsaying that the materials and setting approximated the perfect laboratory and observatory. For those who saw power as the definitive index of the future, there were multiplied figures, and pictures upon pictures. For those who saw energy and price as the foci of all action and guidance there was logic enough not only for the technocrats but for many others. For those who saw land as the real wealth of the nation there was logic enough for the old Jeffersonians, for the dreamers of the new agrarian culture, for the single tax enthusiasts, and for various and sundry others. For all those to whom gold and money were the chief elements in the national fabric there were great bodies of material and evidence in problems of currency stabilization and inflation; fluctuation of the dollar, gold dollar or commodity dollar; silver issue or gold standard; the international flow of gold and money, with its complicating problems of tariff, international trade, and intercultural relationships. The same evidences and backgrounds provided the basis for new pictures of nationalism, featuring the contrast between nationalism and internationalism as being the definitive elements of contemporary society. And once again these materials and backgrounds constituted the basis of conclusion and propaganda on the part of those who believed that there could be no major issue comparable to that of peace and war.

The American picture was rich also in features through which multiple applications of more specialized economic theories were being interpreted and set forth as peculiar instrumentalities in the fabrication of the new plans. Once again an extraordinary inventory, overlapping, interrelated, inseparably tied in with all other backgrounds and other theories: profits and competition; prices and purchasing power; production and distribution; consumers' standards and exchange; "social credit" and national dividends. Again, an incomparable picture of possibilities and eventualities for those who featured the present drama as the supreme test of capitalism, for those who saw in it its doom or for those who saw new opportunities for state capitalism; for those who saw in the present emergency the supreme test of democracy; for those who saw in it democracy's undoing; or for those who saw new and unprecedented opportunities; for those who saw the rise of new governments attaining such composite value and power as had not hitherto been recorded. For those who saw the rise of dictatorship there was abundant evidence, according to every man's several interpretations, to point to the dictatorship of the masses, or of dominant personality, such as Mussolini or Hitler, or of other types yet to be developed through new combinations and permutations of the social elements in the case.

Strangely enough the same background facts, the same framework of inquiry, the same elements of national culture supplied the base for extraordinarily diverse conclusions: that fascism was the way out, that fascism was not the way out; that fascism was approaching, that fascism was impossible. And similarly, revolution was the best way on, revolution was the worst way on; revolution was imminent, revolution was impossible in the American setting. To some the evidence pointed toward complete world chaos; to others world reconstruction; to some toward the destruction of civilization; to others toward new heights of human adequacy. Contributing to these and many other pictures of dilemma were the reputed breakdown of religious and moral sanction, the lack of authentic religious and moral codes, the lack of authentic formal bodies of knowledge, and the consequent inevitable confusion. The saving way out of this was, according to this school of thinkers, to be found only in the revitalization of religion and ethics, the remaking of humanism, the rediscovery of values. And among the evidences for the search after values were the concepts that machines were killing men, that the chief mode of progress was nothing less than tragedy, that there must be a new equilibrium and orientation. Spiritual and mental security and poise were, they said, as important as economic or social security. Finally, there was abundant evidence, according to its several interpretations, to see in the American picture a nation getting better, a nation getting worse; and more particularly to show the real picture of America as one not of good or bad, of better or worse, but one whose dilemmas were centered rather around complexities and difficulties.

A part of this confusion as well as of the panaceanic pattern of social reconstruction so much in vogue was due to the natural incidence of depression and after-war phenomena. Another large part, however, was due to the multiplicity of problems and the imbalance between the world of technology and the world of men. Nevertheless, the very number and complexity of these dilemmas are further testimony to the futility of quick single-track solutions as substitutes for adaptation and adjustment. Rather each problem and each situation, cumulative product of cause and effect, is a constituent and related part of the whole and can be appraised and adjusted only in such relationships. This principle of totality is equally true of the explanation of the past and in the direction of the future. It is in this area of conflict between specialisms and technics, irresponsible intellectuals and "systems," that will be found the testing ground for societal determinism against the new possible technological determinism.

Because of this comprehensive nature and enormity of the American task, it follows that there is an unusually large number and variety of general and specific problems which must be faced before any adequate programs of planning could be drawn up and successfully applied. There is, of course, still the emergency situation, which must be met before the approach to permanent planning can be successfully made. There are also the objectives of developing and training the requisite new leadership and citizenship. There are, then, certain general ideals and principles of American democracy which must be kept continuously in the foreground. There are moreover special scientific problems involved in the quality of the race and the evolution of culture, which unfortunately in the past have most frequently been neglected. Once again there are the special problems of social technology or of ways of attaining the ideals and objectives of the American culture. And as means of attacking these special technical problems there are many specific techniques, samplings of which would indicate both the range of the planning problem and ways of moving forward.

The first essential to the mastery of the emergency is *poise, balance, and sanity*. If it is natural that the bigness and complexity of recent problems here transcended the measure of our understanding and education, it should also be logical that we should strive to develop a leadership which would prevent panic, blind mass emotion and action. If the nation is perhaps ashamed of the things which it has overdone or done wrongly, surely it does not wish to be ashamed more of what it is about to do in the continuing crisis. Where there are doubt and fear there must be, to go alongside of the search after the facts, abundant hope and faith commensurate with the national heritage. Mass emotion and a blind striking out to abolish and to destroy will crowd out the fruits of reconstruction and recovery. There must be also a certain unity of support not always required in normal times. The second emergency problem of *public relief* is one of helping individuals and families literally to survive and to retain their normal status of self-sustaining American citizens. Physical and mental morale undermined will give the nation such tragedy as America has not yet faced. There can be no waiting for final plans, because the blame belongs to the nation, not the people. Commonly estimated to be the most immediate and disturbing emergency problem of the nation is that of *unemployment*. What will happen to a nation which cannot give gainful employment to its people? How long can it last? Likewise, in *farm relief*, the problem of preventing bankruptcy of the nation's chief primary enterprise is of such emergency nature as to threaten the very foundations of Americanism. So, too, *private debts and mortgages* constitute a problem of some sort of equitable adjustment for the unreasonably unfair confiscation of homes and property from thousands of the nation's best citizens. Finally, there is the dilemma of *public debts and balanced budgets,* the practical problem of obtaining at the very present moment enough funds to carry on the decent obligations of public affairs and to meet the obligations of previous commitments now falling due and of maintaining a stable financial equilibrium.

Among the generic problems in the way of attaining the ends of a new democracy, there are many which are still traditional, partly abstract and partly technical. Yet there is opportunity for new focus upon the regional foundation of both cause and effect, past and future. *The distribution of wealth* is essentially a problem of reworking our economic institutions and regional arrangements to the end that the rewards of labor and the resources of Nature may be more equitably distributed and adjusted. *The "new" equalization of opportunity* is in reality a readjustment and expansion of earlier methods made necessary because of the bigness of our civilization and especially because of a complex urban and industrial life in conflict with the past and with natural societies and rural institutions. *The guarantee of security* is a comprehensive social problem involved in the adjustment of labor to technological invention, to machinery production, and to radical changes in occupations and economic conditions, as well as age and equipment levels of the people and their distribution in relation to resources. *The promotion of education and social welfare* is an enlarged problem of equalization arrangements among regions as well as of training for citizenship and leadership and of amelioration that involves children, youth, the socially deficient, the physically handicapped, the future quality of the people. *International relations* assume new problems not only of world community, of nationalism, of war and peace, and of financial equilibrium, but of regional commodities and of tariffs and exports of cotton and wheat and paper pulp and starch. *Group conflict and adjustment* include the threatened conflict between the new labor classes, race and ethnic groups, religions, radicals, conservatives, and all their interregional adjustments. All this means a *re-examination of the Constitution,* a reinterpretation of the theory of powers and functions and especially an adaptation and revitalization of its provisions in the light of regional inequalities, and of many changing conditions in the modern world.

The group of needed special techniques is no less impressive and includes problems which also involve practical ways of attacking the larger problems of readjustment already enumerated. But they require adequate technical procedures well tempered with human values. *Taxation and governmental finance* is essentially a problem of the marginal points between nation and states, between individualism and social obligations, as well as being a technical problem of economics and political science. The problem of *railroads and highway traffic* requires new approaches to a mobile nation, to a new world of decentralization, as well as to financing, on the one hand, and to control and regulation, on the other. *Banking and finance* is a continuation and extension of the effort towards economic security and stability generally estimated as the first essential for economic recovery, but also involves problems of stability and overconcentration of capital wealth. The technical *problem of the dollar* in relation to the gold standard or commodity value is assuming increasingly critical importance. The *control and use of utilities* is the old, all-important problem, the conservation and utilization of power and natural resources in relation to human wealth. The *conservation of natural wealth* has become a societal problem rather than merely an economic one and calls for *regional planning* of a new order. *Social insurance* is a new demand for technical ways of equalizing opportunity and guaranteeing security with reasonable standards of work and living. *Governmental reorganization* is commonly estimated to be fundamental to both immediate recovery and to the stability of the social order. It is a continuation and extension of the movement towards service, efficiency, and economy. There is a new problem which approaches dilemma, namely, that of *optimum production*, which is a problem of balance between production and consumption, with special reference to new modes of financing and distribution, and of new standards of consumption. Closely related to this is the problem of some *agricultural adjustment*, or more authoritative action by the government looking toward the parity of prices as between agriculture and industry, involving fundamental issues of curtailment of production or increase of use. Finally, the ends of *co-operative enterprise* stress as never before the problem of organization and co-operation in agricultural effort and industrial enterprise. Here are testing grounds of the new social order and especially of the centralization and concentration of commerce and industry, and of governmental control and supervision of economic processes. The problem of *state and regional readjustment* represents both a composite approach to all of these, yet also in itself is an increasingly important dilemma involving the relation of federal to state organizations, special state and regional problems, as well as problems of state lines, of consolidation of minor units, and of co-ordinated efforts.

Emerging from this multiplicity and complexity of problems and from the prior critical examination of the organic nature of regionalism, there appear to be four major fundamental problems that transcend all others. These relate to the twofold background which we emphasized in the earlier part of this chapter, namely, the American background and current technological civilization. The first two focus upon the American scene. The first of these is a matter of plain physiography, namely, the continued adjustment and better readaptation of the nation to its geography; of its people to the land and resources through the conservation, development, and utilization of the great basic physical wealth of the nation. This is a major phase of Americanism. The second is the problem of liberty and freedom within the flexible, geographic framework of representative democracy, which must continue to develop, conserve, and give opportunity to every individual and demotic unit through such social arrangements as will develop a richer human culture in a superior civilization. This, too, is a major aspect of "Americanism." Both of these are tangible, definable, and susceptible of flexible adaptation to whatever new social order may emerge. The third problem is one of universal culture seeking to achieve enduring civilization in harmony with the natural heritage. The fourth is the problem of progress which consists in the mastery of the physical, technological, and societal forces, and the resulting human-use ends, through which the continuity of human evolution may be attained.

Now all of these are basic and elemental. They reflect needs of organic structure and totality rather than super-specialized function. Inherent in the framework of regionalism are ample postulates for such evolutionary progress, and implied in its frame of reference is the power and facility for implementing the combined knowledge and skills of the nation and its people. Yet, the essential reality of the new regionalism must be found in the basic consideration that, so far from being a panacea for the artificial reconstruction of the nation, it is the most natural thing in the world. For, regionalism, pointing equally to the past or future, assumes the totality of all environmental factors of nature and of all cultural forces such that there can be no single deterministic force but rather what may be termed societal determinism. Such regionalism manifestly points to balance and equilibrium between and among all the forces and implies a quality culture in a quantity world.

Again, we may characterize regionalism as tool and technique for various objectives of planning and of attaining equilibrium and balance, decentralization and distribution, in particular as these relate to population, to wealth, and to sovereignty. This is of particular importance and vividness in relation to the adjustments between agrarian and urban culture, between natural and human resources, and in other essentials upon which wealth, in its finest sense, and civilization, in its richest implications of a balance of man in harmony with his natural heritage, find their basis.

Regionalism may, however, be featured as symbol and reality of the new frontiers of American life and as current mode of that high motivation which has characterized the American people. This motivation would tend to be of several sorts. First is that of making the nation "regional conscious" instead of "sectional-minded," an objective that is far from being merely academic. Second is the desired objective of making the states less provincial and more regional and national-minded to the end that greater unity and richness of national life may be attained. Third is the contrariwise objective of conserving state and regional autonomy in the ever-encroaching centralization of power and functions of the Federal Government and the consequent trend toward bigness and over-centralization everywhere, with also the natural danger of dictatorships. A fourth is found in the motivation for planning, for looking forward to abundance and to the reality of experience, rather than looking backward or to the futility of utopian abstractions. There is a fifth type of motivation inherent in regionalism, and that is its possibilities for vivid portraiture of the nation, for interpreting the drama of its history and crises, and for creating new interest and new patriotism among the American people. Thus, Lewis Mumford appraises the regional guides of America "as indispensable toward creating that new sense of the regional setting and regional history, without which we cannot have an informed and participating body of citizens who will understand the problems that grow out of their intercourse with the earth and with other groups: citizens who will eventually learn the art of socialized living and regional planning and will make the earth their collective home. . . . They will give to contemporary Americans the opportunity to know and understand intimately their country, as they never had the opportunity, without a lifetime of leisure, to do before."[4] In this and some other respects there may, therefore, be a rich variety of meanings and implications of the subregionality of the nation in art, literature, travel, recreation, folk culture, all constituent parts of the whole. In all of these meanings the keynote of the region as a *constituent part of the whole* in opposition to areal separateness, which is pointed up in our first chapter, is everywhere apparent.

[4] Lewis Mumford, "Writers' Project," *The New Republic*, LXXXXII, No. 1194, p. 307.

BIBLIOGRAPHY

(Exclusive of the more general titles listed in footnotes in Part II)

BOOKS, REPORTS, PROCEEDINGS, PAMPHLETS

Abercrombie, Patrick, and Johnson, T. H. *The Doncaster Regional Planning Scheme.* Liverpool: University Press, 1922.

—— and Kelly, S. R. *Cumbrian Regional Joint Advisory Committee, Cumbrian (England) Regional Planning Scheme.* Liverpool: University Press, 1932.

—— Kelly, S. R., and Fyfe, Theodore. *The Deeside Regional Planning Scheme.* Liverpool: University Press, 1923.

—— and Others. *Sheffield and District Regional Planning Scheme.* Liverpool: University Press, 1931.

Adams, C. C. *Guide to the Study of Animal Ecology.* New York: The Macmillan Company, 1913.

Adams, E. K., and Wood, E. P. *A Five Year Experiment in Training Volunteer Group Leaders, 1922-1927.* New York: Girl Scouts, Inc., 1927.

Adams, James Truslow. *America's Tragedy.* New York: Charles Scribner's Sons, 1934.

—— *The Epic of America.* New York: Little, Brown, and Company, 1931.

—— *Provincial Society, 1690-1763.* A History of American Life Series, III. New York: The Macmillan Company, 1927.

—— Graves, H. S., *et al. New England's Prospect.* New York: American Geographical Society, 1933.

Agar, Herbert. *Land of the Free.* Boston: Houghton Mifflin Company, 1935.

Allee, W. C. *Animal Aggregations: A Study in General Sociology.* Chicago: The University of Chicago Press, 1931.

Ancel, Jacques. *Géopolitique.* Paris: Librairie Delagrave, 1936.

Babcock, K. C. *The Rise of American Nationality.* New York: Harper and Brothers, 1906.

Bailey, L. H. *The Holy Earth.* New York: Charles Scribner's Sons, 1917.

Baker, O. E. (ed.). *Atlas of American Agriculture.* Washington, D. C.: U. S. Department of Agriculture, 1936.

Banbury and District Joint Regional Planning Commission. *The Regional*

Planning of Banbury and District, an Explanatory Memoranaum. Banbury, England: T. F. Thompson, 1913.

Bancroft, H. H. *Histories of the West in Works.* 31 volumes. San Francisco: History Company, 1890.

Banse, Ewald. *Das Buch der Länder: Landschaft und Seele der Erde.* 2 volumes. Berlin: A. Scherl, 1929-1930.

Barrés, Maurice. *Les déracinés.* Paris: Bibliothèque-Charpentier, 1897.

Bassett, E. M. *Zoning: The Laws, Administration, and Court Decisions During the First Twenty Years.* New York: The Russell Sage Foundation, 1936.

Baulig, Henri. *Amérique Septentrionale.* Vol. 13, Géographie Universelle, edited by Paul Vidal de la Blache and L. Gallois. Paris: A. Colin, 1935-1936.

Beard, Charles A., and Smith, G. H. E. *The Idea of National Interest: An Analytical Study of American Foreign Policy.* New York: The Macmillan Company, 1934.

Bennett, H. H. *The Soils and Agriculture of the Southern States.* New York: The Macmillan Company, 1921.

Bernard, L. L. (ed.). *The Fields and Methods of Sociology.* New York: Farrar and Rinehart, 1934.

Betters, P. V. *Recent Federal-City Relations.* Washington, D. C.: U. S. Conference of Mayors, 1936.

Bews, J. W. *Human Ecology.* London: Oxford University Press, 1935.

Boas, Franz. *Anthropology and Modern Life.* New York: W. W. Norton and Company, 1928.

— *The Mind of Primitive Man.* New York: The Macmillan Company, 1931.

Bond, B. W., Jr. *The Civilization of the Old Northwest.* New York: The Macmillan Company, 1934.

Bonn, M. J. *The American Adventure.* New York: John Day Company, 1934.

Borg, C. O. *The Great Southwest.* Santa Ana, California: Fine Arts Press, 1936.

Bowman, Isaiah. *Forest Physiography.* New York: John Wiley and Sons, 1911.

— *Geography in Relation to the Social Sciences.* New York: Charles Scribner's Sons, 1934.

— *The New World Problems in Political Geography.* 4th edition. New York: World Book Company, 1928.

— *The Pioneer Fringe.* New York: American Geographical Society, Research Series No. 13, 1931.

Branch, E. D. *Westward, the Romance of the Frontier.* New York: D. Appleton Company, 1930.

Branford, S. G., and Farquharson, Alexander. *An Introduction to Regional Surveys.* Westminster: The Le Play House Press, 1924.

Branford, Victor. *The Regional Survey as a Method of Social Study.* Oxford: Holywell Press, 1915.
—— and Geddes, Patrick. *The Coming Polity.* London: Williams and Norgate, 1917. New enlarged edition, 1919.
—— and Geddes, Patrick. *Our Social Inheritance.* London: Williams and Norgate, 1919.
Brigham, A. P. *Geographic Influences in American History.* New York: Ginn and Company, 1903.
Brooke, C. E. P. *Climate.* New York: Charles Scribner's Sons, 1930.
Brooks, Van Wyck. *The Flowering of New England.* New York: E. P. Dutton and Company, 1936.
Brun, Charles. *Le régionalisme.* Paris: Bloud et Cie, 1911.
Brunhes, Jean. *Human Geography.* Translated and edited by Isaiah Bowman and Ellwood Dodd. New York: Rand, McNally and Company, 1920.
—— *La géographie de l'histoire.* Paris: Delagrave, 1914.
—— *La géographie humaine.* Paris: Alcan, 1912.
Bryan, P. W. *Man's Adaptation of Nature: Studies of the Cultural Landscape.* New York: Henry Holt and Company, 1935.
Buck, Paul S. *The Road to Reunion, 1865-1900.* Boston: Little, Brown, and Company, 1936.
Buckle, H. T. *History of Civilization in England.* 2 volumes. New York: D. Appleton, 1882.
—— *Introduction to the History of Civilization in England.* (New, revised edition by J. M. Robertson.) London: G. Routledge and Sons, Ltd.; New York: E. P. Dutton and Company, 1904.
Buechel, F. A. *The Commerce of Agriculture.* New York: John Wiley and Sons, 1926.
Buffet, Jean. *Du régionalisme au nationalisme financier.* Paris: Berger-Levrault, 1917.
Bulletin of the American Library Association, Volume 30, No. 11 (November, 1936).
Bunting, W. L. *Where Geography and History Meet.* London and Toronto: J. M. Dent and Sons, 1925.
Burgess, Ernest W. (ed.). *The Urban Community.* Chicago: University of Chicago Press, 1926.
Burgess, Ernest W., and Blumer, Herbert (eds.). *Human Side of Social Planning.* Selected papers from the Proceedings of the American Sociological Society, 1935. Chicago: American Sociological Society, 1936.

Caffey, G. N. *Study of the Soils of the United States.* U. S. Bureau of Soils, Bulletin 85, 1913.
Cambo, F. *La solución autonomista del problema catalán.* Madrid: Estab. tip. de J. Rates, 1918.

Campbell, J. C. *The Southern Highlander and His Home Land.* New York: Russell Sage Foundation, 1921.

Capek, Thomas. *The Czechs (Bohemians) in America.* New York: Houghton Mifflin Company, 1920.

Cauley, T. J. *Agrarianism.* Chapel Hill: The University of North Carolina Press, 1935.

Chaddock, R. E. *Ohio before 1850: A Study of the Early Influence of Pennsylvania and Southern Population in Ohio.* New York: Columbia University Press, 1908.

Chapman, R. N. *Animal Ecology.* New York: McGraw-Hill Book Company, 1931.

Chase, Stuart. *Rich Land, Poor Land.* New York: Whittlesey House, 1936.

Clark, R. C. *The Beginnings of Texas.* Bulletin of the University of Texas, No. 98, Humanistic Series, No. 6. Austin: University of Texas Press, 1907.

Clark University. *Economic Geography.* Graduate School of Geography, 1931.

Clements, F. E. *Plant Physiology and Ecology.* New York: Henry Holt and Company, 1907.

—— *Research Methods in Ecology.* Lincoln, Nebraska: The University Publishing Company, 1905.

Cohnstaedt, Wilhelm. *Administrative Districting in Germany since 1918.* Chicago: Committee on Public Administration, Social Science Research Council, 1935.

Colby, C. C. *Source Book for the Economic Geography of North America.* Chicago: University of Chicago Press, 1916.

Cole, W. E., and Crowe, H. P. *Recent Trends in Rural Planning.* New York: Prentice-Hall, 1937.

Cooper Studies. *Pioneer Settlement.* New York: American Geographical Society, 1932.

Couch, W. T. (ed.). *Culture in the South.* Chapel Hill: The University of North Carolina Press, 1934.

Crane, V. W. *The Southern Frontier, 1670-1732.* Durham, North Carolina: Duke University Press, 1928.

Cronin, F. D., and Beers, H. W. *Areas of Intense Drought Distress, 1930-1936.* Works Progress Administration Bulletin, Series V, No. 1. Washington, D. C.: U. S. Government Printing Office, 1937.

Davidson, Donald. *The Attack on Leviathan: Regionalism and Nationalism in the United States.* Chapel Hill: The University of North Carolina Press, 1938.

Delaisi, F. *Les deux Europes: Europe industrielle et Europe agricole.* Paris: Payot, 1929.

Denison, J. H. *Emotional Currents in American History.* New York: Charles Scribner's Sons, 1932.

Deschanel, Paul. *La décentralisation.* Paris: Berger-Levrault, 1895.
Dexter, E. G. *Weather Influences.* New York: The Macmillan Company, 1904.
Dickinson, R. E., and Howarth, O. J. R. *The Making of Geography.* Oxford: Clarendon Press, 1933.
Dickson, Harris. *The Story of King Cotton.* New York: Funk and Wagnalls, 1937.
Dimock, M. E., and Benson, G. C. S. *Can Interstate Compacts Succeed?* Public Policy Pamphlet No. 22. Chicago: University of Chicago Press, 1937.
Dixon, R. B. *The Building of Cultures.* New York: Charles Scribner's Sons, 1928.
— *The Racial History of Man.* New York: Charles Scribner's Sons, 1923.
Dobie, J. F. *The Flavor of Texas.* Dallas: Dealey and Lowe, 1936.
Dodd, W. E. *The Old South: Struggles for Democracy.* New York: The Macmillan Company, 1937.
— *Woodrow Wilson and His Work.* New York: Peter Smith, 1932.
Duffus, R. L. *Mastering a Metropolis: Planning the Future of the New York Regions.* New York and London: Harper and Brothers, 1930.

Eggan, Fred, *et al. Social Anthropology of North American Tribes.* Chicago: University of Chicago Press, 1937.
Elliott, F. F. *Types of Farming in the United States.* Washington, D. C.: Government Printing Office, 1933.
Elliott, W. Y. *The Need for Constitutional Reform.* New York: Whittlesey House, McGraw-Hill Book Company, 1935.
Elton, Charles. *The Ecology of Animals.* London: Methuen and Company, Ltd., 1933.
Ely, Northcutt. *Oil Conservation Through Interstate Agreement.* Washington, D. C.: U. S. Government Printing Office, 1933.
Ely, R. T., and Morehouse, E. W. *Elements of Land Economics.* New York: The Macmillan Company, 1924.
Engelen, O. D. *Inheriting the Earth, or the Geographical Factor in National Development.* New York: The Macmillan Company, 1922.

Fagg, C. C., and G. E. Hutchings. *An Introduction to Regional Surveying.* Cambridge: University Press, 1930.
Fairgrieve, James. *Geography and World Power.* London: University of London Press, Ltd., 1921.
Faris, John T. *Seeing the Middle West.* Philadelphia: J. B. Lippincott Company, 1923.
Farm Tenancy. Report of the President's Committee, February, 1937. Prepared under the auspices of the National Resources Committee. Washington, D. C.: U. S. Government Printing Office, 1937.

Faust, A. B. *The German Element in the United States.* 2 volumes. New York: Houghton Mifflin Company, 1909.
Fawcett, C. B. *Frontiers: A Study in Political Geography.* London: Oxford University Press, 1918.
Febvre, Lucien. *A Geographical Introduction to History.* New York: Alfred A. Knopf, 1925.
Federal Writers' Project of the Works Progress Administration for the State of Maine. *Maine: A Guide "Down East."* Boston: Houghton Mifflin Company, 1937.
Federal Writers' Project of the Works Progress Administration for the State of Massachusetts. *Massachusetts: A Guide to Its Places and People.* Boston: Houghton Mifflin Company, 1937.
Federal Writers' Project of the Works Progress Administration for the State of Rhode Island. *Rhode Island: A Guide to the Smallest State.* Boston: Houghton Mifflin Company, 1937.
Federal Writers' Project of the Works Progress Administration for the State of Vermont. *Vermont: A Guide to the Green Mountain State.* Boston: Houghton Mifflin Company, 1937.
Fenneman, N. M. *Physiography of Western United States.* 1st ed. New York and London: McGraw-Hill Book Company, 1931.
Finch, V. C., and Baker, O. E. *Geography of the World's Agriculture.* Washington, D. C.: U. S. Department of Agriculture, 1911.
Fleure, H. J. *The Geographical Background of Modern Problems.* New York: Longmans, Green and Company, 1932.
Folsom, J. K. *Culture and Social Progress.* New York: Longmans, Green and Company, 1928.
Fox, D. R. *Sources of Culture in the Middle West.* New York: D. Appleton-Century Company, 1934.
Fryxell, F. M. *The Physiography of the Region of Chicago.* Chicago: University of Chicago Press, 1927.

Geddes, Patrick. *Cities in Evolution.* London: Williams and Norgate, 1915.
—— *Syllabus of a Course of Ten Lectures on Great Cities. Their Place in Geography and Their Relation to Human Development.* London: Southwood, Smith and Company, 1909.
—— *Town Planning in Colombo.* Ceylon: H. R. Cattle, Government Printer, 1921.
—— *Two Steps in Civics: Cities and Town Planning Exhibition and the International Congress of Cities.* Liverpool: The University Press, 1913.
George, H. B. *Relations of Geography to History.* Oxford: Clarendon Press, 1924.
Giddings, Franklin H. *Civilization and Society.* Howard W. Odum, editor. New York: Henry Holt and Company, 1932.
Gilbert, G. C., and Pogue, J. E. *The Energy Resources in North*

America. Washington, D. C.: U. S. Government Printing Office, 1919.

Gist, N. P., and Halbert, L. A. *Urban Society*. New York: Thomas Y. Crowell Company, 1933.

Goldenweiser, A. A. *Early Civilization.* New York: Alfred A. Knopf and Company, 1922.

Gooch, R. K. *Regionalism in France.* University of Virginia, Institute for Research in the Social Sciences, No. 12. New York: The Century Company, 1931.

Grant, Madison. *The Conquest of A Continent or Expansion of Races in America.* New York: Charles Scribner's Sons, 1933.

Gras, N. S. B. *An Introduction to Economic History*. New York: Harper and Brothers, 1922.

Graves, W. B. *Uniform State Action.* Chapel Hill: The University of North Carolina Press, 1934.

Greenwood, A. P. *We Sagebrush Folks.* New York: D. Appleton-Century Company, 1934.

Gregg, Josiah. *The Commerce of the Prairies.* Chicago: R. R. Donnelley and Sons, 1926.

Gregory, J. W. *Human Migration and the Future. A Study of the Causes, Effects and Control of Emigration.* Philadelphia: J. B. Lippincott Company, 1927.

Groves, Ernest R. *The American Woman.* New York: Greenberg, 1937.

Gruening, Ernest (ed.). *These United States: A Symposium.* New York: Boni and Liveright, 1932.

Gulich, S. L. *The American Japanese Problem: A Study of the Racial Relations of the East and West.* New York: Charles Scribner's Sons, 1914.

Guthein, F. A. *Regional Planning by the Federal Government.* Editorial Research Reports, July 10, 1933.

Hacker, L. M., and Kendrick, B. B. *The United States Since 1865.* New York: F. S. Crofts and Company, 1932.

Haddon, A. C., and Quiggin, A. H. *History of Anthropology*. London: Watts and Company, 1910.

Haines, Henry S. *Problems in Railway Regulation.* New York: The Macmillan Company, 1911.

Hall, James. *The West, Its Commerce and Navigation.* Cincinnati: A. W. Derby and Company, 1848.

—— *The West, Its Soils, Surface and Production.* Cincinnati: Derby, Bradley and Company, 1848.

Hann, Julius von. *Handbook of Climatology*. Translated by R. de C. Ward. New York: The Macmillan Company, 1903.

Hauser, Henri. *Le problème du regionalisme.* Paris: Les Presses Universitaires de France, 1924.

Havemeyer, Loomis (ed.). *Conservation of Our Natural Resources.* New York: The Macmillan Company, 1930.

Havighurst, Walter. *Upper Mississippi: A Wilderness Saga.* New York: Farrar and Rinehart, 1937.

Heaton, E. W. *A Regional Geography of Six Continents.* London: Herbert Russell, Book I, 1914; Appendix, 1921; Book IV, 1919; Book V, 1921.

Hedden, W. P. *How Great Cities Are Fed.* New York: D. C. Heath, 1929.

Heer, Clarence. *Income and Wages in the South.* Chapel Hill: University of North Carolina Press, 1930.

Hennessy, Jean. *Le problème du regionalisme.* Carnegie Endowment for International Peace. *Economic and Social History of the World War.* French series. Paris, 1924.

—— *Regions of France.* Paris: G. Crés., 1916.

Herbertson, A. J. *A Handbook of Geography.* 2 volumes. London: A. and C. Black, 1911.

—— and F. D. *Man and His Work.* London: A. and C. Black, 1928.

Hesse, Richard. *Ecological Animal Geography.* New York: John Wiley and Sons, 1937.

Hettner, Alfred. *Die Geographie; ihre Geschichte, ihr Wesen und ihre Methodie.* Breslau: F. Hirt, 1927.

—— *Die Klimate der Erde.* Leipzig and Berlin: B. G. Teubner, 1930.

Hobbs, S. H., Jr. *North Carolina Economic and Social.* Chapel Hill: University of North Carolina Press, 1930.

Hobhouse, L. T., Wheeler, G. C., and Ginsburg, M. *The Material Culture and Social Institutions of the Simpler Peoples.* London: Chapman and Hall, 1930.

Holdich, Sir Thomas. *Political Frontiers and Boundary Making.* London: The Macmillan Company, Ltd., 1916.

Horner, J. T. *Agricultural Marketing.* New York: John Wiley and Sons, 1925.

Howard, Ebenezer. *Garden Cities of Tomorrow.* London: S. Sonnenschien and Company, Ltd., 1922.

Huizinga, G. F. *What the Dutch Have Done in the West of the United States.* Philadelphia: Privately printed, 1909.

Hulbert, A. B. *Frontiers, the Genius of American Nationality.* Boston: Little, Brown and Company, 1929.

—— *Paths of Inland Commerce.* New Haven: Yale University Press, 1920.

—— *Soil. Its Influence on the History of the United States.* New Haven: Yale University Press, 1930.

Humboldt, Alexander. *Aspects of Nature.* Translated by Mrs. E. J. Sabine. London: Longman, Brown, Green and Longman, 1849.

Huntington, Ellsworth. *Civilization and Climate.* New Haven: Yale University Press, 1915.

Huntington, Ellsworth. *Climatic Factors as Illustrated in Arid America.* Washington, D. C.: Carnegie Institute, Publication No. 192, 1914.
—— *The Human Habitat.* New York: D. Van Nostrand Company, 1927.
—— *The Pulse of Progress.* New York: Charles Scribner's Sons, 1926.
——, Williams, F. E., and von Valkenburg, S. *Economic and Social Geography.* New York: John Wiley and Sons, 1933.

Iyenaga, T., and Kenosheo, Sato. *Japan and the California Problem.* New York: Putnam's, 1921.

Jacks, L. P. *My American Friends.* New York: The Macmillan Company, 1933.
Jackson, G. P. *White Spirituals in the Southern Uplands.* Chapel Hill: The University of North Carolina Press, 1933.
James, Harlean (ed.). *American Planning and Civic Annual.* Washington, D. C.: American Planning and Civic Association, 1937.
James, Harlean. *Land Planning in the United States for City, State and Nation.* New York: The Macmillan Company, 1926.
Jillson, W. R. *The Big Sandy Valley, A Regional History Prior to the Year 1850.* Louisville, Kentucky: J. B. Morton and Company, 1930.
Jones, L. R., and Bryan, P. W. *North America.* New York: The Dial Press, 1924.
—— and —— *North America: An Historical, Economic and Regional Geography.* 2nd edition. London: Methuen and Company, Ltd., 1928.
Jones, W. D., and Whittlesey, D. S. *An Introduciton to Economic Geography.* Chicago: University of Chicago Press, 1925.
Junek, O. W. *Isolated Communities.* Cincinnati: The American Book Company, 1937.

Kellog, C. E. *Development and Significance of the Great Soil Groups of the United States.* United States Department of Agriculture, Publication No. 229. Washington, D. C.: U. S. Government Printing Office, 1936.
Kendrew, W. G. *Climate, A Treatise on the Principles of Weather and Climate.* Oxford: Clarendon Press, 1930.
—— *The Climates of the Continents.* 2nd Edition. Oxford: Clarendon Press, 1927.
Kennedy, L. V. *The Negro Peasant Turns Cityward: Effects of Recent Migrations to Northern Centers.* New York: Columbia University Press, 1930.
King, F. H. *Farmers of Forty Centuries.* Madison, Wisconsin: Mrs. F. H. King, 1911.
Kolb, J. H., and Brunner, E. de S. *A Study of Rural Society.* Boston: Houghton Mifflin Company, 1935.

Koller, Armin Hajman. *The Theory of Environment.* Menasha, Wisconsin: George Banta Publishing Company, 1918.

The Land of Better Farms: The Pacific Northwest. Chicago, Burlington and Quincy Railroad, Northern Pacific Railway, Great Northern Railway, 1923.

Larson, L. M. *The Changing West.* Northfield, Minnesota: Norwegian-American Historical Association, 1937.

Laut, A. C. *Pathfinders of the West.* New York: The Macmillan Company, 1904.

Lehman, Lucien. *The American Illusion.* New York: The Century Company, 1931.

Le Play, Frédéric. *La réforme sociale en France.* Paris: H. Plan, 1864. 2 volumes.

Letourneau, C. J. M. *Sociology, Based upon Ethnography.* London: Chapman and Hall, 1893.

Lewis, E. E. *The Mobility of the Negro: A Study in the American Labor Supply.* New York: Columbia University Press, 1931.

Linton, Ralph. *The Study of Man.* New York: D. Appleton-Century Company, 1936.

Lippert, Julius. *The Evolution of Culture.* Translated by George Peter Murdock. New York: The Macmillan Company, 1931.

Location of Federal Reserve Districts. Senate Document 485, Sixty-third Congress, Second Session.

Lockwood, Lucy. *In Search of America.* New York: Thomas Y. Crowell Company, 1930.

Lorwin, L. S. *The Problem of Economic Planning, 1931 World Economic Congress,* Section II, 3 (under the Auspices of the International Industrial Relations Association), The Hague, Holland.

Lowie, R. H. *An Introduction to Cultural Anthropology.* New York: Farrar and Rinehart, 1934.

Lowrie, S. H. *Culture Conflicts in Texas, 1821-1835.* New York: Columbia University Press, 1932.

Lundberg, Ferdinand. *America's 60 Families.* New York: The Vanguard Press, 1937.

Lynd, R. S., and H. M. *Middletown.* New York: Harcourt, Brace and Company, 1929.

MacDonald, A. F. *Federal Aid.* New York: Thomas Y. Crowell Company, 1928.

MacKaye, Benton. *Employment and Natural Resources.* Washington: U. S. Government Printing Office, 1919.

—— *The New Exploration: A Philosophy of Regional Planning.* New York: Harcourt, Brace and Company, 1928.

Marbut, C. F., Bennett, H. H., Lapham, J. E., and Lapham, M. H. *Soils of the United States.* Washington, D. C.: United States Department of Agriculture, Bureau of Soils, Bulletin 96, 1913.

Marett, R. R. *Psychology and Folk-Lore.* London: Methuen and Company, 1920.

Marsh, G. P. *The Earth as Modified by Human Action.* London: Low and Searle, 1874; New York: Charles Scribner's Sons, 1898.

Martonne, E. de. *Geographical Regions of France.* Translated by H. C. Brintnall. London: W. Heinemann, Ltd., 1933.

McAdie, A. G. *Man and Weather.* Cambridge: Harvard University Press, 1926.

McConnell, W. J. *Social Cleavages in Texas: A Study of the Proposed Division of the State.* New York: Columbia University Press, 1925.

McKenzie, R. D. *The Metropolitan Community.* New York: McGraw-Hill Book Company, 1932.

McLean, W. H. *Regional and Town Planning, in Principle and Practice.* London: Crosby, Lockwood and Sons, 1930.

McWilliams, Carey. *The New Regionalism in American Literature.* Seattle: University of Washington Book Store, 1930.

Merriam, C. H. *Life Zones and Crop Zones of the United States.* Washington, D. C.: United States Department of Agriculture, Division of Biology, Bulletin 10, 1898.

Mill, H. R. *The Realm of Nature.* New York: Charles Scribner's Sons, 1896.

Miller, G. J., and Parkins, A. E. *Geography of North America.* New York: John Wiley and Sons, 1928.

Millikan, R. A. *Science and the New Civilization.* New York: Charles Scribner's Sons, 1930.

Molyneaux, Peter. *What Economic Nationalism Means.* World Affairs Pamphlet, No. 4. New York: Foreign Policy Association and World Peace Foundation, 1934.

Monette, J. W. *History of the Valley of the Mississippi.* New York: Harper Brothers, 1846.

Moore, Harry Estill. *What Is Regionalism?* Chapel Hill: The University of North Carolina Press, 1937.

Morison, S. E., and Commager, H. S. *The Growth of the American Republic.* 2 vols. New York: Oxford University Press, 1937.

Mukerjee, Radhakamal. *Regional Sociology.* New York: The Century Company, 1926.

Mulhauser, R., and Huus, R. O. *A Bibliography on Regional Government.* Cleveland: Western Reserve University, 1928.

Mumford, Lewis. *The Culture of Cities.* New York: Harcourt, Brace and Company, 1938.

— *Technics and Civilization.* New York: Harcourt, Brace and Company, 1934.

Munro, W. B. *The Invisible Government.* New York: The Macmillan Company, 1928.

National Resources Board. *A Report on National Planning and Public Works in Relation to Natural Resources.* Washington, D. C.: U. S. Government Printing Office, 1934.

National Resources Committee. *Drainage Basin Problems and Programs*, December 1936. Washington, D. C.: United States Government Printing Office, 1937.

—— *Regional Planning, Part I,–Pacific Northwest*, May 1936. Washington, D. C.: United States Government Printing Office, 1936.

—— *Regional Planning, Part II,–St. Louis Region*, June 1936. Washington, D. C.: United States Government Printing Office, 1936.

—— *Regional Planning, Part III,–New England*, July 1936. Washington, D. C.: United States Government Printing Office, 1936.

—— *Regional Factors in National Planning and Development*, December 2, 1935. Washington, D. C.: U. S. Government Printing Office, 1935.

—— Research Committee on Urbanism. *Interim Report to the National Resources Committee*, July 1936. (Mimeographed.)

—— *Status of City and County Planning in the United States*, May 15, 1937.

Newbigin, M. I. *Man and His Conquest of Nature.* London: A. and C. Black, 1922. 3rd edition.

—— *The Mediterranean Lands. An Introductory Study in Human and Historical Geography.* New York: Alfred A. Knopf, 1924.

—— *Modern Geography.* New York: Henry Holt and Company, 1911.

—— *A New Regional Geography of the World.* New York: Harcourt, Brace and Company, 1929.

New Horizons in Planning. Proceedings of the National Planning Conference Held at Detroit, Michigan, June 1-3, 1937. Chicago: American Society of Planning Officials, 1937.

Obermaier, Jugo. *El hombre fosil.* Madrid, 1916. Translated by C. D. Matthew. New Haven: Yale University Press, 1924.

Odum, Howard W. *An American Epoch.* New York: Henry Holt and Company, 1930.

—— *The Regional Approach to National Social Planning.* New York: Foreign Policy Association and Chapel Hill: The University of North Carolina Press, 1935.

—— *Southern Regions of the United States.* Chapel Hill: The University of North Carolina Press, 1936.

—— and Jocher, Katharine. *An Introduction to Social Research.* New York: Henry Holt and Company, 1929.

Ogburn, W. F. *Social Characteristics of Cities.* Chicago: International City Managers' Association, 1937.

Ogilvie, A. G. (ed.). *Great Britain: Essays in Regional Geography.* Cambridge: University Press, 1928.

Ormsby, H. *France: A Regional and Economic Geography.* New York: E. P. Dutton and Company, 1931.

Park, R. E., Burgess, E. W., and McKenzie, R. D. *The City*. Chicago: University of Chicago Press, 1925.

Parkins, A. E., and Whitaker, J. R. (eds.). *Our Natural Resources and Their Conservation.* New York: John Wiley and Sons; London: Chapman and Hall, Ltd., 1936.

Paullin, C. O., and Wright, J. K. (eds.). *Atlas of the Historical Geography of the United States.* Carnegie Institute of Washington and the American Geographic Society of New York, 1932.

Paxson, F. L. *History of the American Frontier, 1763-1893.* Boston: Houghton Mifflin Company, 1924.

Pearse, A. S. *Animal Ecology*. New York: The McGraw-Hill Book Company, 1926.

Pearse, Arthur. *Environment and Life*. Baltimore: C. C. Thomas, 1930.

Peate, I. C. (ed.). *Studies in Regional Consciousness and Environment.* London: Oxford University Press, 1930.

Penck, Albrecht. *Morphologie der Erdoberflache.* Stuttgart: J. Englehorn, 1894.

Peschel, Oscar. *Geschichte der Erdkunde.* Munich: R. Oldenbourg, 1877-1878.

Pierre, South Dakota, and Vicinity, Guide to. Compiled by the Federal Writers' Project, W.P.A., State Publishing Company, 1937.

Planning for City, State, Region and Nation. Proceedings of the Joint Conference on Planning (American City Planning Institute, American Planning and Civic Association, American Society of Planning Officials) May 4, 5, and 6, 1936, Richmond, Virginia. Chicago: American Society of Planning Officials, 1936.

Pomfret, J. E. *The Geographical Pattern of Mankind.* New York: D. Appleton-Century Company, 1935.

President's Research Committee on Social Trends. *Recent Social Trends in the United States.* 2 vols. New York: The McGraw-Hill Book Company, 1933.

Prevet, F. *Le régionalisme économique.* Paris: Recueil Sirey, 1929.

Price, E. B. *Study of Regional Areas in Federal Administration: Exploratory Study of the Farm Credit Administration.* Washington, D. C.: Brookings Institution, 1934.

Quiett, G. C. *They Built the West.* New York: D. Appleton-Century Company, 1934.

Ralph, Julian. *Our Great West: A Study of the Present Conditions and Future Possibilities of the New Commonwealths and Capitols of the United States.* New York: Harper and Brothers, 1893.

Ratzel, Friedrich. *Anthropogeographie.* Stuttgart: J. Engelhorn nachf., 1921-1922.

—— *Politische Geographie.* Munich and Leipzig: R. Oldenbourg, 1897.

Ratzel, Friedrich. *Stadte-und-Culturbilder aus Nordamerika.* Leipzig: F. A. Brockhaus, 1876.
—— *Volkerkunde.* Leipzig: Bibliographisches Institut, 1894.
Redfield, Robert. *Tepotzlan.* Chicago: The University of Chicago Press, 1930.
Richardson, R. N., and Rister, C. C., *The Greater Southwest.* Glendale, California: The Arthur H. Clark Company, 1934.
Riegel, Robert E. *America Moves West.* New York: Henry Holt and Company, 1930.
Ringel, F. J. *America as Americans See It.* New York: The Literary Guild, 1932.
Robbins, Lionel. *Economic Planning and International Order.* New York: The Macmillan Company, 1937.
Robertson, J. M. *Evolution of States.* London: Watts and Company, 1912.
Roosevelt, Theodore. *Winning of the West.* 4 vols. New York: G. P. Putnam's Sons, 1889-1910.
Russel, R. R. *Economic Aspects of Southern Sectionalism.* Urbana: University of Illinois Press, 1924.

Sauer, C. O. *Aboriginal Population of Northwestern Mexico.* Ibero-Americana: 10. Berkeley: University of California Press, 1935.
—— *The Geography of the Ozark Highlands.* Chicago: Geographical Society of Chicago, 1920.
—— *Geography of the Pennyroyal.* Frankfort, Kentucky: The Kentucky Geological Survey, 1927.
—— *The Morphology of Landscape.* University of California Publications in Geography. Vol. II, No. 2, 1925.
Schafer, Joseph. *The Social History of American Agriculture.* New York: The Macmillan Company, 1936.
Schimper, A. F. W. *Plant Geography.* Translated by Fisher. Oxford: Clarendon Press, 1930.
Schrieke, B. *Alien Americans.* New York: Viking Press, 1936.
Semple, Ellen Churchill. *American History and Its Geographic Conditions.* Boston: Houghton Mifflin Company, 1903.
—— *The Geography of the Mediterranean Region.* New York: Henry Holt and Company, 1931.
—— *Influences of Geographic Environment.* New York: Henry Holt and Company, 1911. (On the basis of Ratzel's System of Anthropology.)
Shaler, N. S. *Nature and Man in America.* New York: Charles Scribner's Sons, 1891.
Shannon, J. B. *A Survey of the Natural Resources and Population Trends of Kentucky River Valleys.* (Mimeographed.) Studies in Regionalism in Kentucky, No. 1, 1937.
Smith, G. E. *The Diffusion of Culture.* London: Watts and Company, 1933.

Smith, J. R. *American Lands and Peoples.* Chicago: John C. Winston Company, 1932.

—— *Human Geography.* 2 vols. Chicago: The John C. Winston Company, 1921-1922.

—— *Industrial and Commercial Geography.* New York: Henry Holt and Company, 1913.

—— *Men and Resources: A Study of North America and Its Place in World Geography.* New York: Harcourt, Brace and Company, 1937.

—— *North America: Its Peoples and the Resources, Development, and Prospects as an Agricultural, Industrial, and Commercial Area.* New York: Harcourt, Brace and Company, 1925.

Spengler, Oswald. *Decline of the West.* Translated by Charles F. Atkinson. New York: Alfred A. Knopf Company, 1926-1928.

Stamp, L. D. *The World, A General Geography.* New York: Longmans, Green and Company, 1929.

Stanbery, V. B. *An Approach to Regional Planning.* (Mimeographed.) Oregon State Planning Board, October 25, 1935.

Taeuber, Conrad, and Taylor, C. C. *The People of the Drought States.* Washington, D. C.: Works Progress Administration, 1937.

Tansley, A. G. *Practical Plant Ecology: A Guide for Beginners in Field Study of Plant Communities.* London: George Allen and Unwin, Ltd., 1923.

Tennessee Valley Authority, 1933-1937. Washington, D. C.: U. S. Government Printing Office, 1937.

Thomas, Franklin. *The Environmental Basis of Society.* New York: The Century Company, 1925.

Turner, F. J. *The Frontier in American History.* New York: Henry Holt and Company, 1920.

—— *The Significance of Sections in American History.* New York: Henry Holt and Company, 1932.

—— *The United States, 1830-1850, The Nation and Its Sections.* New York: Henry Holt and Company, 1935.

Unwin, Raymond. *Town Planning in Practice.* London: T. Fisher Unwin, Ltd., 1920.

Vance, R. B. *Human Factors in Cotton Culture.* Chapel Hill: The University of North Carolina Press, 1929.

—— *Human Geography of the South.* Chapel Hill: The University of North Carolina Press, 1932.

—— *Regional Reconstruction: A Way Out for the South.* New York: Foreign Policy Association, and Chapel Hill: The University of North Carolina Press, 1935.

Van Hise, C. R. *The Conservation of Natural Resources.* New York: The Macmillan Company, 1913.

— *The Conservation of Natural Resources in the United States.* Based on Van Hise and edited by Loomis Havemeyer and others. New York: The Macmillan Company, 1930.

Vidal de la Blache, P. M. J. *Principles of Human Geography.* Edited by Emmanuel de Martonne; translated by Millicent Todd Bingham. New York: Henry Holt and Company, 1926.

Volney, C. F. *View of the Climate and Soil of the United States of America.* London: J. Johnson, 1804.

von Hellwald, Friedrich. *Die Erde und ihre Volker: Ein geographisches Handbuch.* 2 vols. Stuttgart: 1877.

Walker, C. R. *The American City.* New York: Farrar and Rinehart, 1937.

Ward, R. de C. *Climate Considered Especially in Relation to Man.* New York: G. P. Putnam's Sons, 1918.

— *The Climates of the United States.* Boston: Ginn and Company, 1925.

Warming, Eug. *Oecology of Plants, An Introduction to the Study of Plant-Communities.* London: Oxford University Press, 1925.

Webb, W. P. *Divided We Stand: The Crisis of a Frontierless Democracy.* New York: Farrar and Rinehart, 1937.

— *The Great Plains.* Boston: Ginn and Company, 1931.

The Western Range. 74th Congress, 2nd Session, Senate Document No. 199. Washington, D. C.: United States Government Printing Office, 1936.

Whitbeck, R. H., and Thomas, O. J. *The Geographic Factor: Its Role in Life and Civilization.* New York: The Century Company, 1932.

White, C. L., and Renner, G. T. *Geography: An Introduction to Human Ecology.* New York: D. Appleton-Century Company, 1936.

Whitney, Milton. *Soils and Civilization.* New York: D. Van Nostrand Company, 1925.

— *Soils of the United States.* U. S. Bureau of Soils, Bulletin No. 55. Washington, D. C.: United States Government Printing Office, 1909.

— *Use of Soils East of the Great Plains Region.* U. S. D. A. Bureau of Soils, Bulletin 78. Washington, D. C.: United States Government Printing Office, 1911.

Willey, M. M., and Rice, S. A. *Communication Agencies and Social Life.* New York: McGraw-Hill Book Company, 1933.

Wilson, C. M. *Roots of America: A Travelogue of American Personalities.* New York: Funk and Wagnalls Company, 1936.

Wilson, G. L. *Coordinated Motor-Rail-Steamship Transportation.* New York: D. Appleton and Company, 1930.

Winsor, Justin. *The Mississippi Basin.* Boston: Houghton Mifflin Company, 1895.

Wissler, Clark. *An Introduction to Social Anthropology*. New York: Henry Holt and Company, 1929.
—— *Man and Culture*. New York: Thomas Y. Crowell Company, 1923.
—— *North American Indians of the Plains*. Handbook Series, No. 1, American Museum of Natural History, Third Edition, New York, 1927.
—— *The Relation of Nature to Man in Aboriginal America*. London: Oxford University Press, 1926.
Wolfanger, L. A. *The Major Soil Divisions of the United States*. New York: John Wiley and Sons, 1930.
Woofter, T. J., Jr. *Black Yoemanry*. New York: Henry Holt and Company, 1930.

Zimmermann, E. W. *World Resources and Industries*. New York: Harper and Brothers, 1933.

ARTICLES

Adams, Charles. "The Relation of General Ecology to Human Ecology." *Ecology*, 16, pp. 316-335 (July 1935).
Adams, Thomas. "Forecast: The Regional Community of the Future." American Society of Civil Engineers, *Transactions*, pp. 1146-1180 (1928).
—— "Industrial Decentralization As a Cause for Regional Planning." *Engineering News Record*, 85, pp. 31-32 (July 1, 1920).
—— "Regional Planning in Relation to Public Administration." *National Municipal Review*, 15, pp. 35-42 (January 1926).
—— "Social Objectives of Regional Planning." *National Municipal Review*, 15, pp. 79-87 (February 1926).
Aitkin, B. "Regional Survey of Mexico: a Study of a Mixed and Hybrid Population." *Eugenics Review*, 15, pp. 330-334 (April 1923).
American Civic Association. "Regional Planning in the United States." Ser. 4 (April 1929).
Antsiferov, N. "The Application of Regional Study to History." *Regional Study*, 5, No. 6, pp. 321-338 (1928).
Aronovici, C. "Let the Cities Perish." *Survey*, 68, pp. 437-440 (October 1, 1932).
—— "Regional Planning Versus Metropolitanism." *Scholastic*, 24, pp. 11-13 (March 17, 1934).
Ascher, C. S. "Public Tools for Regional Planning." *Survey*, 68, pp. 472-473 (October 1, 1932).
—— "Regionalism, Charting the Future." *Survey*, 66, pp. 460-461 (August 15, 1931).
—— "Regionalism, a New Approach to the Good Life." *National Municipal Review*, 20, pp. 592-596 (October 1931).

Bailey, T. A. "The West and Radical Legislation, 1890-1930." *American Journal of Sociology*, 38, pp. 603-611 (January 1933).

Baker, D. M. "Community Planning with Uncle Sam; the Southwest Gets Ready for Regional Planning and to Make a Part of the Big National Plan." *Southern California Business*, pp. 10-11 (February 1934).

Baker, J. E. "Regionalism in the Middle West." *American Review*, 4, pp. 603-614 (March 1935).

— "Regionalism: Pro and Con—Four Arguments for Regionalism." *Saturday Review of Literature*, 15, No. 5, pp. 3, 4, 14 (November 28, 1936).

Baker, O. E. "Agricultural Regions of North America." *Economic Geography*, 2, pp. 459-493 (October 1926); 3, pp. 50-86 (January 1927); 3, pp. 309-339 (July 1927); 4, pp. 44-73 (January 1928); 4, pp. 399-433 (October 1928); 5, pp. 36-69 (January 1929); 6, pp. 166-190 (April 1930).

— "The Agriculture of the Great Plains Region." *Annals of the Association of American Geographers*, 13, No. 3, pp. 109-167 (September 1923).

— "Land Utilization in the United States. Geographic Aspects of the Problem." *Geographical Review*, 13, pp. 1-26 (January 1923).

Balfour, Henry. "The Geographical Study of Folklore." *Folklore*, 35, pp. 16-25 (March 31, 1924).

Barrows, E. M. "United Regions of America, a New American Nation." *New Outlook*, 161, pp. 17-21 (May 1933).

Barrows, H. H. "Geography as Human Ecology." *Annals of the Association of American Geographers*, 13, pp. 1-14 (March 1923).

Beard, C. A. "The City's Place in Civilization." *Survey*, 61, pp. 213-215 (November 15, 1928).

— "Some Aspects of Regional Planning." *American Political Science Review*, 20, No. 2, pp. 273-283 (May 1926).

— "Some Regional Realities." *Survey*, 56, pp. 85-87 (April 15, 1926).

Beath, P. R. "Regionalism: Pro and Con—Four Fallacies of Regionalism." *Saturday Review of Literature*, 15, No. 5, pp. 3, 4, 14, 16 (November 28, 1936).

Beaufoy, S. L. G. "Regional Planning." *Town Planning Review*, 15, pp. 83-104 (November 1932); pp. 188-214 (May 1933).

Bernard, L. L. "A Classification of Environments." *American Journal of Sociology*, 31, pp. 318-332 (November 1925).

Black, R. V. N. "A Few Governmental Principles of Regional Planning as Observed in the Philadelphia Tri-State District." *American City*, 36, pp. 673-676 (May 1926).

Bone, H. A. "Geographic Problems in American History." *Mississippi Valley Historical Review*, supplement, pp. 450-453 (May 1919).

"The Boom in Regionalism." (Editorial) *Saturday Review of Literature*, 10, p. 606 (April 17, 1934).

Botkin, B. A. "Regionalism: Cult or Culture?" *English Journal*, 25, No. 3, pp. 181-185 (March 1936).

—— "Regionalism: The Next Step." *Space*, 1, pp. 86-88.

—— "We Talk about Regionalism—North, East, South and West." *Frontier*, pp. 1-11 (May 1933).

Brocard, Lucien. "Regional Economy and Economic Regionalism." Translated by F. Cyril James from an article appearing in *Revue Économique Internationale* (November 1931) and reprinted in translation in *Annals of the American Academy of Political and Social Science*, 162, pp. 81-92 (July 1932).

Brooks, E. C., and L. M. "A Decade of 'Planning' Literature." *Social Forces*, 12, pp. 427-459 (March 1934).

—— and —— "Five Years of 'Planning' Literature." *Social Forces*, 11, pp. 430-465 (March 1933).

Brown, E. F. "The Tennessee Valley Idea." *Current History*. 40, pp. 410-417 (July 1934).

Bruce, A. A. "The Compacts and Agreements of States with One Another and with Foreign Powers." *Minnesota Law Review*, 2, No. 7, pp. 500-516 (June 1918).

Bruere, R. W. "Giant Power, Region Builder." *Survey Graphic*, 54, pp. 161-164 (May 1, 1925).

Buck, S. J. "The Settlement of Oklahoma." Wisconsin Academy of Sciences, Arts, and Letters: *Transactions*, 15, Part 2, pp. 325-380, 1907.

Burgess, E. W. "The New Community and Its Future." *Annals of the American Academy of Political and Social Science*, 149, pp. 157-164 (May 1930).

—— "Social Planning and the Mores." *Publication of the American Sociological Society*, 29, No. 3, pp. 1-18 (August 1935).

Buttenheim, H. S. "Trends in Present-Day City and Regional Planning in the United States." *City Planning*, 9, pp. 73-86 (April 1933).

—— "Trends in Present-Day Regional Planning in the United States." *City Planning*, 10, pp. 62-77 (April 1934).

Byington, M. F. "Pittsburgh Studies Itself." *Survey Graphic*, 27, No. 2, pp. 75-79 (February 1938).

Calrow, C. J. "Interstate Cooperation." *National Municipal Review*, 25, pp. 445-451 (August 1936).

Carpenter, Niles. "Nature and Origins of the French Regionalist Movement." *Publications of the American Sociological Society*, 24, pp. 23-32 (May 1930).

Chapman, John. "San Antonio." *Southwest Review*, 22, No. 1, pp. 16-40 (Autumn 1936).

Cheney, C. H. "Progress of City and Regional Planning in 1931." *Municipal Index*, *1932*, pp. 122-126, Section 2.

Clark, Delbert. "Nine Groups Instead of the 48 States." *New York Times Magazine* (April 21, 1935).

Clark, H. F. "Planning in America." *Journal of the National Education Association*, 21, pp. 85-87 (March 1932).

Clark, J. P. "Little Americas: Innovations in Government by Interstate Compacts." *Survey Graphic*, 25, pp. 36-38 (January 1936).

Comey, A. C. "What Is National Planning?" *City Planning*, 9, pp. 164-167 (October 1933).

"Communications." *The Sociological Review*, 24, No. 2, pp. 197-198 (April-July 1932).

Cottrell, E. A. "The Metropolitan Water District of Southern California." *American Political Science Review*, 26, pp. 695-697 (August 1932).

Crane, J. L., Jr. "Decentralization–Eventually but not Now." *Annals of the American Academy of Political and Social Science*, 133, pp. 234-240 (September 1927).

Crane, Jacob. "Large Scale Regional Planning. The Unit: Watershed or States." *American City*, 49, pp. 60-61 (January 1934).

Crawford, A. W. "Cultural Opportunities in Regional Planning." American Society of Civil Engineers, *Transactions*, 92, No. 1683, pp. 1132-1145 (1928).

—— "Regional Planning in a New Light." *American Magazine of Art*, 18, No. 2, pp. 70-75 (February 1927).

Crouch, W. W. "Extra-territorial Powers of Cities as Factors in California Metropolitan Government." *American Political Science Review*, 31, pp. 286-291 (April 1937).

Dalzell, A. G. "The Need for Regional Planning." *Town Planning*, 8, pp. 64-67 (June 1929).

Davidson, Donald. "The Political Economy of Regionalism." *American Review*, 6, pp. 410-434 (February 1936).

—— "Regionalism and Nationalism in American Literature." *American Review*, 5, No. 1, pp. 48-61 (April 1935).

—— "Where Regionalism and Sectionalism Meet." *Social Forces*, 13, No. 1, pp. 23-31 (October 1934).

Dawson, J. M. "Keeping up with Culture in Texas and the Southwest." *Social Forces*, 10, No. 2, pp. 176-183 (December 1931).

Delano, J. "Regional Planning Next?" *National Municipal Review*, 13, pp. 141-148 (March 1924).

Dewey, John. "Americanism and Localism." *Dial*, 68, pp. 684-688 (June 1920).

Dice, L. R. "Biotic Areas and Ecologic Habitats as Units for the Statement of Animal and Plant Distribution." *Science*, n.s. 55, pp. 335-338 (March 31, 1922).

Dodd, A. M. "Interstate Compacts." *United States Law Review*, 70, pp. 557-578 (October 1936).

Donovan, W. J. "State Compacts as a Method of Settling Problems Common to Several States." *University of Pennsylvania Law Review*, 80, pp. 5-16 (November 1931).

Dryer, C. R. "Natural Economic Regions." *Annals of the Association of American Geographers*, 5, pp. 121-125, 1915.

Dykstra, C. A. "If the City Fails, America Fails." *Survey Graphic*, 26, No. 12, p. 663 (December 1937).

Egger, R. A. "New Proposal for Regional Government and Planning, New Jersey: With Comment from the Regional Plan Association." *American City*, 43, pp. 115-117 (April 1930).

Eliot, C. W. "National Planning." *City Planning*, 10, pp. 103-111 (July 1934).

Elton, C. S. "Animal Ecology." *Encyclopædia Britannica*, 7, (14th edition), pp. 915-924, 1932.

"The Failure of the States." *New Republic*, 9, pp. 170-172 (December 16, 1916).

Fairlie, J. A. "Administrative Regions in Great Britain." *American Political Science Review*, 31, pp. 937-941 (October 1937).

Fawcett, C. B. "Regional Planning in England and Wales." International Geographical Congress, July, 1928, *Proceedings*, pp. 453-461 (1930).

Fenneman, N. M. "Physiographic Boundaries within the United States." *Annals of the Association of American Geographers*, 4, pp. 84-134 (1914).

—— "Physiographic Divisions of the United States." *Annals of the Association of American Geographers*, 6, pp. 19-98 (1916).

—— "Physiographic Divisions of the United States." *Annals of the Association of American Geographers*, 18, pp. 261-353 (December 1928).

Fesler, J. W. "Federal Administrative Regions." *American Political Science Review*, 30, pp. 257-268 (April 1936).

—— "Standardization of Federal Administrative Regions." *Social Forces*, 15, pp. 12-21 (October 1936).

Fletcher, J. G. "Regionalism and Folk Art." *Southwest Review*, 19, No. 4, pp. 429-434 (July 1934).

Fleure, H. J. "France—A Regional Interpretation." *Scottish Geographical Magazine*, 32, pp. 519-534 (November 1916).

—— "Human Regions." *Scottish Geographical Magazine*, 35, pp. 94-105 (March 1919).

—— "Regional Balance of Racial Evolution." *Nature*, 118, pp. 380-383 (September 11, 1926).

Fohmann, K. B. "Helping Our Youth to Think in Terms of Regions." *City Planning*, 9, pp. 168-171 (October 1933).

Ford, G. B. "Regional and Metropolitan Planning." *American City*, 28, p. 614 (June 1923).

Frank, W. "Re-discovery of America." *New Republic*, 53, pp. 89-91, 136-138, 187-189, 240-243, 291-293, 344-347; 54, pp. 64-66 (December 14-21, 1927; January 4, 18, February 1, 15, 29, 1928).

Frankfurter, Felix, and Landis, J. M. "The Compact Clause of the Constitution–A Study in Interstate Adjustments." *Yale Law Journal*, 34, No. 7, pp. 685-758 (May 1925).

Fuller, B. "East and West, a Study of Differences." *Living Age*, 272, pp. 32-40 (January 6, 1912).

Garner, J. W. "Administrative Reforms in France." *American Political Science Review*, 13, pp. 17-46 (February 1919).

Geddes, Patrick. "Mapping of Life." *Sociological Review*, 16, pp. 193-203 (July 1924).

Gerould, Katharine Fullerton. "Our Northwestern States." *Harper's Magazine*, 150, pp. 412-428 (March 1925).

Goldenweiser, A. A. "Culture and Environment." *American Journal of Sociology*, 21, pp. 628-633 (March 1916).

—— "Diffusionism and the American School of Historical Ethnology." *American Journal of Sociology*, 31, No. 1, pp. 19-38 (July 1925).

Gras, N. S. B. "Development of Metropolitan Economy in Europe and America." *American Historical Review*, 27, pp. 695-708 (July 1922).

—— "Regionalism and Nationalism." *Foreign Affairs*, 7, pp. 454-467 (April 1929).

—— "The Rise of the Metropolitan Community." *Publications of the American Sociological Society*, 20, pp. 155-163, 1925.

Graves, W. B. "The Future of the American States." *American Political Science Review*, 30, pp. 24-50 (February 1936).

Gray, James. "The Minnesota Muse." *Saturday Review of Literature*, 16, No. 7, pp. 3, 4, 14 (June 12, 1937).

Greber, J. "Aesthetic and Sociological Aspects of City and Regional Planning." *American Philosophical Society Proceedings*, 74, No. 1, pp. 15-19, 1934.

Greeley, General A. W. "Rainfall Types of the United States." *National Geographic Magazine*, 5, pp. 45-58 (April 29, 1893).

Gutheim, F. A. "Regional Planning by the Federal Government." (Editorial.) *Research Reports*, 7, pp. 23-29 (July 10, 1933).

Hacker, L. R. "Sections or Classes?" (Review of Turner's "The Significance of Sections in American History.") *Nation*, 137, pp. 108-110 (July 26, 1933).

Hadcliffe, G. L. "Some Governmental Aspects of Regional Planning." *American Philosophical Society Proceedings*, 74, No. 1, pp. 1-13, 1934.

Hall, R. B. "The Geographic Region: A Résumé." *Annals of the As-*

sociation of American Geographers, 25, No. 1, pp. 122-136 (March 1935).

Harris, G. M. "Regional Planning in Germany." *Town and Country Planning*, 2, pp. 61-63 (March 1934).

Harrison, S. M. "Round Table on Regional Planning–Some Regional Problems and Methods of Their Study." *American Political Science Review*, 20, No. 1, pp. 156-163 (February 1926).

Hartshorne, Richard. "Recent Developments in Political Geography." *American Political Science Review*, 29, pp. 785-804, 943-966 (October, December 1935).

—— and Dickens, S. N. "A Classification of the Agricultural Regions of Europe and North America on a Uniform Statistical Basis." *Annals of the Association of American Geographers*, 25, pp. 99-120 (June 1935).

Hartsough, Mildred. "The Concept of Regionalism as Applied to Western Germany." *Publications of the American Sociological Society*, 24, No. 2, pp. 12-22 (May 1930).

Harvey, D. E. "Programme of Polish Regionalism." *Sociological Review*, 24, pp. 197-199 (April 1932).

Hayes, E. C. "Effects of Geographic Conditions upon Social Realities." *American Journal of Sociology*, 19, pp. 813-824 (May 1914).

Hayes, Z. M. "Bibliography of Regional Planning." *Bulletin of Bibliography*, 13, pp. 65-69 (September 1927).

Heath, M. S. "The Prospect for Optimum Regional Production in the Southern Regions." *Social Forces*, 13, No. 1, pp. 31-36 (October 1934).

Herbertson, A. J. "The Major Natural Regions: An Essay in Systematic Geography." *Geographical Journal*, 25, No. 3, pp. 300-312 (March 1905).

—— "A New Science of Geography." *Scientific American Supplement*, 72, pp. 66-67 (July 29, 1911).

Herring, H. L. "Early Industrial Development in the South." *Annals of the American Academy of Political and Social Science*, 153, pp. 1-10 (January 1931).

Hintze, Hedwig. "Regionalism." *Encyclopaedia of the Social Sciences*, 13, pp. 208-218.

Holmes, R. H. "A Study in the Origins of Distinguished Living Americans." *American Journal of Sociology*, 34, pp. 670-685 (January 1929).

Holmes, W. H. "Areas of American Culture, Characterization as an Aid in the Study of the Antiquities." *American Anthropologist*, New Series, 16, pp. 413-446 (July 1914).

Horgan, Paul. "About the Southwest. A Panorama of Neuva Granada." *Southwest Review*, 18, No. 4, pp. 329-359 (July 1933).

Howland, L. "Provincial or National?" *Scribner's*, 43, pp. 450-455 (April 1908).

Hubbard, H. V. "Planning the City and the Region, Then and Now." *American City*, 43, pp. 99-100 (September 1930).

Hubbard, T. K. "Brief Survey of City and Regional Planning in the United States, 1929." *City Planning*, 6, No. 3, pp. 199-224 (July 1930).

—— "Brief Review of City and Regional Planning in the United States." *National Municipal Review*, 14, pp. 307-314 (May 1925); 15, pp. 342-349 (January 1926).

Hughes, E. C. "The Ecological Aspect of Institutions." *American Sociological Review*, 1, No. 2, pp. 180-189 (April 1936).

Hunt, E. E. "An Approach to State Planning." *Social Forces*, 6, pp. 111-117 (September 1927).

Huntington, Ellsworth. "The Handicap of Poor Land." *Economic Geography*, 2, No. 3, pp. 335-357 (July 1926).

—— "New Science of Geography." *Yale Review*, New Series, 2, pp. 82-96 (October 1912).

Huxley, J. S. "Climate and Human History." *Atlantic Monthly*, 145, pp. 512-522 (April 1930).

Hypes, J. L. "Geography, A Social Determinant." *Journal of Rural Education*, 4, pp. 193-204 (January 1925).

Ickes, H. L. "Saving the Good Earth; The Mississippi Valley Committee and Its Plan." *Survey Graphic*, 23, pp. 52-59 (February 1934).

James, Harlean. "The Cost of Regional Planning." *Journal of Land and Public Utility Economics*, 5, pp. 303-310 (August 1929).

Jefferson, Mark. "Some Considerations on the Geographical Provinces of the United States." *Annals of the Association of American Geographers*, 7, pp. 3-15, 1917.

Joerg, W. L. G. "The Subdivisions of North America into Natural Regions, A Preliminary Inquiry." *Annals of the Association of American Geographers*, 4, pp. 55-83, 1914.

Jones, H. M. "Is There a Southern Renaissance?" *Virginia Quarterly Review*, 6, No. 2, pp. 184-197 (April 1930).

Jones, Idwal. "Letters on the Pacific Rim." *Saturday Review of Literature*, 15, No. 14, pp. 3, 4, 15 (January 30, 1937).

Jones, W. D. "Procedures in Investigating Human Occupance of a Region." *Annals of the Association of American Geographers*, 24, pp. 93-107 (June 1934).

Kehr, C. "City and Regional Planning: Review of a Nation Plan." *Bulletin of Pan American Union*, 61, pp. 269-271 (March 1927).

Keir, Malcolm. "Economic Factors in the Location of Manufacturing Industries." *Annals of the American Academy of Political and Social Science*, 97, pp. 83-92 (September 1921).

Kelly, F. F. "Menace of Localism." *Yale Review*, New Series, 9, pp. 379-393 (January 1920).

Kendrick, B. B. "A Southern Confederation of Learning." *Southwest Review*, 19, pp. 182-195 (January 1934).

Kendrick, B. B., Jr. "Peace-Time Regulation as a Precedent for National Planning." *Social Forces*, 11, No. 4, pp. 574-578 (May 1933).

Kent, F. R. "Sectionalism in America." *Spectator*, 135, pp. 296-297 (August 22, 1925).

Keyserling, Hermann. "Genius Loci." *Atlantic Monthly*, 144, pp. 302-311 (September 1929).

Klugh, A. B. "A Common System of Classification in Plant and Animal Ecology." *Ecology*, 4, pp. 366-377 (October 1923).

Knight, Melvin. "Commercial Routes." *Encyclopaedia of the Social Sciences*, 4, pp. 19-24.

Knowles, Morris. "Governmental Organization to Make Regional Plans Effective." *Proceedings of National Housing Association*, 10, pp. 217-228, 1929.

Kroeber, A. L. "American Culture and the Northwest Coast." *American Anthropologist*, 25, No. 1, pp. 1-20 (January 1923).

—— "Culture Area." *Encyclopaedia of the Social Sciences*, 4, pp. 646-647.

Langley, J. M. "Why Regional Planning?" *New Horizons in Planning.* (Proceedings of the National Planning Conference, June 1937), pp. 150-151.

Laski, H. J. "The Problem of Administrative Areas." *Smith College Studies in History*, 4, No. 1, 1918.

Leland, S. E. "Coordination of Federal, State, and Local Fiscal Systems." *Municipal Finance* (August 1933).

"Le Regionalisme Français." *Spectator*, 152, p. 537 (April 6, 1934).

Lewis, B. G. "Regionalism, A Plan for Uniting the States More Effectively." *The Forum*, 89, pp. 136-141 (March 1933).

Lively, C. E. "Social Planning and the Sociology of Subregions." *Rural Sociology*, 2, No. 3, pp. 287-298 (September 1937).

Lorwin, L. L. "Social Aspects of the Planning State." *The American Political Science Review*, 28, No. 1, pp. 16-22 (February 1934).

"Louisville: A Study of Economic Geography." *Journal of School Geography*, 4, pp. 361-370 (December 1920).

Lowrie, S. G. "Governing Our Metropolitan Areas." *University of Cincinnati Law Review*, 5, No. 2, pp. 186-196 (March 1931).

Mack, Bryan. "Oklahoma—Forty Years Young." *Review of Reviews*, 80, pp. 132-140 (September 1929).

Mackaye, Benton. "Regional Planning." *Sociological Review*, 20, No. 4, pp. 293-299 (October 1928).

—— "Tennessee: Seed of a National Plan." *Survey Graphic*, 22, pp. 251-254 (May 1933).

Mackinder, H. J. "Human Habitat." *Scottish Geographical Magazine*, 47, pp. 321-335 (November 1931).

Mackmurdo, A. H. "Regional Social Unit." *Sociological Review*, 24, pp. 14-23 (January 1932).

Macleod, Norman. "Notes on Regionalism." *Sewanee Review*, 39, pp. 456-459 (October-December 1931).

Marett, R. R. "Jersey: Suggestions Towards a Civic and Regional Survey." *Sociological Review*, 24, pp. 233-247 (April 1932).

Matherly, W. J. "The Emergence of the Metropolitan Community in the South." *Social Forces*, 14, No. 3, pp. 311-325 (March 1936).

— "The Urban Development of the South." *Southern Economic Journal*, 1, No. 4, pp. 3-26 (February 1935).

Maxey, C. C. "The Political Integration of Metropolitan Communities." *National Municipal Review*, 11, pp. 229-253 (August 1922).

McKenzie, R. D. "The Ecological Approach to the Study of the Human Community." *American Journal of Sociology*, 30, pp. 287-301 (November 1924).

— "The Scope of Human Ecology." *Papers and Proceedings of the American Sociological Society*, 20, pp. 141-154 (July 1926).

McKinley, C. "Portland, Oregon Seeks to Simplify Her Regional Government." *National Municipal Review*, 16, pp. 293-295 (May 1927).

McWilliams, Carey. "Localism in American Criticism." *Southwest Review*, 19, No. 4, pp. 410-428 (July 1934).

Merriam, C. E. "Federal Government Recognizes the Cities." *National Municipal Review*, 23, pp. 107-109 (February 1934).

— "Planning Agencies in America." *American Political Science Review*, 29, pp. 197-211 (April 1935).

Merriam, C. H. "The Geographic Distribution of Life in North America." *Smithsonian Institution Annual Report*, 1891, pp. 365-415, Washington, 1893.

Moore, Barrington. "The Scope of Ecology." *Ecology*, 1, No. 1, pp. 3-5 (January 1920).

Mukerjee, Radhakamal. "The Broken Balance of Man and Region." *Sociology and Social Research*, 17, No. 5, pp. 403-408 (May-June 1933).

— "The Concepts of Balance and Organization in Social Ecology." *Sociology and Social Research*, 16, No. 6, pp. 503-516 (July-August 1932).

— "The Concepts of Distribution and Succession in Social Ecology." *Social Forces*, 11, pp. 1-7 (October 1932).

— "The Criterion of Optimum Population." *American Journal of Sociology*, 38, No. 5, pp. 688-698 (March 1933).

— "The Ecological Outlook in Sociology." *American Journal of Sociology*, 38, No. 3, pp. 349-355 (November 1932).

— "Ecological Un-balance of Man." *Sociological Review*, 25, No. 3, pp. 233-243 (October 1933).

Mukerjee, Radhakamal. "The Processes of Regional Balance." *Sociological Review*, 23, No. 3, pp. 173-181 (October 1931).
—— "Regional Balance of Man." *American Journal of Sociology*, 36, No. 3, pp. 455-460 (November 1930).
Mumford, Lewis. "Origins of the American Mind." *American Mercury*, 8, pp. 345-354 (July 1926).
—— "Orozco in New England." *New Republic*, 80, pp. 231-235 (October 10, 1934).
—— "Regionalism and Irregionalism." *Sociological Review*, 19, pp. 277-288 (October 1927); 20, pp. 18-33, 131-141 (April 1928).
—— "Regional Planning Schemes." *Journal of the American Institute of Architects*, 11, pp. 404-405 (October 1923).
—— "Regions—To Live In." *Survey Graphic*, 54, pp. 151-152 (May 1, 1925).
—— "Relation of Nationalism and Culture." *Sociological Review*, 14, pp. 315-319 (October 1922).
—— "The Theory and Practice of Regionalism." *Sociological Review*, 20, pp. 18-33, 131-141 (January-April 1928).
Munro, W. B. "Do We Need Regional Governments?" *Forum*, 79, pp. 108-112 (January 1928).
Murchison, C. T. "Nationalism and the South." *Virginia Quarterly Review*, 10, pp. 1-15 (January 1934).

"Nationalism and Sectionalism." *Independent*, 65, pp. 1624-1626 (December 31, 1908).
Neuberger, R. L. "The New Oregon Trail." *Collier's*, 99, No. 13, pp. 14-15, 38 (March 27, 1937).
Nichols, G. E. "A Working Basis for the Ecological Classification of Plant Communities." *Ecology*, 4, pp. 11-23 (January 1923), and pp. 154-179 (April 1923).
Nolan, John. "Regional Planning." *Encyclopaedia of the Social Sciences*, 13, pp. 205-208.

Odum, Howard W. "The Case for Regional National Social Planning." *Social Forces*, 13, No. 1, pp. 6-23 (October 1934).
—— "Folk and Regional Conflict as a Field of Sociological Study." *Publications of the American Sociological Society*, 25, No. 2, pp. 1-17 (May 1931).
—— "Notes on the Study of Regional and Folk Society." *Social Forces*, 10, pp. 164-175 (December 1931).
—— "Notes on the Technicways in Contemporary Society." *American Sociological Review*, 2, No. 3, pp. 336-346 (June 1937).
—— "Regionalism Versus Sectionalism in the South's Place in the National Economy." *Social Forces*, 12, pp. 338-354 (March 1934).
—— "Realistic Premises for Regional Planning Objectives." *Plan Age*, 2, No. 3, pp. 7-23 (March 1936).

Odum, Howard W. "A Sociological Approach to National Social Planning: A Syllabus." *Sociology and Social Research*, 19, No. 4, pp. 303-313 (March-April 1935).

— and Becker, Donald. "Planning the Southeast." *Plan Age*, 2, No. 3, pp. 1-6 (March 1936).

Ogburn, W. F. "Regions." *Social Forces*, 15, pp. 6-11 (October 1936).

— "Social Characteristics of Cities. VII, Urban Resemblances and Regional Differences." *Public Management*, 18, pp. 200-203 (July 1936).

Ogg, W. G. "Soil Classification and Soil Surveys; Extract." *Scottish Geographical Magazine*, 43, pp. 193-203 (July 1927).

Owsley, F. L. "Pillars of Agrarianism." *American Review*, 4, pp. 529-547 (March 1935).

Park, R. E. "Social Planning and Human Nature." *Publication of the American Sociological Society*, 29, No. 3, pp. 19-28 (August 1935).

— "Succession, an Ecological Concept." *American Sociological Review*, 1, No. 2, pp. 171-179 (April 1936).

— "Urbanization as Measured by Newspaper Circulation." *American Journal of Sociology*, 35, pp. 60-79 (July 1929).

Parsons, P. A. "The Northwest Regional Planning Conference." *Commonwealth Review*, 16, pp. 1-6 (March 1934).

"Passing of Sectionalism." *New Republic*, 27, pp. 60-63 (June 15, 1921).

Patten, S. N. "The Decay of State and Local Governments." *Annals of the American Academy of Political and Social Science*, 1, pp. 26-42 (July 1890).

Peattie, Roderick. "The Consequences of Provincialism." *Journal of Geography*, 28, No. 8, pp. 327-333 (November 1929).

— "New Geography: The Study of a Region's Domination of a People." *Educational Review*, 58, pp. 420-430 (December 1919).

Pipkin, C. W. "Legislation and Social Economic Planning." *Southwest Review*, 18, pp. 207-224 (Spring 1933).

— "Southern Philosophy of States' Rights." *Southwest Review*, 19, pp. 175-182 (Winter 1934).

Pitt-Rivers, G. H. L. F. "Regional Planning in Relation to Population Movement." *Population*, 2, No. 2, pp. 31-41.

Powell, J. W. "Physiographic Regions of the United States." *National Geographic Monographs*, 1, pp. 65-100 (1895).

Pritchett, C. H. "Regional Authorities through Interstate Compacts." *Social Forces*, 14, No. 2, pp. 200-210 (December 1935).

Quinn, J. A. "Ecological Versus Social Interaction." *Sociology and Social Research*, 18, pp. 565-570 (July 1934).

Ransom, J. C. "The Aesthetics of Regionalism." *American Review*, 2, pp. 290-310 (January 1934).

Ratzel, Friedrich. "Studies in Political Areas." Translated by Ellen Churchill Semple. *American Journal of Sociology*, 3, pp. 297-313 (November 1897); 3, pp. 449-463 (January 1898); 4, pp. 366-379 (November 1898).

Reclus, Elisee. "The Evolution of Cities." *Living Age*, 204, No. 2646, pp. 707-720 (March 23, 1895).

"A Reconsideration of the Nature of Interstate Compacts." *Columbia Law Review*, 35, pp. 76-87 (January 1935).

Redfield, Robert. "The Regional Aspect of Culture." *Publications of the American Sociological Society*, 24, pp. 33-41 (May 1930).

Redway, J. W. "Effects of Topography on Economic Development." *Gunton's Magazine*, 19, pp. 135-141 (August 1900).

Reed, T. H. "How a Planned Region Shall be Governed." *American City*, 33, pp. 20-22 (July 1925).

—— "Region, a New Government Unit: The Problem of Metropolitan Areas." *National Municipal Review*, 14, pp. 417-423 (July 1925).

—— "What Government Should a Region Have?" *National Municipal Review*, 15, pp. 95-99 (February 1926).

"Regional Community: a New Plan of Relating Masses of Population to the Land." *Survey Graphic*, 54, pp. 129-176 (May 1, 1925).

"Regional Planning and Unemployment." *New Statesman*, 36, pp. 545-546 (February 14, 1931).

"Regional Town Planning Progress in England." *American City*, 30, No. 4, p. 431 (April 1924).

Renner, G. T. "The Statistical Approach to Regions." *Annals of the Association of American Geographers*, 25, pp. 137-145 (September 1935).

Richardson, R. N. "Some Historical Factors Contributing to the Problems of the Great Plains." *The Southwestern Social Science Quarterly*, 18, No. 1, pp. 1-14 (June 1937).

Ridgeway, William. "The Application of Zoological Laws to Man." *Nature*, 78, pp. 525-533 (September 24, 1908).

Roach, H. G. "Sectionalism in Congress, 1870-1890." *American Political Science Review*, 19, pp. 500-526 (August 1925).

Robinson, E. E. "Recent Manifestations of Sectionalism." *American Journal of Sociology*, 19, pp. 446-467 (January 1914).

Roosevelt, Franklin D. "Growing Up by Plan." *Survey Graphic*, 67, pp. 483-485 (February 1, 1932).

Rosenquist, C. M., and Moore, Harry Estill. "The Bases of Urbanism in Texas." *Southwestern Social Science Quarterly*, 14, pp. 109-119 (September 1933).

Ross, E. A. "Sectionalism and Its Avoidance." *Social Forces*, 2, pp. 484-491 (May 1924).

Sauer, C. O. "Cultural Geography." *Encyclopaedia of the Social Sciences*, 6, pp. 621-624.

Sauer, C. O. "Mapping the Utilization of the Land." *Geographical Review*, 8, pp. 47-54 (July 1919).

—— "Notes on the Geographic Significance of Soils." *Journal of Geography*, 21, pp. 187-190 (May 1922).

—— "The Survey Method in Geography and Its Objectives." *Annals of the Association of American Geographers*, 14, No. 1, pp. 17-33 (March 1924).

Semple, E. C. "The Anglo-Saxons of the Kentucky Mountains." *Bulletin of the American Geographical Society*, 42, No. 8, pp. 561-594 (1910).

Shaler, N. S. "The Peculiarities of the South." *North American Review*, 151, pp. 477-488 (October 1890).

Shaw, Albert. "How Railroads Adapt Themselves to National Conditions." *Proceedings of the Academy of Political Science*, 10, No. 1, pp. 97-100 (July 1922).

Shaw, Desmond. "American City Civilization; The Natural Divisions of the United States." *Century*, 108, No. 4, pp. 548-555 (August 1924).

Slocum, S. E. "Geographic Aspects of Culture." *Popular Science Monthly*, 76, pp. 158-169 (February 1910).

Smith, Henry. "The Dilemma of Agrarianism." *Southwest Review*, 19, No. 3, pp. 215-232 (April 1934).

Smith, R. G. "Concept of the Culture Area." *Social Forces*, 7, pp. 421-423 (March 1929).

Speck, F. G. "Culture Problems in Northeastern North America." *Proceedings of the American Philosophical Society*, 65, pp. 272-311 (1926).

Spinden, H. J. "The Origin and Distribution of Agriculture in America." *Proceedings*, 19th International Congress of Americanists, Washington, pp. 269-276 (1915).

Strong, H. M. "Regionalism, Its Cultural Significance." *Economic Geography*, 12, pp. 392-412 (October 1936).

Strong, W. D. "An Analysis of Southwestern Society." *American Anthropologist*, 29, pp. 1-61 (January 1927).

Swanton, J. R. "Notes on the Cultural Province of the Southeast." *American Anthropologist*, 37, pp. 373-385 (July 1935).

"A Symposium on Regional Planning." *Survey Graphic*, Regionalism Number (May 1925).

Tate, Allen. "Regionalism and Sectionalism." *New Republic*, 59, pp. 158-161 (December 23, 1931).

Taylor, Griffith. "The Ecological Basis of Anthropology." *Ecology*, 15, pp. 223-242 (July 1934).

Taylor, T. G. "Climatic Cycles and Evolution." *Geographical Review*, 8, pp. 289-328 (December 1919).

—— "The Geographers Aid in Nation Planning." *Scottish Geographical Magazine*, 48, pp. 1-20 (January 1932).

Taylor, W. P. "What Is Ecology and What Good Is It?" *Ecology* 17, No. 3, pp. 333-346 (July 1936).

"Tennessee Valley Plan." *New Republic*, 74, pp. 4-6 (February 15, 1933).

Thompson, W. H. "Somerset Regional Survey and Regional Planning Proposals." *Town Planning Institute Journal*, 20, pp. 107-110 (February 1934).

Thompson, W. S. "The Future of the Large City." *American Mercury*, 20, pp. 327-337 (July 1930).

Townroe, B. S. "Progress of Regional Planning." *Spectator*, 145, p. 304 (September 6, 1930).

— "Regional Planning." *Outlook* (London), 61, pp. 402-405 (March 31, 1928).

Trotter, S. "Atlantic Forest Region of North America." *Popular Science Monthly*, 75, pp. 370-392 (October 1909).

Turner, F. J. "Geographic Influences in American Political History." *Bulletin of the American Geographic Society*, 46, pp. 591-595 (August 1914).

— "Geographic Sectionalism in American History." *Annals of the Association of American Geographers*, 16, No. 2, pp. 85-93 (June 1926).

— "The Problem of the West." *Atlantic Monthly*, 78, pp. 289-297, 1896.

— "Sectionalism in America." *American Journal of Sociology*, 13, pp. 661-675 (May 1908).

— "Sections and Nation." *Yale Review*, New Series, 12, pp. 1-21 (October 1922).

— "Significance of the Frontier in American History." *Annual Report of the American Historical Association*, 1893, pp. 199-227, Washington, 1894.

— "Significance of Sections in American History." *Wisconsin Magazine of History*, 8, pp. 254-280 (March 1925).

"Twelve Planning Regions Established." *American City*, 49, No. 4, p. 81 (April 1934).

Unstead, J. F. "A Synthetic Method of Determining Geographical Regions." *Geographical Journal*, 48, No. 3, pp. 230-249 (September 1916).

Vance, R. B. "Concept of the Region." *Social Forces*, 8, pp. 202-218 (December 1929).

— "Cotton Culture and Social Life and Institutions of the South." *Publications of the American Sociological Society*, 23, pp. 51-59, 1928.

— "Implications of the Concept 'Region and Regional Planning.'" *Publication of the American Sociological Society*, 29, No. 3, pp. 85-93 (August 1935).

Vance, R. B. "Planning the Southern Economy." *Southwest Review*, 20, No. 2, pp. 111-123 (January 1935).

—— "What of Submarginal Areas in Regional Planning?" *Social Forces*, 12, pp. 315-329 (March 1934).

Van Cleef, E. "Philosophy and Geography and Geographical Regions." *Geographical Review*, 22, pp. 497-498 (July 1932).

Viles, Jonas. "Sections and Sectionalism in a Border State." *Mississippi Valley Historical Review*, 21, pp. 3-22 (June 1934).

Vincent, M. J. "Regionalism and Fiction." *Social Forces*, 14, No. 3, pp. 335-340 (March 1936).

Ward, R. de C. "The Climatic Factor in Man's Physical Environment." *Scientific Monthly*, 30, No. 2, pp. 170-183 (February 1930).

—— "Arable Land in the United States." *Geographical Review*, 8, p. 55 (July 1919).

—— "The Literature of Climatology." *Annals of the Association of American Geographers*, 21, pp. 34-51 (March 1931).

—— "A New Classification of Climates." *Geographical Review*, 8, pp. 188-191 (September 1919).

—— "The Weather Element in American Climates." *Annals of the Association of American Geographers*, 4, pp. 3-54, 1914.

Warren, Austin. "Regional Retrospection." *The American Review*, 8, No. 2, pp. 245-251 (December 1936).

Waterman, T. T. "Culture Horizons in the Southwest." *American Anthropologist*, 31, No. 3, pp. 367-400 (July 1929).

—— "Subdivisions of the Human Race and Their Distribution." *American Anthropologist*, 26, pp. 474-490 (October 1924).

Wells, H. G. "Anticipations: The Probable Diffusion of Great Cities." *Fortnightly Review*, 75, pp. 925-938 (May 1901).

West, H. L. "Two Republics in One." *North American Review*, 162, pp. 509-511, 1896.

"What, Why, and How of Regional Planning." *American City*, 34, pp. 527-528 (May 1926).

Whitaker, J. R. "Regional Interdependence." *Journal of Geography*, 31, pp. 164-165 (April 1932).

Whitbeck, R. H. "Facts and Fiction in Geography by Natural Regions." *Journal of Geography*, 22, pp. 86-94 (March 1923).

White, W. A. "Racy of the Soil" (Review of Arthur Pound's *Once a Wilderness*). *Saturday Review of Literature*, 10, No. 38, p. 607 (April 7, 1934).

Whitnall, C. B. "Argument for Regional Planning." *American City*, 29, pp. 36-38 (July 1923).

Wilgus, W. J., and Adams, T. "Forecast of the Regional Community." *American City*, 35, pp. 617-620 (November 1926).

Willey, M. M. "Some Limits of the Culture Area Concept." *Social Forces*, 10, pp. 28-31 (October 1931).

Willey, M. M. "The Validity of the Culture Area Concept." *American Journal of Sociology*, 35, pp. 204-219 (September 1929).
—— and Herskovits, M. J. "The Cultural Approach to Sociology." *American Journal of Sociology*, 29, pp. 188-199 (September 1923).
Wirth, Louis. "Localism, Regionalism, and Centralization." *The American Journal of Sociology*, 42, No. 4, pp. 493-509 (January 1937).
—— "The Prospects of Regional Research in Relation to Social Planning." *Publication of the American Sociological Society*, 29, No. 3, pp. 107-114 (August 1935).
Wissler, Clark. "The Culture Area Concept as a Research Lead." *American Journal of Sociology*, 33, pp. 894-900 (May 1928).
—— "The Culture Area Concept in Social Anthropology." *American Journal of Sociology*, 32, pp. 881-891 (May 1927).
—— "The Relation of Nature to Man as Illustrated by the North American Indian." *Ecology*, 5, No. 4, pp. 311-318 (October 1924).
Wolfanger, L. A. "Economic Geography of the Gray-brownerths of the Eastern United States." *Geographical Review*, 21, pp. 276-296 (April 1931).
Woods, C. A. "A Criticism of Wissler's North American Culture Areas." *American Anthropologist*, 36, pp. 517-523 (October 1934).
Woofter, T. J., Jr. "Southern Population and Social Planning." *Social Forces*, 14, No. 1, pp. 16-22 (October 1935).
—— "The Subregions of the Southeast." *Social Forces*, 13, No. 1, pp. 43-50 (October 1934).
—— "The Tennessee Basin." *American Journal of Sociology*, 39, pp. 809-817 (May 1934).
—— "Tennessee Valley Regional Plan." *Social Forces*, 12, pp. 329-338 (March 1934).
Wright, J. K. "Sections and National Growth." *Geographical Review*, 22, pp. 353-360 (July 1932).

Zimmermann, E. W. "Natural Resources." *Encyclopaedia of the Social Sciences*, 11, pp. 290-299.
—— "The Resources of the South." *South Atlantic Quarterly*, 32, pp. 213-226 (July 1933).

INDEX